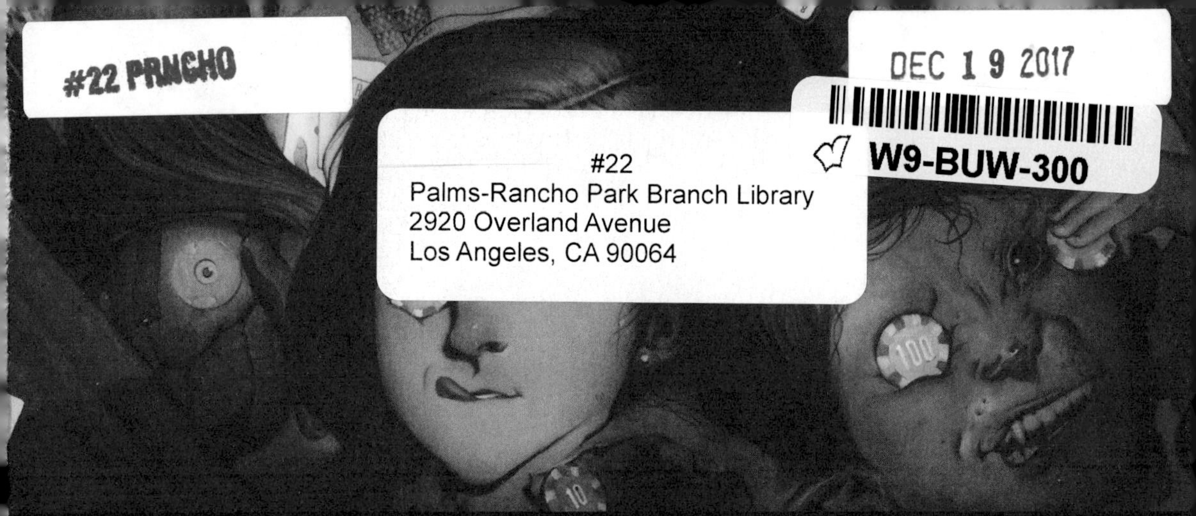

FABLES:
THE GREAT FABLES CROSSOVER

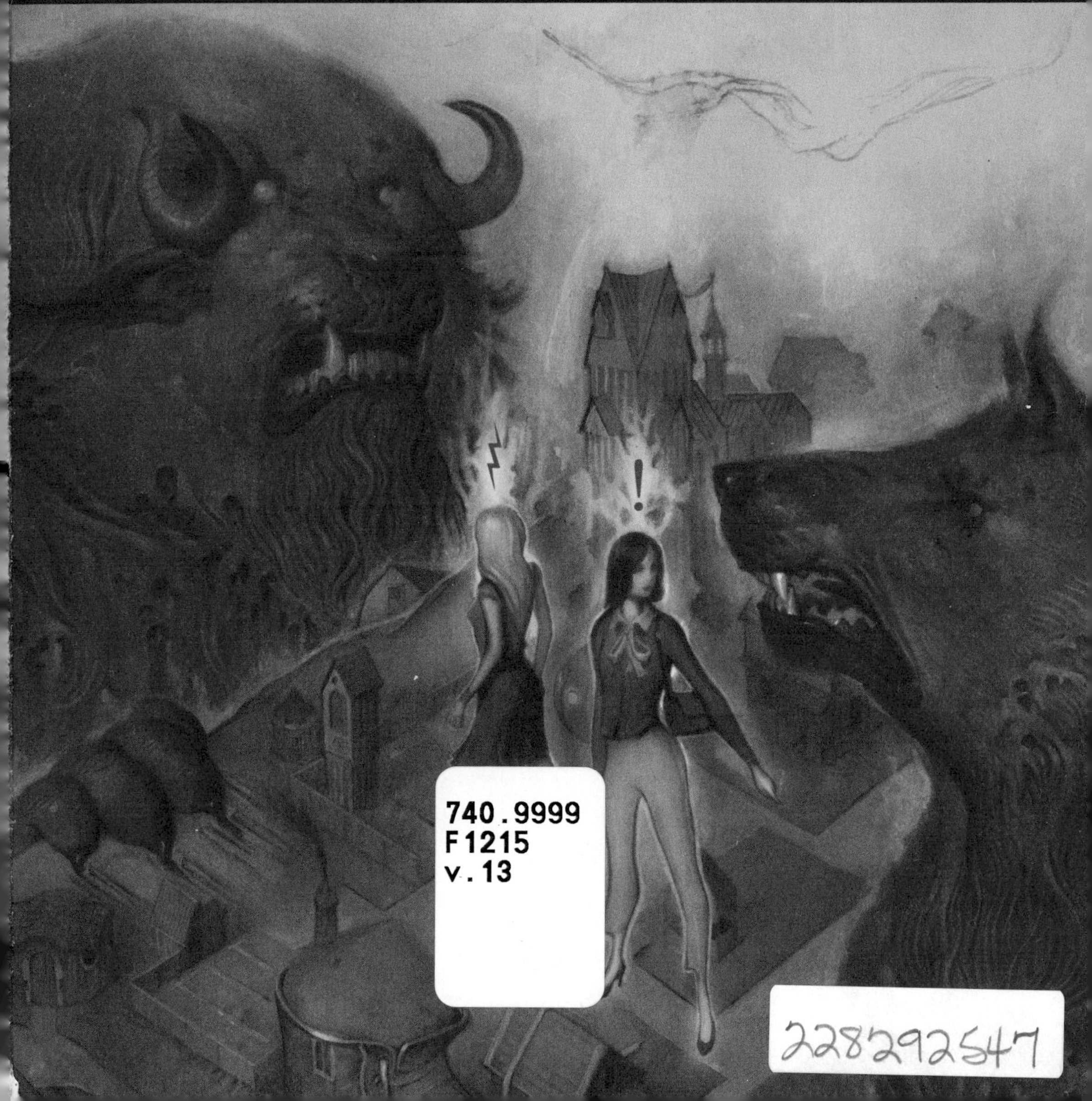

FABLES:
THE GREAT FABLES CROSSOVER

FABLES CREATED BY BILL WILLINGHAM

Bill Willingham and Matthew Sturges
writers

Mark Buckingham
Tony Akins
Russ Braun
Andrew Pepoy
José Marzán, Jr.
Dan Green
artists

Lee Loughridge
Daniel Vozzo
colorists

Todd Klein
letterer

Brian Bolland
Mark Buckingham
Joao Ruas
original series covers

Shelly Bond
Angela Rufino
Editors – Original Series

Scott Nybakken
Editor

Robbin Brosterman
Design Director – Books

Shelly Bond
Executive Editor – Vertigo

Hank Kanalz
Senior VP – Vertigo and Integrated
Publishing

Diane Nelson
President

Dan DiDio and Jim Lee
Co-Publishers

Geoff Johns
Chief Creative Officer

Amit Desai
Senior VP – Marketing and Franchise
Management

Amy Genkins
Senior VP – Business and Legal Affairs

Nairi Gardiner
Senior VP – Finance

Jeff Boison
VP – Publishing Planning

Mark Chiarello
VP – Art Direction and Design

John Cunningham
VP – Marketing

Terri Cunningham
VP – Editorial Administration

Larry Ganem
VP – Talent Relations and Services

Alison Gill
Senior VP – Manufacturing and Operations

Jay Kogan
VP – Business and Legal Affairs, Publishing

Jack Mahan
VP – Business Affairs, Talent

Nick Napolitano
VP – Manufacturing Administration

Sue Pohja
VP – Book Sales

Fred Ruiz
VP – Manufacturing Operations

Courtney Simmons
Senior VP – Publicity

Bob Wayne
Senior VP – Sales

*For Bill and Shelly — thanks for this opportunity,
not to mention the many others. And for Bucky —
a comic book writer's dream come true.*
— Matthew Sturges

*For all my old friends back in Clevedon,
especially for Andrew, Tom, Darren & Kev.*
— Mark Buckingham

*For the debaser, the harbinger
and for fiat and the killer-of-clones.
For the meta-wizard, for the staticCreep and
all the shifters of the shapes within
and around us... and to the page
ever being turned.*
— Tony Akins

Cover illustration by Brian Bolland
Logo design by Brainchild Studios/NYC

FABLES: THE GREAT FABLES CROSSOVER
Published by DC Comics. Cover and compilation
Copyright © 2010 DC Comics. All Rights Reserved.
Originally published in single magazine form as
FABLES 83-85, JACK OF FABLES 33-35 and THE
LITERALS 1-3. Copyright © 2009 Bill Willingham and
DC Comics. All Rights Reserved. All characters, their
distinctive likenesses and related elements featured
in this publication are trademarks of Bill Willingham.
VERTIGO is a trademark of DC Comics. The stories,
characters and incidents featured in this publication
are entirely fictional. DC Comics does not read or
accept unsolicited submissions of ideas,
stories or artwork.
DC Comics, 1700 Broadway, New York, NY 10019
A Warner Bros. Entertainment Company.
Printed in Canada. Fifth Printing.
ISBN: 978-1-4012-2572-8

Library of Congress Cataloging-in-Publication Data

Willingham, Bill.
  Fables. Vol. 13, The great fables crossover / Bill
Willingham, Matthew Sturges, Mark Buckingham, Russ
Braun, Tony Akins, Andrew Pepoy, José Marzán, Jr.
    p. cm.
  "Originally published in single magazine form as
Fables 83-85, Jack of Fables 33-35 and The Literals 1-3."
  ISBN 978-1-4012-2572-8 (alk. paper)
  1. Graphic novels. I. Sturges, Matthew. II
Buckingham, Mark. III. Braun, Russell. IV. Akins, Tony.
V. Pepoy, Andrew. VI. Marzán, José. VII. Title. VIII. Title:
Great Fables crossover.
  PN6727.W52F396 2012
  741.5'973--dc23
                                        2012024699

Table of Contents

WHO'S WHO IN FABLETOWN

STINKY

A somewhat curmudgeonly pillar of the non-human Fables community.

CLARA

A dragon in crow's clothing.

SNOW WHITE

The former deputy mayor of Fabletown and wife of Bigby Wolf.

FRAU TOTENKINDER

Fabletown's most powerful witch and a reformed child cooker.

JACK OF THE TALES

Also known as Little Jack Horner, Jack the Giant Killer, and by countless other responsibility-evading aliases.

GARY, THE PATHETIC FALLACY

A timid, warm-hearted fellow, and also one of the fantastically powerful Literals.

KEVIN THORNE

Gary's son, Mr. Revise's father, and a danger to the entire universe.

HANSEL

A wicked Fable who collaborated with the Adversary in the war to liberate the Homelands.

BEAUTY AND THE BEAST

Fabletown's husband-and-wife tag team of deputy mayor and sheriff.

BIGBY

The Big Bad Wolf of house-blowing fame, now a respected husband and father.

KING COLE

The current mayor of Fabletown — or at least what's left of it.

GRIMBLE

A fearsome bridge troll disguised as a dozy security guard.

THE PAGE SISTERS

Mr. Revise's trusted assistants, lately much abused by Literal and Fable alike

MR. REVISE

An enemy of magic in general and Fables in particular, he is, despite appearances, Gary's grandson.

SAM

A speedy fellow whose politically incorrect nature nearly cost him his existence.

ROSE RED

Snow White's sister, currently in a deep depression.

THE STORY SO FAR

Following their victory over Geppetto's empire, Fabletown has been hit by an escalating series of unfortunate events — most recently the destruction of their home base in New York City and the death of the heroic Boy Blue. A terrible evil, it seems, is loose in the world, and the free Fables must regroup quickly if they are to have a hope of standing against it. But if they think things are bad now, just wait until they hear the news that the exiled Jack Horner and his band of misfits are about to deliver...

THE GREAT FABLES CROSSOVER

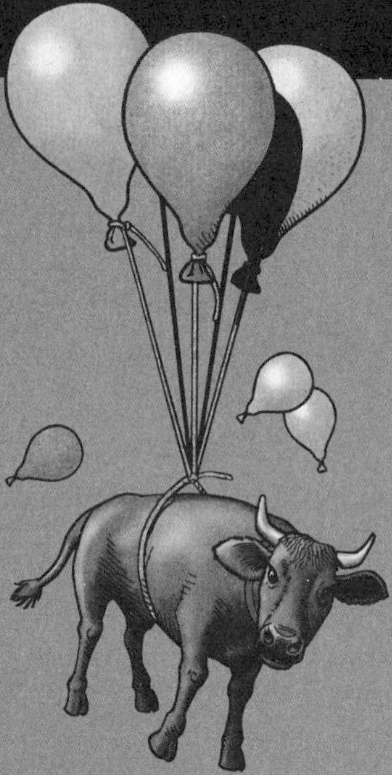

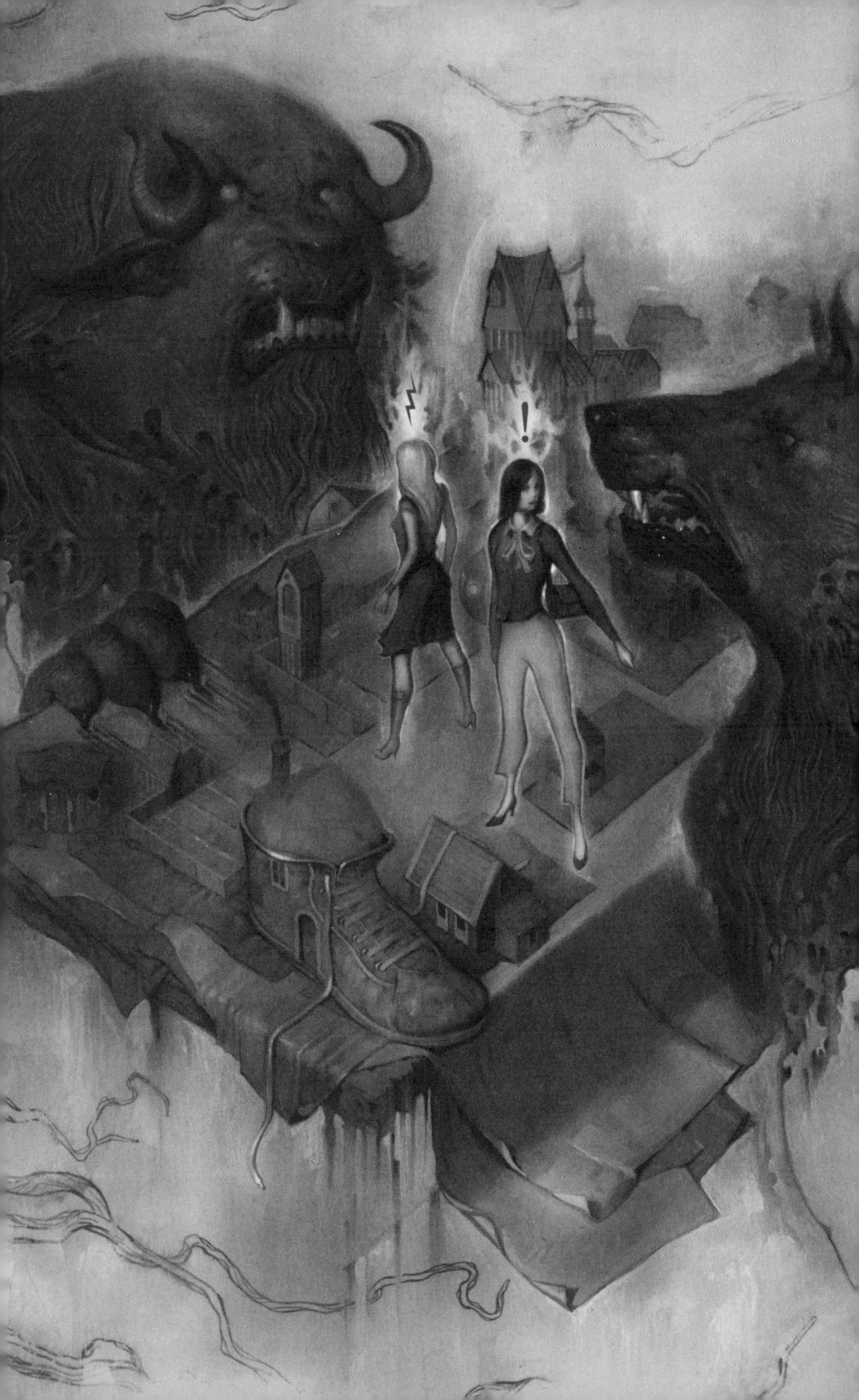

*"Who can gauge all the ways in which
the gods who've created you craft your life?"*

The Great FABLES Crossover

part 1 of 9

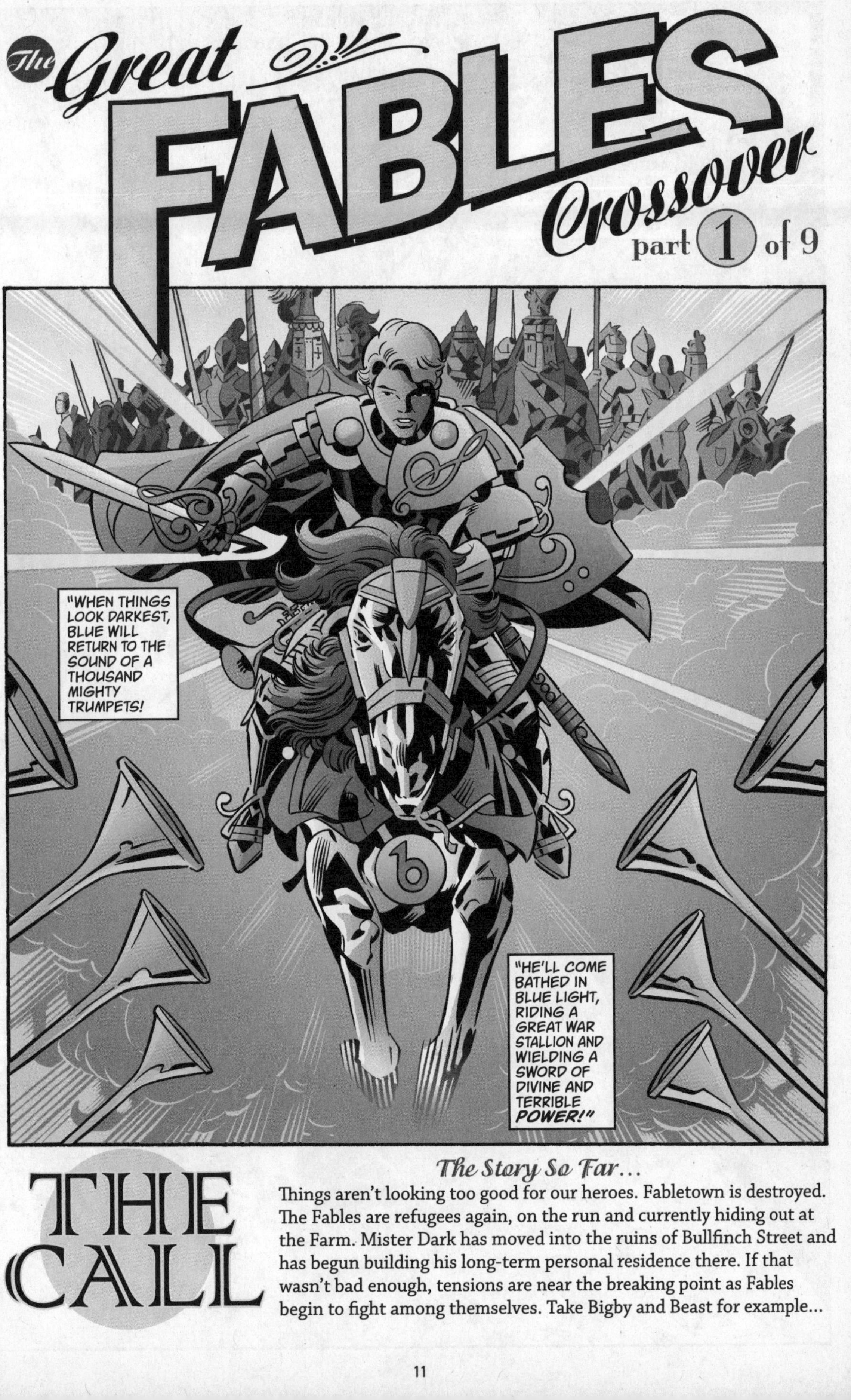
"WHEN THINGS LOOK DARKEST, BLUE WILL RETURN TO THE SOUND OF A THOUSAND MIGHTY TRUMPETS!
"HE'LL COME BATHED IN BLUE LIGHT, RIDING A GREAT WAR STALLION AND WIELDING A SWORD OF DIVINE AND TERRIBLE *POWER!*"

THE CALL

The Story So Far...

Things aren't looking too good for our heroes. Fabletown is destroyed. The Fables are refugees again, on the run and currently hiding out at the Farm. Mister Dark has moved into the ruins of Bullfinch Street and has begun building his long-term personal residence there. If that wasn't bad enough, tensions are near the breaking point as Fables begin to fight among themselves. Take Bigby and Beast for example...

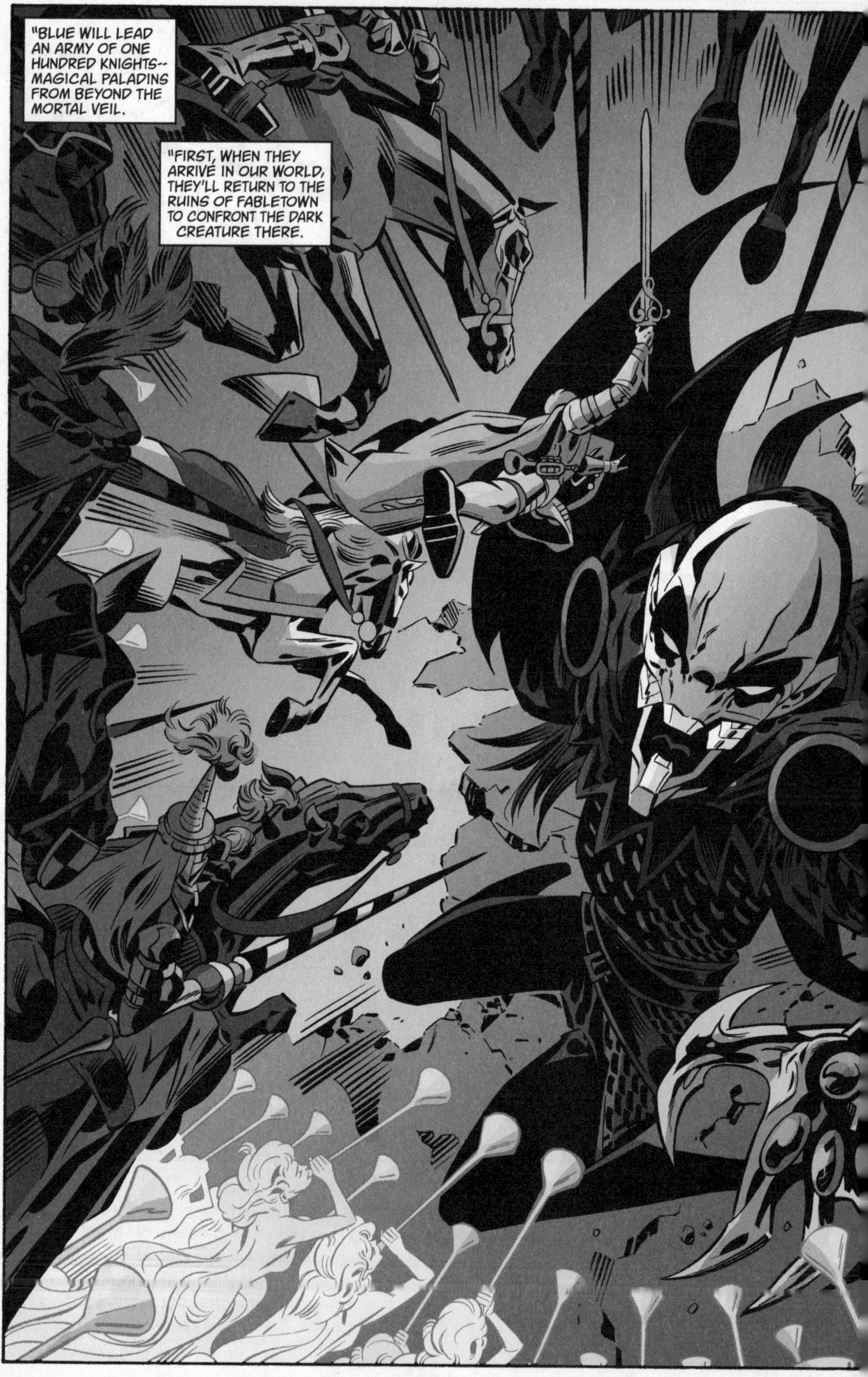
"BLUE WILL LEAD AN ARMY OF ONE HUNDRED KNIGHTS-- MAGICAL PALADINS FROM BEYOND THE MORTAL VEIL.
"FIRST, WHEN THEY ARRIVE IN OUR WORLD, THEY'LL RETURN TO THE RUINS OF FABLETOWN TO CONFRONT THE DARK CREATURE THERE.

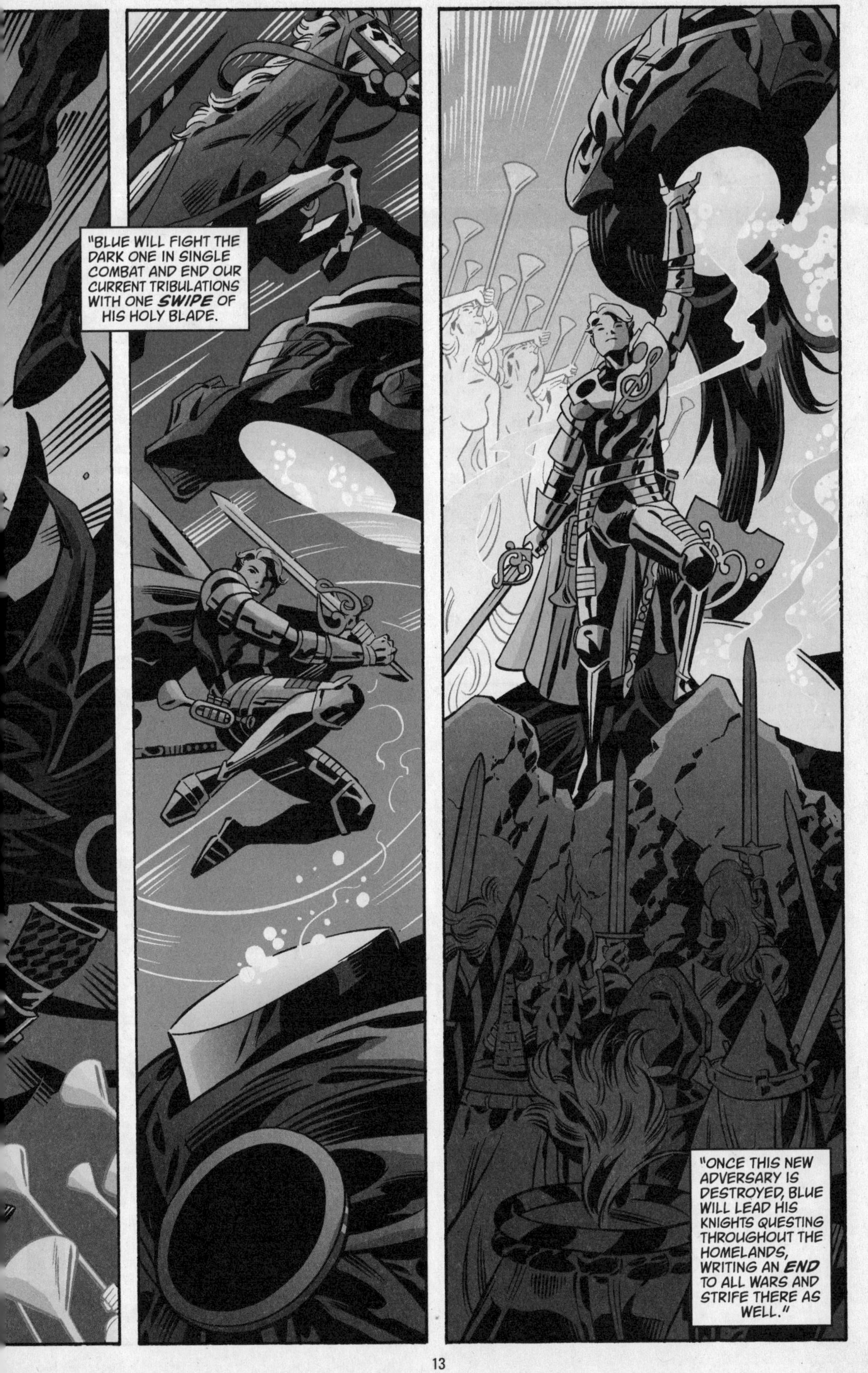
"BLUE WILL FIGHT THE DARK ONE IN SINGLE COMBAT AND END OUR CURRENT TRIBULATIONS WITH ONE SWIPE OF HIS HOLY BLADE.
"ONCE THIS NEW ADVERSARY IS DESTROYED, BLUE WILL LEAD HIS KNIGHTS QUESTING THROUGHOUT THE HOMELANDS, WRITING AN END TO ALL WARS AND STRIFE THERE AS WELL."

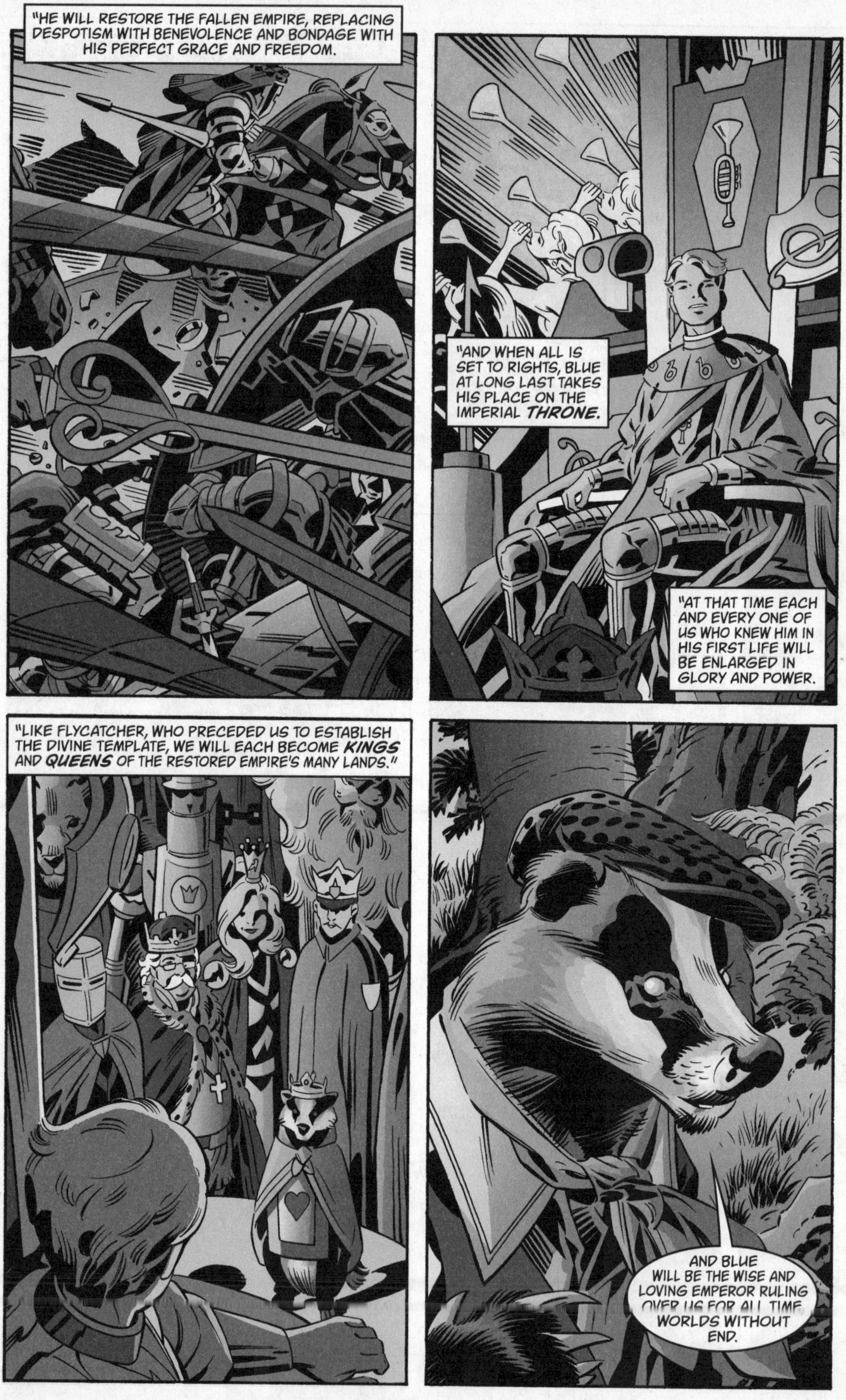
"HE WILL RESTORE THE FALLEN EMPIRE, REPLACING DESPOTISM WITH BENEVOLENCE AND BONDAGE WITH HIS PERFECT GRACE AND FREEDOM.
"AND WHEN ALL IS SET TO RIGHTS, BLUE AT LONG LAST TAKES HIS PLACE ON THE IMPERIAL THRONE.
"AT THAT TIME EACH AND EVERY ONE OF US WHO KNEW HIM IN HIS FIRST LIFE WILL BE ENLARGED IN GLORY AND POWER.
"LIKE FLYCATCHER, WHO PRECEDED US TO ESTABLISH THE DIVINE TEMPLATE, WE WILL EACH BECOME KINGS AND QUEENS OF THE RESTORED EMPIRE'S MANY LANDS."
AND BLUE WILL BE THE WISE AND LOVING EMPEROR RULING OVER US FOR ALL TIME, WORLDS WITHOUT END.

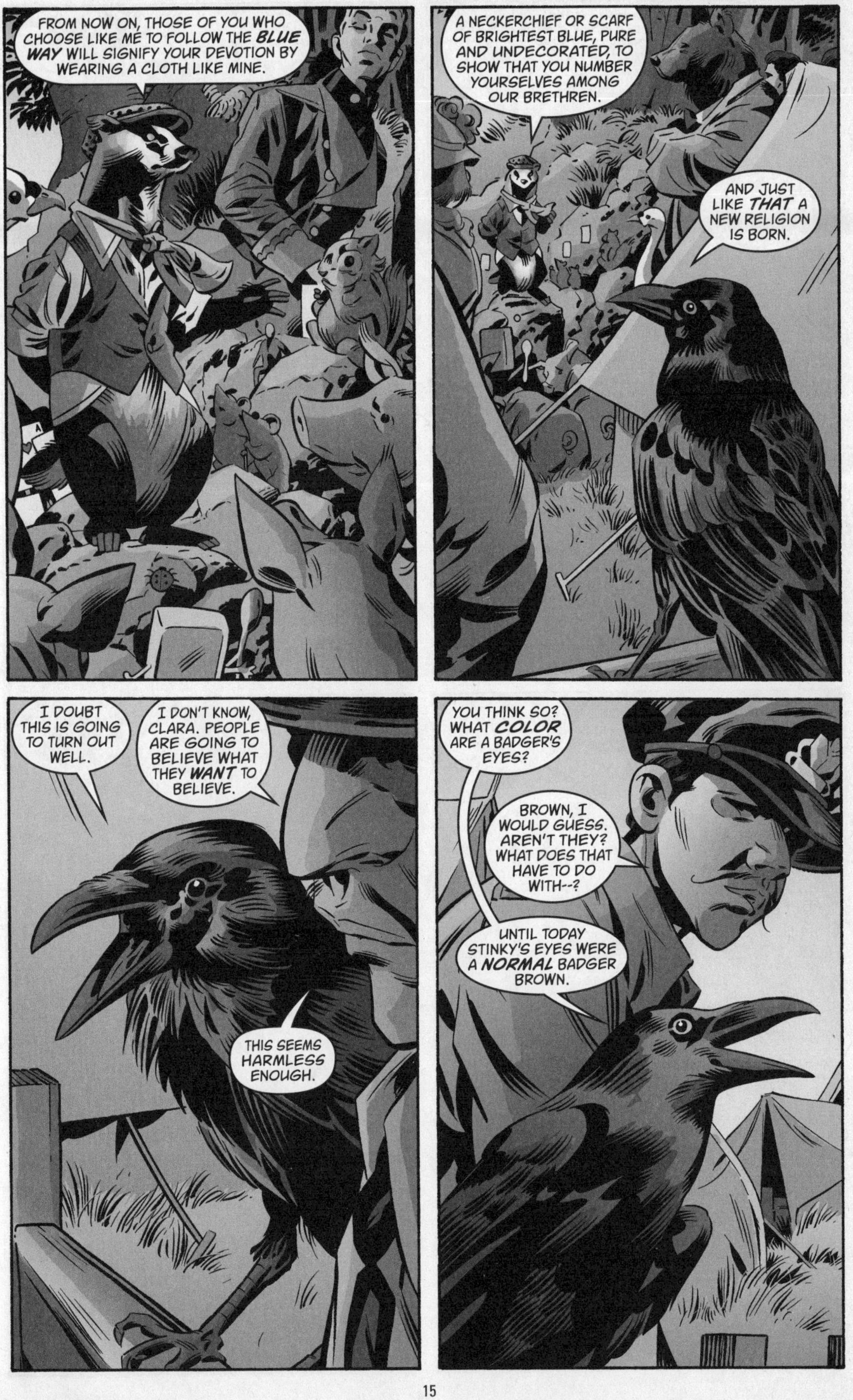
FROM NOW ON, THOSE OF YOU WHO CHOOSE LIKE ME TO FOLLOW THE BLUE WAY WILL SIGNIFY YOUR DEVOTION BY WEARING A CLOTH LIKE MINE.
A NECKERCHIEF OR SCARF OF BRIGHTEST BLUE, PURE AND UNDECORATED, TO SHOW THAT YOU NUMBER YOURSELVES AMONG OUR BRETHREN.
AND JUST LIKE THAT A NEW RELIGION IS BORN.
I DOUBT THIS IS GOING TO TURN OUT WELL.
I DON'T KNOW, CLARA. PEOPLE ARE GOING TO BELIEVE WHAT THEY WANT TO BELIEVE.
THIS SEEMS HARMLESS ENOUGH.
YOU THINK SO? WHAT COLOR ARE A BADGER'S EYES?
BROWN, I WOULD GUESS. AREN'T THEY? WHAT DOES THAT HAVE TO DO WITH--?
UNTIL TODAY STINKY'S EYES WERE A NORMAL BADGER BROWN.

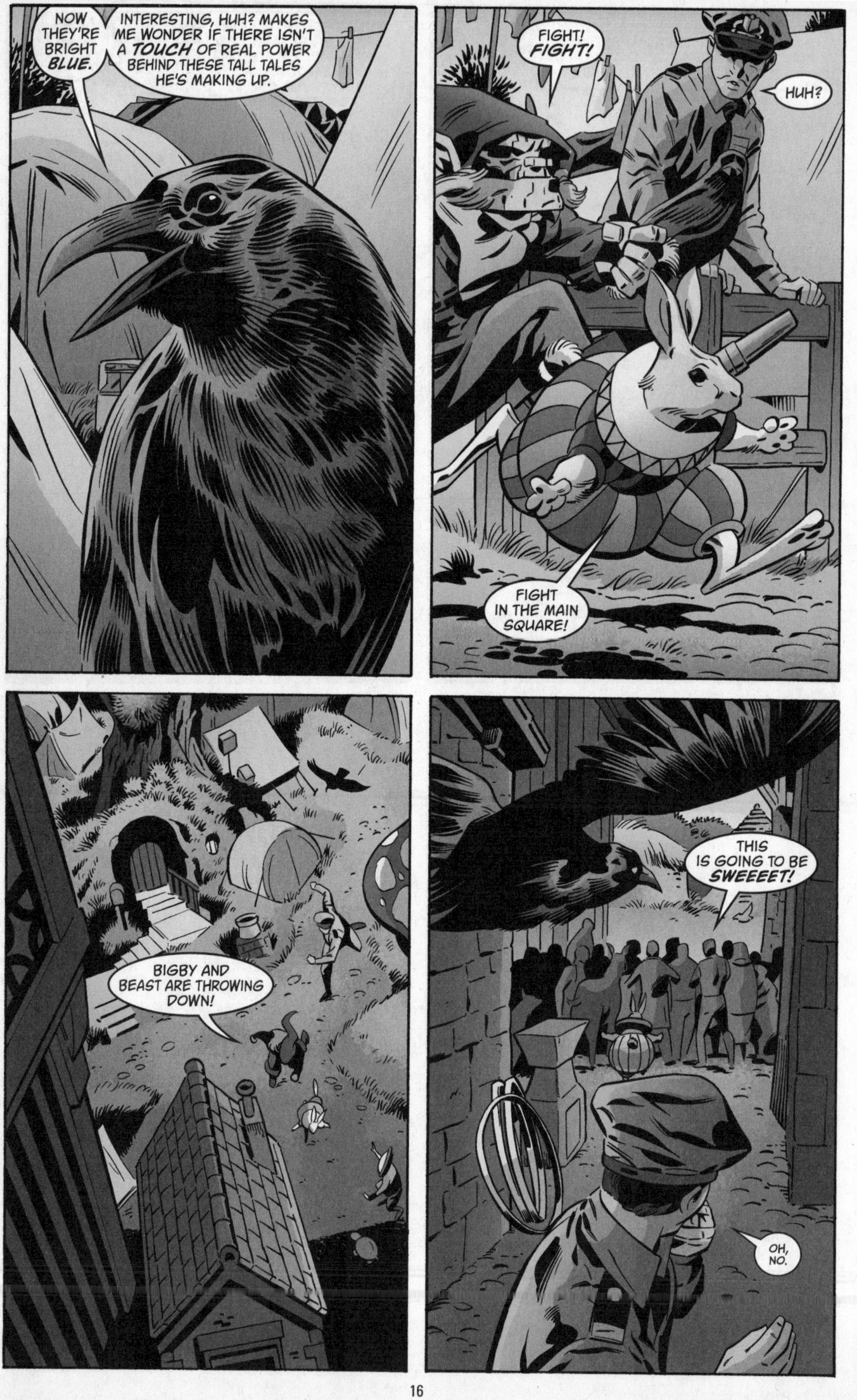
NOW THEY'RE BRIGHT BLUE.
INTERESTING, HUH? MAKES ME WONDER IF THERE ISN'T A TOUCH OF REAL POWER BEHIND THESE TALL TALES HE'S MAKING UP.
FIGHT! FIGHT!
HUH?
FIGHT IN THE MAIN SQUARE!
BIGBY AND BEAST ARE THROWING DOWN!
THIS IS GOING TO BE SWEEEET!
OH, NO.

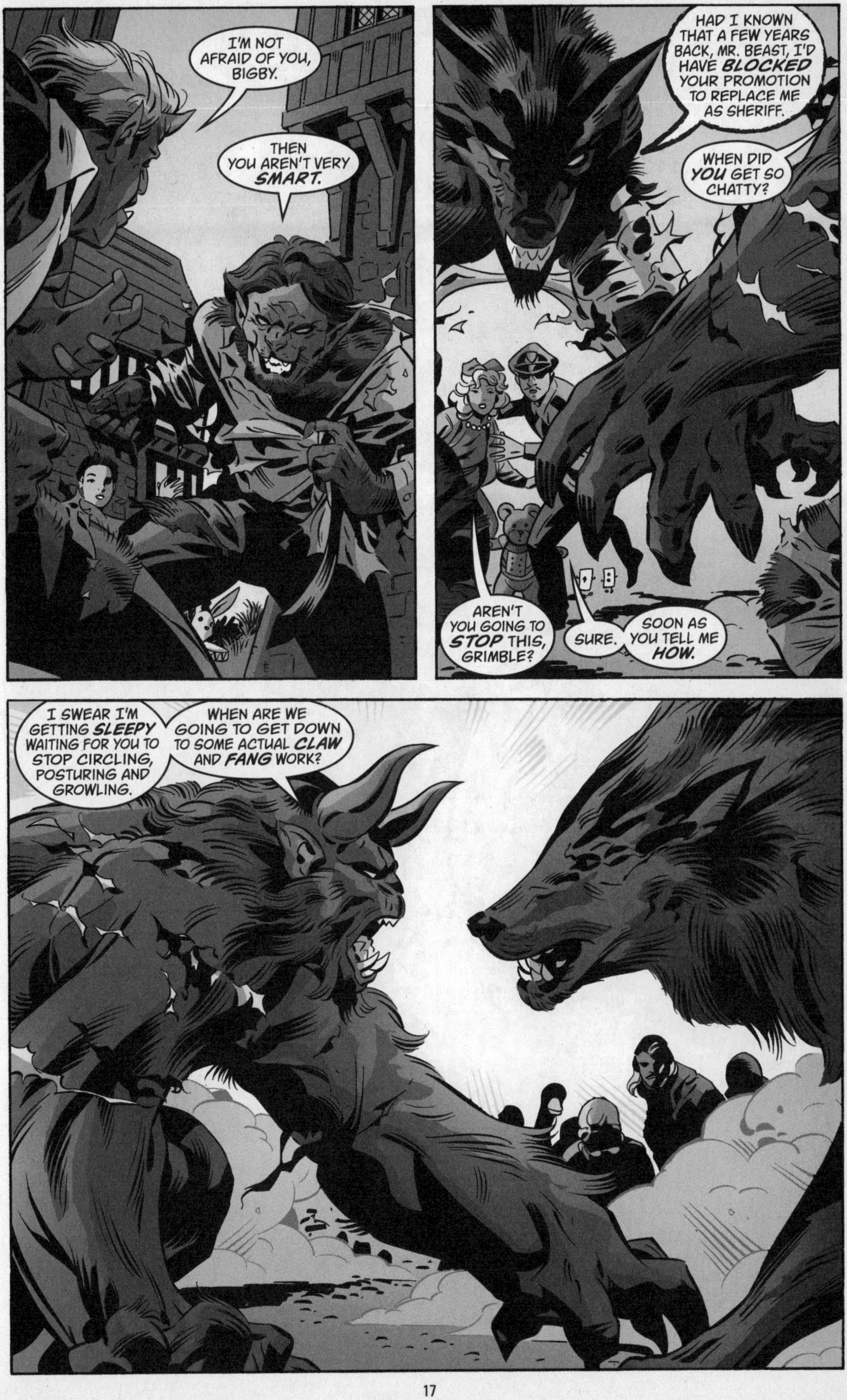
I'M NOT AFRAID OF YOU, BIGBY.
THEN YOU AREN'T VERY SMART.
HAD I KNOWN THAT A FEW YEARS BACK, MR. BEAST, I'D HAVE BLOCKED YOUR PROMOTION TO REPLACE ME AS SHERIFF.
WHEN DID YOU GET SO CHATTY?
AREN'T YOU GOING TO STOP THIS, GRIMBLE?
SURE.
SOON AS YOU TELL ME HOW.
I SWEAR I'M GETTING SLEEPY WAITING FOR YOU TO STOP CIRCLING, POSTURING AND GROWLING.
WHEN ARE WE GOING TO GET DOWN TO SOME ACTUAL CLAW AND FANG WORK?

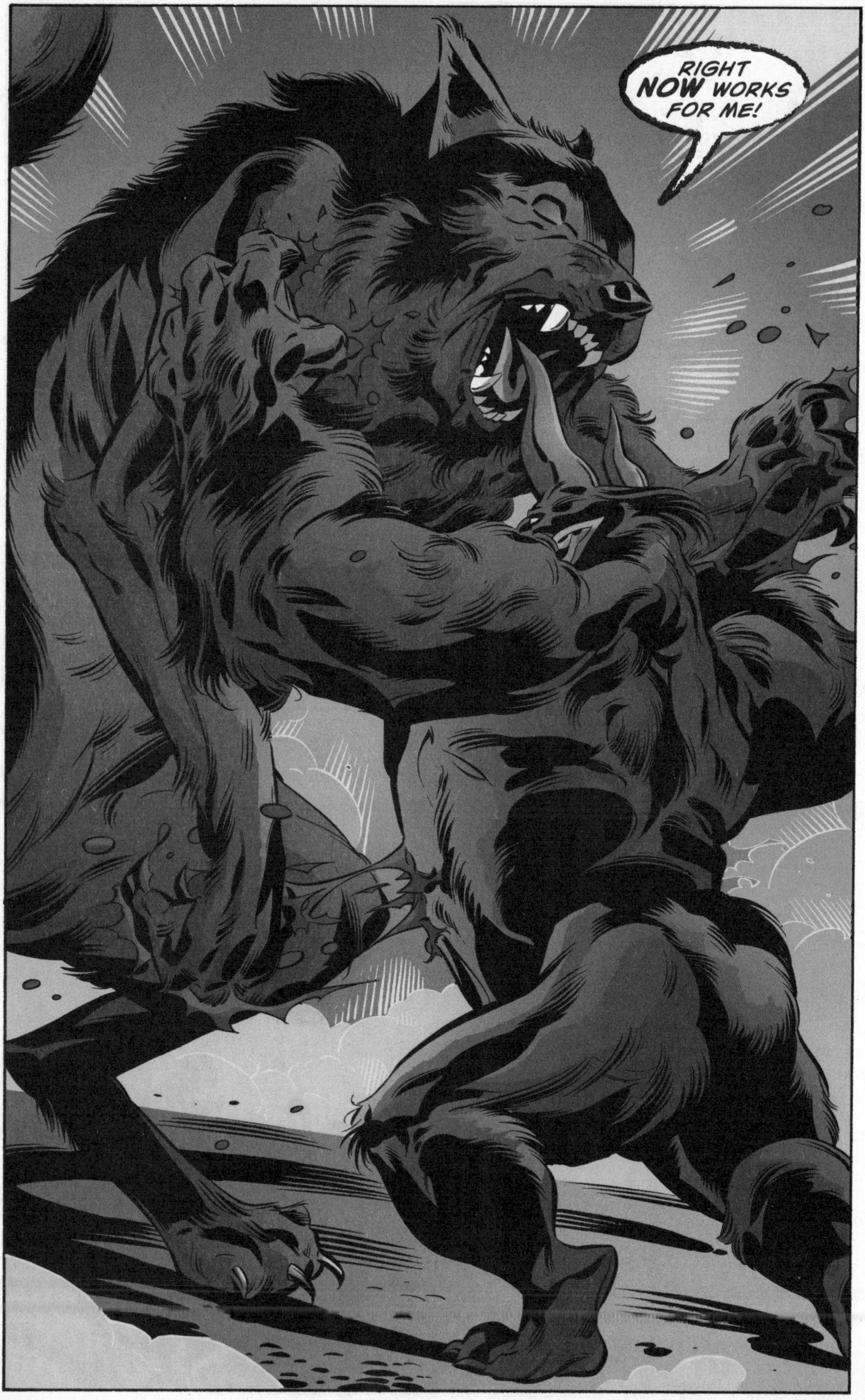
RIGHT NOW WORKS FOR ME!

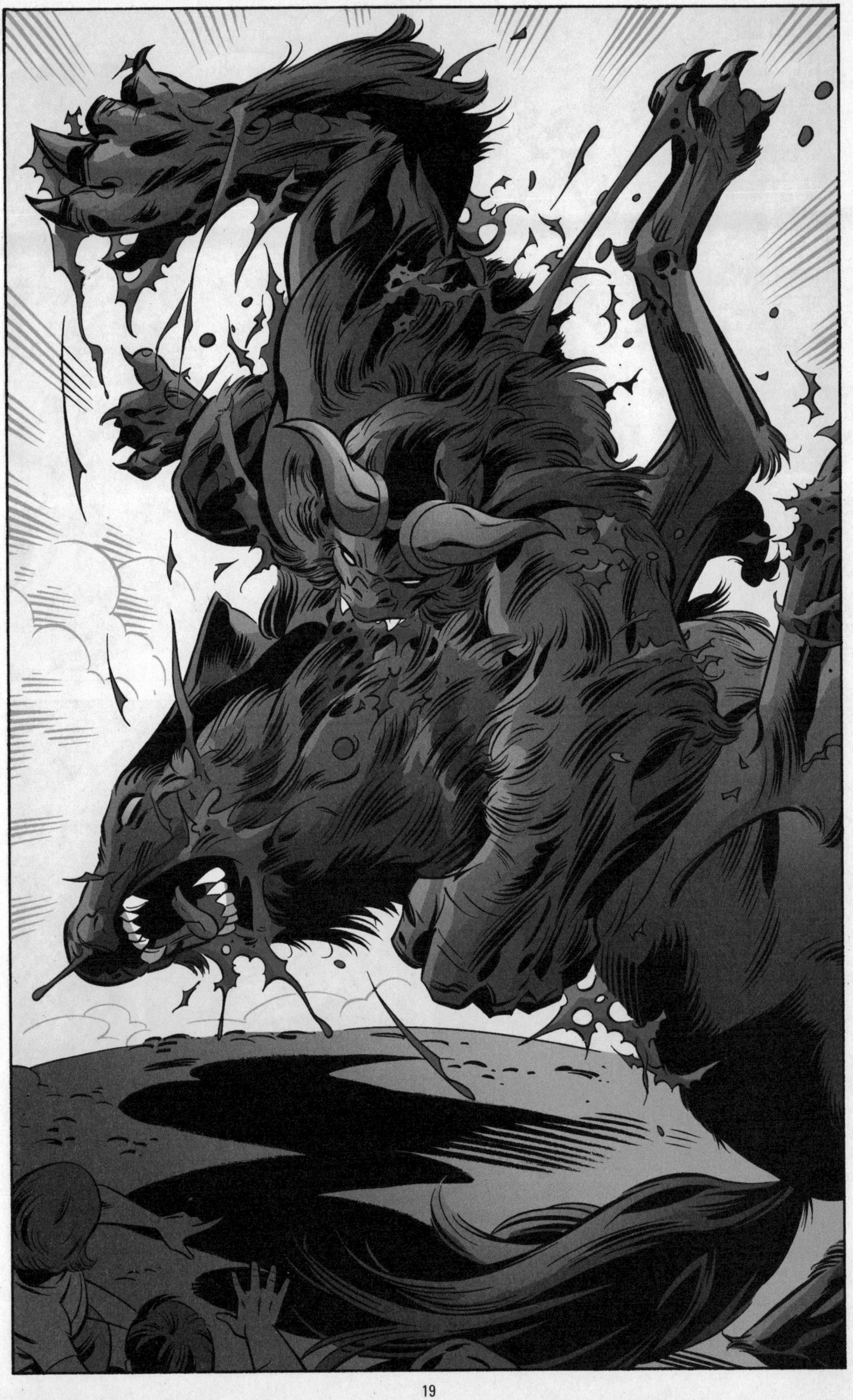

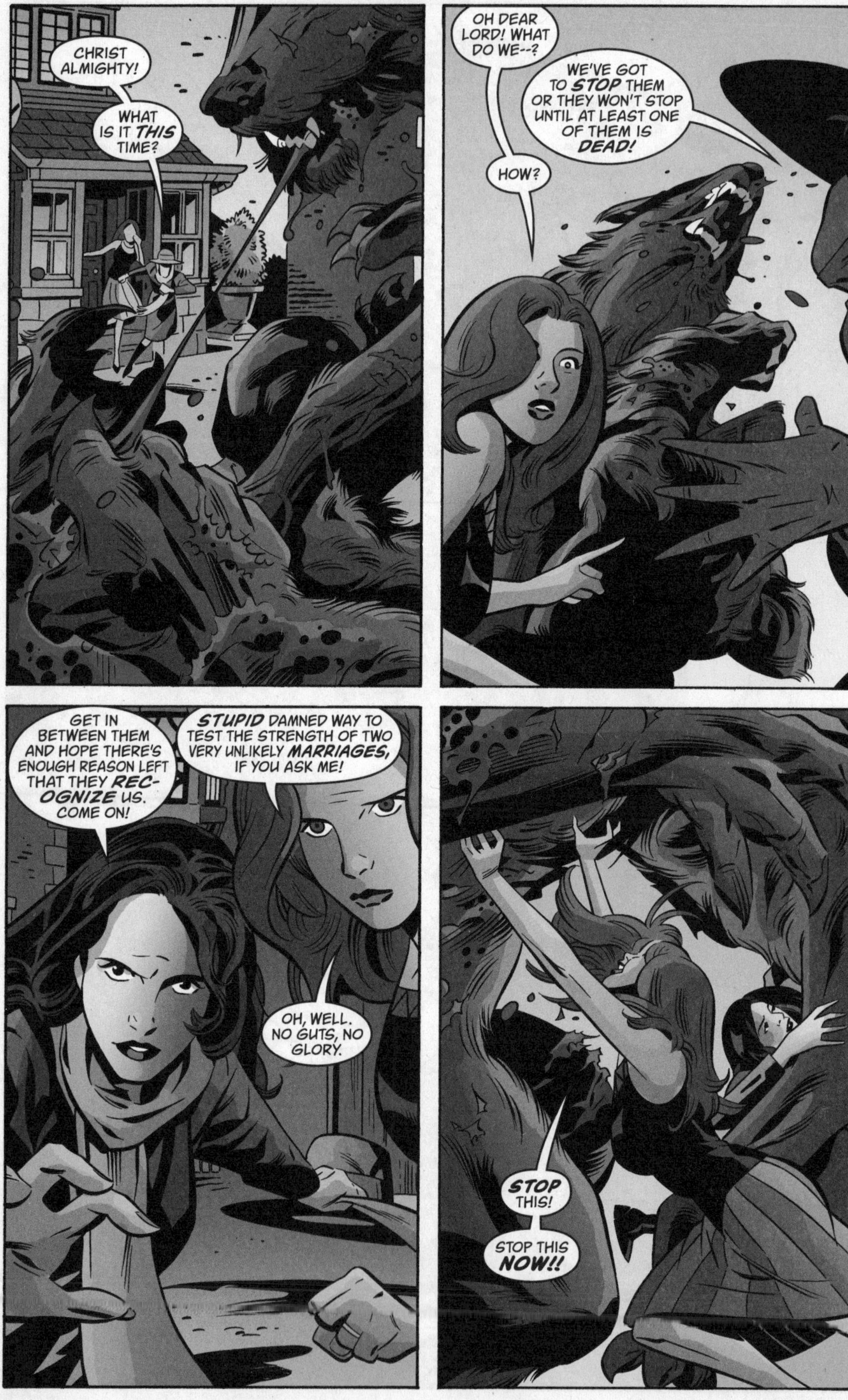
CHRIST ALMIGHTY!
WHAT IS IT THIS TIME?
OH DEAR LORD! WHAT DO WE--?
WE'VE GOT TO STOP THEM OR THEY WON'T STOP UNTIL AT LEAST ONE OF THEM IS DEAD!
HOW?
GET IN BETWEEN THEM AND HOPE THERE'S ENOUGH REASON LEFT THAT THEY RECOGNIZE US. COME ON!
STUPID DAMNED WAY TO TEST THE STRENGTH OF TWO VERY UNLIKELY MARRIAGES, IF YOU ASK ME!
OH, WELL. NO GUTS, NO GLORY.
STOP THIS!
STOP THIS NOW!!

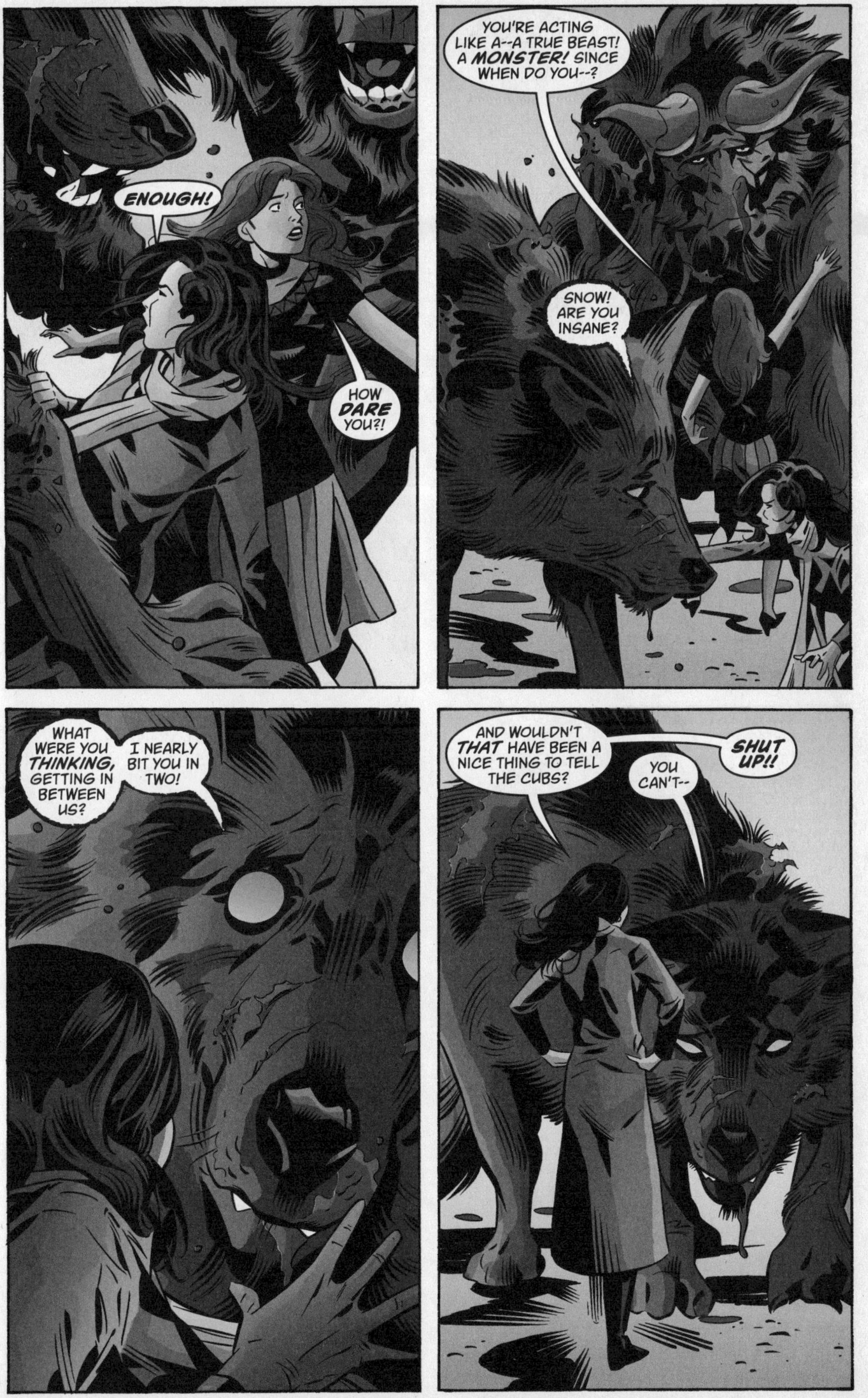
ENOUGH!
HOW DARE YOU?!
YOU'RE ACTING LIKE A--A TRUE BEAST! A MONSTER! SINCE WHEN DO YOU--?
SNOW! ARE YOU INSANE?
WHAT WERE YOU THINKING, GETTING IN BETWEEN US?
I NEARLY BIT YOU IN TWO!
AND WOULDN'T THAT HAVE BEEN A NICE THING TO TELL THE CUBS?
YOU CAN'T--
SHUT UP!!

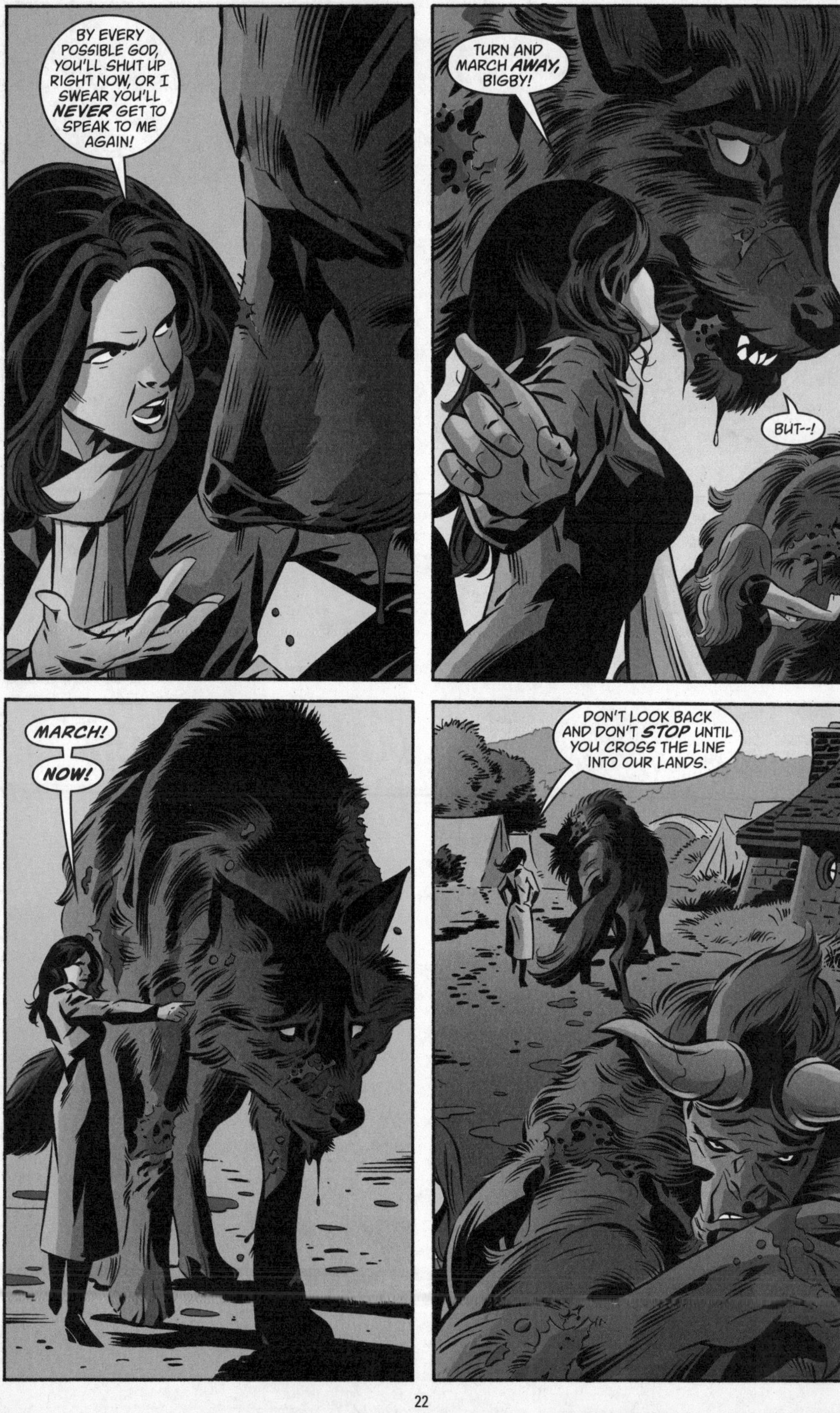
BY EVERY POSSIBLE GOD, YOU'LL SHUT UP RIGHT NOW, OR I SWEAR YOU'LL NEVER GET TO SPEAK TO ME AGAIN!
TURN AND MARCH AWAY, BIGBY!
BUT--!
MARCH!
NOW!
DON'T LOOK BACK AND DON'T STOP UNTIL YOU CROSS THE LINE INTO OUR LANDS.

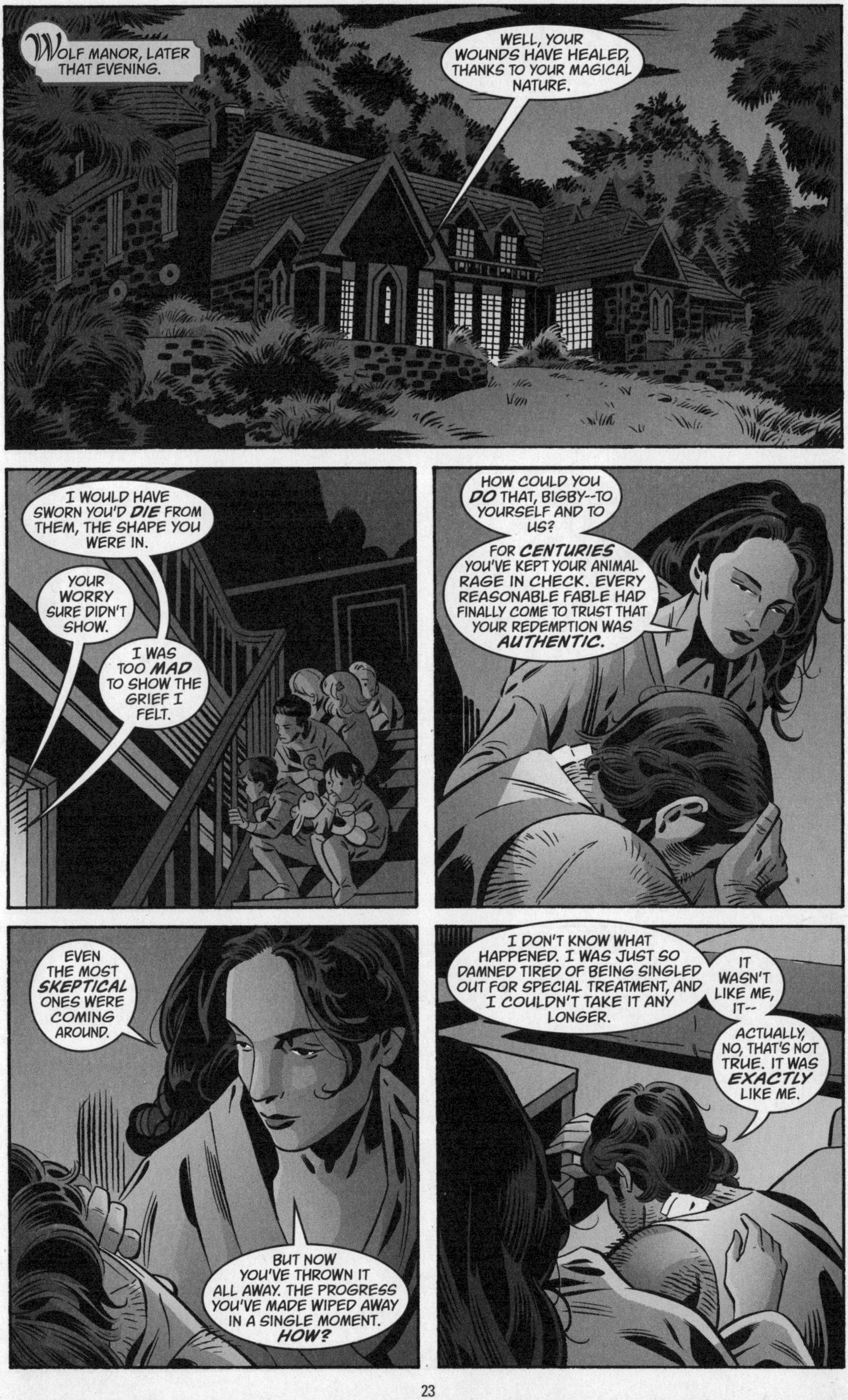
WOLF MANOR, LATER THAT EVENING.
WELL, YOUR WOUNDS HAVE HEALED, THANKS TO YOUR MAGICAL NATURE.
I WOULD HAVE SWORN YOU'D DIE FROM THEM, THE SHAPE YOU WERE IN.
YOUR WORRY SURE DIDN'T SHOW.
I WAS TOO MAD TO SHOW THE GRIEF I FELT.
HOW COULD YOU DO THAT, BIGBY--TO YOURSELF AND TO US?
FOR CENTURIES YOU'VE KEPT YOUR ANIMAL RAGE IN CHECK. EVERY REASONABLE FABLE HAD FINALLY COME TO TRUST THAT YOUR REDEMPTION WAS AUTHENTIC.
EVEN THE MOST SKEPTICAL ONES WERE COMING AROUND.
BUT NOW YOU'VE THROWN IT ALL AWAY. THE PROGRESS YOU'VE MADE WIPED AWAY IN A SINGLE MOMENT. HOW?
I DON'T KNOW WHAT HAPPENED. I WAS JUST SO DAMNED TIRED OF BEING SINGLED OUT FOR SPECIAL TREATMENT, AND I COULDN'T TAKE IT ANY LONGER.
IT WASN'T LIKE ME, IT--
ACTUALLY, NO, THAT'S NOT TRUE. IT WAS EXACTLY LIKE ME.

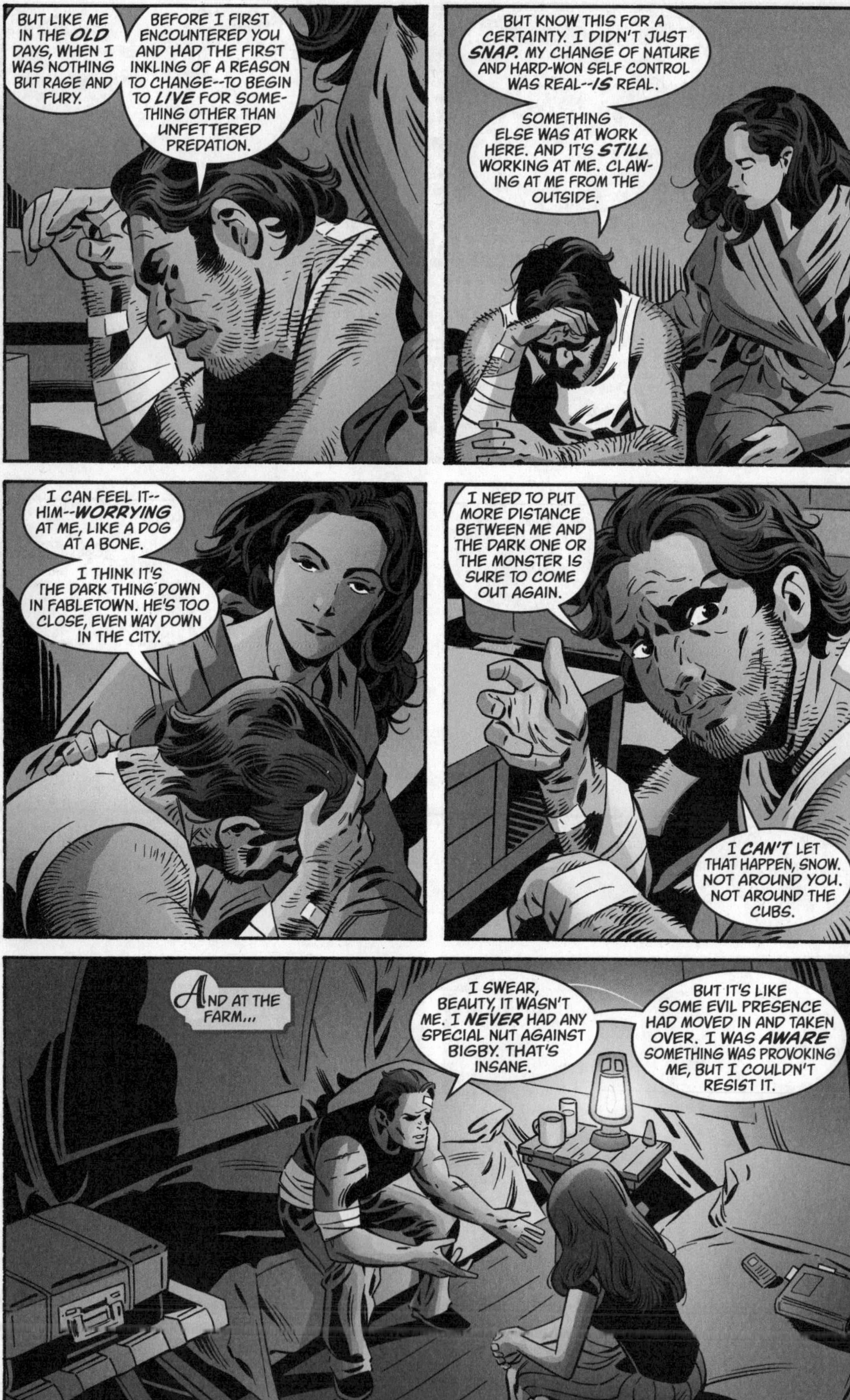

BUT LIKE ME IN THE *OLD* DAYS, WHEN I WAS NOTHING BUT RAGE AND FURY.
BEFORE I FIRST ENCOUNTERED YOU AND HAD THE FIRST INKLING OF A REASON TO CHANGE--TO BEGIN TO *LIVE* FOR SOMETHING OTHER THAN UNFETTERED PREDATION.
BUT KNOW THIS FOR A CERTAINTY. I DIDN'T JUST *SNAP.* MY CHANGE OF NATURE AND HARD-WON SELF CONTROL WAS REAL--*IS* REAL.
SOMETHING ELSE WAS AT WORK HERE. AND IT'S *STILL* WORKING AT ME. CLAWING AT ME FROM THE OUTSIDE.
I CAN FEEL IT--HIM--*WORRYING* AT ME, LIKE A DOG AT A BONE.
I THINK IT'S THE DARK THING DOWN IN FABLETOWN. HE'S TOO CLOSE, EVEN WAY DOWN IN THE CITY.
I NEED TO PUT MORE DISTANCE BETWEEN ME AND THE DARK ONE OR THE MONSTER IS SURE TO COME OUT AGAIN.
I *CAN'T* LET THAT HAPPEN, SNOW. NOT AROUND YOU. NOT AROUND THE CUBS.
AND AT THE FARM...
I SWEAR, BEAUTY, IT WASN'T ME. I *NEVER* HAD ANY SPECIAL NUT AGAINST BIGBY. THAT'S INSANE.
BUT IT'S LIKE SOME EVIL PRESENCE HAD MOVED IN AND TAKEN OVER. I WAS *AWARE* SOMETHING WAS PROVOKING ME, BUT I COULDN'T RESIST IT.

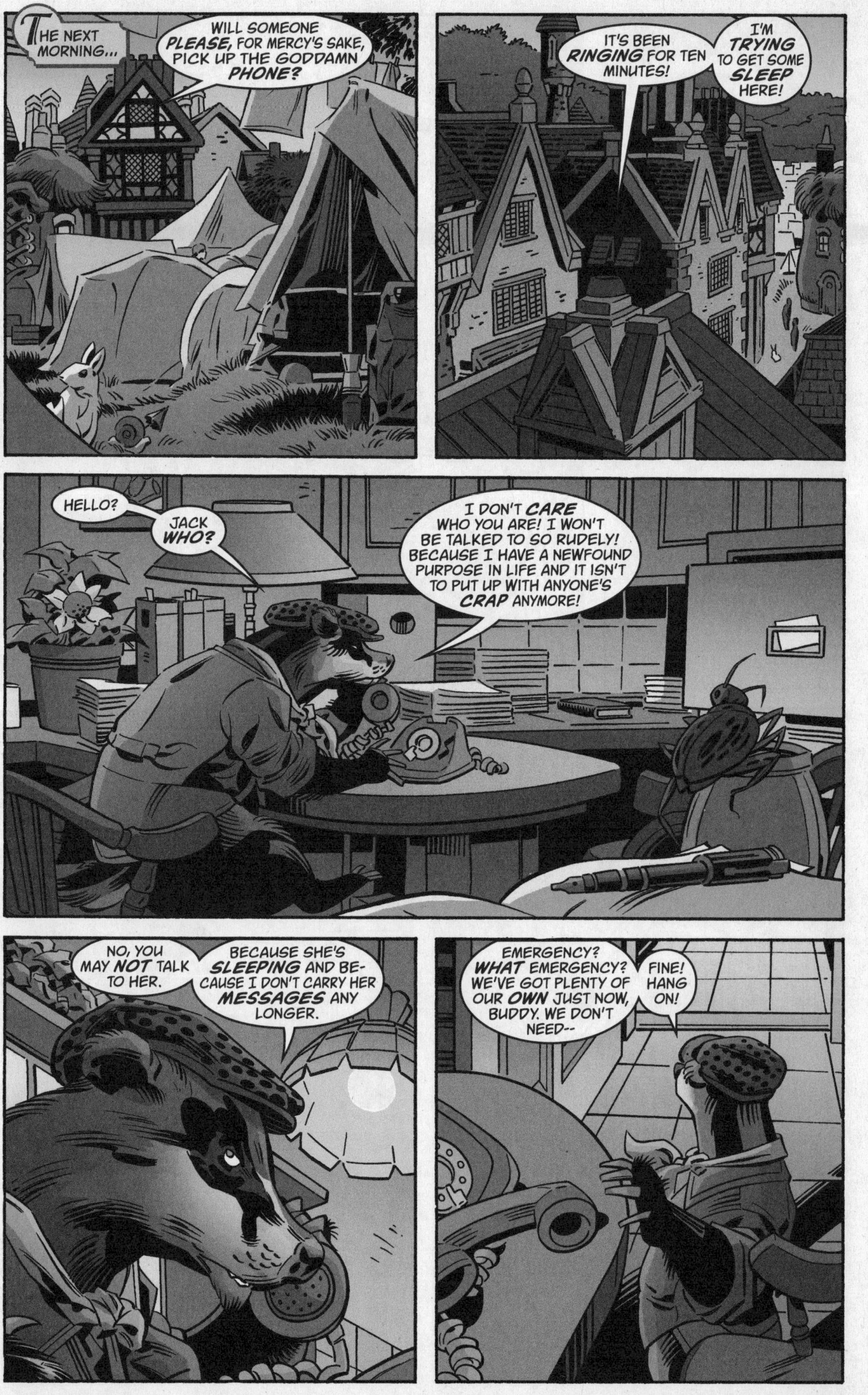

THE NEXT MORNING...
WILL SOMEONE PLEASE, FOR MERCY'S SAKE, PICK UP THE GODDAMN PHONE?
IT'S BEEN RINGING FOR TEN MINUTES!
I'M TRYING TO GET SOME SLEEP HERE!
HELLO?
JACK WHO?
I DON'T CARE WHO YOU ARE! I WON'T BE TALKED TO SO RUDELY! BECAUSE I HAVE A NEWFOUND PURPOSE IN LIFE AND IT ISN'T TO PUT UP WITH ANYONE'S CRAP ANYMORE!
NO, YOU MAY NOT TALK TO HER.
BECAUSE SHE'S SLEEPING AND BECAUSE I DON'T CARRY HER MESSAGES ANY LONGER.
EMERGENCY? WHAT EMERGENCY? WE'VE GOT PLENTY OF OUR OWN JUST NOW, BUDDY. WE DON'T NEED--
FINE! HANG ON!

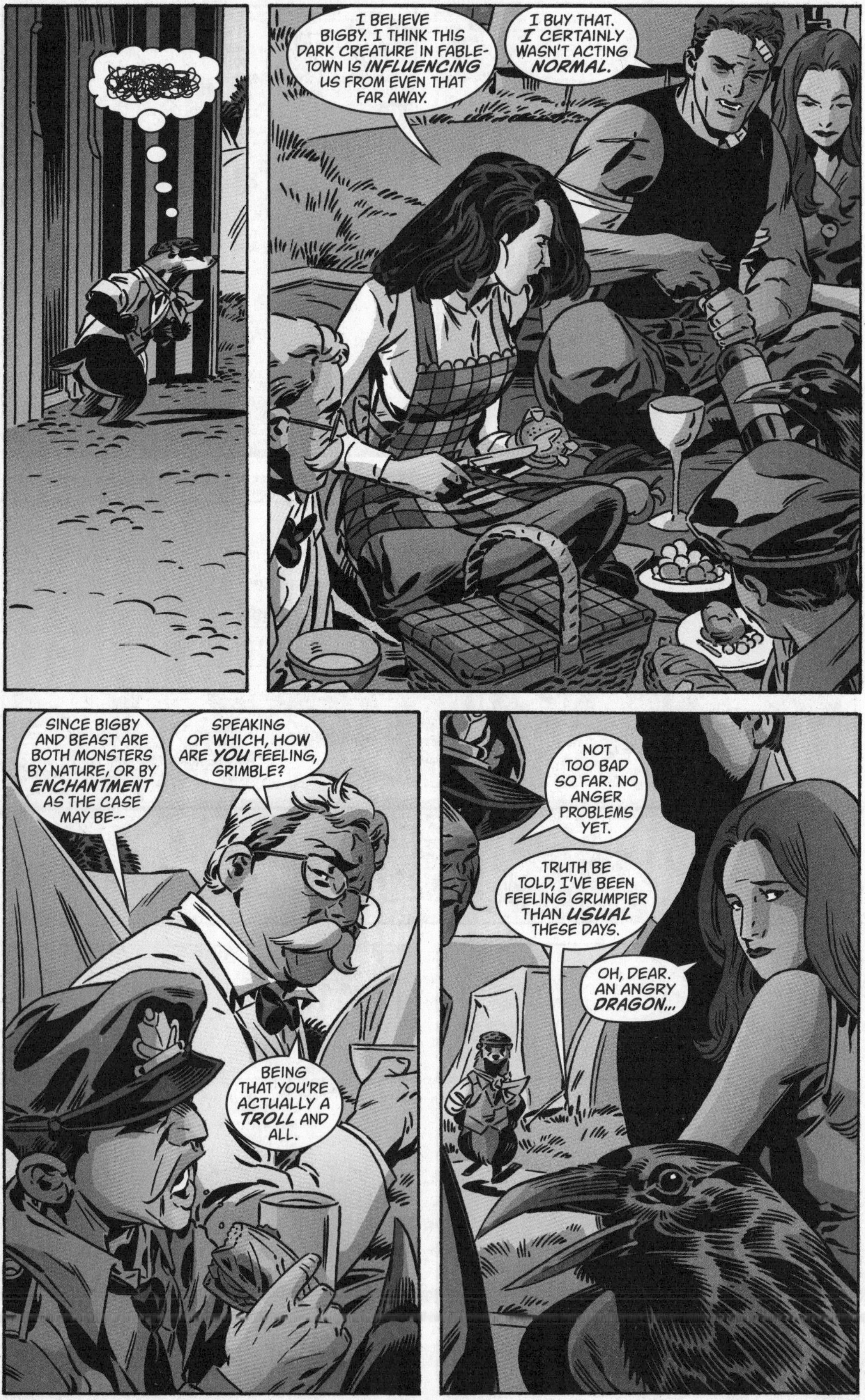
I BELIEVE BIGBY. I THINK THIS DARK CREATURE IN FABLE-TOWN IS *INFLUENCING* US FROM EVEN THAT FAR AWAY.
I BUY THAT. *I* CERTAINLY WASN'T ACTING *NORMAL.*
SINCE BIGBY AND BEAST ARE BOTH MONSTERS BY NATURE, OR BY *ENCHANTMENT* AS THE CASE MAY BE--
SPEAKING OF WHICH, HOW ARE *YOU* FEELING, GRIMBLE?
BEING THAT YOU'RE ACTUALLY A *TROLL* AND ALL.
NOT TOO BAD SO FAR. NO ANGER PROBLEMS YET.
TRUTH BE TOLD, I'VE BEEN FEELING GRUMPIER THAN *USUAL* THESE DAYS.
OH, DEAR. AN ANGRY *DRAGON...*

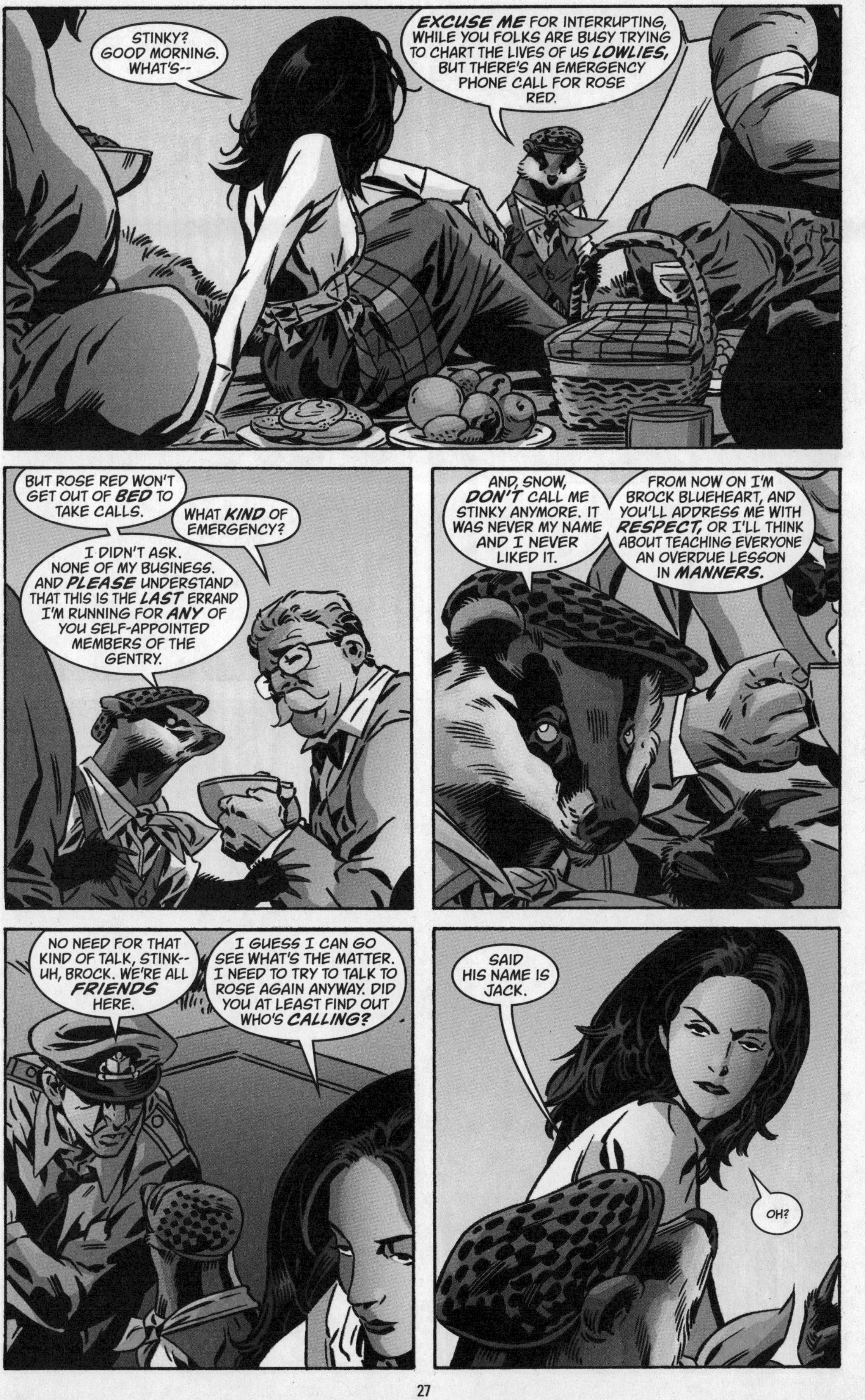
STINKY? GOOD MORNING. WHAT'S--
EXCUSE ME FOR INTERRUPTING, WHILE YOU FOLKS ARE BUSY TRYING TO CHART THE LIVES OF US LOWLIES, BUT THERE'S AN EMERGENCY PHONE CALL FOR ROSE RED.
BUT ROSE RED WON'T GET OUT OF BED TO TAKE CALLS.
WHAT KIND OF EMERGENCY?
I DIDN'T ASK. NONE OF MY BUSINESS. AND PLEASE UNDERSTAND THAT THIS IS THE LAST ERRAND I'M RUNNING FOR ANY OF YOU SELF-APPOINTED MEMBERS OF THE GENTRY.
AND, SNOW, DON'T CALL ME STINKY ANYMORE. IT WAS NEVER MY NAME AND I NEVER LIKED IT.
FROM NOW ON I'M BROCK BLUEHEART, AND YOU'LL ADDRESS ME WITH RESPECT, OR I'LL THINK ABOUT TEACHING EVERYONE AN OVERDUE LESSON IN MANNERS.
NO NEED FOR THAT KIND OF TALK, STINK-- UH, BROCK. WE'RE ALL FRIENDS HERE.
I GUESS I CAN GO SEE WHAT'S THE MATTER. I NEED TO TRY TO TALK TO ROSE AGAIN ANYWAY. DID YOU AT LEAST FIND OUT WHO'S CALLING?
SAID HIS NAME IS JACK.
OH?

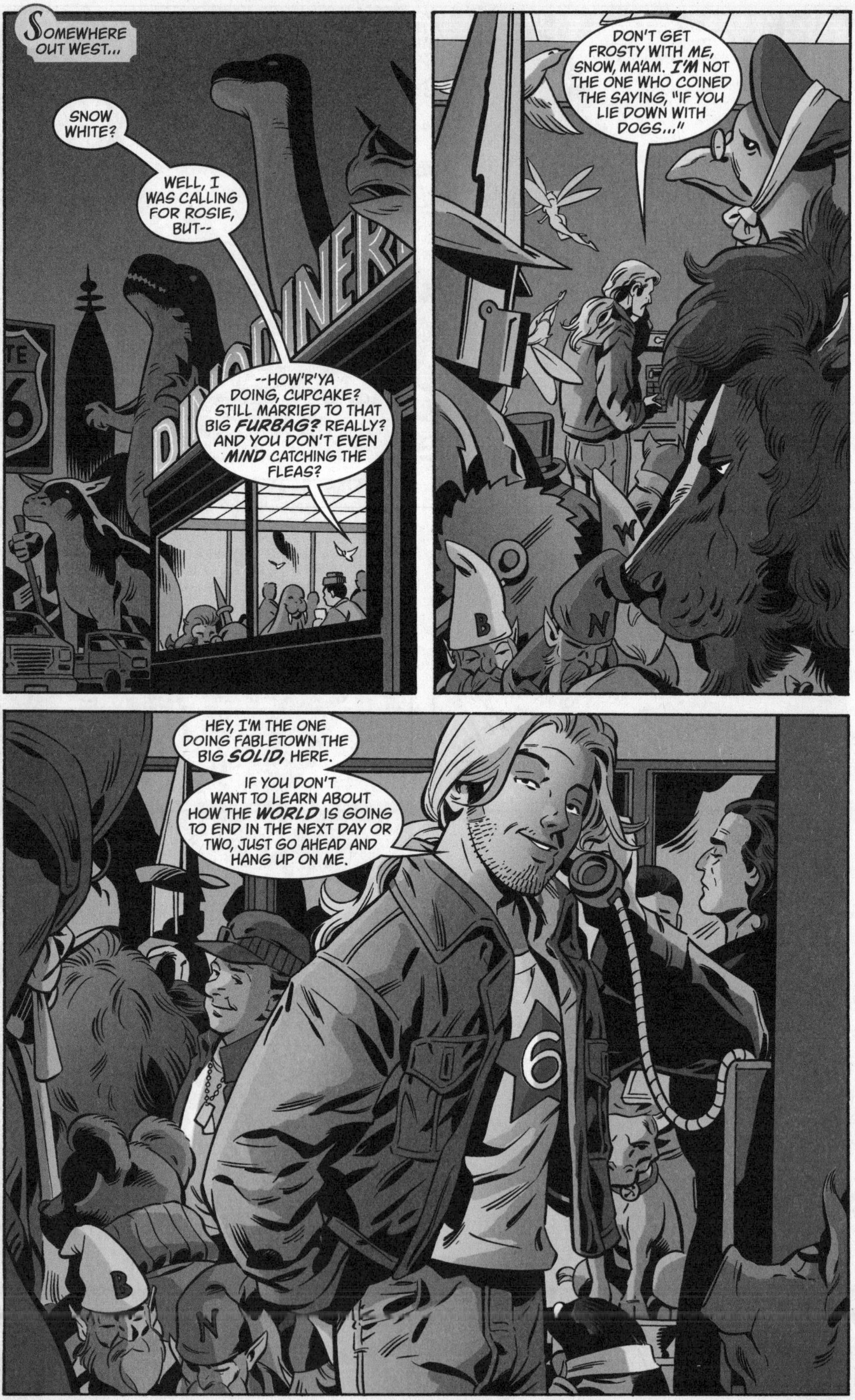
SOMEWHERE OUT WEST...
SNOW WHITE?
WELL, I WAS CALLING FOR ROSIE, BUT--
--HOW'R'YA DOING, CUPCAKE? STILL MARRIED TO THAT BIG FURBAG? REALLY? AND YOU DON'T EVEN MIND CATCHING THE FLEAS?
DINO DINER
DON'T GET FROSTY WITH ME, SNOW, MA'AM. I'M NOT THE ONE WHO COINED THE SAYING, "IF YOU LIE DOWN WITH DOGS..."
HEY, I'M THE ONE DOING FABLETOWN THE BIG SOLID, HERE.
IF YOU DON'T WANT TO LEARN ABOUT HOW THE WORLD IS GOING TO END IN THE NEXT DAY OR TWO, JUST GO AHEAD AND HANG UP ON ME.

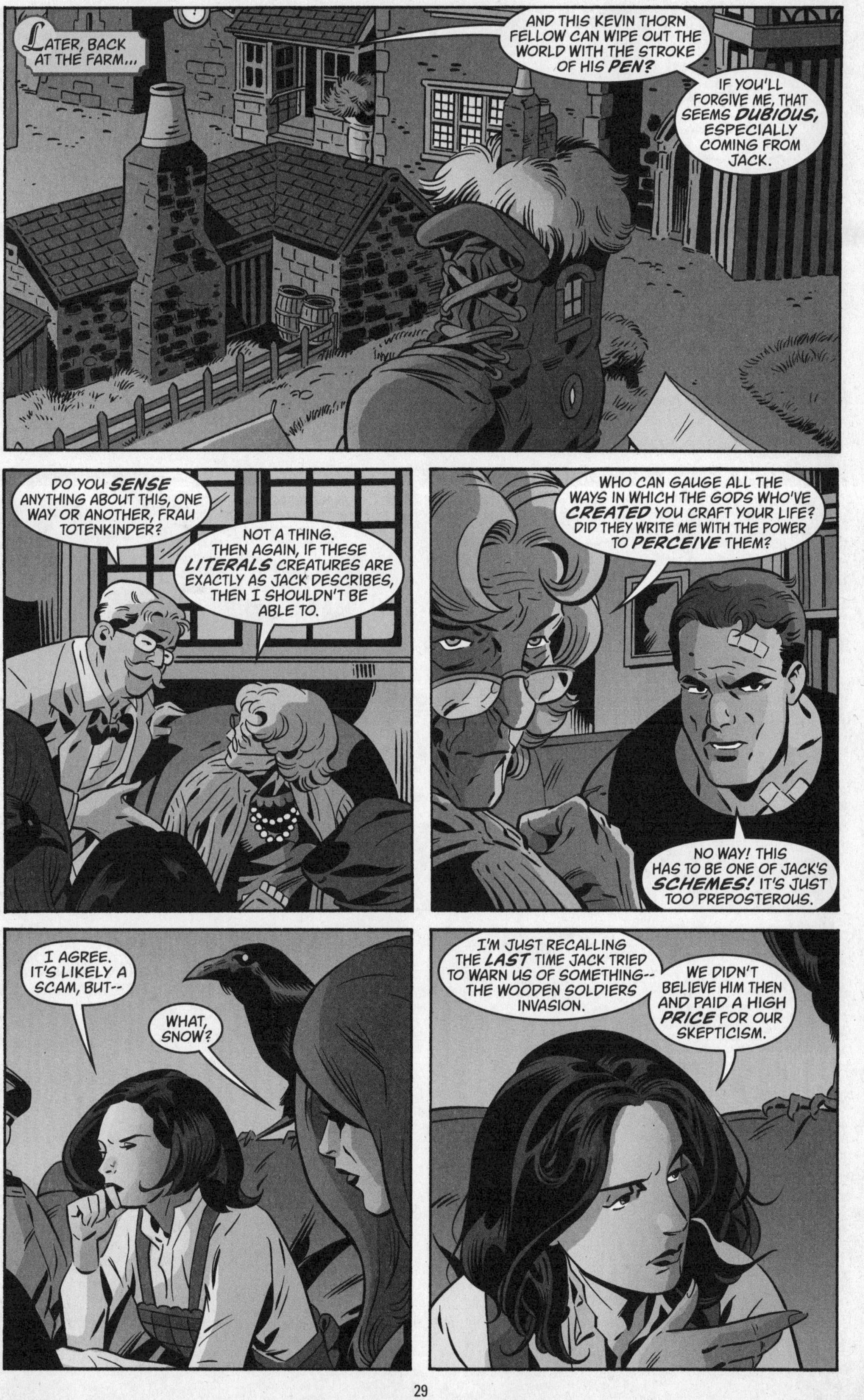
LATER, BACK AT THE FARM...
AND THIS KEVIN THORN FELLOW CAN WIPE OUT THE WORLD WITH THE STROKE OF HIS PEN?
IF YOU'LL FORGIVE ME, THAT SEEMS DUBIOUS, ESPECIALLY COMING FROM JACK.
DO YOU SENSE ANYTHING ABOUT THIS, ONE WAY OR ANOTHER, FRAU TOTENKINDER?
NOT A THING. THEN AGAIN, IF THESE LITERALS CREATURES ARE EXACTLY AS JACK DESCRIBES, THEN I SHOULDN'T BE ABLE TO.
WHO CAN GAUGE ALL THE WAYS IN WHICH THE GODS WHO'VE CREATED YOU CRAFT YOUR LIFE? DID THEY WRITE ME WITH THE POWER TO PERCEIVE THEM?
NO WAY! THIS HAS TO BE ONE OF JACK'S SCHEMES! IT'S JUST TOO PREPOSTEROUS.
I AGREE. IT'S LIKELY A SCAM, BUT--
WHAT, SNOW?
I'M JUST RECALLING THE LAST TIME JACK TRIED TO WARN US OF SOMETHING-- THE WOODEN SOLDIERS INVASION.
WE DIDN'T BELIEVE HIM THEN AND PAID A HIGH PRICE FOR OUR SKEPTICISM.

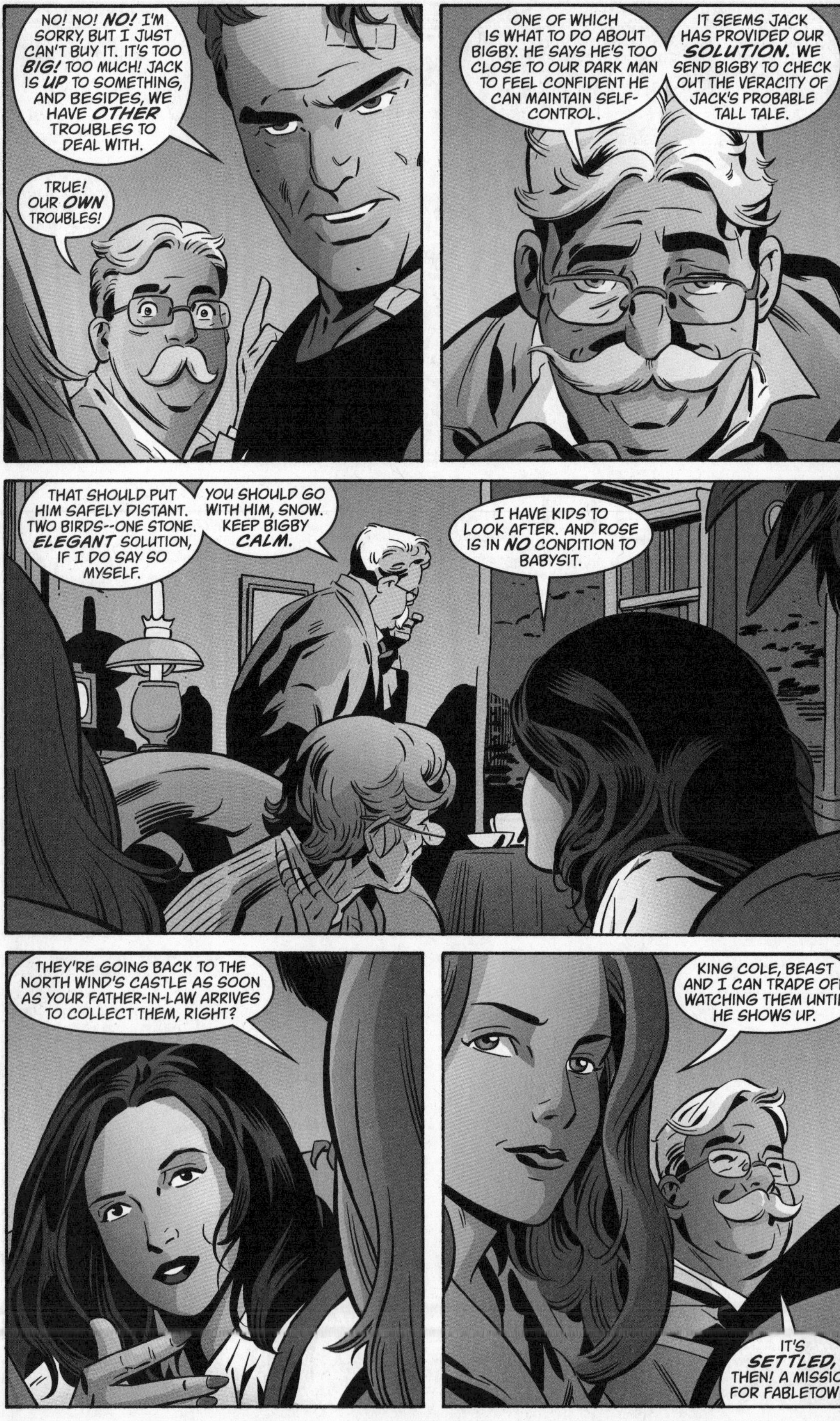
NO! NO! NO! I'M SORRY, BUT I JUST CAN'T BUY IT. IT'S TOO BIG! TOO MUCH! JACK IS UP TO SOMETHING, AND BESIDES, WE HAVE OTHER TROUBLES TO DEAL WITH.
TRUE! OUR OWN TROUBLES!
ONE OF WHICH IS WHAT TO DO ABOUT BIGBY. HE SAYS HE'S TOO CLOSE TO OUR DARK MAN TO FEEL CONFIDENT HE CAN MAINTAIN SELF-CONTROL.
IT SEEMS JACK HAS PROVIDED OUR SOLUTION. WE SEND BIGBY TO CHECK OUT THE VERACITY OF JACK'S PROBABLE TALL TALE.
THAT SHOULD PUT HIM SAFELY DISTANT. TWO BIRDS--ONE STONE. ELEGANT SOLUTION, IF I DO SAY SO MYSELF.
YOU SHOULD GO WITH HIM, SNOW. KEEP BIGBY CALM.
I HAVE KIDS TO LOOK AFTER. AND ROSE IS IN NO CONDITION TO BABYSIT.
THEY'RE GOING BACK TO THE NORTH WIND'S CASTLE AS SOON AS YOUR FATHER-IN-LAW ARRIVES TO COLLECT THEM, RIGHT?
KING COLE, BEAST AND I CAN TRADE OFF WATCHING THEM UNTIL HE SHOWS UP.
IT'S SETTLED, THEN! A MISSION FOR FABLETOWN!

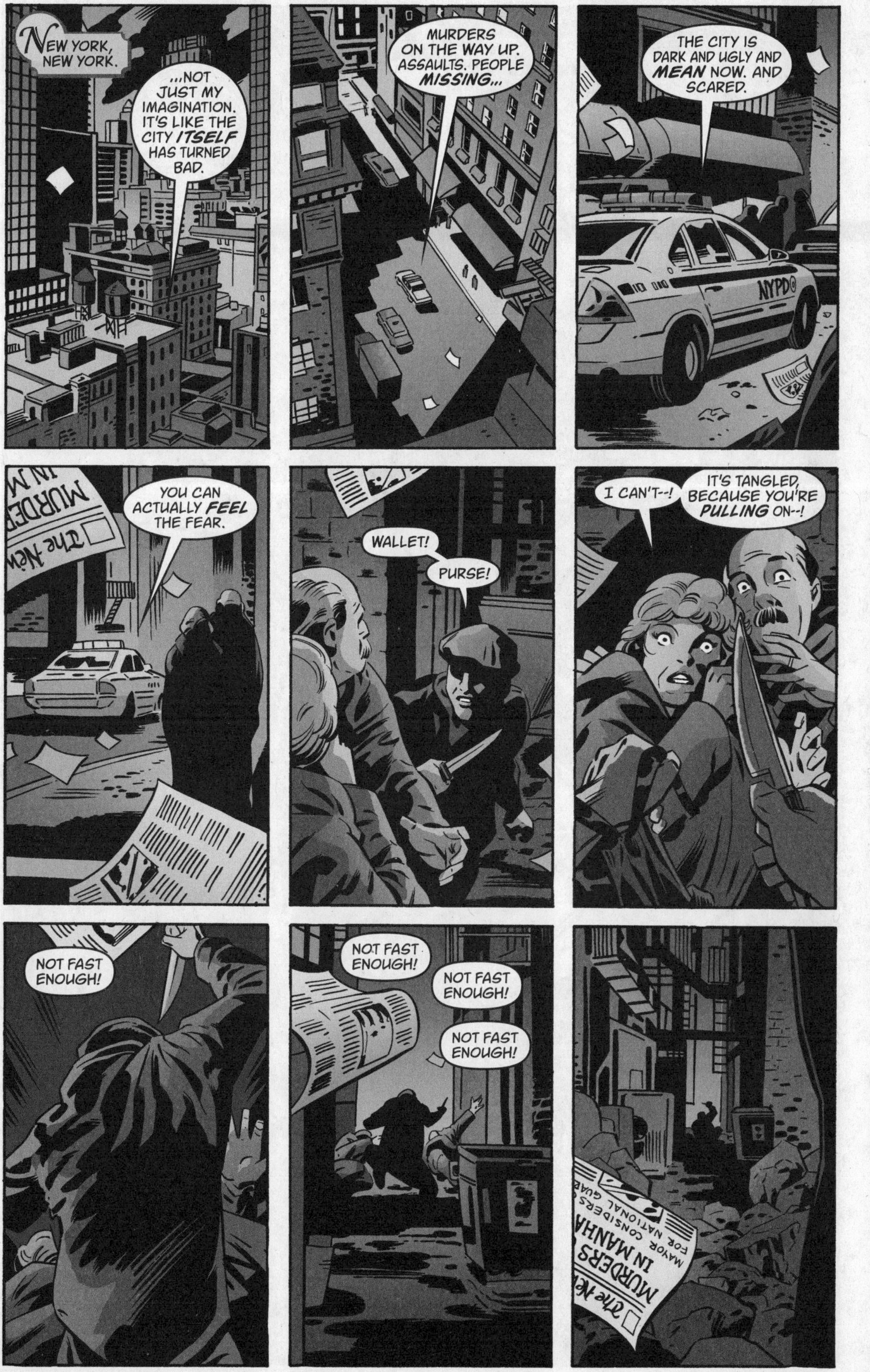
NEW YORK, NEW YORK.
...NOT JUST MY IMAGINATION. IT'S LIKE THE CITY ITSELF HAS TURNED BAD.
MURDERS ON THE WAY UP. ASSAULTS. PEOPLE MISSING...
THE CITY IS DARK AND UGLY AND MEAN NOW. AND SCARED.
YOU CAN ACTUALLY FEEL THE FEAR.
WALLET!
PURSE!
I CAN'T--!
IT'S TANGLED, BECAUSE YOU'RE PULLING ON--!
NOT FAST ENOUGH!
NOT FAST ENOUGH!
NOT FAST ENOUGH!
NOT FAST ENOUGH!
NYPD

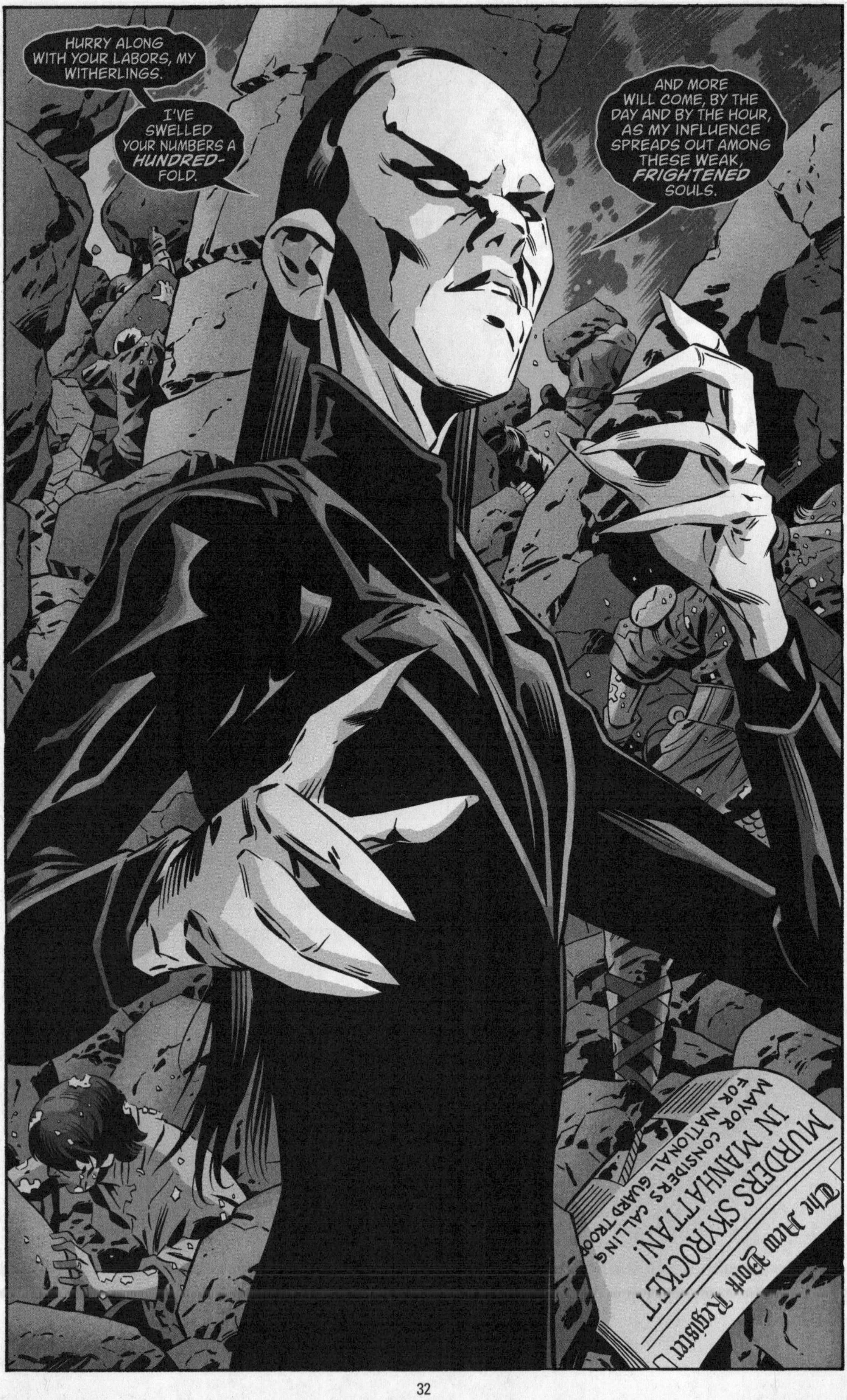
HURRY ALONG WITH YOUR LABORS, MY WITHERLINGS.
I'VE SWELLED YOUR NUMBERS A HUNDRED-FOLD.
AND MORE WILL COME, BY THE DAY AND BY THE HOUR, AS MY INFLUENCE SPREADS OUT AMONG THESE WEAK, FRIGHTENED SOULS.
The New York Register
MURDERS SKYROCKET IN MANHATTAN!
MAYOR CONSIDERS CALLING FOR NATIONAL GUARD TROOP

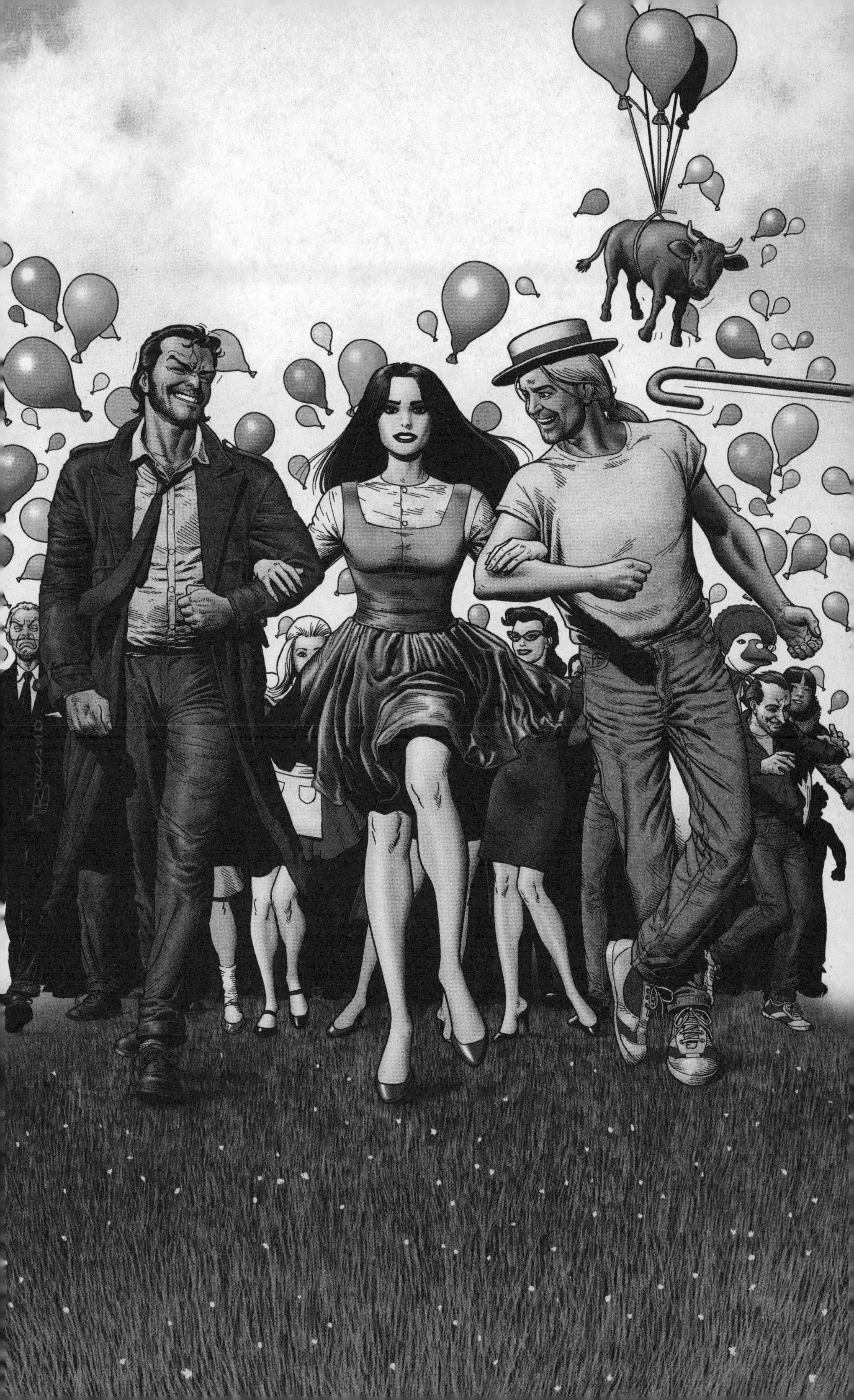

*"Just who are the Literals and which one
might decide to rewrite the universe?"*

The Great FABLES Crossover part 2 of 9

SOMEWHERE ALONG HISTORIC ROUTE 66...
ROUTE 66
DINO DINER
AND I'M TELLING YOU, QUIT CALLING ME HALF-BREED!
BUT IT'S AN ACCURATE TERM, JACK, AND NOT MEANT IN A DEROGATORY SENSE. YOU ARE HALF FABLE AND HALF LITERAL.
I BELIEVE THE TERM JACK WOULD PREFER IS "MONGREL."

SWAP MEET

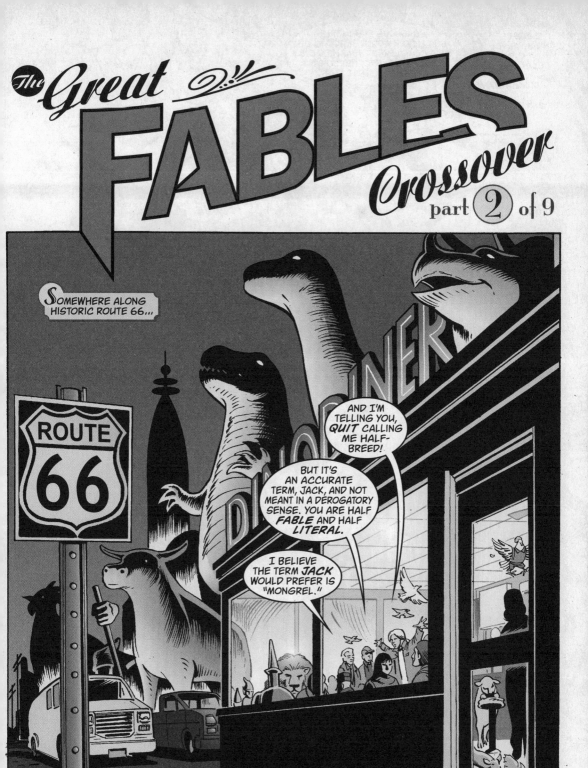

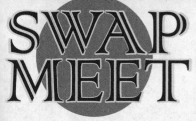

The Story So Far... So I finally got around to cluing in those pea-brains in Fabletown about the existence of the Literals, and do I get so much as a thank you? So much as a by-your-leave? Fat chance. Instead they turn around and spend the rest of the issue talking about a bunch of stuff that has nothing whatsoever to do with the Big Fables Crossover—which is fitting, since it should have been called the Big Jack Crossover to begin with. But what do you expect from a bunch of rank amateurs?

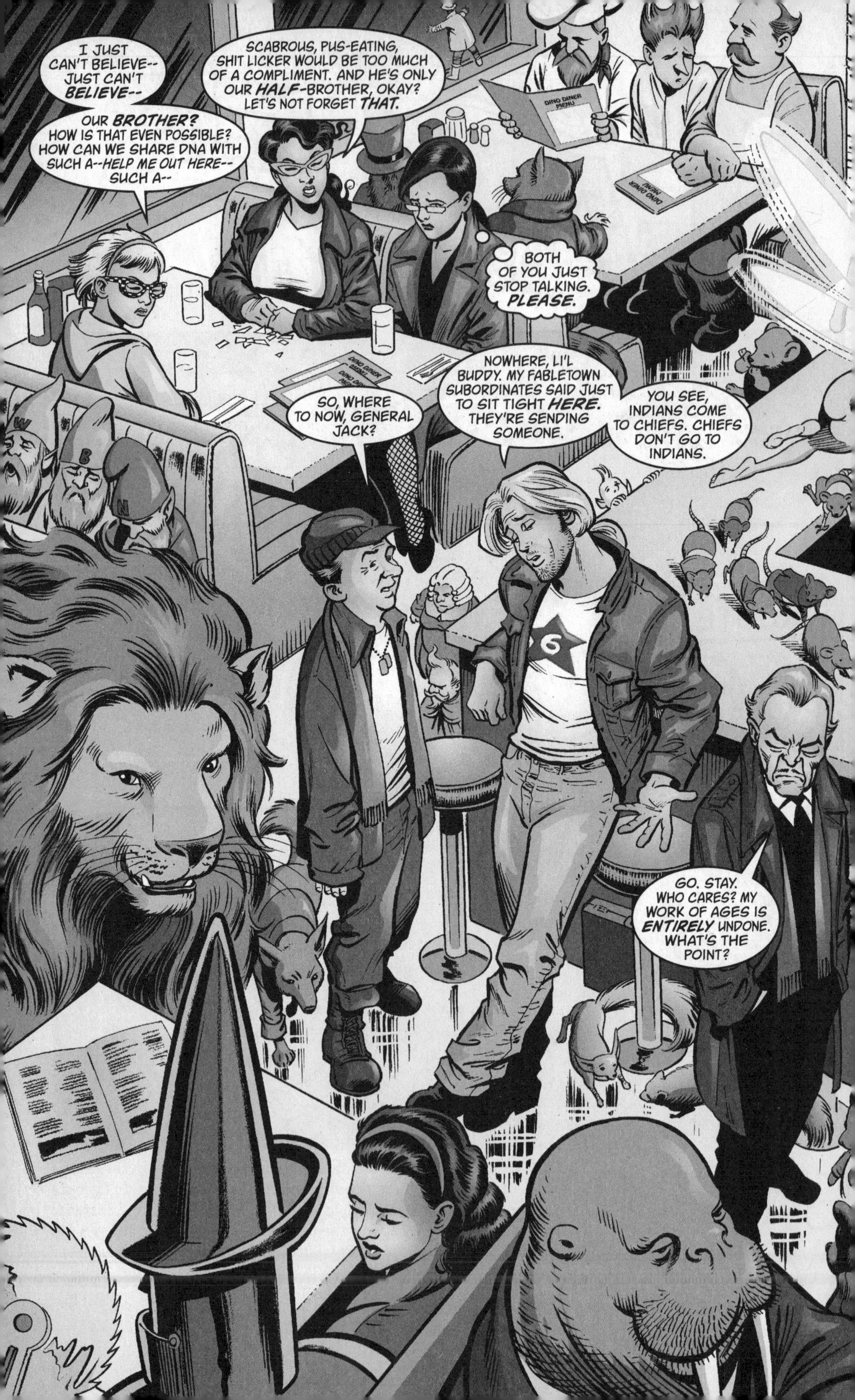
I JUST CAN'T BELIEVE-- JUST CAN'T BELIEVE--
SCABROUS, PUS-EATING, SHIT LICKER WOULD BE TOO MUCH OF A COMPLIMENT. AND HE'S ONLY OUR HALF-BROTHER, OKAY? LET'S NOT FORGET THAT.
OUR BROTHER? HOW IS THAT EVEN POSSIBLE? HOW CAN WE SHARE DNA WITH SUCH A--HELP ME OUT HERE-- SUCH A--
BOTH OF YOU JUST STOP TALKING. PLEASE.
DINO DINER MENU
SO, WHERE TO NOW, GENERAL JACK?
NOWHERE, LI'L BUDDY. MY FABLETOWN SUBORDINATES SAID JUST TO SIT TIGHT HERE. THEY'RE SENDING SOMEONE.
YOU SEE, INDIANS COME TO CHIEFS. CHIEFS DON'T GO TO INDIANS.
GO. STAY. WHO CARES? MY WORK OF AGES IS ENTIRELY UNDONE. WHAT'S THE POINT?

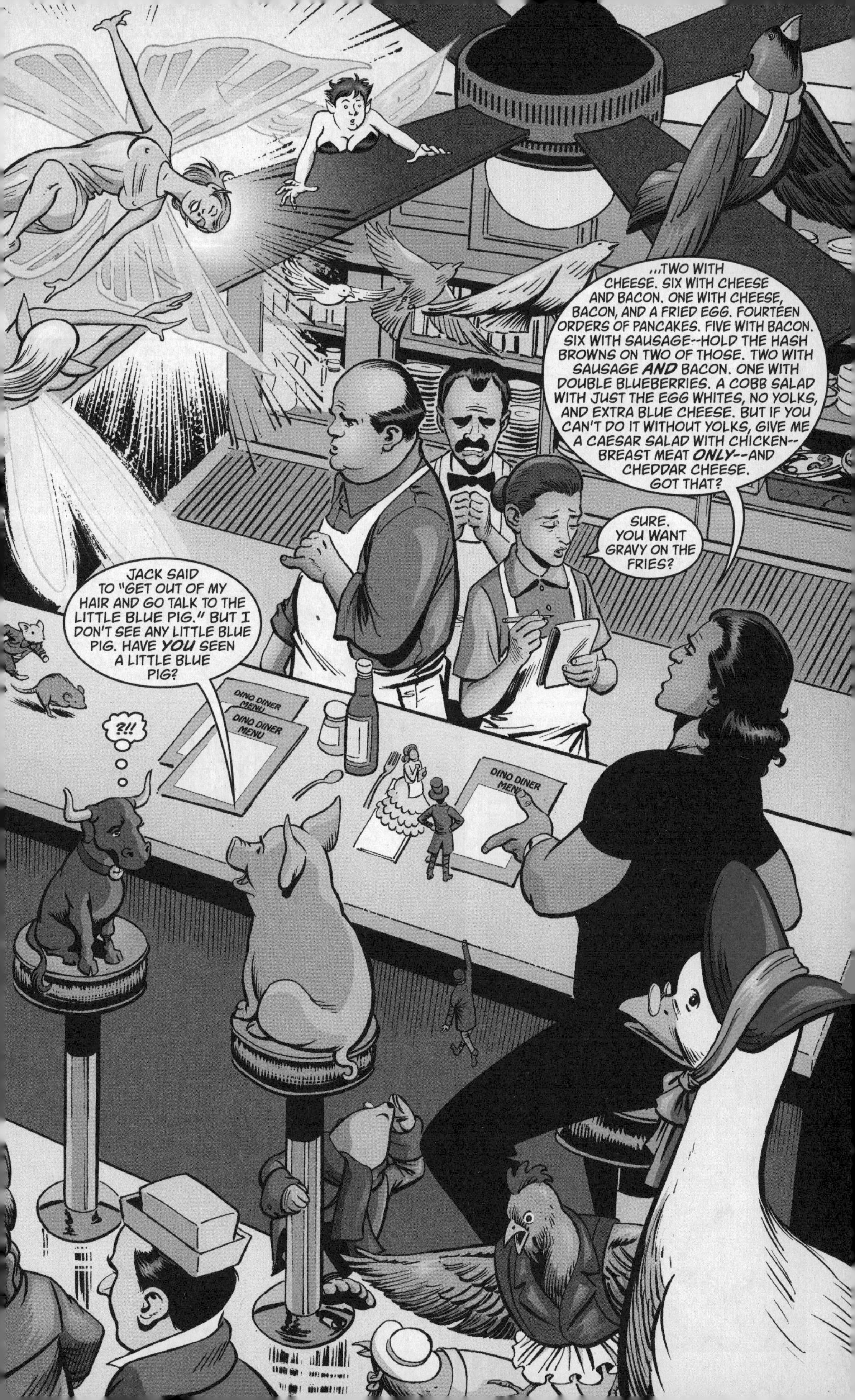
...TWO WITH CHEESE. SIX WITH CHEESE AND BACON. ONE WITH CHEESE, BACON, AND A FRIED EGG. FOURTEEN ORDERS OF PANCAKES. FIVE WITH BACON. SIX WITH SAUSAGE--HOLD THE HASH BROWNS ON TWO OF THOSE. TWO WITH SAUSAGE *AND* BACON. ONE WITH DOUBLE BLUEBERRIES. A COBB SALAD WITH JUST THE EGG WHITES, NO YOLKS, AND EXTRA BLUE CHEESE. BUT IF YOU CAN'T DO IT WITHOUT YOLKS, GIVE ME A CAESAR SALAD WITH CHICKEN--BREAST MEAT *ONLY*--AND CHEDDAR CHEESE. GOT THAT?
SURE. YOU WANT GRAVY ON THE FRIES?
JACK SAID TO "GET OUT OF MY HAIR AND GO TALK TO THE LITTLE BLUE PIG." BUT I DON'T SEE ANY LITTLE BLUE PIG. HAVE *YOU* SEEN A LITTLE BLUE PIG?
?!!
DINO DINER MENU
DINO DINER MENU
DINO DINER MENU

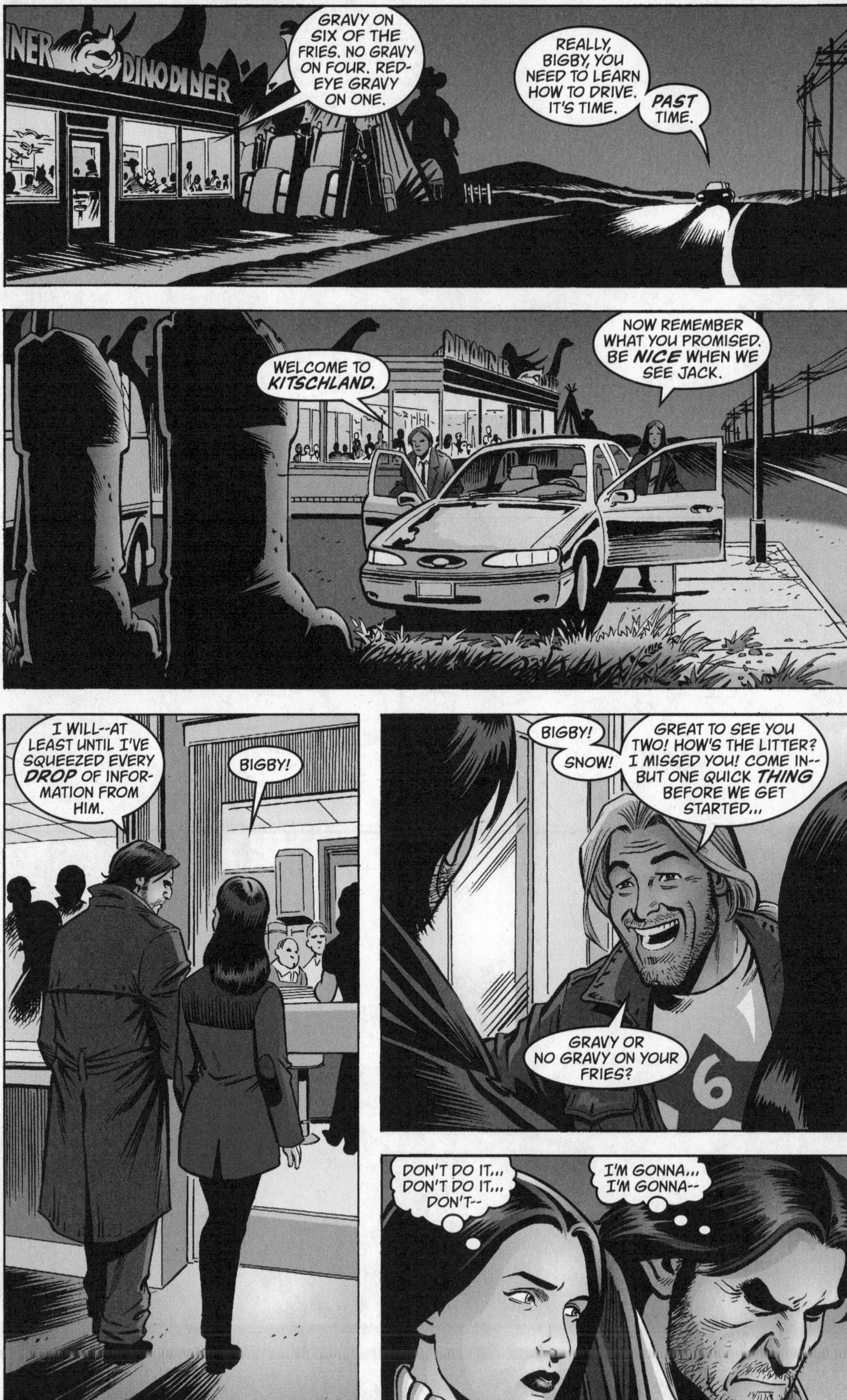
GRAVY ON SIX OF THE FRIES. NO GRAVY ON FOUR. RED-EYE GRAVY ON ONE.
REALLY, BIGBY, YOU NEED TO LEARN HOW TO DRIVE. IT'S TIME.
PAST TIME.
DINO DINER
WELCOME TO KITSCHLAND.
NOW REMEMBER WHAT YOU PROMISED. BE NICE WHEN WE SEE JACK.
I WILL--AT LEAST UNTIL I'VE SQUEEZED EVERY DROP OF INFORMATION FROM HIM.
BIGBY!
BIGBY!
SNOW!
GREAT TO SEE YOU TWO! HOW'S THE LITTER? I MISSED YOU! COME IN--BUT ONE QUICK THING BEFORE WE GET STARTED...
GRAVY OR NO GRAVY ON YOUR FRIES?
DON'T DO IT... DON'T DO IT... DON'T--
I'M GONNA... I'M GONNA--

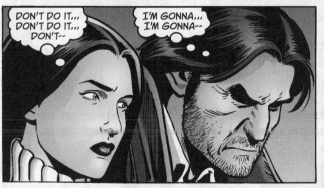

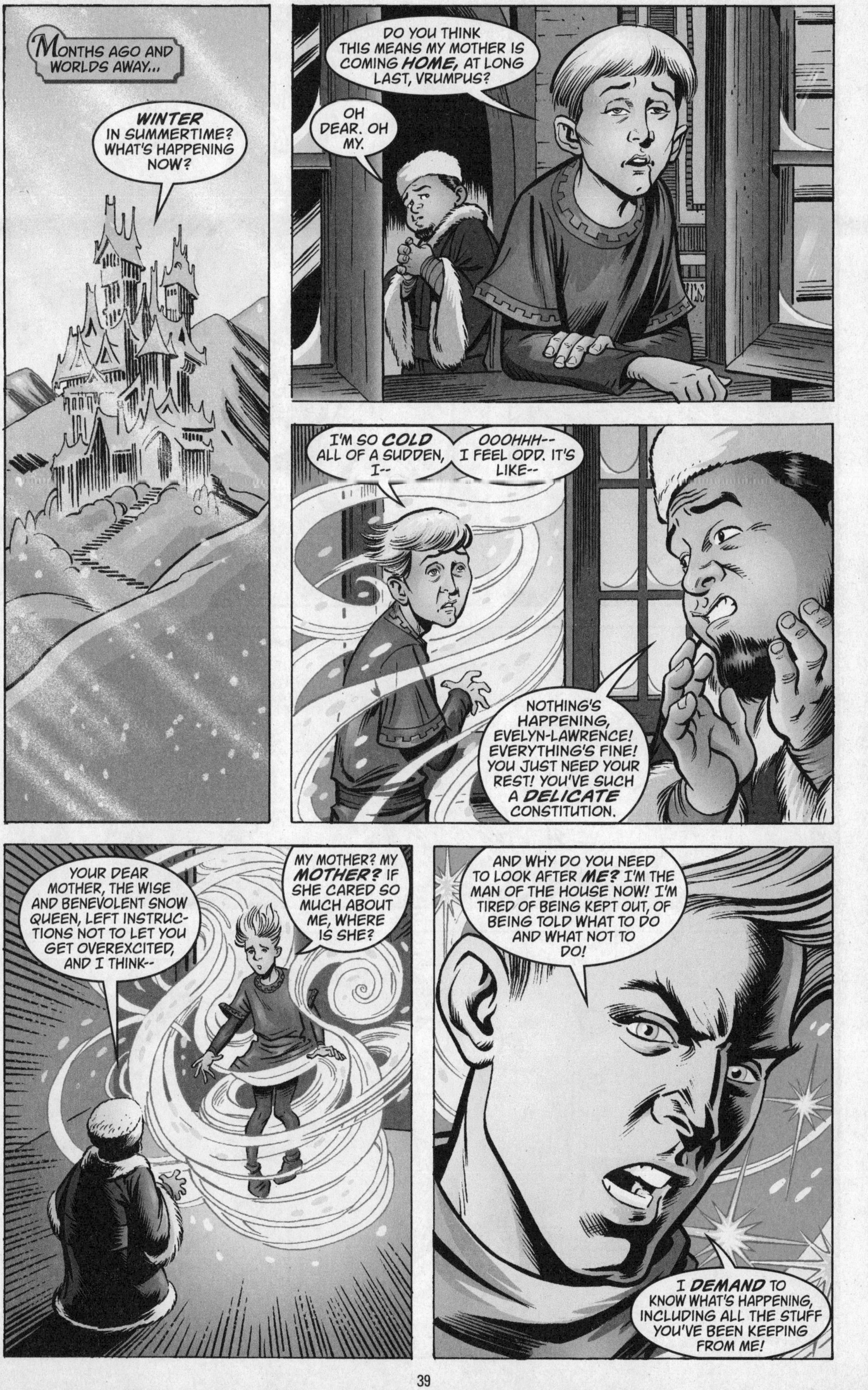
MONTHS AGO AND WORLDS AWAY...
WINTER IN SUMMERTIME? WHAT'S HAPPENING NOW?
DO YOU THINK THIS MEANS MY MOTHER IS COMING HOME, AT LONG LAST, VRUMPUS?
OH DEAR. OH MY.
I'M SO COLD ALL OF A SUDDEN, I--
OOOHHH-- I FEEL ODD. IT'S LIKE--
NOTHING'S HAPPENING, EVELYN-LAWRENCE! EVERYTHING'S FINE! YOU JUST NEED YOUR REST! YOU'VE SUCH A DELICATE CONSTITUTION.
YOUR DEAR MOTHER, THE WISE AND BENEVOLENT SNOW QUEEN, LEFT INSTRUCTIONS NOT TO LET YOU GET OVEREXCITED, AND I THINK--
MY MOTHER? MY MOTHER? IF SHE CARED SO MUCH ABOUT ME, WHERE IS SHE?
AND WHY DO YOU NEED TO LOOK AFTER ME? I'M THE MAN OF THE HOUSE NOW! I'M TIRED OF BEING KEPT OUT, OF BEING TOLD WHAT TO DO AND WHAT NOT TO DO!
I DEMAND TO KNOW WHAT'S HAPPENING, INCLUDING ALL THE STUFF YOU'VE BEEN KEEPING FROM ME!

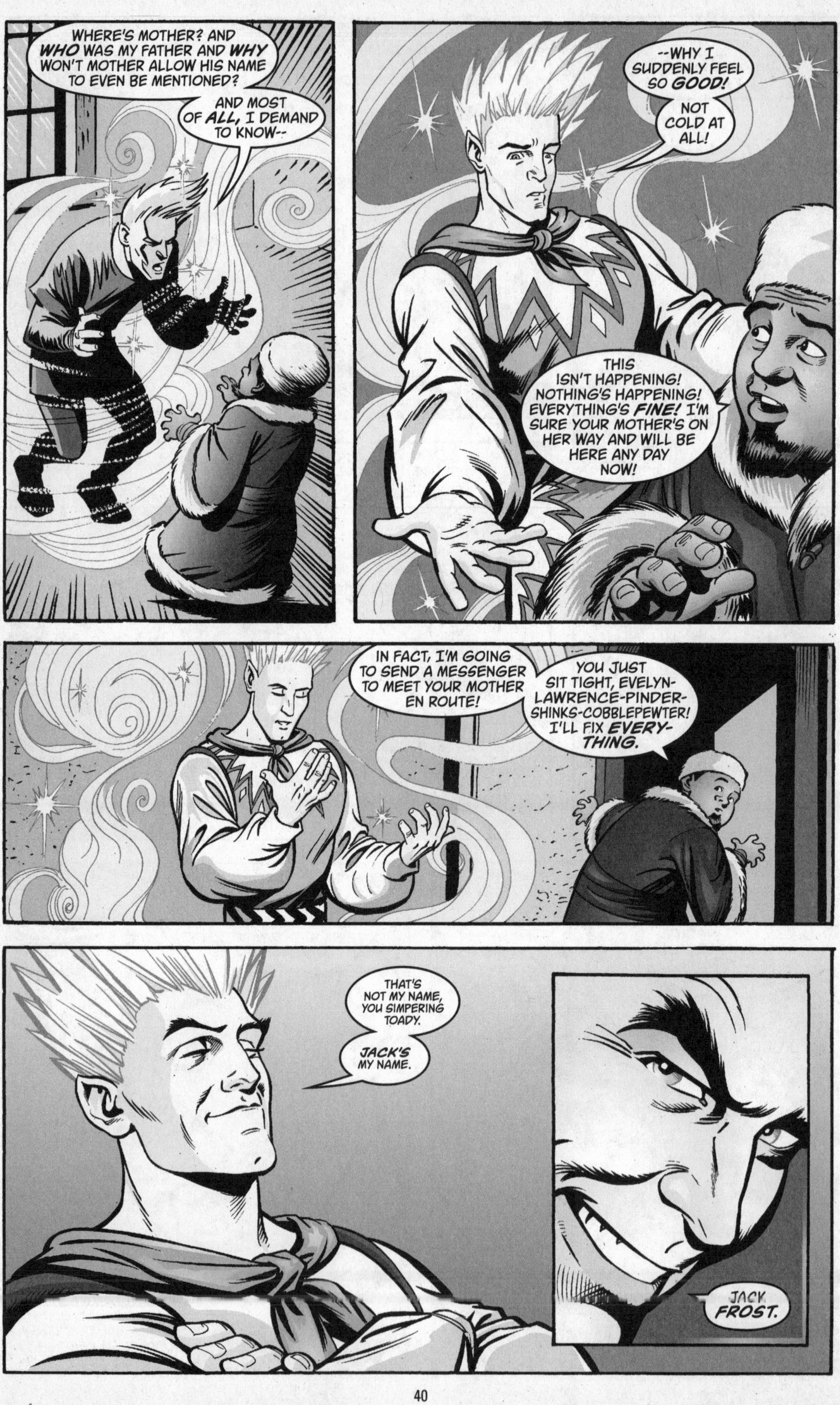
WHERE'S MOTHER? AND WHO WAS MY FATHER AND WHY WON'T MOTHER ALLOW HIS NAME TO EVEN BE MENTIONED?
AND MOST OF ALL, I DEMAND TO KNOW--
--WHY I SUDDENLY FEEL SO GOOD!
NOT COLD AT ALL!
THIS ISN'T HAPPENING! NOTHING'S HAPPENING! EVERYTHING'S FINE! I'M SURE YOUR MOTHER'S ON HER WAY AND WILL BE HERE ANY DAY NOW!
IN FACT, I'M GOING TO SEND A MESSENGER TO MEET YOUR MOTHER EN ROUTE!
YOU JUST SIT TIGHT, EVELYN-LAWRENCE-PINDER-SHINKS-COBBLEPEWTER! I'LL FIX EVERY-THING.
THAT'S NOT MY NAME, YOU SIMPERING TOADY.
JACK'S MY NAME.
JACK FROST.

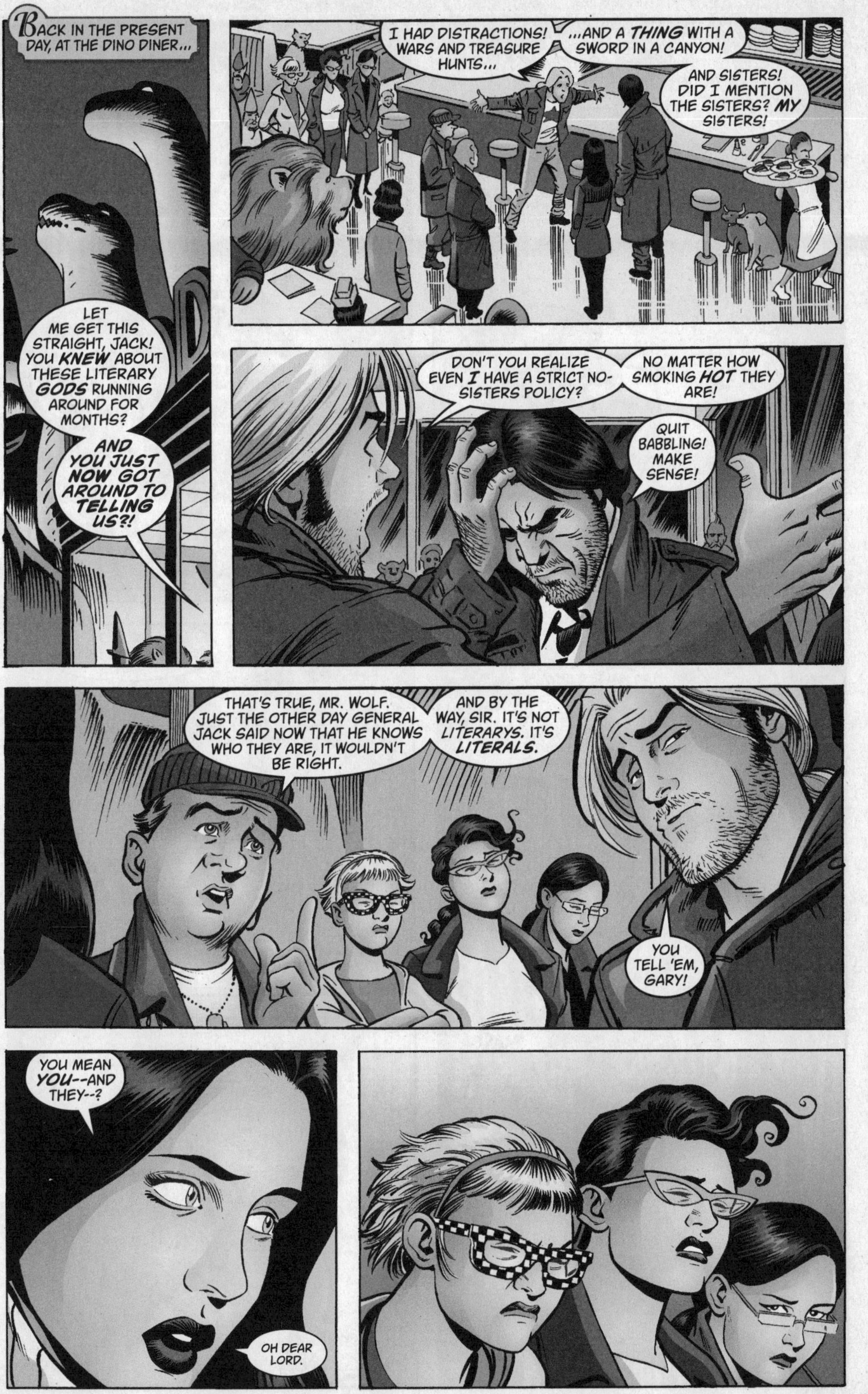
BACK IN THE PRESENT DAY, AT THE DINO DINER...
I HAD DISTRACTIONS! WARS AND TREASURE HUNTS...
...AND A THING WITH A SWORD IN A CANYON!
AND SISTERS! DID I MENTION THE SISTERS? MY SISTERS!
LET ME GET THIS STRAIGHT, JACK! YOU KNEW ABOUT THESE LITERARY GODS RUNNING AROUND FOR MONTHS?
AND YOU JUST NOW GOT AROUND TO TELLING US?!
DON'T YOU REALIZE EVEN I HAVE A STRICT NO-SISTERS POLICY?
NO MATTER HOW SMOKING HOT THEY ARE!
QUIT BABBLING! MAKE SENSE!
THAT'S TRUE, MR. WOLF. JUST THE OTHER DAY GENERAL JACK SAID NOW THAT HE KNOWS WHO THEY ARE, IT WOULDN'T BE RIGHT.
AND BY THE WAY, SIR. IT'S NOT LITERARYS. IT'S LITERALS.
YOU TELL 'EM, GARY!
YOU MEAN YOU--AND THEY--?
OH DEAR LORD.

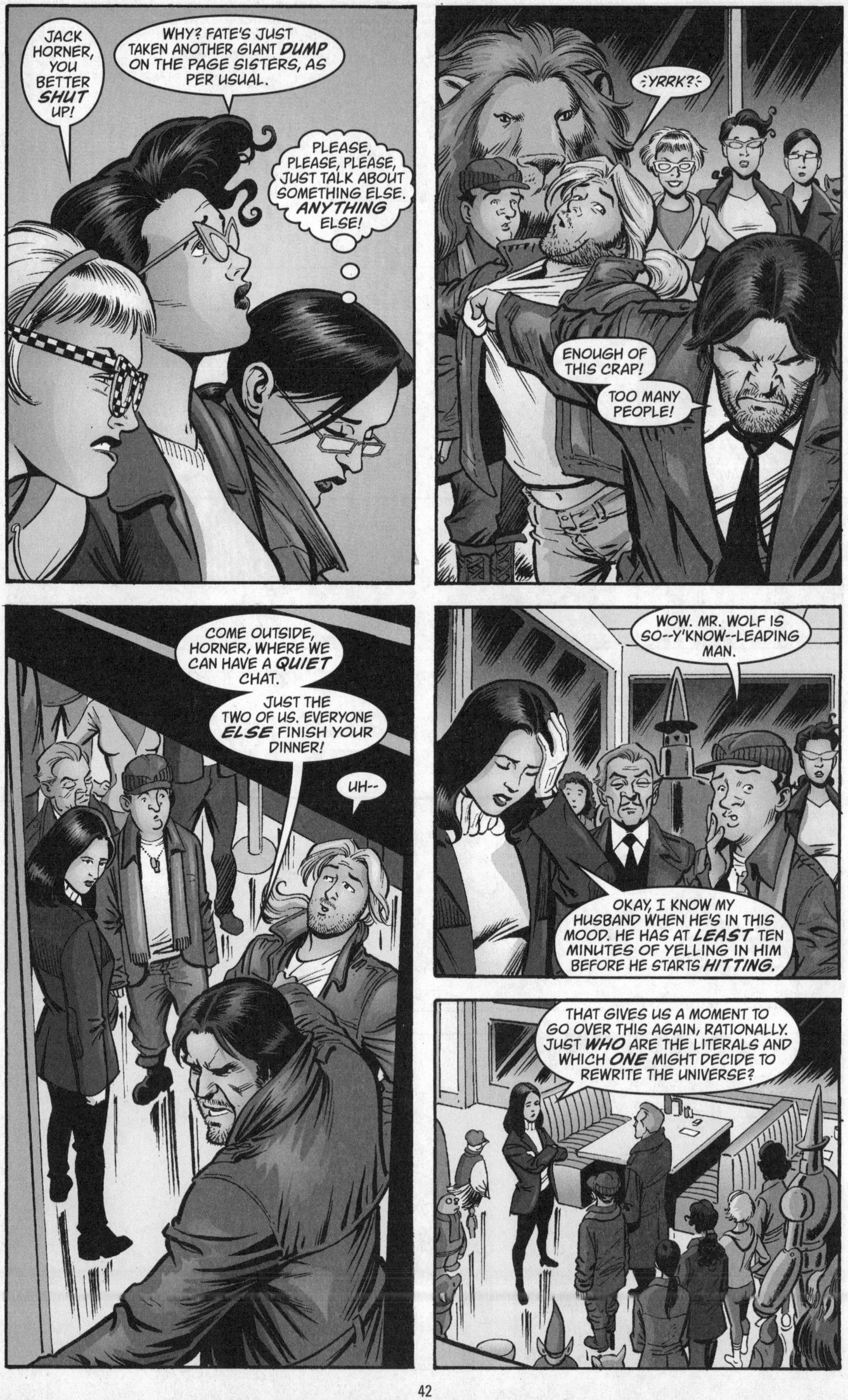
JACK HORNER, YOU BETTER SHUT UP!
WHY? FATE'S JUST TAKEN ANOTHER GIANT DUMP ON THE PAGE SISTERS, AS PER USUAL.
PLEASE, PLEASE, PLEASE, JUST TALK ABOUT SOMETHING ELSE. ANYTHING ELSE!
YRRK?
ENOUGH OF THIS CRAP!
TOO MANY PEOPLE!
COME OUTSIDE, HORNER, WHERE WE CAN HAVE A QUIET CHAT.
JUST THE TWO OF US. EVERYONE ELSE FINISH YOUR DINNER!
UH--
WOW. MR. WOLF IS SO--Y'KNOW--LEADING MAN.
OKAY, I KNOW MY HUSBAND WHEN HE'S IN THIS MOOD. HE HAS AT LEAST TEN MINUTES OF YELLING IN HIM BEFORE HE STARTS HITTING.
THAT GIVES US A MOMENT TO GO OVER THIS AGAIN, RATIONALLY. JUST WHO ARE THE LITERALS AND WHICH ONE MIGHT DECIDE TO REWRITE THE UNIVERSE?

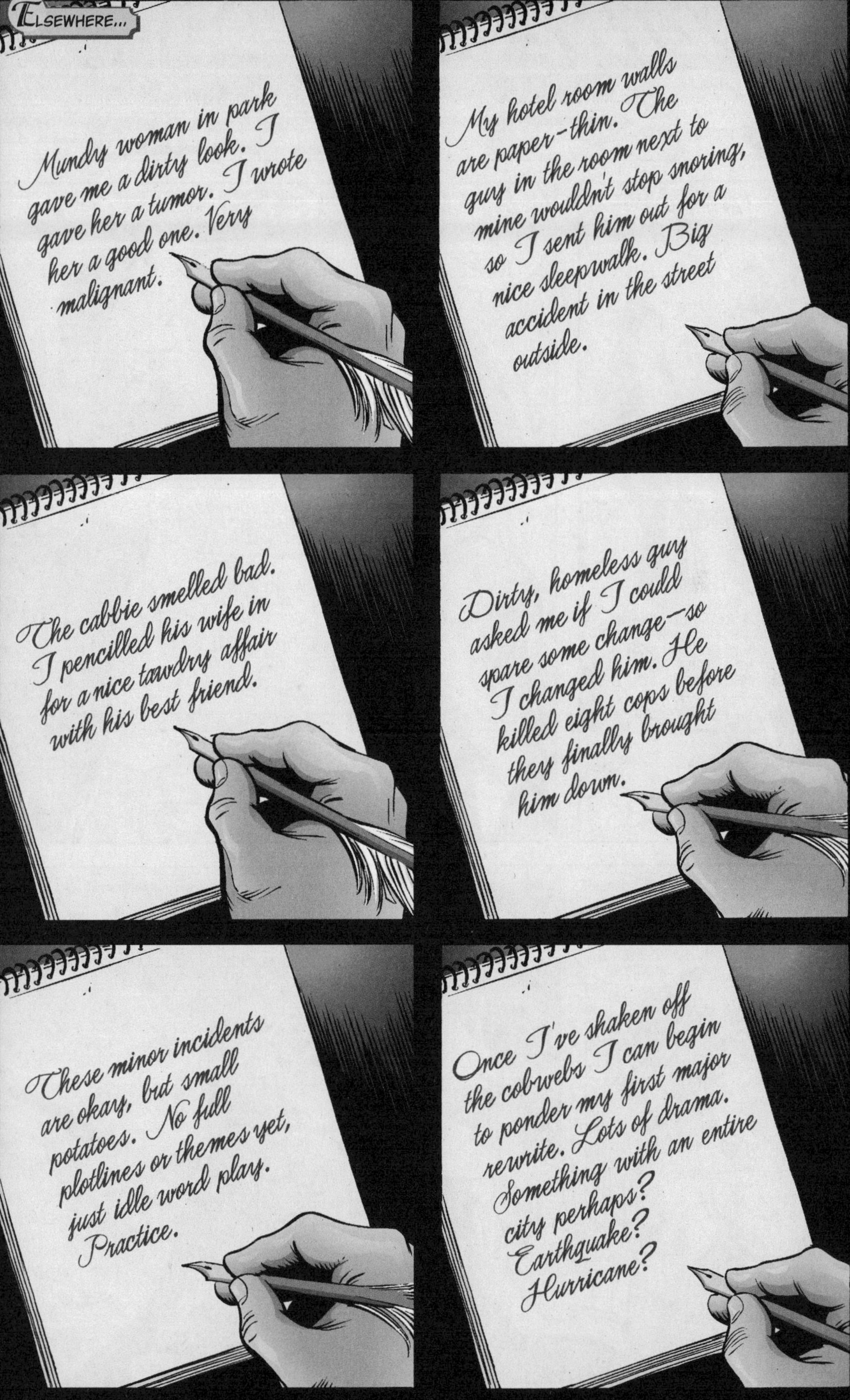
ELSEWHERE...
Mundy woman in park gave me a dirty look. I gave her a tumor. I wrote her a good one. Very malignant.
My hotel room walls are paper-thin. The guy in the room next to mine wouldn't stop snoring, so I sent him out for a nice sleepwalk. Big accident in the street outside.
The cabbie smelled bad. I pencilled his wife in for a nice tawdry affair with his best friend.
Dirty, homeless guy asked me if I could spare some change—so I changed him. He killed eight cops before they finally brought him down.
These minor incidents are okay, but small potatoes. No full plotlines or themes yet, just idle word play. Practice.
Once I've shaken off the cobwebs I can begin to ponder my first major rewrite. Lots of drama. Something with an entire city perhaps? Earthquake? Hurricane?

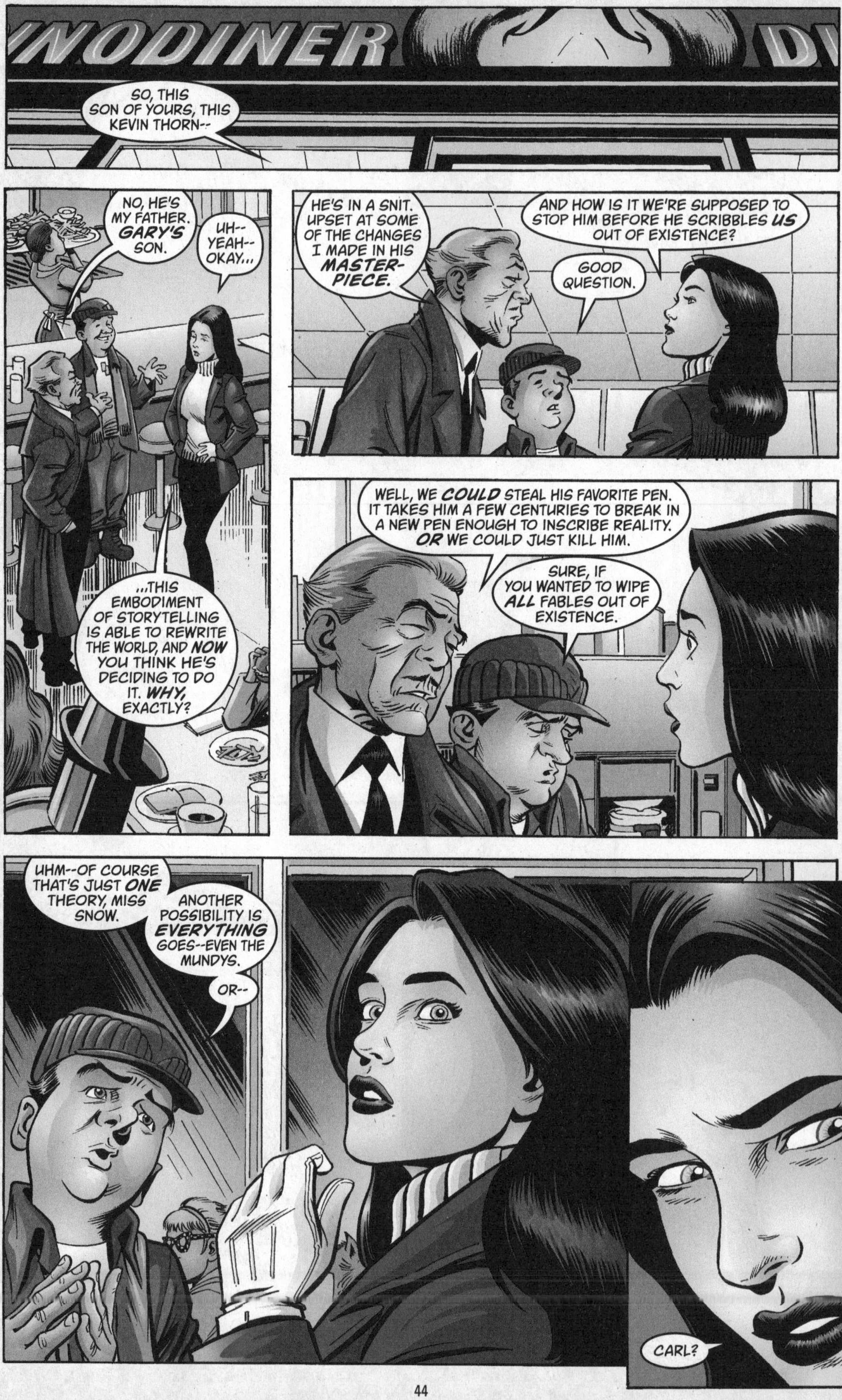

NODINER
SO, THIS SON OF YOURS, THIS KEVIN THORN--
NO, HE'S MY FATHER. GARY'S SON.
UH--YEAH--OKAY...
...THIS EMBODIMENT OF STORYTELLING IS ABLE TO REWRITE THE WORLD, AND NOW YOU THINK HE'S DECIDING TO DO IT. WHY, EXACTLY?
HE'S IN A SNIT. UPSET AT SOME OF THE CHANGES I MADE IN HIS MASTER-PIECE.
AND HOW IS IT WE'RE SUPPOSED TO STOP HIM BEFORE HE SCRIBBLES US OUT OF EXISTENCE?
GOOD QUESTION.
WELL, WE COULD STEAL HIS FAVORITE PEN. IT TAKES HIM A FEW CENTURIES TO BREAK IN A NEW PEN ENOUGH TO INSCRIBE REALITY. OR WE COULD JUST KILL HIM.
SURE, IF YOU WANTED TO WIPE ALL FABLES OUT OF EXISTENCE.
UHM--OF COURSE THAT'S JUST ONE THEORY, MISS SNOW.
ANOTHER POSSIBILITY IS EVERYTHING GOES--EVEN THE MUNDYS.
OR--
CARL?

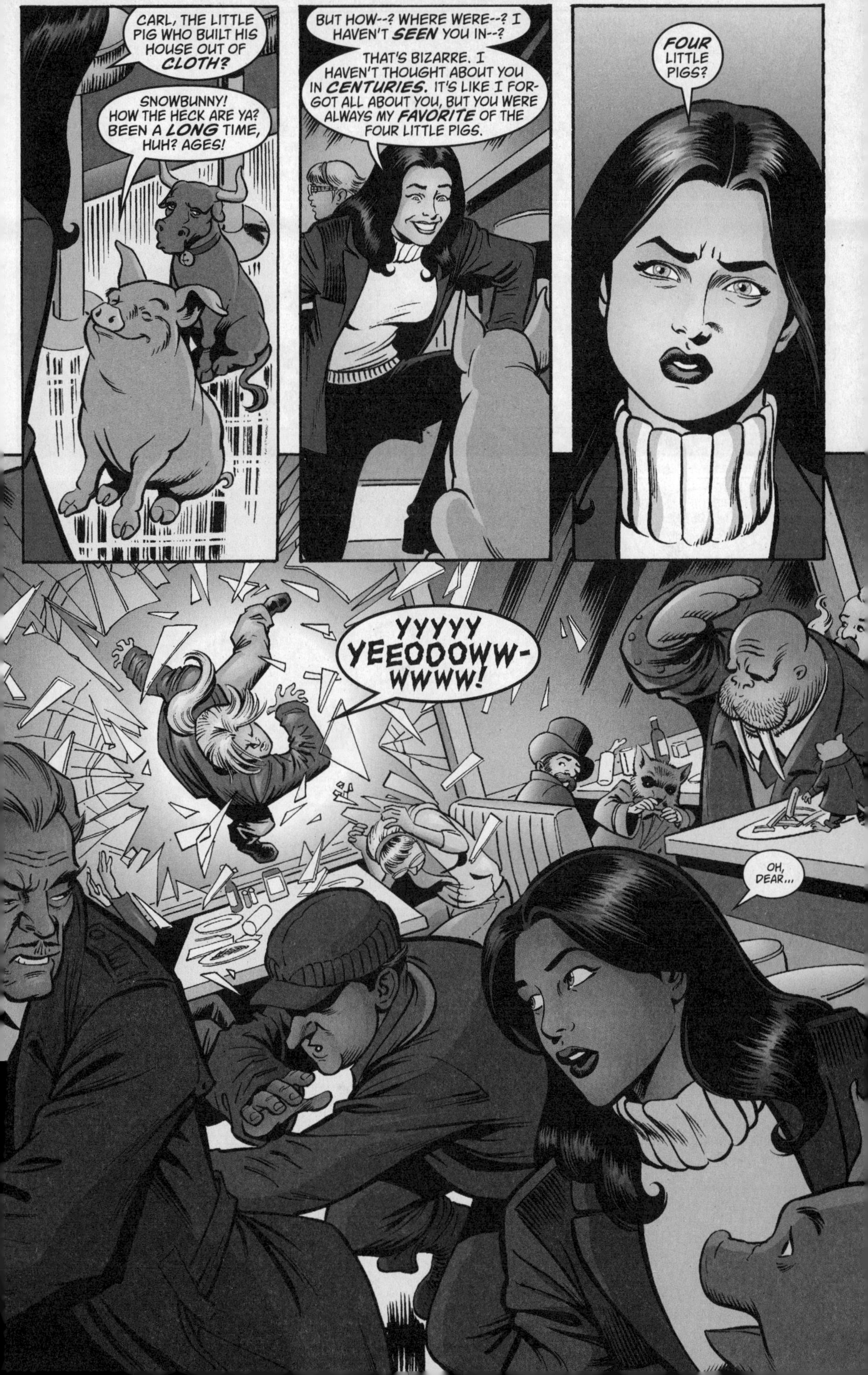
CARL, THE LITTLE PIG WHO BUILT HIS HOUSE OUT OF CLOTH?
SNOWBUNNY! HOW THE HECK ARE YA? BEEN A LONG TIME, HUH? AGES!
BUT HOW--? WHERE WERE--? I HAVEN'T SEEN YOU IN--?
THAT'S BIZARRE. I HAVEN'T THOUGHT ABOUT YOU IN CENTURIES. IT'S LIKE I FORGOT ALL ABOUT YOU, BUT YOU WERE ALWAYS MY FAVORITE OF THE FOUR LITTLE PIGS.
FOUR LITTLE PIGS?
YYYYY YEEOOOWW-WWWW!
OH, DEAR...

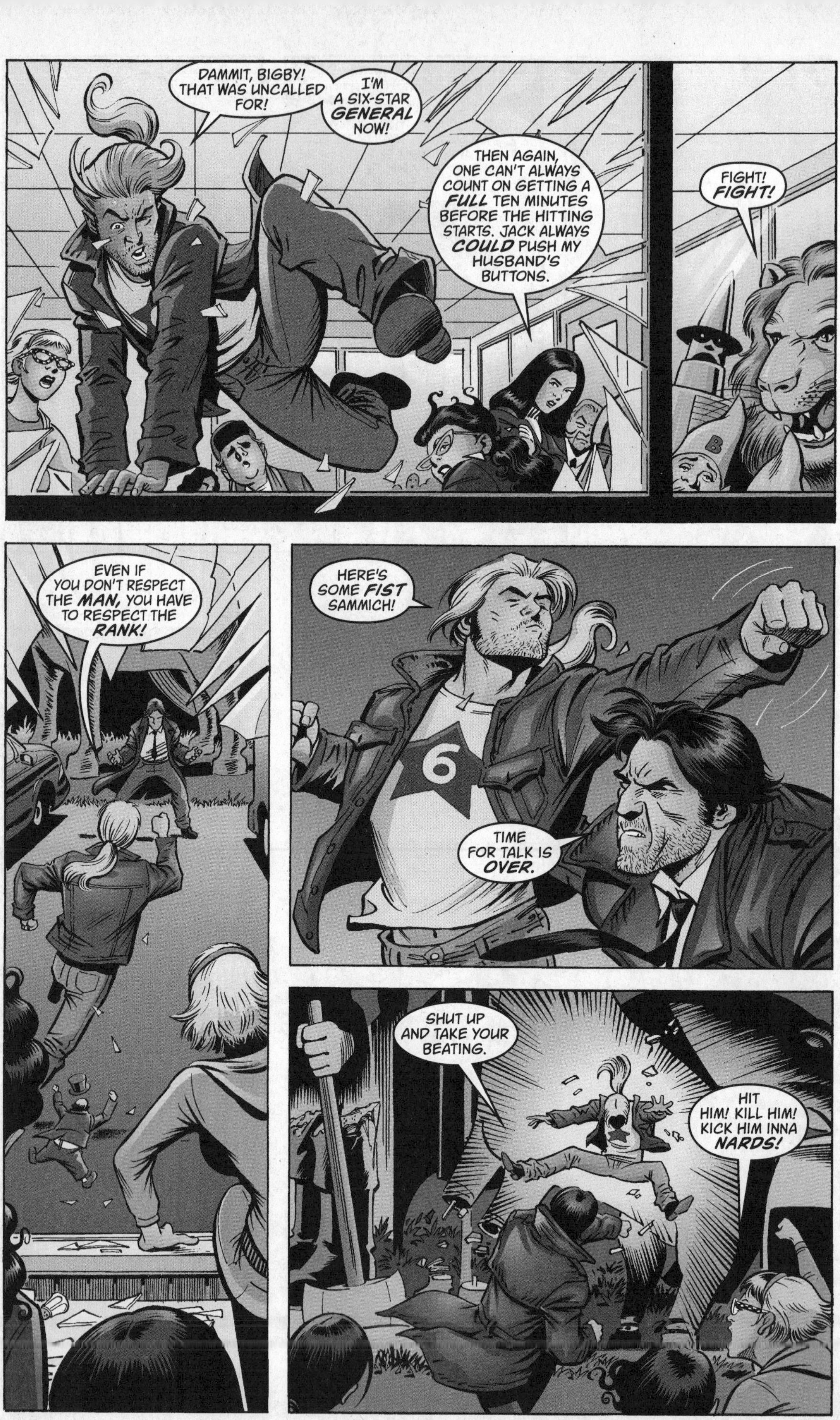
DAMMIT, BIGBY! THAT WAS UNCALLED FOR!
I'M A SIX-STAR GENERAL NOW!
THEN AGAIN, ONE CAN'T ALWAYS COUNT ON GETTING A FULL TEN MINUTES BEFORE THE HITTING STARTS. JACK ALWAYS COULD PUSH MY HUSBAND'S BUTTONS.
FIGHT! FIGHT!
EVEN IF YOU DON'T RESPECT THE MAN, YOU HAVE TO RESPECT THE RANK!
HERE'S SOME FIST SAMMICH!
6
TIME FOR TALK IS OVER.
SHUT UP AND TAKE YOUR BEATING.
HIT HIM! KILL HIM! KICK HIM INNA NARDS!

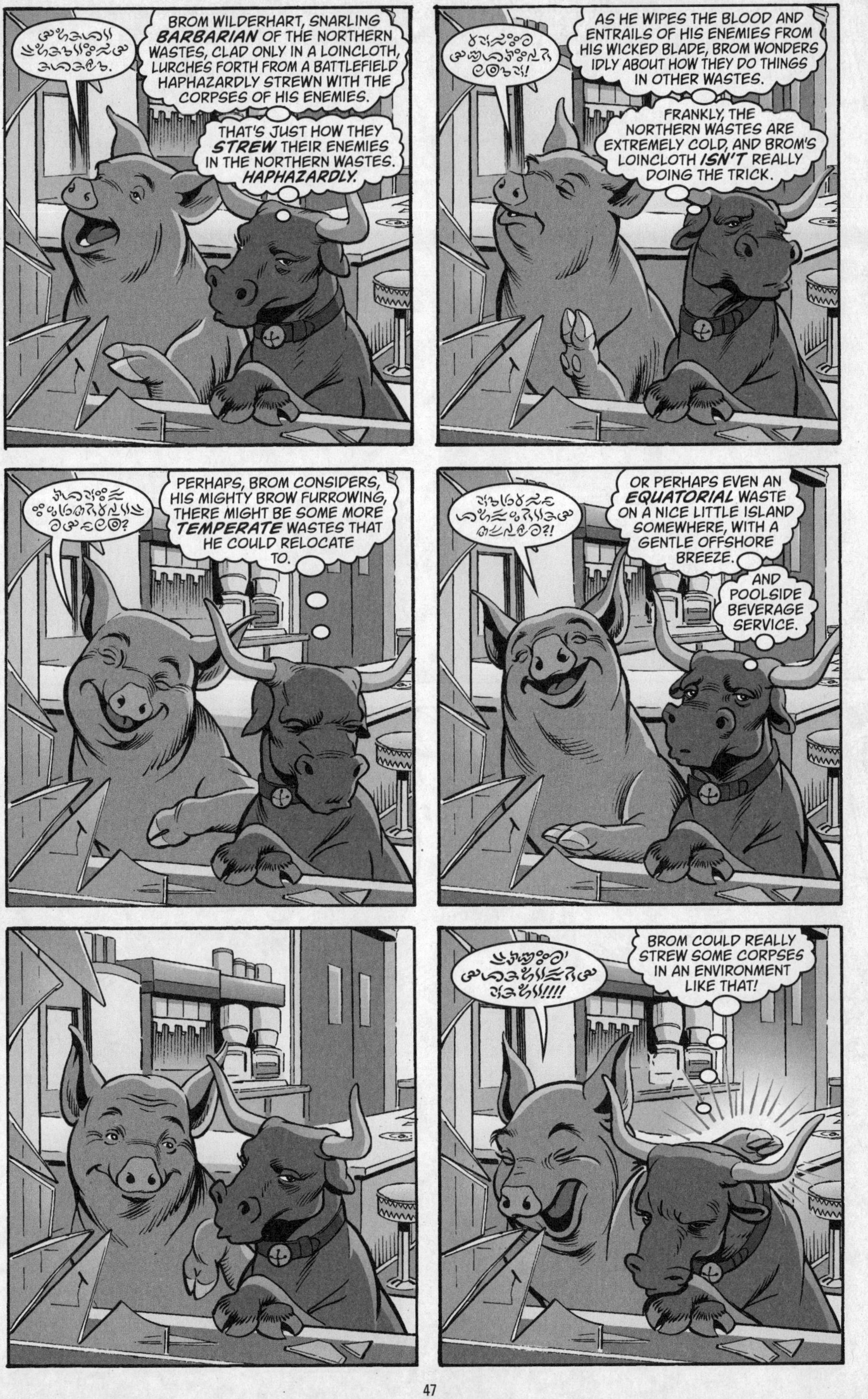

BROM WILDERHART, SNARLING BARBARIAN OF THE NORTHERN WASTES, CLAD ONLY IN A LOINCLOTH, LURCHES FORTH FROM A BATTLEFIELD HAPHAZARDLY STREWN WITH THE CORPSES OF HIS ENEMIES.
THAT'S JUST HOW THEY STREW THEIR ENEMIES IN THE NORTHERN WASTES. HAPHAZARDLY.
AS HE WIPES THE BLOOD AND ENTRAILS OF HIS ENEMIES FROM HIS WICKED BLADE, BROM WONDERS IDLY ABOUT HOW THEY DO THINGS IN OTHER WASTES.
FRANKLY, THE NORTHERN WASTES ARE EXTREMELY COLD, AND BROM'S LOINCLOTH ISN'T REALLY DOING THE TRICK.
PERHAPS, BROM CONSIDERS, HIS MIGHTY BROW FURROWING, THERE MIGHT BE SOME MORE TEMPERATE WASTES THAT HE COULD RELOCATE TO.
OR PERHAPS EVEN AN EQUATORIAL WASTE ON A NICE LITTLE ISLAND SOMEWHERE, WITH A GENTLE OFFSHORE BREEZE.
AND POOLSIDE BEVERAGE SERVICE.
BROM COULD REALLY STREW SOME CORPSES IN AN ENVIRONMENT LIKE THAT!

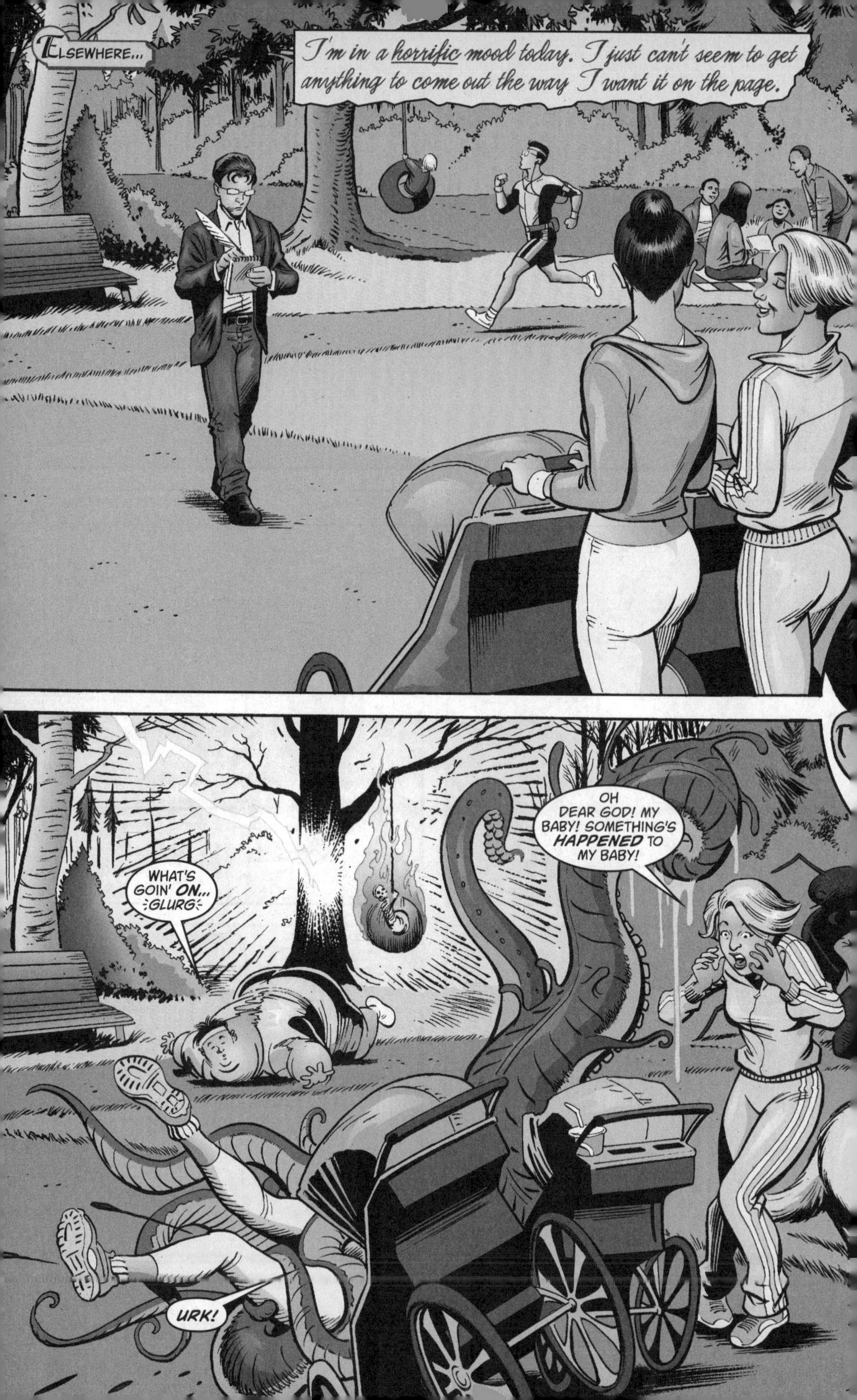
ELSEWHERE...
I'm in a horrific mood today. I just can't seem to get anything to come out the way I want it on the page.
WHAT'S GOIN' ON... GLURG
OH DEAR GOD! MY BABY! SOMETHING'S HAPPENED TO MY BABY!
URK!

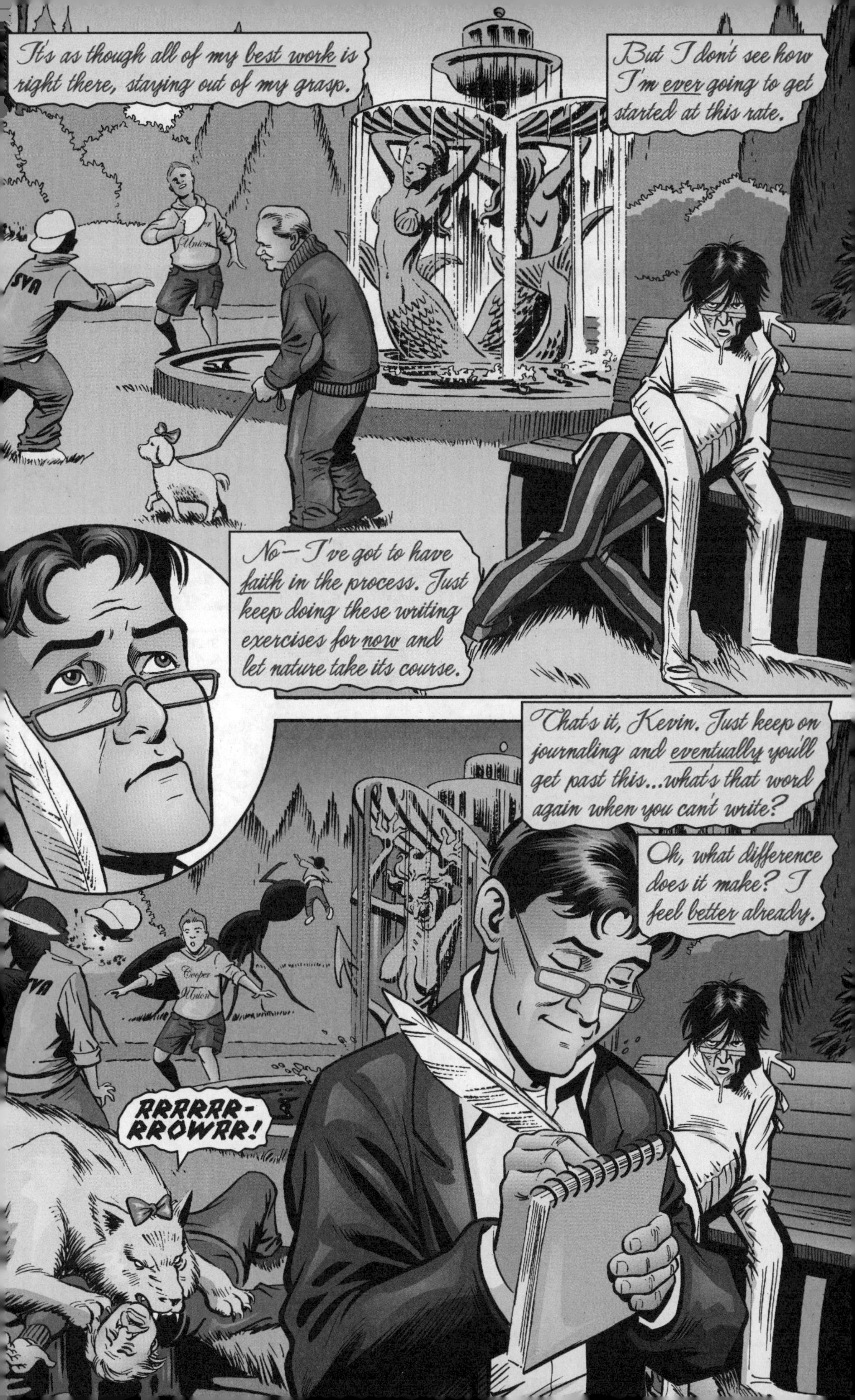
It's as though all of my best work is right there, staying out of my grasp.
But I don't see how I'm ever going to get started at this rate.
Union
No—I've got to have faith in the process. Just keep doing these writing exercises for now and let nature take its course.
That's it, Kevin. Just keep on journaling and eventually you'll get past this...what's that word again when you can't write?
Oh, what difference does it make? I feel better already.
SVA
Cooper Union
RRRRRR-RROWRR!

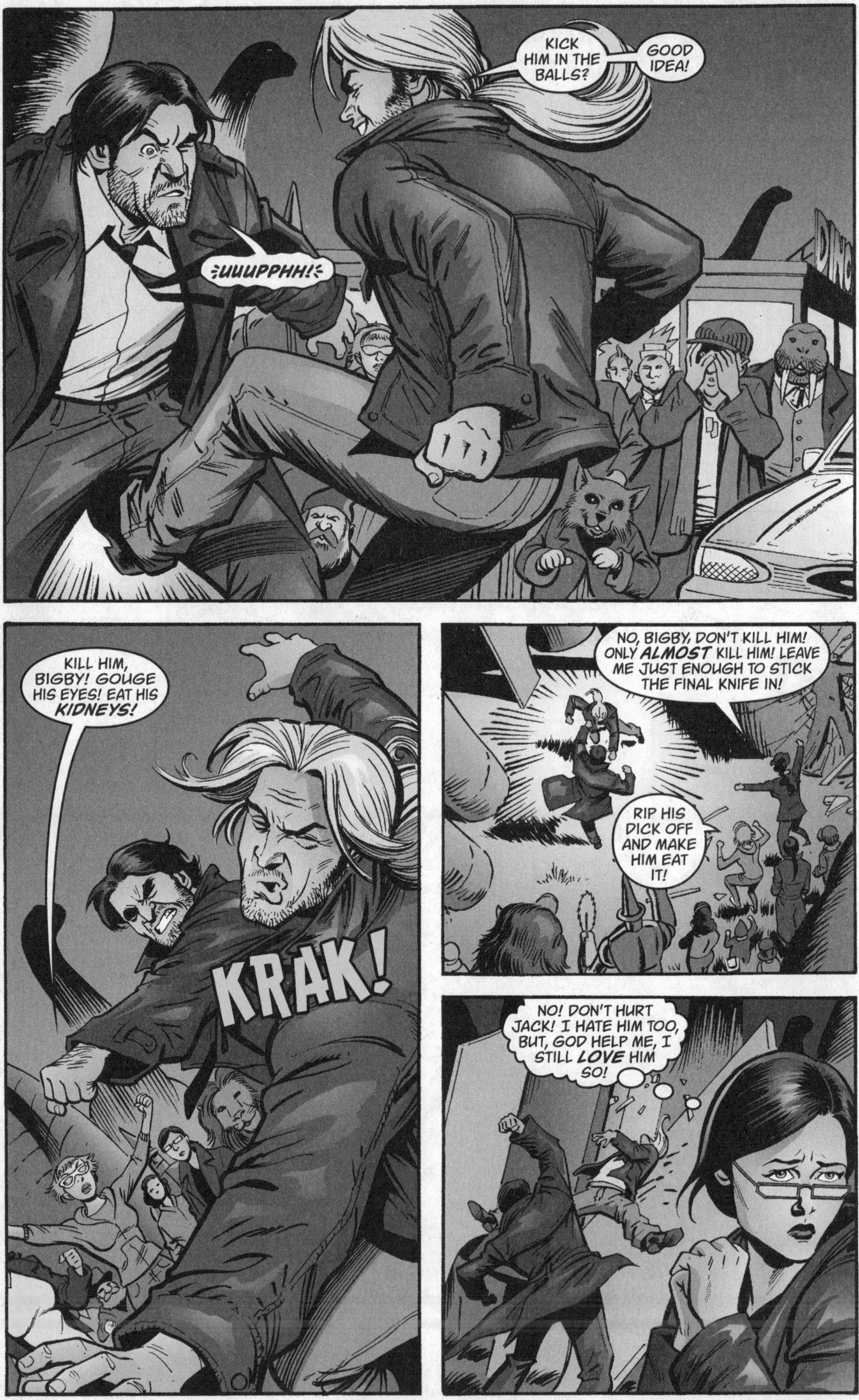
KICK HIM IN THE BALLS?
GOOD IDEA!
UUUPPHH!
KILL HIM, BIGBY! GOUGE HIS EYES! EAT HIS KIDNEYS!
KRAK!
NO, BIGBY, DON'T KILL HIM! ONLY ALMOST KILL HIM! LEAVE ME JUST ENOUGH TO STICK THE FINAL KNIFE IN!
RIP HIS DICK OFF AND MAKE HIM EAT IT!
NO! DON'T HURT JACK! I HATE HIM TOO, BUT, GOD HELP ME, I STILL LOVE HIM SO!

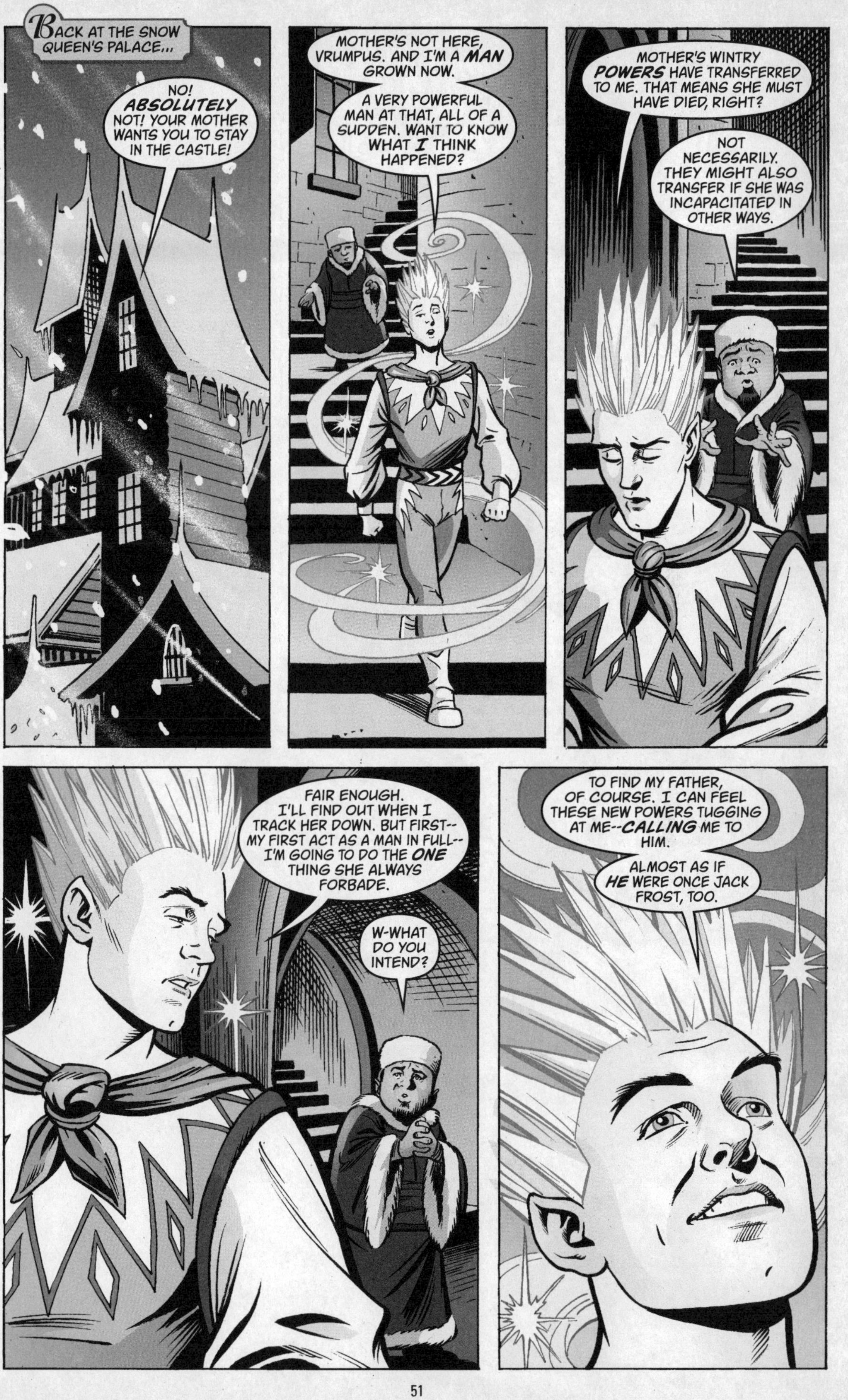
BACK AT THE SNOW QUEEN'S PALACE...
NO! ABSOLUTELY NOT! YOUR MOTHER WANTS YOU TO STAY IN THE CASTLE!
MOTHER'S NOT HERE, VRUMPUS. AND I'M A MAN GROWN NOW.
A VERY POWERFUL MAN AT THAT, ALL OF A SUDDEN. WANT TO KNOW WHAT I THINK HAPPENED?
MOTHER'S WINTRY POWERS HAVE TRANSFERRED TO ME. THAT MEANS SHE MUST HAVE DIED, RIGHT?
NOT NECESSARILY. THEY MIGHT ALSO TRANSFER IF SHE WAS INCAPACITATED IN OTHER WAYS.
FAIR ENOUGH. I'LL FIND OUT WHEN I TRACK HER DOWN. BUT FIRST-- MY FIRST ACT AS A MAN IN FULL-- I'M GOING TO DO THE ONE THING SHE ALWAYS FORBADE.
W-WHAT DO YOU INTEND?
TO FIND MY FATHER, OF COURSE. I CAN FEEL THESE NEW POWERS TUGGING AT ME--CALLING ME TO HIM.
ALMOST AS IF HE WERE ONCE JACK FROST, TOO.

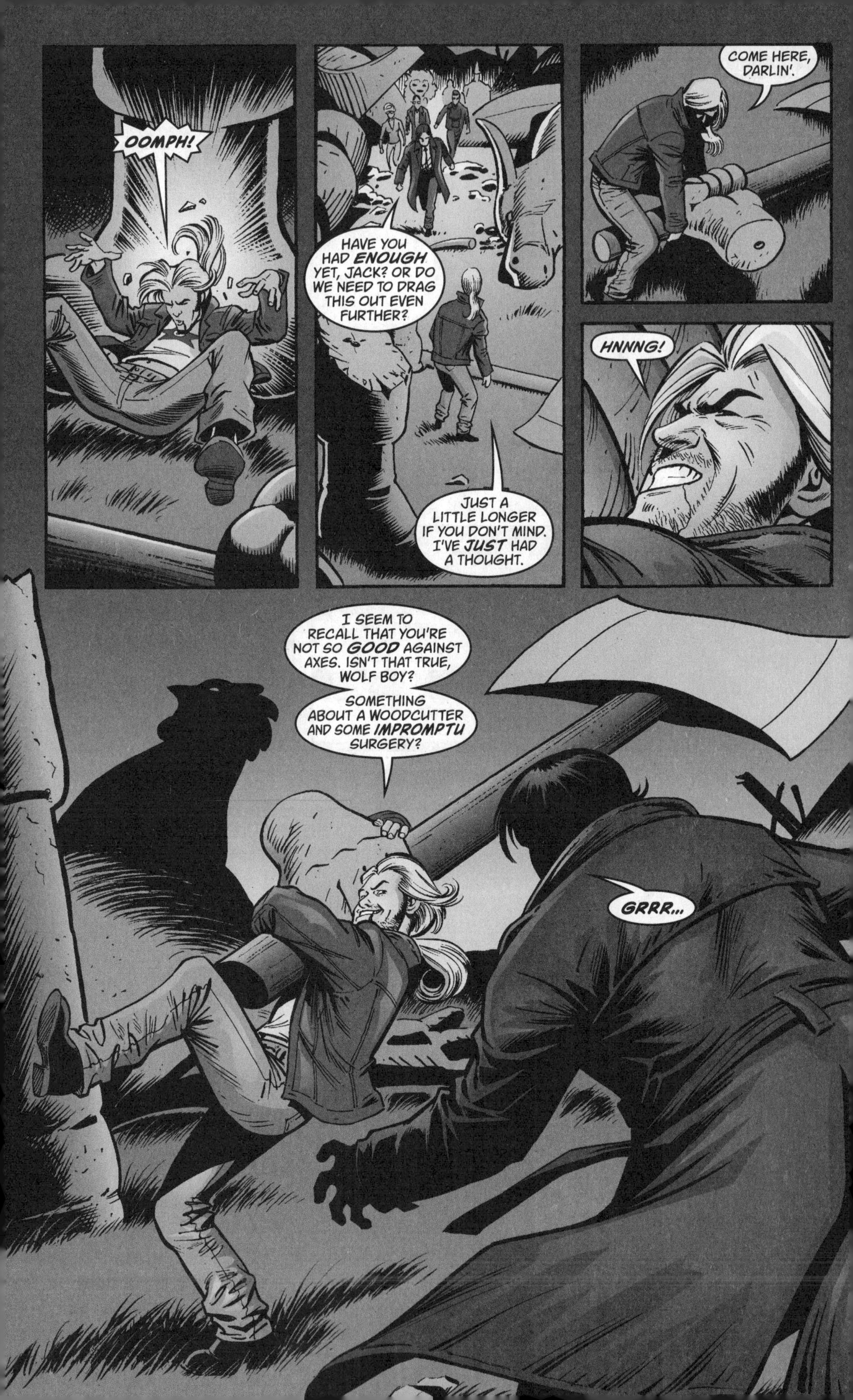
OOMPH!
HAVE YOU HAD ENOUGH YET, JACK? OR DO WE NEED TO DRAG THIS OUT EVEN FURTHER?
JUST A LITTLE LONGER IF YOU DON'T MIND. I'VE JUST HAD A THOUGHT.
COME HERE, DARLIN'.
HNNNG!
I SEEM TO RECALL THAT YOU'RE NOT SO GOOD AGAINST AXES. ISN'T THAT TRUE, WOLF BOY?
SOMETHING ABOUT A WOODCUTTER AND SOME IMPROMPTU SURGERY?
GRRR...

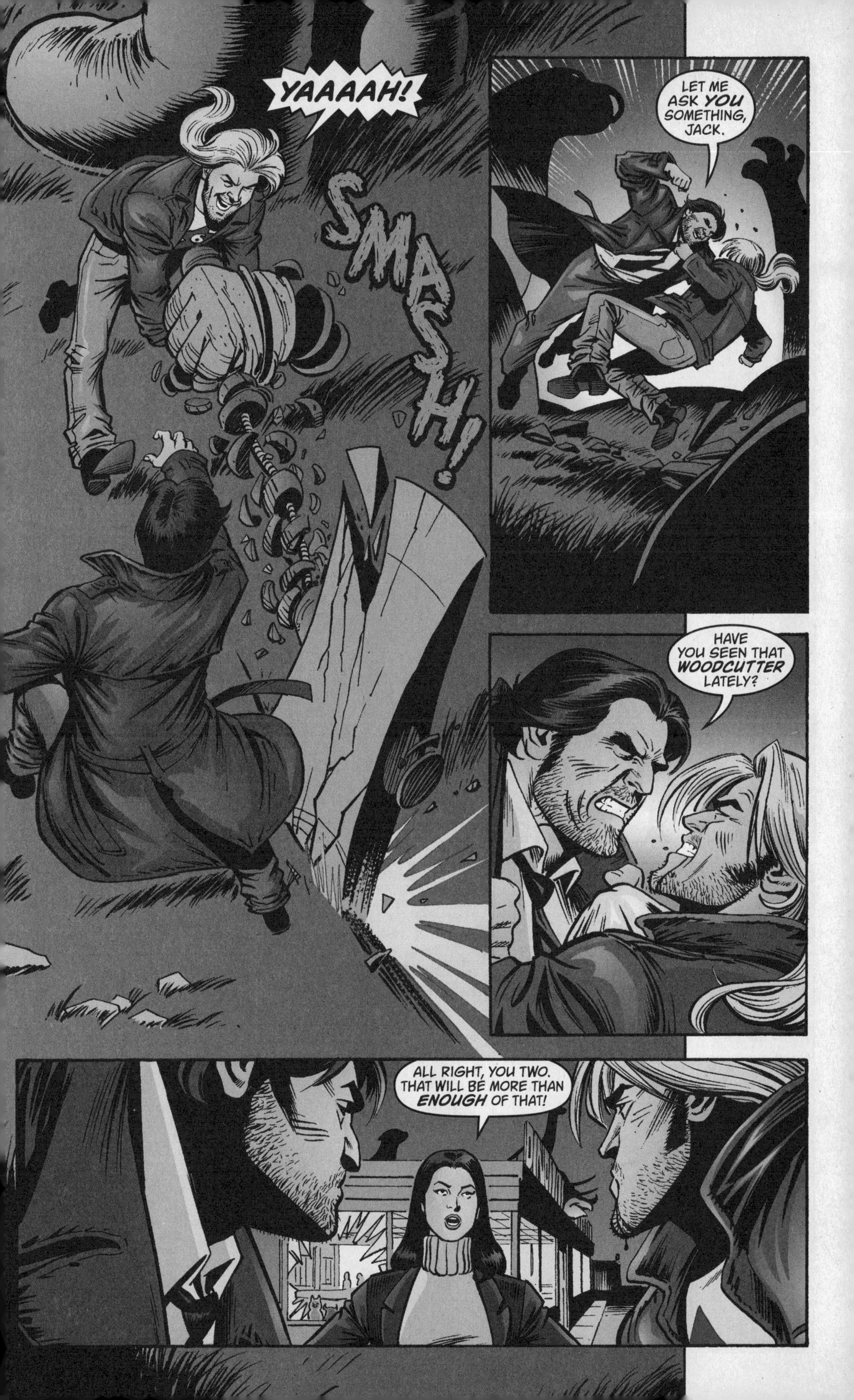
YAAAAH!
SMASH!
LET ME ASK YOU SOMETHING, JACK.
HAVE YOU SEEN THAT WOODCUTTER LATELY?
ALL RIGHT, YOU TWO. THAT WILL BE MORE THAN ENOUGH OF THAT!

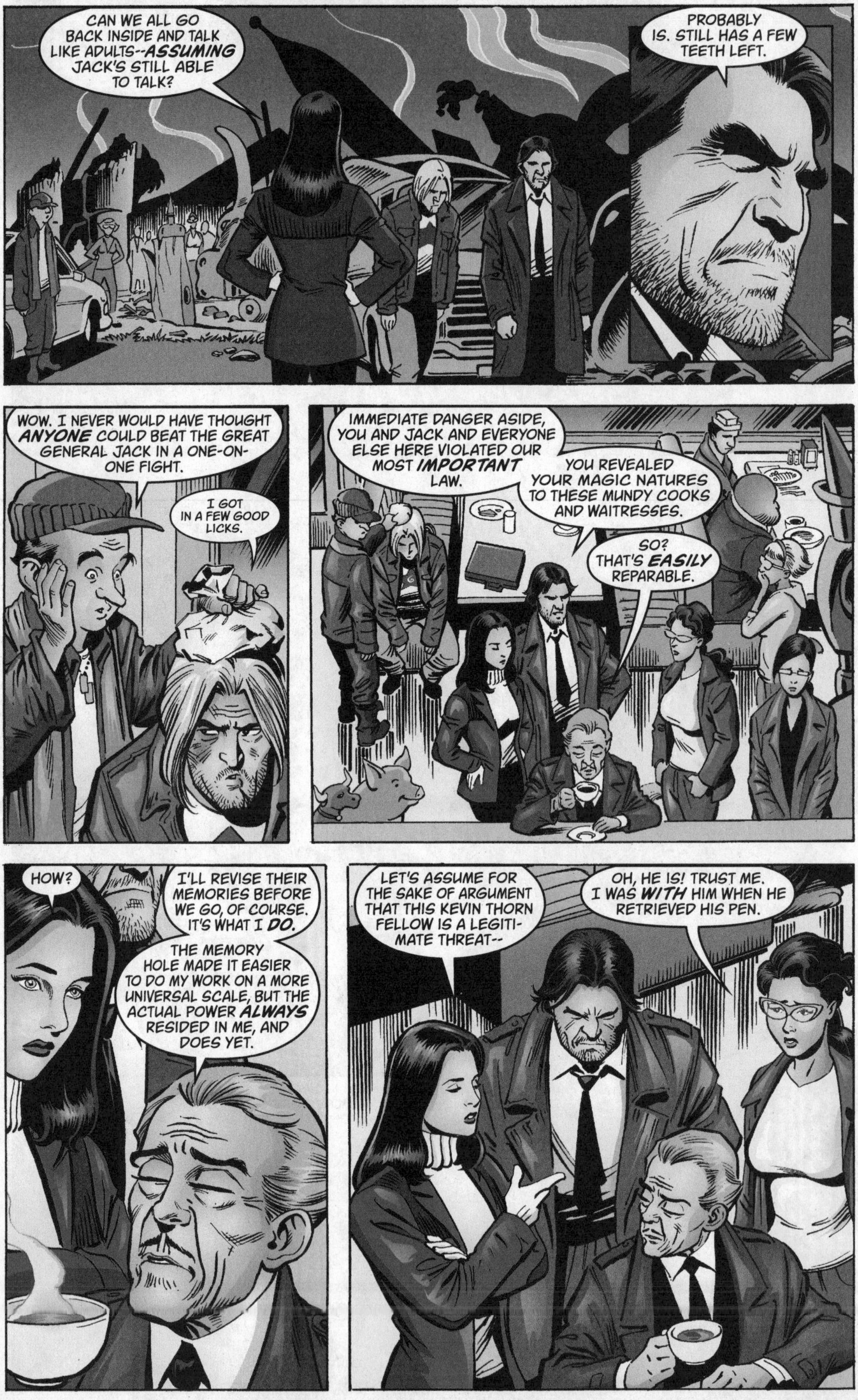
CAN WE ALL GO BACK INSIDE AND TALK LIKE ADULTS--ASSUMING JACK'S STILL ABLE TO TALK?
PROBABLY IS. STILL HAS A FEW TEETH LEFT.
WOW. I NEVER WOULD HAVE THOUGHT ANYONE COULD BEAT THE GREAT GENERAL JACK IN A ONE-ON-ONE FIGHT.
I GOT IN A FEW GOOD LICKS.
IMMEDIATE DANGER ASIDE, YOU AND JACK AND EVERYONE ELSE HERE VIOLATED OUR MOST IMPORTANT LAW.
YOU REVEALED YOUR MAGIC NATURES TO THESE MUNDY COOKS AND WAITRESSES.
SO? THAT'S EASILY REPARABLE.
HOW?
I'LL REVISE THEIR MEMORIES BEFORE WE GO, OF COURSE. IT'S WHAT I DO.
THE MEMORY HOLE MADE IT EASIER TO DO MY WORK ON A MORE UNIVERSAL SCALE, BUT THE ACTUAL POWER ALWAYS RESIDED IN ME, AND DOES YET.
LET'S ASSUME FOR THE SAKE OF ARGUMENT THAT THIS KEVIN THORN FELLOW IS A LEGITIMATE THREAT--
OH, HE IS! TRUST ME. I WAS WITH HIM WHEN HE RETRIEVED HIS PEN.

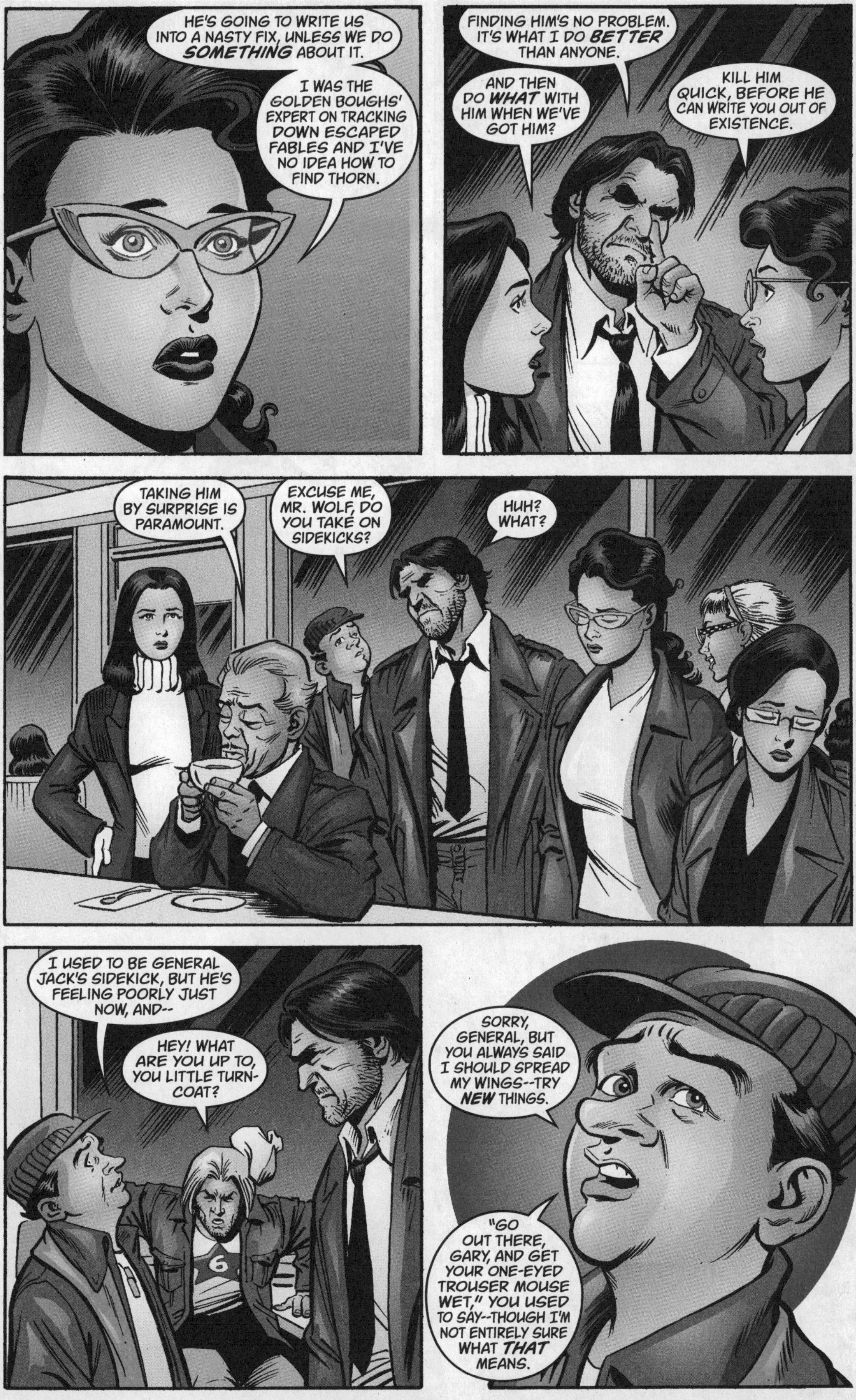
HE'S GOING TO WRITE US INTO A NASTY FIX, UNLESS WE DO SOMETHING ABOUT IT.
I WAS THE GOLDEN BOUGHS' EXPERT ON TRACKING DOWN ESCAPED FABLES AND I'VE NO IDEA HOW TO FIND THORN.
FINDING HIM'S NO PROBLEM. IT'S WHAT I DO BETTER THAN ANYONE.
AND THEN DO WHAT WITH HIM WHEN WE'VE GOT HIM?
KILL HIM QUICK, BEFORE HE CAN WRITE YOU OUT OF EXISTENCE.
TAKING HIM BY SURPRISE IS PARAMOUNT.
EXCUSE ME, MR. WOLF, DO YOU TAKE ON SIDEKICKS?
HUH? WHAT?
I USED TO BE GENERAL JACK'S SIDEKICK, BUT HE'S FEELING POORLY JUST NOW, AND--
HEY! WHAT ARE YOU UP TO, YOU LITTLE TURN-COAT?
SORRY, GENERAL, BUT YOU ALWAYS SAID I SHOULD SPREAD MY WINGS--TRY NEW THINGS.
"GO OUT THERE, GARY, AND GET YOUR ONE-EYED TROUSER MOUSE WET," YOU USED TO SAY--THOUGH I'M NOT ENTIRELY SURE WHAT THAT MEANS.

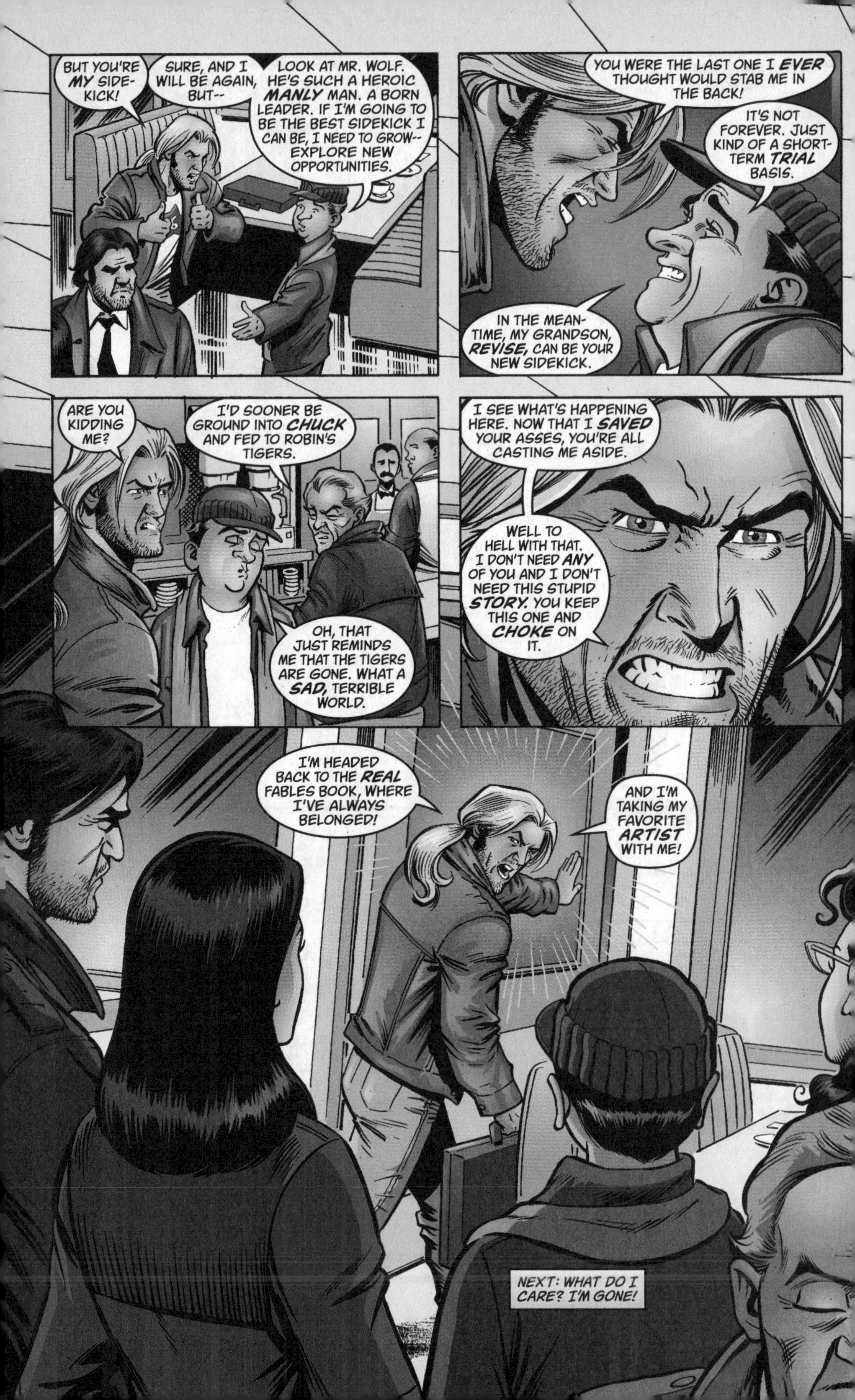
BUT YOU'RE MY SIDE-KICK!
SURE, AND I WILL BE AGAIN, BUT--
LOOK AT MR. WOLF. HE'S SUCH A HEROIC MANLY MAN. A BORN LEADER. IF I'M GOING TO BE THE BEST SIDEKICK I CAN BE, I NEED TO GROW--EXPLORE NEW OPPORTUNITIES.
YOU WERE THE LAST ONE I EVER THOUGHT WOULD STAB ME IN THE BACK!
IT'S NOT FOREVER. JUST KIND OF A SHORT-TERM TRIAL BASIS.
IN THE MEAN-TIME, MY GRANDSON, REVISE, CAN BE YOUR NEW SIDEKICK.
ARE YOU KIDDING ME?
I'D SOONER BE GROUND INTO CHUCK AND FED TO ROBIN'S TIGERS.
OH, THAT JUST REMINDS ME THAT THE TIGERS ARE GONE. WHAT A SAD, TERRIBLE WORLD.
I SEE WHAT'S HAPPENING HERE. NOW THAT I SAVED YOUR ASSES, YOU'RE ALL CASTING ME ASIDE.
WELL TO HELL WITH THAT. I DON'T NEED ANY OF YOU AND I DON'T NEED THIS STUPID STORY. YOU KEEP THIS ONE AND CHOKE ON IT.
I'M HEADED BACK TO THE REAL FABLES BOOK, WHERE I'VE ALWAYS BELONGED!
AND I'M TAKING MY FAVORITE ARTIST WITH ME!
NEXT: WHAT DO I CARE? I'M GONE!

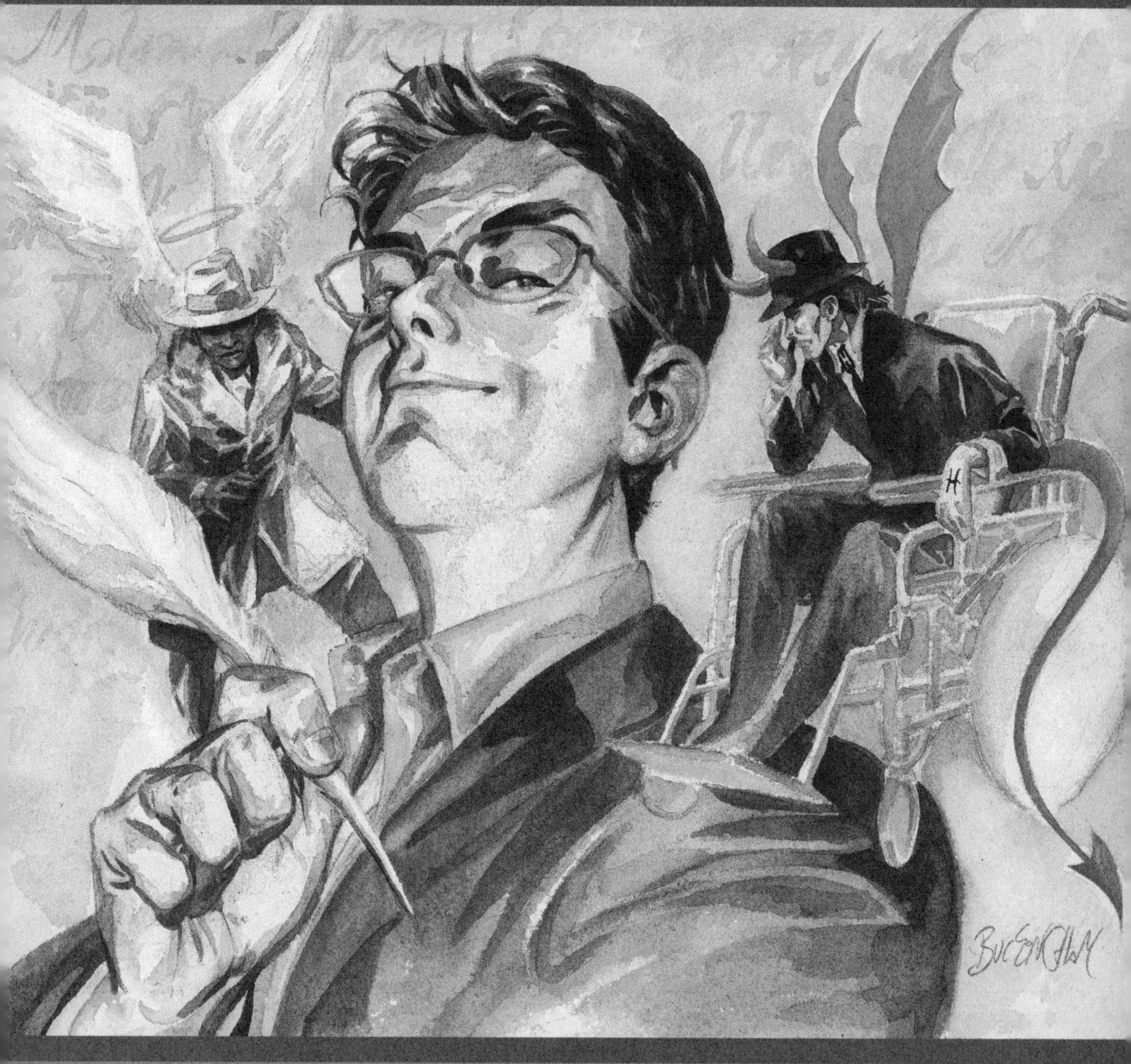

"I see it now. A final judgment passed on this depraved and fallen universe."

The Great FABLES Crossover

part 3 of 9

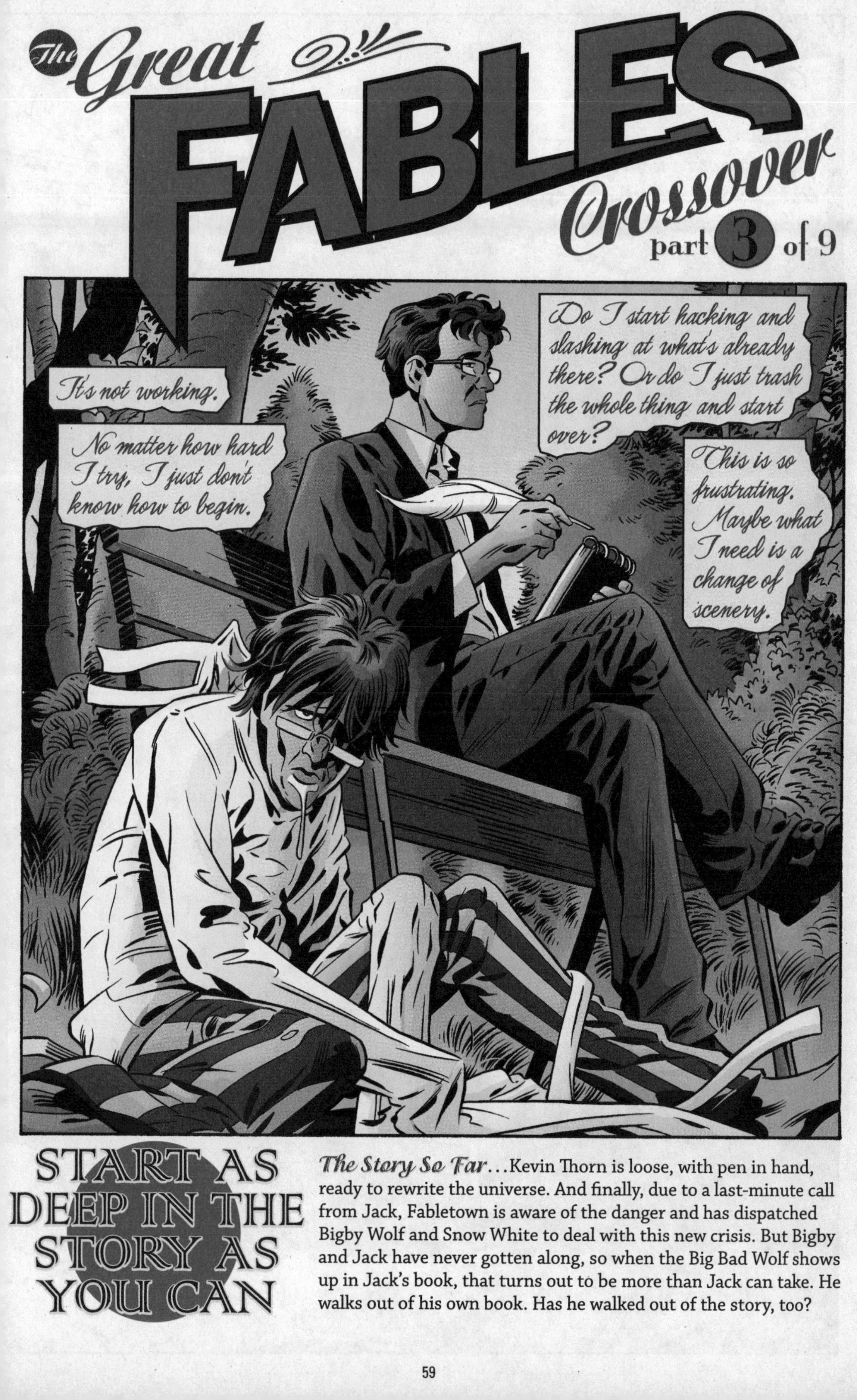
It's not working.
No matter how hard I try, I just don't know how to begin.
Do I start hacking and slashing at what's already there? Or do I just trash the whole thing and start over?
This is so frustrating. Maybe what I need is a change of scenery.

START AS DEEP IN THE STORY AS YOU CAN

The Story So Far...Kevin Thorn is loose, with pen in hand, ready to rewrite the universe. And finally, due to a last-minute call from Jack, Fabletown is aware of the danger and has dispatched Bigby Wolf and Snow White to deal with this new crisis. But Bigby and Jack have never gotten along, so when the Big Bad Wolf shows up in Jack's book, that turns out to be more than Jack can take. He walks out of his own book. Has he walked out of the story, too?

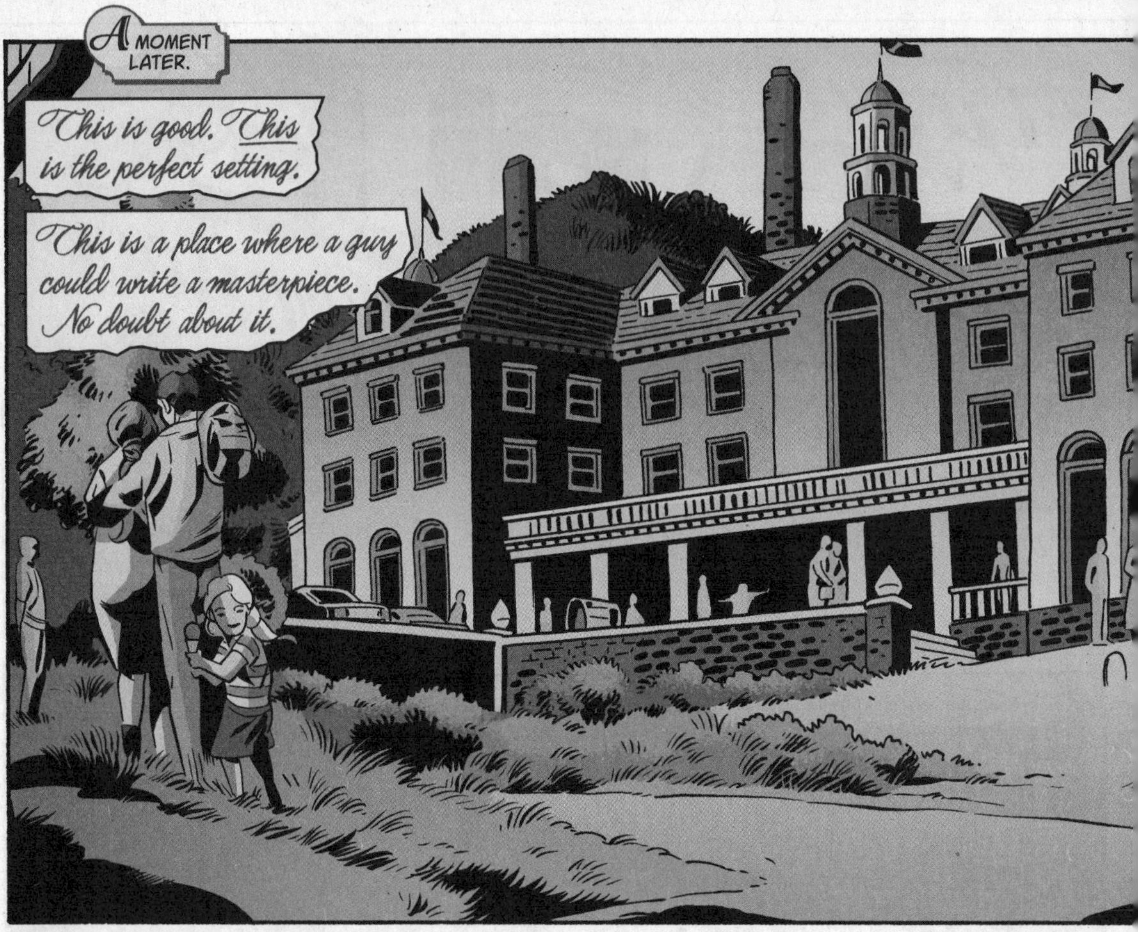
A MOMENT LATER.
This is good. This is the perfect setting.
This is a place where a guy could write a masterpiece. No doubt about it.

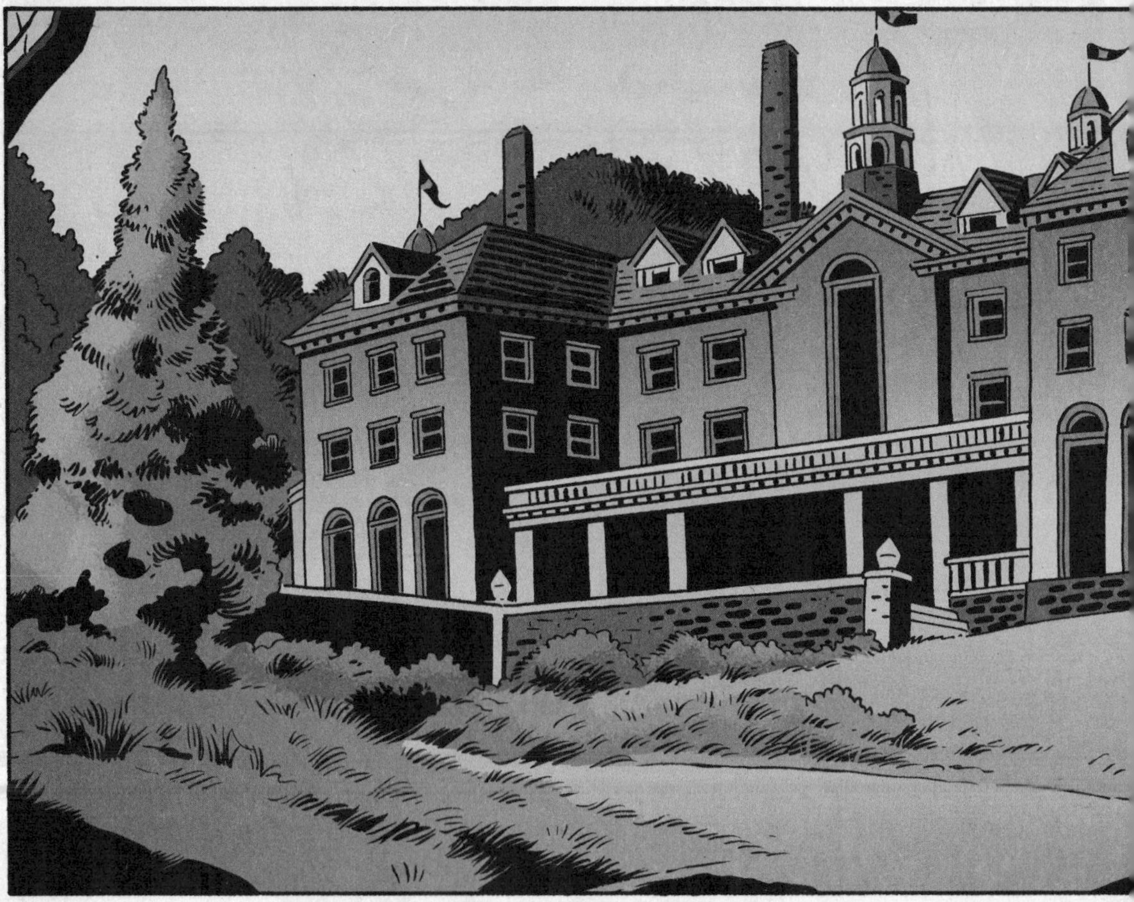

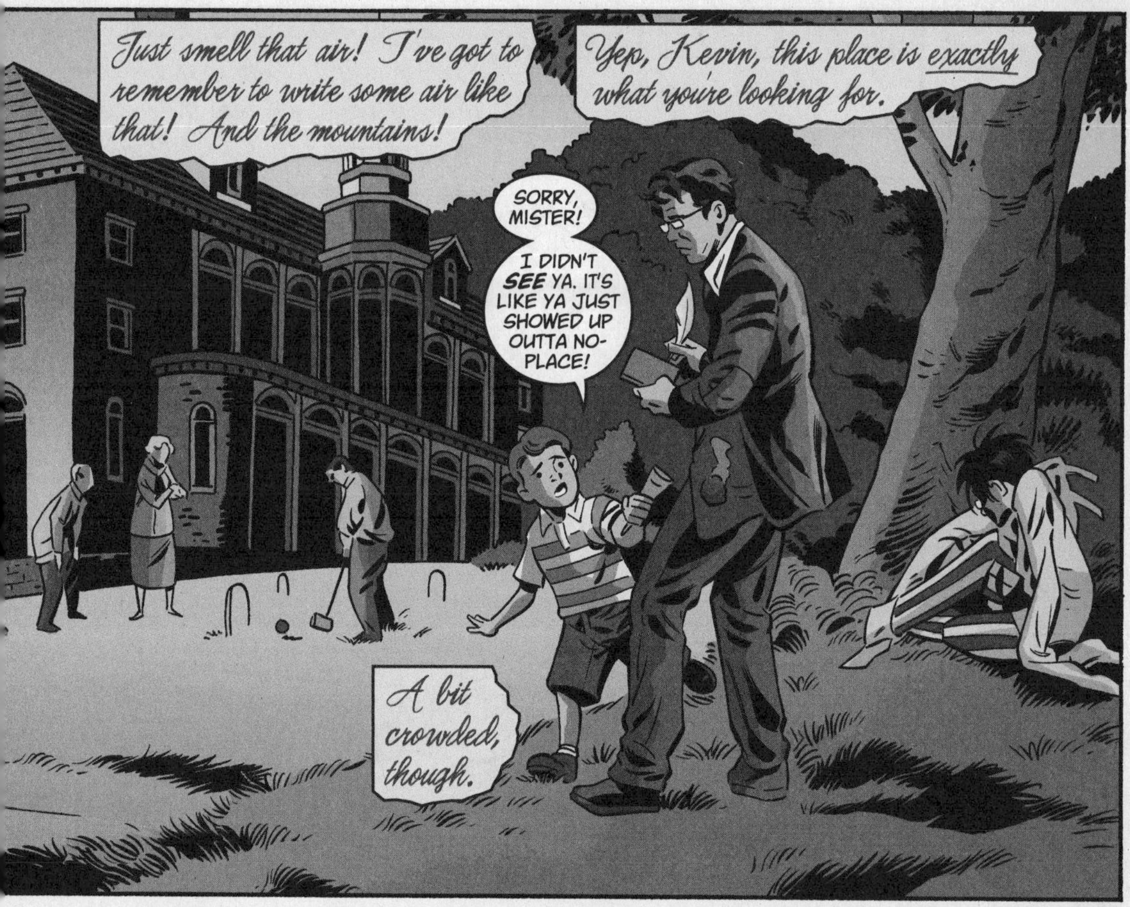
Just smell that air! I've got to remember to write some air like that! And the mountains!
Yep, Kevin, this place is exactly what you're looking for.
SORRY, MISTER!
I DIDN'T SEE YA. IT'S LIKE YA JUST SHOWED UP OUTTA NO-PLACE!
A bit crowded, though.

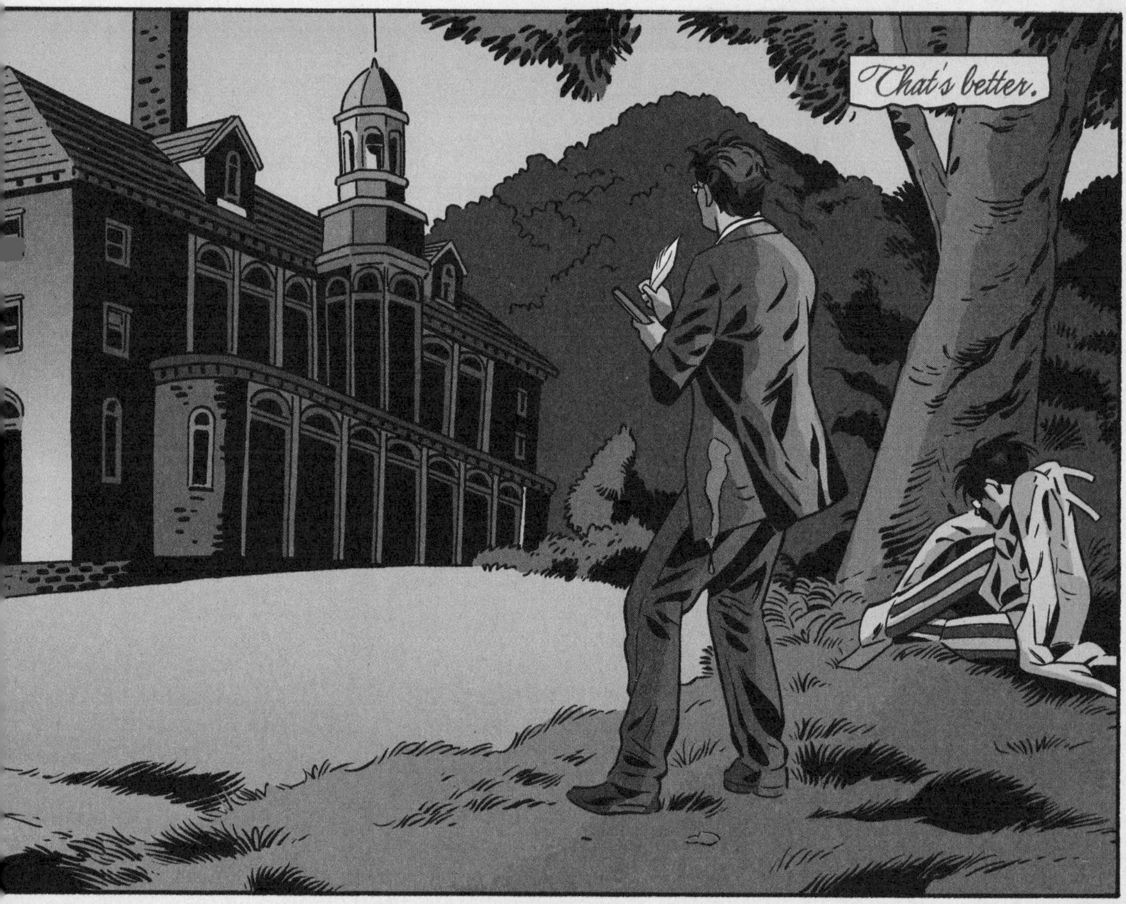
That's better.

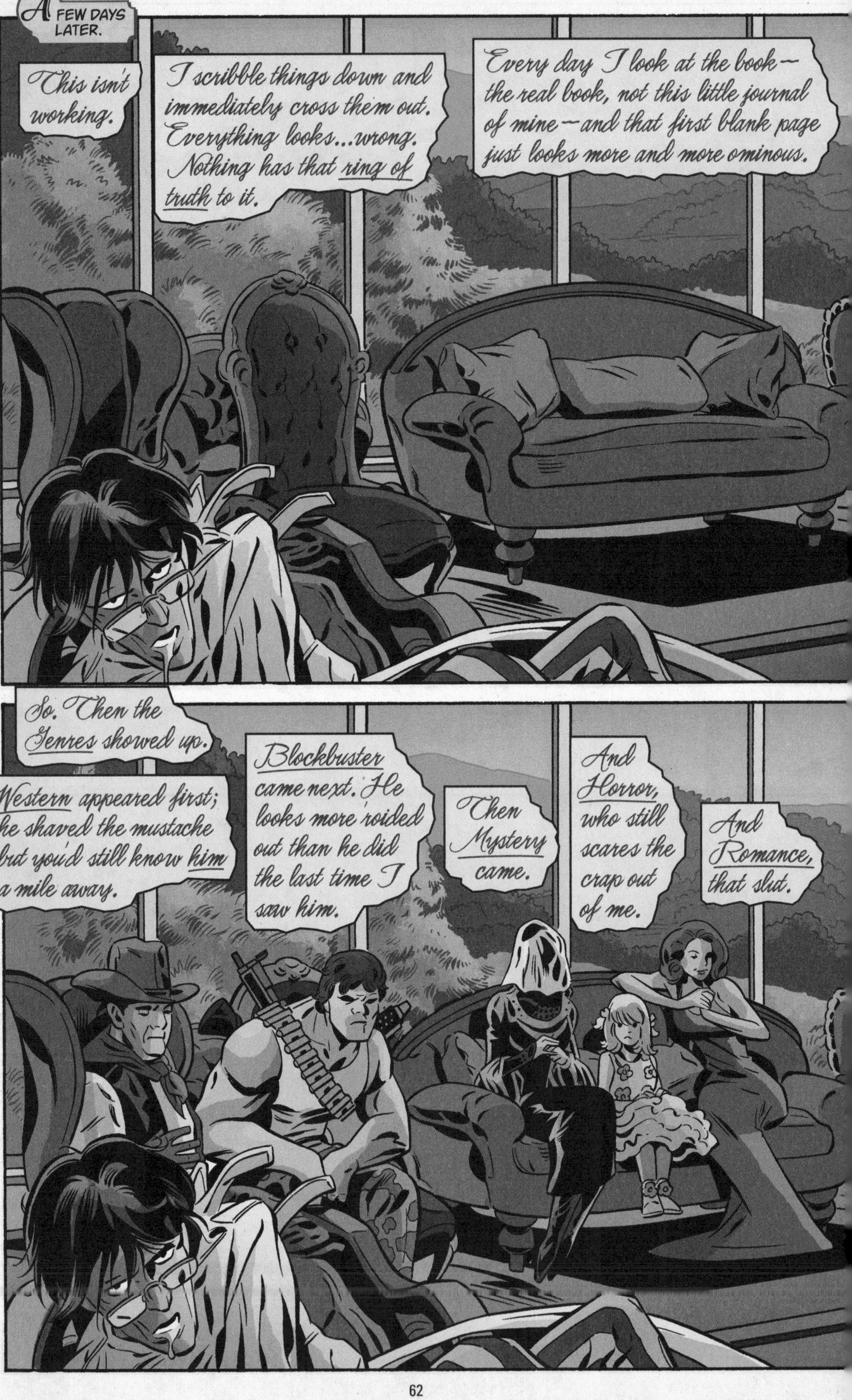
A FEW DAYS LATER.
This isn't working.
I scribble things down and immediately cross them out. Everything looks...wrong. Nothing has that ring of truth to it.
Every day I look at the book—the real book, not this little journal of mine—and that first blank page just looks more and more ominous.
So. Then the Genres showed up.
Western appeared first; he shaved the mustache but you'd still know him a mile away.
Blockbuster came next. He looks more 'roided out than he did the last time I saw him.
Then Mystery came.
And Horror, who still scares the crap out of me.
And Romance, that slut.

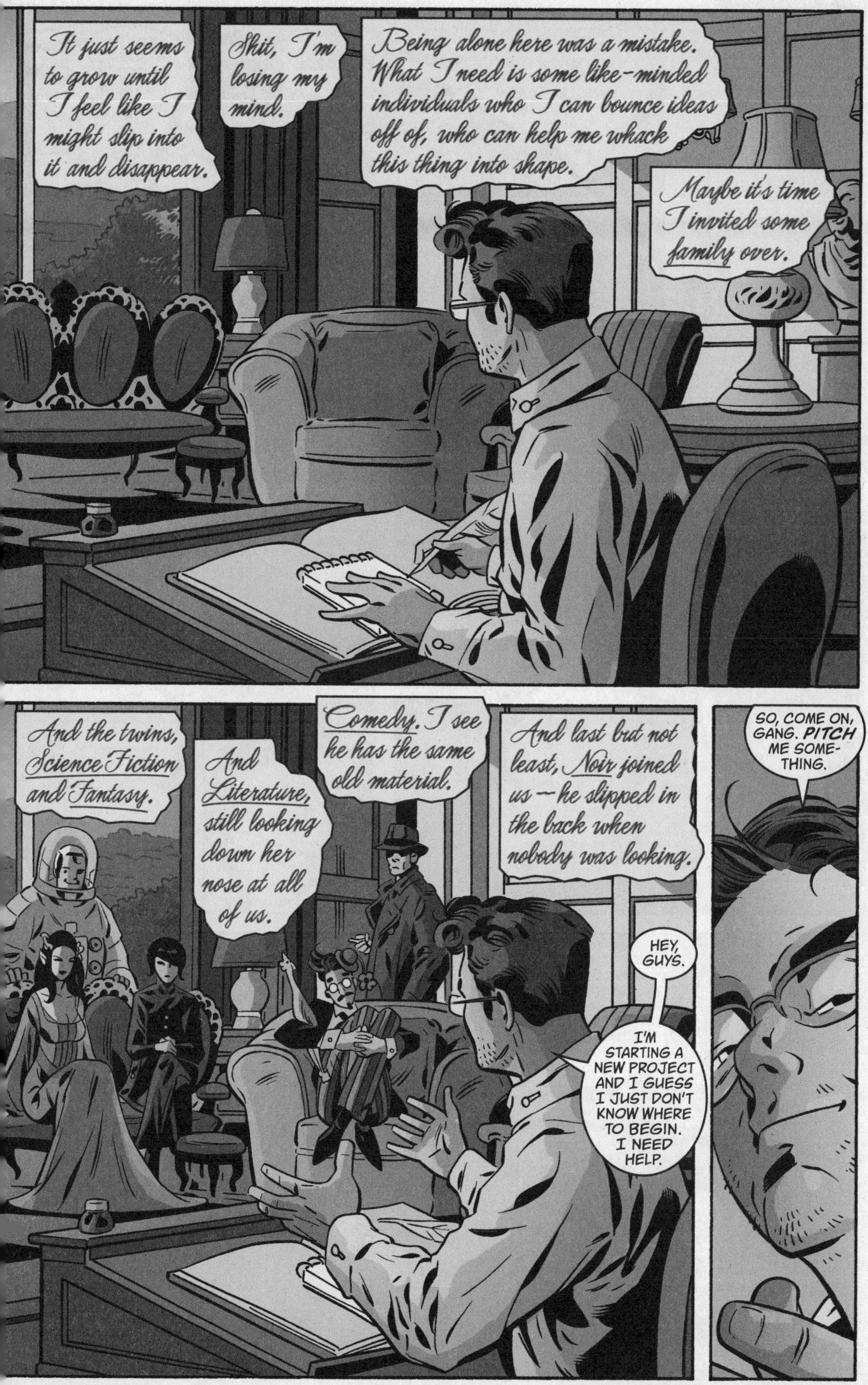
It just seems to grow until I feel like I might slip into it and disappear.
Shit, I'm losing my mind.
Being alone here was a mistake. What I need is some like-minded individuals who I can bounce ideas off of, who can help me whack this thing into shape.
Maybe it's time I invited some family over.
And the twins, Science Fiction and Fantasy.
And Literature, still looking down her nose at all of us.
Comedy. I see he has the same old material.
And last but not least, Noir joined us — he slipped in the back when nobody was looking.
HEY, GUYS.
I'M STARTING A NEW PROJECT AND I GUESS I JUST DON'T KNOW WHERE TO BEGIN. I NEED HELP.
SO, COME ON, GANG. PITCH ME SOMETHING.

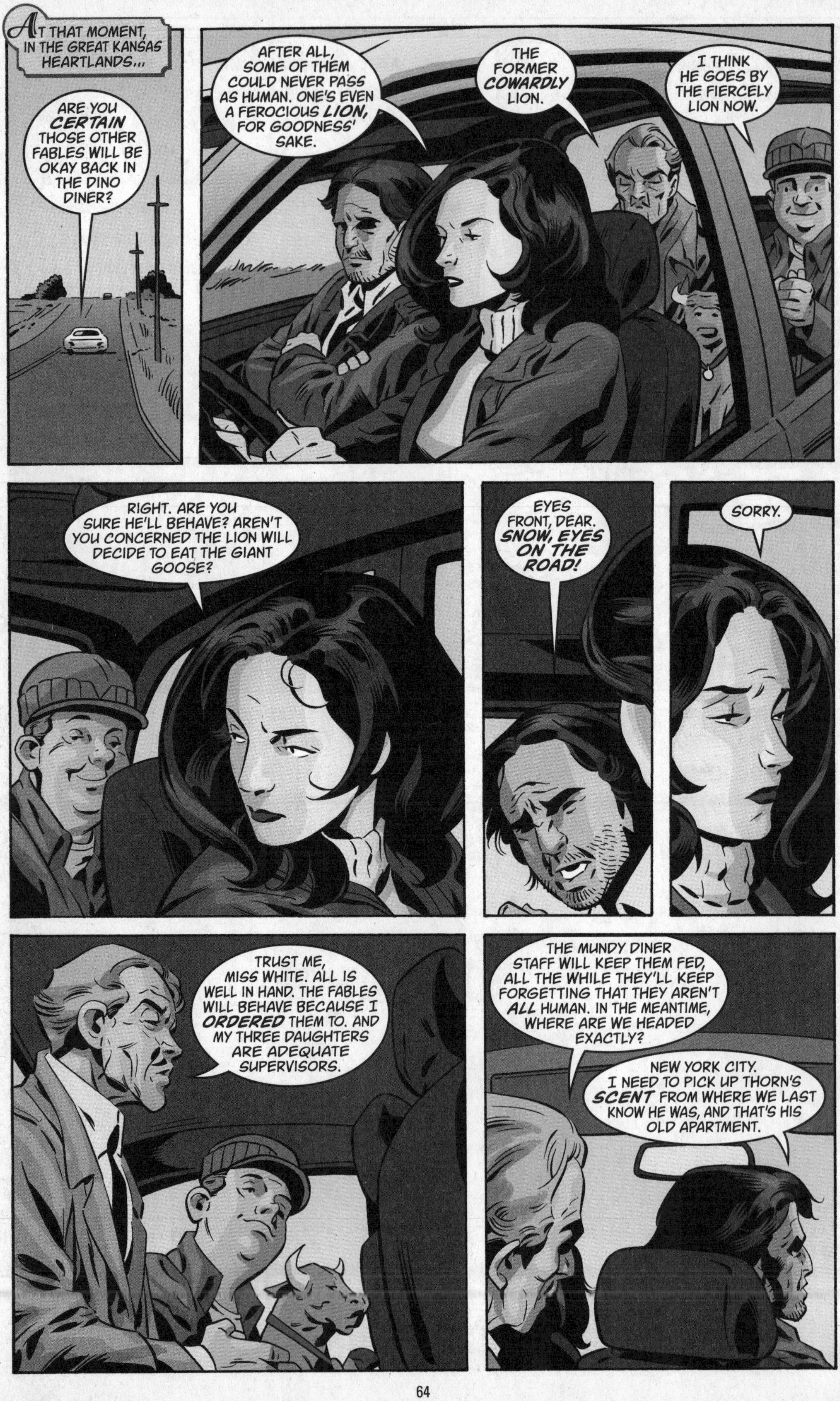
AT THAT MOMENT, IN THE GREAT KANSAS HEARTLANDS...
ARE YOU CERTAIN THOSE OTHER FABLES WILL BE OKAY BACK IN THE DINO DINER?
AFTER ALL, SOME OF THEM COULD NEVER PASS AS HUMAN. ONE'S EVEN A FEROCIOUS LION, FOR GOODNESS' SAKE.
THE FORMER COWARDLY LION.
I THINK HE GOES BY THE FIERCELY LION NOW.
RIGHT. ARE YOU SURE HE'LL BEHAVE? AREN'T YOU CONCERNED THE LION WILL DECIDE TO EAT THE GIANT GOOSE?
EYES FRONT, DEAR. SNOW, EYES ON THE ROAD!
SORRY.
TRUST ME, MISS WHITE. ALL IS WELL IN HAND. THE FABLES WILL BEHAVE BECAUSE I ORDERED THEM TO. AND MY THREE DAUGHTERS ARE ADEQUATE SUPERVISORS.
THE MUNDY DINER STAFF WILL KEEP THEM FED, ALL THE WHILE THEY'LL KEEP FORGETTING THAT THEY AREN'T ALL HUMAN. IN THE MEANTIME, WHERE ARE WE HEADED EXACTLY?
NEW YORK CITY. I NEED TO PICK UP THORN'S SCENT FROM WHERE WE LAST KNOW HE WAS, AND THAT'S HIS OLD APARTMENT.

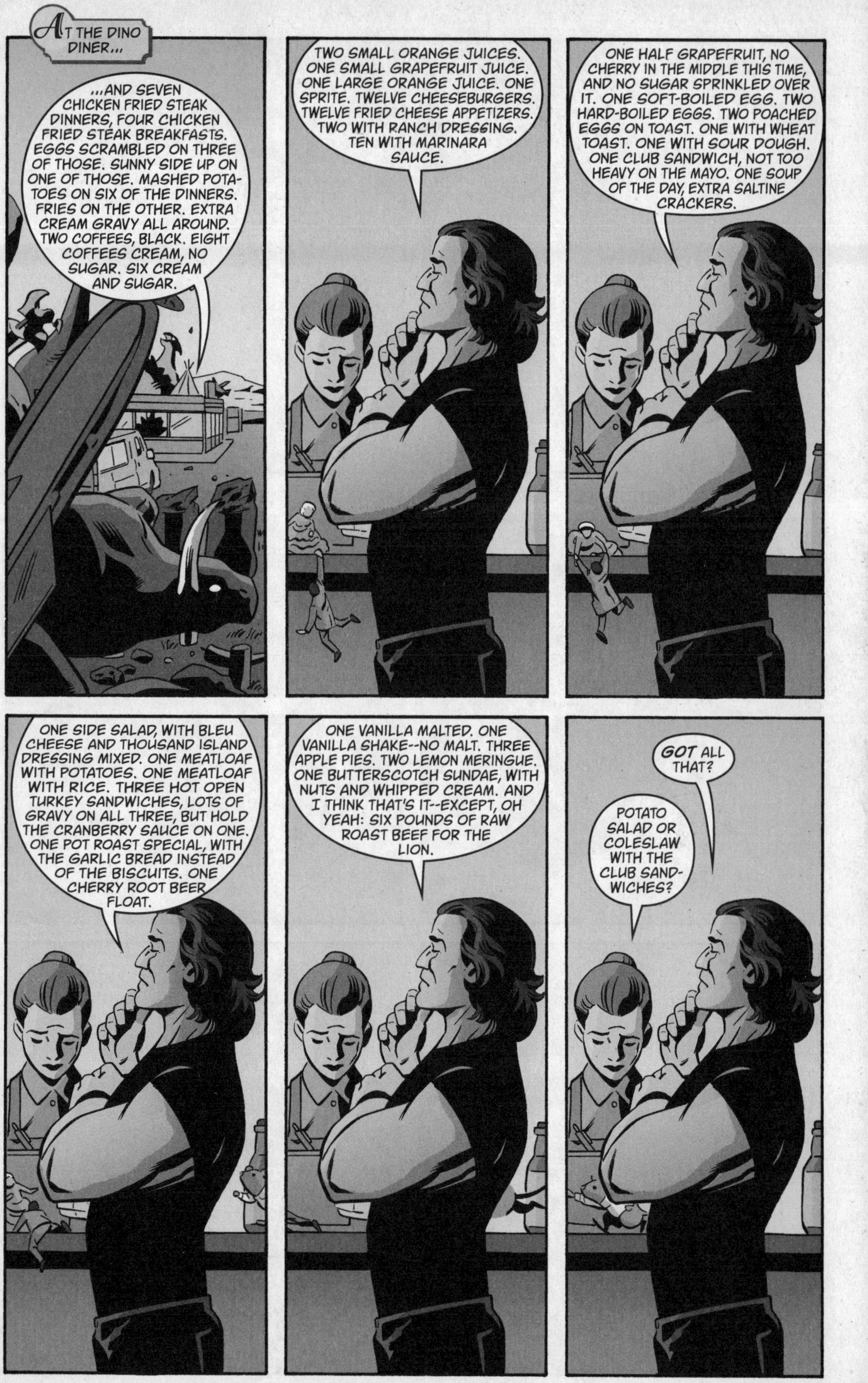
AT THE DINO DINER...
...AND SEVEN CHICKEN FRIED STEAK DINNERS, FOUR CHICKEN FRIED STEAK BREAKFASTS. EGGS SCRAMBLED ON THREE OF THOSE. SUNNY SIDE UP ON ONE OF THOSE. MASHED POTATOES ON SIX OF THE DINNERS. FRIES ON THE OTHER. EXTRA CREAM GRAVY ALL AROUND. TWO COFFEES, BLACK. EIGHT COFFEES CREAM, NO SUGAR. SIX CREAM AND SUGAR.
TWO SMALL ORANGE JUICES. ONE SMALL GRAPEFRUIT JUICE. ONE LARGE ORANGE JUICE. ONE SPRITE. TWELVE CHEESEBURGERS. TWELVE FRIED CHEESE APPETIZERS. TWO WITH RANCH DRESSING. TEN WITH MARINARA SAUCE.
ONE HALF GRAPEFRUIT, NO CHERRY IN THE MIDDLE THIS TIME, AND NO SUGAR SPRINKLED OVER IT. ONE SOFT-BOILED EGG. TWO HARD-BOILED EGGS. TWO POACHED EGGS ON TOAST. ONE WITH WHEAT TOAST. ONE WITH SOUR DOUGH. ONE CLUB SANDWICH, NOT TOO HEAVY ON THE MAYO. ONE SOUP OF THE DAY, EXTRA SALTINE CRACKERS.
ONE SIDE SALAD, WITH BLEU CHEESE AND THOUSAND ISLAND DRESSING MIXED. ONE MEATLOAF WITH POTATOES. ONE MEATLOAF WITH RICE. THREE HOT OPEN TURKEY SANDWICHES, LOTS OF GRAVY ON ALL THREE, BUT HOLD THE CRANBERRY SAUCE ON ONE. ONE POT ROAST SPECIAL, WITH THE GARLIC BREAD INSTEAD OF THE BISCUITS. ONE CHERRY ROOT BEER FLOAT.
ONE VANILLA MALTED. ONE VANILLA SHAKE--NO MALT. THREE APPLE PIES. TWO LEMON MERINGUE. ONE BUTTERSCOTCH SUNDAE, WITH NUTS AND WHIPPED CREAM. AND I THINK THAT'S IT--EXCEPT, OH YEAH: SIX POUNDS OF RAW ROAST BEEF FOR THE LION.
GOT ALL THAT?
POTATO SALAD OR COLESLAW WITH THE CLUB SANDWICHES?

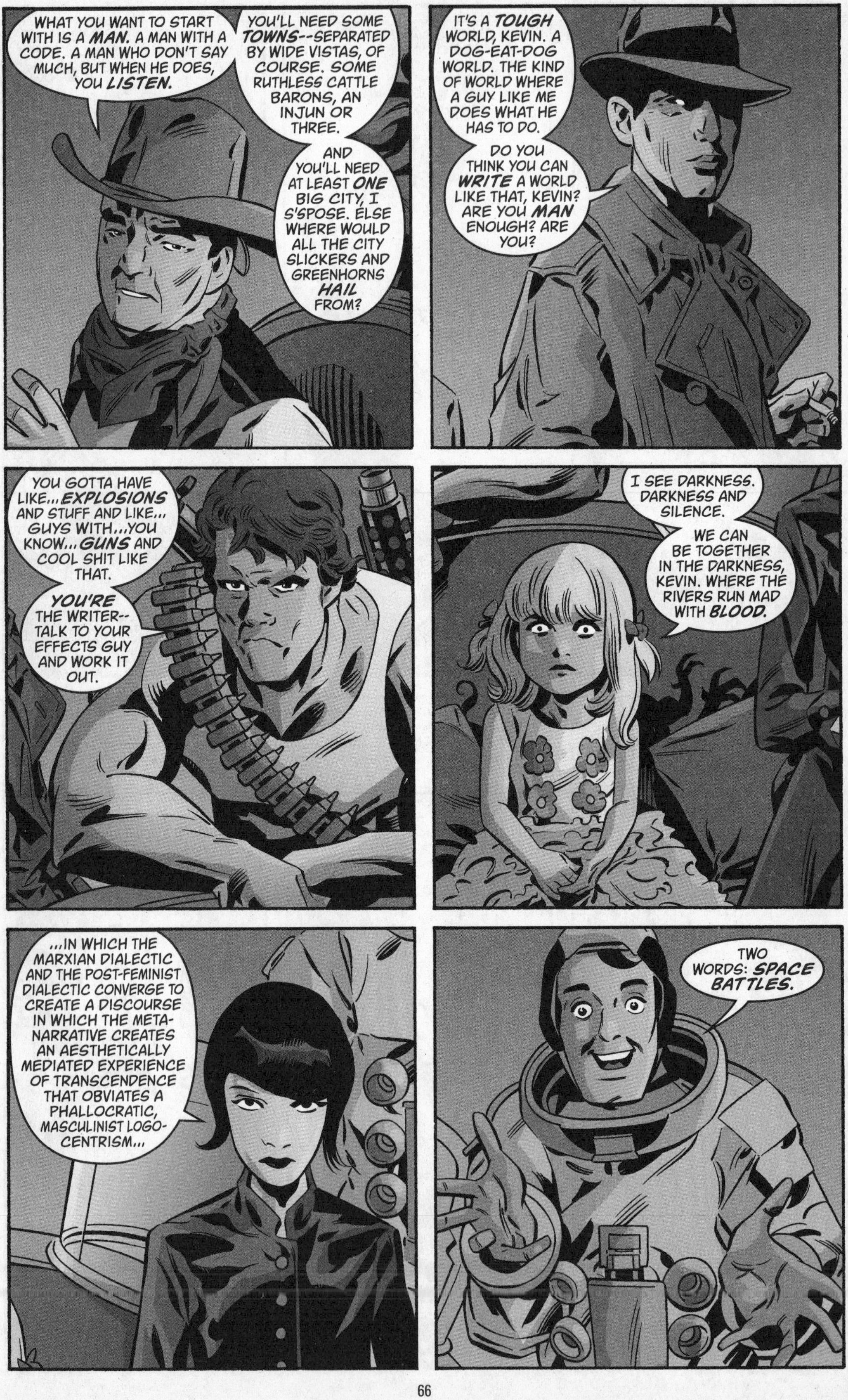
WHAT YOU WANT TO START WITH IS A MAN. A MAN WITH A CODE. A MAN WHO DON'T SAY MUCH, BUT WHEN HE DOES, YOU LISTEN.
YOU'LL NEED SOME TOWNS--SEPARATED BY WIDE VISTAS, OF COURSE. SOME RUTHLESS CATTLE BARONS, AN INJUN OR THREE.
AND YOU'LL NEED AT LEAST ONE BIG CITY, I S'SPOSE. ELSE WHERE WOULD ALL THE CITY SLICKERS AND GREENHORNS HAIL FROM?
IT'S A TOUGH WORLD, KEVIN. A DOG-EAT-DOG WORLD. THE KIND OF WORLD WHERE A GUY LIKE ME DOES WHAT HE HAS TO DO.
DO YOU THINK YOU CAN WRITE A WORLD LIKE THAT, KEVIN? ARE YOU MAN ENOUGH? ARE YOU?
YOU GOTTA HAVE LIKE...EXPLOSIONS AND STUFF AND LIKE... GUYS WITH...YOU KNOW...GUNS AND COOL SHIT LIKE THAT.
YOU'RE THE WRITER-- TALK TO YOUR EFFECTS GUY AND WORK IT OUT.
I SEE DARKNESS. DARKNESS AND SILENCE.
WE CAN BE TOGETHER IN THE DARKNESS, KEVIN. WHERE THE RIVERS RUN MAD WITH BLOOD.
...IN WHICH THE MARXIAN DIALECTIC AND THE POST-FEMINIST DIALECTIC CONVERGE TO CREATE A DISCOURSE IN WHICH THE META-NARRATIVE CREATES AN AESTHETICALLY MEDIATED EXPERIENCE OF TRANSCENDENCE THAT OBVIATES A PHALLOCRATIC, MASCULINIST LOGO-CENTRISM...
TWO WORDS: SPACE BATTLES.

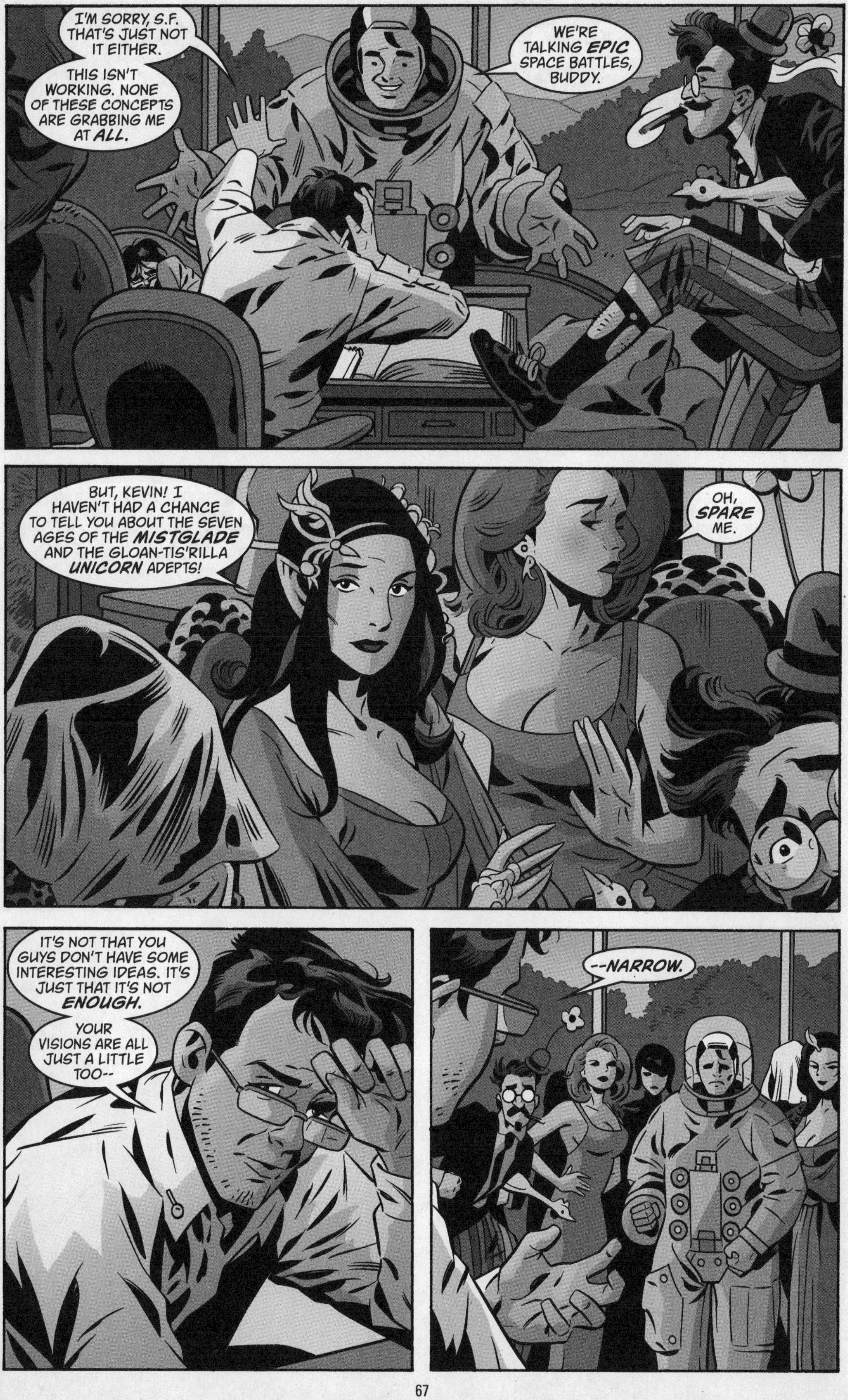
I'M SORRY, S.F. THAT'S JUST NOT IT EITHER.
THIS ISN'T WORKING. NONE OF THESE CONCEPTS ARE GRABBING ME AT ALL.
WE'RE TALKING EPIC SPACE BATTLES, BUDDY.
BUT, KEVIN! I HAVEN'T HAD A CHANCE TO TELL YOU ABOUT THE SEVEN AGES OF THE MISTGLADE AND THE GLOAN-TIS'RILLA UNICORN ADEPTS!
OH, SPARE ME.
IT'S NOT THAT YOU GUYS DON'T HAVE SOME INTERESTING IDEAS. IT'S JUST THAT IT'S NOT ENOUGH.
YOUR VISIONS ARE ALL JUST A LITTLE TOO--
--NARROW.

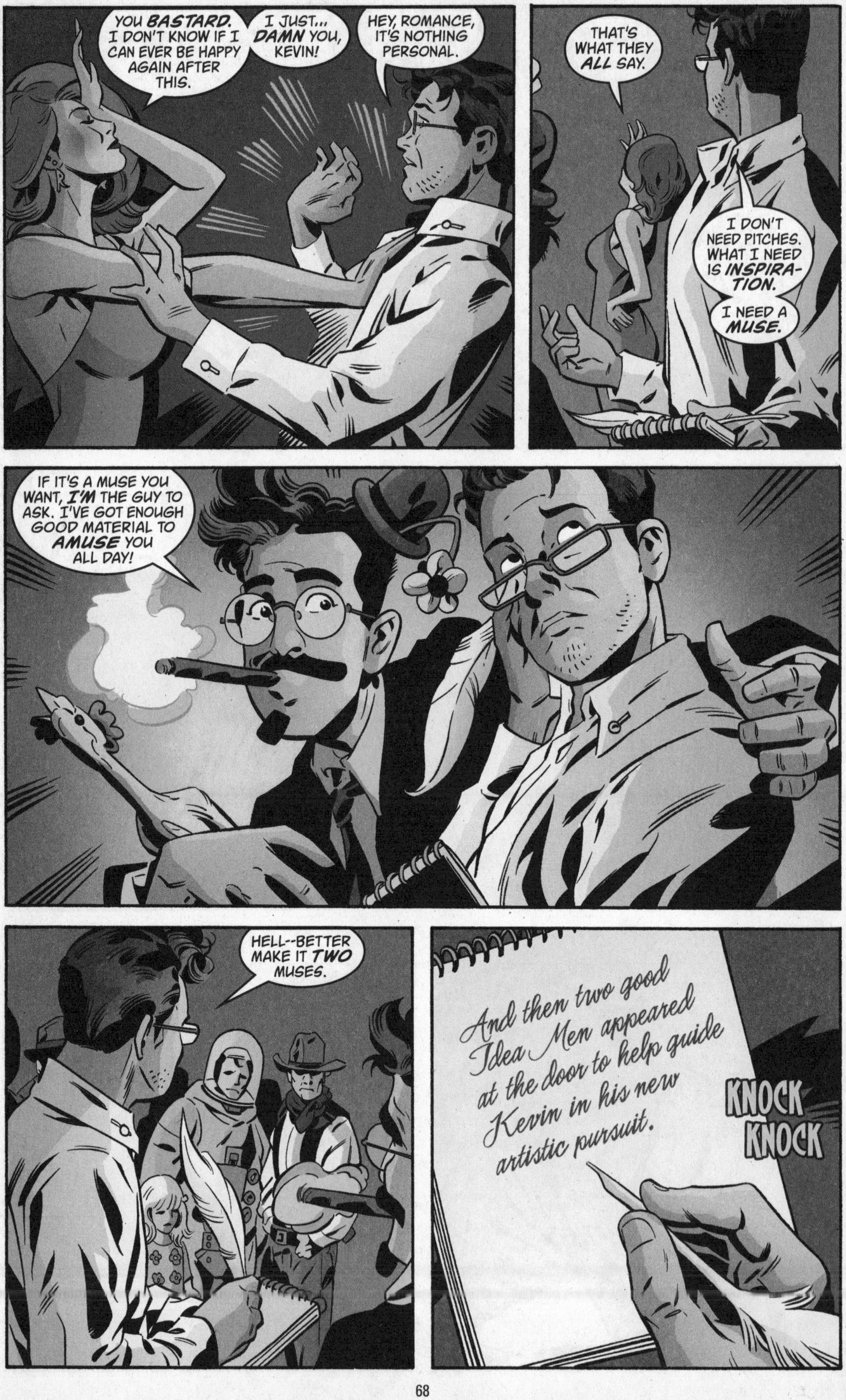
YOU BASTARD. I DON'T KNOW IF I CAN EVER BE HAPPY AGAIN AFTER THIS.
I JUST... DAMN YOU, KEVIN!
HEY, ROMANCE, IT'S NOTHING PERSONAL.
THAT'S WHAT THEY ALL SAY.
I DON'T NEED PITCHES. WHAT I NEED IS INSPIRA-TION.
I NEED A MUSE.
IF IT'S A MUSE YOU WANT, I'M THE GUY TO ASK. I'VE GOT ENOUGH GOOD MATERIAL TO AMUSE YOU ALL DAY!
HELL--BETTER MAKE IT TWO MUSES.
And then two good Idea Men appeared at the door to help guide Kevin in his new artistic pursuit.
KNOCK
KNOCK

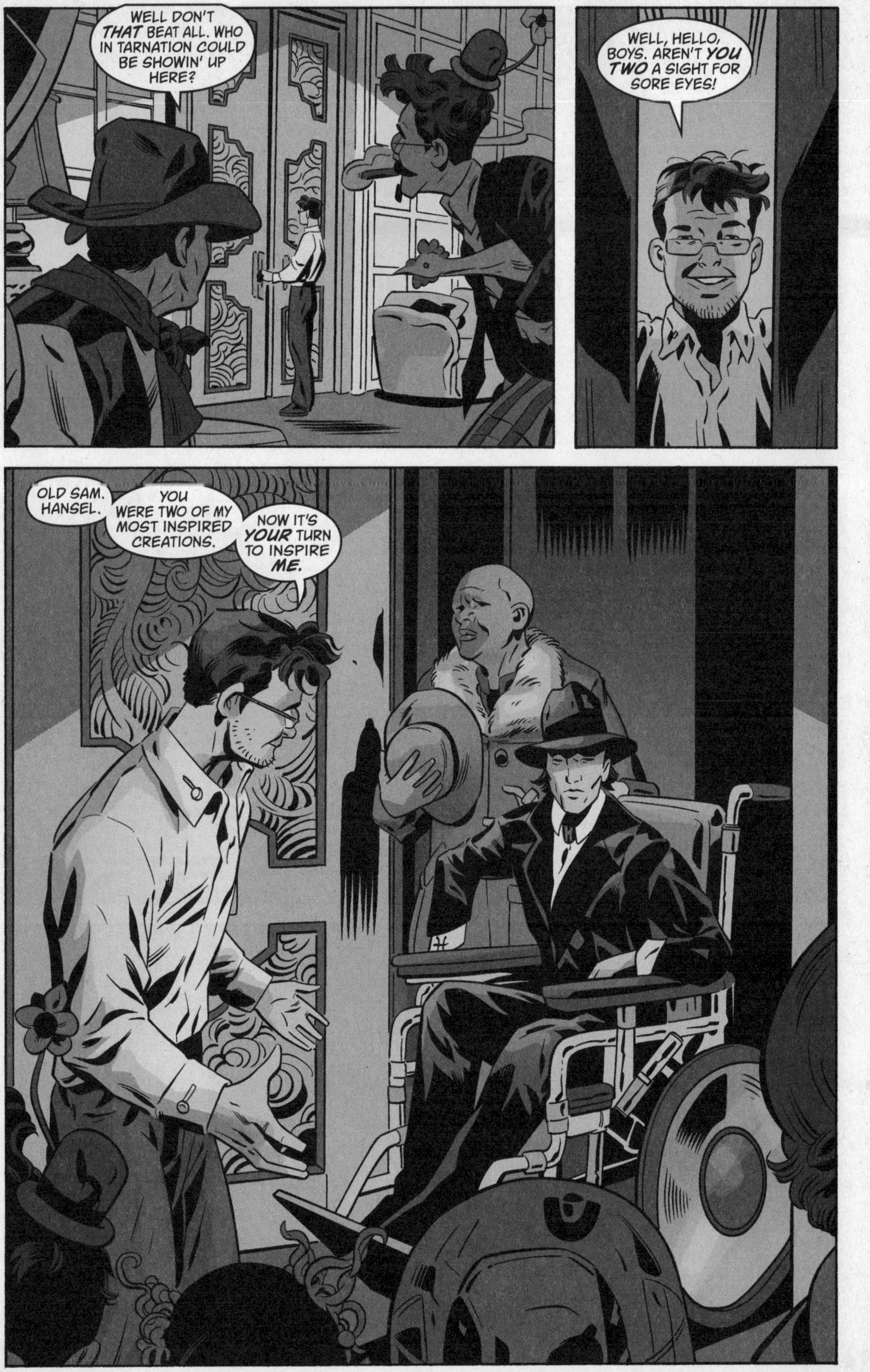
WELL DON'T THAT BEAT ALL. WHO IN TARNATION COULD BE SHOWIN' UP HERE?
WELL, HELLO, BOYS. AREN'T YOU TWO A SIGHT FOR SORE EYES!
OLD SAM. HANSEL.
YOU WERE TWO OF MY MOST INSPIRED CREATIONS.
NOW IT'S YOUR TURN TO INSPIRE ME.

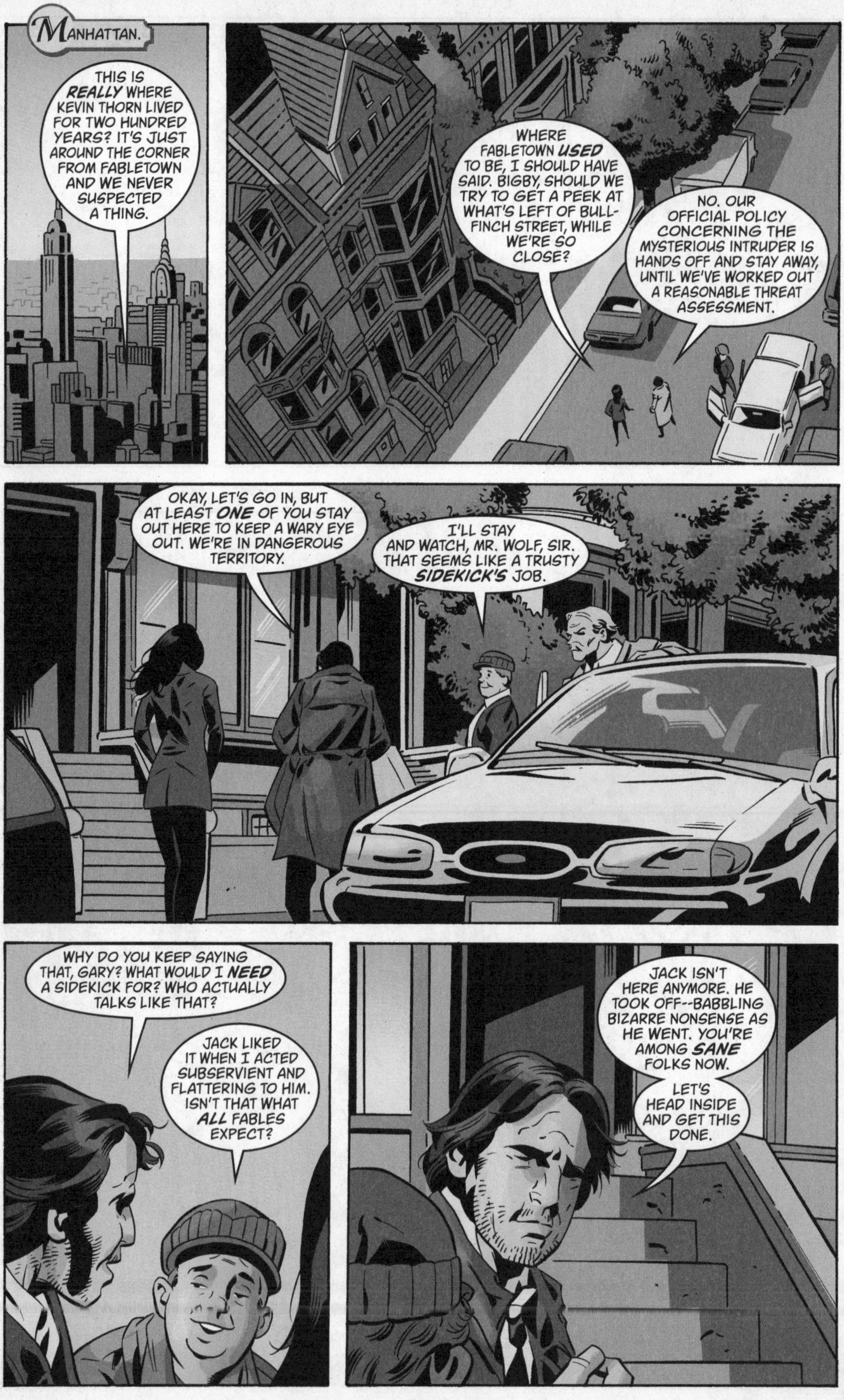
MANHATTAN.
THIS IS REALLY WHERE KEVIN THORN LIVED FOR TWO HUNDRED YEARS? IT'S JUST AROUND THE CORNER FROM FABLETOWN AND WE NEVER SUSPECTED A THING.
WHERE FABLETOWN USED TO BE, I SHOULD HAVE SAID. BIGBY, SHOULD WE TRY TO GET A PEEK AT WHAT'S LEFT OF BULL-FINCH STREET, WHILE WE'RE SO CLOSE?
NO. OUR OFFICIAL POLICY CONCERNING THE MYSTERIOUS INTRUDER IS HANDS OFF AND STAY AWAY, UNTIL WE'VE WORKED OUT A REASONABLE THREAT ASSESSMENT.
OKAY, LET'S GO IN, BUT AT LEAST ONE OF YOU STAY OUT HERE TO KEEP A WARY EYE OUT. WE'RE IN DANGEROUS TERRITORY.
I'LL STAY AND WATCH, MR. WOLF, SIR. THAT SEEMS LIKE A TRUSTY SIDEKICK'S JOB.
WHY DO YOU KEEP SAYING THAT, GARY? WHAT WOULD I NEED A SIDEKICK FOR? WHO ACTUALLY TALKS LIKE THAT?
JACK LIKED IT WHEN I ACTED SUBSERVIENT AND FLATTERING TO HIM. ISN'T THAT WHAT ALL FABLES EXPECT?
JACK ISN'T HERE ANYMORE. HE TOOK OFF--BABBLING BIZARRE NONSENSE AS HE WENT. YOU'RE AMONG SANE FOLKS NOW.
LET'S HEAD INSIDE AND GET THIS DONE.

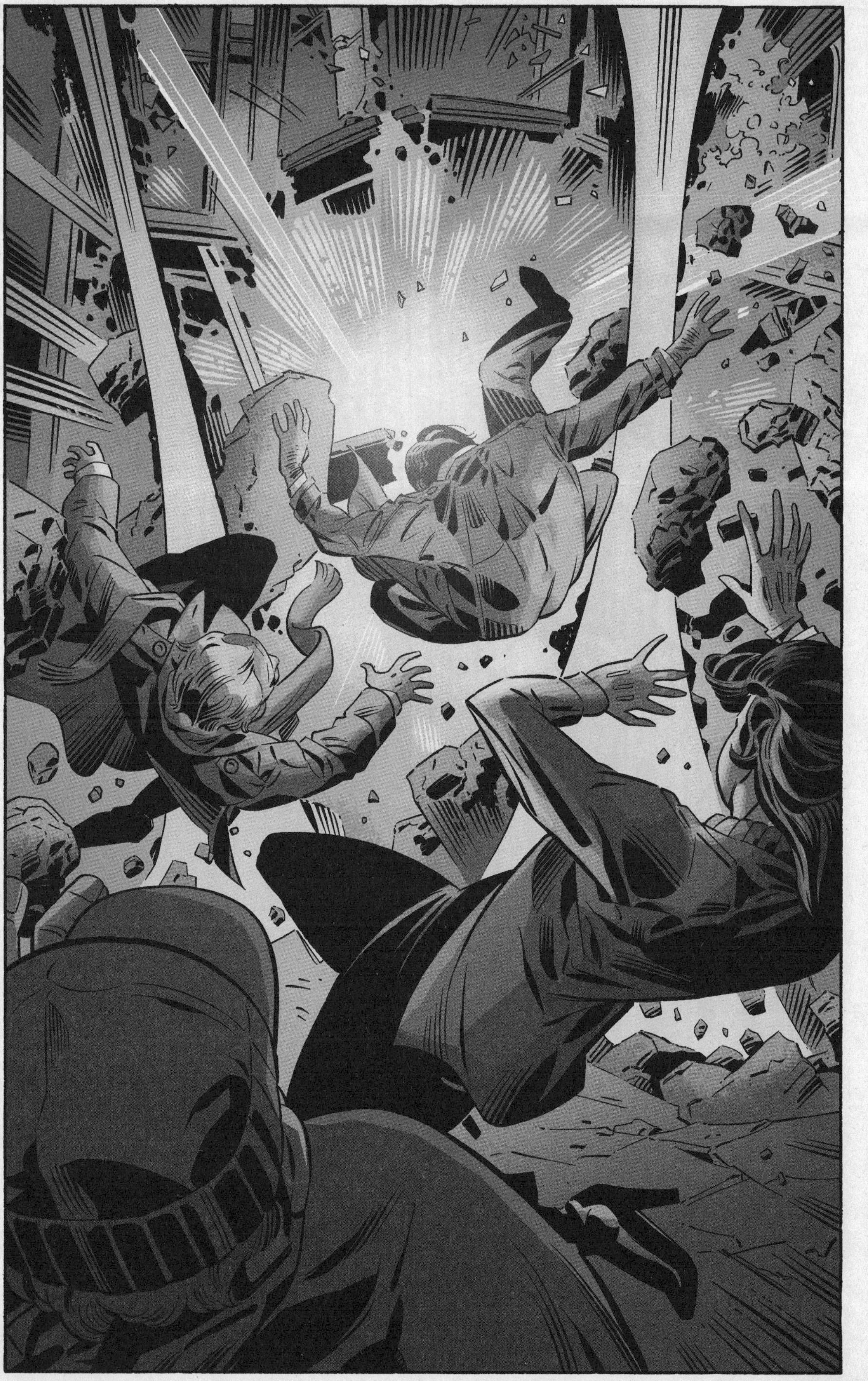

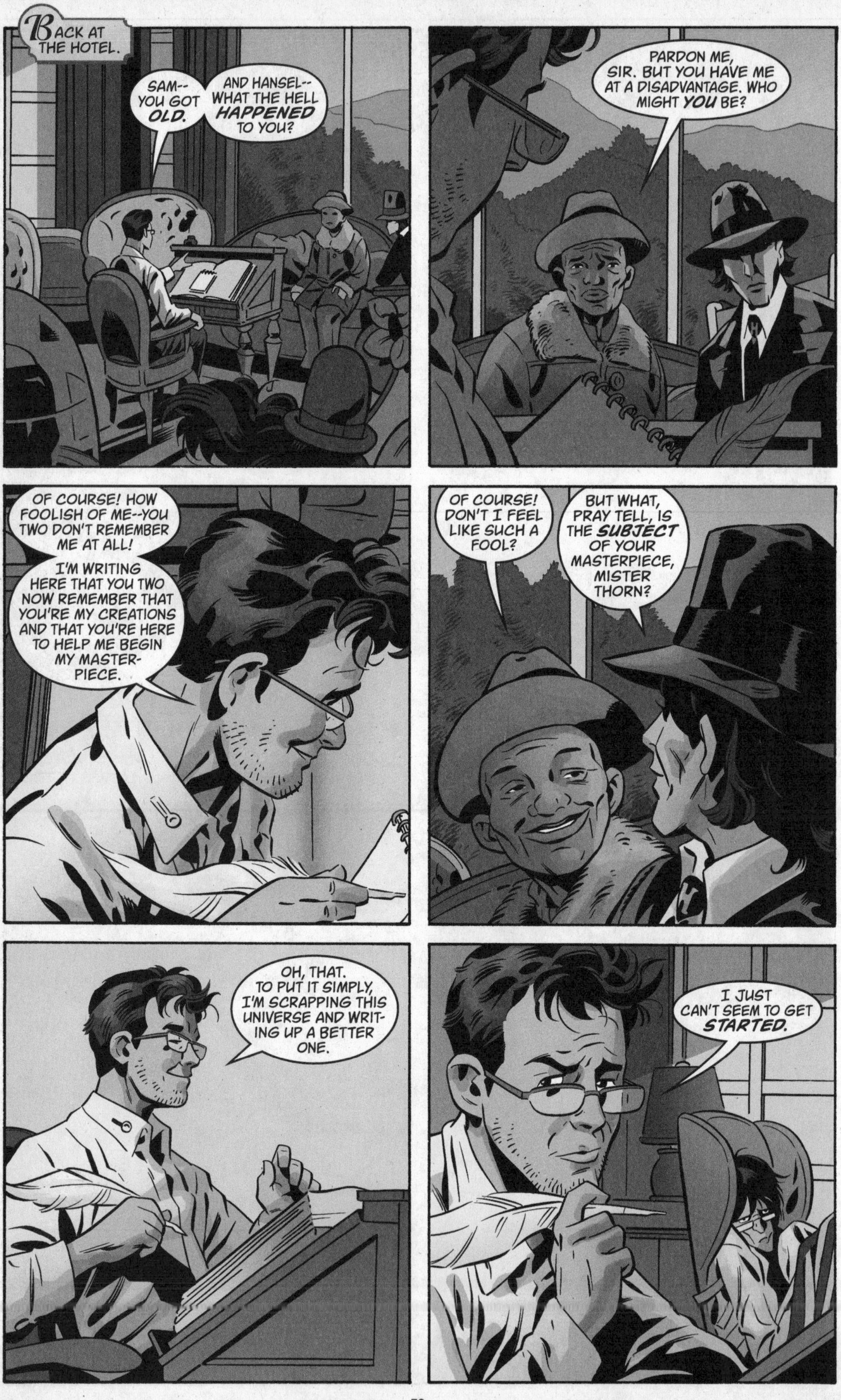
BACK AT THE HOTEL.
SAM-- YOU GOT OLD.
AND HANSEL-- WHAT THE HELL HAPPENED TO YOU?
PARDON ME, SIR. BUT YOU HAVE ME AT A DISADVANTAGE. WHO MIGHT YOU BE?
OF COURSE! HOW FOOLISH OF ME--YOU TWO DON'T REMEMBER ME AT ALL!
I'M WRITING HERE THAT YOU TWO NOW REMEMBER THAT YOU'RE MY CREATIONS AND THAT YOU'RE HERE TO HELP ME BEGIN MY MASTER-PIECE.
OF COURSE! DON'T I FEEL LIKE SUCH A FOOL?
BUT WHAT, PRAY TELL, IS THE SUBJECT OF YOUR MASTERPIECE, MISTER THORN?
OH, THAT. TO PUT IT SIMPLY, I'M SCRAPPING THIS UNIVERSE AND WRIT-ING UP A BETTER ONE.
I JUST CAN'T SEEM TO GET STARTED.

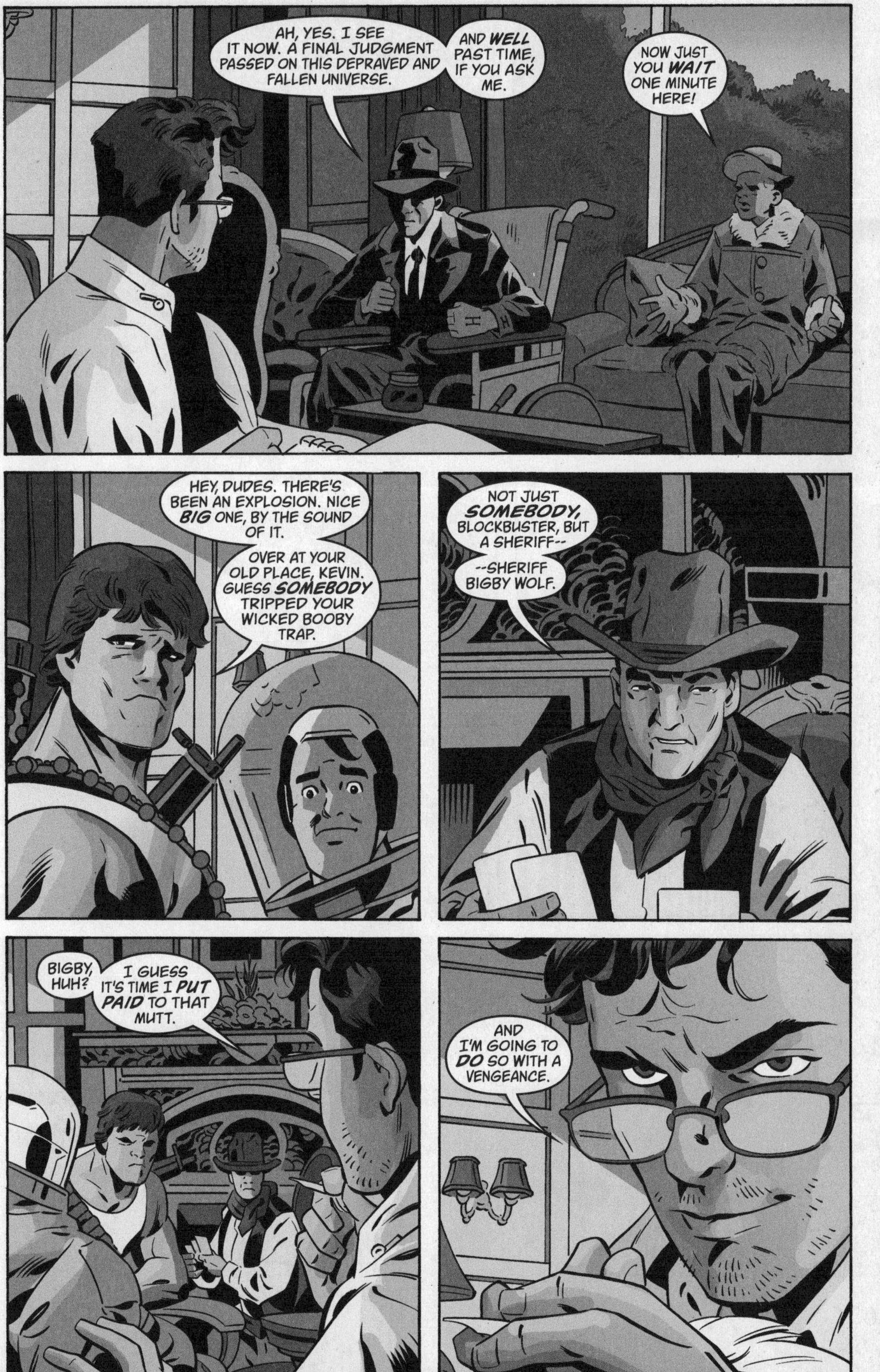
AH, YES. I SEE IT NOW. A FINAL JUDGMENT PASSED ON THIS DEPRAVED AND FALLEN UNIVERSE.
AND WELL PAST TIME, IF YOU ASK ME.
NOW JUST YOU WAIT ONE MINUTE HERE!
HEY, DUDES. THERE'S BEEN AN EXPLOSION. NICE BIG ONE, BY THE SOUND OF IT.
OVER AT YOUR OLD PLACE, KEVIN. GUESS SOMEBODY TRIPPED YOUR WICKED BOOBY TRAP.
NOT JUST SOMEBODY, BLOCKBUSTER, BUT A SHERIFF--
--SHERIFF BIGBY WOLF.
BIGBY, HUH?
I GUESS IT'S TIME I PUT PAID TO THAT MUTT.
AND I'M GOING TO DO SO WITH A VENGEANCE.

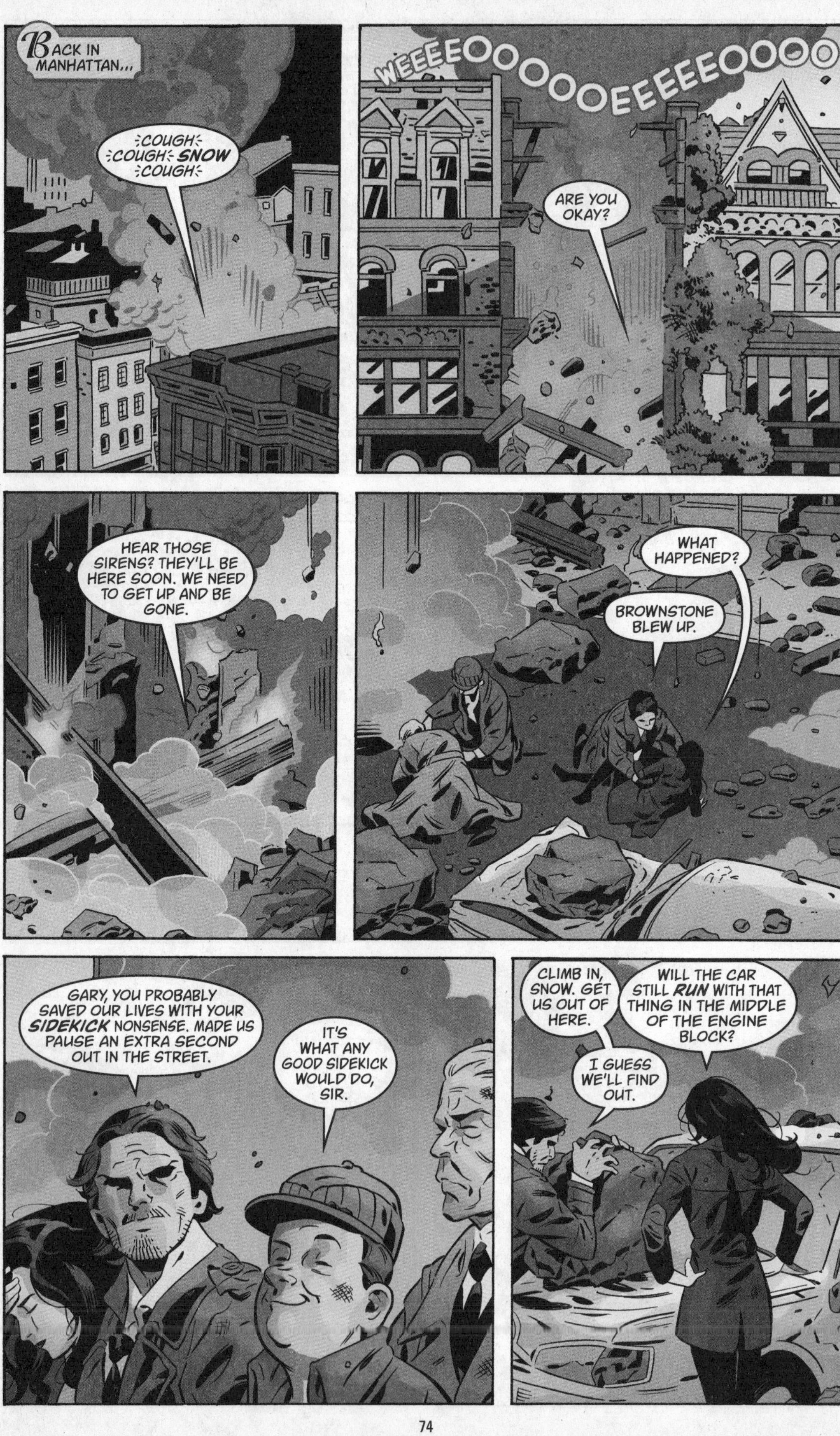

BACK IN MANHATTAN...
COUGH COUGH SNOW COUGH
WEEEEOOOOOOEEEEEOOOO
ARE YOU OKAY?
HEAR THOSE SIRENS? THEY'LL BE HERE SOON. WE NEED TO GET UP AND BE GONE.
WHAT HAPPENED?
BROWNSTONE BLEW UP.
GARY, YOU PROBABLY SAVED OUR LIVES WITH YOUR SIDEKICK NONSENSE. MADE US PAUSE AN EXTRA SECOND OUT IN THE STREET.
IT'S WHAT ANY GOOD SIDEKICK WOULD DO, SIR.
CLIMB IN, SNOW. GET US OUT OF HERE.
WILL THE CAR STILL RUN WITH THAT THING IN THE MIDDLE OF THE ENGINE BLOCK?
I GUESS WE'LL FIND OUT.

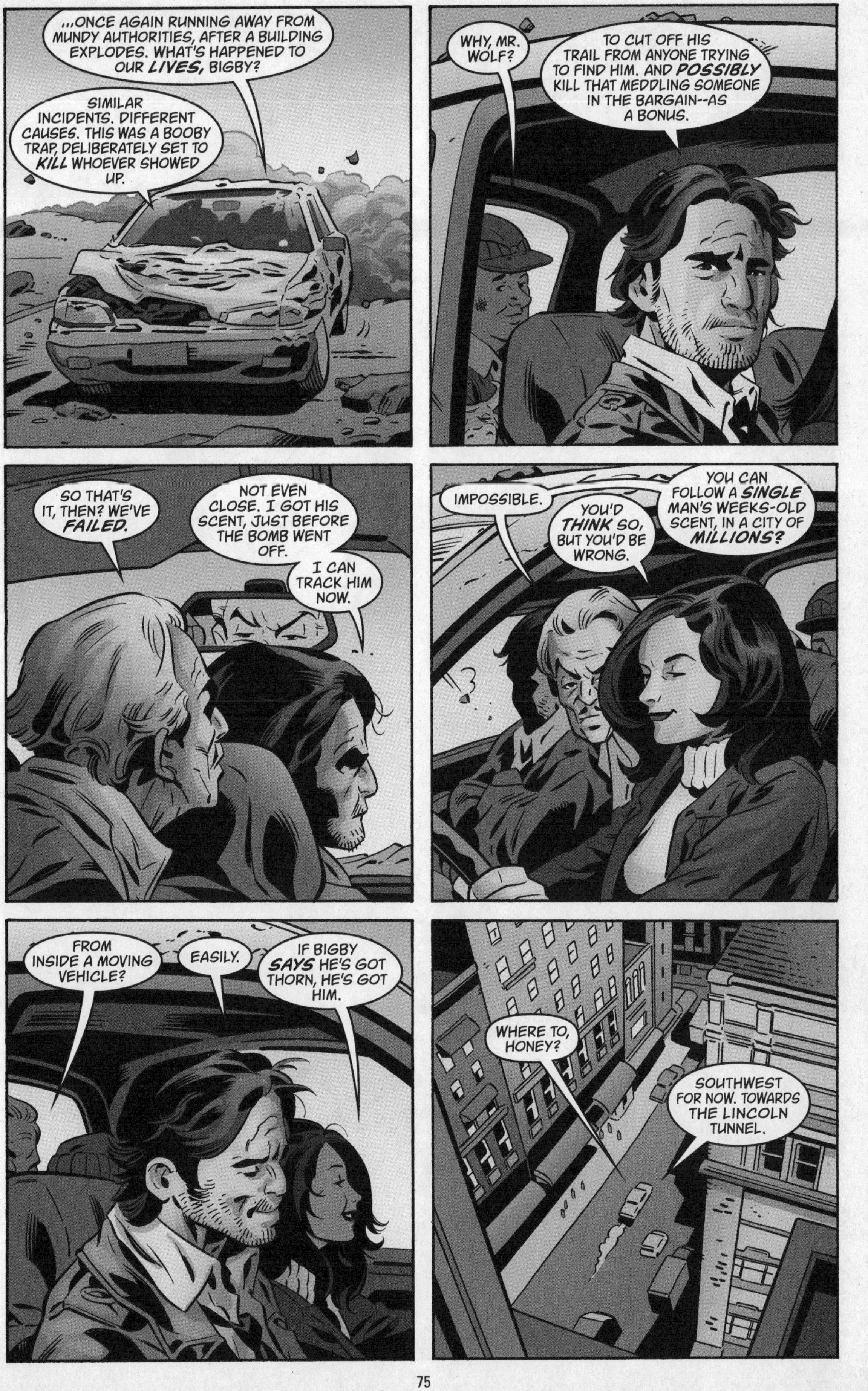

...ONCE AGAIN RUNNING AWAY FROM MUNDY AUTHORITIES, AFTER A BUILDING EXPLODES. WHAT'S HAPPENED TO OUR LIVES, BIGBY?
SIMILAR INCIDENTS. DIFFERENT CAUSES. THIS WAS A BOOBY TRAP, DELIBERATELY SET TO KILL WHOEVER SHOWED UP.
WHY, MR. WOLF?
TO CUT OFF HIS TRAIL FROM ANYONE TRYING TO FIND HIM. AND POSSIBLY KILL THAT MEDDLING SOMEONE IN THE BARGAIN--AS A BONUS.
SO THAT'S IT, THEN? WE'VE FAILED.
NOT EVEN CLOSE. I GOT HIS SCENT, JUST BEFORE THE BOMB WENT OFF.
I CAN TRACK HIM NOW.
IMPOSSIBLE.
YOU'D THINK SO, BUT YOU'D BE WRONG.
YOU CAN FOLLOW A SINGLE MAN'S WEEKS-OLD SCENT, IN A CITY OF MILLIONS?
FROM INSIDE A MOVING VEHICLE?
EASILY.
IF BIGBY SAYS HE'S GOT THORN, HE'S GOT HIM.
WHERE TO, HONEY?
SOUTHWEST FOR NOW. TOWARDS THE LINCOLN TUNNEL.

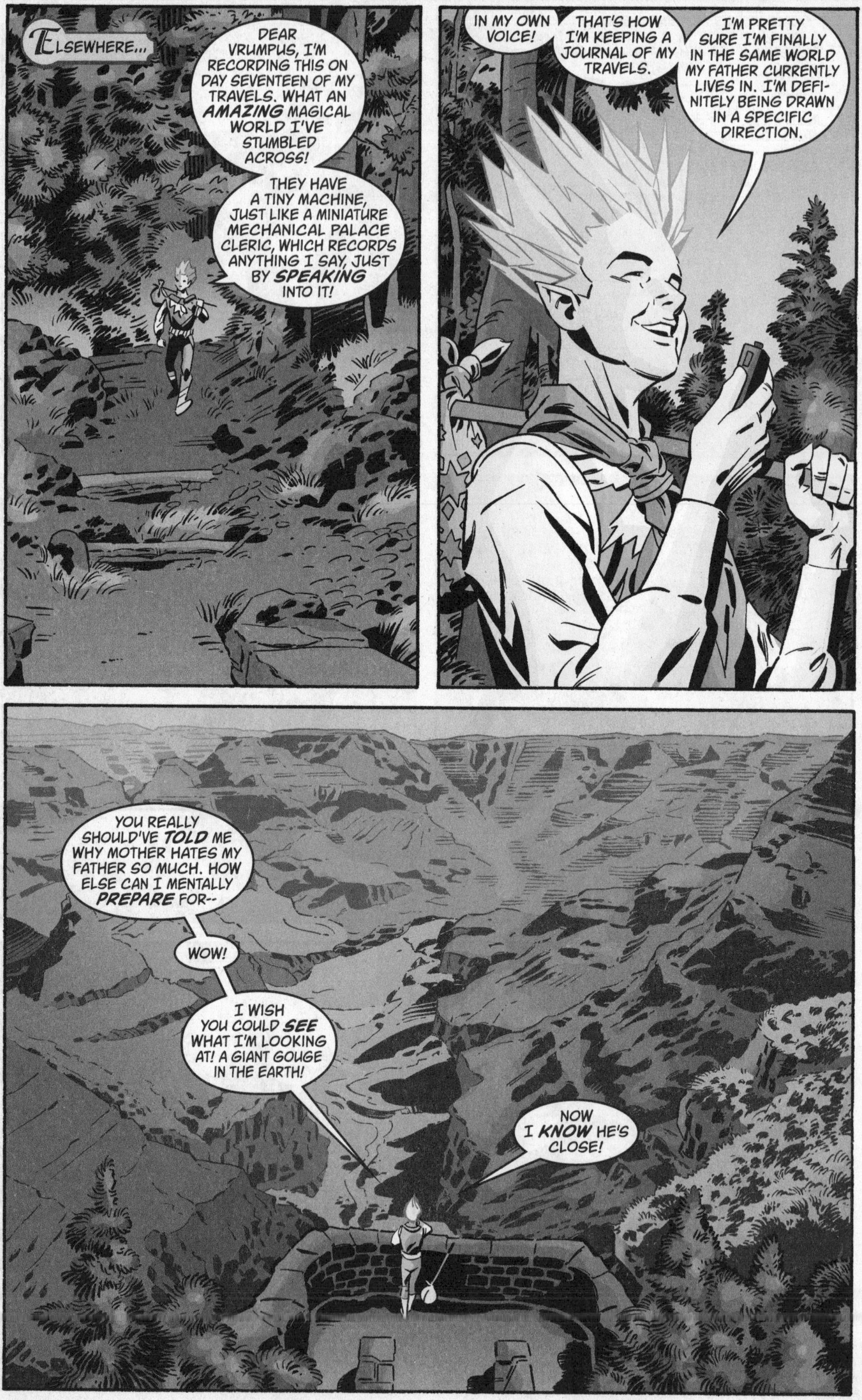
ELSEWHERE...
DEAR VRUMPUS, I'M RECORDING THIS ON DAY SEVENTEEN OF MY TRAVELS. WHAT AN AMAZING MAGICAL WORLD I'VE STUMBLED ACROSS!
THEY HAVE A TINY MACHINE, JUST LIKE A MINIATURE MECHANICAL PALACE CLERIC, WHICH RECORDS ANYTHING I SAY, JUST BY SPEAKING INTO IT!
IN MY OWN VOICE!
THAT'S HOW I'M KEEPING A JOURNAL OF MY TRAVELS.
I'M PRETTY SURE I'M FINALLY IN THE SAME WORLD MY FATHER CURRENTLY LIVES IN. I'M DEFINITELY BEING DRAWN IN A SPECIFIC DIRECTION.
YOU REALLY SHOULD'VE TOLD ME WHY MOTHER HATES MY FATHER SO MUCH. HOW ELSE CAN I MENTALLY PREPARE FOR--
WOW!
I WISH YOU COULD SEE WHAT I'M LOOKING AT! A GIANT GOUGE IN THE EARTH!
NOW I KNOW HE'S CLOSE!

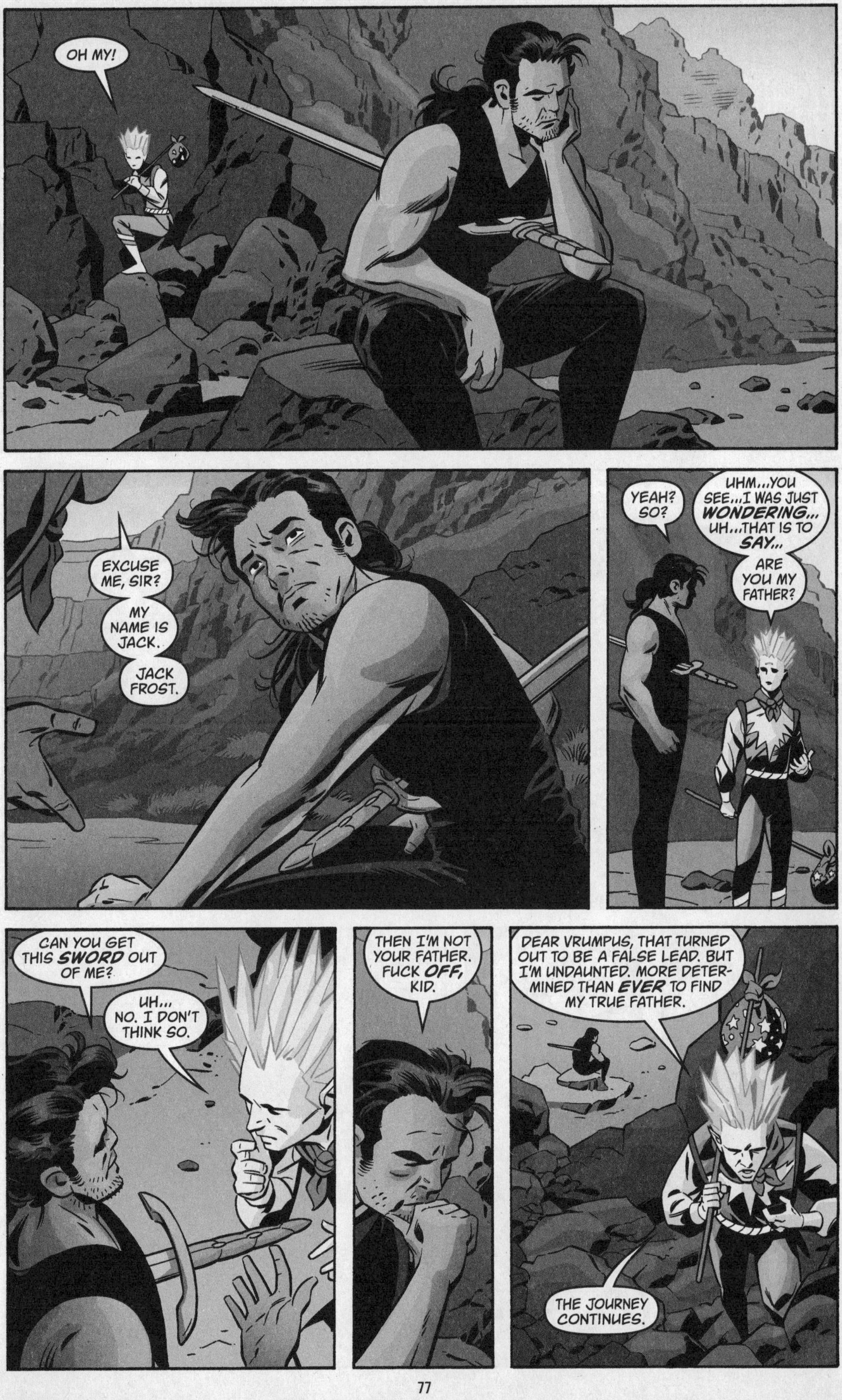
OH MY!
EXCUSE ME, SIR?
MY NAME IS JACK.
JACK FROST.
YEAH? SO?
UHM...YOU SEE...I WAS JUST WONDERING... UH...THAT IS TO SAY...
ARE YOU MY FATHER?
CAN YOU GET THIS SWORD OUT OF ME?
UH... NO. I DON'T THINK SO.
THEN I'M NOT YOUR FATHER. FUCK OFF, KID.
DEAR VRUMPUS, THAT TURNED OUT TO BE A FALSE LEAD. BUT I'M UNDAUNTED. MORE DETERMINED THAN EVER TO FIND MY TRUE FATHER.
THE JOURNEY CONTINUES.

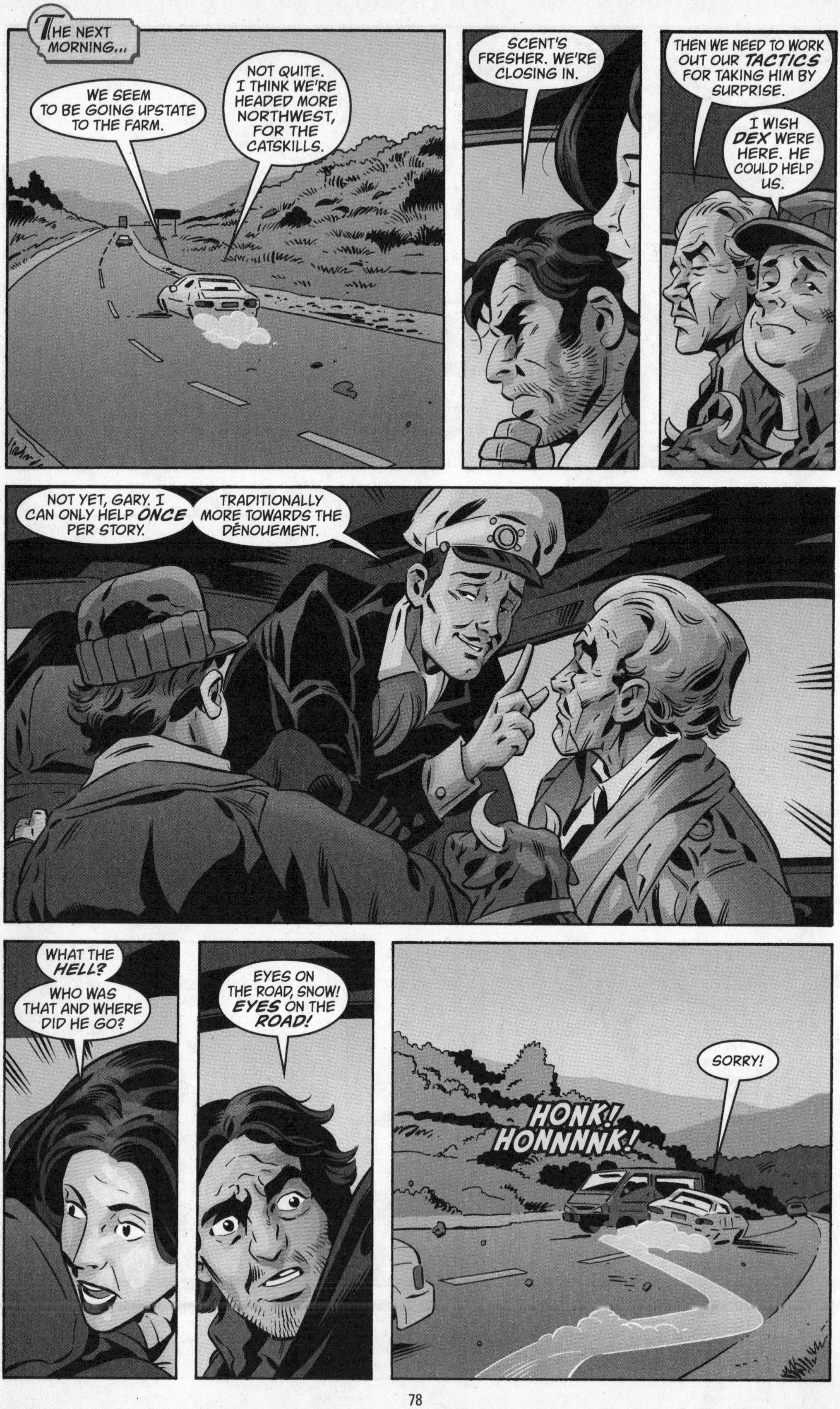
THE NEXT MORNING...
WE SEEM TO BE GOING UPSTATE TO THE FARM.
NOT QUITE. I THINK WE'RE HEADED MORE NORTHWEST, FOR THE CATSKILLS.
SCENT'S FRESHER. WE'RE CLOSING IN.
THEN WE NEED TO WORK OUT OUR TACTICS FOR TAKING HIM BY SURPRISE.
I WISH DEX WERE HERE. HE COULD HELP US.
NOT YET, GARY. I CAN ONLY HELP ONCE PER STORY.
TRADITIONALLY MORE TOWARDS THE DÉNOUEMENT.
WHAT THE HELL? WHO WAS THAT AND WHERE DID HE GO?
EYES ON THE ROAD, SNOW! EYES ON THE ROAD!
HONK! HONNNNK!
SORRY!

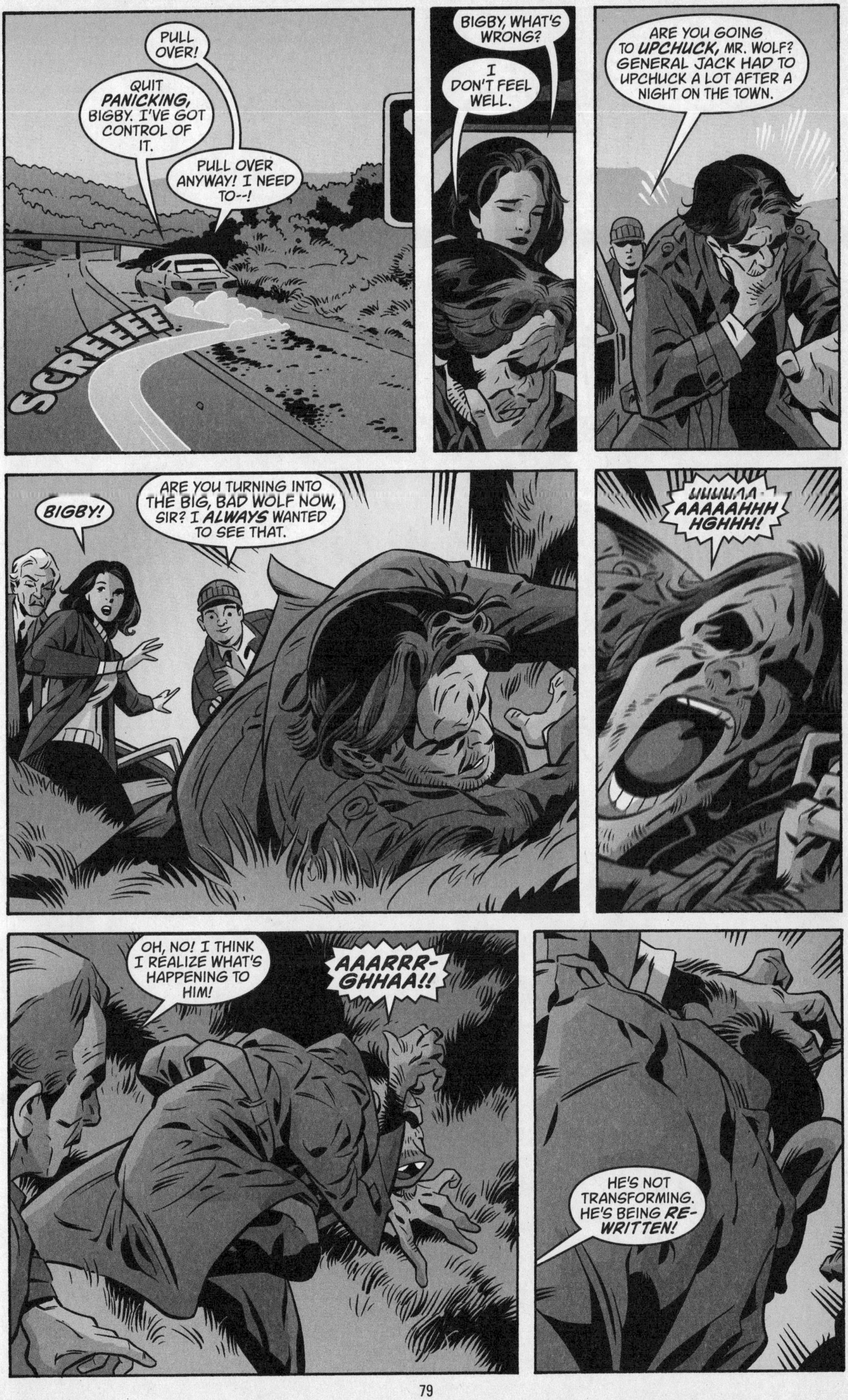
PULL OVER!
QUIT PANICKING, BIGBY. I'VE GOT CONTROL OF IT.
PULL OVER ANYWAY! I NEED TO--!
SCREEEE
BIGBY, WHAT'S WRONG?
I DON'T FEEL WELL.
ARE YOU GOING TO UPCHUCK, MR. WOLF? GENERAL JACK HAD TO UPCHUCK A LOT AFTER A NIGHT ON THE TOWN.
BIGBY!
ARE YOU TURNING INTO THE BIG, BAD WOLF NOW, SIR? I ALWAYS WANTED TO SEE THAT.
UUUUAA AAAAAHHH HGHHH!
OH, NO! I THINK I REALIZE WHAT'S HAPPENING TO HIM!
AAARRR-GHHAA!!
HE'S NOT TRANSFORMING. HE'S BEING RE-WRITTEN!

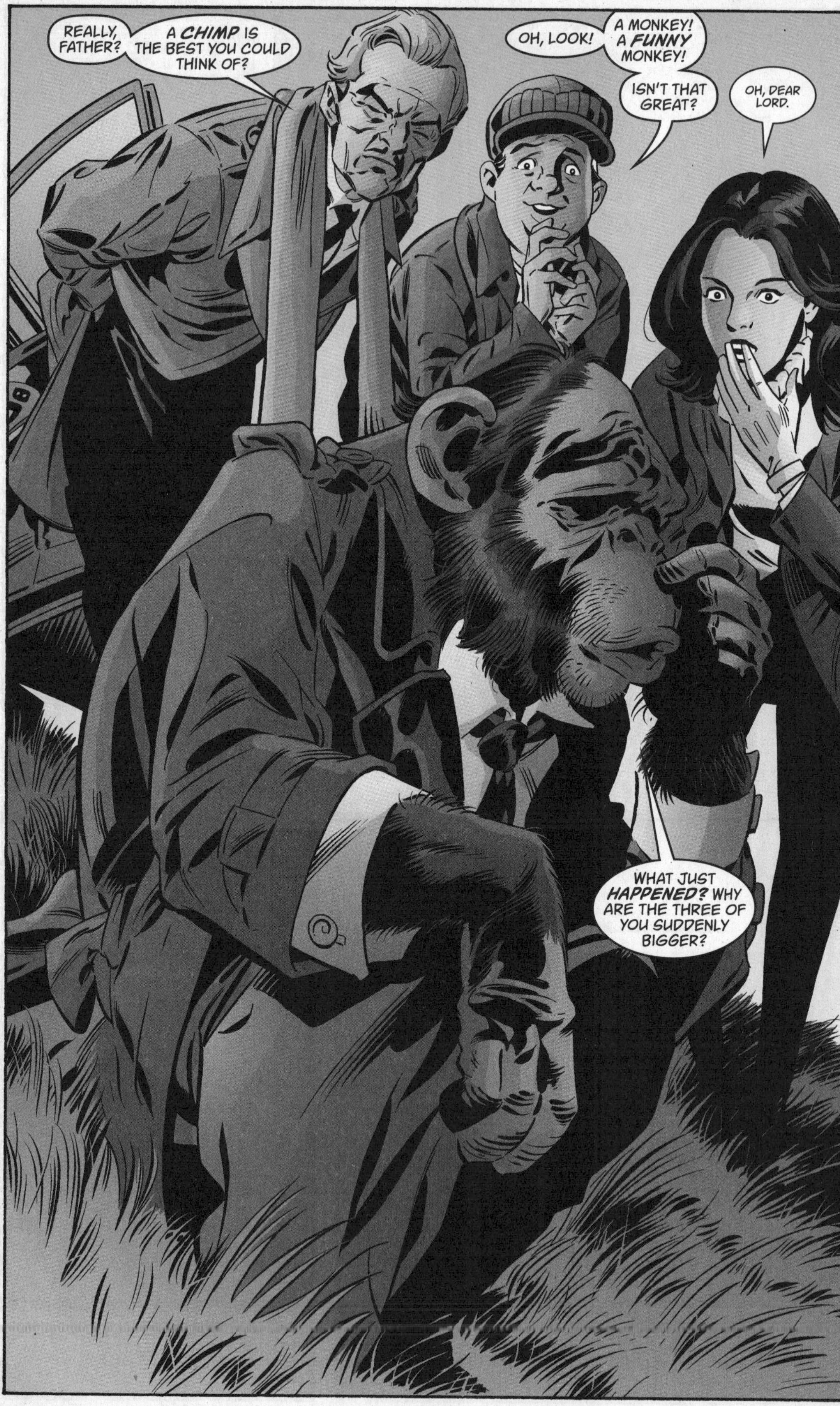
REALLY, FATHER?
A *CHIMP* IS THE BEST YOU COULD THINK OF?
OH, LOOK!
A MONKEY! A *FUNNY* MONKEY!
ISN'T THAT GREAT?
OH, DEAR LORD.
WHAT JUST *HAPPENED?* WHY ARE THE THREE OF YOU SUDDENLY BIGGER?

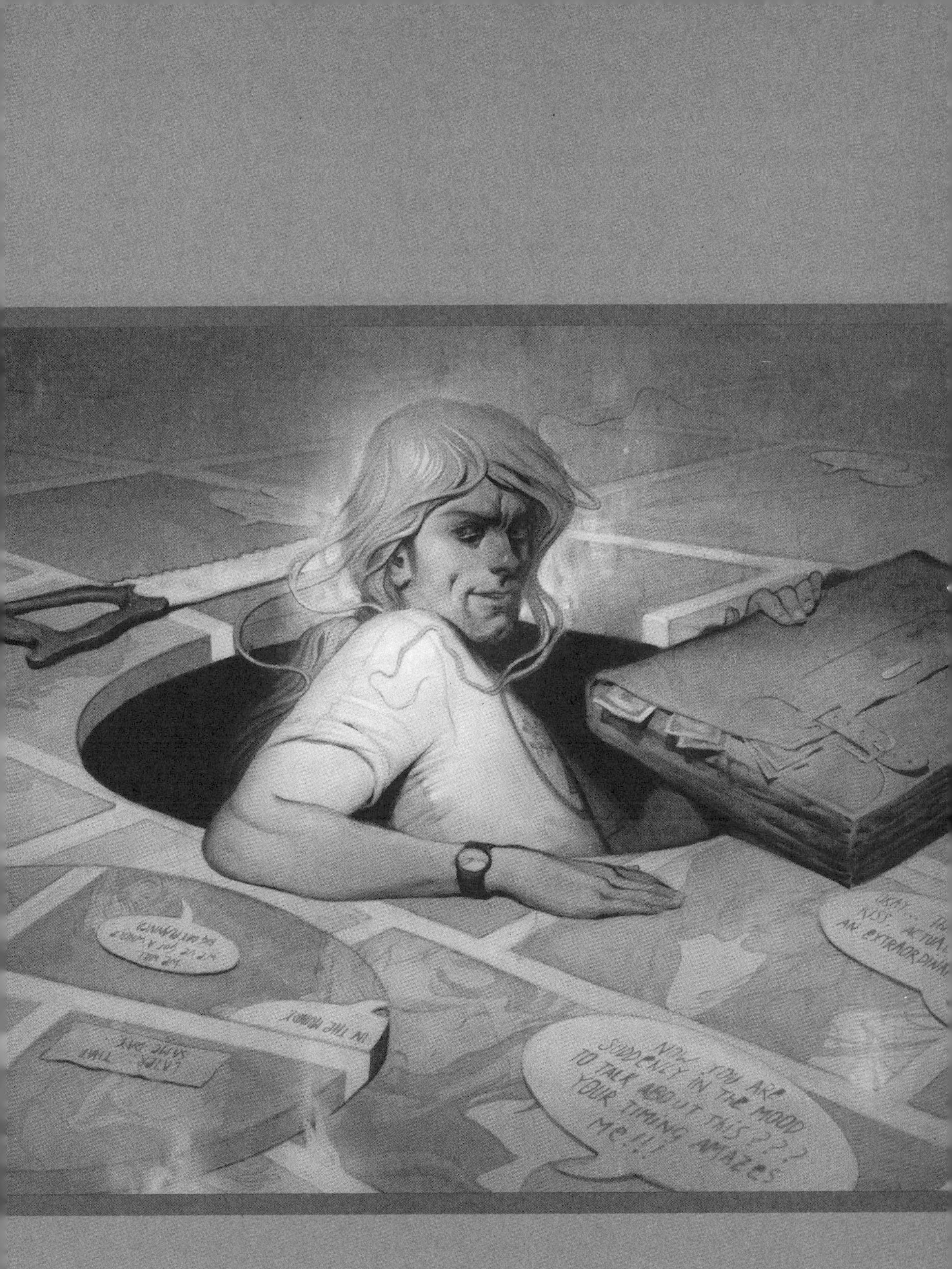
LATER. THAT SAME DAY.
IN THE MOOD.
NOW YOU ARE SUDDENLY IN THE MOOD TO TALK ABOUT THIS??? YOUR TIMING AMAZES ME!!!

"The fact that I let you back into my bed
is the proof that I've hit rock bottom."

The Great FABLES Crossover part 4 of 9

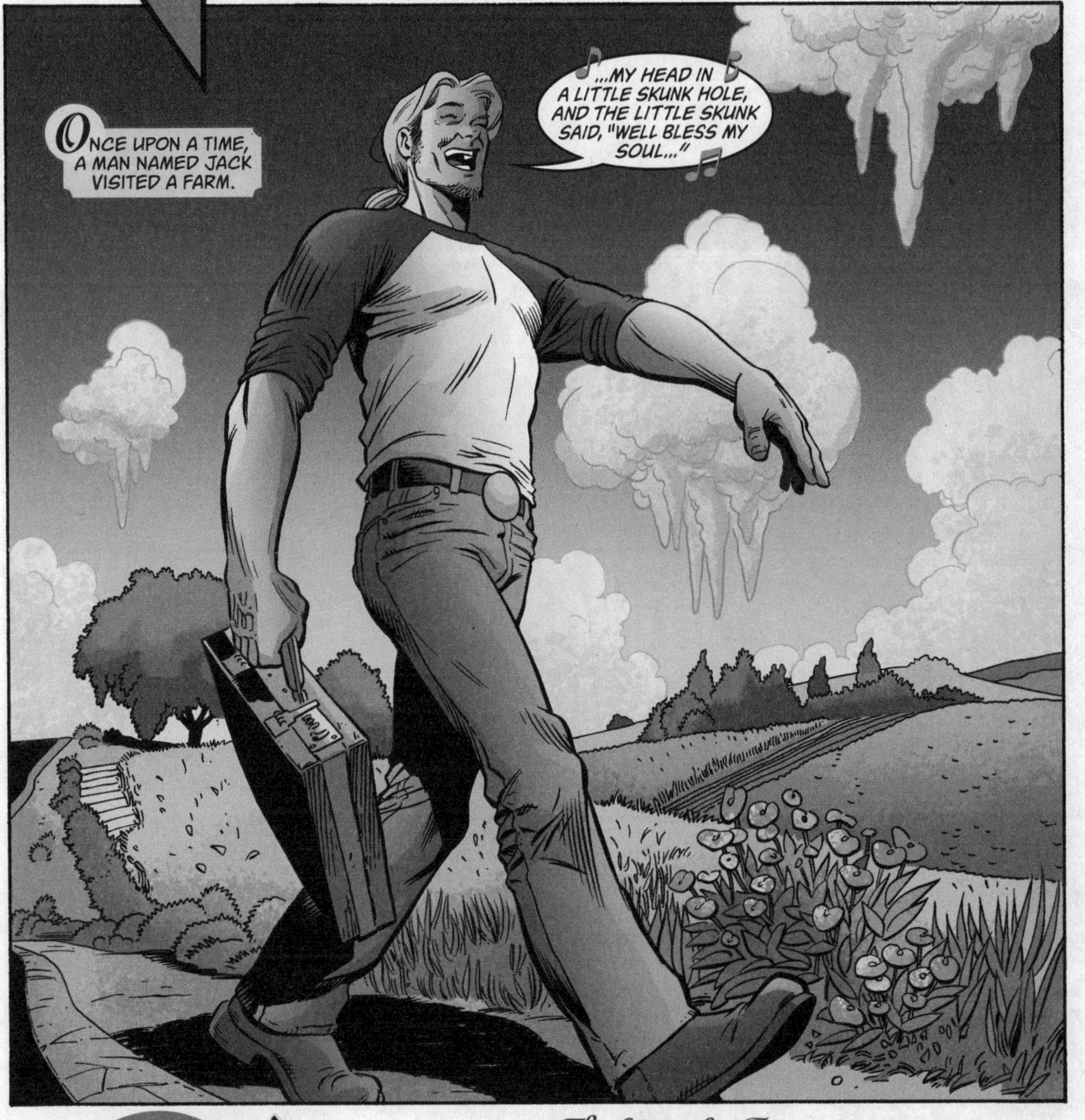

ONCE UPON A TIME, A MAN NAMED JACK VISITED A FARM.
...MY HEAD IN A LITTLE SKUNK HOLE, AND THE LITTLE SKUNK SAID, "WELL BLESS MY SOUL..."

JACK'S BACK

The Story So Far...

Fabletown is no more and the refugee Fables have too many pressing troubles to spend much time worrying about Kevin Thorn and the chance he might want to rewrite the universe. Sending Bigby and Snow to investigate should be enough. Besides, Kevin Thorn is probably just another damned lie cooked up by Jack Horner, isn't he? And speaking of Jack, who's that coming down the road?

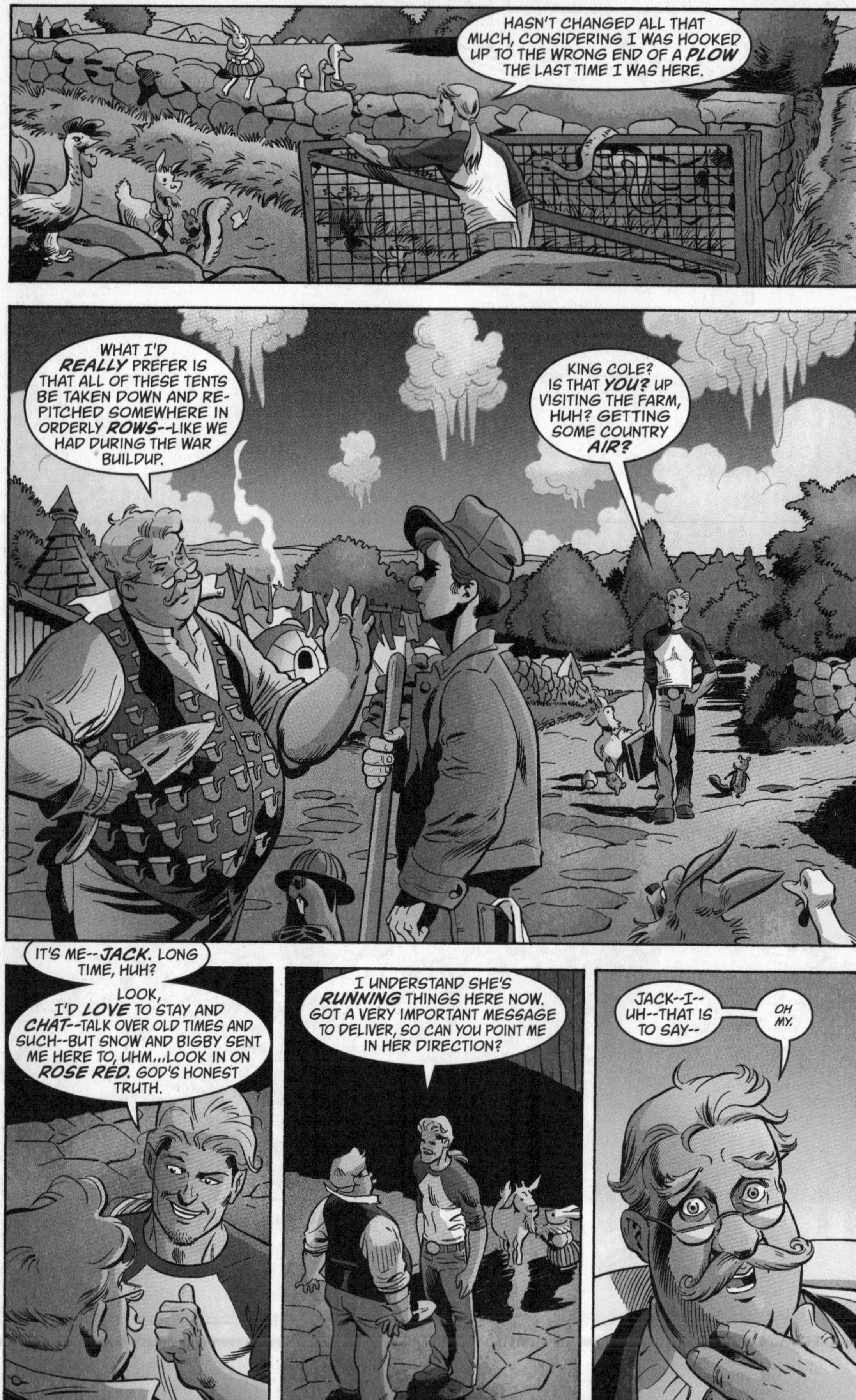
HASN'T CHANGED ALL THAT MUCH, CONSIDERING I WAS HOOKED UP TO THE WRONG END OF A PLOW THE LAST TIME I WAS HERE.
WHAT I'D REALLY PREFER IS THAT ALL OF THESE TENTS BE TAKEN DOWN AND RE-PITCHED SOMEWHERE IN ORDERLY ROWS--LIKE WE HAD DURING THE WAR BUILDUP.
KING COLE? IS THAT YOU? UP VISITING THE FARM, HUH? GETTING SOME COUNTRY AIR?
IT'S ME--JACK. LONG TIME, HUH?
LOOK, I'D LOVE TO STAY AND CHAT--TALK OVER OLD TIMES AND SUCH--BUT SNOW AND BIGBY SENT ME HERE TO, UHM...LOOK IN ON ROSE RED. GOD'S HONEST TRUTH.
I UNDERSTAND SHE'S RUNNING THINGS HERE NOW. GOT A VERY IMPORTANT MESSAGE TO DELIVER, SO CAN YOU POINT ME IN HER DIRECTION?
JACK--I--UH--THAT IS TO SAY--
OH MY.

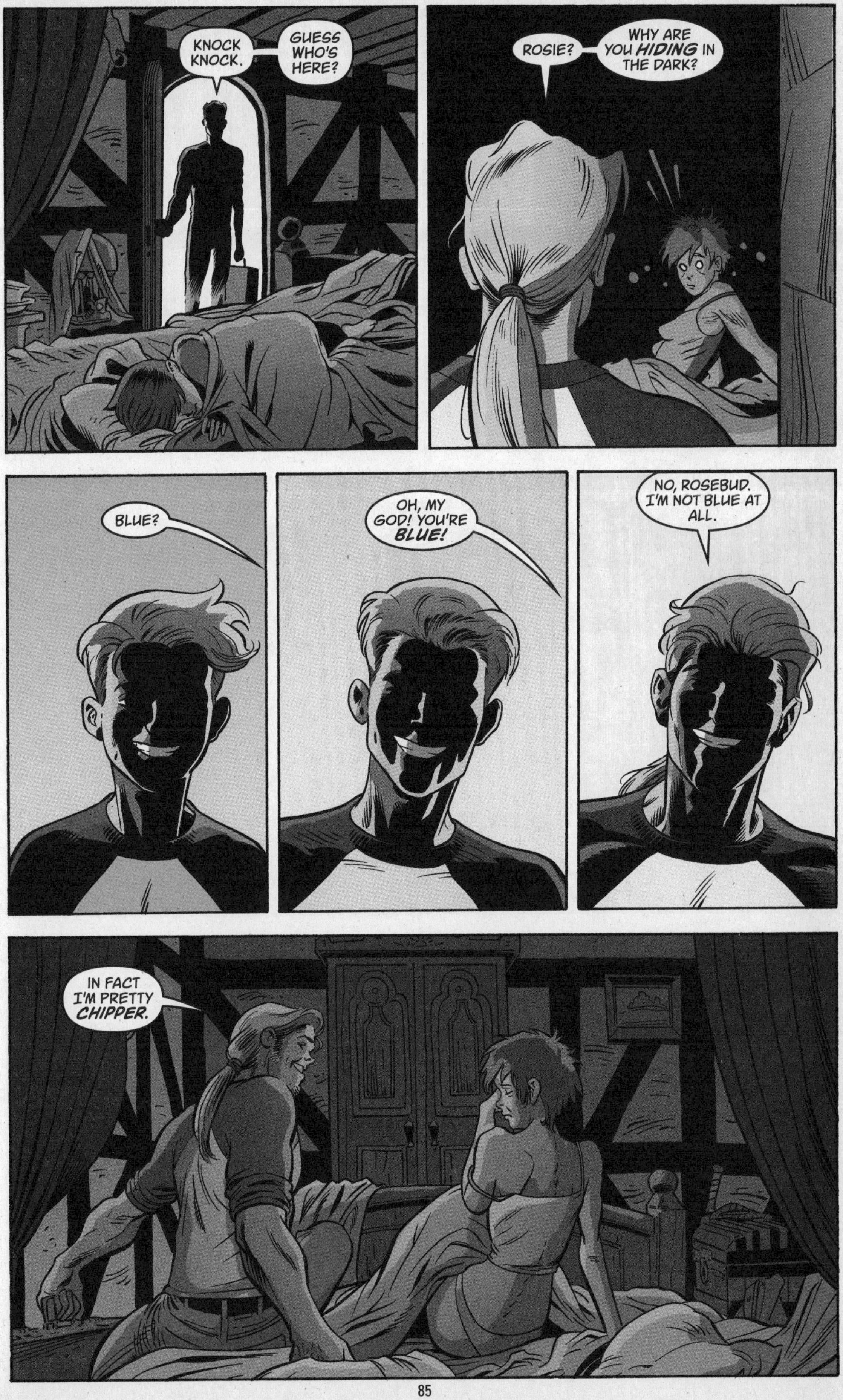
KNOCK KNOCK.
GUESS WHO'S HERE?
ROSIE?
WHY ARE YOU HIDING IN THE DARK?
BLUE?
OH, MY GOD! YOU'RE BLUE!
NO, ROSEBUD. I'M NOT BLUE AT ALL.
IN FACT I'M PRETTY CHIPPER.

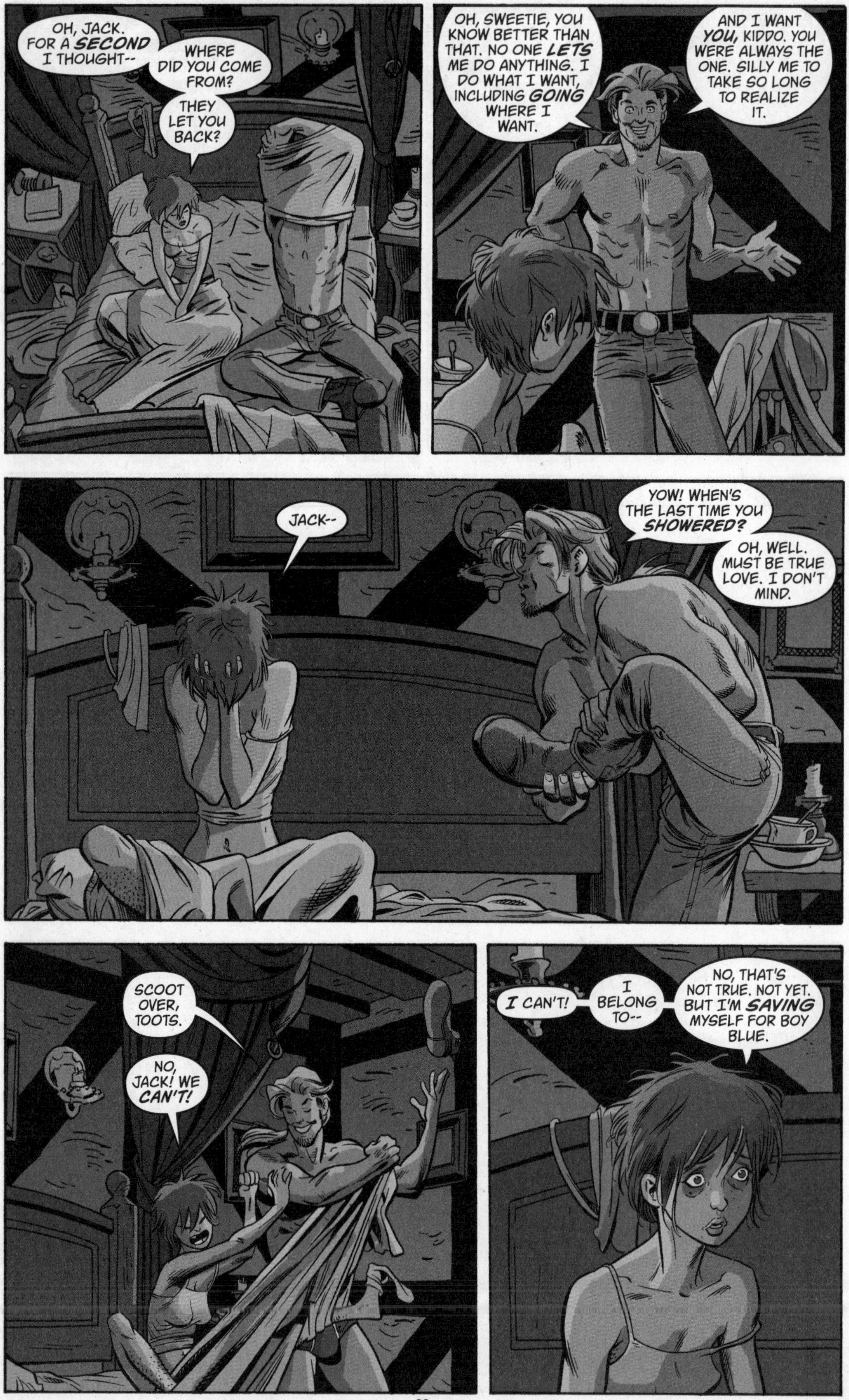
OH, JACK. FOR A SECOND I THOUGHT--
WHERE DID YOU COME FROM?
THEY LET YOU BACK?
OH, SWEETIE, YOU KNOW BETTER THAN THAT. NO ONE LETS ME DO ANYTHING. I DO WHAT I WANT, INCLUDING GOING WHERE I WANT.
AND I WANT YOU, KIDDO. YOU WERE ALWAYS THE ONE. SILLY ME TO TAKE SO LONG TO REALIZE IT.
JACK--
YOW! WHEN'S THE LAST TIME YOU SHOWERED?
OH, WELL. MUST BE TRUE LOVE. I DON'T MIND.
SCOOT OVER, TOOTS.
NO, JACK! WE CAN'T!
I CAN'T!
I BELONG TO--
NO, THAT'S NOT TRUE. NOT YET. BUT I'M SAVING MYSELF FOR BOY BLUE.

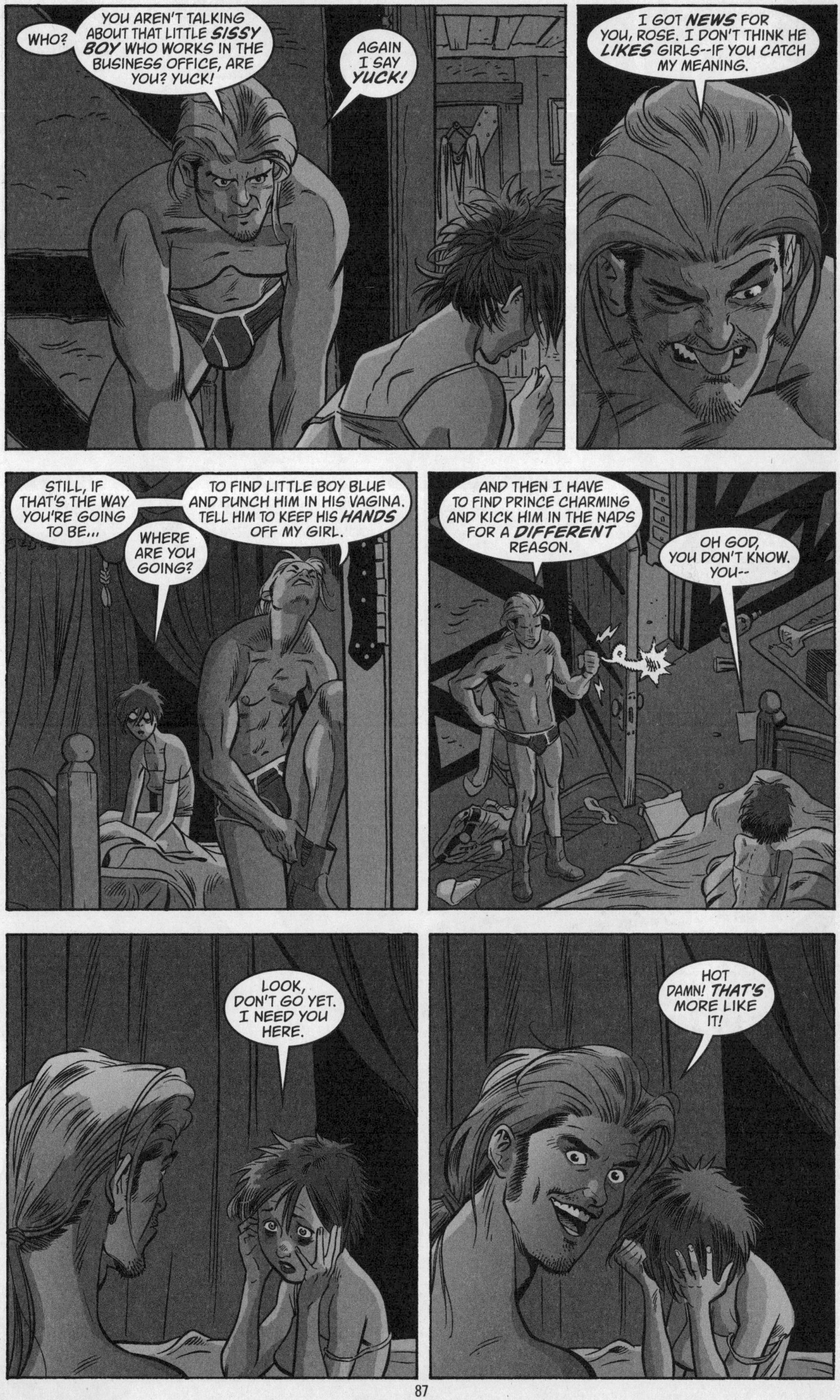
WHO?
YOU AREN'T TALKING ABOUT THAT LITTLE SISSY BOY WHO WORKS IN THE BUSINESS OFFICE, ARE YOU? YUCK!
AGAIN I SAY YUCK!
I GOT NEWS FOR YOU, ROSE. I DON'T THINK HE LIKES GIRLS--IF YOU CATCH MY MEANING.
STILL, IF THAT'S THE WAY YOU'RE GOING TO BE...
WHERE ARE YOU GOING?
TO FIND LITTLE BOY BLUE AND PUNCH HIM IN HIS VAGINA. TELL HIM TO KEEP HIS HANDS OFF MY GIRL.
AND THEN I HAVE TO FIND PRINCE CHARMING AND KICK HIM IN THE NADS FOR A DIFFERENT REASON.
OH GOD, YOU DON'T KNOW. YOU--
LOOK, DON'T GO YET. I NEED YOU HERE.
HOT DAMN! THAT'S MORE LIKE IT!

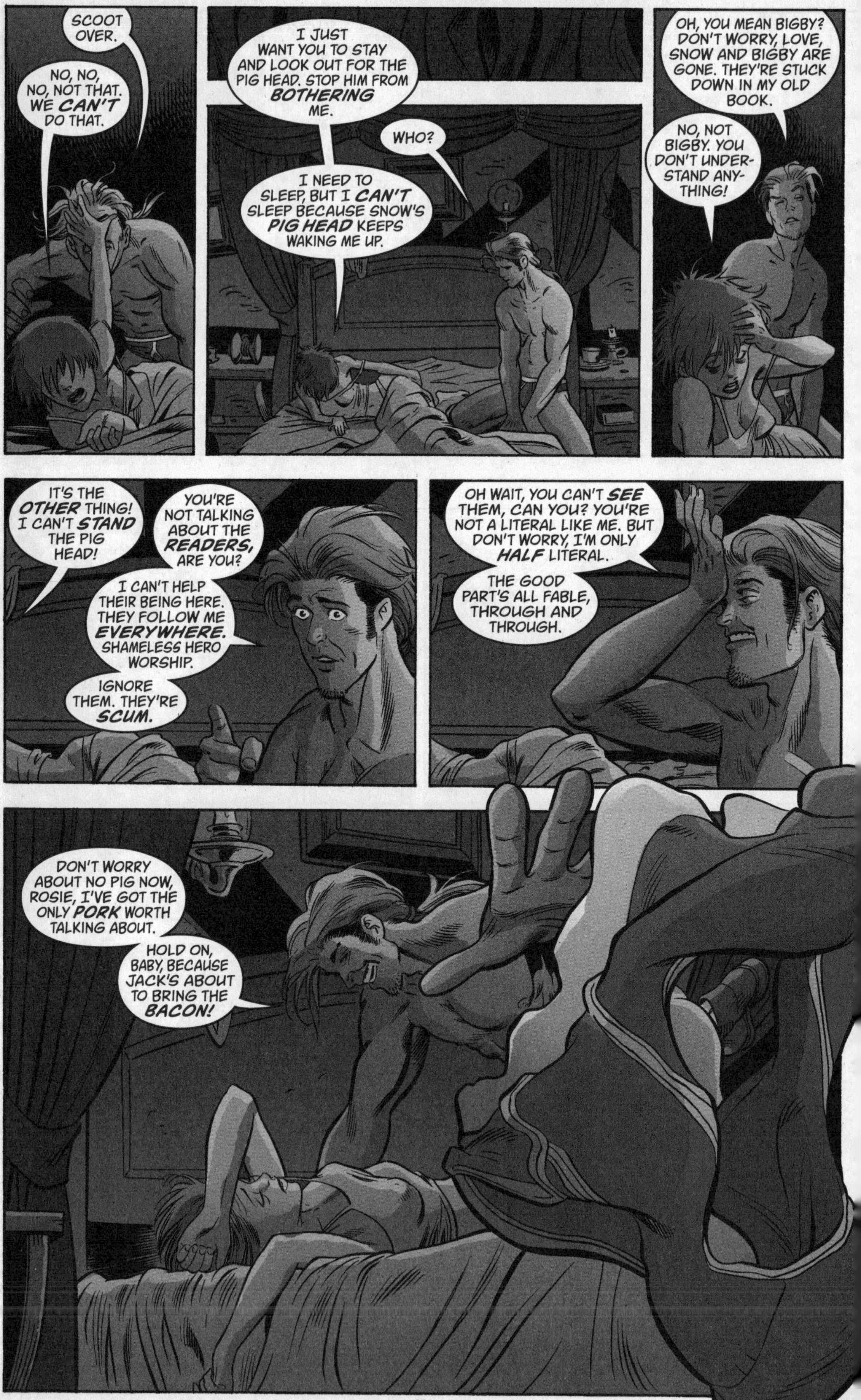
SCOOT OVER.
NO, NO, NO, NOT THAT. WE CAN'T DO THAT.
I JUST WANT YOU TO STAY AND LOOK OUT FOR THE PIG HEAD. STOP HIM FROM BOTHERING ME.
WHO?
I NEED TO SLEEP, BUT I CAN'T SLEEP BECAUSE SNOW'S PIG HEAD KEEPS WAKING ME UP.
OH, YOU MEAN BIGBY? DON'T WORRY, LOVE, SNOW AND BIGBY ARE GONE. THEY'RE STUCK DOWN IN MY OLD BOOK.
NO, NOT BIGBY. YOU DON'T UNDERSTAND ANYTHING!
IT'S THE OTHER THING! I CAN'T STAND THE PIG HEAD!
YOU'RE NOT TALKING ABOUT THE READERS, ARE YOU?
I CAN'T HELP THEIR BEING HERE. THEY FOLLOW ME EVERYWHERE. SHAMELESS HERO WORSHIP.
IGNORE THEM. THEY'RE SCUM.
OH WAIT, YOU CAN'T SEE THEM, CAN YOU? YOU'RE NOT A LITERAL LIKE ME. BUT DON'T WORRY, I'M ONLY HALF LITERAL.
THE GOOD PART'S ALL FABLE, THROUGH AND THROUGH.
DON'T WORRY ABOUT NO PIG NOW, ROSIE, I'VE GOT THE ONLY PORK WORTH TALKING ABOUT.
HOLD ON, BABY, BECAUSE JACK'S ABOUT TO BRING THE BACON!

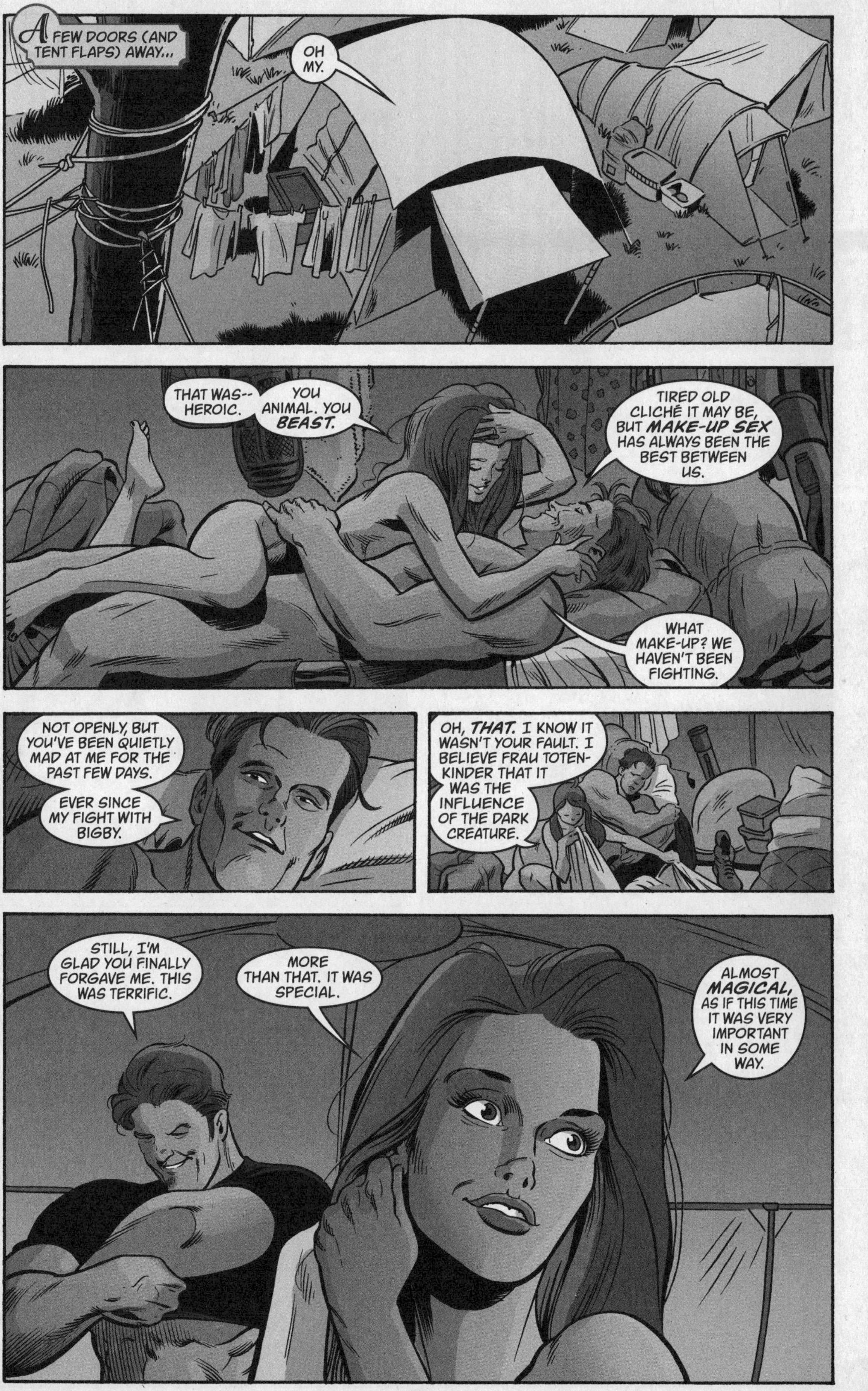
A FEW DOORS (AND TENT FLAPS) AWAY...
OH MY.
THAT WAS-- HEROIC.
YOU ANIMAL. YOU BEAST.
TIRED OLD CLICHÉ IT MAY BE, BUT MAKE-UP SEX HAS ALWAYS BEEN THE BEST BETWEEN US.
WHAT MAKE-UP? WE HAVEN'T BEEN FIGHTING.
NOT OPENLY, BUT YOU'VE BEEN QUIETLY MAD AT ME FOR THE PAST FEW DAYS.
EVER SINCE MY FIGHT WITH BIGBY.
OH, THAT. I KNOW IT WASN'T YOUR FAULT. I BELIEVE FRAU TOTENKINDER THAT IT WAS THE INFLUENCE OF THE DARK CREATURE.
STILL, I'M GLAD YOU FINALLY FORGAVE ME. THIS WAS TERRIFIC.
MORE THAN THAT. IT WAS SPECIAL.
ALMOST MAGICAL, AS IF THIS TIME IT WAS VERY IMPORTANT IN SOME WAY.

MEANWHILE, BACK AT THE MAIN HOUSE...

OH, BLUE! OH, BLUE! OH, *BLUE!*

SEE? THAT'S WHY I *CALLED* YOU HERE, STINKY!

OH, BLUE! OH, BLUE! OH, BLUE! OH, *BLUE!* OH, *BLUE!* YES! YES! YES! YES! OH, BLUE! OH, BLUE! OH, BLUE! OH, BLUE! YES! YES! YES! OH, BLUE! YES! *YES!* YES! *OH, BLUE!* OH, BLUE! OH, BLUE! *BLUE!* OH, BLUE! YES! YES! YES! OH, BLUE! YES! OH, BLUE! OH, BLUE! YES! YES! BLUE! OH, BLUE! YES! *YES!* OH, BLUE! BLUE! YES! *YES!*

WE COULD HEAR IT ALL THE WAY TO THE STABLES!

OH, *BLUE!* OH, *BLUE!* OH, *BLUE!* OH, *BLUE!* YES! YES! YES! OH, *BLUE!* YES! OH, BLUE! OH, BLUE! OH, BLUE! OH, *BLUE!* YES! *YES!* OH, *BLUE!*

DON'T CALL ME *STINKY* ANY-MORE!

I'M BROCK BLUEHEART NOW! I SHOULDN'T HAVE TO KEEP *CORRECTING* YOU.

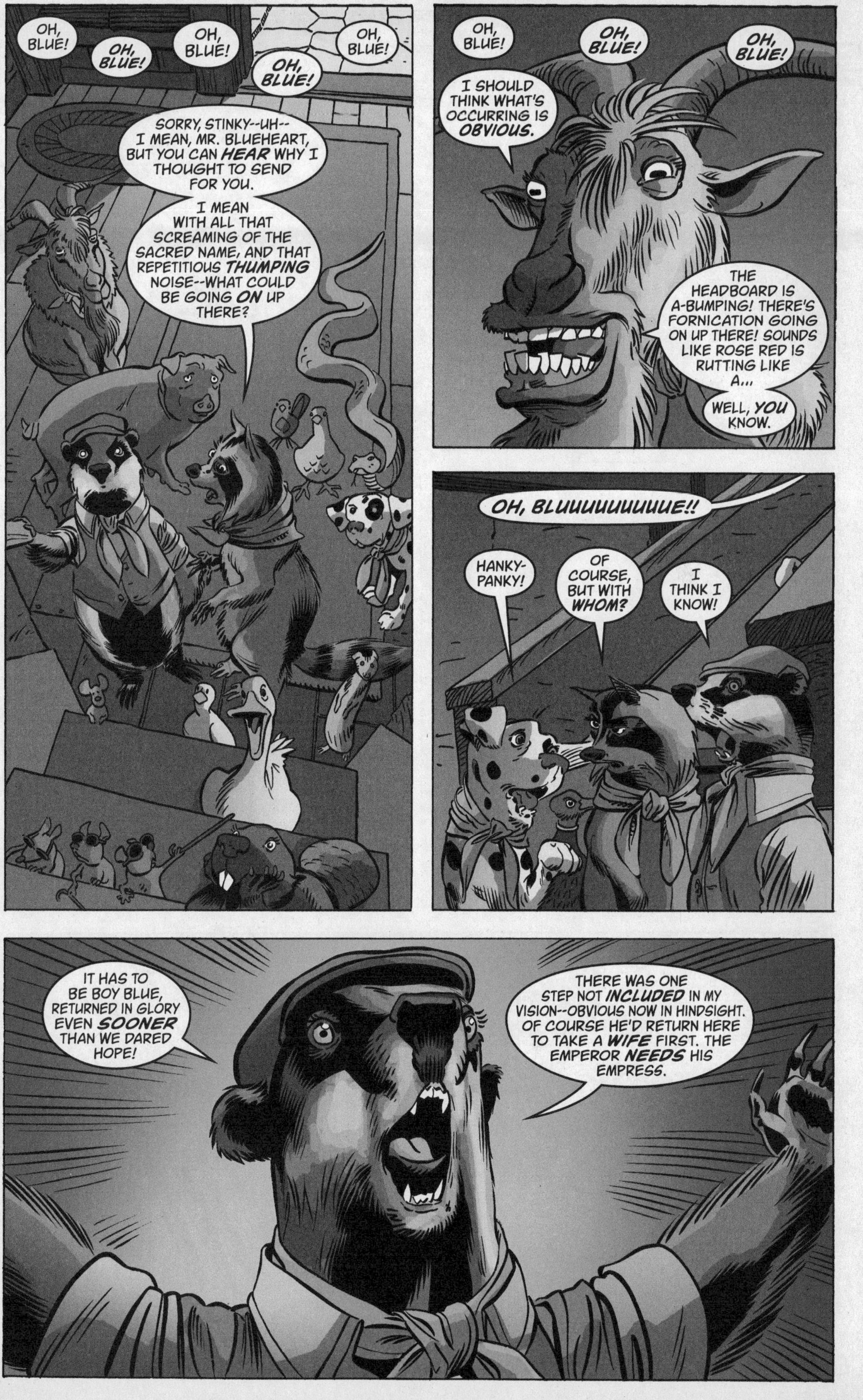
OH, BLUE!
OH, BLUE!
OH, BLUE!
OH, BLUE!
OH, BLUE!
SORRY, STINKY--UH-- I MEAN, MR. BLUEHEART, BUT YOU CAN **HEAR** WHY I THOUGHT TO SEND FOR YOU.
I MEAN WITH ALL THAT SCREAMING OF THE SACRED NAME, AND THAT REPETITIOUS **THUMPING** NOISE--WHAT COULD BE GOING **ON** UP THERE?
OH, BLUE!
OH, BLUE!
OH, BLUE!
I SHOULD THINK WHAT'S OCCURRING IS **OBVIOUS.**
THE HEADBOARD IS A-BUMPING! THERE'S FORNICATION GOING ON UP THERE! SOUNDS LIKE ROSE RED IS RUTTING LIKE A...
WELL, **YOU** KNOW.
OH, BLUUUUUUUUUE!!
HANKY-PANKY!
OF COURSE, BUT WITH **WHOM?**
I THINK I KNOW!
IT HAS TO BE BOY BLUE, RETURNED IN GLORY EVEN **SOONER** THAN WE DARED HOPE!
THERE WAS ONE STEP NOT **INCLUDED** IN MY VISION--OBVIOUS NOW IN HINDSIGHT. OF COURSE HE'D RETURN HERE TO TAKE A **WIFE** FIRST. THE EMPEROR **NEEDS** HIS EMPRESS.

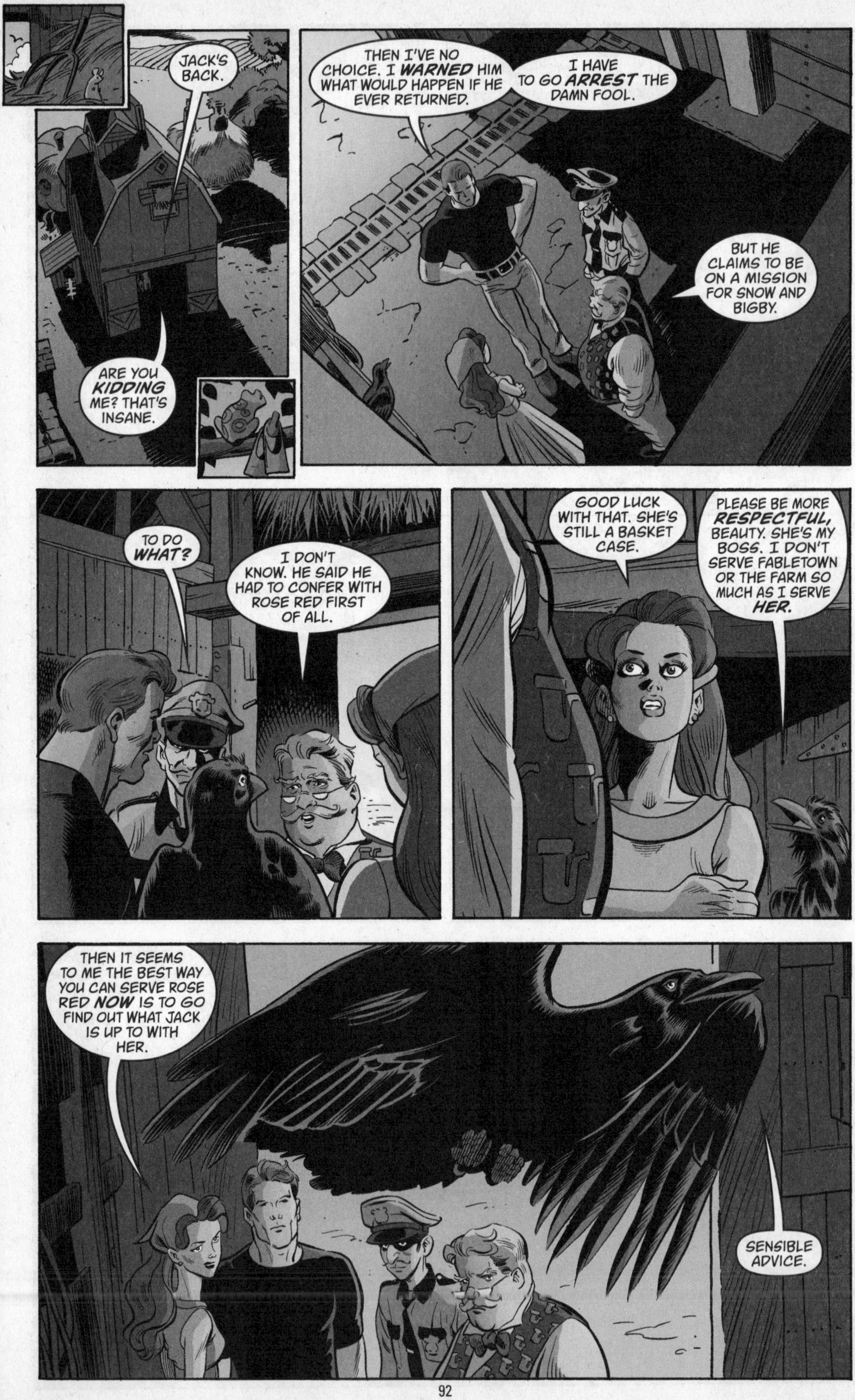
JACK'S BACK.
ARE YOU KIDDING ME? THAT'S INSANE.
THEN I'VE NO CHOICE. I WARNED HIM WHAT WOULD HAPPEN IF HE EVER RETURNED.
I HAVE TO GO ARREST THE DAMN FOOL.
BUT HE CLAIMS TO BE ON A MISSION FOR SNOW AND BIGBY.
TO DO WHAT?
I DON'T KNOW. HE SAID HE HAD TO CONFER WITH ROSE RED FIRST OF ALL.
GOOD LUCK WITH THAT. SHE'S STILL A BASKET CASE.
PLEASE BE MORE RESPECTFUL, BEAUTY. SHE'S MY BOSS. I DON'T SERVE FABLETOWN OR THE FARM SO MUCH AS I SERVE HER.
THEN IT SEEMS TO ME THE BEST WAY YOU CAN SERVE ROSE RED NOW IS TO GO FIND OUT WHAT JACK IS UP TO WITH HER.
SENSIBLE ADVICE.

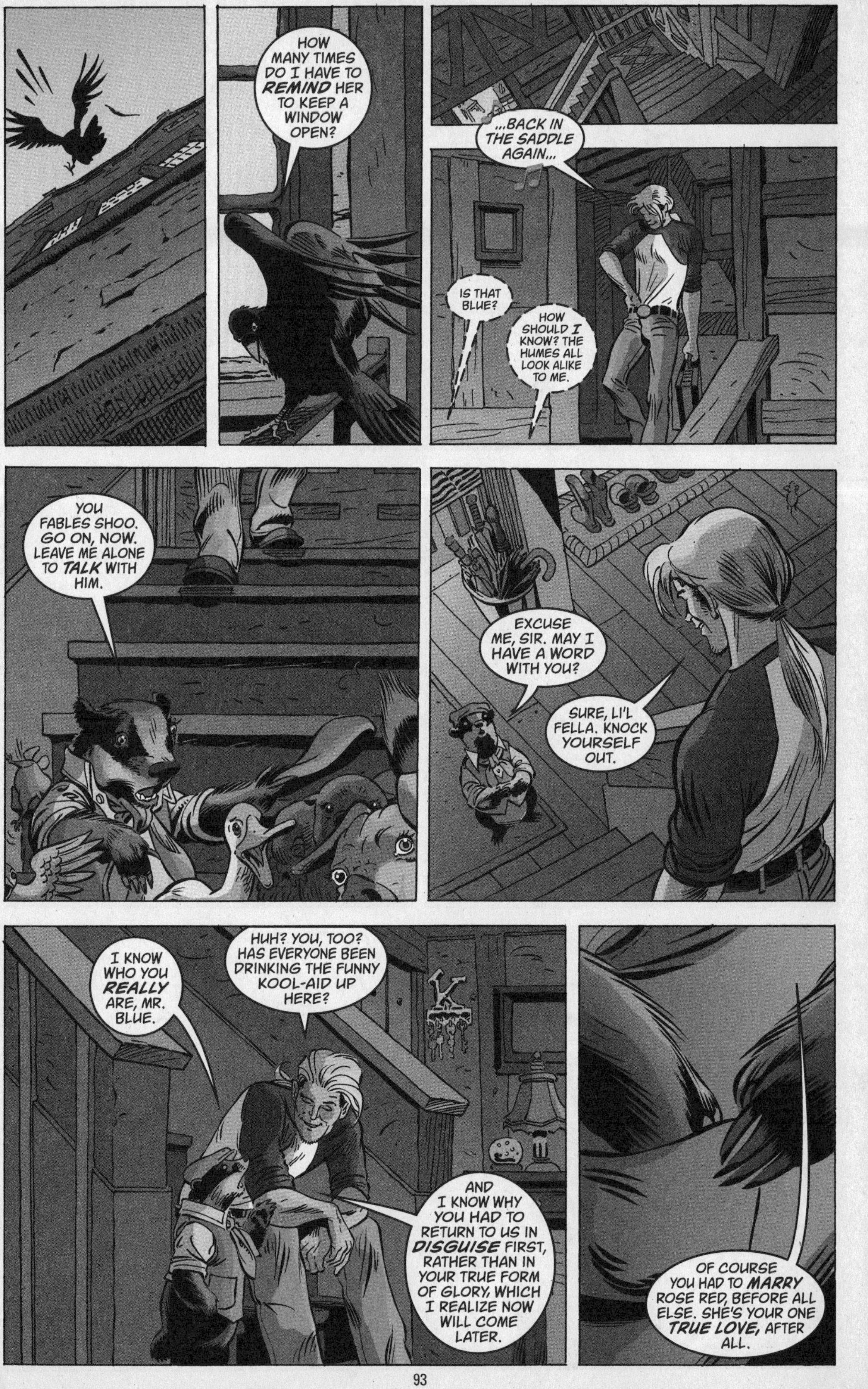
HOW MANY TIMES DO I HAVE TO REMIND HER TO KEEP A WINDOW OPEN?
...BACK IN THE SADDLE AGAIN...
IS THAT BLUE?
HOW SHOULD I KNOW? THE HUMES ALL LOOK ALIKE TO ME.
YOU FABLES SHOO. GO ON, NOW. LEAVE ME ALONE TO TALK WITH HIM.
EXCUSE ME, SIR. MAY I HAVE A WORD WITH YOU?
SURE, LI'L FELLA. KNOCK YOURSELF OUT.
I KNOW WHO YOU REALLY ARE, MR. BLUE.
HUH? YOU, TOO? HAS EVERYONE BEEN DRINKING THE FUNNY KOOL-AID UP HERE?
AND I KNOW WHY YOU HAD TO RETURN TO US IN DISGUISE FIRST, RATHER THAN IN YOUR TRUE FORM OF GLORY, WHICH I REALIZE NOW WILL COME LATER.
OF COURSE YOU HAD TO MARRY ROSE RED, BEFORE ALL ELSE. SHE'S YOUR ONE TRUE LOVE, AFTER ALL.

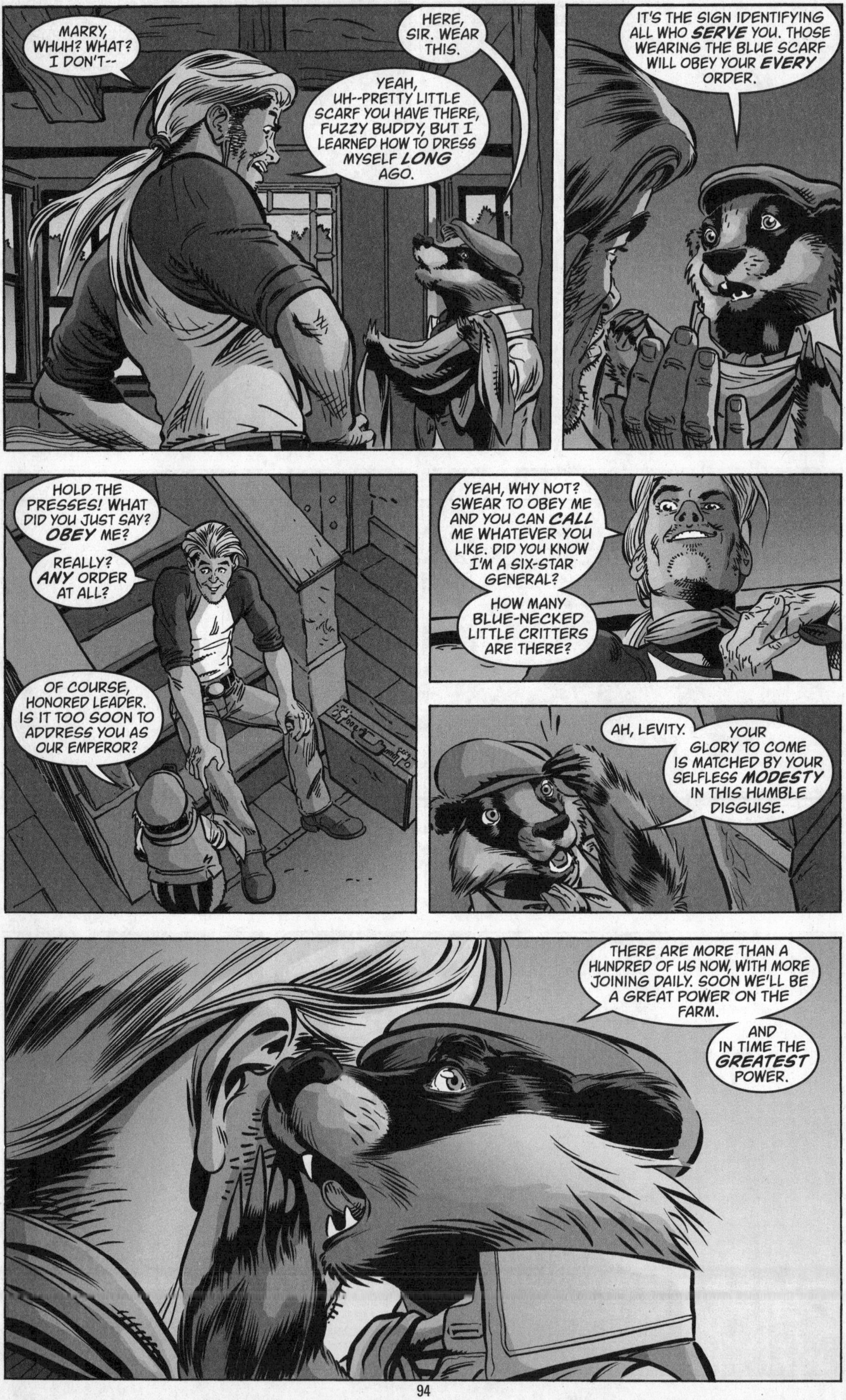
MARRY, WHUH? WHAT? I DON'T--
HERE, SIR. WEAR THIS.
YEAH, UH--PRETTY LITTLE SCARF YOU HAVE THERE, FUZZY BUDDY, BUT I LEARNED HOW TO DRESS MYSELF LONG AGO.
IT'S THE SIGN IDENTIFYING ALL WHO SERVE YOU. THOSE WEARING THE BLUE SCARF WILL OBEY YOUR EVERY ORDER.
HOLD THE PRESSES! WHAT DID YOU JUST SAY? OBEY ME?
REALLY? ANY ORDER AT ALL?
OF COURSE, HONORED LEADER. IS IT TOO SOON TO ADDRESS YOU AS OUR EMPEROR?
YEAH, WHY NOT? SWEAR TO OBEY ME AND YOU CAN CALL ME WHATEVER YOU LIKE. DID YOU KNOW I'M A SIX-STAR GENERAL?
HOW MANY BLUE-NECKED LITTLE CRITTERS ARE THERE?
AH, LEVITY.
YOUR GLORY TO COME IS MATCHED BY YOUR SELFLESS MODESTY IN THIS HUMBLE DISGUISE.
THERE ARE MORE THAN A HUNDRED OF US NOW, WITH MORE JOINING DAILY. SOON WE'LL BE A GREAT POWER ON THE FARM.
AND IN TIME THE GREATEST POWER.

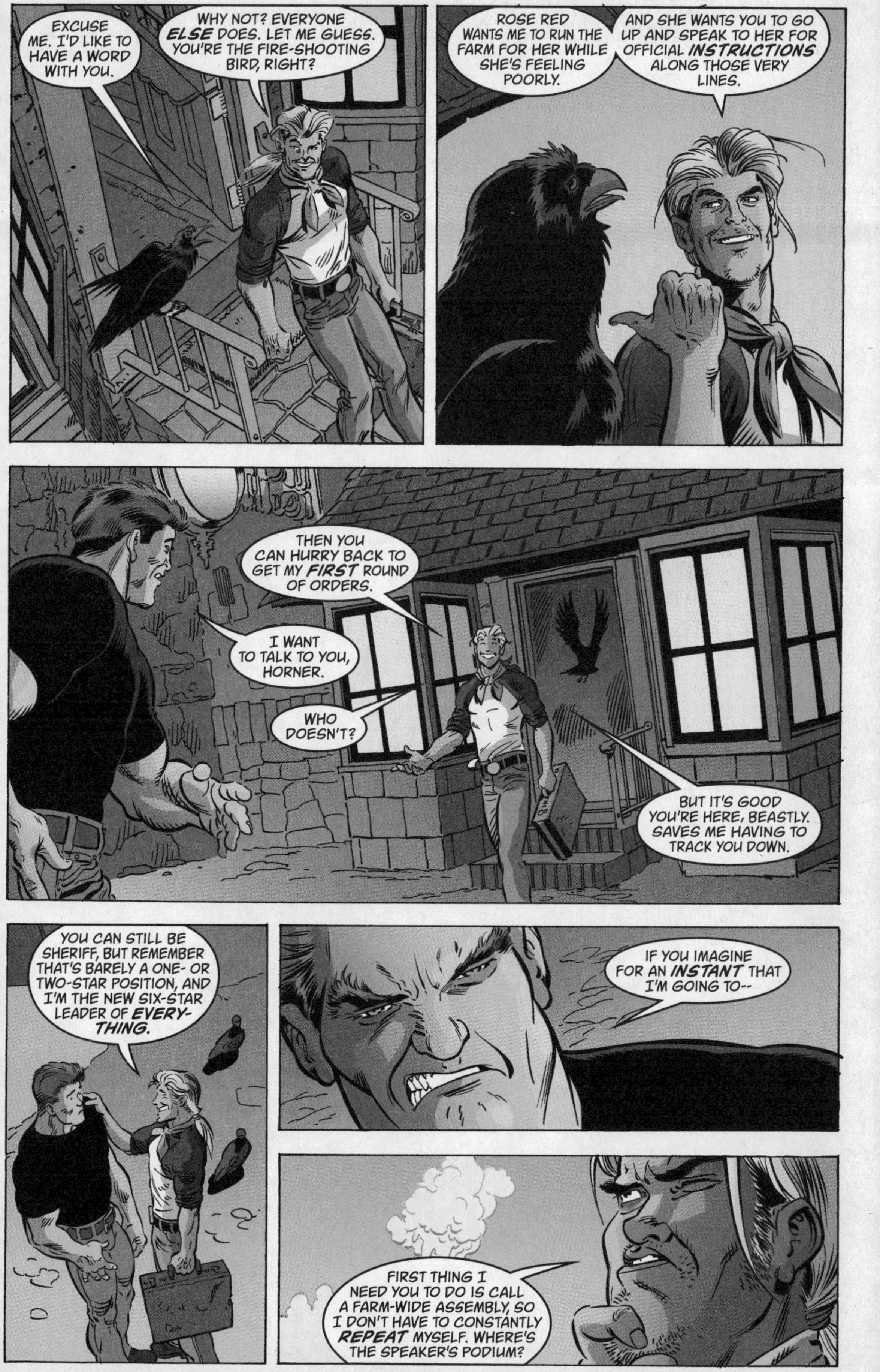
EXCUSE ME. I'D LIKE TO HAVE A WORD WITH YOU.
WHY NOT? EVERYONE ELSE DOES. LET ME GUESS. YOU'RE THE FIRE-SHOOTING BIRD, RIGHT?
ROSE RED WANTS ME TO RUN THE FARM FOR HER WHILE SHE'S FEELING POORLY.
AND SHE WANTS YOU TO GO UP AND SPEAK TO HER FOR OFFICIAL INSTRUCTIONS ALONG THOSE VERY LINES.
THEN YOU CAN HURRY BACK TO GET MY FIRST ROUND OF ORDERS.
I WANT TO TALK TO YOU, HORNER.
WHO DOESN'T?
BUT IT'S GOOD YOU'RE HERE, BEASTLY. SAVES ME HAVING TO TRACK YOU DOWN.
YOU CAN STILL BE SHERIFF, BUT REMEMBER THAT'S BARELY A ONE- OR TWO-STAR POSITION, AND I'M THE NEW SIX-STAR LEADER OF EVERY-THING.
IF YOU IMAGINE FOR AN INSTANT THAT I'M GOING TO--
FIRST THING I NEED YOU TO DO IS CALL A FARM-WIDE ASSEMBLY, SO I DON'T HAVE TO CONSTANTLY REPEAT MYSELF. WHERE'S THE SPEAKER'S PODIUM?

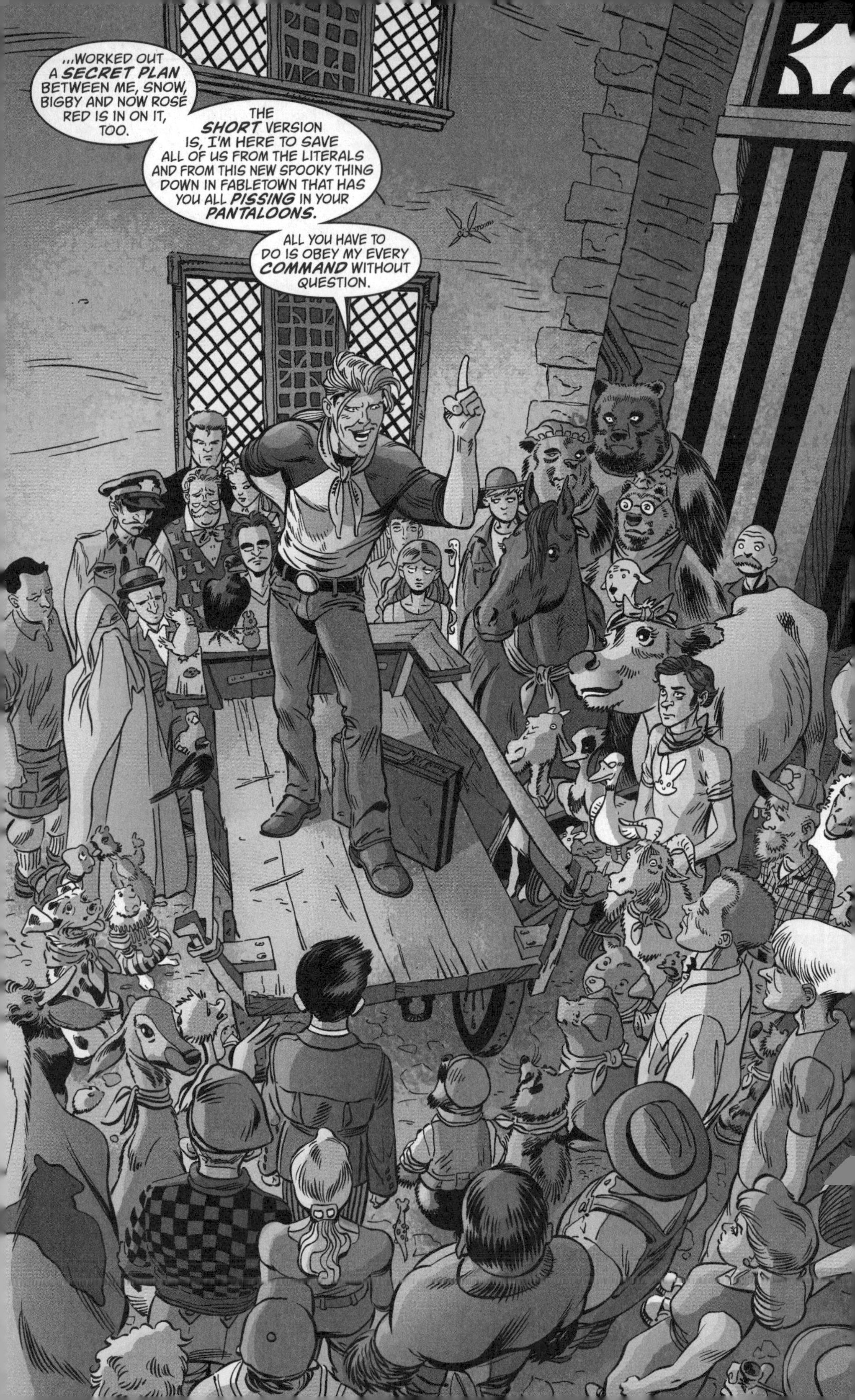
...WORKED OUT A **SECRET PLAN** BETWEEN ME, SNOW, BIGBY AND NOW ROSE RED IS IN ON IT, TOO.
THE **SHORT** VERSION IS, I'M HERE TO SAVE ALL OF US FROM THE LITERALS AND FROM THIS NEW SPOOKY THING DOWN IN FABLETOWN THAT HAS YOU ALL **PISSING** IN YOUR **PANTALOONS**.
ALL YOU HAVE TO DO IS OBEY MY EVERY **COMMAND** WITHOUT QUESTION.

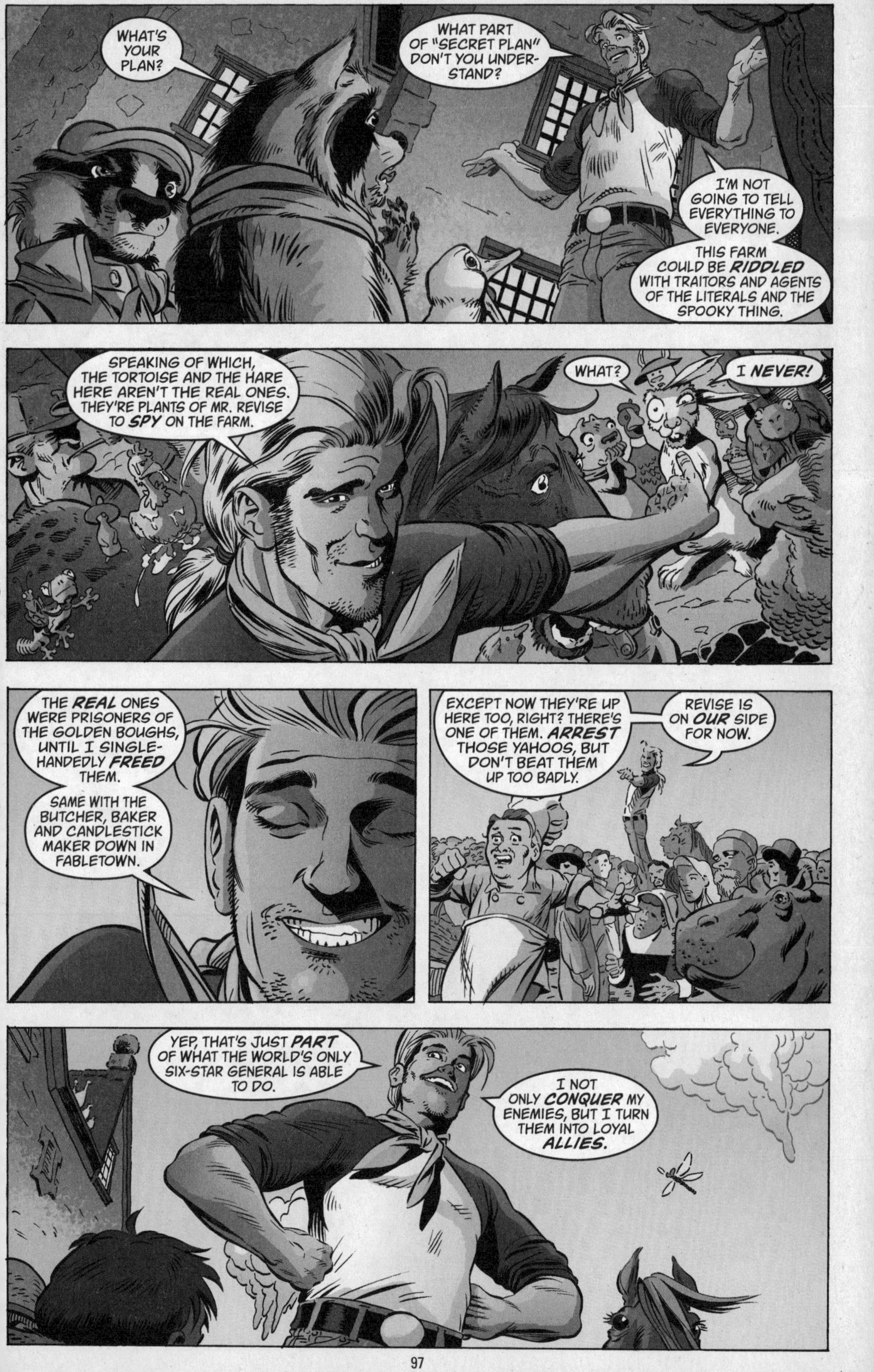
WHAT'S YOUR PLAN?
WHAT PART OF "SECRET PLAN" DON'T YOU UNDERSTAND?
I'M NOT GOING TO TELL EVERYTHING TO EVERYONE.
THIS FARM COULD BE RIDDLED WITH TRAITORS AND AGENTS OF THE LITERALS AND THE SPOOKY THING.
SPEAKING OF WHICH, THE TORTOISE AND THE HARE HERE AREN'T THE REAL ONES. THEY'RE PLANTS OF MR. REVISE TO SPY ON THE FARM.
WHAT?
I NEVER!
THE REAL ONES WERE PRISONERS OF THE GOLDEN BOUGHS, UNTIL I SINGLE-HANDEDLY FREED THEM.
SAME WITH THE BUTCHER, BAKER AND CANDLESTICK MAKER DOWN IN FABLETOWN.
EXCEPT NOW THEY'RE UP HERE TOO, RIGHT? THERE'S ONE OF THEM. ARREST THOSE YAHOOS, BUT DON'T BEAT THEM UP TOO BADLY.
REVISE IS ON OUR SIDE FOR NOW.
YEP, THAT'S JUST PART OF WHAT THE WORLD'S ONLY SIX-STAR GENERAL IS ABLE TO DO.
I NOT ONLY CONQUER MY ENEMIES, BUT I TURN THEM INTO LOYAL ALLIES.

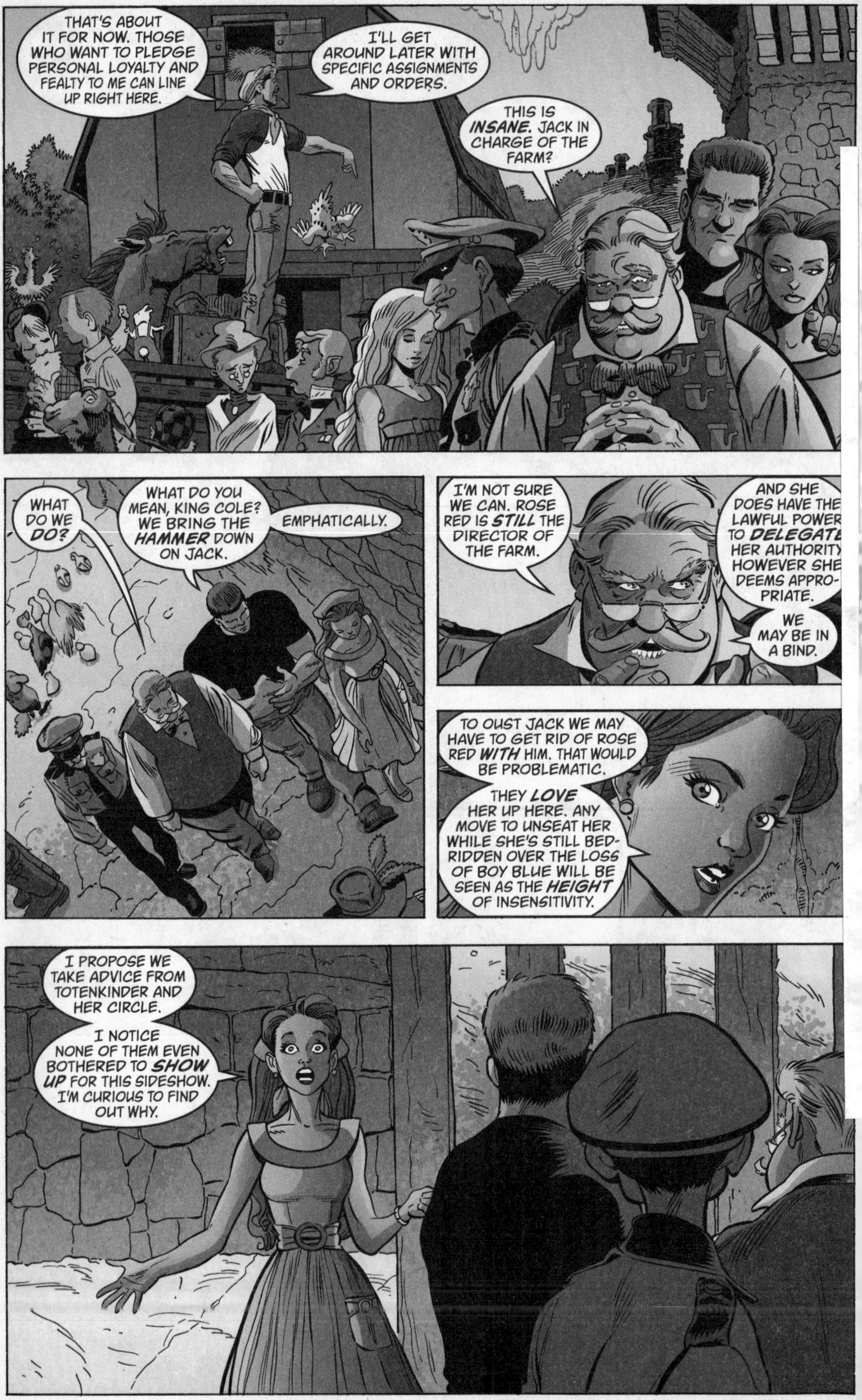
THAT'S ABOUT IT FOR NOW. THOSE WHO WANT TO PLEDGE PERSONAL LOYALTY AND FEALTY TO ME CAN LINE UP RIGHT HERE.
I'LL GET AROUND LATER WITH SPECIFIC ASSIGNMENTS AND ORDERS.
THIS IS INSANE. JACK IN CHARGE OF THE FARM?
WHAT DO WE DO?
WHAT DO YOU MEAN, KING COLE? WE BRING THE HAMMER DOWN ON JACK.
EMPHATICALLY.
I'M NOT SURE WE CAN. ROSE RED IS STILL THE DIRECTOR OF THE FARM.
AND SHE DOES HAVE THE LAWFUL POWER TO DELEGATE HER AUTHORITY HOWEVER SHE DEEMS APPRO-PRIATE.
WE MAY BE IN A BIND.
TO OUST JACK WE MAY HAVE TO GET RID OF ROSE RED WITH HIM. THAT WOULD BE PROBLEMATIC.
THEY LOVE HER UP HERE. ANY MOVE TO UNSEAT HER WHILE SHE'S STILL BED-RIDDEN OVER THE LOSS OF BOY BLUE WILL BE SEEN AS THE HEIGHT OF INSENSITIVITY.
I PROPOSE WE TAKE ADVICE FROM TOTENKINDER AND HER CIRCLE.
I NOTICE NONE OF THEM EVEN BOTHERED TO SHOW UP FOR THIS SIDESHOW. I'M CURIOUS TO FIND OUT WHY.

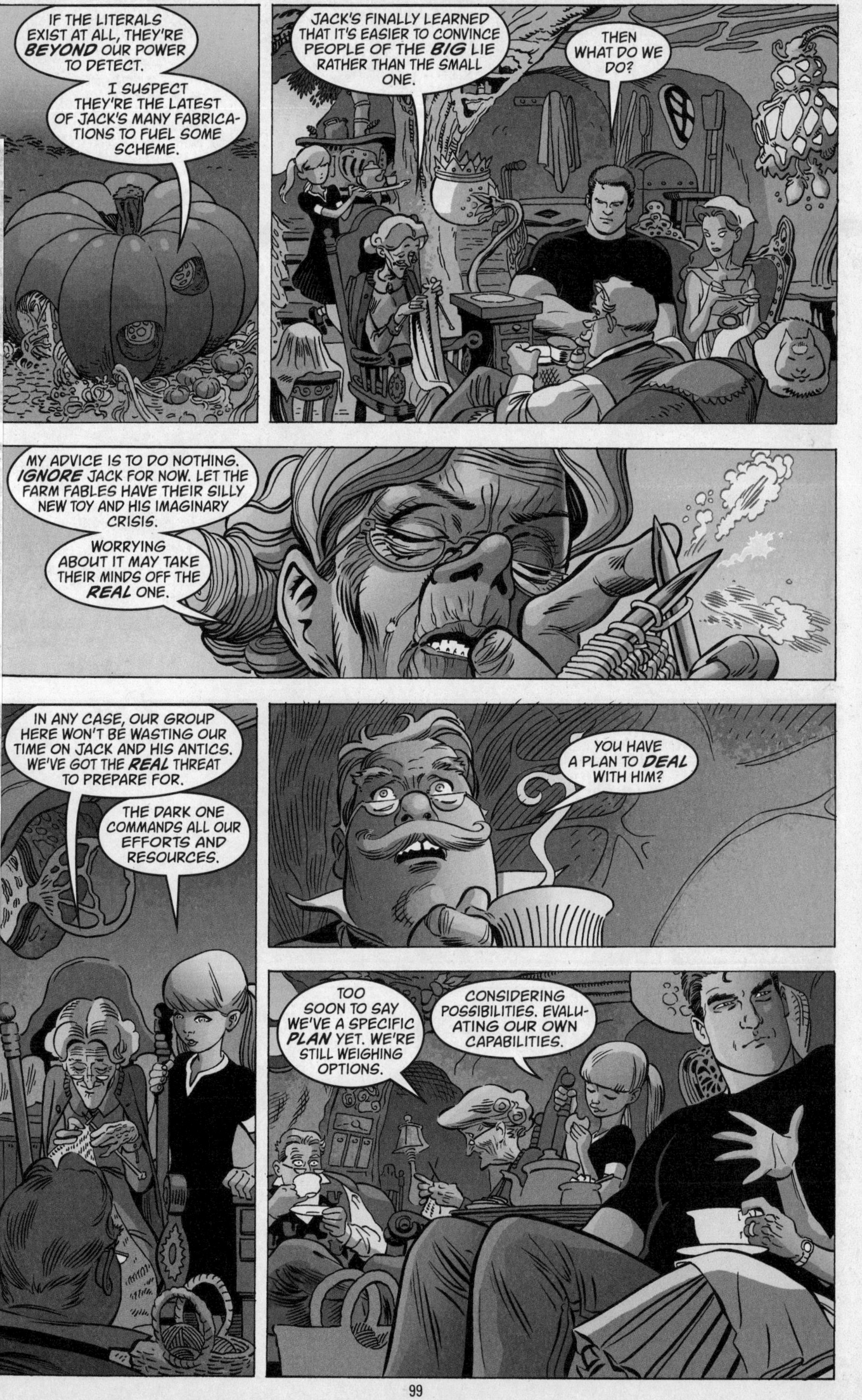
IF THE LITERALS EXIST AT ALL, THEY'RE BEYOND OUR POWER TO DETECT.
I SUSPECT THEY'RE THE LATEST OF JACK'S MANY FABRICA-TIONS TO FUEL SOME SCHEME.
JACK'S FINALLY LEARNED THAT IT'S EASIER TO CONVINCE PEOPLE OF THE BIG LIE RATHER THAN THE SMALL ONE.
THEN WHAT DO WE DO?
MY ADVICE IS TO DO NOTHING. IGNORE JACK FOR NOW. LET THE FARM FABLES HAVE THEIR SILLY NEW TOY AND HIS IMAGINARY CRISIS.
WORRYING ABOUT IT MAY TAKE THEIR MINDS OFF THE REAL ONE.
IN ANY CASE, OUR GROUP HERE WON'T BE WASTING OUR TIME ON JACK AND HIS ANTICS. WE'VE GOT THE REAL THREAT TO PREPARE FOR.
THE DARK ONE COMMANDS ALL OUR EFFORTS AND RESOURCES.
YOU HAVE A PLAN TO DEAL WITH HIM?
TOO SOON TO SAY WE'VE A SPECIFIC PLAN YET. WE'RE STILL WEIGHING OPTIONS.
CONSIDERING POSSIBILITIES. EVALU-ATING OUR OWN CAPABILITIES.

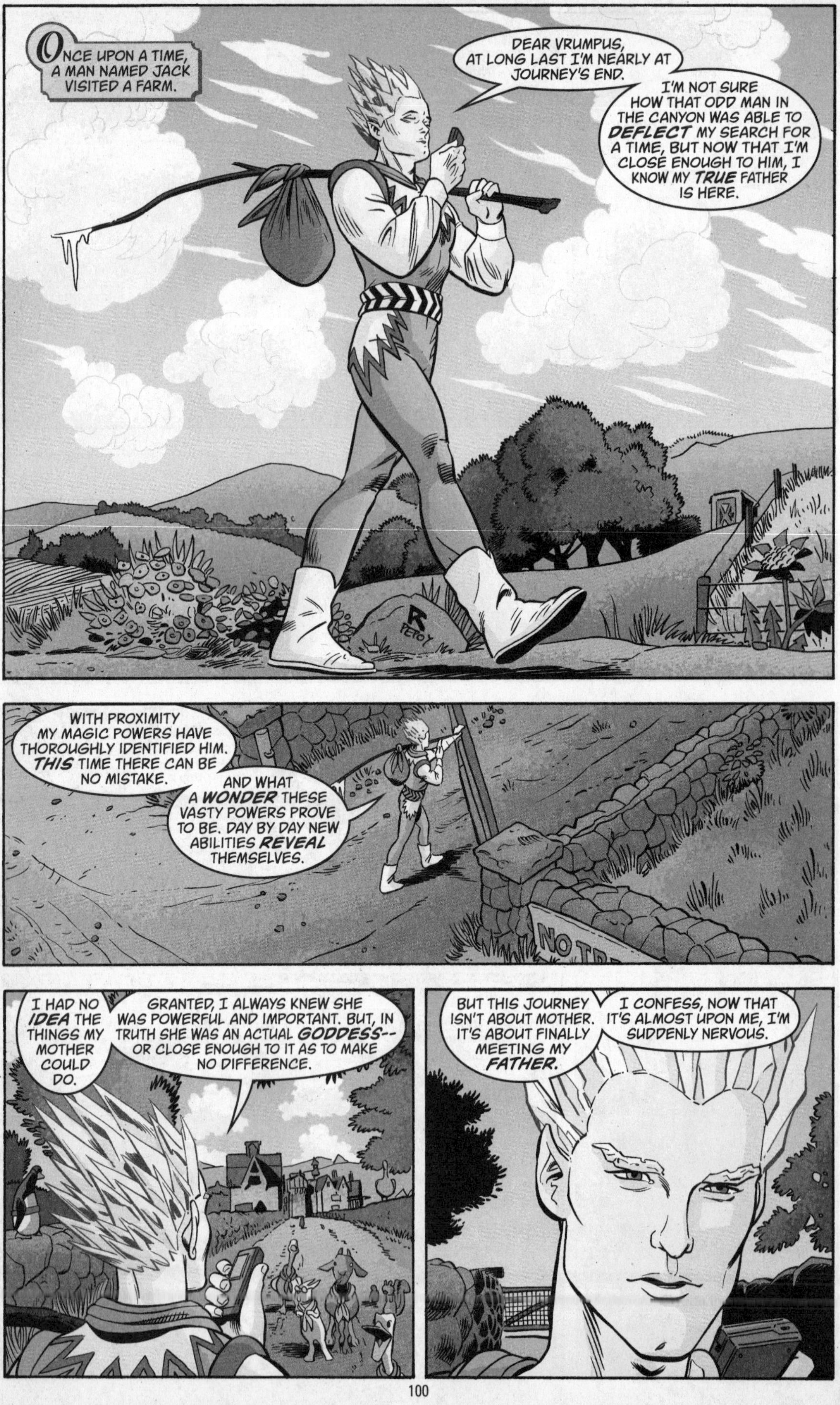
ONCE UPON A TIME, A MAN NAMED JACK VISITED A FARM.
DEAR VRUMPUS, AT LONG LAST I'M NEARLY AT JOURNEY'S END.
I'M NOT SURE HOW THAT ODD MAN IN THE CANYON WAS ABLE TO DEFLECT MY SEARCH FOR A TIME, BUT NOW THAT I'M CLOSE ENOUGH TO HIM, I KNOW MY TRUE FATHER IS HERE.
WITH PROXIMITY MY MAGIC POWERS HAVE THOROUGHLY IDENTIFIED HIM. THIS TIME THERE CAN BE NO MISTAKE.
AND WHAT A WONDER THESE VASTY POWERS PROVE TO BE. DAY BY DAY NEW ABILITIES REVEAL THEMSELVES.
NO TR
I HAD NO IDEA THE THINGS MY MOTHER COULD DO.
GRANTED, I ALWAYS KNEW SHE WAS POWERFUL AND IMPORTANT. BUT, IN TRUTH SHE WAS AN ACTUAL GODDESS-- OR CLOSE ENOUGH TO IT AS TO MAKE NO DIFFERENCE.
BUT THIS JOURNEY ISN'T ABOUT MOTHER. IT'S ABOUT FINALLY MEETING MY FATHER.
I CONFESS, NOW THAT IT'S ALMOST UPON ME, I'M SUDDENLY NERVOUS.

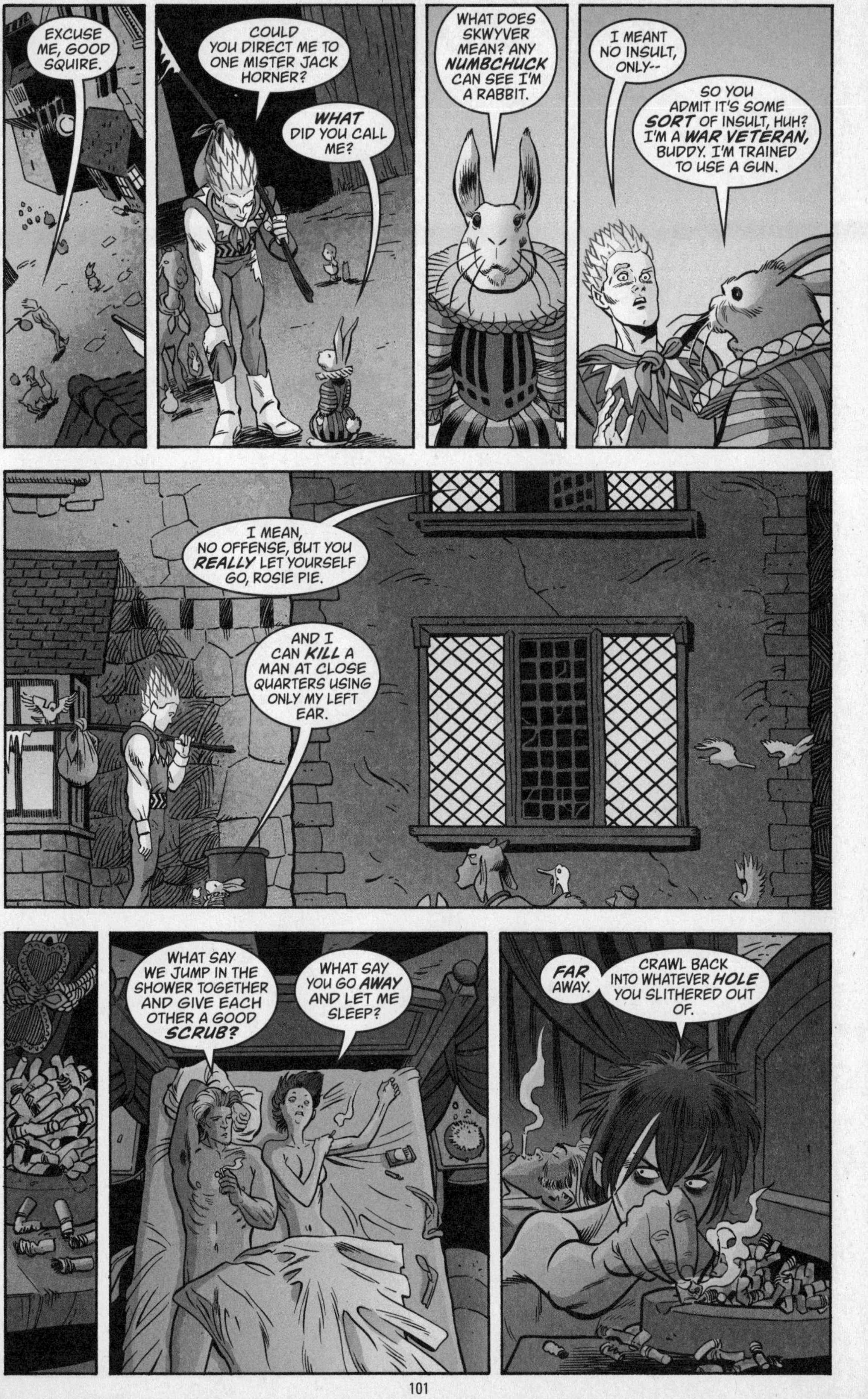
EXCUSE ME, GOOD SQUIRE.
COULD YOU DIRECT ME TO ONE MISTER JACK HORNER?
WHAT DID YOU CALL ME?
WHAT DOES SKWYVER MEAN? ANY NUMBCHUCK CAN SEE I'M A RABBIT.
I MEANT NO INSULT, ONLY--
SO YOU ADMIT IT'S SOME SORT OF INSULT, HUH? I'M A WAR VETERAN, BUDDY. I'M TRAINED TO USE A GUN.
I MEAN, NO OFFENSE, BUT YOU REALLY LET YOURSELF GO, ROSIE PIE.
AND I CAN KILL A MAN AT CLOSE QUARTERS USING ONLY MY LEFT EAR.
WHAT SAY WE JUMP IN THE SHOWER TOGETHER AND GIVE EACH OTHER A GOOD SCRUB?
WHAT SAY YOU GO AWAY AND LET ME SLEEP?
FAR AWAY.
CRAWL BACK INTO WHATEVER HOLE YOU SLITHERED OUT OF.

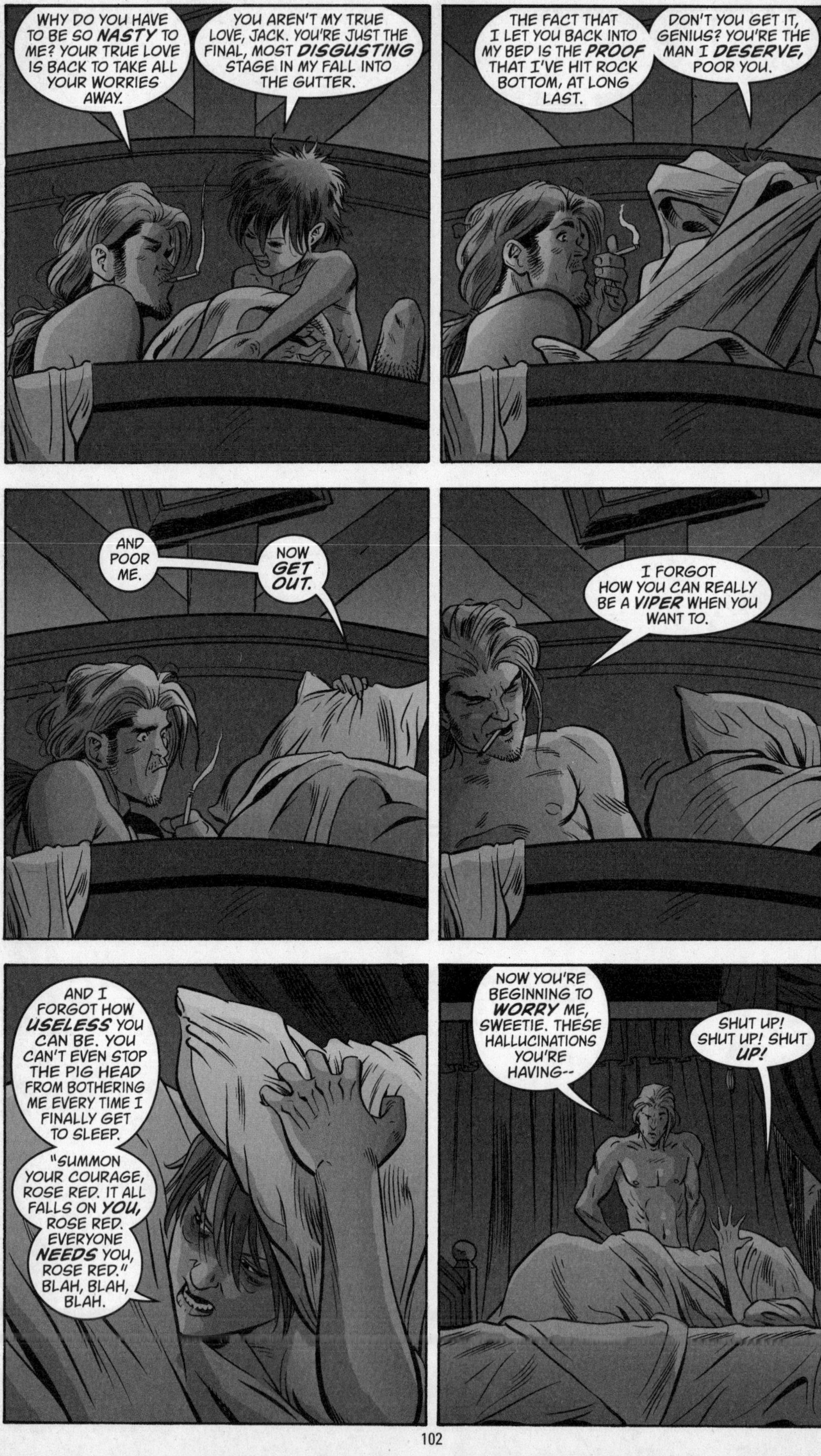
WHY DO YOU HAVE TO BE SO NASTY TO ME? YOUR TRUE LOVE IS BACK TO TAKE ALL YOUR WORRIES AWAY.
YOU AREN'T MY TRUE LOVE, JACK. YOU'RE JUST THE FINAL, MOST DISGUSTING STAGE IN MY FALL INTO THE GUTTER.
THE FACT THAT I LET YOU BACK INTO MY BED IS THE PROOF THAT I'VE HIT ROCK BOTTOM, AT LONG LAST.
DON'T YOU GET IT, GENIUS? YOU'RE THE MAN I DESERVE, POOR YOU.
AND POOR ME.
NOW GET OUT.
I FORGOT HOW YOU CAN REALLY BE A VIPER WHEN YOU WANT TO.
AND I FORGOT HOW USELESS YOU CAN BE. YOU CAN'T EVEN STOP THE PIG HEAD FROM BOTHERING ME EVERY TIME I FINALLY GET TO SLEEP.
"SUMMON YOUR COURAGE, ROSE RED. IT ALL FALLS ON YOU, ROSE RED. EVERYONE NEEDS YOU, ROSE RED." BLAH, BLAH, BLAH.
NOW YOU'RE BEGINNING TO WORRY ME, SWEETIE. THESE HALLUCINATIONS YOU'RE HAVING--
SHUT UP! SHUT UP! SHUT UP!

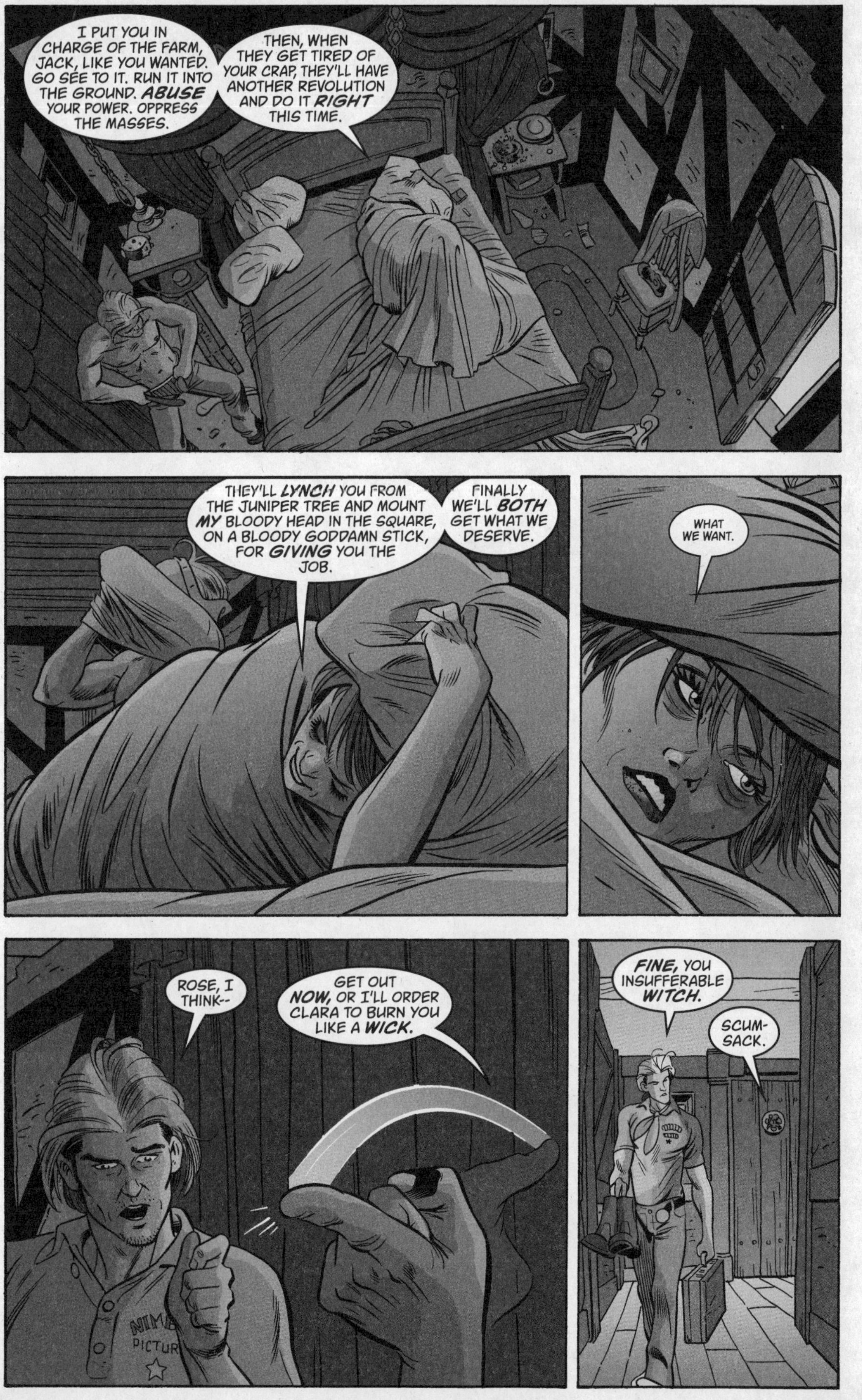
I PUT YOU IN CHARGE OF THE FARM, JACK, LIKE YOU WANTED. GO SEE TO IT. RUN IT INTO THE GROUND. ABUSE YOUR POWER. OPPRESS THE MASSES.
THEN, WHEN THEY GET TIRED OF YOUR CRAP, THEY'LL HAVE ANOTHER REVOLUTION AND DO IT RIGHT THIS TIME.
THEY'LL LYNCH YOU FROM THE JUNIPER TREE AND MOUNT MY BLOODY HEAD IN THE SQUARE, ON A BLOODY GODDAMN STICK, FOR GIVING YOU THE JOB.
FINALLY WE'LL BOTH GET WHAT WE DESERVE.
WHAT WE WANT.
ROSE, I THINK--
GET OUT NOW, OR I'LL ORDER CLARA TO BURN YOU LIKE A WICK.
FINE, YOU INSUFFERABLE WITCH.
SCUM-SACK.

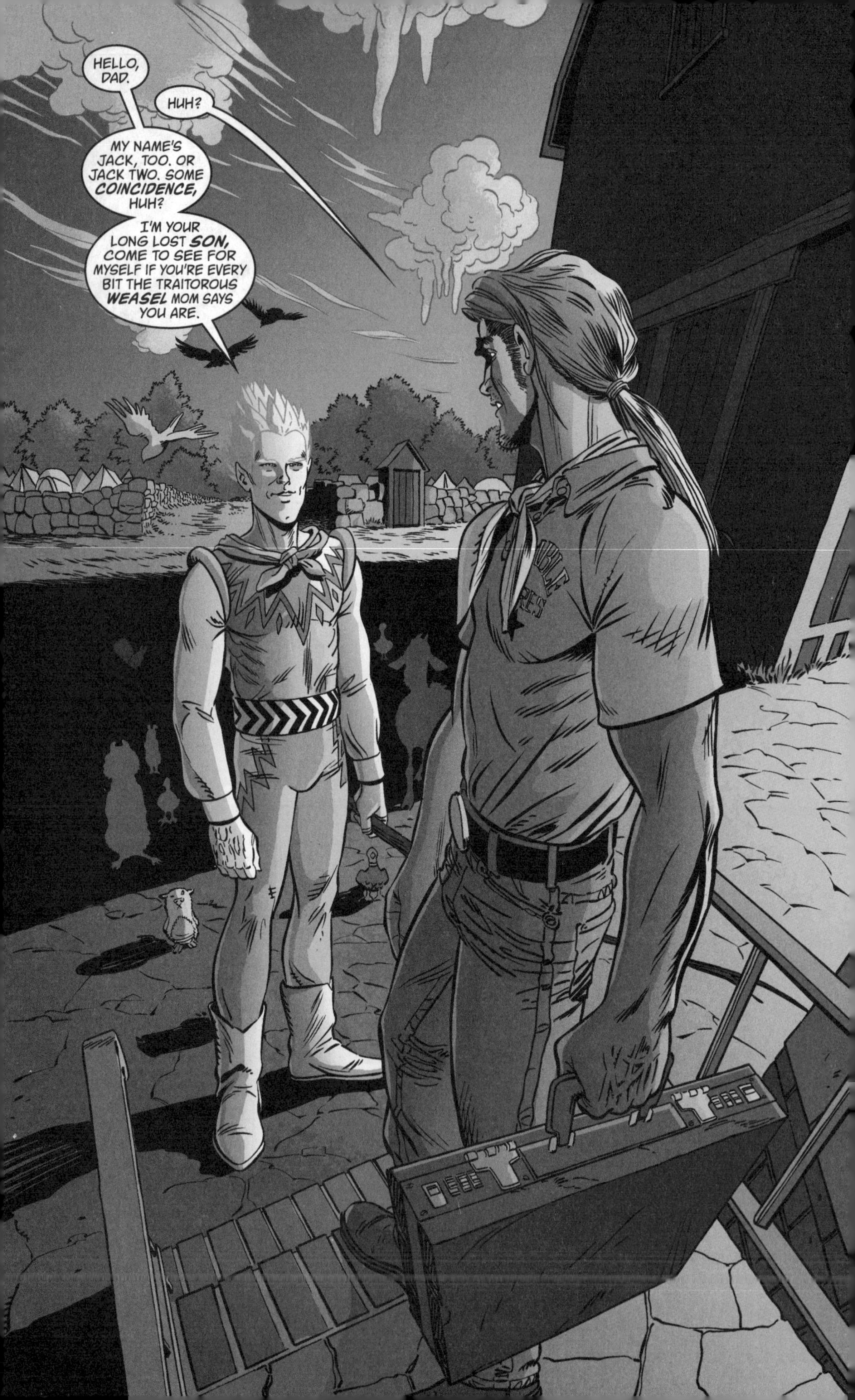
HELLO, DAD.
HUH?
MY NAME'S JACK, TOO. OR JACK TWO. SOME COINCIDENCE, HUH?
I'M YOUR LONG LOST SON, COME TO SEE FOR MYSELF IF YOU'RE EVERY BIT THE TRAITOROUS WEASEL MOM SAYS YOU ARE.

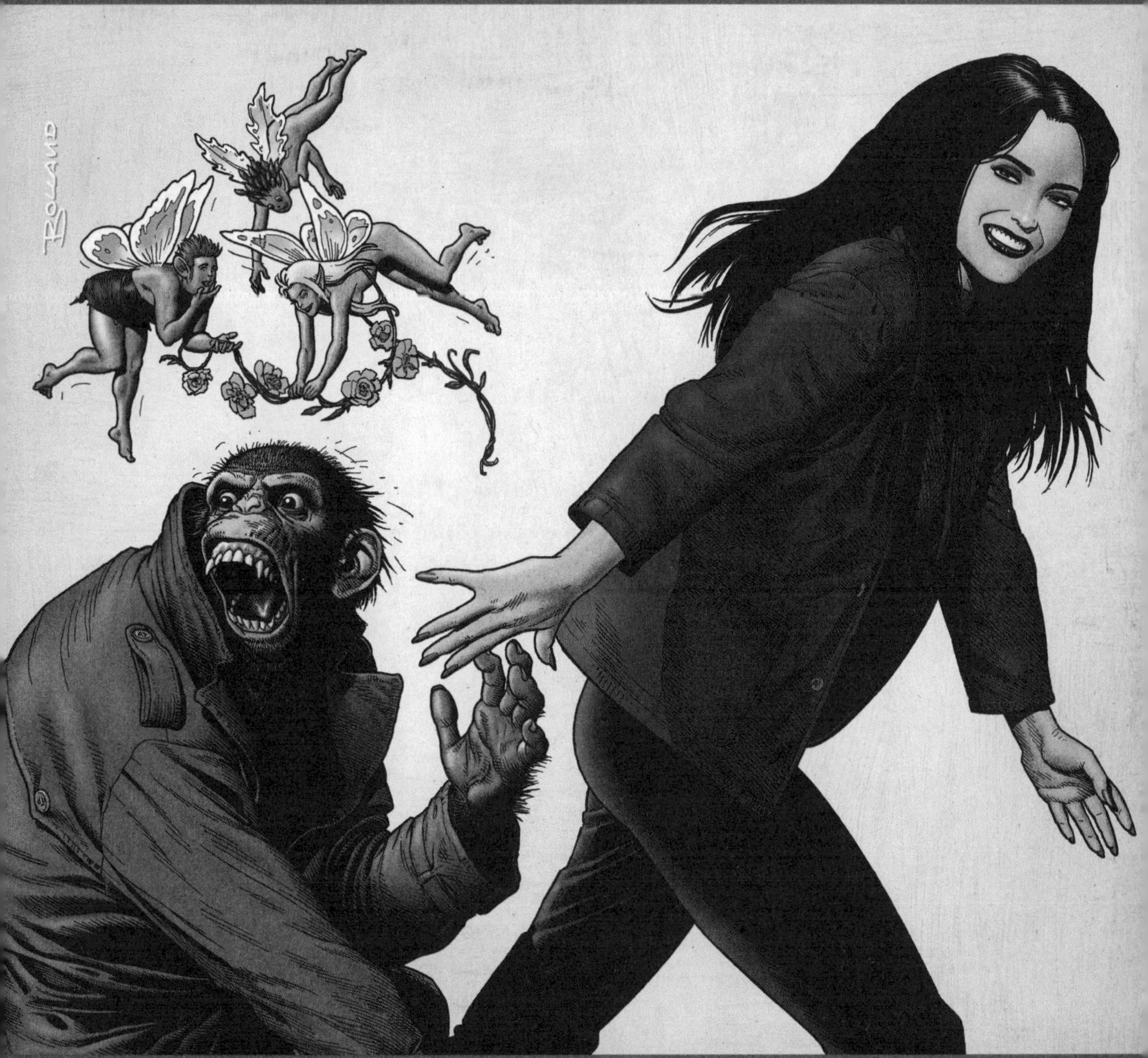
BOLLAND

"Even if we don't stand a chance,
it's better to go down fighting."

The Great FABLES Crossover part 5 of 9

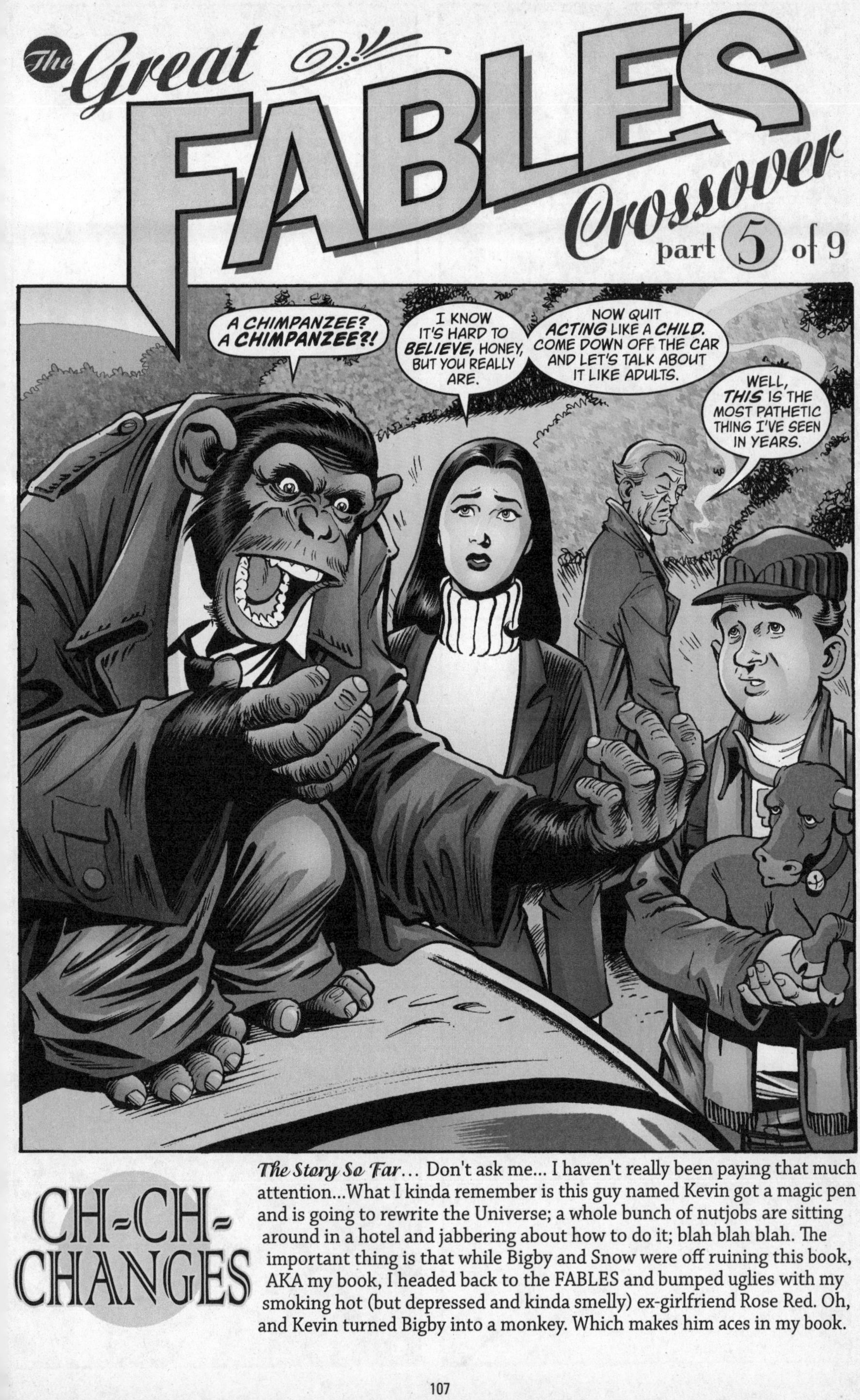
A CHIMPANZEE? A CHIMPANZEE?!
I KNOW IT'S HARD TO BELIEVE, HONEY, BUT YOU REALLY ARE.
NOW QUIT ACTING LIKE A CHILD. COME DOWN OFF THE CAR AND LET'S TALK ABOUT IT LIKE ADULTS.
WELL, THIS IS THE MOST PATHETIC THING I'VE SEEN IN YEARS.

CH-CH-CHANGES

The Story So Far... Don't ask me... I haven't really been paying that much attention...What I kinda remember is this guy named Kevin got a magic pen and is going to rewrite the Universe; a whole bunch of nutjobs are sitting around in a hotel and jabbering about how to do it; blah blah blah. The important thing is that while Bigby and Snow were off ruining this book, AKA my book, I headed back to the FABLES and bumped uglies with my smoking hot (but depressed and kinda smelly) ex-girlfriend Rose Red. Oh, and Kevin turned Bigby into a monkey. Which makes him aces in my book.

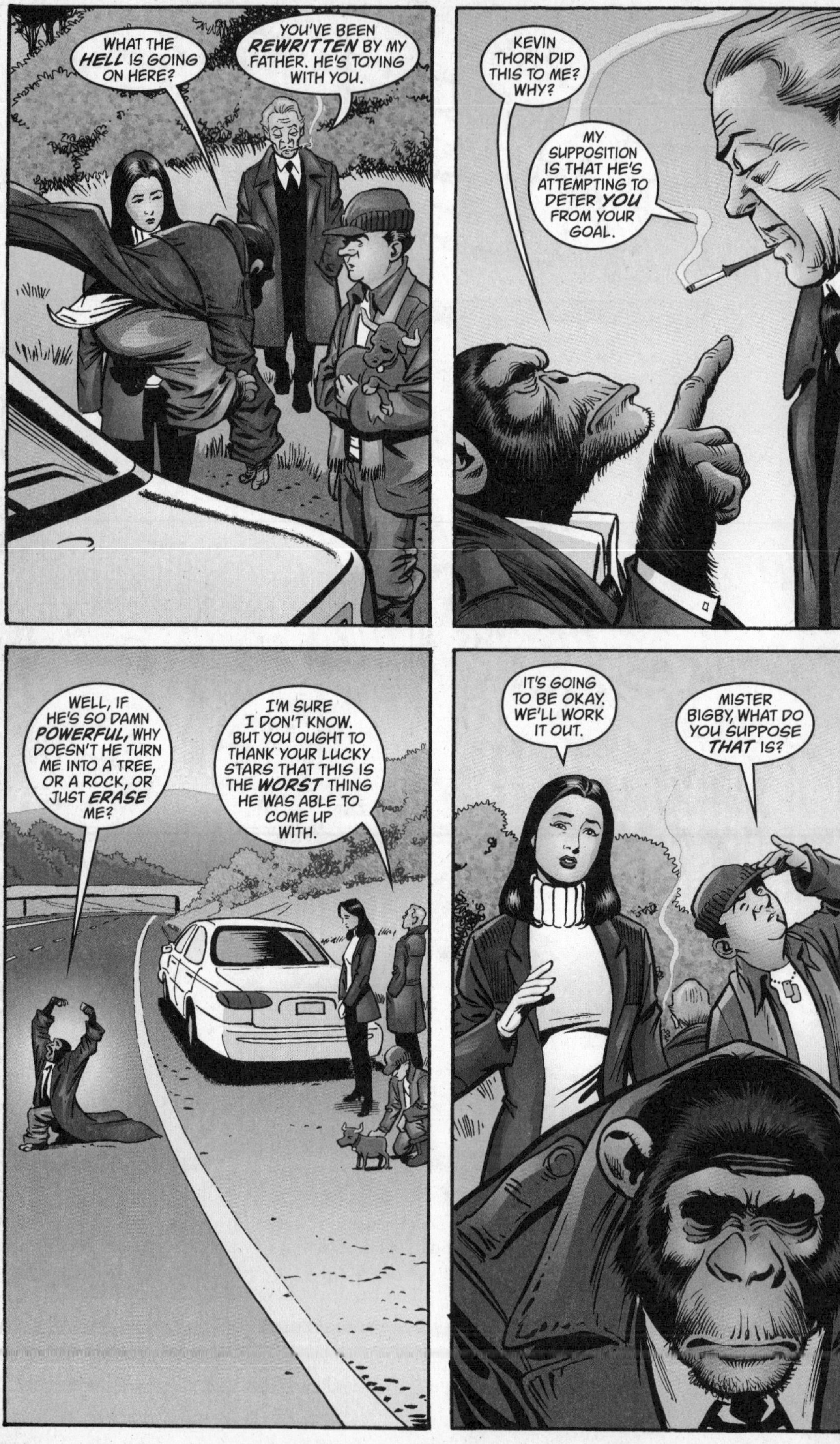
WHAT THE HELL IS GOING ON HERE?
YOU'VE BEEN REWRITTEN BY MY FATHER. HE'S TOYING WITH YOU.
KEVIN THORN DID THIS TO ME? WHY?
MY SUPPOSITION IS THAT HE'S ATTEMPTING TO DETER YOU FROM YOUR GOAL.
WELL, IF HE'S SO DAMN POWERFUL, WHY DOESN'T HE TURN ME INTO A TREE, OR A ROCK, OR JUST ERASE ME?
I'M SURE I DON'T KNOW. BUT YOU OUGHT TO THANK YOUR LUCKY STARS THAT THIS IS THE WORST THING HE WAS ABLE TO COME UP WITH.
IT'S GOING TO BE OKAY. WE'LL WORK IT OUT.
MISTER BIGBY, WHAT DO YOU SUPPOSE THAT IS?

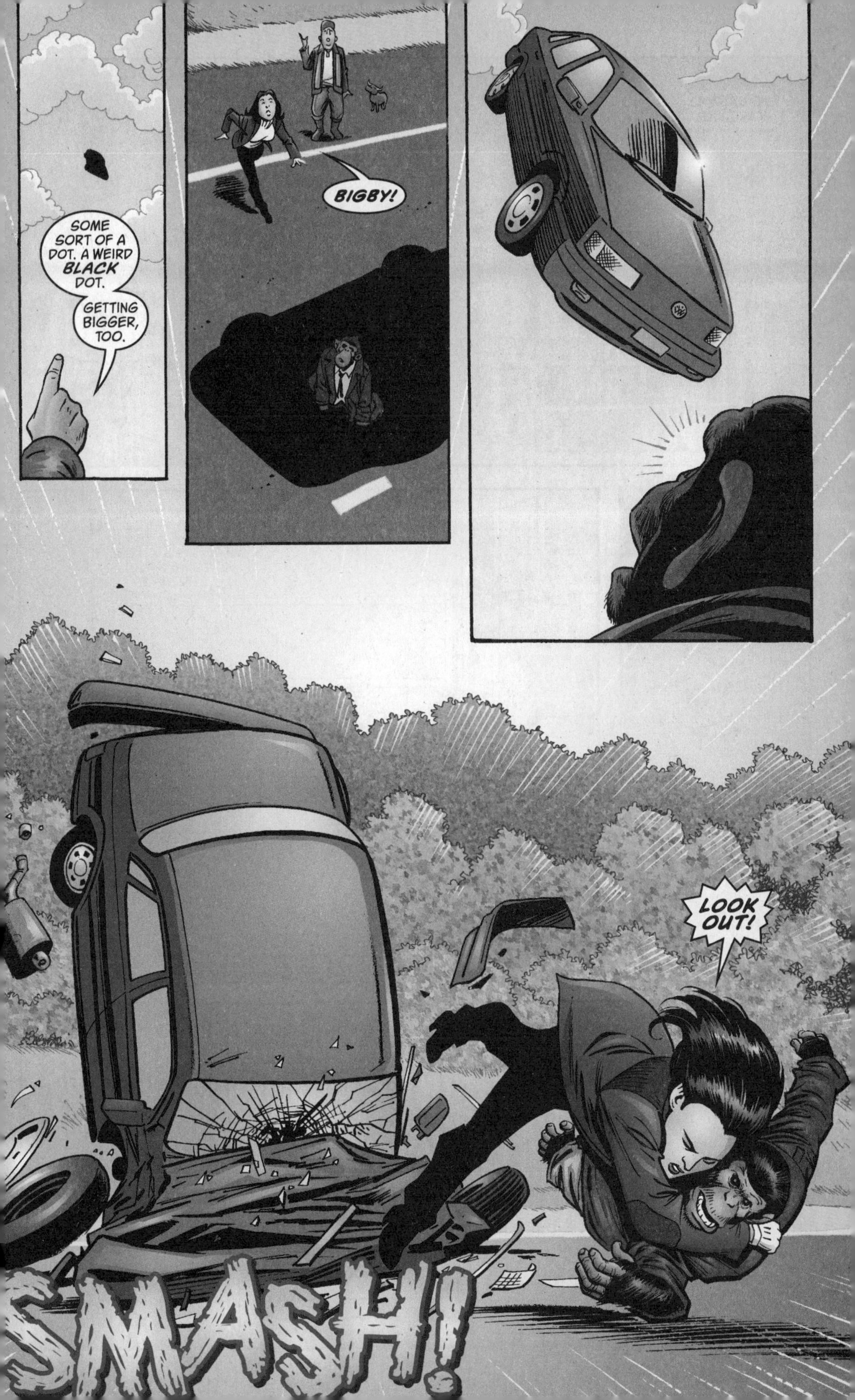
SOME SORT OF A DOT. A WEIRD BLACK DOT.
GETTING BIGGER, TOO.
BIGBY!
LOOK OUT!
SMASH!

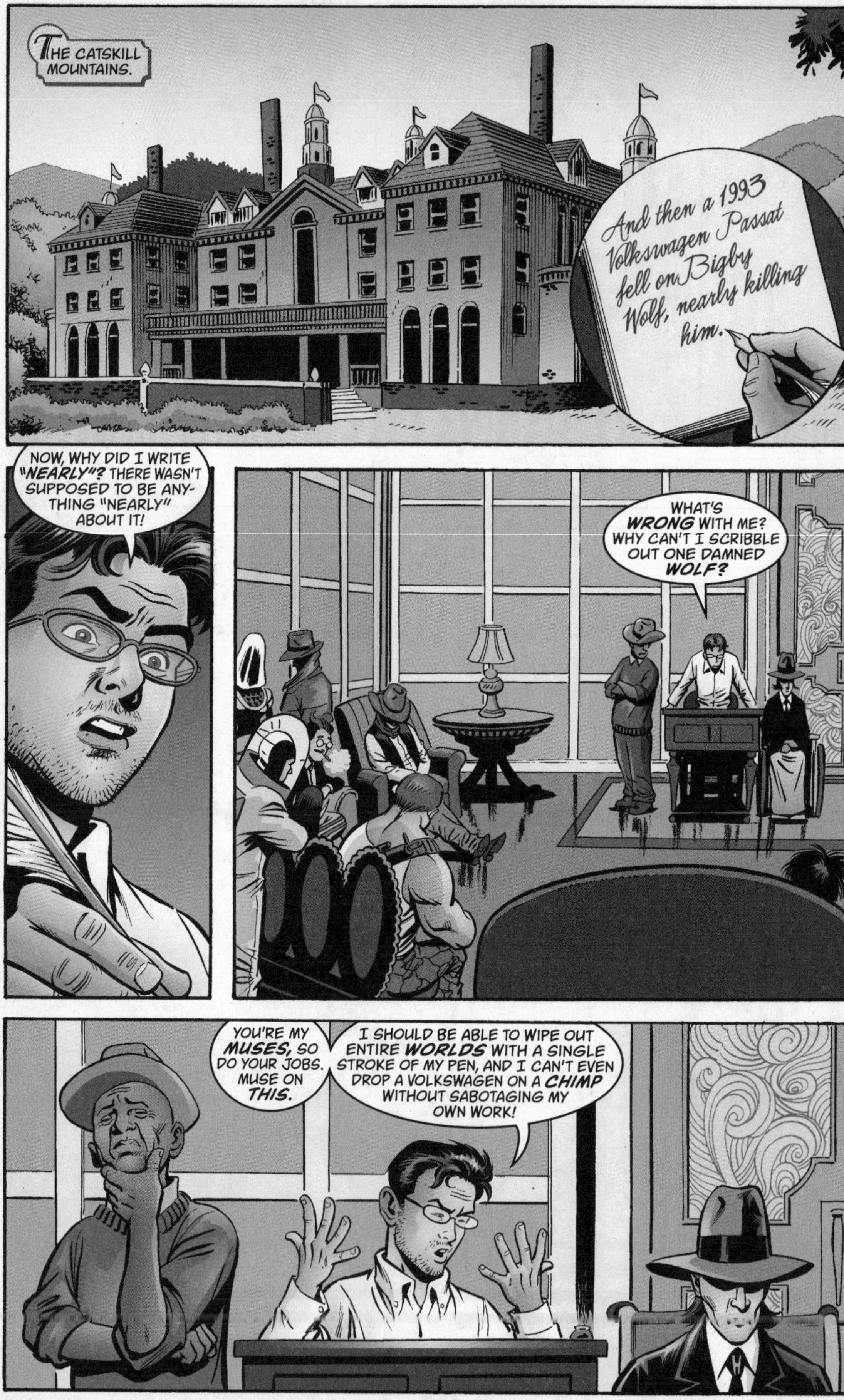
THE CATSKILL MOUNTAINS.
And then a 1993 Volkswagen Passat fell on Bigby Wolf, nearly killing him.
NOW, WHY DID I WRITE "NEARLY"? THERE WASN'T SUPPOSED TO BE ANYTHING "NEARLY" ABOUT IT!
WHAT'S WRONG WITH ME? WHY CAN'T I SCRIBBLE OUT ONE DAMNED WOLF?
YOU'RE MY MUSES, SO DO YOUR JOBS. MUSE ON THIS.
I SHOULD BE ABLE TO WIPE OUT ENTIRE WORLDS WITH A SINGLE STROKE OF MY PEN, AND I CAN'T EVEN DROP A VOLKSWAGEN ON A CHIMP WITHOUT SABOTAGING MY OWN WORK!

I CONDUCTED THOROUGH OPPOSITION **RESEARCH** ON BIGBY WOLF WHEN I WAS ASSIGNED TO SPY ON FABLETOWN.

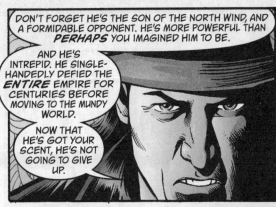

DON'T FORGET HE'S THE SON OF THE NORTH WIND, AND A FORMIDABLE OPPONENT. HE'S MORE POWERFUL THAN **PERHAPS** YOU IMAGINED HIM TO BE.

AND HE'S INTREPID. HE SINGLE-HANDEDLY DEFIED THE **ENTIRE** EMPIRE FOR CENTURIES BEFORE MOVING TO THE MUNDY WORLD.

NOW THAT HE'S GOT YOUR SCENT, HE'S NOT GOING TO GIVE UP.

THAT'S RIDICULOUS, HANSEL! I **INVENTED** HIM!

I HEAR YOU--BUT IT SEEMS HE'S HIS **OWN** MAN NOW.

YOU MIGHT HAVE MADE HIM UP, BUT HE'S HAD A WHOLE MESS OF YEARS TO MAKE **HIMSELF** UP SINCE THEN. I RECKON HE'S GOTTEN POWERFULLY AUTONOMOUS.

NO, SAM, NO! IT DOESN'T MATTER HOW **POWERFUL** HE'S BECOME. THAT'S LIKE BEING THE BIGGEST TURKEY AT A TURKEY SHOOT.

THE TURKEY STILL GETS **SHOT.**

I KNOW I'M PROBABLY WASTING MY TIME, BUT DO ANY OF YOU **FREELOADERS** HAVE A BRIGHT IDEA?

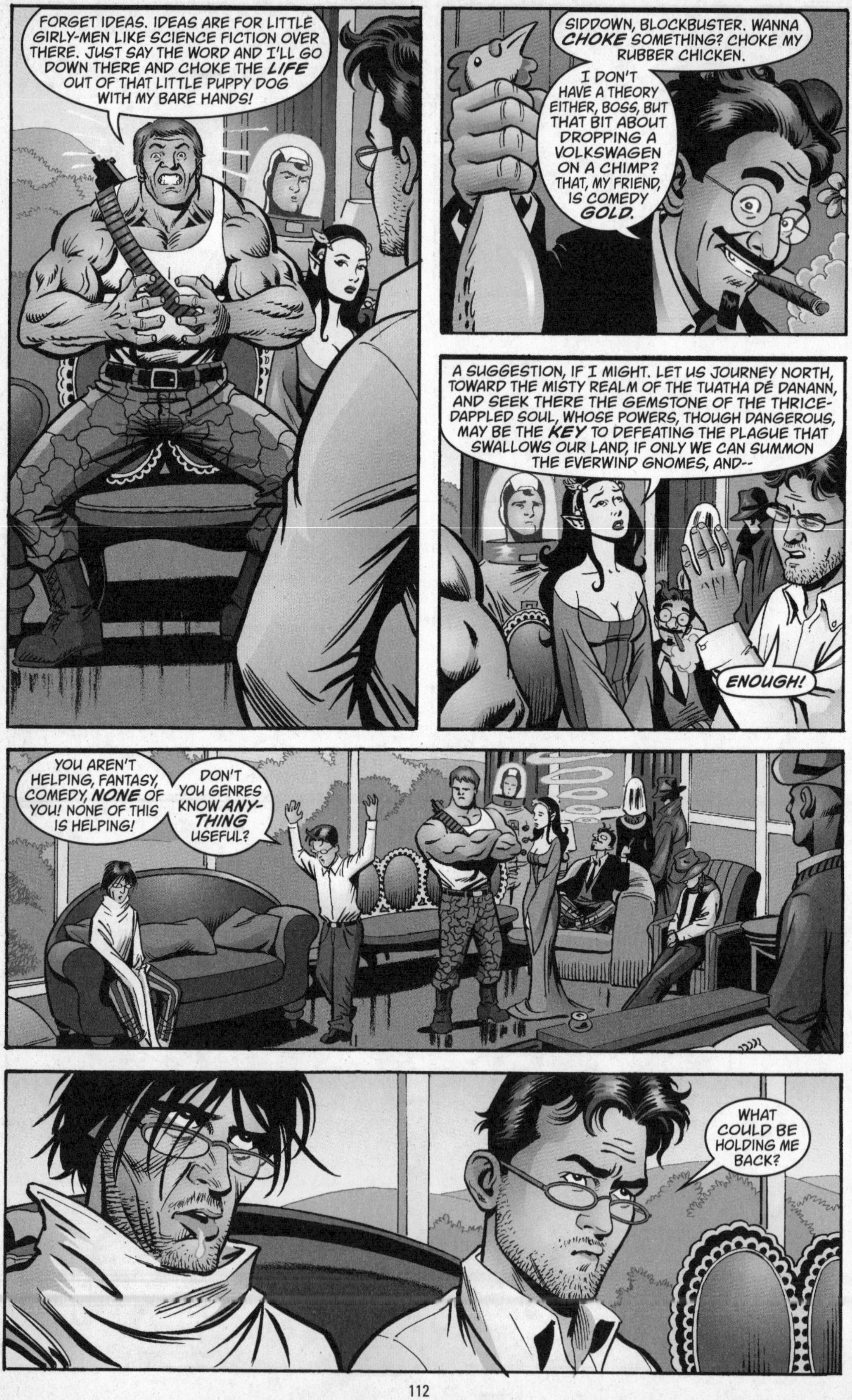
FORGET IDEAS. IDEAS ARE FOR LITTLE GIRLY-MEN LIKE SCIENCE FICTION OVER THERE. JUST SAY THE WORD AND I'LL GO DOWN THERE AND CHOKE THE LIFE OUT OF THAT LITTLE PUPPY DOG WITH MY BARE HANDS!
SIDDOWN, BLOCKBUSTER. WANNA CHOKE SOMETHING? CHOKE MY RUBBER CHICKEN.
I DON'T HAVE A THEORY EITHER, BOSS, BUT THAT BIT ABOUT DROPPING A VOLKSWAGEN ON A CHIMP? THAT, MY FRIEND, IS COMEDY GOLD.
A SUGGESTION, IF I MIGHT. LET US JOURNEY NORTH, TOWARD THE MISTY REALM OF THE TUATHA DÉ DANANN, AND SEEK THERE THE GEMSTONE OF THE THRICE-DAPPLED SOUL, WHOSE POWERS, THOUGH DANGEROUS, MAY BE THE KEY TO DEFEATING THE PLAGUE THAT SWALLOWS OUR LAND, IF ONLY WE CAN SUMMON THE EVERWIND GNOMES, AND--
ENOUGH!
YOU AREN'T HELPING, FANTASY, COMEDY, NONE OF YOU! NONE OF THIS IS HELPING!
DON'T YOU GENRES KNOW ANYTHING USEFUL?
WHAT COULD BE HOLDING ME BACK?

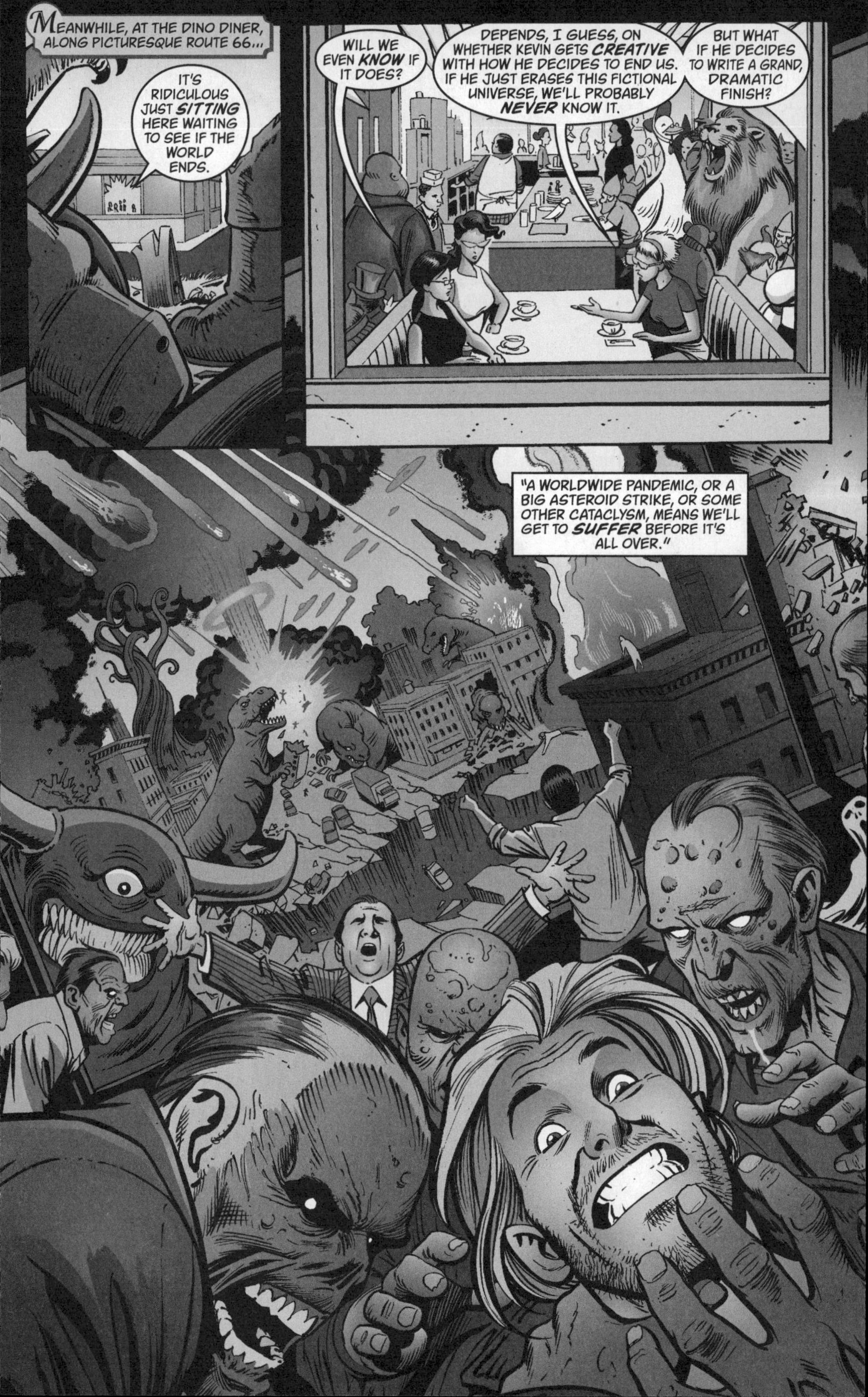
MEANWHILE, AT THE DINO DINER, ALONG PICTURESQUE ROUTE 66...
IT'S RIDICULOUS JUST **SITTING** HERE WAITING TO SEE IF THE WORLD ENDS.
WILL WE EVEN **KNOW** IF IT DOES?
DEPENDS, I GUESS, ON WHETHER KEVIN GETS **CREATIVE** WITH HOW HE DECIDES TO END US. IF HE JUST ERASES THIS FICTIONAL UNIVERSE, WE'LL PROBABLY **NEVER** KNOW IT.
BUT WHAT IF HE DECIDES TO WRITE A GRAND, DRAMATIC FINISH?
"A WORLDWIDE PANDEMIC, OR A BIG ASTEROID STRIKE, OR SOME OTHER CATACLYSM, MEANS WE'LL GET TO **SUFFER** BEFORE IT'S ALL OVER."

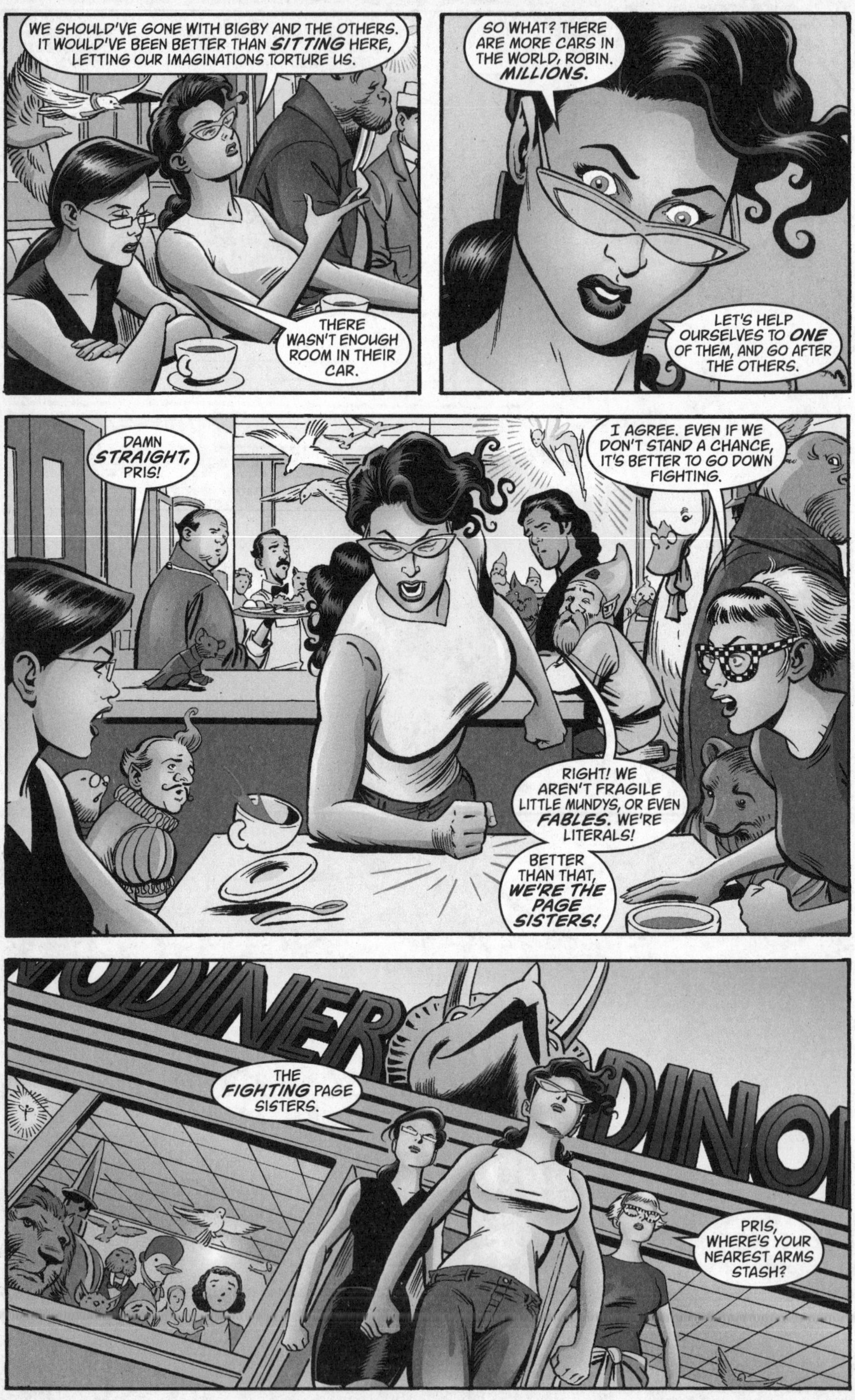
WE SHOULD'VE GONE WITH BIGBY AND THE OTHERS. IT WOULD'VE BEEN BETTER THAN *SITTING* HERE, LETTING OUR IMAGINATIONS TORTURE US.
THERE WASN'T ENOUGH ROOM IN THEIR CAR.
SO WHAT? THERE ARE MORE CARS IN THE WORLD, ROBIN. ***MILLIONS.***
LET'S HELP OURSELVES TO ***ONE*** OF THEM, AND GO AFTER THE OTHERS.
DAMN ***STRAIGHT,*** PRIS!
I AGREE. EVEN IF WE DON'T STAND A CHANCE, IT'S BETTER TO GO DOWN FIGHTING.
RIGHT! WE AREN'T FRAGILE LITTLE MUNDYS, OR EVEN ***FABLES.*** WE'RE LITERALS!
BETTER THAN THAT, ***WE'RE THE PAGE SISTERS!***
DINER
THE ***FIGHTING*** PAGE SISTERS.
PRIS, WHERE'S YOUR NEAREST ARMS STASH?

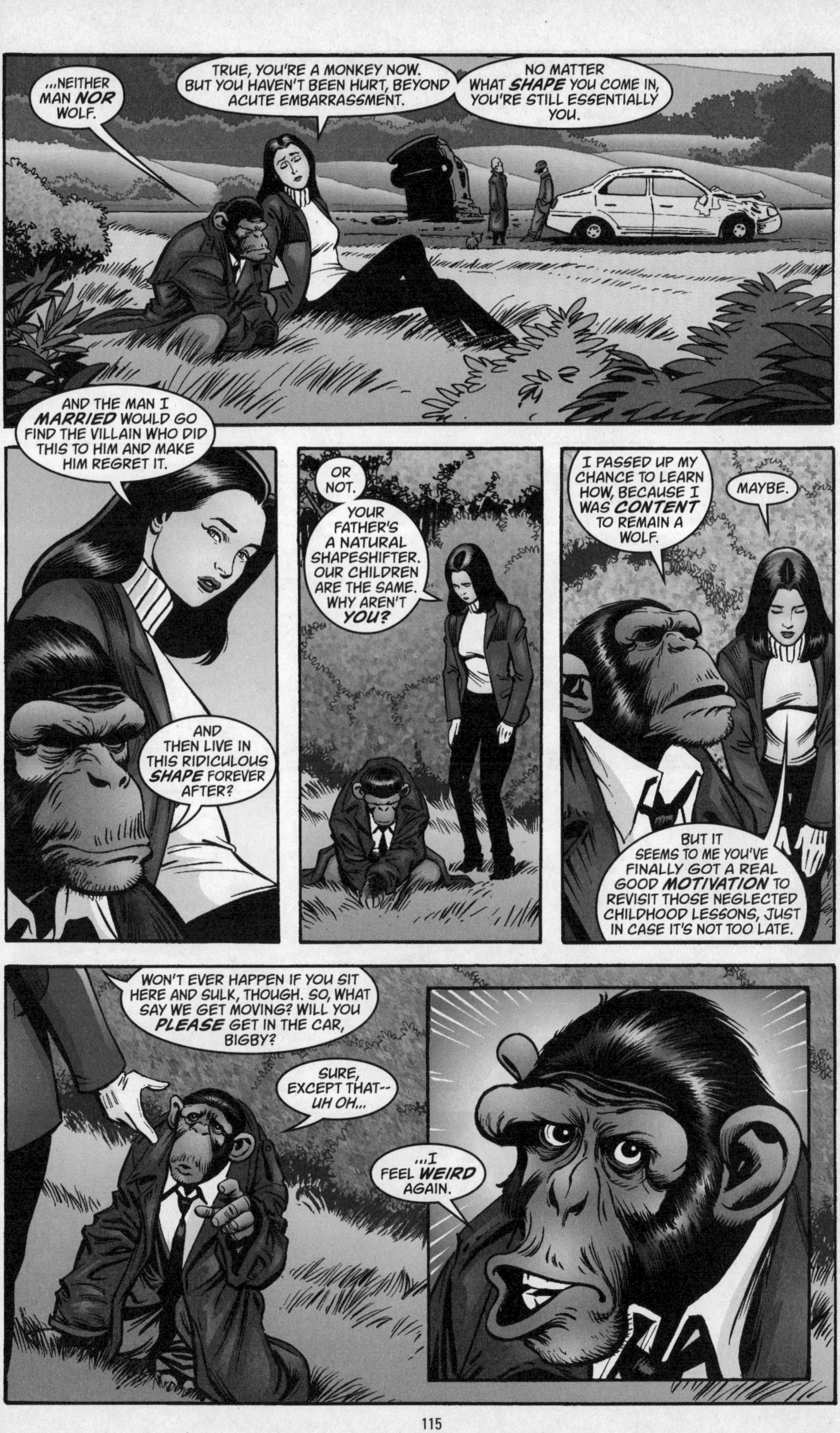
...NEITHER MAN NOR WOLF.
TRUE, YOU'RE A MONKEY NOW. BUT YOU HAVEN'T BEEN HURT, BEYOND ACUTE EMBARRASSMENT.
NO MATTER WHAT SHAPE YOU COME IN, YOU'RE STILL ESSENTIALLY YOU.
AND THE MAN I MARRIED WOULD GO FIND THE VILLAIN WHO DID THIS TO HIM AND MAKE HIM REGRET IT.
AND THEN LIVE IN THIS RIDICULOUS SHAPE FOREVER AFTER?
OR NOT.
YOUR FATHER'S A NATURAL SHAPESHIFTER. OUR CHILDREN ARE THE SAME. WHY AREN'T YOU?
I PASSED UP MY CHANCE TO LEARN HOW, BECAUSE I WAS CONTENT TO REMAIN A WOLF.
MAYBE.
BUT IT SEEMS TO ME YOU'VE FINALLY GOT A REAL GOOD MOTIVATION TO REVISIT THOSE NEGLECTED CHILDHOOD LESSONS, JUST IN CASE IT'S NOT TOO LATE.
WON'T EVER HAPPEN IF YOU SIT HERE AND SULK, THOUGH. SO, WHAT SAY WE GET MOVING? WILL YOU PLEASE GET IN THE CAR, BIGBY?
SURE, EXCEPT THAT-- UH OH...
...I FEEL WEIRD AGAIN.

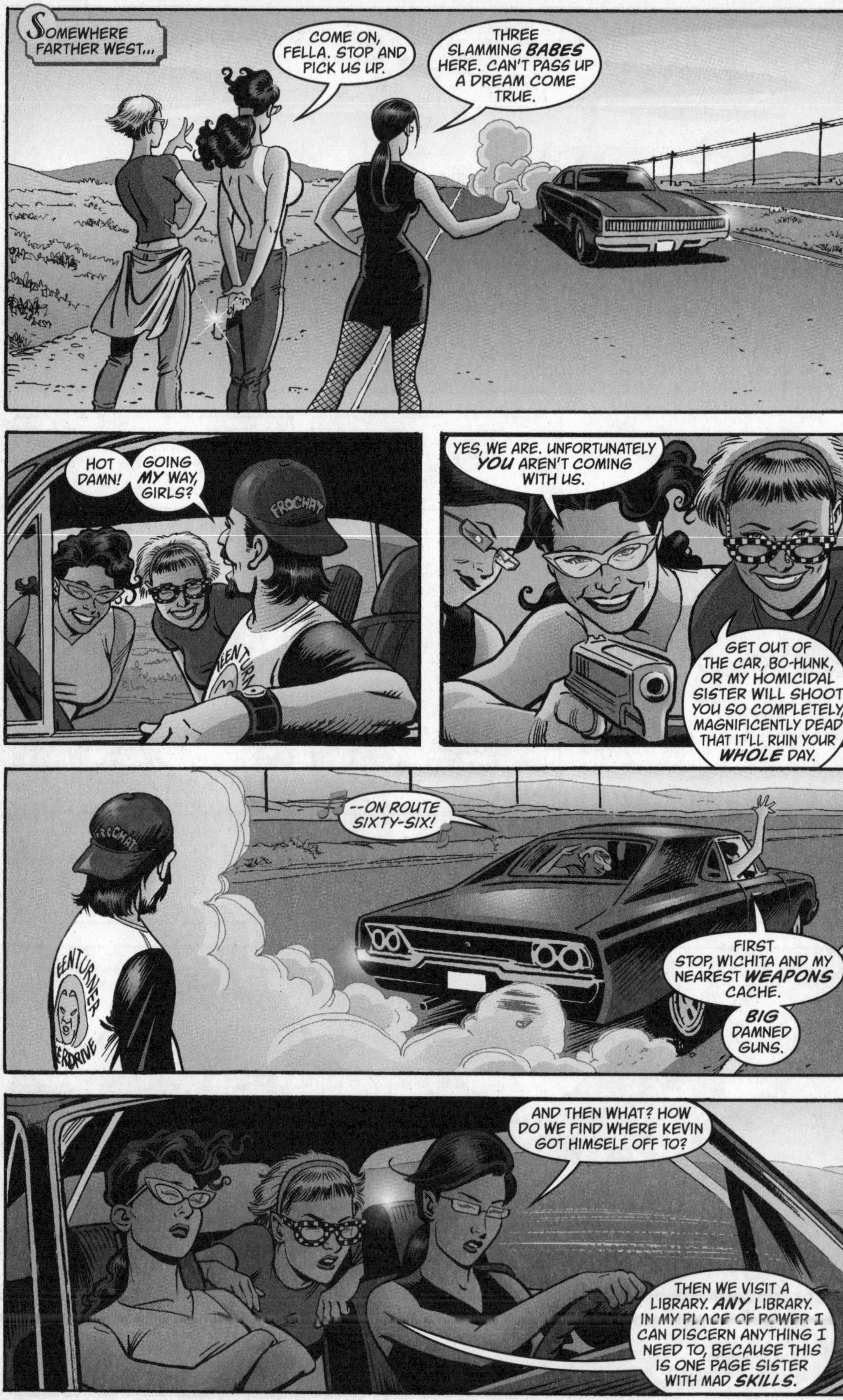
SOMEWHERE FARTHER WEST...
COME ON, FELLA. STOP AND PICK US UP.
THREE SLAMMING BABES HERE. CAN'T PASS UP A DREAM COME TRUE.
HOT DAMN!
GOING MY WAY, GIRLS?
FROCHAT
YES, WE ARE. UNFORTUNATELY YOU AREN'T COMING WITH US.
GET OUT OF THE CAR, BO-HUNK, OR MY HOMICIDAL SISTER WILL SHOOT YOU SO COMPLETELY, MAGNIFICENTLY DEAD THAT IT'LL RUIN YOUR WHOLE DAY.
--ON ROUTE SIXTY-SIX!
FIRST STOP, WICHITA AND MY NEAREST WEAPONS CACHE.
BIG DAMNED GUNS.
AND THEN WHAT? HOW DO WE FIND WHERE KEVIN GOT HIMSELF OFF TO?
THEN WE VISIT A LIBRARY. ANY LIBRARY. IN MY PLACE OF POWER I CAN DISCERN ANYTHING I NEED TO, BECAUSE THIS IS ONE PAGE SISTER WITH MAD SKILLS.

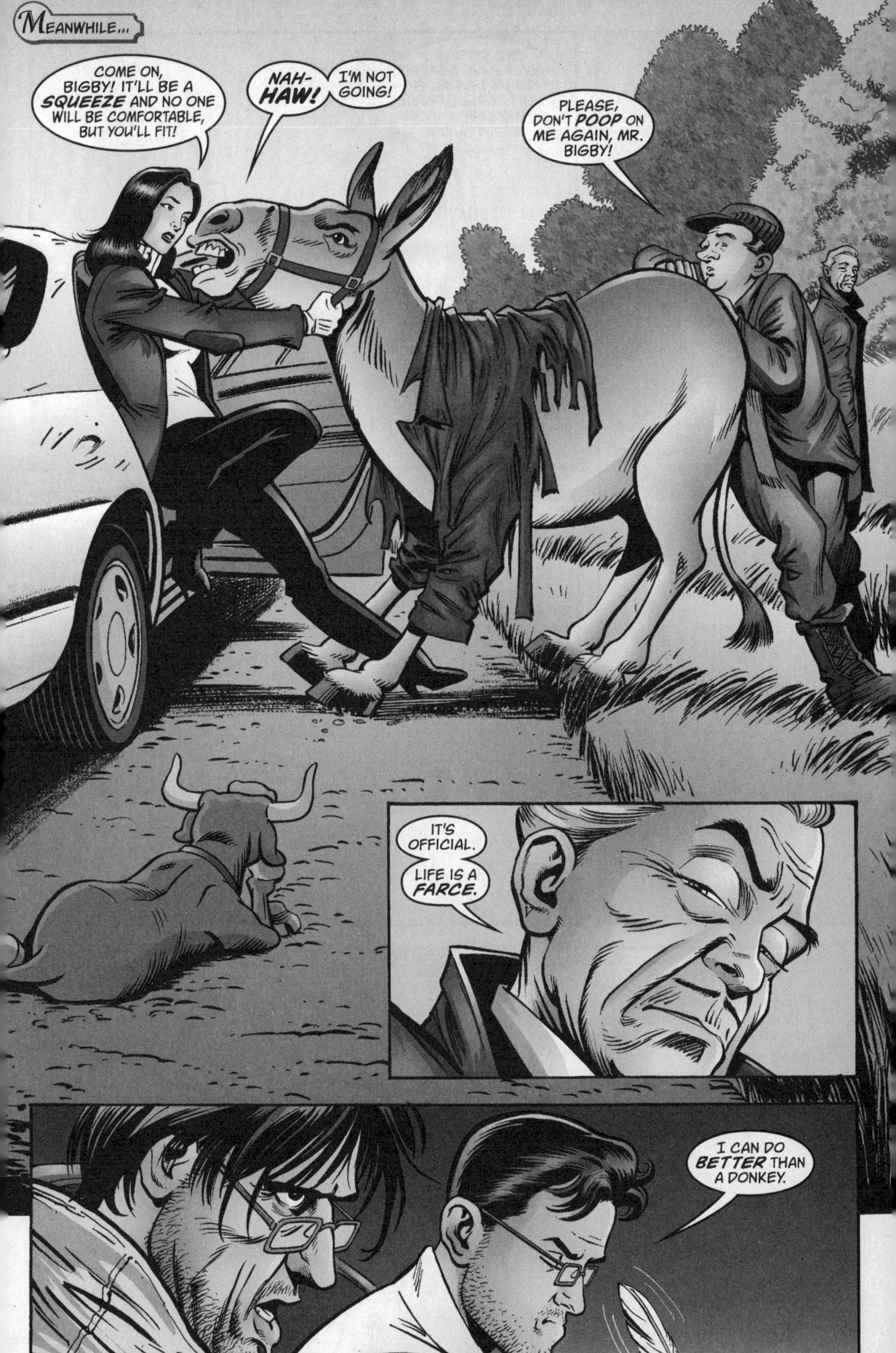
MEANWHILE...
COME ON, BIGBY! IT'LL BE A SQUEEZE AND NO ONE WILL BE COMFORTABLE, BUT YOU'LL FIT!
NAH-HAW!
I'M NOT GOING!
PLEASE, DON'T POOP ON ME AGAIN, MR. BIGBY!
IT'S OFFICIAL.
LIFE IS A FARCE.
I CAN DO BETTER THAN A DONKEY.

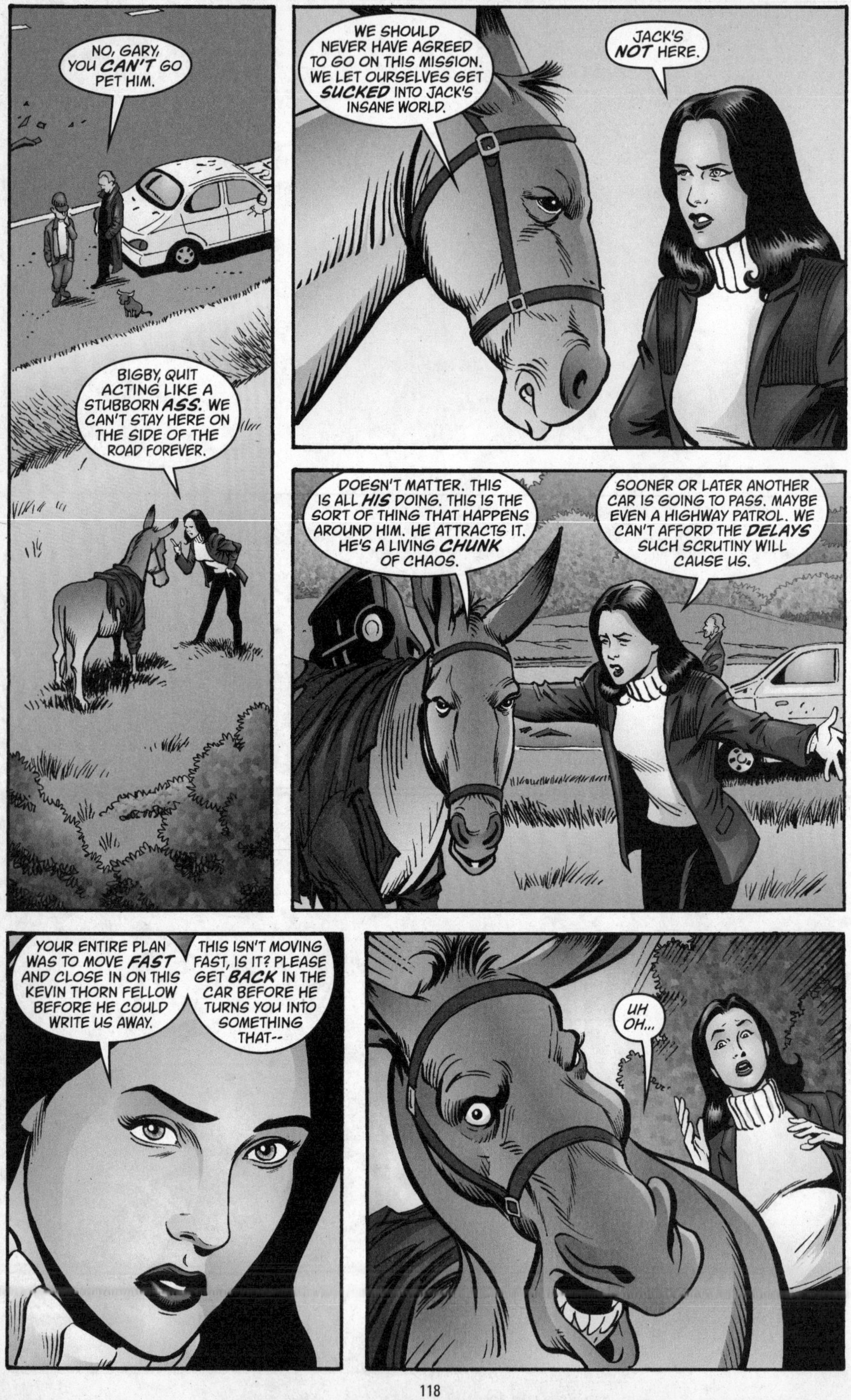
NO, GARY, YOU CAN'T GO PET HIM.
BIGBY, QUIT ACTING LIKE A STUBBORN ASS. WE CAN'T STAY HERE ON THE SIDE OF THE ROAD FOREVER.
WE SHOULD NEVER HAVE AGREED TO GO ON THIS MISSION. WE LET OURSELVES GET SUCKED INTO JACK'S INSANE WORLD.
JACK'S NOT HERE.
DOESN'T MATTER. THIS IS ALL HIS DOING. THIS IS THE SORT OF THING THAT HAPPENS AROUND HIM. HE ATTRACTS IT. HE'S A LIVING CHUNK OF CHAOS.
SOONER OR LATER ANOTHER CAR IS GOING TO PASS. MAYBE EVEN A HIGHWAY PATROL. WE CAN'T AFFORD THE DELAYS SUCH SCRUTINY WILL CAUSE US.
YOUR ENTIRE PLAN WAS TO MOVE FAST AND CLOSE IN ON THIS KEVIN THORN FELLOW BEFORE HE COULD WRITE US AWAY.
THIS ISN'T MOVING FAST, IS IT? PLEASE GET BACK IN THE CAR BEFORE HE TURNS YOU INTO SOMETHING THAT--
UH OH...

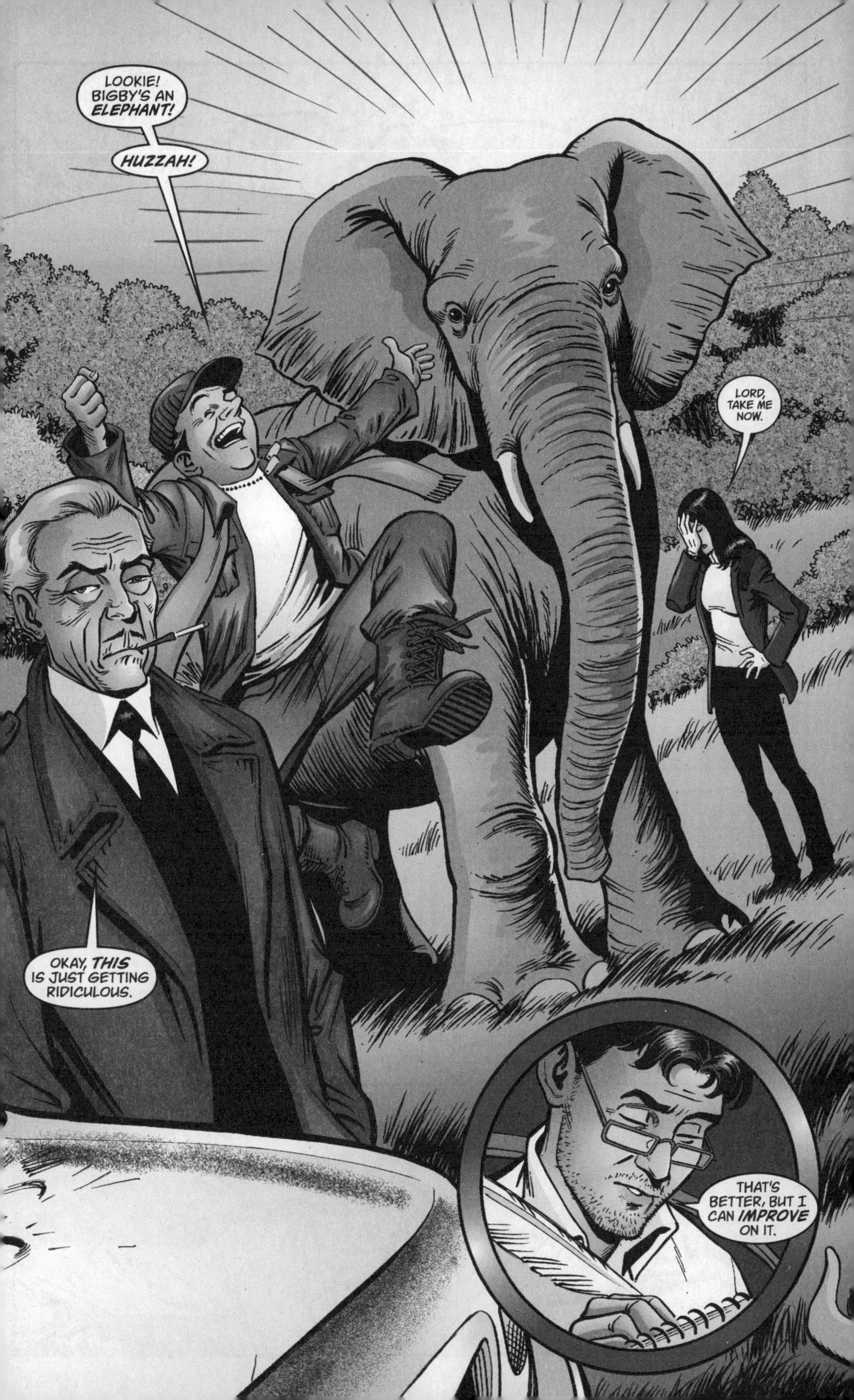
LOOKIE! BIGBY'S AN *ELEPHANT!*
HUZZAH!
LORD, TAKE ME NOW.
OKAY, *THIS* IS JUST GETTING RIDICULOUS.
THAT'S BETTER, BUT I CAN *IMPROVE* ON IT.

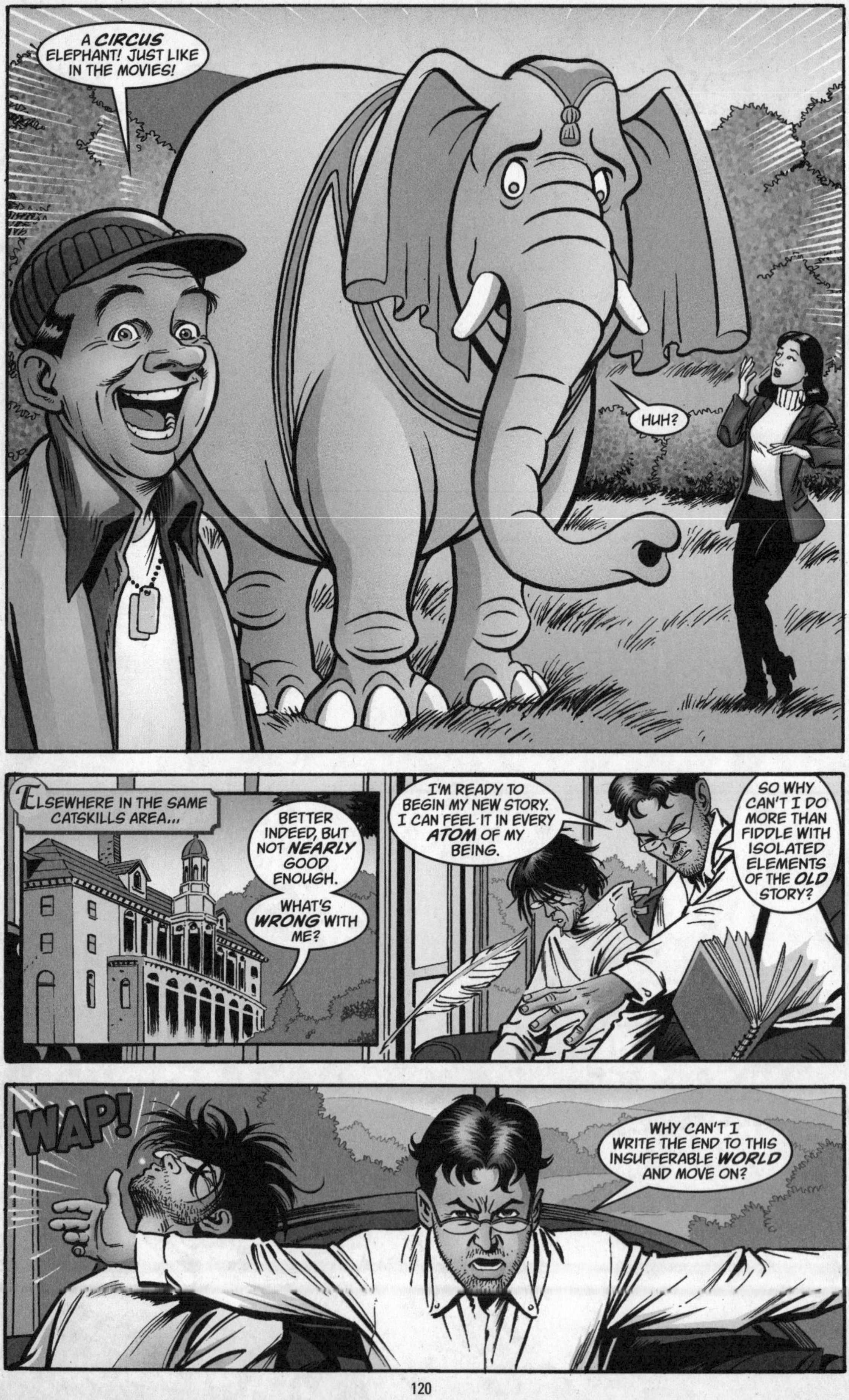
A CIRCUS ELEPHANT! JUST LIKE IN THE MOVIES!
HUH?
ELSEWHERE IN THE SAME CATSKILLS AREA...
BETTER INDEED, BUT NOT NEARLY GOOD ENOUGH.
WHAT'S WRONG WITH ME?
I'M READY TO BEGIN MY NEW STORY. I CAN FEEL IT IN EVERY ATOM OF MY BEING.
SO WHY CAN'T I DO MORE THAN FIDDLE WITH ISOLATED ELEMENTS OF THE OLD STORY?
WAP!
WHY CAN'T I WRITE THE END TO THIS INSUFFERABLE WORLD AND MOVE ON?

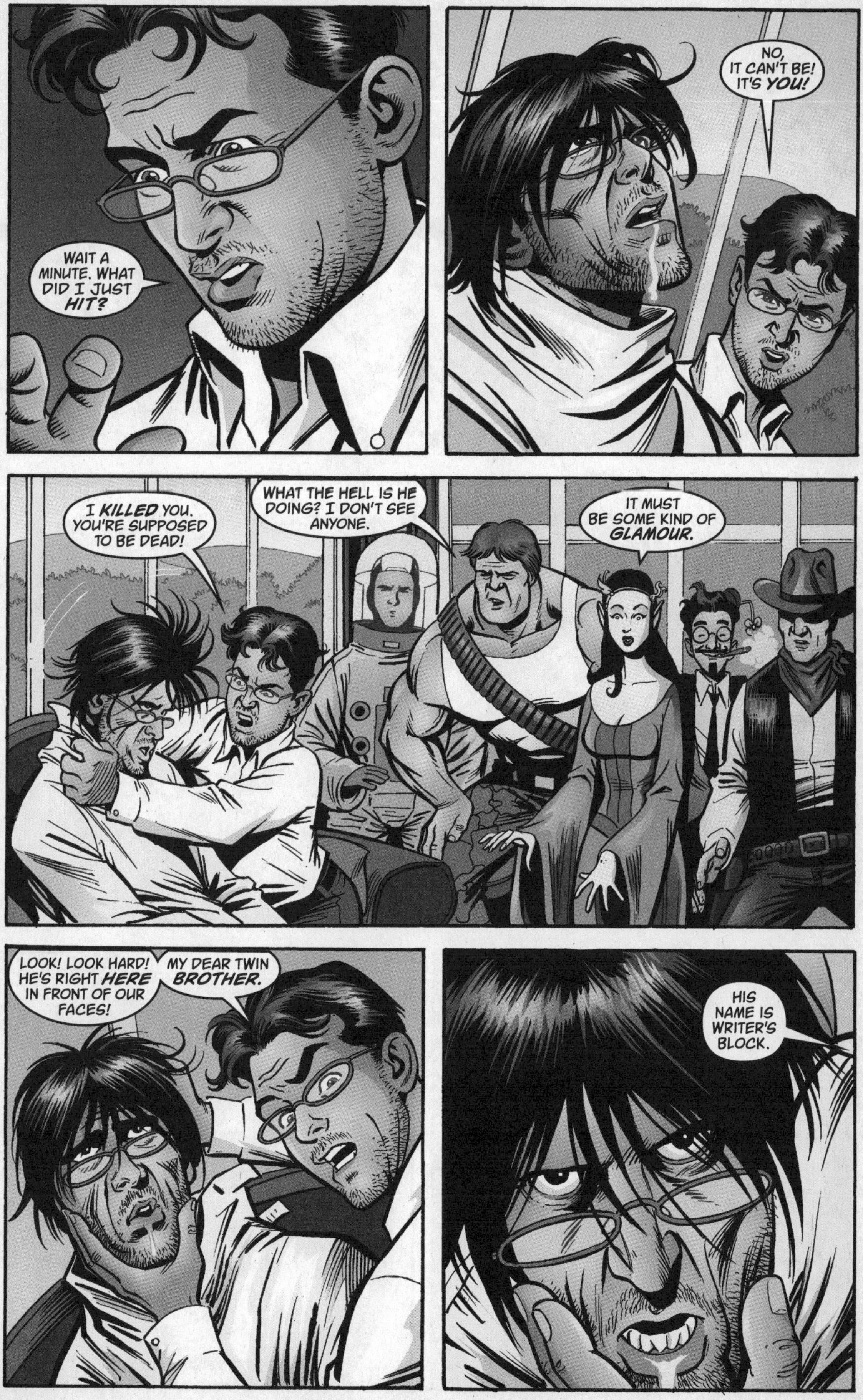
WAIT A MINUTE. WHAT DID I JUST HIT?
NO, IT CAN'T BE! IT'S YOU!
I KILLED YOU. YOU'RE SUPPOSED TO BE DEAD!
WHAT THE HELL IS HE DOING? I DON'T SEE ANYONE.
IT MUST BE SOME KIND OF GLAMOUR.
LOOK! LOOK HARD! HE'S RIGHT HERE IN FRONT OF OUR FACES!
MY DEAR TWIN BROTHER.
HIS NAME IS WRITER'S BLOCK.

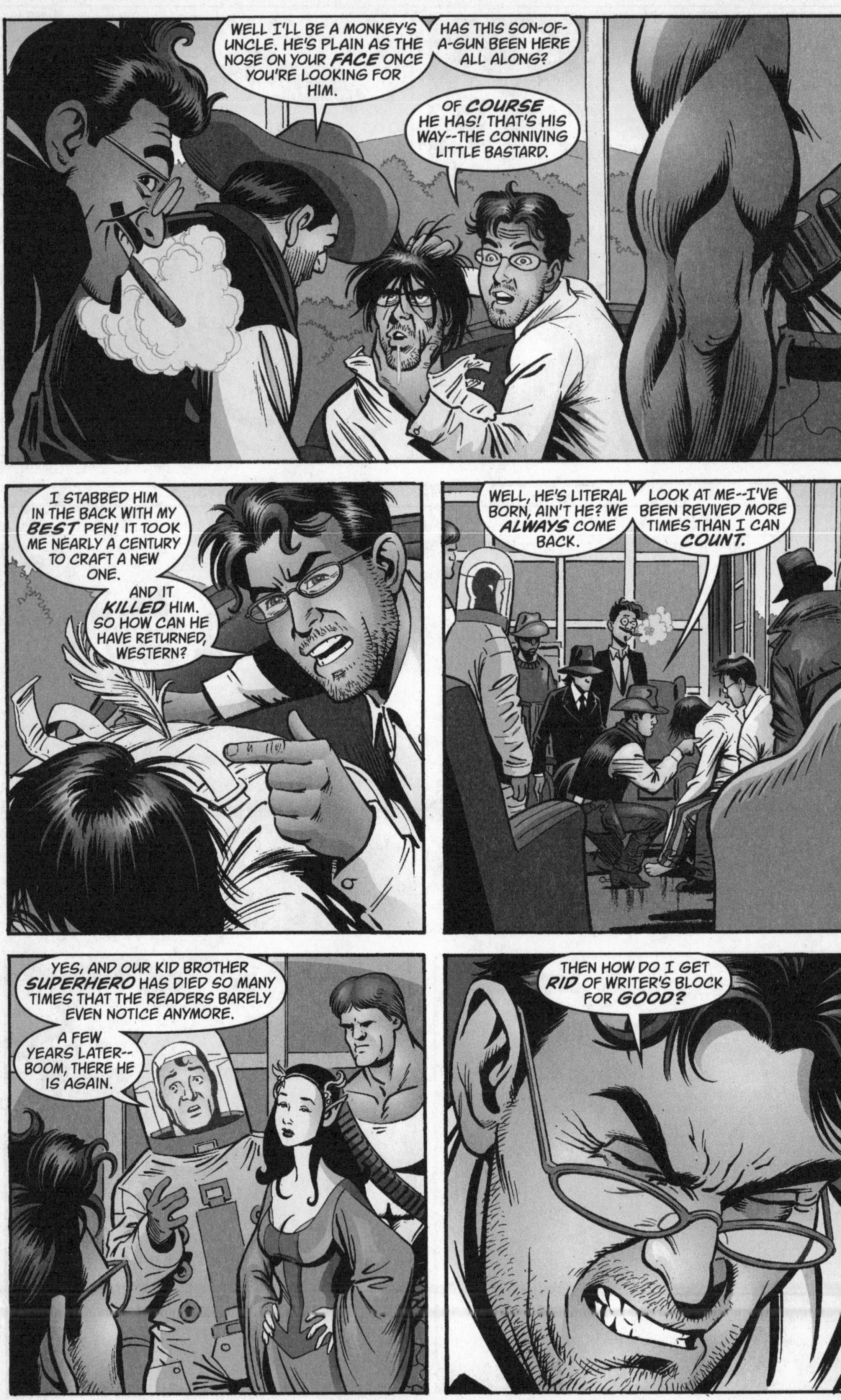
WELL I'LL BE A MONKEY'S UNCLE. HE'S PLAIN AS THE NOSE ON YOUR FACE ONCE YOU'RE LOOKING FOR HIM.
HAS THIS SON-OF-A-GUN BEEN HERE ALL ALONG?
OF COURSE HE HAS! THAT'S HIS WAY--THE CONNIVING LITTLE BASTARD.
I STABBED HIM IN THE BACK WITH MY BEST PEN! IT TOOK ME NEARLY A CENTURY TO CRAFT A NEW ONE.
AND IT KILLED HIM. SO HOW CAN HE HAVE RETURNED, WESTERN?
WELL, HE'S LITERAL BORN, AIN'T HE? WE ALWAYS COME BACK.
LOOK AT ME--I'VE BEEN REVIVED MORE TIMES THAN I CAN COUNT.
YES, AND OUR KID BROTHER SUPERHERO HAS DIED SO MANY TIMES THAT THE READERS BARELY EVEN NOTICE ANYMORE.
A FEW YEARS LATER--BOOM, THERE HE IS AGAIN.
THEN HOW DO I GET RID OF WRITER'S BLOCK FOR GOOD?

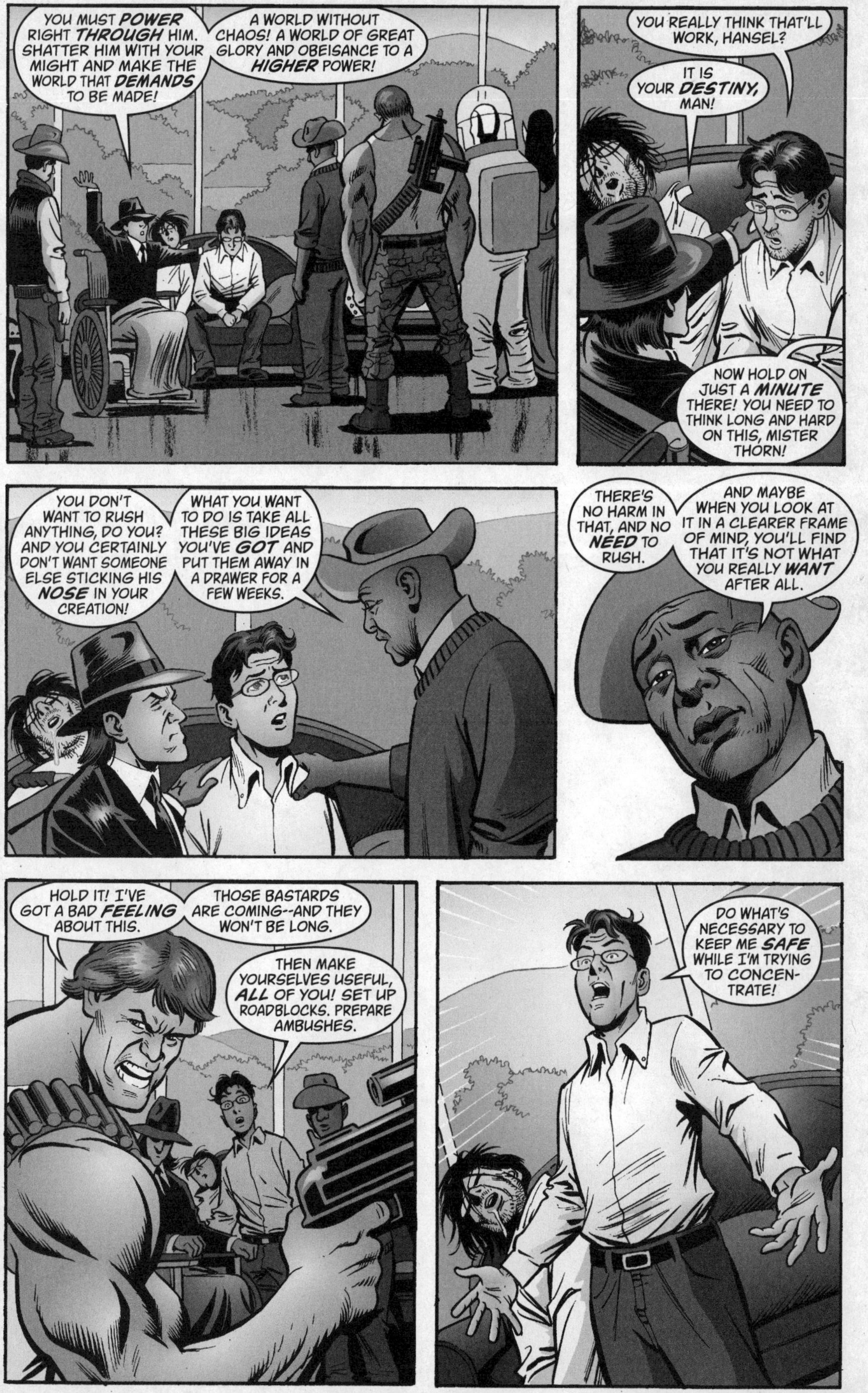
YOU MUST POWER RIGHT THROUGH HIM. SHATTER HIM WITH YOUR MIGHT AND MAKE THE WORLD THAT DEMANDS TO BE MADE!
A WORLD WITHOUT CHAOS! A WORLD OF GREAT GLORY AND OBEISANCE TO A HIGHER POWER!
YOU REALLY THINK THAT'LL WORK, HANSEL?
IT IS YOUR DESTINY, MAN!
NOW HOLD ON JUST A MINUTE THERE! YOU NEED TO THINK LONG AND HARD ON THIS, MISTER THORN!
YOU DON'T WANT TO RUSH ANYTHING, DO YOU? AND YOU CERTAINLY DON'T WANT SOMEONE ELSE STICKING HIS NOSE IN YOUR CREATION!
WHAT YOU WANT TO DO IS TAKE ALL THESE BIG IDEAS YOU'VE GOT AND PUT THEM AWAY IN A DRAWER FOR A FEW WEEKS.
THERE'S NO HARM IN THAT, AND NO NEED TO RUSH.
AND MAYBE WHEN YOU LOOK AT IT IN A CLEARER FRAME OF MIND, YOU'LL FIND THAT IT'S NOT WHAT YOU REALLY WANT AFTER ALL.
HOLD IT! I'VE GOT A BAD FEELING ABOUT THIS.
THOSE BASTARDS ARE COMING--AND THEY WON'T BE LONG.
THEN MAKE YOURSELVES USEFUL, ALL OF YOU! SET UP ROADBLOCKS. PREPARE AMBUSHES.
DO WHAT'S NECESSARY TO KEEP ME SAFE WHILE I'M TRYING TO CONCEN-TRATE!

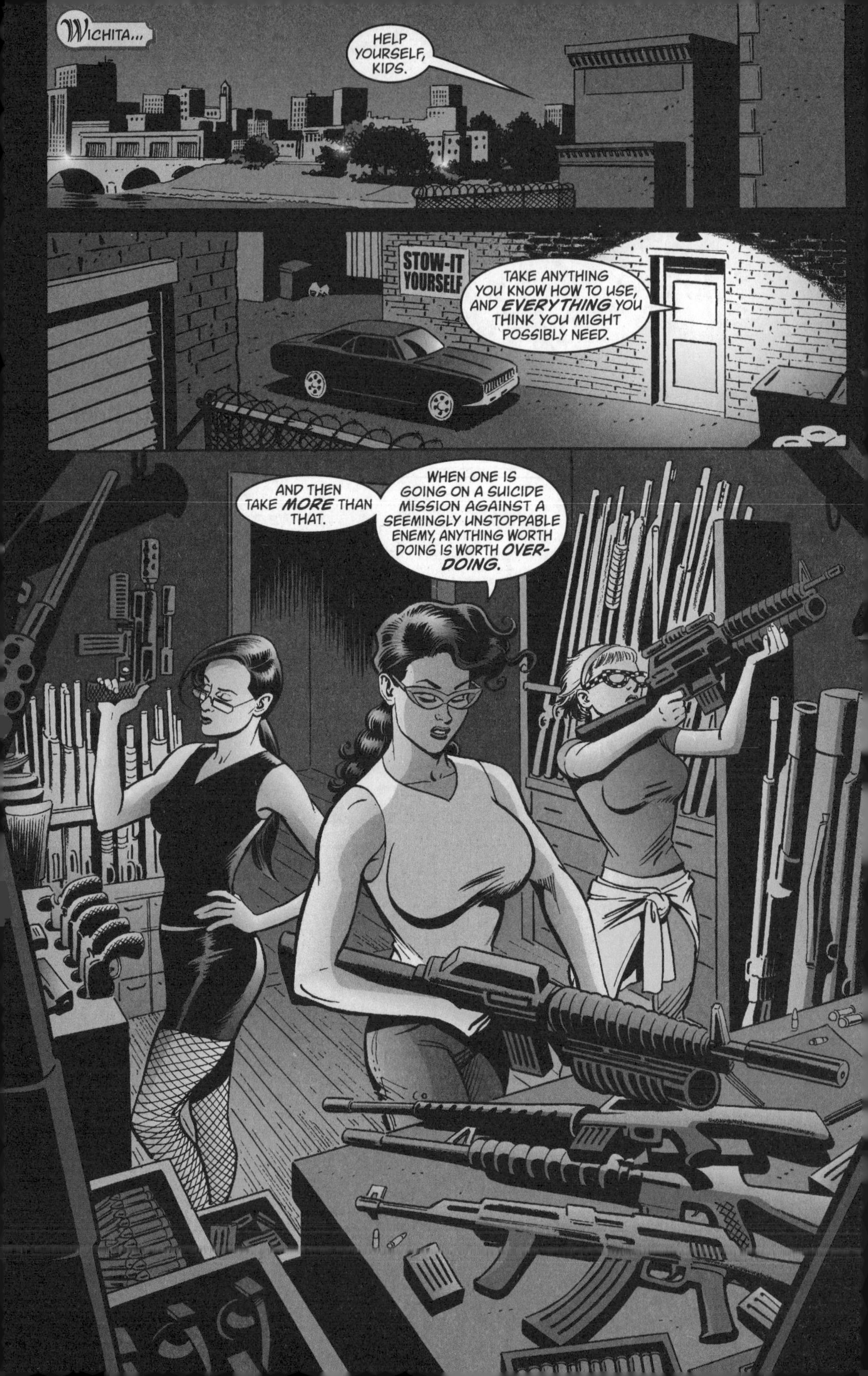
WICHITA...
HELP YOURSELF, KIDS.
STOW-IT YOURSELF
TAKE ANYTHING YOU KNOW HOW TO USE, AND EVERYTHING YOU THINK YOU MIGHT POSSIBLY NEED.
AND THEN TAKE MORE THAN THAT.
WHEN ONE IS GOING ON A SUICIDE MISSION AGAINST A SEEMINGLY UNSTOPPABLE ENEMY, ANYTHING WORTH DOING IS WORTH OVER-DOING.

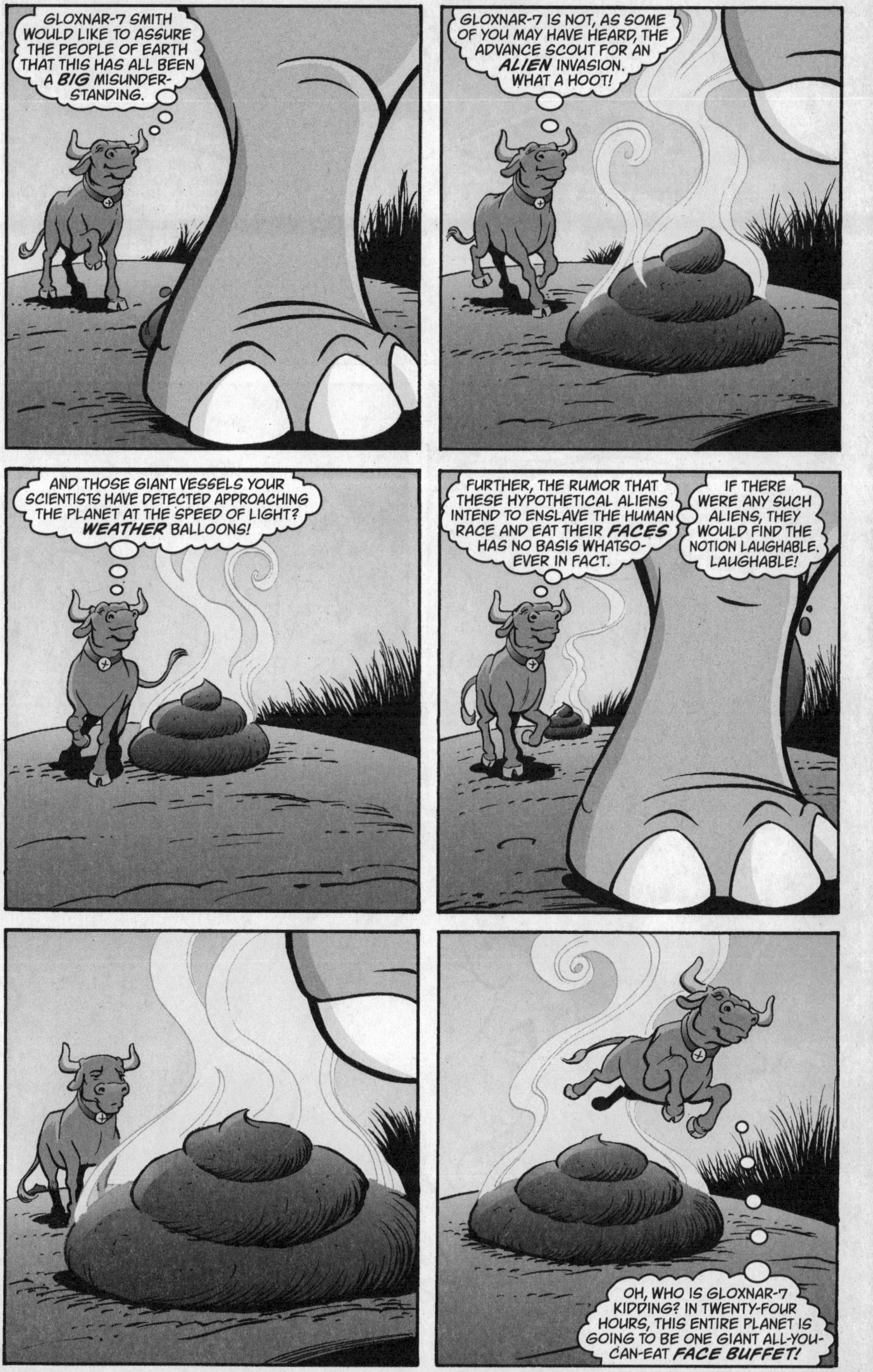
GLOXNAR-7 SMITH WOULD LIKE TO ASSURE THE PEOPLE OF EARTH THAT THIS HAS ALL BEEN A BIG MISUNDER-STANDING.
GLOXNAR-7 IS NOT, AS SOME OF YOU MAY HAVE HEARD, THE ADVANCE SCOUT FOR AN ALIEN INVASION. WHAT A HOOT!
AND THOSE GIANT VESSELS YOUR SCIENTISTS HAVE DETECTED APPROACHING THE PLANET AT THE SPEED OF LIGHT? WEATHER BALLOONS!
FURTHER, THE RUMOR THAT THESE HYPOTHETICAL ALIENS INTEND TO ENSLAVE THE HUMAN RACE AND EAT THEIR FACES HAS NO BASIS WHATSO-EVER IN FACT.
IF THERE WERE ANY SUCH ALIENS, THEY WOULD FIND THE NOTION LAUGHABLE. LAUGHABLE!
OH, WHO IS GLOXNAR-7 KIDDING? IN TWENTY-FOUR HOURS, THIS ENTIRE PLANET IS GOING TO BE ONE GIANT ALL-YOU-CAN-EAT FACE BUFFET!

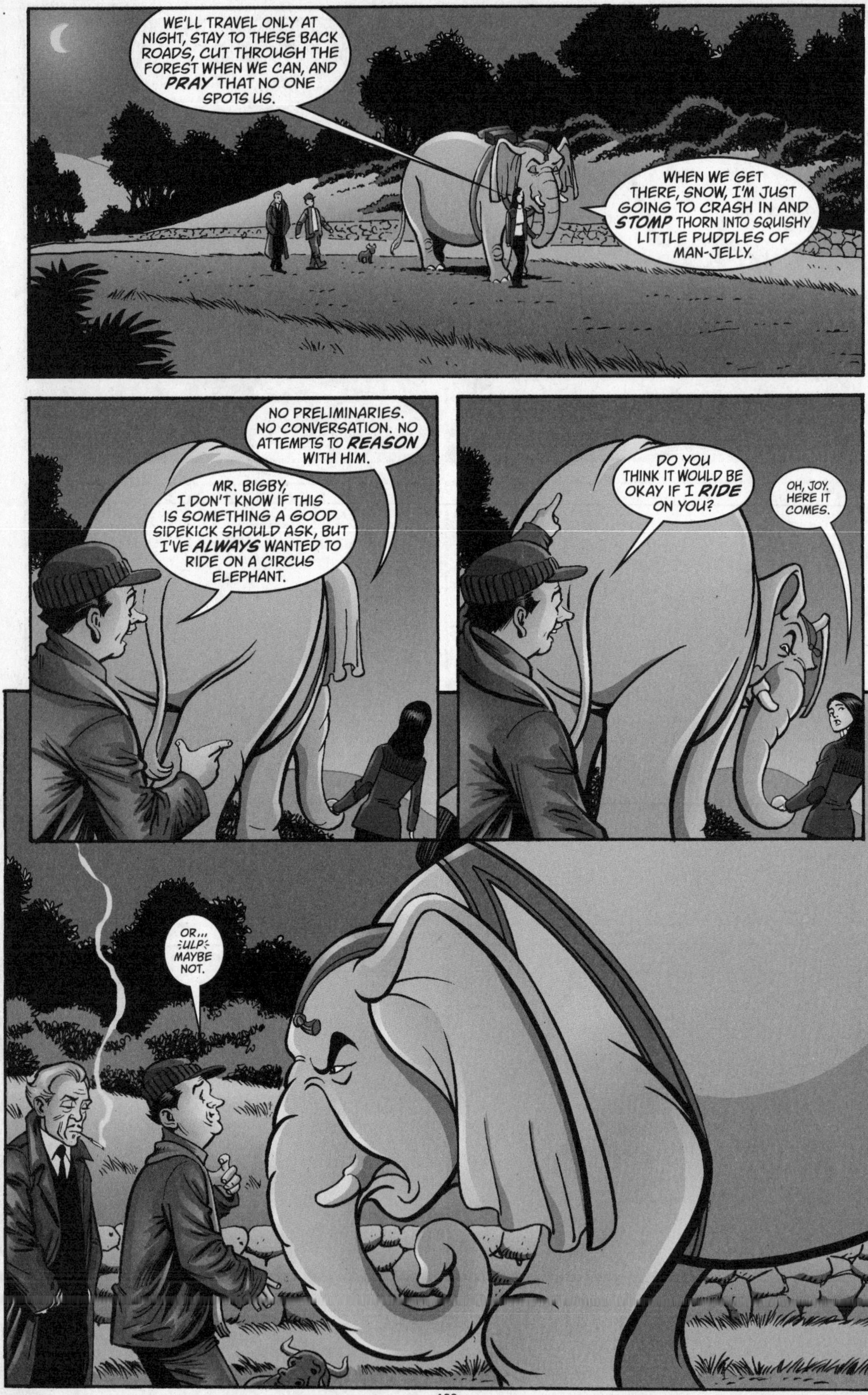
WE'LL TRAVEL ONLY AT NIGHT, STAY TO THESE BACK ROADS, CUT THROUGH THE FOREST WHEN WE CAN, AND PRAY THAT NO ONE SPOTS US.
WHEN WE GET THERE, SNOW, I'M JUST GOING TO CRASH IN AND STOMP THORN INTO SQUISHY LITTLE PUDDLES OF MAN-JELLY.
NO PRELIMINARIES. NO CONVERSATION. NO ATTEMPTS TO REASON WITH HIM.
MR. BIGBY, I DON'T KNOW IF THIS IS SOMETHING A GOOD SIDEKICK SHOULD ASK, BUT I'VE ALWAYS WANTED TO RIDE ON A CIRCUS ELEPHANT.
DO YOU THINK IT WOULD BE OKAY IF I RIDE ON YOU?
OH, JOY. HERE IT COMES.
OR... ULP MAYBE NOT.

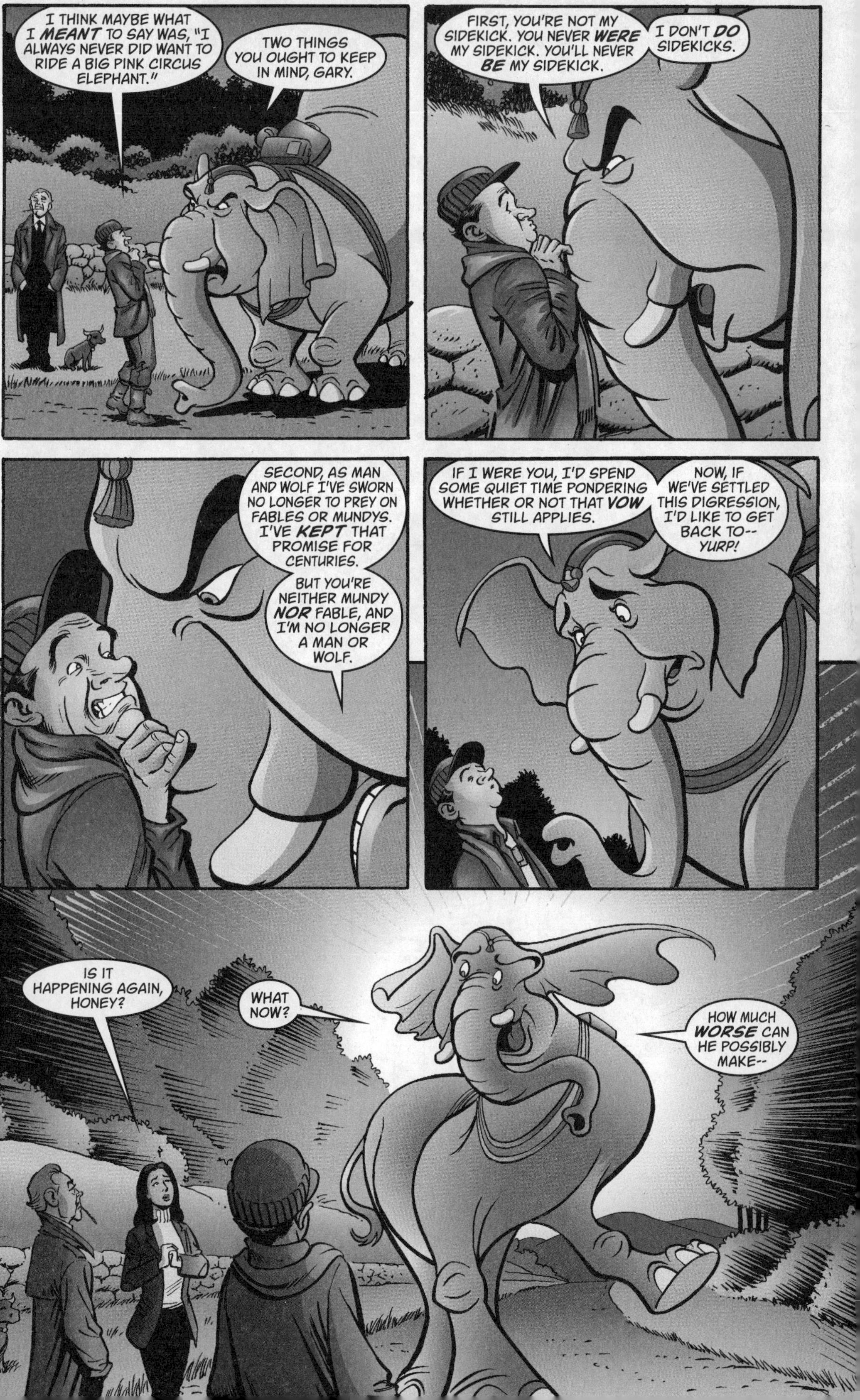
I THINK MAYBE WHAT I MEANT TO SAY WAS, "I ALWAYS NEVER DID WANT TO RIDE A BIG PINK CIRCUS ELEPHANT."
TWO THINGS YOU OUGHT TO KEEP IN MIND, GARY.
FIRST, YOU'RE NOT MY SIDEKICK. YOU NEVER WERE MY SIDEKICK. YOU'LL NEVER BE MY SIDEKICK.
I DON'T DO SIDEKICKS.
SECOND, AS MAN AND WOLF I'VE SWORN NO LONGER TO PREY ON FABLES OR MUNDYS. I'VE KEPT THAT PROMISE FOR CENTURIES.
BUT YOU'RE NEITHER MUNDY NOR FABLE, AND I'M NO LONGER A MAN OR WOLF.
IF I WERE YOU, I'D SPEND SOME QUIET TIME PONDERING WHETHER OR NOT THAT VOW STILL APPLIES.
NOW, IF WE'VE SETTLED THIS DIGRESSION, I'D LIKE TO GET BACK TO-- YURP!
IS IT HAPPENING AGAIN, HONEY?
WHAT NOW?
HOW MUCH WORSE CAN HE POSSIBLY MAKE--

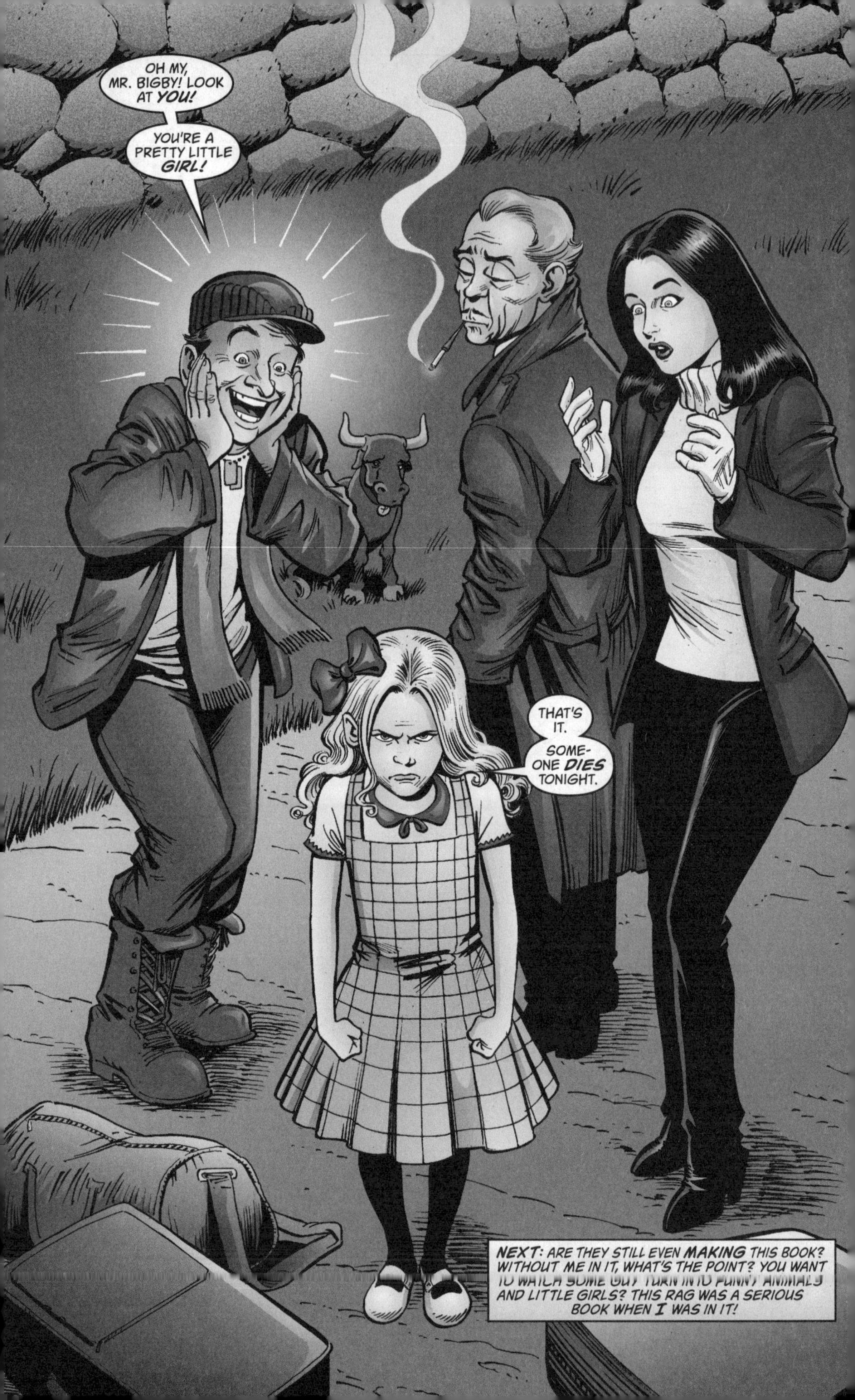
OH MY, MR. BIGBY! LOOK AT YOU!
YOU'RE A PRETTY LITTLE GIRL!
THAT'S IT.
SOME-ONE DIES TONIGHT.
NEXT: ARE THEY STILL EVEN MAKING THIS BOOK? WITHOUT ME IN IT, WHAT'S THE POINT? YOU WANT TO WATCH SOME GUY TURN INTO FUNNY ANIMALS AND LITTLE GIRLS? THIS RAG WAS A SERIOUS BOOK WHEN I WAS IN IT!

*"Sometimes the only way to deal with a recalcitrant
relative is with a good sound bludgeoning."*

The Great FABLES Crossover
part 6 of 9

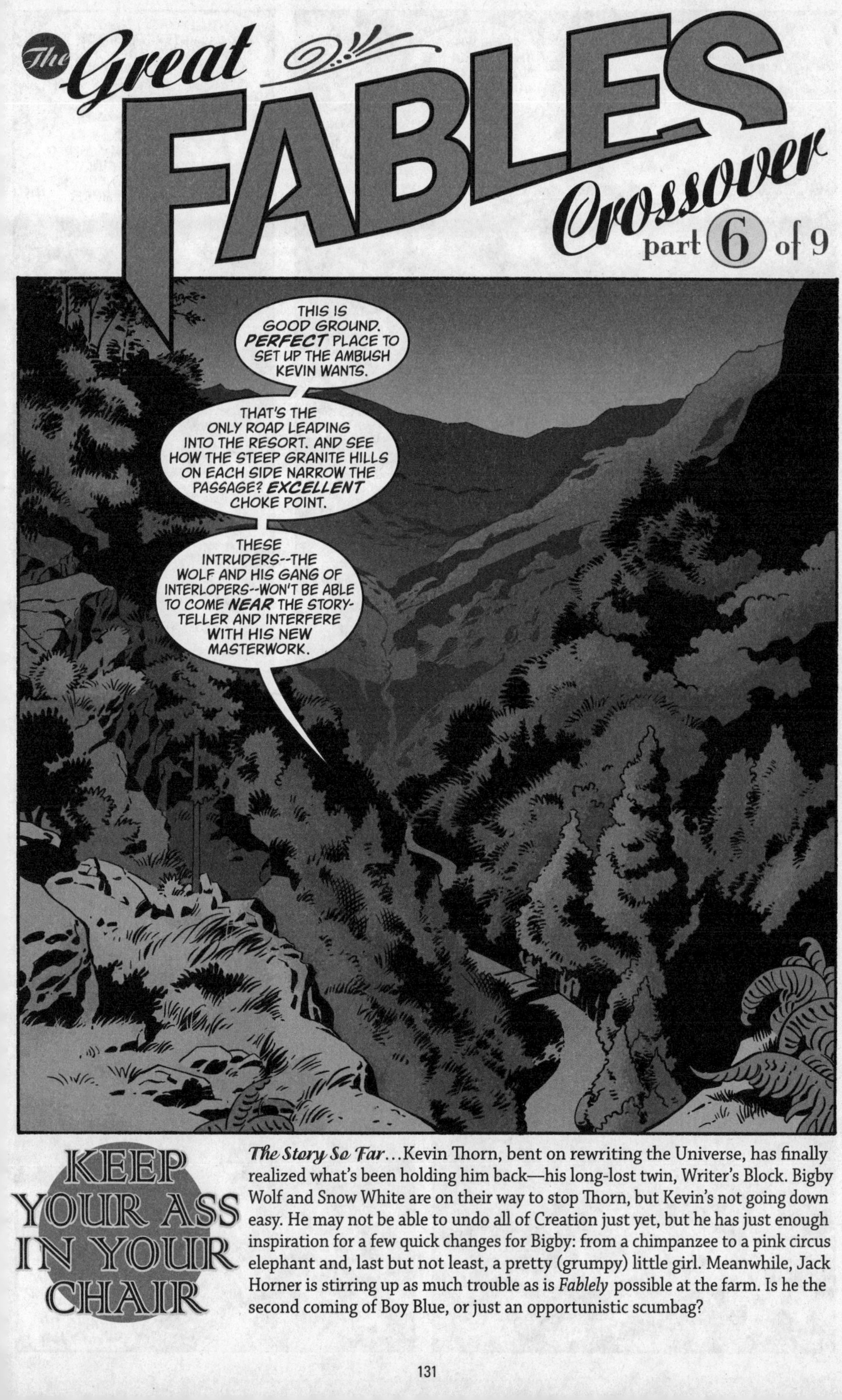
THIS IS GOOD GROUND. PERFECT PLACE TO SET UP THE AMBUSH KEVIN WANTS.
THAT'S THE ONLY ROAD LEADING INTO THE RESORT. AND SEE HOW THE STEEP GRANITE HILLS ON EACH SIDE NARROW THE PASSAGE? EXCELLENT CHOKE POINT.
THESE INTRUDERS--THE WOLF AND HIS GANG OF INTERLOPERS--WON'T BE ABLE TO COME NEAR THE STORY-TELLER AND INTERFERE WITH HIS NEW MASTERWORK.

KEEP YOUR ASS IN YOUR CHAIR

The Story So Far...Kevin Thorn, bent on rewriting the Universe, has finally realized what's been holding him back—his long-lost twin, Writer's Block. Bigby Wolf and Snow White are on their way to stop Thorn, but Kevin's not going down easy. He may not be able to undo all of Creation just yet, but he has just enough inspiration for a few quick changes for Bigby: from a chimpanzee to a pink circus elephant and, last but not least, a pretty (grumpy) little girl. Meanwhile, Jack Horner is stirring up as much trouble as is *Fablely* possible at the farm. Is he the second coming of Boy Blue, or just an opportunistic scumbag?

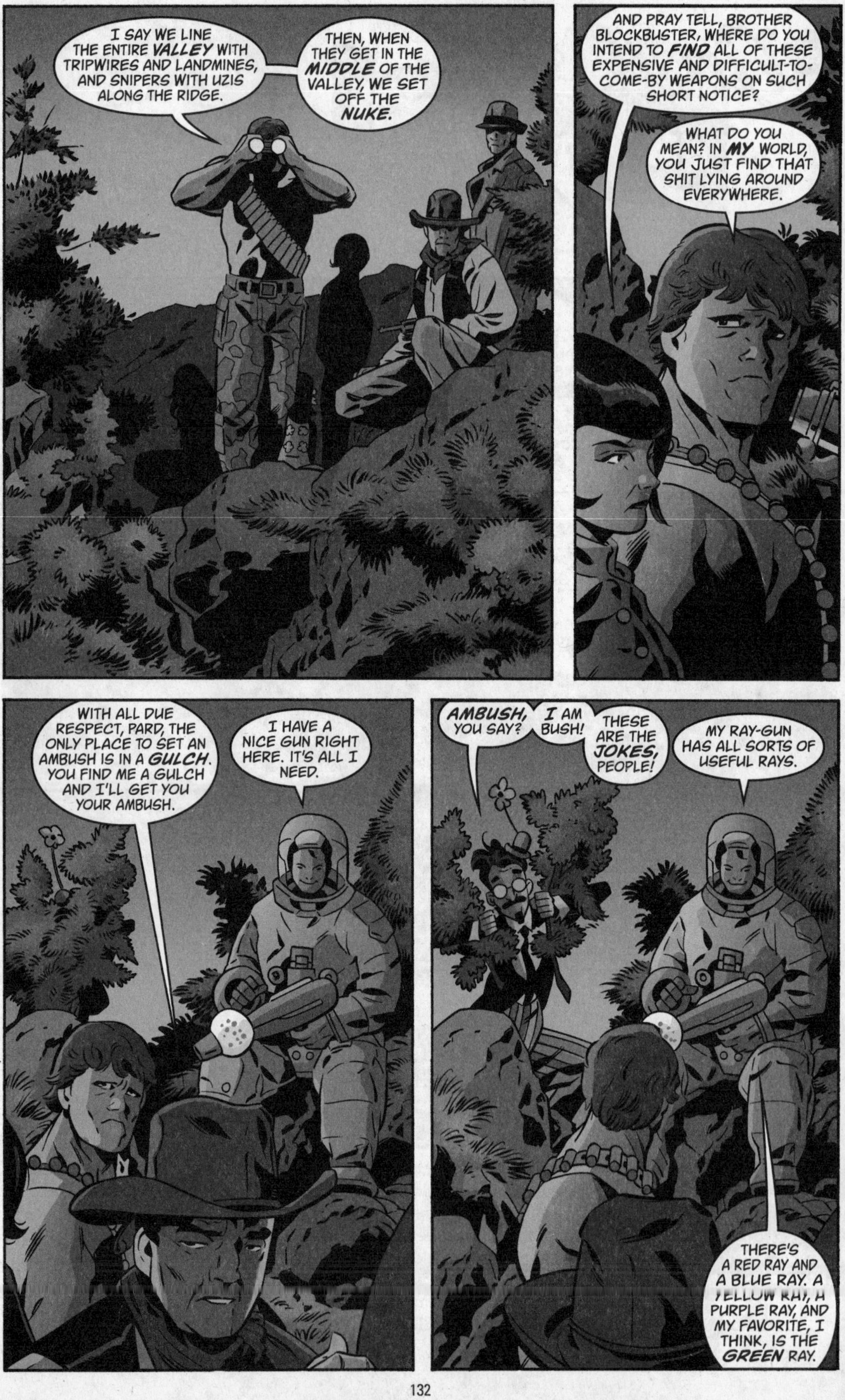

I SAY WE LINE THE ENTIRE VALLEY WITH TRIPWIRES AND LANDMINES, AND SNIPERS WITH UZIS ALONG THE RIDGE.
THEN, WHEN THEY GET IN THE MIDDLE OF THE VALLEY, WE SET OFF THE NUKE.
AND PRAY TELL, BROTHER BLOCKBUSTER, WHERE DO YOU INTEND TO FIND ALL OF THESE EXPENSIVE AND DIFFICULT-TO-COME-BY WEAPONS ON SUCH SHORT NOTICE?
WHAT DO YOU MEAN? IN MY WORLD, YOU JUST FIND THAT SHIT LYING AROUND EVERYWHERE.
WITH ALL DUE RESPECT, PARD, THE ONLY PLACE TO SET AN AMBUSH IS IN A GULCH. YOU FIND ME A GULCH AND I'LL GET YOU YOUR AMBUSH.
I HAVE A NICE GUN RIGHT HERE. IT'S ALL I NEED.
AMBUSH, YOU SAY?
I AM BUSH!
THESE ARE THE JOKES, PEOPLE!
MY RAY-GUN HAS ALL SORTS OF USEFUL RAYS.
THERE'S A RED RAY AND A BLUE RAY. A YELLOW RAY, A PURPLE RAY, AND MY FAVORITE, I THINK, IS THE GREEN RAY.

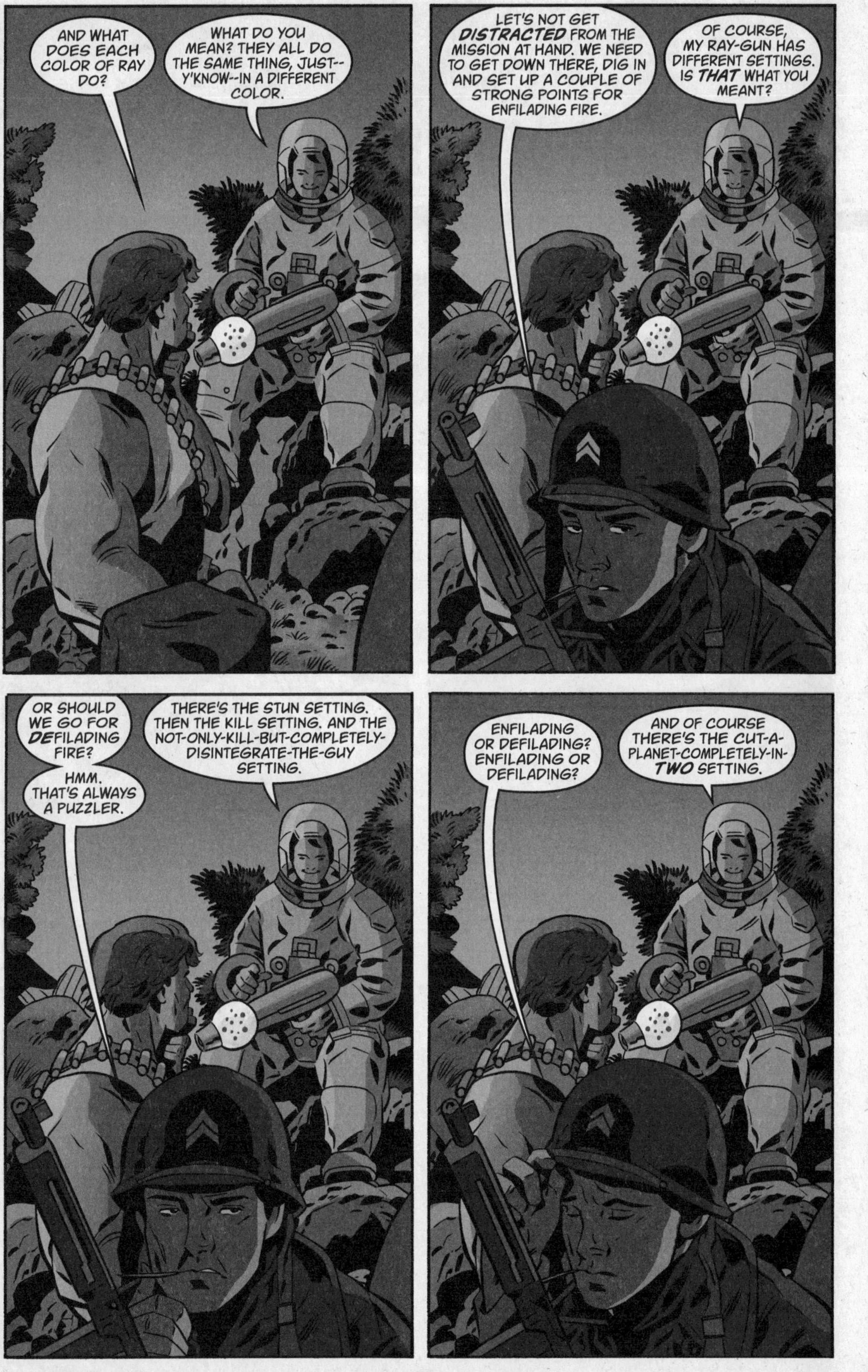
AND WHAT DOES EACH COLOR OF RAY DO?
WHAT DO YOU MEAN? THEY ALL DO THE SAME THING, JUST--Y'KNOW--IN A DIFFERENT COLOR.
LET'S NOT GET DISTRACTED FROM THE MISSION AT HAND. WE NEED TO GET DOWN THERE, DIG IN AND SET UP A COUPLE OF STRONG POINTS FOR ENFILADING FIRE.
OF COURSE, MY RAY-GUN HAS DIFFERENT SETTINGS. IS THAT WHAT YOU MEANT?
OR SHOULD WE GO FOR DEFILADING FIRE?
HMM. THAT'S ALWAYS A PUZZLER.
THERE'S THE STUN SETTING. THEN THE KILL SETTING. AND THE NOT-ONLY-KILL-BUT-COMPLETELY-DISINTEGRATE-THE-GUY SETTING.
ENFILADING OR DEFILADING? ENFILADING OR DEFILADING?
AND OF COURSE THERE'S THE CUT-A-PLANET-COMPLETELY-IN-TWO SETTING.

At that moment, scant miles distant...

DON'T YOU GET IT? I'M TRYING TO REMAKE THE *WORLD* HERE!

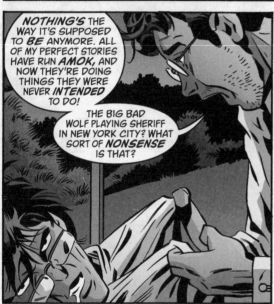

NOTHING'S THE WAY IT'S SUPPOSED TO *BE* ANYMORE. ALL OF MY PERFECT STORIES HAVE RUN *AMOK,* AND NOW THEY'RE DOING THINGS THEY WERE NEVER *INTENDED* TO DO!

THE BIG BAD WOLF PLAYING SHERIFF IN NEW YORK CITY? WHAT SORT OF *NONSENSE* IS THAT?

GEPPETTO AS THE LEADER OF A GIANT EVIL EMPIRE? *GEPPETTO?* ALL HE WAS SUPPOSED TO DO WAS MAKE THAT LITTLE KID WITH THE NOSE INTO A *REAL* BOY!

HOW ABOUT THIS: HOW ABOUT YOU JUST *STEP ASIDE* FOR A BIT AND LET ME GET STARTED? JUST *FIVE MINUTES* TO LET ME END THE WORLD!

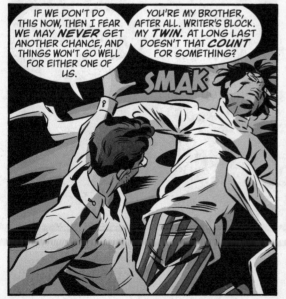

IF WE DON'T DO THIS NOW, THEN I FEAR WE MAY *NEVER* GET ANOTHER CHANCE, AND THINGS WON'T GO WELL FOR EITHER ONE OF US.

YOU'RE MY BROTHER, AFTER ALL. WRITER'S BLOCK. MY *TWIN.* AT LONG LAST DOESN'T THAT *COUNT* FOR SOMETHING?

SMAK

DO YOU UNDERSTAND A *WORD* I'M SAYING? IS THERE ANYBODY *IN* THERE?

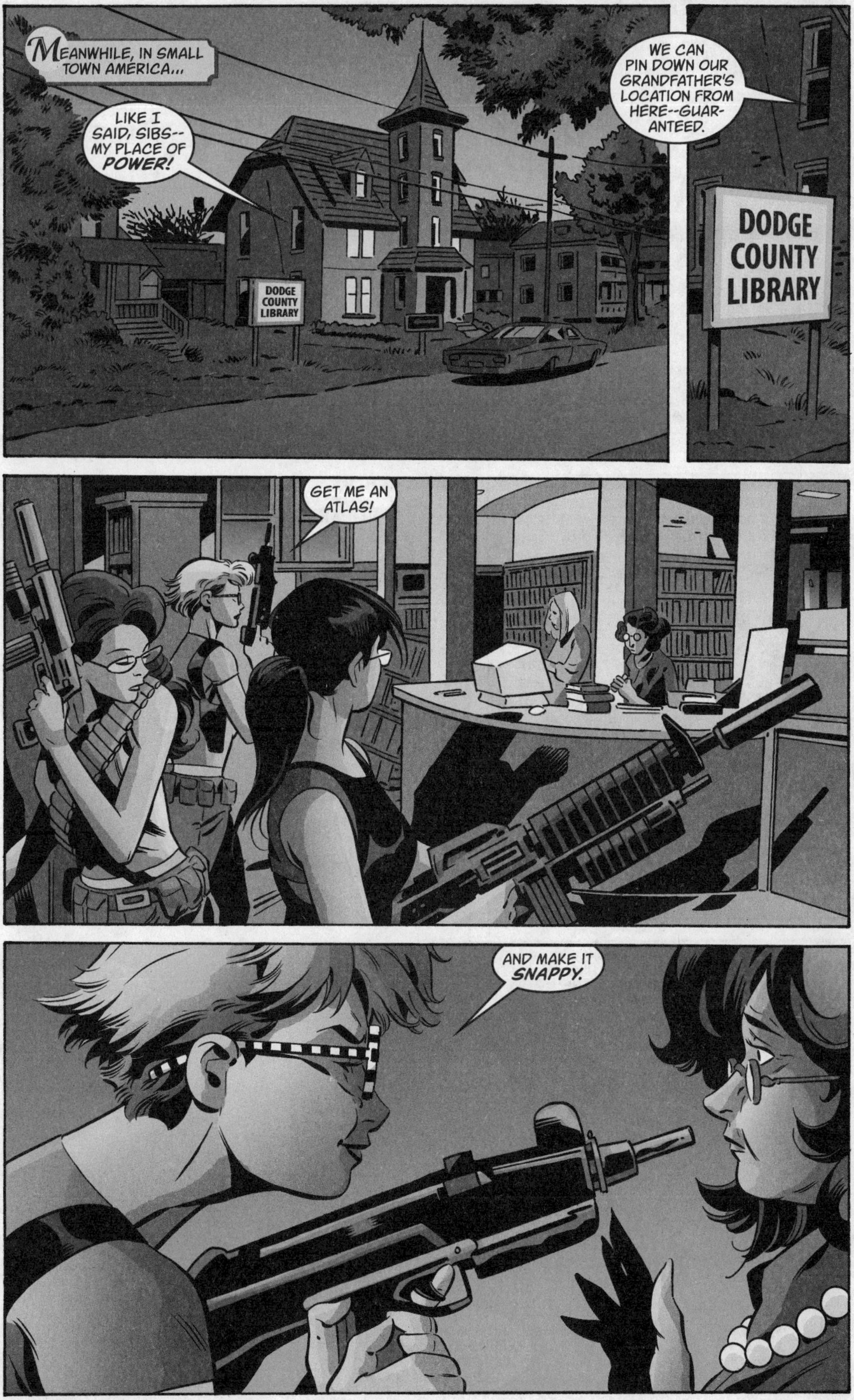
MEANWHILE, IN SMALL TOWN AMERICA...
LIKE I SAID, SIBS-- MY PLACE OF POWER!
DODGE COUNTY LIBRARY
WE CAN PIN DOWN OUR GRANDFATHER'S LOCATION FROM HERE--GUARANTEED.
DODGE COUNTY LIBRARY
GET ME AN ATLAS!
AND MAKE IT SNAPPY.

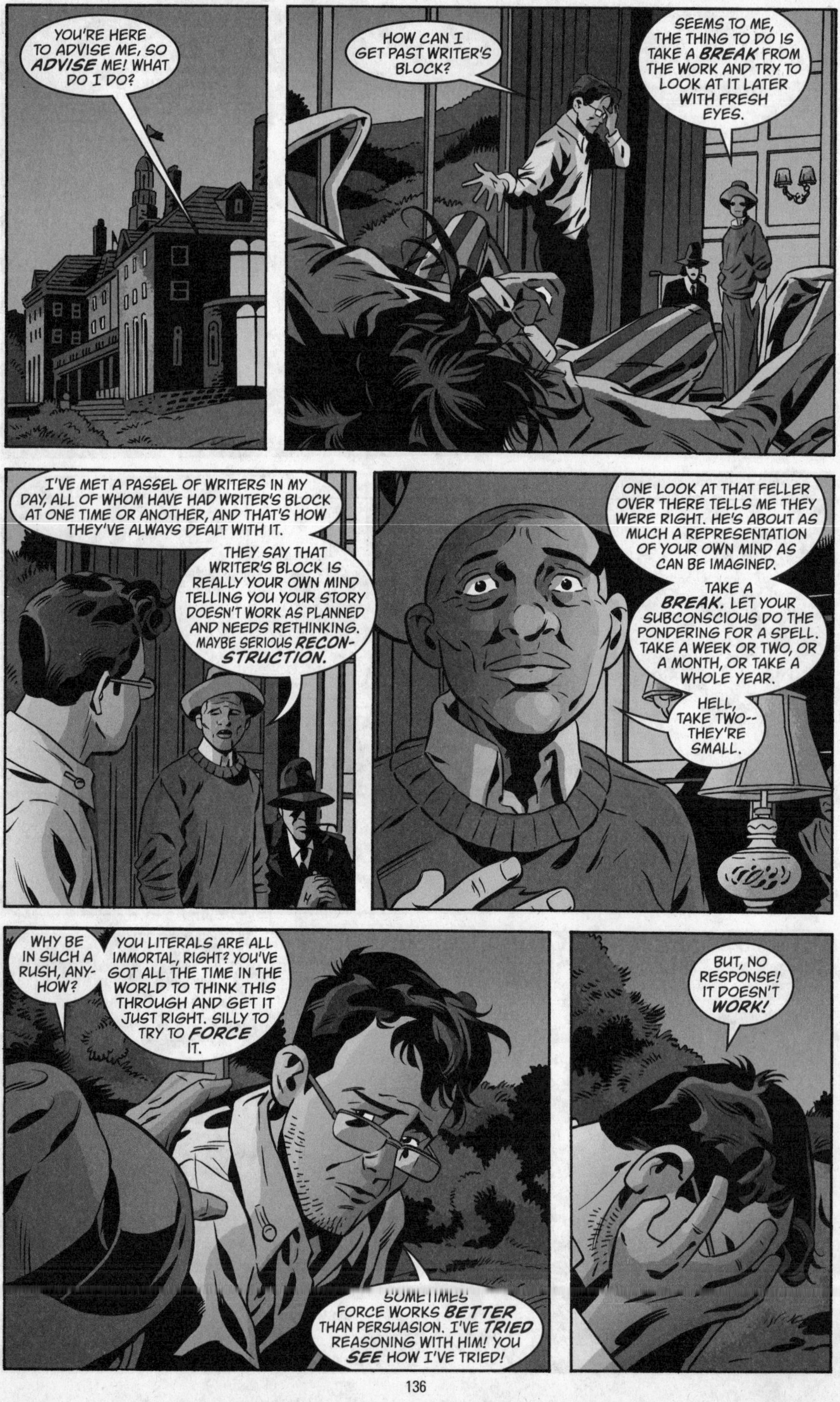

YOU'RE HERE TO ADVISE ME, SO ADVISE ME! WHAT DO I DO?
HOW CAN I GET PAST WRITER'S BLOCK?
SEEMS TO ME, THE THING TO DO IS TAKE A BREAK FROM THE WORK AND TRY TO LOOK AT IT LATER WITH FRESH EYES.
I'VE MET A PASSEL OF WRITERS IN MY DAY, ALL OF WHOM HAVE HAD WRITER'S BLOCK AT ONE TIME OR ANOTHER, AND THAT'S HOW THEY'VE ALWAYS DEALT WITH IT.
THEY SAY THAT WRITER'S BLOCK IS REALLY YOUR OWN MIND TELLING YOU YOUR STORY DOESN'T WORK AS PLANNED AND NEEDS RETHINKING. MAYBE SERIOUS RECON-STRUCTION.
ONE LOOK AT THAT FELLER OVER THERE TELLS ME THEY WERE RIGHT. HE'S ABOUT AS MUCH A REPRESENTATION OF YOUR OWN MIND AS CAN BE IMAGINED.
TAKE A BREAK. LET YOUR SUBCONSCIOUS DO THE PONDERING FOR A SPELL. TAKE A WEEK OR TWO, OR A MONTH, OR TAKE A WHOLE YEAR.
HELL, TAKE TWO-- THEY'RE SMALL.
WHY BE IN SUCH A RUSH, ANY-HOW?
YOU LITERALS ARE ALL IMMORTAL, RIGHT? YOU'VE GOT ALL THE TIME IN THE WORLD TO THINK THIS THROUGH AND GET IT JUST RIGHT. SILLY TO TRY TO FORCE IT.
SOMETIMES FORCE WORKS BETTER THAN PERSUASION. I'VE TRIED REASONING WITH HIM! YOU SEE HOW I'VE TRIED!
BUT, NO RESPONSE! IT DOESN'T WORK!

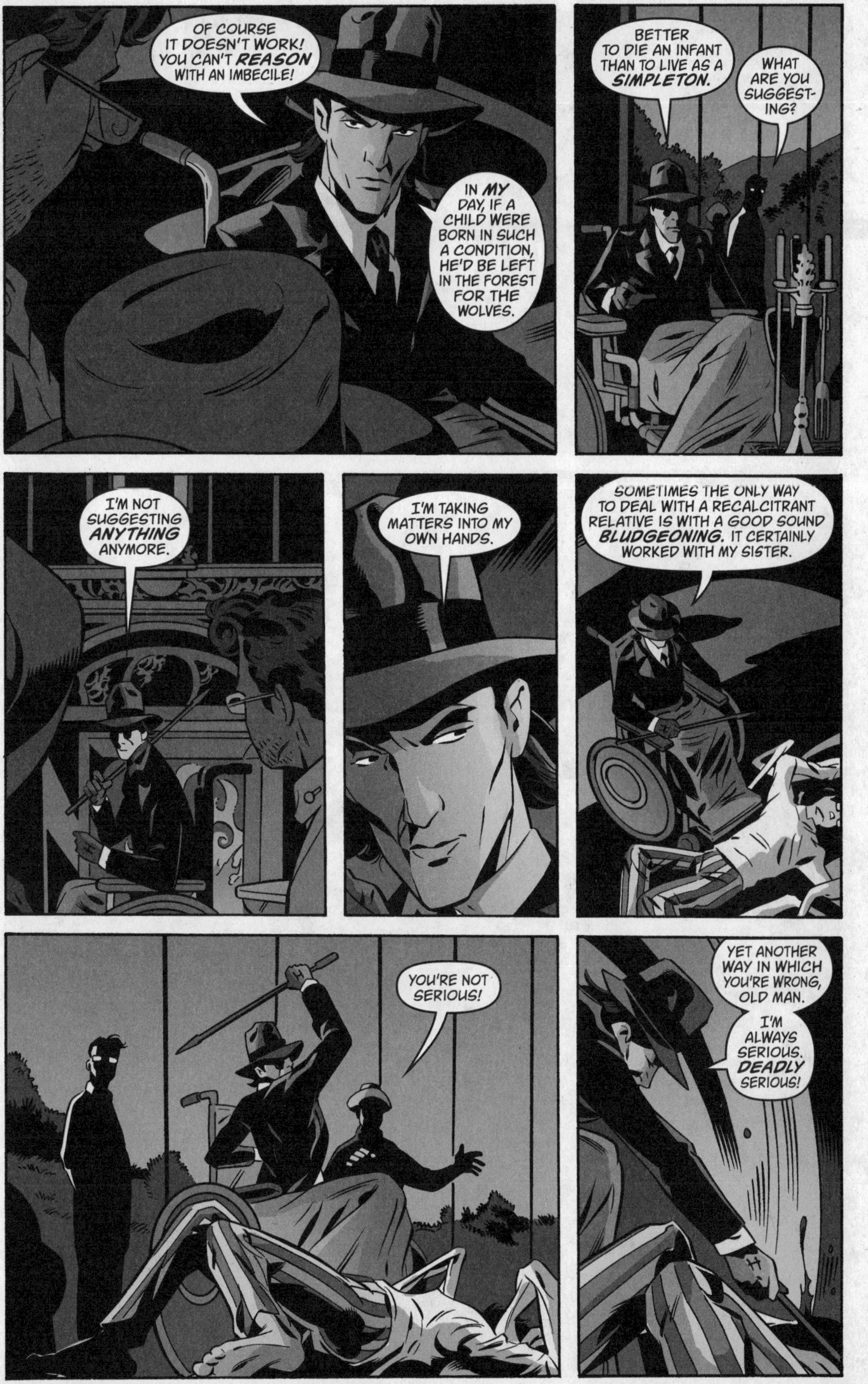
OF COURSE IT DOESN'T WORK! YOU CAN'T REASON WITH AN IMBECILE!
IN MY DAY, IF A CHILD WERE BORN IN SUCH A CONDITION, HE'D BE LEFT IN THE FOREST FOR THE WOLVES.
BETTER TO DIE AN INFANT THAN TO LIVE AS A SIMPLETON.
WHAT ARE YOU SUGGESTING?
I'M NOT SUGGESTING ANYTHING ANYMORE.
I'M TAKING MATTERS INTO MY OWN HANDS.
SOMETIMES THE ONLY WAY TO DEAL WITH A RECALCITRANT RELATIVE IS WITH A GOOD SOUND BLUDGEONING. IT CERTAINLY WORKED WITH MY SISTER.
YOU'RE NOT SERIOUS!
YET ANOTHER WAY IN WHICH YOU'RE WRONG, OLD MAN.
I'M ALWAYS SERIOUS. DEADLY SERIOUS!

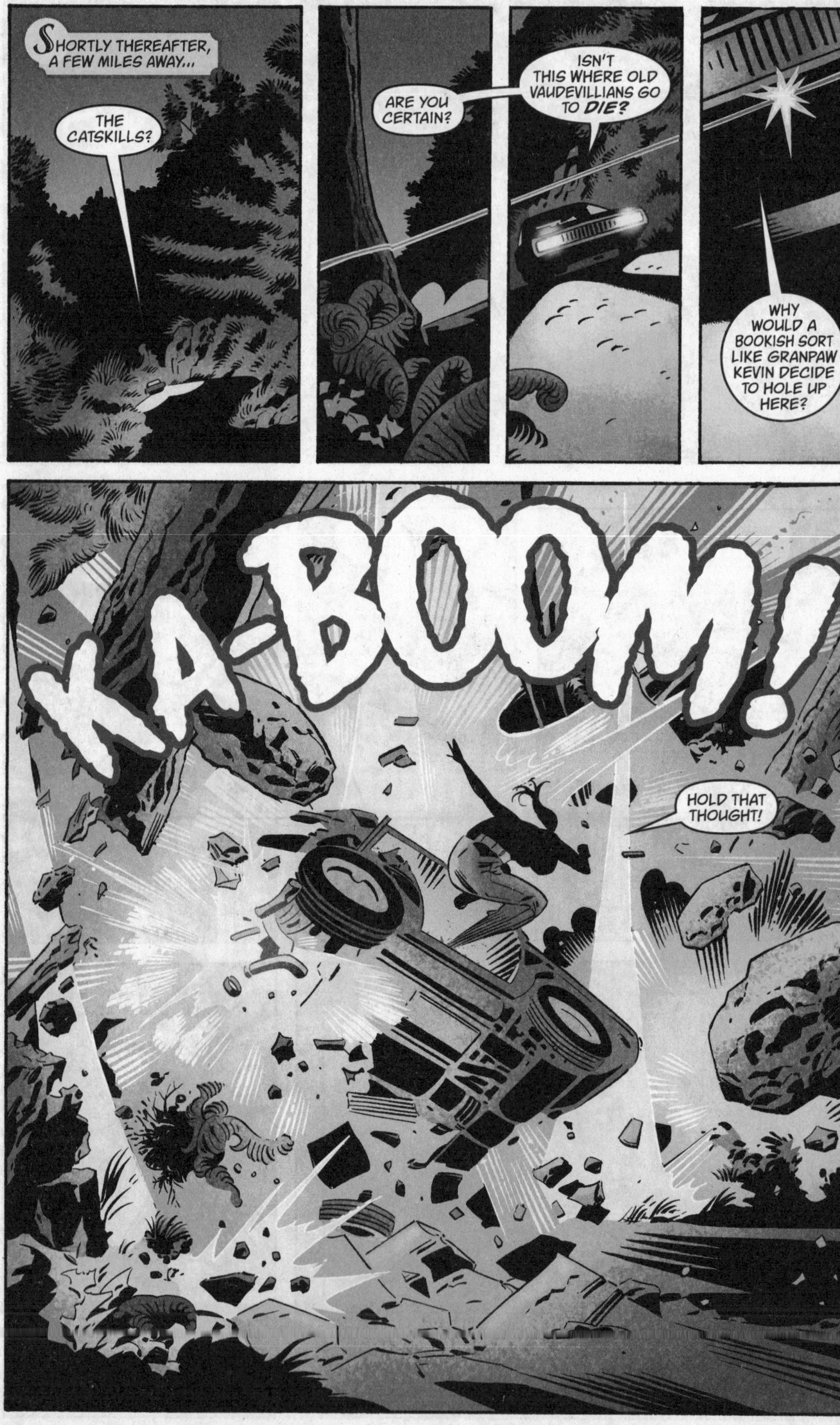
SHORTLY THEREAFTER, A FEW MILES AWAY...
THE CATSKILLS?
ARE YOU CERTAIN?
ISN'T THIS WHERE OLD VAUDEVILLIANS GO TO *DIE?*
WHY WOULD A BOOKISH SORT LIKE GRANPAW KEVIN DECIDE TO HOLE UP HERE?
KA-BOOM!
HOLD THAT THOUGHT!

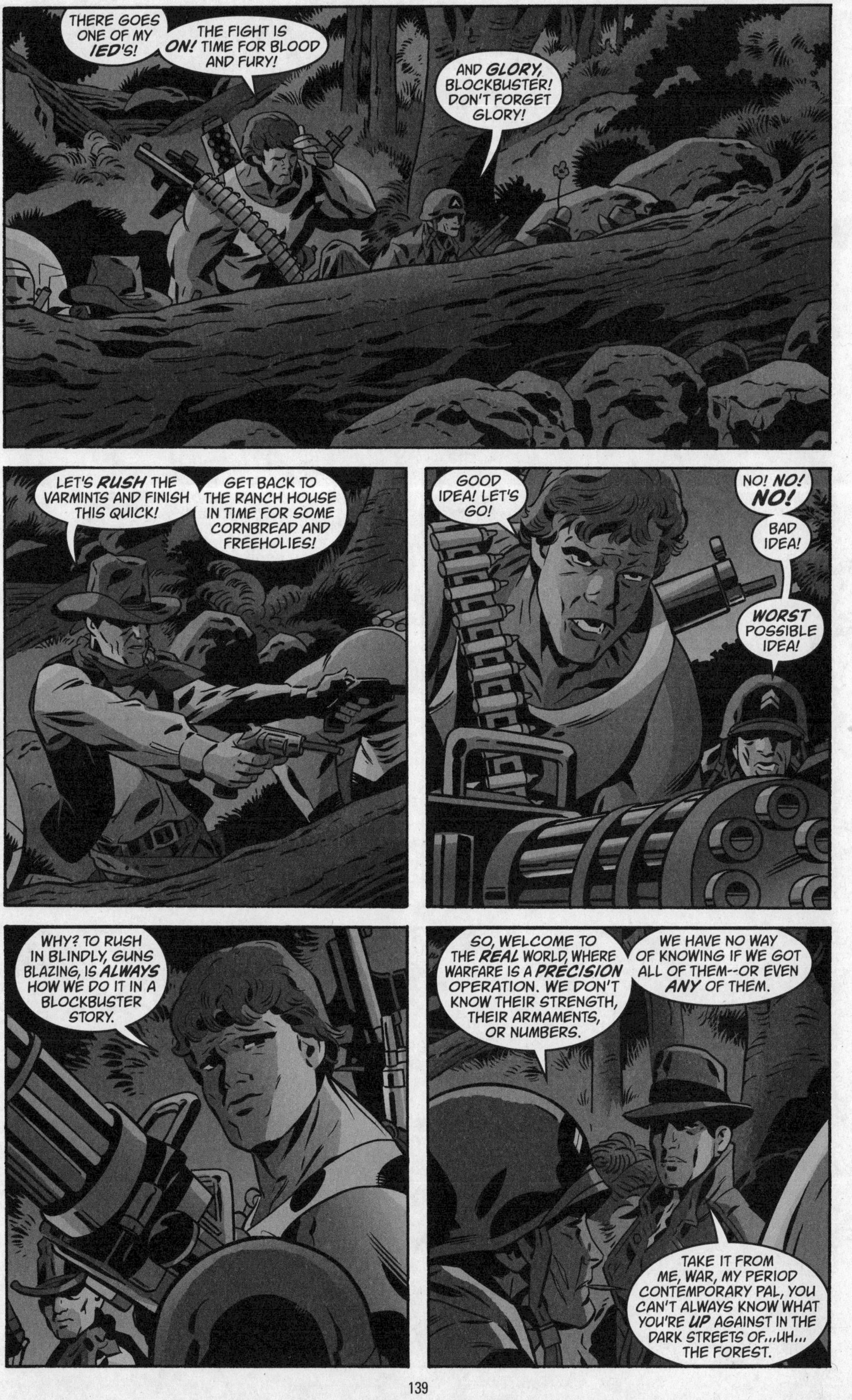
THERE GOES ONE OF MY IED'S!
THE FIGHT IS ON! TIME FOR BLOOD AND FURY!
AND GLORY, BLOCKBUSTER! DON'T FORGET GLORY!
LET'S RUSH THE VARMINTS AND FINISH THIS QUICK!
GET BACK TO THE RANCH HOUSE IN TIME FOR SOME CORNBREAD AND FREEHOLIES!
GOOD IDEA! LET'S GO!
NO! NO! NO!
BAD IDEA!
WORST POSSIBLE IDEA!
WHY? TO RUSH IN BLINDLY, GUNS BLAZING, IS ALWAYS HOW WE DO IT IN A BLOCKBUSTER STORY.
SO, WELCOME TO THE REAL WORLD, WHERE WARFARE IS A PRÉCISION OPERATION. WE DON'T KNOW THEIR STRENGTH, THEIR ARMAMENTS, OR NUMBERS.
WE HAVE NO WAY OF KNOWING IF WE GOT ALL OF THEM--OR EVEN ANY OF THEM.
TAKE IT FROM ME, WAR, MY PERIOD CONTEMPORARY PAL, YOU CAN'T ALWAYS KNOW WHAT YOU'RE UP AGAINST IN THE DARK STREETS OF...UH... THE FOREST.

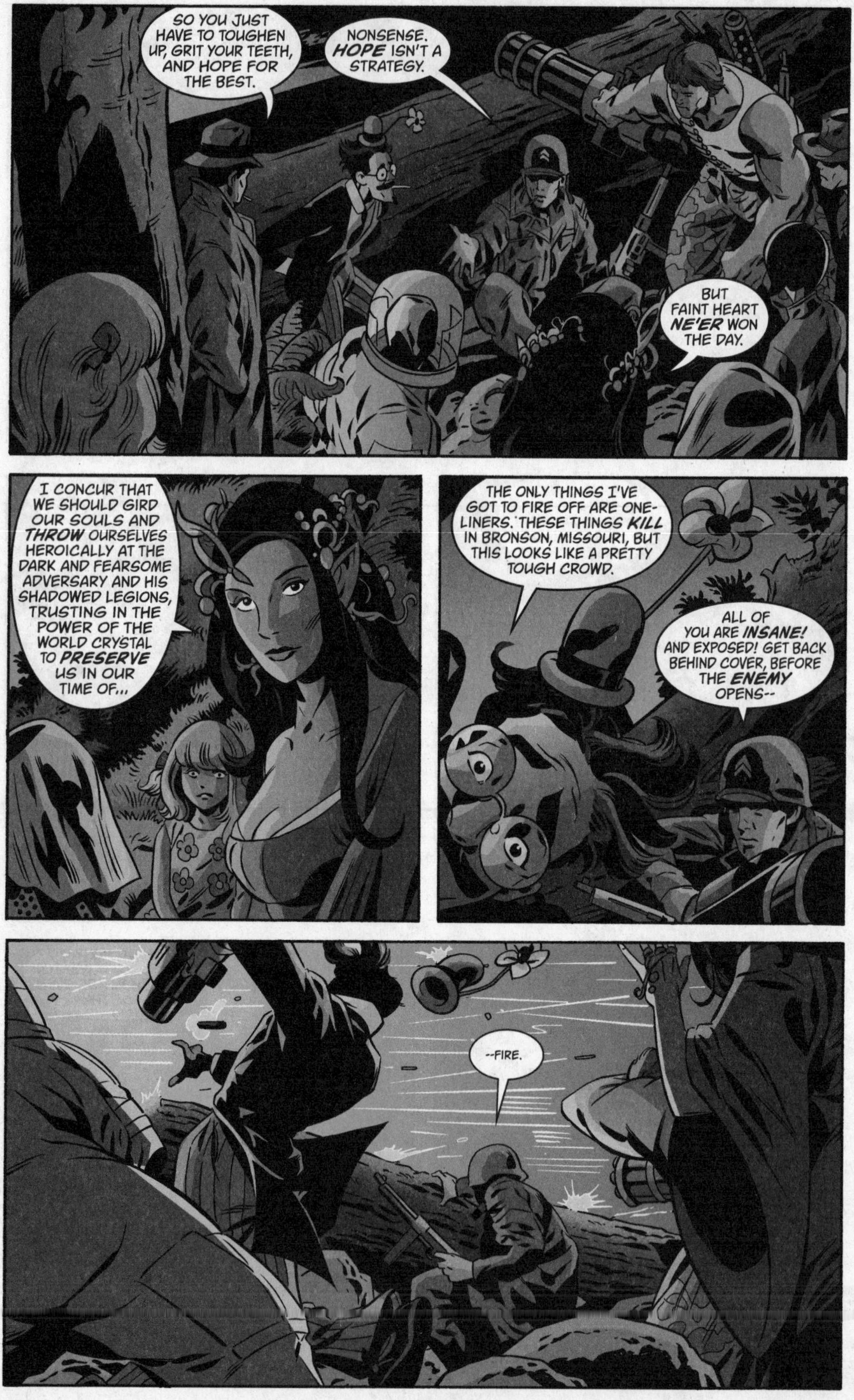
SO YOU JUST HAVE TO TOUGHEN UP, GRIT YOUR TEETH, AND HOPE FOR THE BEST.
NONSENSE. HOPE ISN'T A STRATEGY.
BUT FAINT HEART NE'ER WON THE DAY.
I CONCUR THAT WE SHOULD GIRD OUR SOULS AND THROW OURSELVES HEROICALLY AT THE DARK AND FEARSOME ADVERSARY AND HIS SHADOWED LEGIONS, TRUSTING IN THE POWER OF THE WORLD CRYSTAL TO PRESERVE US IN OUR TIME OF...
THE ONLY THINGS I'VE GOT TO FIRE OFF ARE ONE-LINERS. THESE THINGS KILL IN BRONSON, MISSOURI, BUT THIS LOOKS LIKE A PRETTY TOUGH CROWD.
ALL OF YOU ARE INSANE! AND EXPOSED! GET BACK BEHIND COVER, BEFORE THE ENEMY OPENS--
--FIRE.

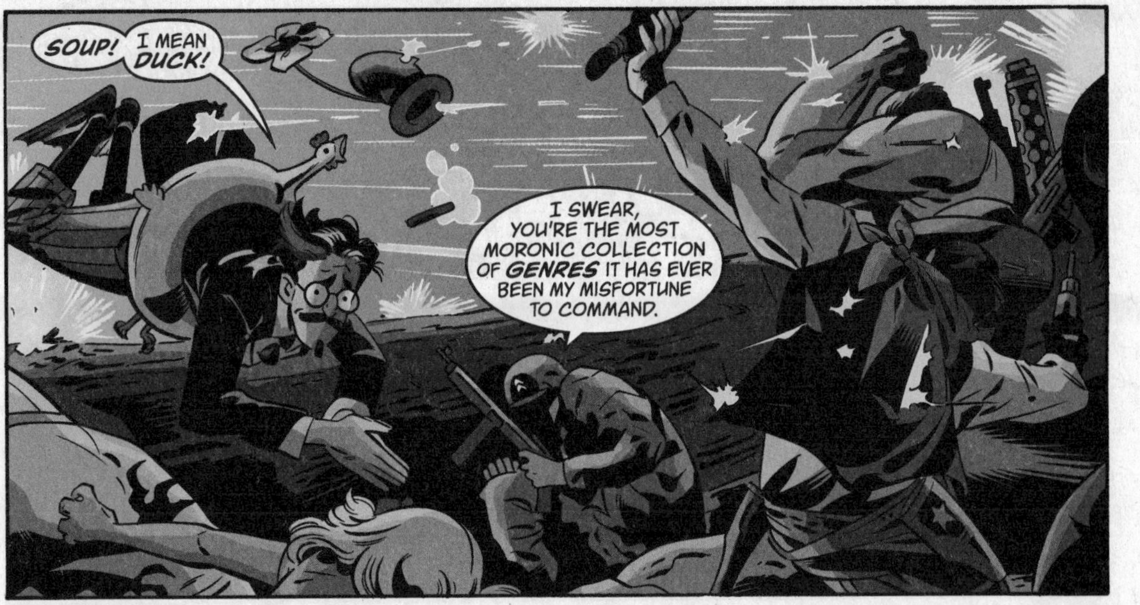
SOUP! I MEAN DUCK!
I SWEAR, YOU'RE THE MOST MORONIC COLLECTION OF GENRES IT HAS EVER BEEN MY MISFORTUNE TO COMMAND.

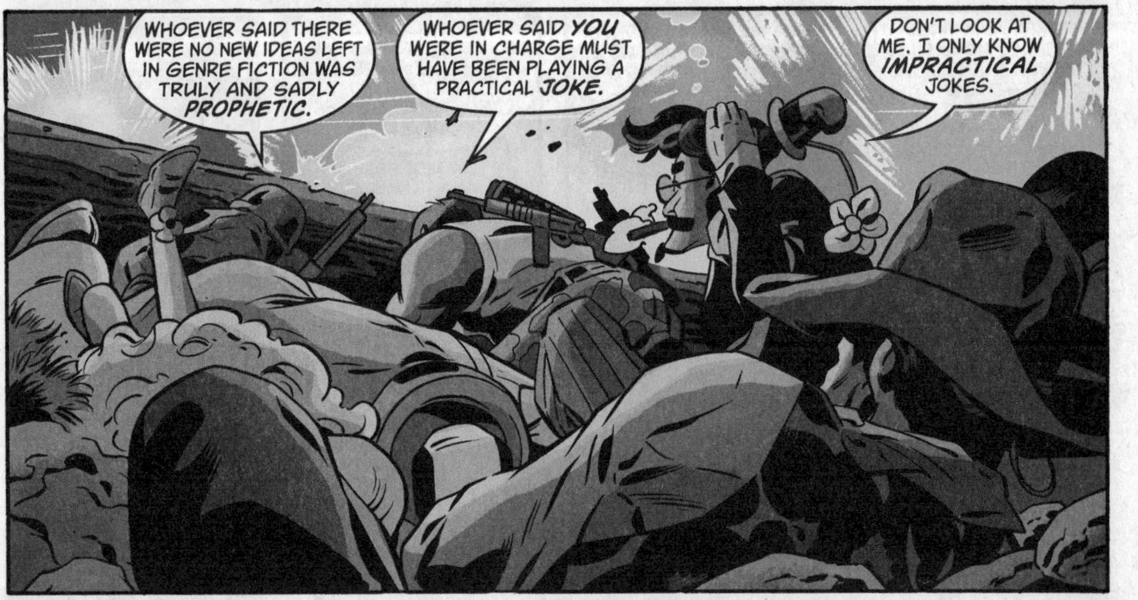
WHOEVER SAID THERE WERE NO NEW IDEAS LEFT IN GENRE FICTION WAS TRULY AND SADLY PROPHETIC.
WHOEVER SAID YOU WERE IN CHARGE MUST HAVE BEEN PLAYING A PRACTICAL JOKE.
DON'T LOOK AT ME. I ONLY KNOW IMPRACTICAL JOKES.

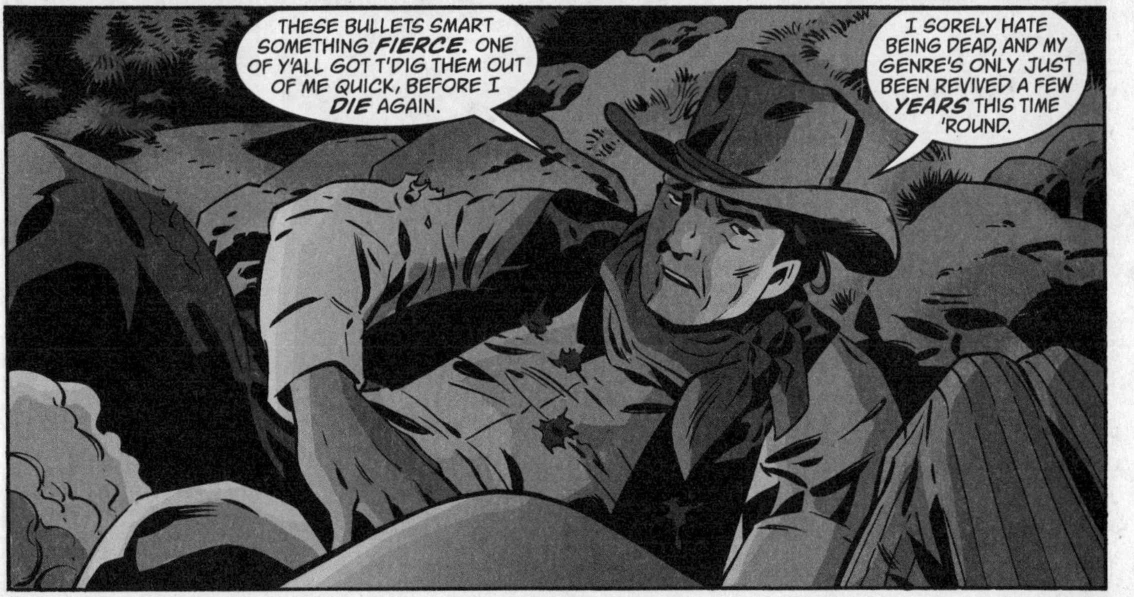
THESE BULLETS SMART SOMETHING FIERCE. ONE OF Y'ALL GOT T'DIG THEM OUT OF ME QUICK, BEFORE I DIE AGAIN.
I SORELY HATE BEING DEAD, AND MY GENRE'S ONLY JUST BEEN REVIVED A FEW YEARS THIS TIME 'ROUND.

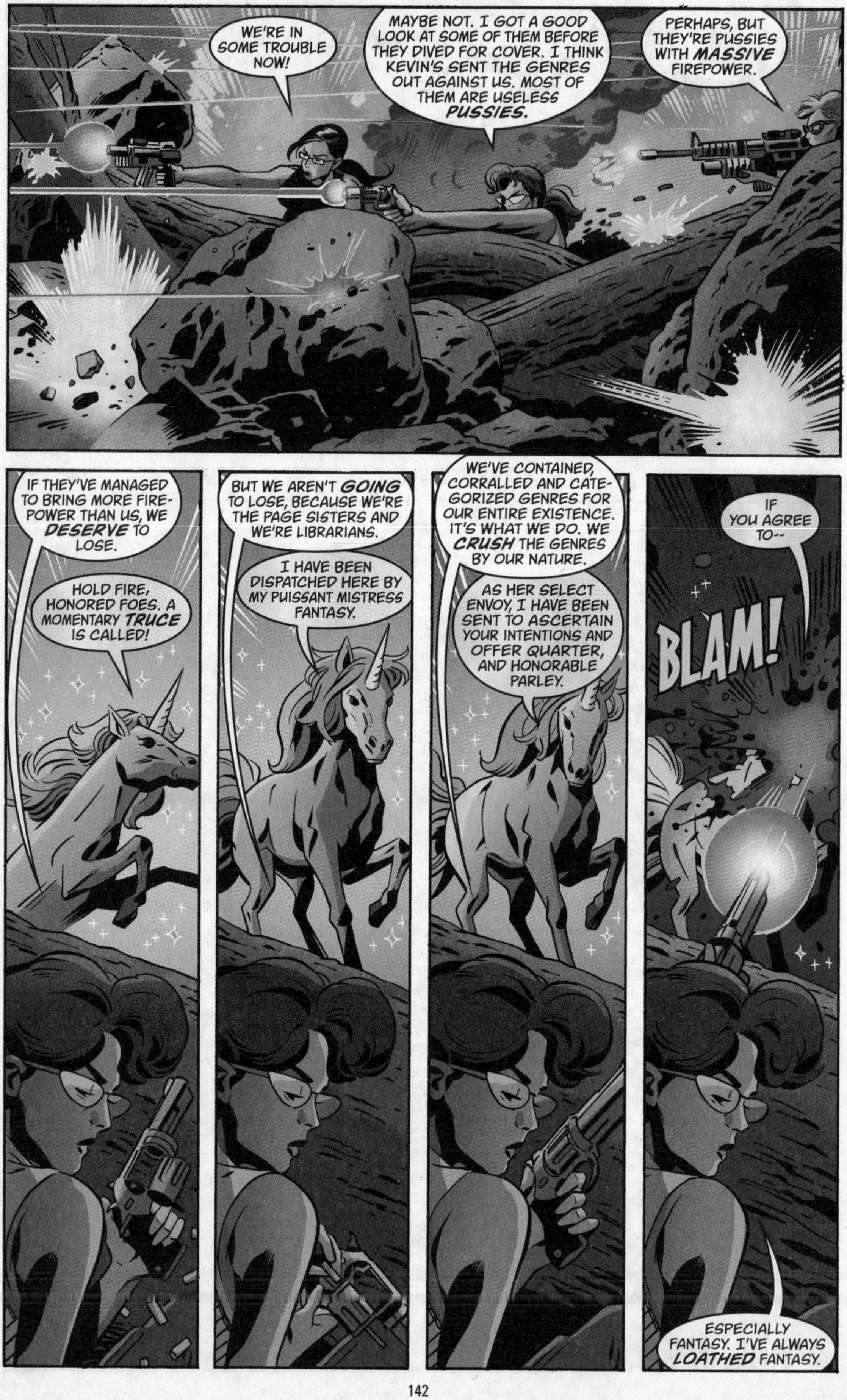
WE'RE IN SOME TROUBLE NOW!
MAYBE NOT. I GOT A GOOD LOOK AT SOME OF THEM BEFORE THEY DIVED FOR COVER. I THINK KEVIN'S SENT THE GENRES OUT AGAINST US. MOST OF THEM ARE USELESS PUSSIES.
PERHAPS, BUT THEY'RE PUSSIES WITH MASSIVE FIREPOWER.
IF THEY'VE MANAGED TO BRING MORE FIRE-POWER THAN US, WE DESERVE TO LOSE.
HOLD FIRE, HONORED FOES. A MOMENTARY TRUCE IS CALLED!
BUT WE AREN'T GOING TO LOSE, BECAUSE WE'RE THE PAGE SISTERS AND WE'RE LIBRARIANS.
I HAVE BEEN DISPATCHED HERE BY MY PUISSANT MISTRESS FANTASY.
WE'VE CONTAINED, CORRALLED AND CATE-GORIZED GENRES FOR OUR ENTIRE EXISTENCE. IT'S WHAT WE DO. WE CRUSH THE GENRES BY OUR NATURE.
AS HER SELECT ENVOY, I HAVE BEEN SENT TO ASCERTAIN YOUR INTENTIONS AND OFFER QUARTER, AND HONORABLE PARLEY.
IF YOU AGREE TO--
BLAM!
ESPECIALLY FANTASY. I'VE ALWAYS LOATHED FANTASY.

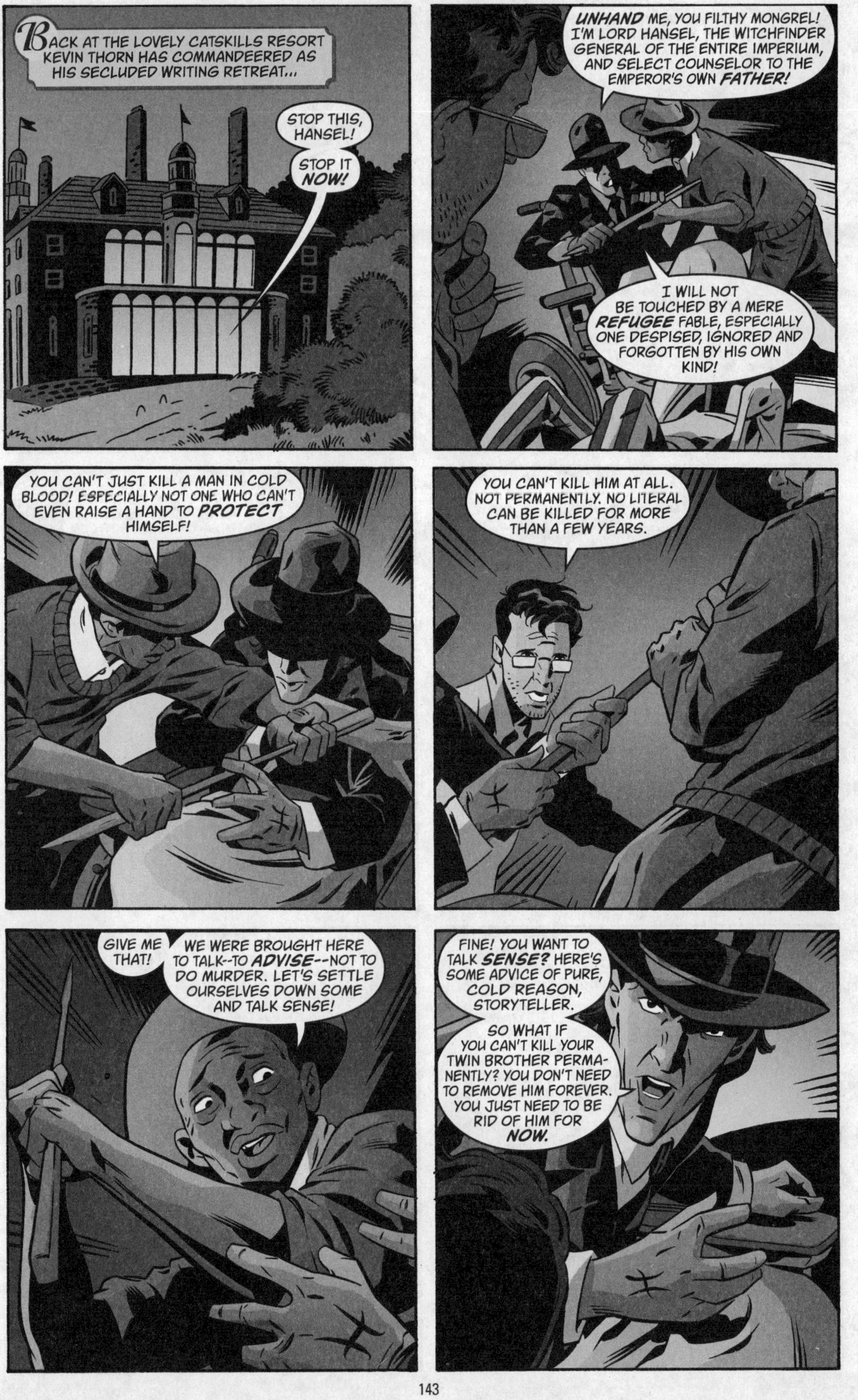
BACK AT THE LOVELY CATSKILLS RESORT KEVIN THORN HAS COMMANDEERED AS HIS SECLUDED WRITING RETREAT...
STOP THIS, HANSEL!
STOP IT NOW!
UNHAND ME, YOU FILTHY MONGREL! I'M LORD HANSEL, THE WITCHFINDER GENERAL OF THE ENTIRE IMPERIUM, AND SELECT COUNSELOR TO THE EMPEROR'S OWN FATHER!
I WILL NOT BE TOUCHED BY A MERE REFUGEE FABLE, ESPECIALLY ONE DESPISED, IGNORED AND FORGOTTEN BY HIS OWN KIND!
YOU CAN'T JUST KILL A MAN IN COLD BLOOD! ESPECIALLY NOT ONE WHO CAN'T EVEN RAISE A HAND TO PROTECT HIMSELF!
YOU CAN'T KILL HIM AT ALL. NOT PERMANENTLY. NO LITERAL CAN BE KILLED FOR MORE THAN A FEW YEARS.
GIVE ME THAT!
WE WERE BROUGHT HERE TO TALK--TO ADVISE--NOT TO DO MURDER. LET'S SETTLE OURSELVES DOWN SOME AND TALK SENSE!
FINE! YOU WANT TO TALK SENSE? HERE'S SOME ADVICE OF PURE, COLD REASON, STORYTELLER.
SO WHAT IF YOU CAN'T KILL YOUR TWIN BROTHER PERMANENTLY? YOU DON'T NEED TO REMOVE HIM FOREVER. YOU JUST NEED TO BE RID OF HIM FOR NOW.

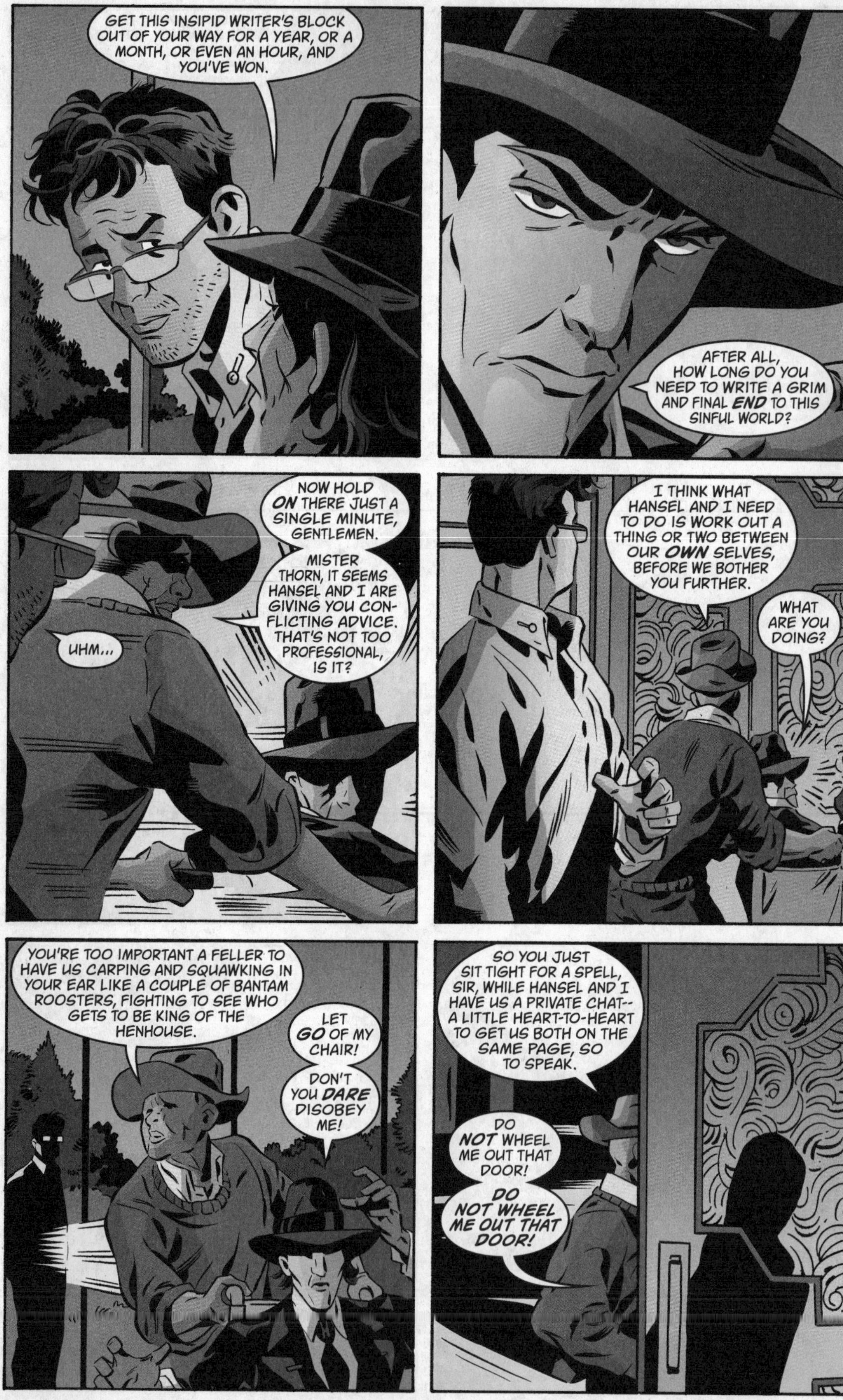
GET THIS INSIPID WRITER'S BLOCK OUT OF YOUR WAY FOR A YEAR, OR A MONTH, OR EVEN AN HOUR, AND YOU'VE WON.
AFTER ALL, HOW LONG DO YOU NEED TO WRITE A GRIM AND FINAL END TO THIS SINFUL WORLD?
NOW HOLD ON THERE JUST A SINGLE MINUTE, GENTLEMEN.
MISTER THORN, IT SEEMS HANSEL AND I ARE GIVING YOU CONFLICTING ADVICE. THAT'S NOT TOO PROFESSIONAL, IS IT?
UHM...
I THINK WHAT HANSEL AND I NEED TO DO IS WORK OUT A THING OR TWO BETWEEN OUR OWN SELVES, BEFORE WE BOTHER YOU FURTHER.
WHAT ARE YOU DOING?
YOU'RE TOO IMPORTANT A FELLER TO HAVE US CARPING AND SQUAWKING IN YOUR EAR LIKE A COUPLE OF BANTAM ROOSTERS, FIGHTING TO SEE WHO GETS TO BE KING OF THE HENHOUSE.
LET GO OF MY CHAIR!
DON'T YOU DARE DISOBEY ME!
SO YOU JUST SIT TIGHT FOR A SPELL, SIR, WHILE HANSEL AND I HAVE US A PRIVATE CHAT--A LITTLE HEART-TO-HEART TO GET US BOTH ON THE SAME PAGE, SO TO SPEAK.
DO NOT WHEEL ME OUT THAT DOOR!
DO NOT WHEEL ME OUT THAT DOOR!

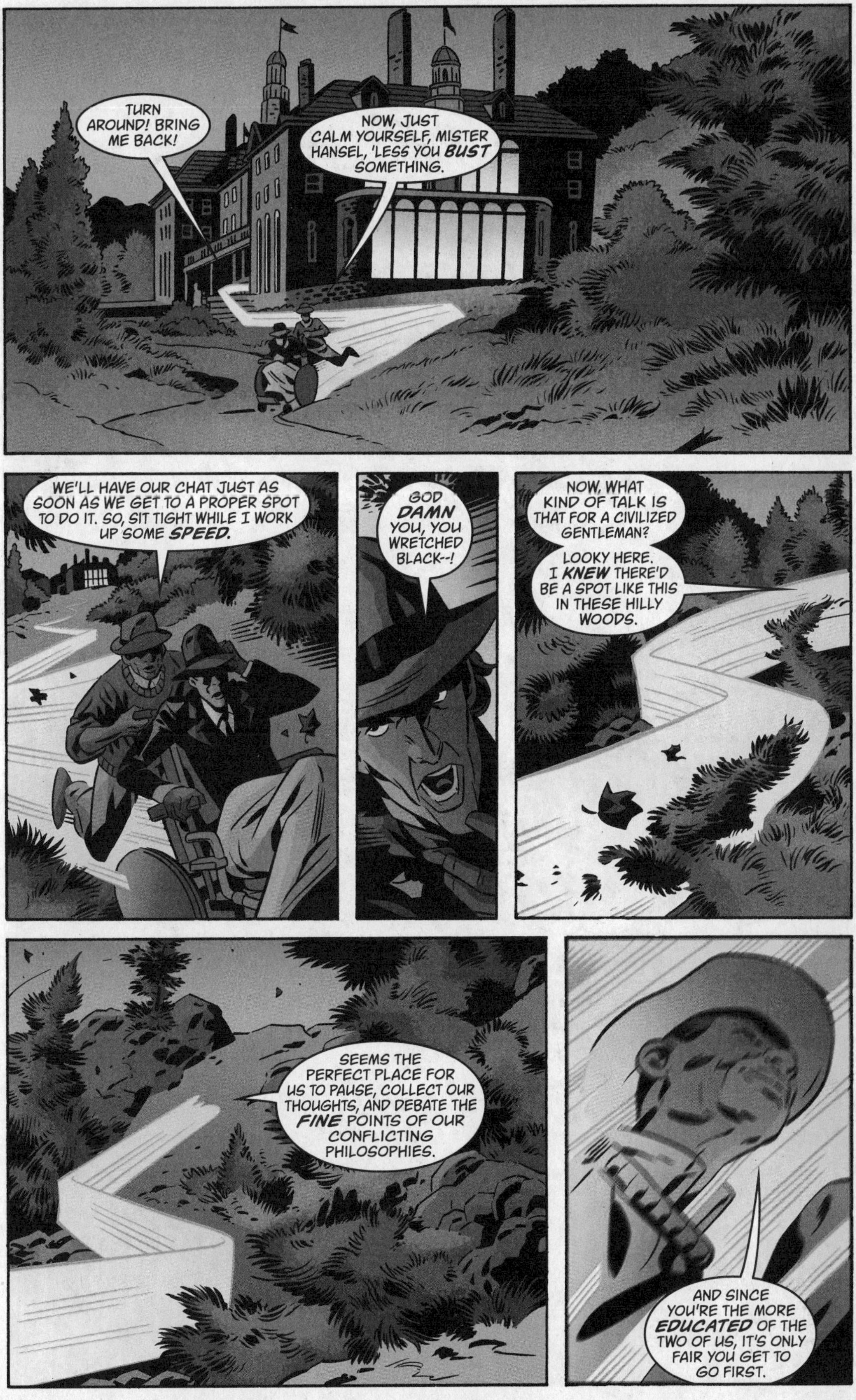
TURN AROUND! BRING ME BACK!
NOW, JUST CALM YOURSELF, MISTER HANSEL, 'LESS YOU BUST SOMETHING.
WE'LL HAVE OUR CHAT JUST AS SOON AS WE GET TO A PROPER SPOT TO DO IT. SO, SIT TIGHT WHILE I WORK UP SOME SPEED.
GOD DAMN YOU, YOU WRETCHED BLACK--!
NOW, WHAT KIND OF TALK IS THAT FOR A CIVILIZED GENTLEMAN?
LOOKY HERE. I KNEW THERE'D BE A SPOT LIKE THIS IN THESE HILLY WOODS.
SEEMS THE PERFECT PLACE FOR US TO PAUSE, COLLECT OUR THOUGHTS, AND DEBATE THE FINE POINTS OF OUR CONFLICTING PHILOSOPHIES.
AND SINCE YOU'RE THE MORE EDUCATED OF THE TWO OF US, IT'S ONLY FAIR YOU GET TO GO FIRST.

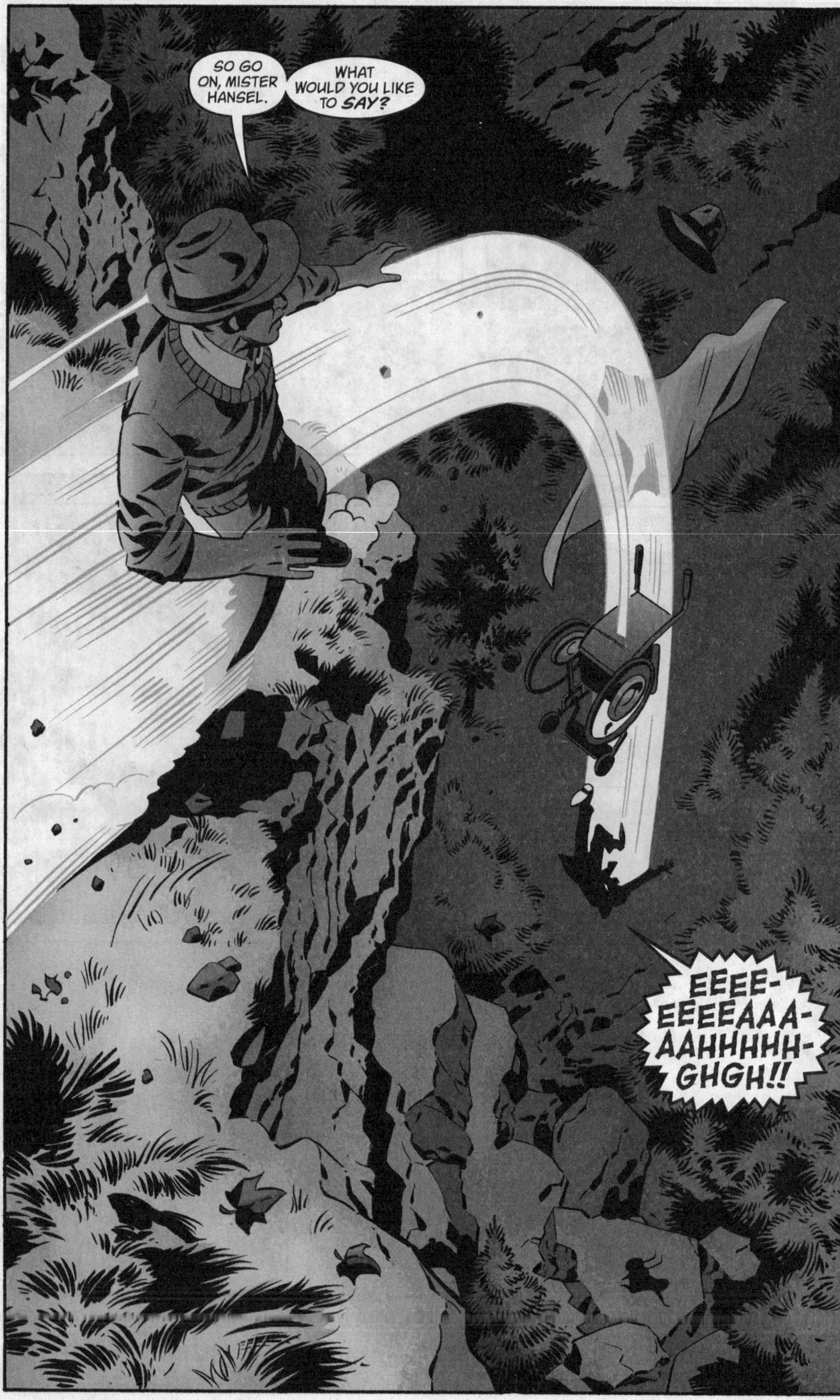
SO GO ON, MISTER HANSEL.
WHAT WOULD YOU LIKE TO SAY?
EEEE-EEEEAAA-AAHHHHH-GHGH!!

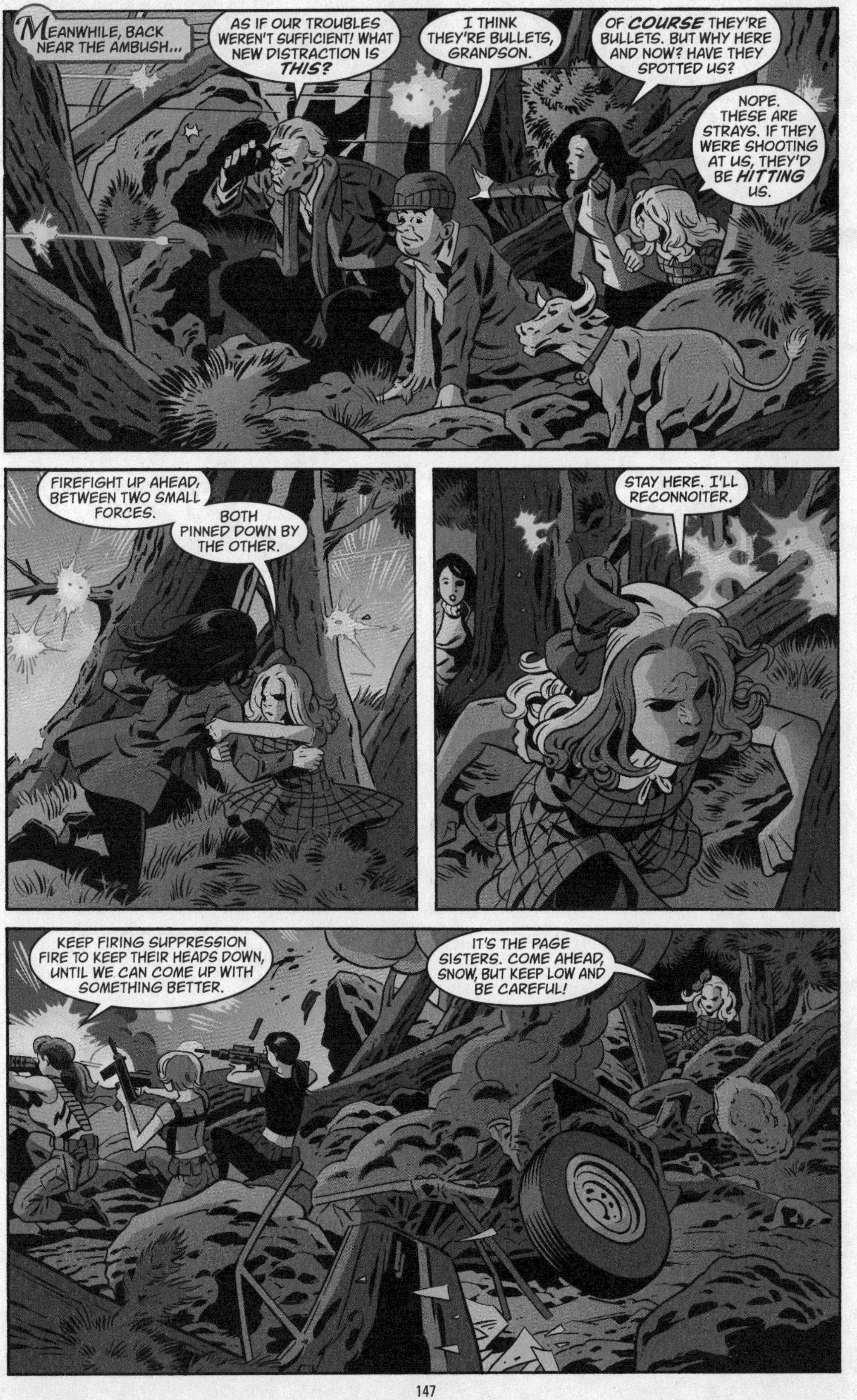
MEANWHILE, BACK NEAR THE AMBUSH...
AS IF OUR TROUBLES WEREN'T SUFFICIENT! WHAT NEW DISTRACTION IS *THIS?*
I THINK THEY'RE BULLETS, GRANDSON.
OF *COURSE* THEY'RE BULLETS. BUT WHY HERE AND NOW? HAVE THEY SPOTTED US?
NOPE. THESE ARE STRAYS. IF THEY WERE SHOOTING AT US, THEY'D BE *HITTING* US.
FIREFIGHT UP AHEAD, BETWEEN TWO SMALL FORCES.
BOTH PINNED DOWN BY THE OTHER.
STAY HERE. I'LL RECONNOITER.
KEEP FIRING SUPPRESSION FIRE TO KEEP THEIR HEADS DOWN, UNTIL WE CAN COME UP WITH SOMETHING BETTER.
IT'S THE PAGE SISTERS. COME AHEAD, SNOW, BUT KEEP LOW AND BE CAREFUL!

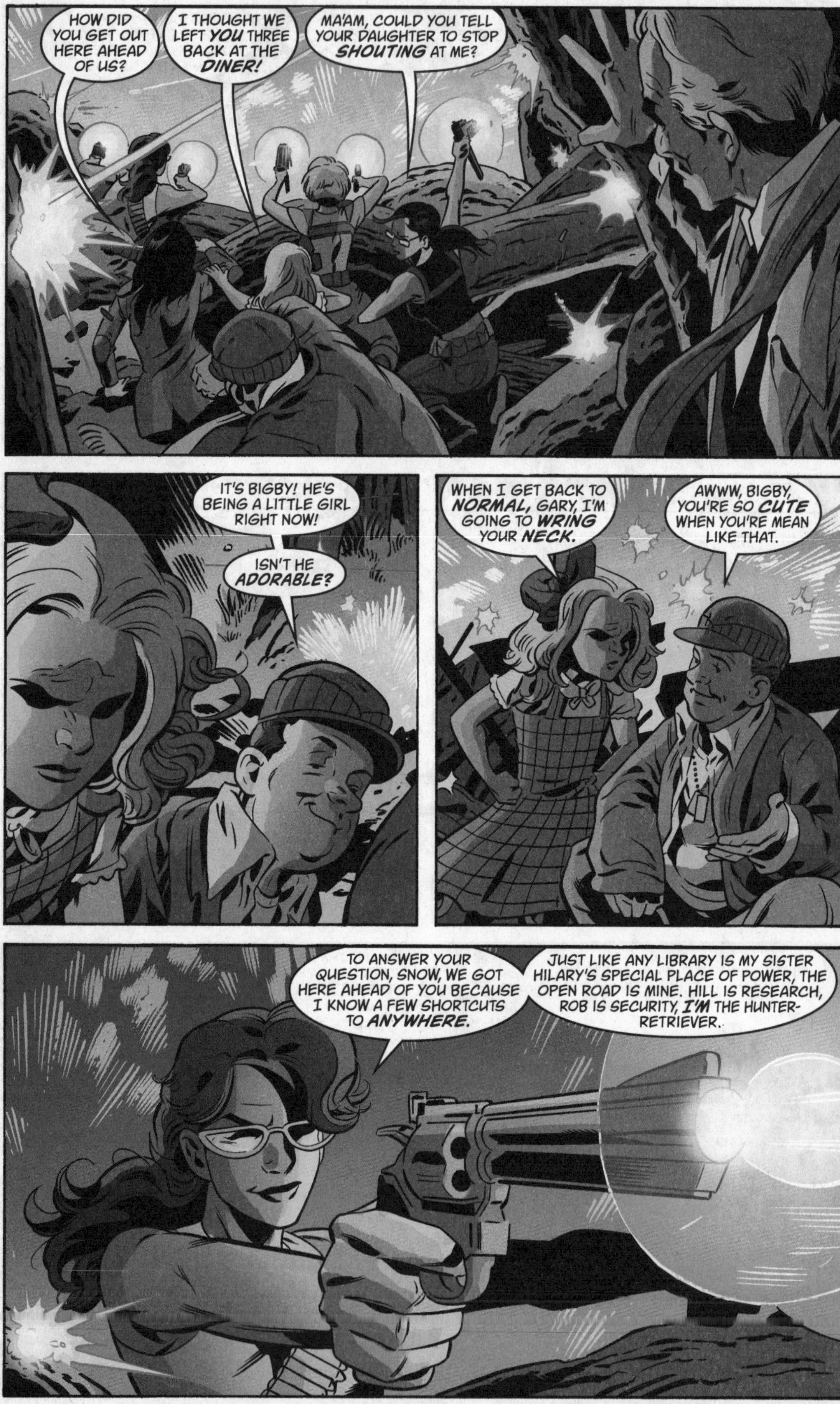
HOW DID YOU GET OUT HERE AHEAD OF US?
I THOUGHT WE LEFT YOU THREE BACK AT THE DINER!
MA'AM, COULD YOU TELL YOUR DAUGHTER TO STOP SHOUTING AT ME?
IT'S BIGBY! HE'S BEING A LITTLE GIRL RIGHT NOW!
ISN'T HE ADORABLE?
WHEN I GET BACK TO NORMAL, GARY, I'M GOING TO WRING YOUR NECK.
AWWW, BIGBY, YOU'RE SO CUTE WHEN YOU'RE MEAN LIKE THAT.
TO ANSWER YOUR QUESTION, SNOW, WE GOT HERE AHEAD OF YOU BECAUSE I KNOW A FEW SHORTCUTS TO ANYWHERE.
JUST LIKE ANY LIBRARY IS MY SISTER HILARY'S SPECIAL PLACE OF POWER, THE OPEN ROAD IS MINE. HILL IS RESEARCH, ROB IS SECURITY, I'M THE HUNTER-RETRIEVER.

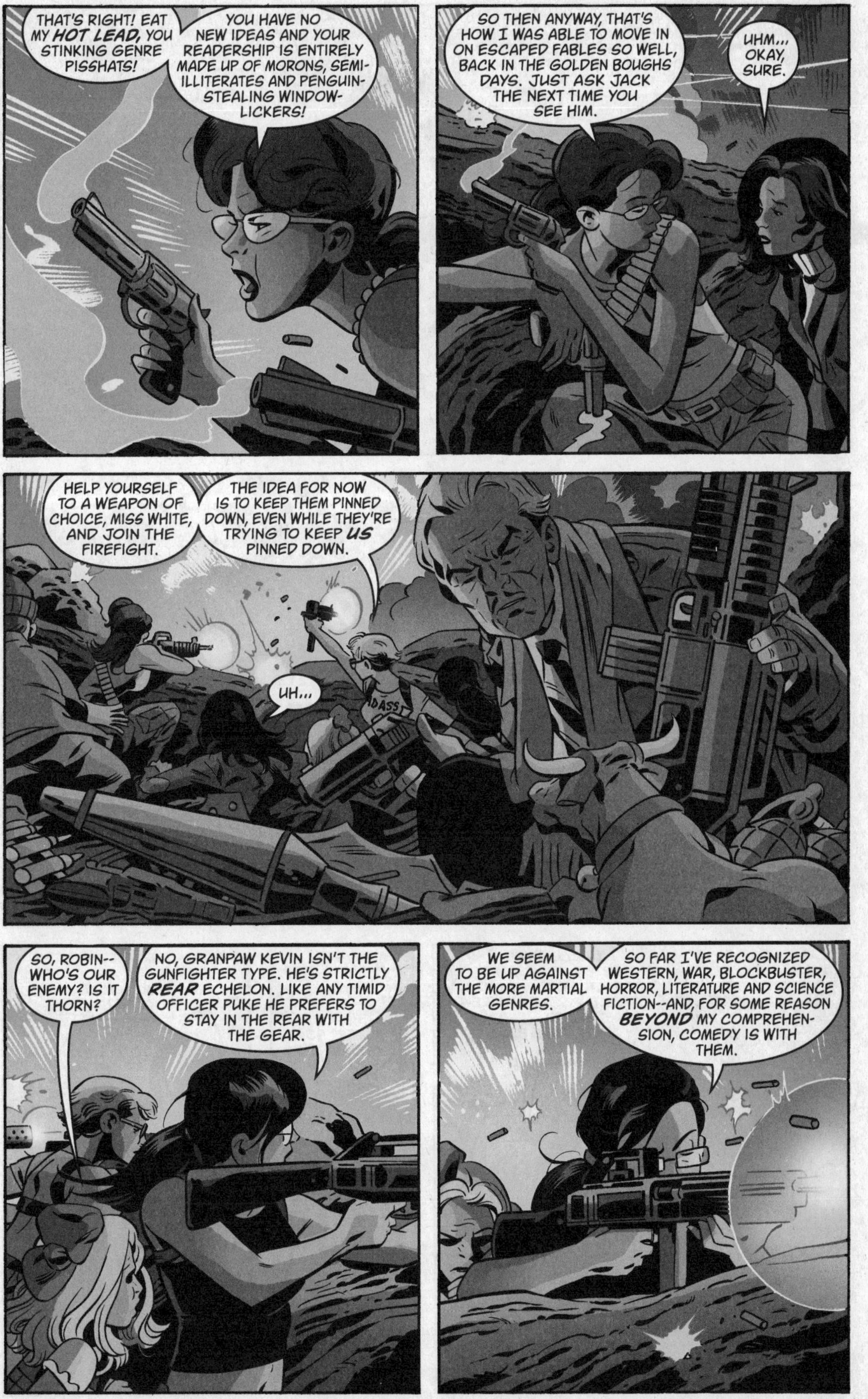
THAT'S RIGHT! EAT MY HOT LEAD, YOU STINKING GENRE PISSHATS!
YOU HAVE NO NEW IDEAS AND YOUR READERSHIP IS ENTIRELY MADE UP OF MORONS, SEMI-ILLITERATES AND PENGUIN-STEALING WINDOW-LICKERS!
SO THEN ANYWAY, THAT'S HOW I WAS ABLE TO MOVE IN ON ESCAPED FABLES SO WELL, BACK IN THE GOLDEN BOUGHS DAYS. JUST ASK JACK THE NEXT TIME YOU SEE HIM.
UHM... OKAY, SURE.
HELP YOURSELF TO A WEAPON OF CHOICE, MISS WHITE, AND JOIN THE FIREFIGHT.
THE IDEA FOR NOW IS TO KEEP THEM PINNED DOWN, EVEN WHILE THEY'RE TRYING TO KEEP US PINNED DOWN.
UH...
SO, ROBIN-- WHO'S OUR ENEMY? IS IT THORN?
NO, GRANPAW KEVIN ISN'T THE GUNFIGHTER TYPE. HE'S STRICTLY REAR ECHELON. LIKE ANY TIMID OFFICER PUKE HE PREFERS TO STAY IN THE REAR WITH THE GEAR.
WE SEEM TO BE UP AGAINST THE MORE MARTIAL GENRES.
SO FAR I'VE RECOGNIZED WESTERN, WAR, BLOCKBUSTER, HORROR, LITERATURE AND SCIENCE FICTION--AND, FOR SOME REASON BEYOND MY COMPREHENSION, COMEDY IS WITH THEM.

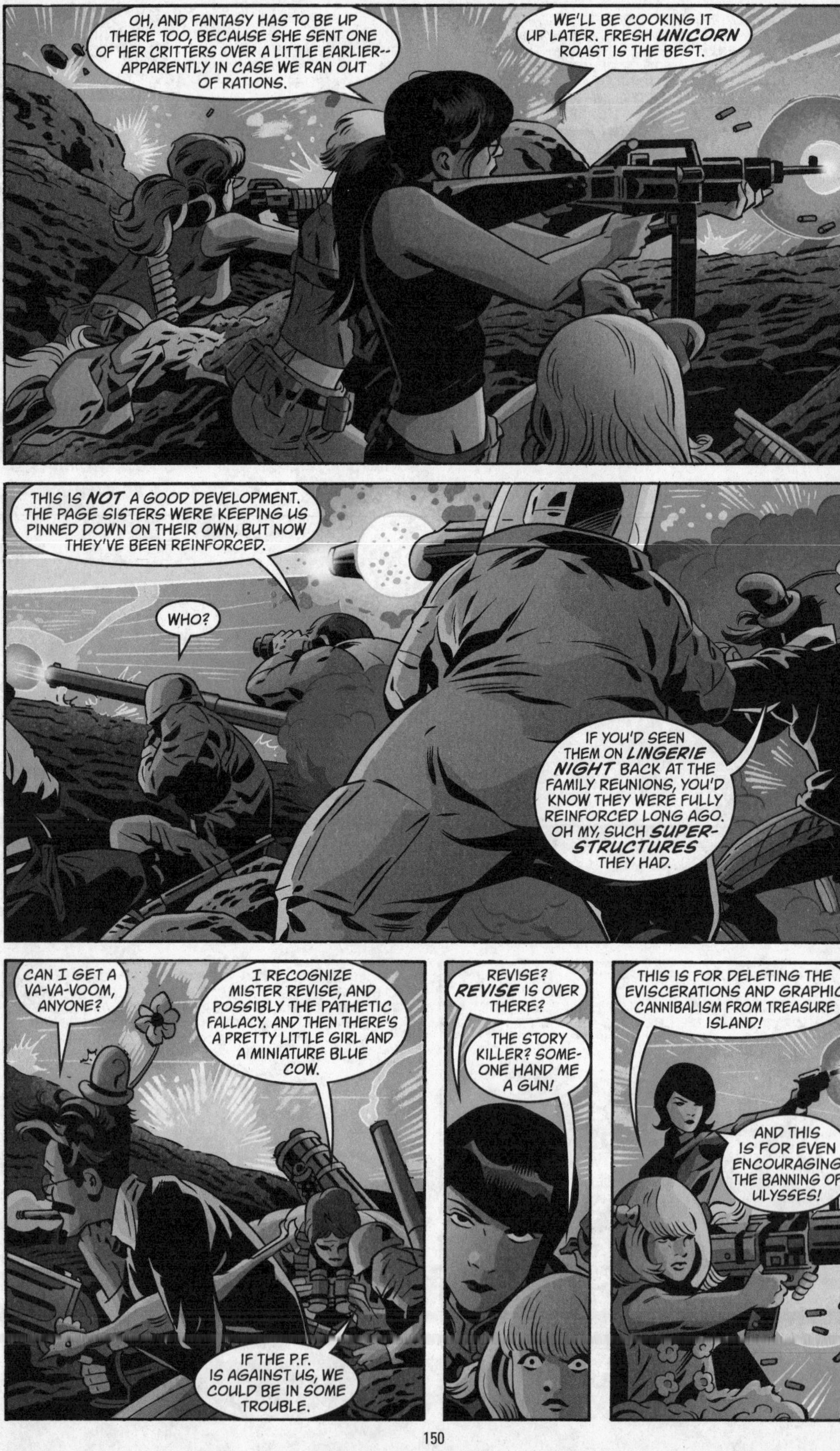
OH, AND FANTASY HAS TO BE UP THERE TOO, BECAUSE SHE SENT ONE OF HER CRITTERS OVER A LITTLE EARLIER-- APPARENTLY IN CASE WE RAN OUT OF RATIONS.
WE'LL BE COOKING IT UP LATER. FRESH UNICORN ROAST IS THE BEST.
THIS IS NOT A GOOD DEVELOPMENT. THE PAGE SISTERS WERE KEEPING US PINNED DOWN ON THEIR OWN, BUT NOW THEY'VE BEEN REINFORCED.
WHO?
IF YOU'D SEEN THEM ON LINGERIE NIGHT BACK AT THE FAMILY REUNIONS, YOU'D KNOW THEY WERE FULLY REINFORCED LONG AGO. OH MY, SUCH SUPER-STRUCTURES THEY HAD.
CAN I GET A VA-VA-VOOM, ANYONE?
I RECOGNIZE MISTER REVISE, AND POSSIBLY THE PATHETIC FALLACY. AND THEN THERE'S A PRETTY LITTLE GIRL AND A MINIATURE BLUE COW.
IF THE P.F. IS AGAINST US, WE COULD BE IN SOME TROUBLE.
REVISE? REVISE IS OVER THERE?
THE STORY KILLER? SOME-ONE HAND ME A GUN!
THIS IS FOR DELETING THE EVISCERATIONS AND GRAPHIC CANNIBALISM FROM TREASURE ISLAND!
AND THIS IS FOR EVEN ENCOURAGING THE BANNING OF ULYSSES!

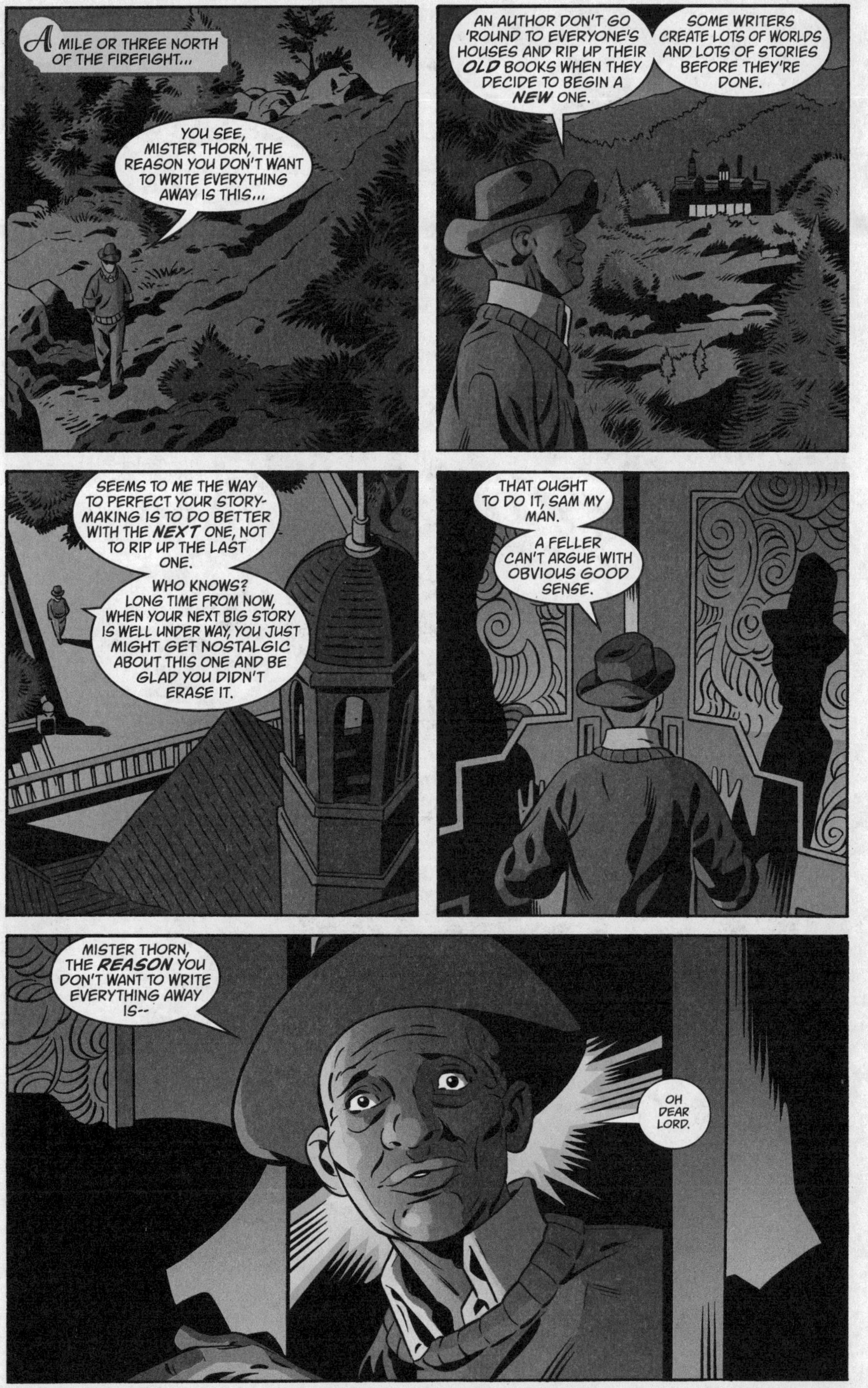
A MILE OR THREE NORTH OF THE FIREFIGHT...
YOU SEE, MISTER THORN, THE REASON YOU DON'T WANT TO WRITE EVERYTHING AWAY IS THIS...
AN AUTHOR DON'T GO 'ROUND TO EVERYONE'S HOUSES AND RIP UP THEIR OLD BOOKS WHEN THEY DECIDE TO BEGIN A NEW ONE.
SOME WRITERS CREATE LOTS OF WORLDS AND LOTS OF STORIES BEFORE THEY'RE DONE.
SEEMS TO ME THE WAY TO PERFECT YOUR STORY-MAKING IS TO DO BETTER WITH THE NEXT ONE, NOT TO RIP UP THE LAST ONE.
WHO KNOWS? LONG TIME FROM NOW, WHEN YOUR NEXT BIG STORY IS WELL UNDER WAY, YOU JUST MIGHT GET NOSTALGIC ABOUT THIS ONE AND BE GLAD YOU DIDN'T ERASE IT.
THAT OUGHT TO DO IT, SAM MY MAN.
A FELLER CAN'T ARGUE WITH OBVIOUS GOOD SENSE.
MISTER THORN, THE REASON YOU DON'T WANT TO WRITE EVERYTHING AWAY IS--
OH DEAR LORD.

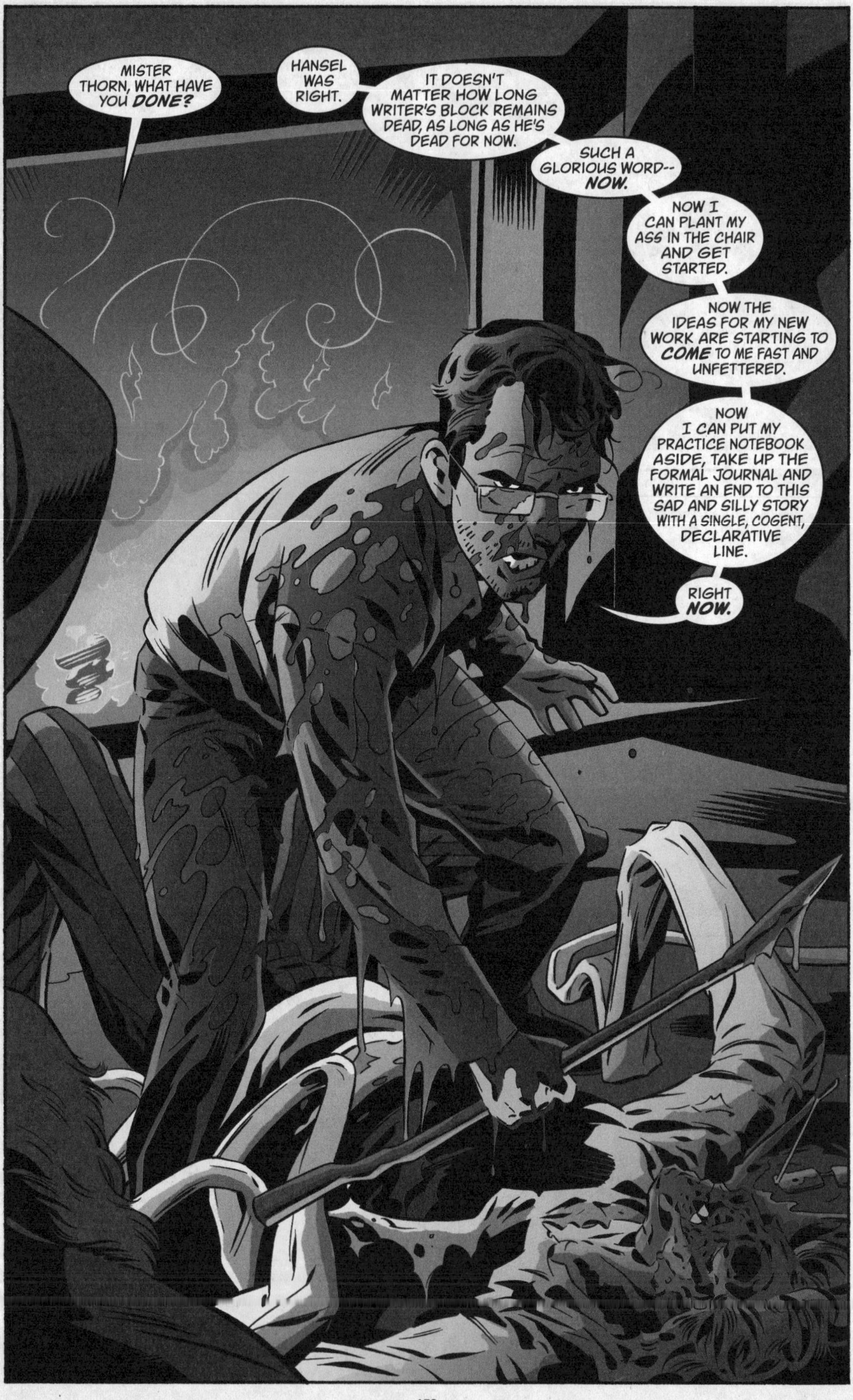
MISTER THORN, WHAT HAVE YOU DONE?
HANSEL WAS RIGHT.
IT DOESN'T MATTER HOW LONG WRITER'S BLOCK REMAINS DEAD, AS LONG AS HE'S DEAD FOR NOW.
SUCH A GLORIOUS WORD-- NOW.
NOW I CAN PLANT MY ASS IN THE CHAIR AND GET STARTED.
NOW THE IDEAS FOR MY NEW WORK ARE STARTING TO COME TO ME FAST AND UNFETTERED.
NOW I CAN PUT MY PRACTICE NOTEBOOK ASIDE, TAKE UP THE FORMAL JOURNAL AND WRITE AN END TO THIS SAD AND SILLY STORY WITH A SINGLE, COGENT, DECLARATIVE LINE.
RIGHT NOW.

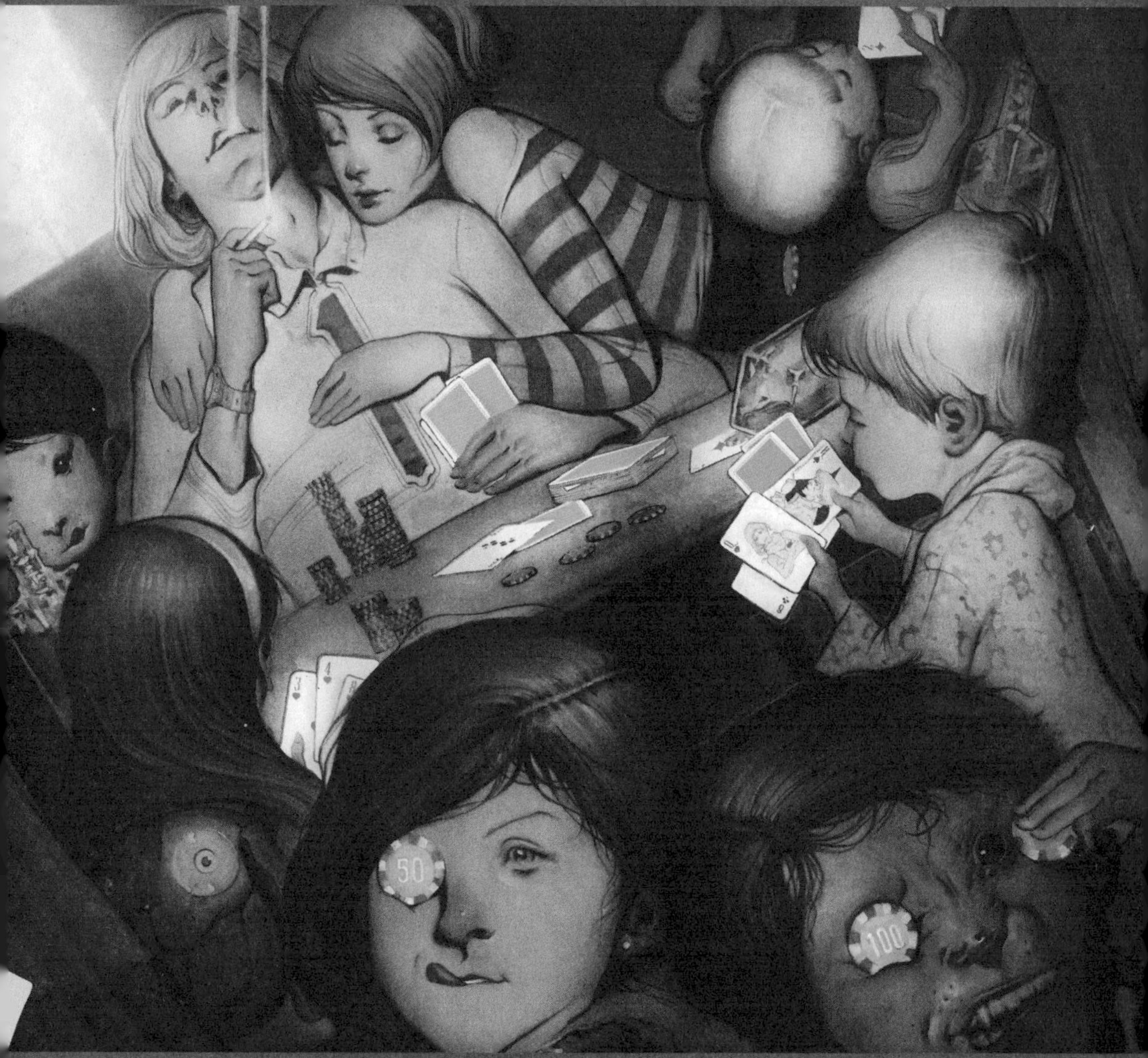
50
100

"He still has to pay for impersonating our savior.
We'll lynch him for purely doctrinal purposes."

The Great FABLES Crossover part 7 of 9

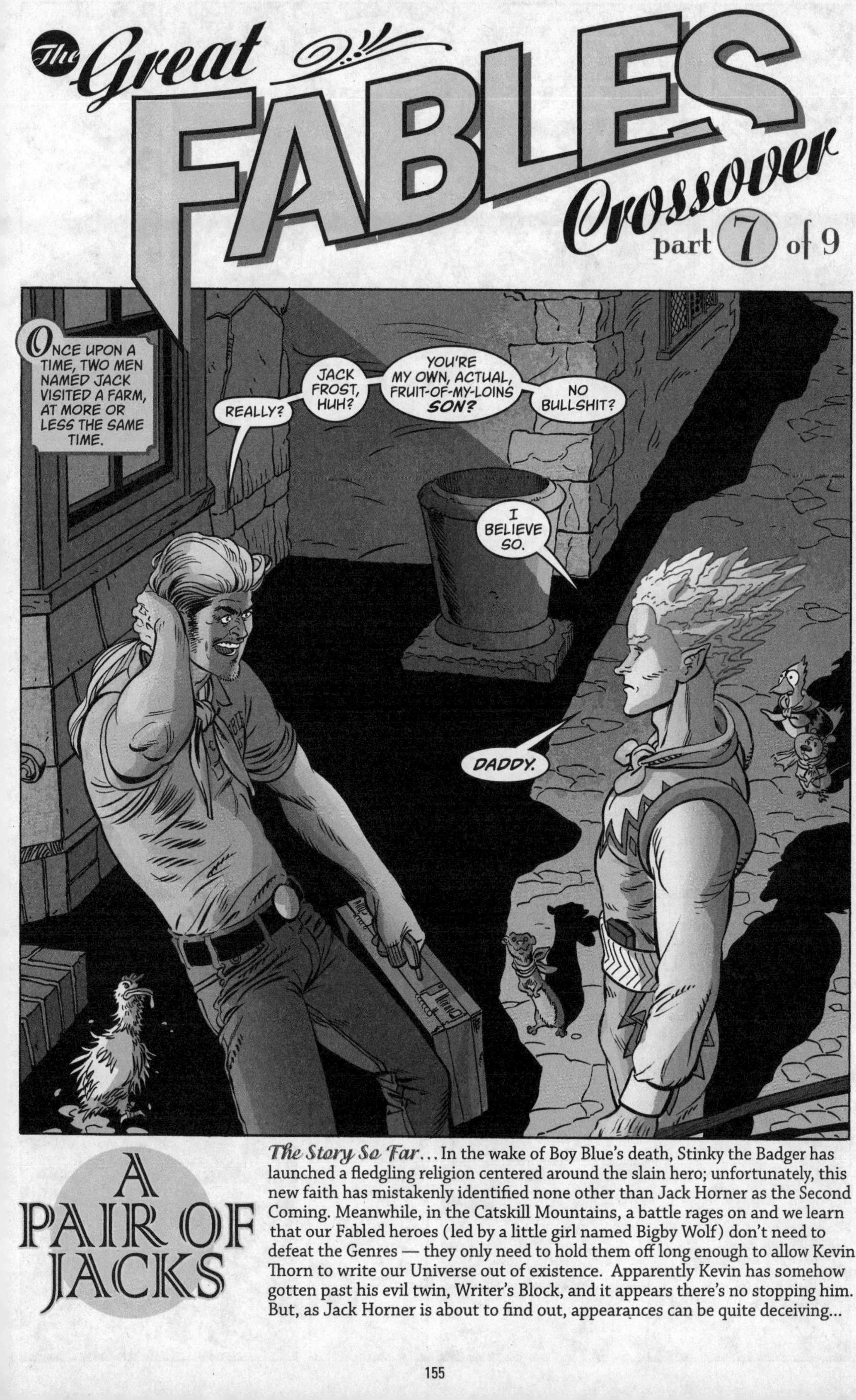
ONCE UPON A TIME, TWO MEN NAMED JACK VISITED A FARM, AT MORE OR LESS THE SAME TIME.
REALLY?
JACK FROST, HUH?
YOU'RE MY OWN, ACTUAL, FRUIT-OF-MY-LOINS SON?
NO BULLSHIT?
I BELIEVE SO.
DADDY.

A PAIR OF JACKS

The Story So Far... In the wake of Boy Blue's death, Stinky the Badger has launched a fledgling religion centered around the slain hero; unfortunately, this new faith has mistakenly identified none other than Jack Horner as the Second Coming. Meanwhile, in the Catskill Mountains, a battle rages on and we learn that our Fabled heroes (led by a little girl named Bigby Wolf) don't need to defeat the Genres — they only need to hold them off long enough to allow Kevin Thorn to write our Universe out of existence. Apparently Kevin has somehow gotten past his evil twin, Writer's Block, and it appears there's no stopping him. But, as Jack Horner is about to find out, appearances can be quite deceiving...

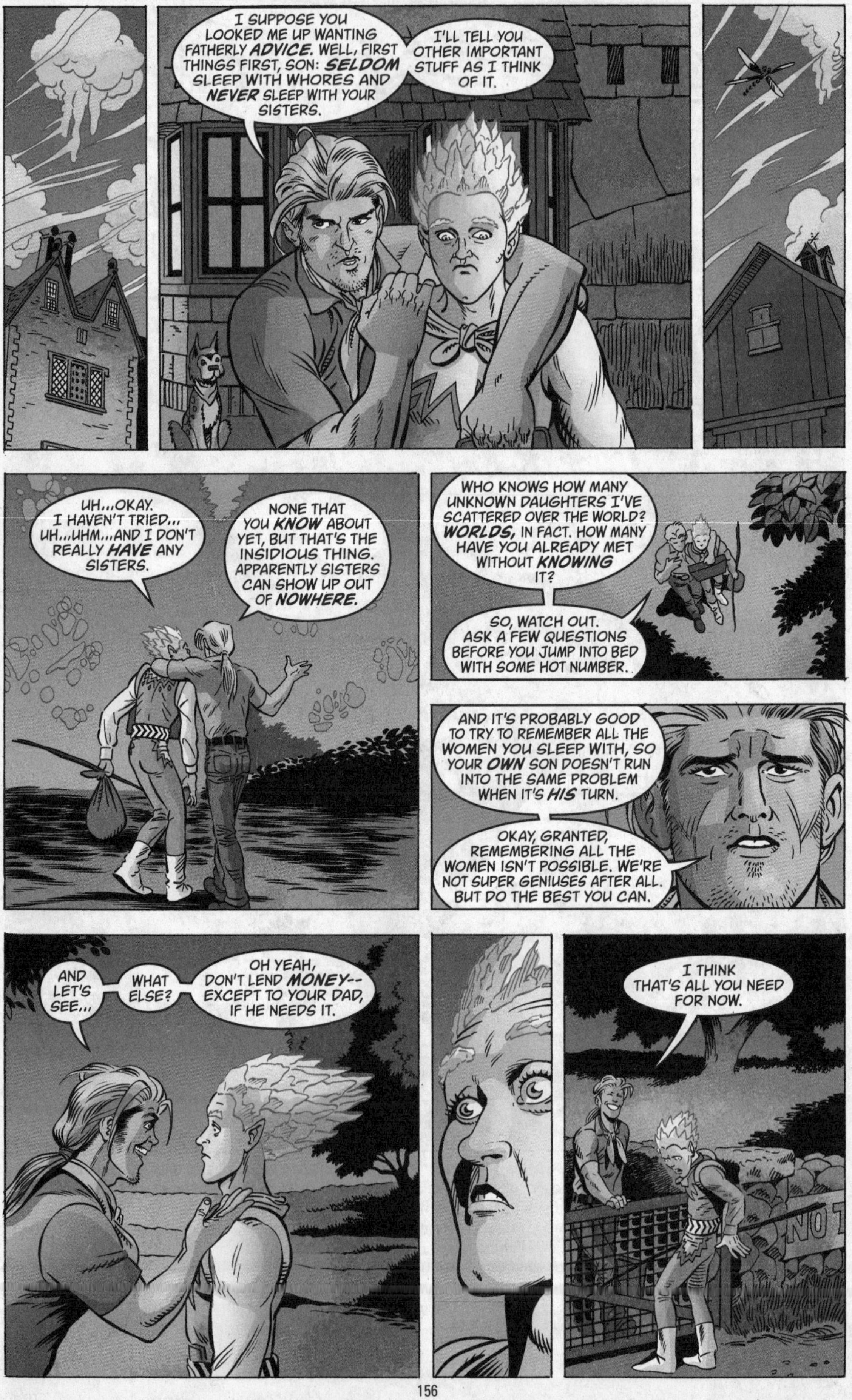
I SUPPOSE YOU LOOKED ME UP WANTING FATHERLY ADVICE. WELL, FIRST THINGS FIRST, SON: SELDOM SLEEP WITH WHORES AND NEVER SLEEP WITH YOUR SISTERS.
I'LL TELL YOU OTHER IMPORTANT STUFF AS I THINK OF IT.
UH...OKAY. I HAVEN'T TRIED... UH...UHM...AND I DON'T REALLY HAVE ANY SISTERS.
NONE THAT YOU KNOW ABOUT YET, BUT THAT'S THE INSIDIOUS THING. APPARENTLY SISTERS CAN SHOW UP OUT OF NOWHERE.
WHO KNOWS HOW MANY UNKNOWN DAUGHTERS I'VE SCATTERED OVER THE WORLD? WORLDS, IN FACT. HOW MANY HAVE YOU ALREADY MET WITHOUT KNOWING IT?
SO, WATCH OUT. ASK A FEW QUESTIONS BEFORE YOU JUMP INTO BED WITH SOME HOT NUMBER.
AND IT'S PROBABLY GOOD TO TRY TO REMEMBER ALL THE WOMEN YOU SLEEP WITH, SO YOUR OWN SON DOESN'T RUN INTO THE SAME PROBLEM WHEN IT'S HIS TURN.
OKAY, GRANTED, REMEMBERING ALL THE WOMEN ISN'T POSSIBLE. WE'RE NOT SUPER GENIUSES AFTER ALL. BUT DO THE BEST YOU CAN.
AND LET'S SEE...
WHAT ELSE?
OH YEAH, DON'T LEND MONEY-- EXCEPT TO YOUR DAD, IF HE NEEDS IT.
I THINK THAT'S ALL YOU NEED FOR NOW.
NO T

NICE OF YOU TO DROP BY, KID. *WRITE* FROM TIME TO TIME. LET YOUR OLD MAN KNOW HOW YOU'RE DOING.

BE *CAREFUL* OUT THERE ON THE WIDE, WILD ROAD.

BUT--I DIDN'T--WE *NEVER*--

BUT I DIDN'T GET TO SAY ANY OF THE THINGS I CAME TO SAY.

YOU JUST SORT OF TOOK CHARGE OF THE CONVERSATION AND--

YOU STOP RIGHT *THERE,* DADDY!

I'M NOT DONE *TALKING* TO YOU, AND I'M NOT GOING *ANYWHERE* UNTIL I *DO!*

WHAT ELSE DO YOU *NEED,* FOR CRAP'S SAKE? I ACKNOWLEDGED YOU AS MY SON. I PASSED ALONG SOME HARD-WON FATHERLY WISDOM. WHAT MORE COULD YOU *WANT?*

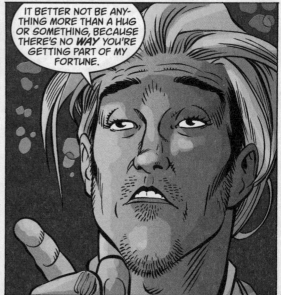

IT BETTER NOT BE ANYTHING MORE THAN A HUG OR SOMETHING, BECAUSE THERE'S NO *WAY* YOU'RE GETTING PART OF MY FORTUNE.

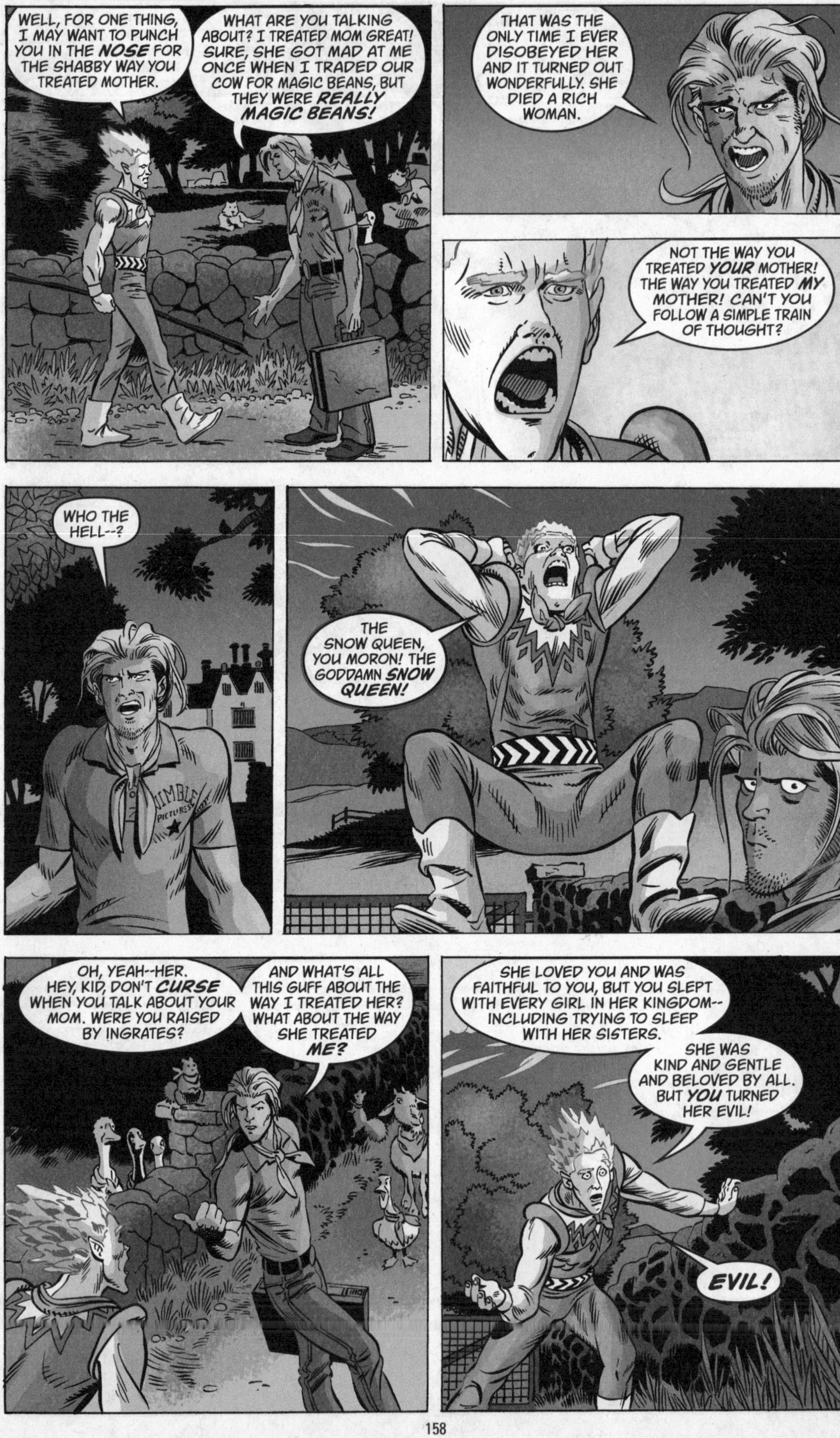
WELL, FOR ONE THING, I MAY WANT TO PUNCH YOU IN THE NOSE FOR THE SHABBY WAY YOU TREATED MOTHER.
WHAT ARE YOU TALKING ABOUT? I TREATED MOM GREAT! SURE, SHE GOT MAD AT ME ONCE WHEN I TRADED OUR COW FOR MAGIC BEANS, BUT THEY WERE REALLY MAGIC BEANS!
THAT WAS THE ONLY TIME I EVER DISOBEYED HER AND IT TURNED OUT WONDERFULLY. SHE DIED A RICH WOMAN.
NOT THE WAY YOU TREATED YOUR MOTHER! THE WAY YOU TREATED MY MOTHER! CAN'T YOU FOLLOW A SIMPLE TRAIN OF THOUGHT?
WHO THE HELL--?
THE SNOW QUEEN, YOU MORON! THE GODDAMN SNOW QUEEN!
OH, YEAH--HER. HEY, KID, DON'T CURSE WHEN YOU TALK ABOUT YOUR MOM. WERE YOU RAISED BY INGRATES?
AND WHAT'S ALL THIS GUFF ABOUT THE WAY I TREATED HER? WHAT ABOUT THE WAY SHE TREATED ME?
SHE LOVED YOU AND WAS FAITHFUL TO YOU, BUT YOU SLEPT WITH EVERY GIRL IN HER KINGDOM-- INCLUDING TRYING TO SLEEP WITH HER SISTERS.
SHE WAS KIND AND GENTLE AND BELOVED BY ALL. BUT YOU TURNED HER EVIL!
EVIL!

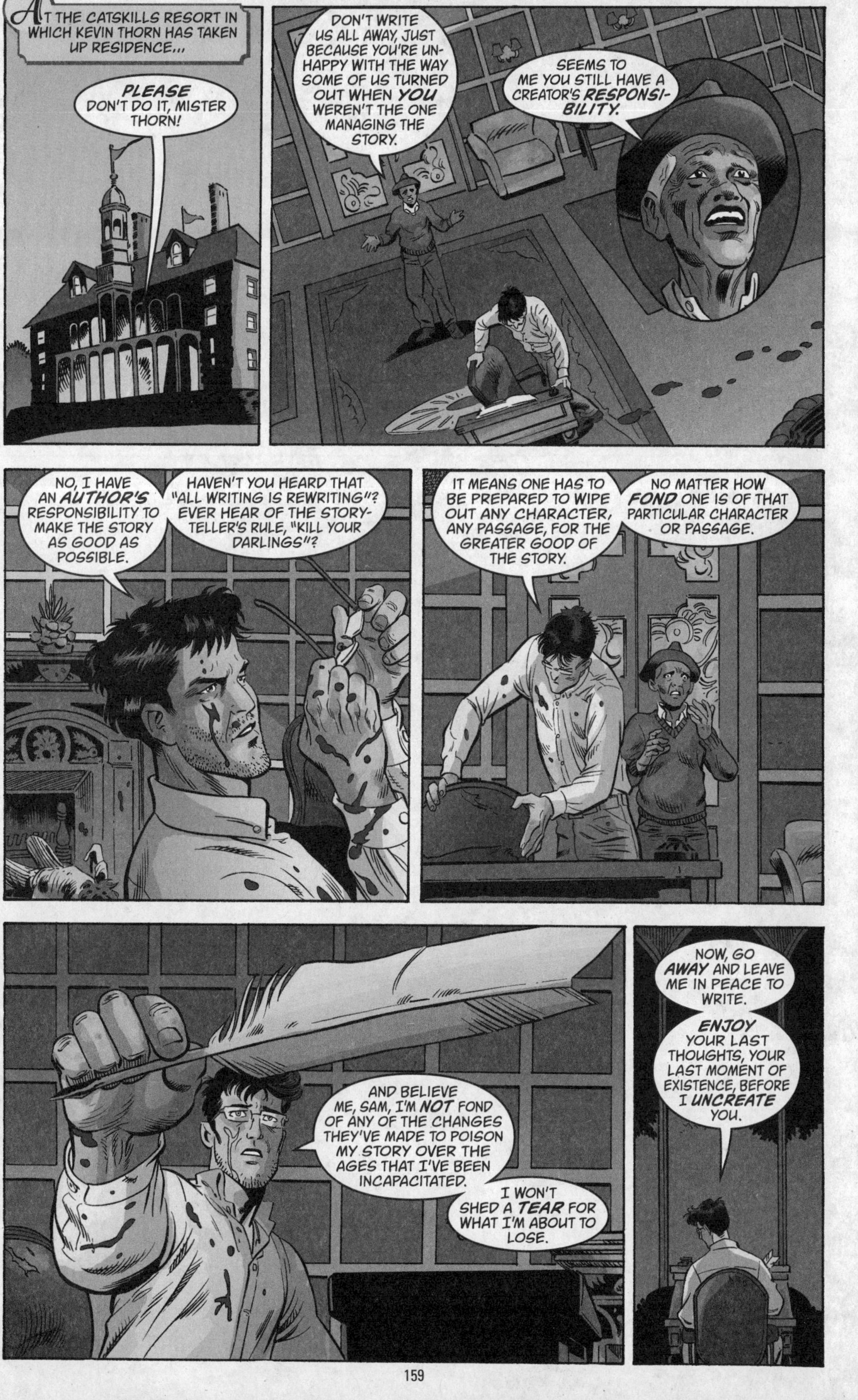
AT THE CATSKILLS RESORT IN WHICH KEVIN THORN HAS TAKEN UP RESIDENCE...
PLEASE DON'T DO IT, MISTER THORN!
DON'T WRITE US ALL AWAY, JUST BECAUSE YOU'RE UNHAPPY WITH THE WAY SOME OF US TURNED OUT WHEN YOU WEREN'T THE ONE MANAGING THE STORY.
SEEMS TO ME YOU STILL HAVE A CREATOR'S RESPONSIBILITY.
NO, I HAVE AN AUTHOR'S RESPONSIBILITY TO MAKE THE STORY AS GOOD AS POSSIBLE.
HAVEN'T YOU HEARD THAT "ALL WRITING IS REWRITING"? EVER HEAR OF THE STORYTELLER'S RULE, "KILL YOUR DARLINGS"?
IT MEANS ONE HAS TO BE PREPARED TO WIPE OUT ANY CHARACTER, ANY PASSAGE, FOR THE GREATER GOOD OF THE STORY.
NO MATTER HOW FOND ONE IS OF THAT PARTICULAR CHARACTER OR PASSAGE.
AND BELIEVE ME, SAM, I'M NOT FOND OF ANY OF THE CHANGES THEY'VE MADE TO POISON MY STORY OVER THE AGES THAT I'VE BEEN INCAPACITATED.
I WON'T SHED A TEAR FOR WHAT I'M ABOUT TO LOSE.
NOW, GO AWAY AND LEAVE ME IN PEACE TO WRITE.
ENJOY YOUR LAST THOUGHTS, YOUR LAST MOMENT OF EXISTENCE, BEFORE I UNCREATE YOU.

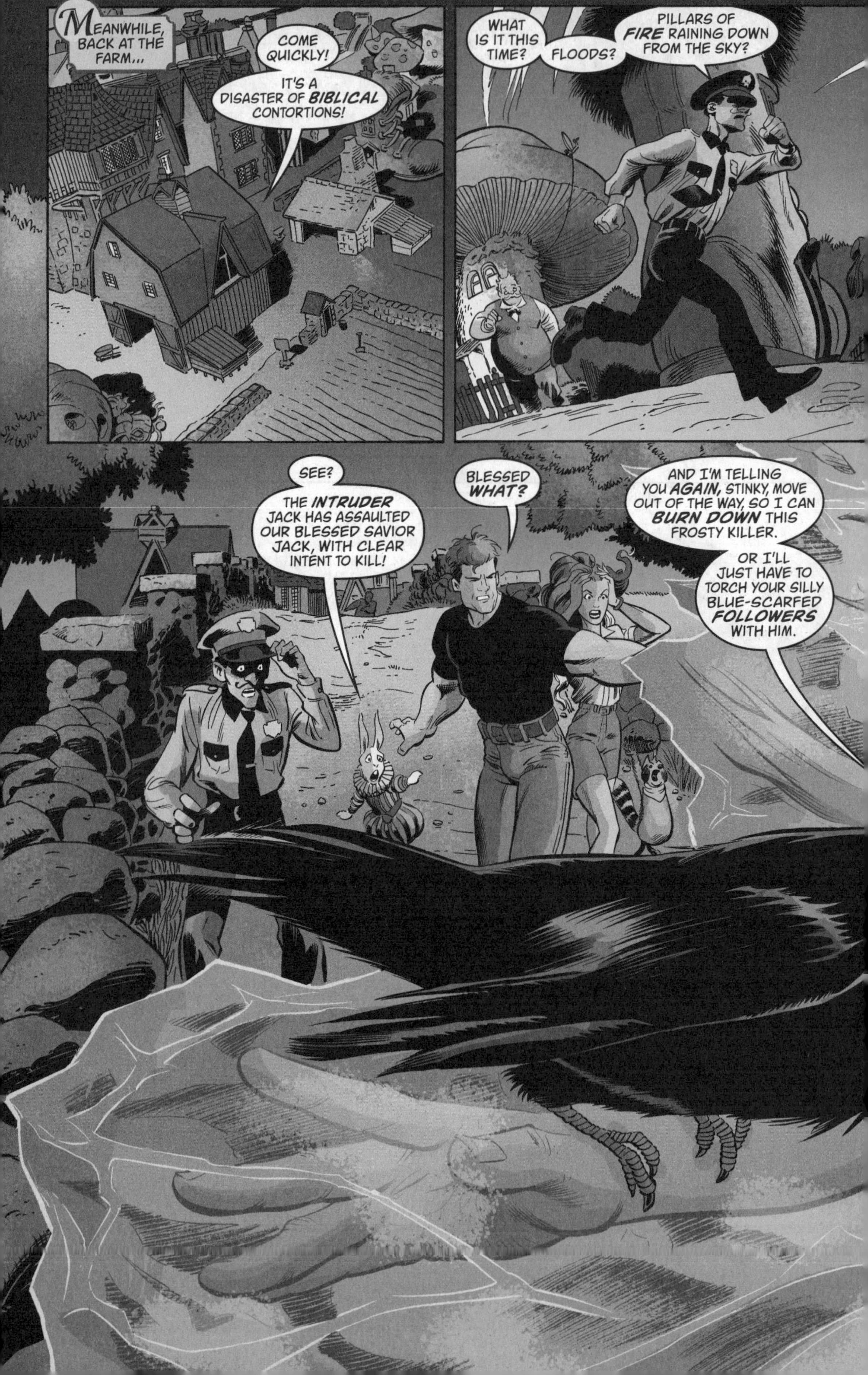
MEANWHILE, BACK AT THE FARM...
COME QUICKLY!
IT'S A DISASTER OF BIBLICAL CONTORTIONS!
WHAT IS IT THIS TIME?
FLOODS?
PILLARS OF FIRE RAINING DOWN FROM THE SKY?
SEE?
THE INTRUDER JACK HAS ASSAULTED OUR BLESSED SAVIOR JACK, WITH CLEAR INTENT TO KILL!
BLESSED WHAT?
AND I'M TELLING YOU AGAIN, STINKY, MOVE OUT OF THE WAY, SO I CAN BURN DOWN THIS FROSTY KILLER.
OR I'LL JUST HAVE TO TORCH YOUR SILLY BLUE-SCARFED FOLLOWERS WITH HIM.

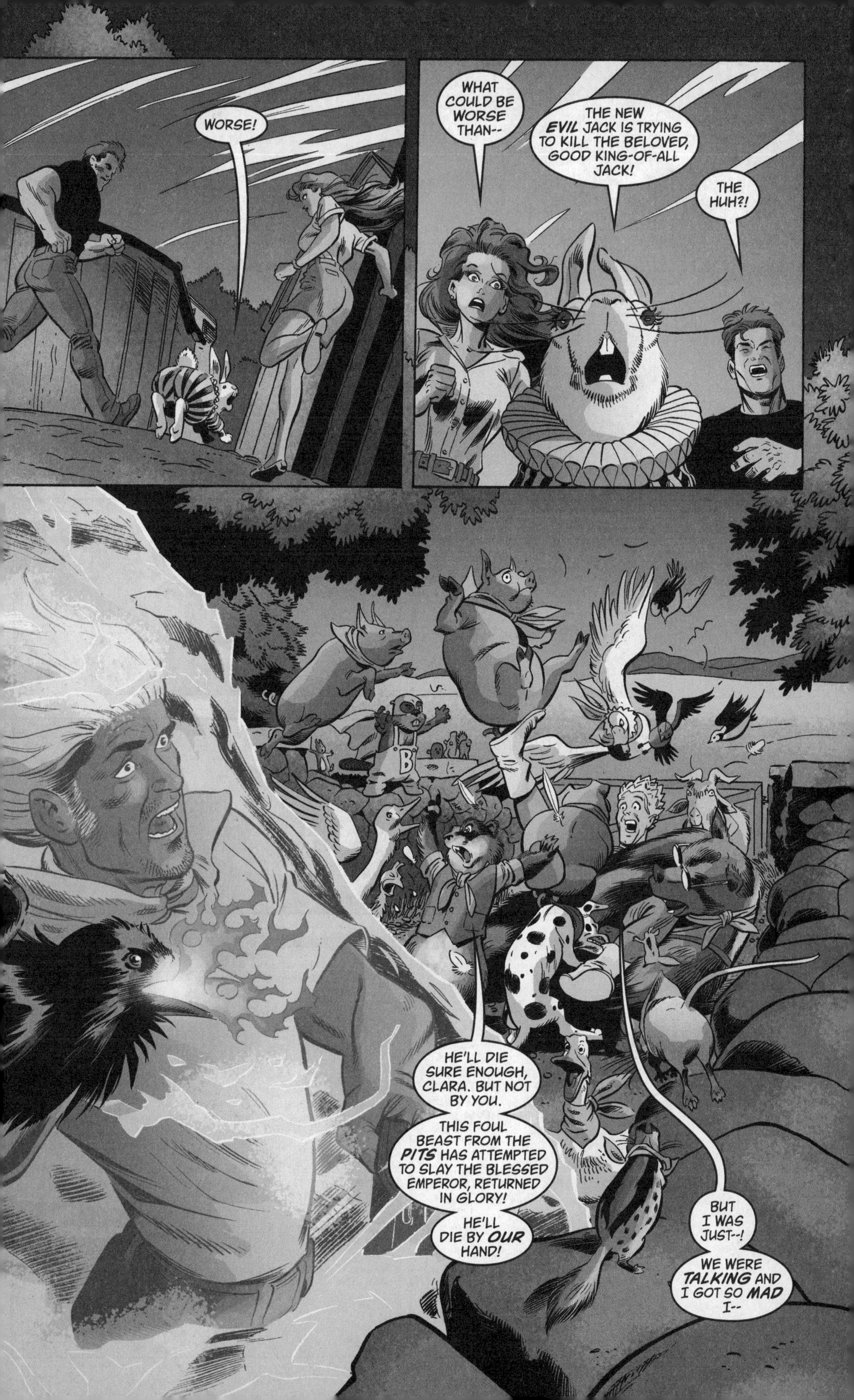
WORSE!
WHAT COULD BE WORSE THAN--
THE NEW EVIL JACK IS TRYING TO KILL THE BELOVED, GOOD KING-OF-ALL JACK!
THE HUH?!
HE'LL DIE SURE ENOUGH, CLARA. BUT NOT BY YOU.
THIS FOUL BEAST FROM THE PITS HAS ATTEMPTED TO SLAY THE BLESSED EMPEROR, RETURNED IN GLORY!
HE'LL DIE BY OUR HAND!
BUT I WAS JUST--!
WE WERE TALKING AND I GOT SO MAD I--

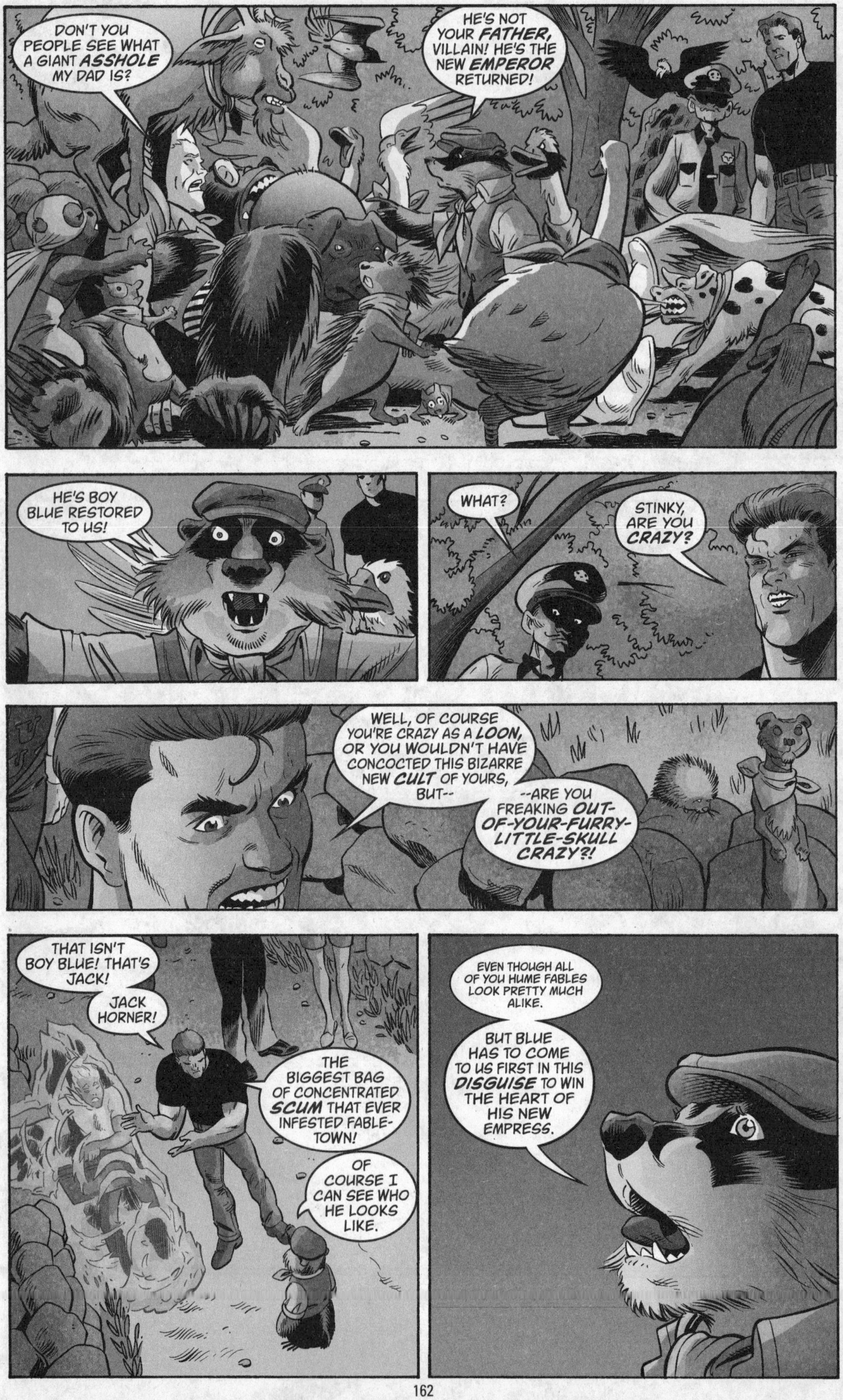
DON'T YOU PEOPLE SEE WHAT A GIANT ASSHOLE MY DAD IS?
HE'S NOT YOUR FATHER, VILLAIN! HE'S THE NEW EMPEROR RETURNED!
HE'S BOY BLUE RESTORED TO US!
WHAT?
STINKY, ARE YOU CRAZY?
WELL, OF COURSE YOU'RE CRAZY AS A LOON, OR YOU WOULDN'T HAVE CONCOCTED THIS BIZARRE NEW CULT OF YOURS, BUT--
--ARE YOU FREAKING OUT-OF-YOUR-FURRY-LITTLE-SKULL CRAZY?!
THAT ISN'T BOY BLUE! THAT'S JACK!
JACK HORNER!
THE BIGGEST BAG OF CONCENTRATED SCUM THAT EVER INFESTED FABLE-TOWN!
OF COURSE I CAN SEE WHO HE LOOKS LIKE.
EVEN THOUGH ALL OF YOU HUME FABLES LOOK PRETTY MUCH ALIKE.
BUT BLUE HAS TO COME TO US FIRST IN THIS DISGUISE TO WIN THE HEART OF HIS NEW EMPRESS.

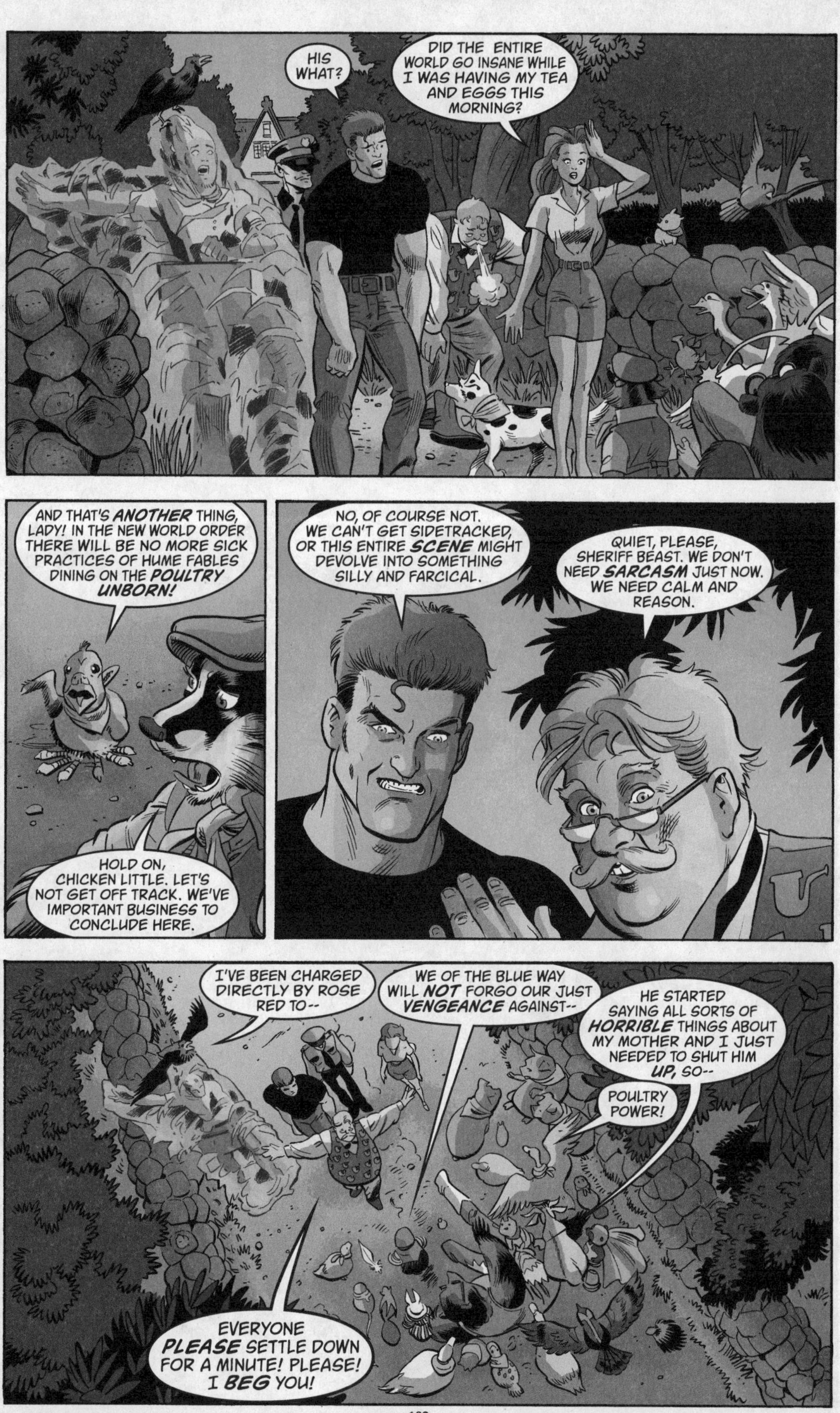
HIS WHAT?
DID THE ENTIRE WORLD GO INSANE WHILE I WAS HAVING MY TEA AND EGGS THIS MORNING?
AND THAT'S ANOTHER THING, LADY! IN THE NEW WORLD ORDER THERE WILL BE NO MORE SICK PRACTICES OF HUME FABLES DINING ON THE POULTRY UNBORN!
HOLD ON, CHICKEN LITTLE. LET'S NOT GET OFF TRACK. WE'VE IMPORTANT BUSINESS TO CONCLUDE HERE.
NO, OF COURSE NOT. WE CAN'T GET SIDETRACKED, OR THIS ENTIRE SCENE MIGHT DEVOLVE INTO SOMETHING SILLY AND FARCICAL.
QUIET, PLEASE, SHERIFF BEAST. WE DON'T NEED SARCASM JUST NOW. WE NEED CALM AND REASON.
I'VE BEEN CHARGED DIRECTLY BY ROSE RED TO--
WE OF THE BLUE WAY WILL NOT FORGO OUR JUST VENGEANCE AGAINST--
HE STARTED SAYING ALL SORTS OF HORRIBLE THINGS ABOUT MY MOTHER AND I JUST NEEDED TO SHUT HIM UP, SO--
POULTRY POWER!
EVERYONE PLEASE SETTLE DOWN FOR A MINUTE! PLEASE! I BEG YOU!

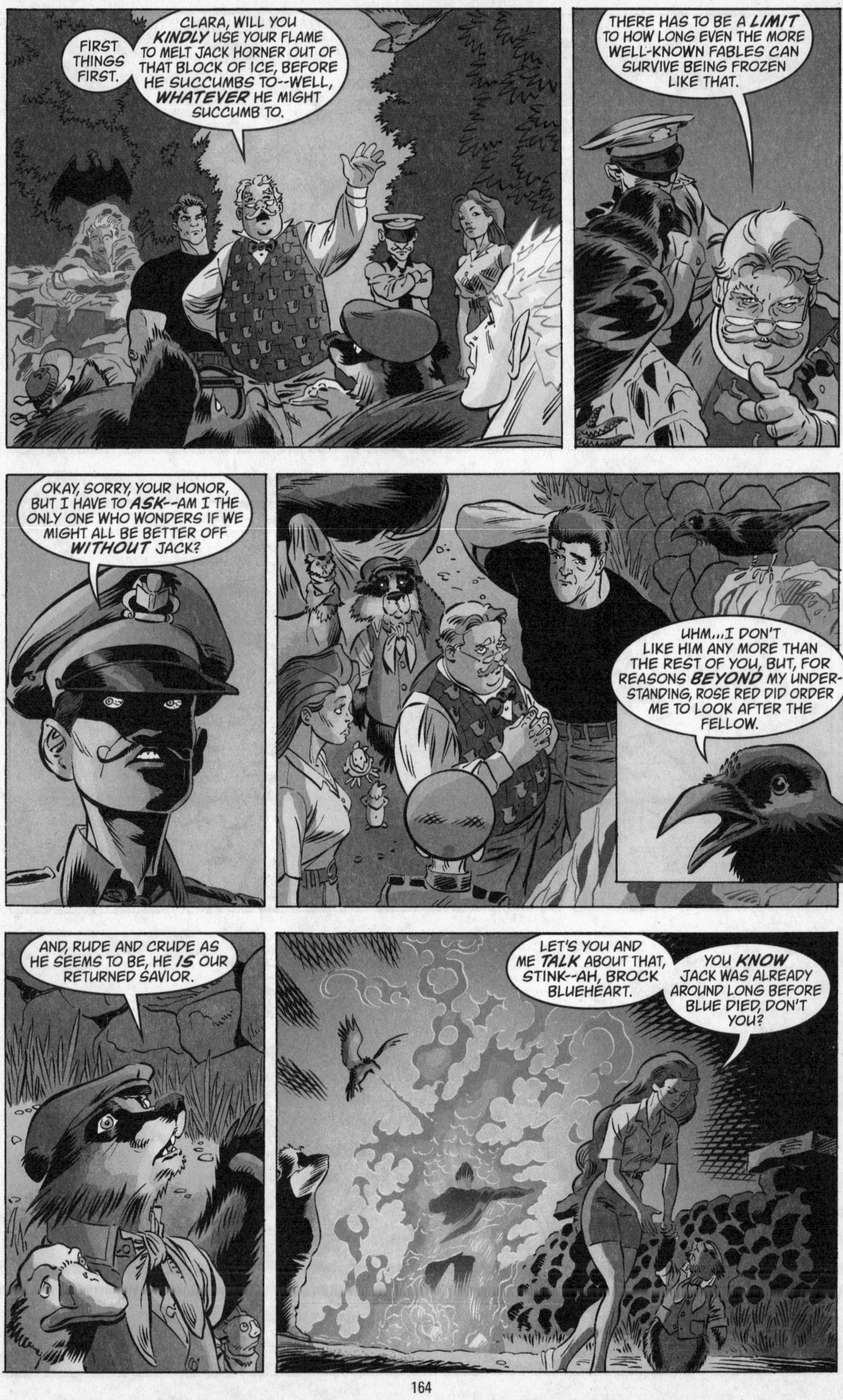
FIRST THINGS FIRST.
CLARA, WILL YOU KINDLY USE YOUR FLAME TO MELT JACK HORNER OUT OF THAT BLOCK OF ICE, BEFORE HE SUCCUMBS TO--WELL, WHATEVER HE MIGHT SUCCUMB TO.
THERE HAS TO BE A LIMIT TO HOW LONG EVEN THE MORE WELL-KNOWN FABLES CAN SURVIVE BEING FROZEN LIKE THAT.
OKAY, SORRY, YOUR HONOR, BUT I HAVE TO ASK--AM I THE ONLY ONE WHO WONDERS IF WE MIGHT ALL BE BETTER OFF WITHOUT JACK?
UHM...I DON'T LIKE HIM ANY MORE THAN THE REST OF YOU, BUT, FOR REASONS BEYOND MY UNDER-STANDING, ROSE RED DID ORDER ME TO LOOK AFTER THE FELLOW.
AND, RUDE AND CRUDE AS HE SEEMS TO BE, HE IS OUR RETURNED SAVIOR.
LET'S YOU AND ME TALK ABOUT THAT, STINK--AH, BROCK BLUEHEART.
YOU KNOW JACK WAS ALREADY AROUND LONG BEFORE BLUE DIED, DON'T YOU?

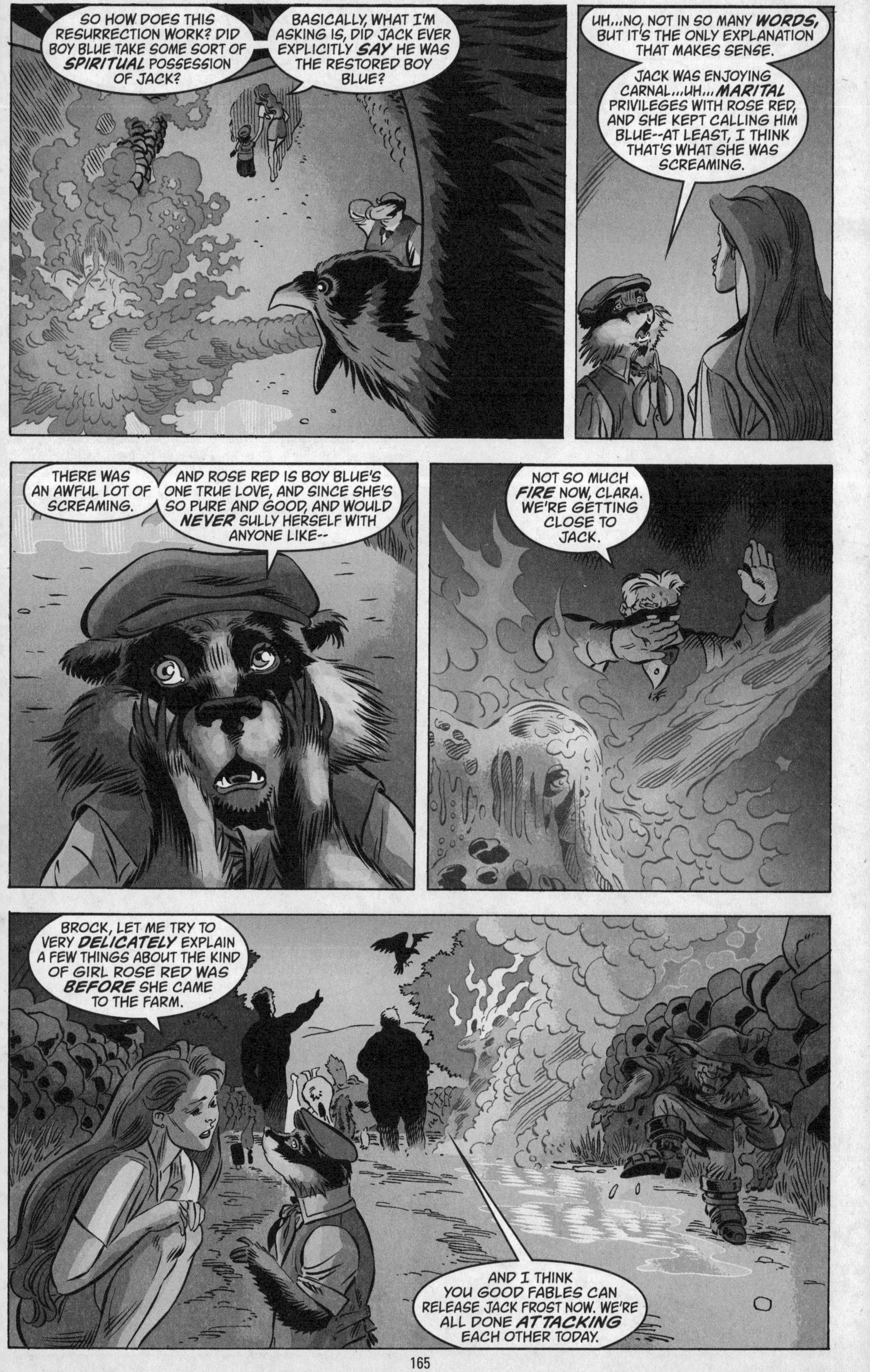
SO HOW DOES THIS RESURRECTION WORK? DID BOY BLUE TAKE SOME SORT OF SPIRITUAL POSSESSION OF JACK?
BASICALLY, WHAT I'M ASKING IS, DID JACK EVER EXPLICITLY SAY HE WAS THE RESTORED BOY BLUE?
UH...NO, NOT IN SO MANY WORDS, BUT IT'S THE ONLY EXPLANATION THAT MAKES SENSE.
JACK WAS ENJOYING CARNAL...UH...MARITAL PRIVILEGES WITH ROSE RED, AND SHE KEPT CALLING HIM BLUE--AT LEAST, I THINK THAT'S WHAT SHE WAS SCREAMING.
THERE WAS AN AWFUL LOT OF SCREAMING.
AND ROSE RED IS BOY BLUE'S ONE TRUE LOVE, AND SINCE SHE'S SO PURE AND GOOD, AND WOULD NEVER SULLY HERSELF WITH ANYONE LIKE--
NOT SO MUCH FIRE NOW, CLARA. WE'RE GETTING CLOSE TO JACK.
BROCK, LET ME TRY TO VERY DELICATELY EXPLAIN A FEW THINGS ABOUT THE KIND OF GIRL ROSE RED WAS BEFORE SHE CAME TO THE FARM.
AND I THINK YOU GOOD FABLES CAN RELEASE JACK FROST NOW. WE'RE ALL DONE ATTACKING EACH OTHER TODAY.

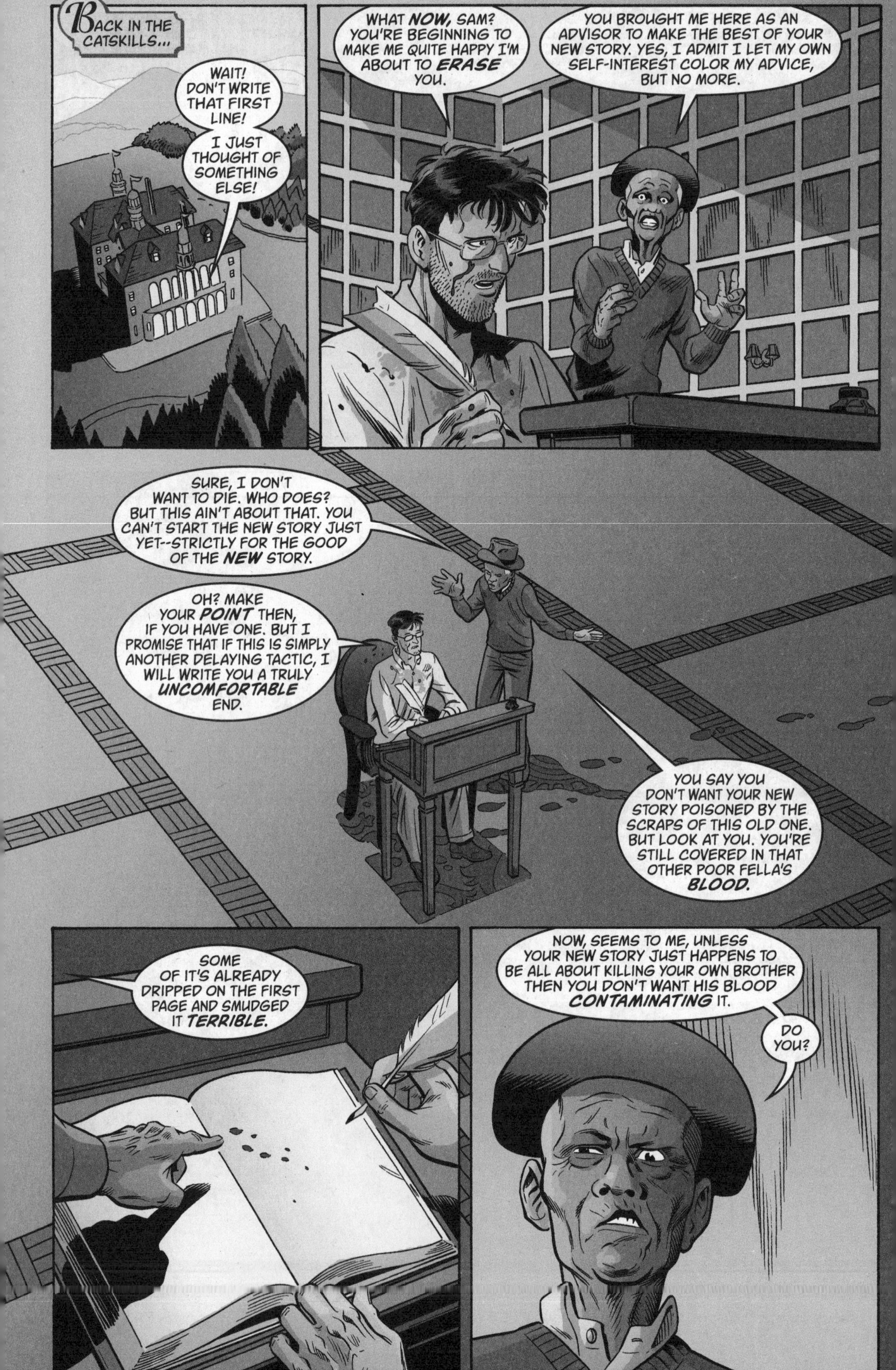
BACK IN THE CATSKILLS...
WAIT! DON'T WRITE THAT FIRST LINE!
I JUST THOUGHT OF SOMETHING ELSE!
WHAT NOW, SAM? YOU'RE BEGINNING TO MAKE ME QUITE HAPPY I'M ABOUT TO ERASE YOU.
YOU BROUGHT ME HERE AS AN ADVISOR TO MAKE THE BEST OF YOUR NEW STORY. YES, I ADMIT I LET MY OWN SELF-INTEREST COLOR MY ADVICE, BUT NO MORE.
SURE, I DON'T WANT TO DIE. WHO DOES? BUT THIS AIN'T ABOUT THAT. YOU CAN'T START THE NEW STORY JUST YET--STRICTLY FOR THE GOOD OF THE NEW STORY.
OH? MAKE YOUR POINT THEN, IF YOU HAVE ONE. BUT I PROMISE THAT IF THIS IS SIMPLY ANOTHER DELAYING TACTIC, I WILL WRITE YOU A TRULY UNCOMFORTABLE END.
YOU SAY YOU DON'T WANT YOUR NEW STORY POISONED BY THE SCRAPS OF THIS OLD ONE. BUT LOOK AT YOU. YOU'RE STILL COVERED IN THAT OTHER POOR FELLA'S BLOOD.
SOME OF IT'S ALREADY DRIPPED ON THE FIRST PAGE AND SMUDGED IT TERRIBLE.
NOW, SEEMS TO ME, UNLESS YOUR NEW STORY JUST HAPPENS TO BE ALL ABOUT KILLING YOUR OWN BROTHER THEN YOU DON'T WANT HIS BLOOD CONTAMINATING IT.
DO YOU?

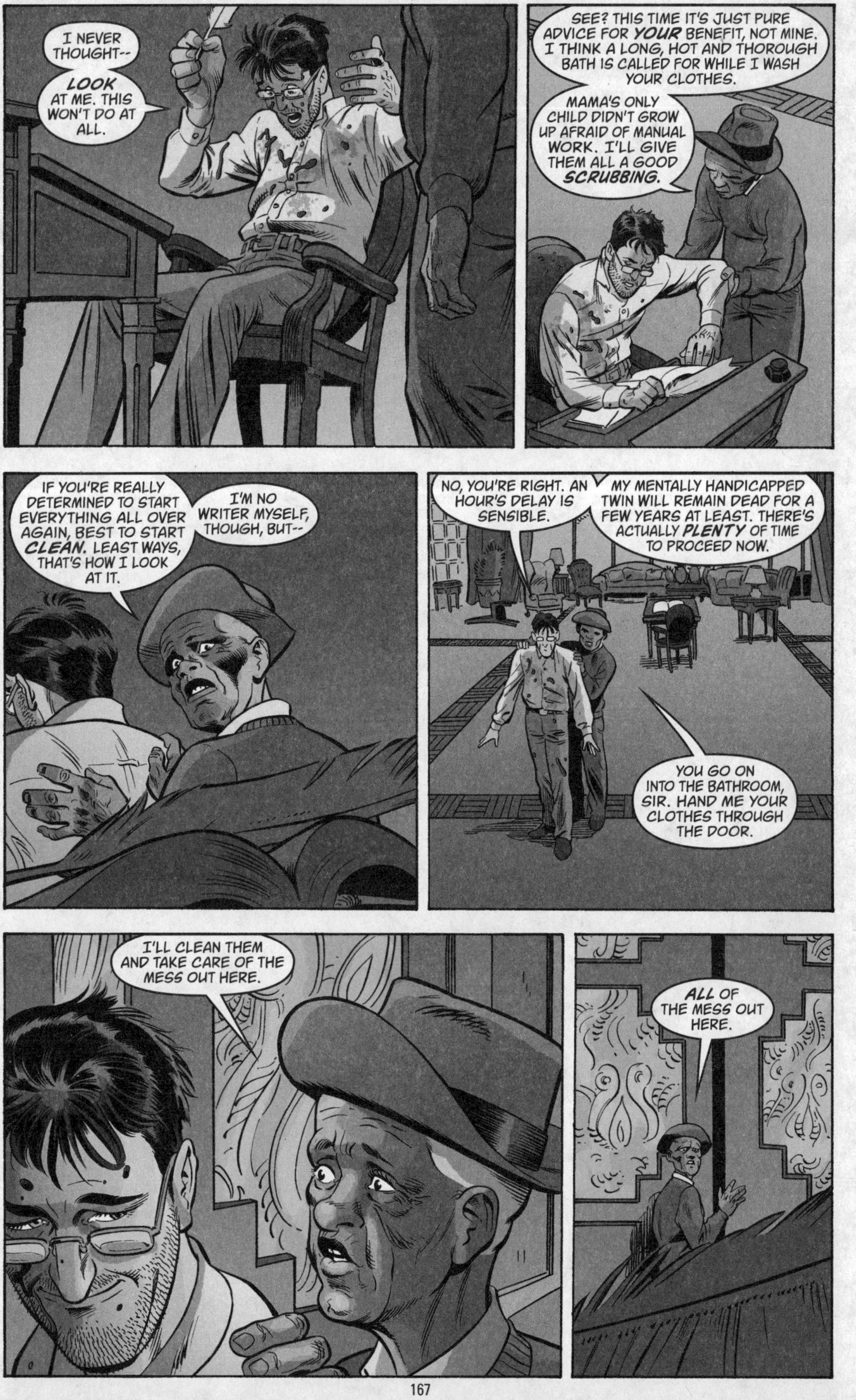
I NEVER THOUGHT--
LOOK AT ME. THIS WON'T DO AT ALL.
SEE? THIS TIME IT'S JUST PURE ADVICE FOR YOUR BENEFIT, NOT MINE. I THINK A LONG, HOT AND THOROUGH BATH IS CALLED FOR WHILE I WASH YOUR CLOTHES.
MAMA'S ONLY CHILD DIDN'T GROW UP AFRAID OF MANUAL WORK. I'LL GIVE THEM ALL A GOOD SCRUBBING.
IF YOU'RE REALLY DETERMINED TO START EVERYTHING ALL OVER AGAIN, BEST TO START CLEAN. LEAST WAYS, THAT'S HOW I LOOK AT IT.
I'M NO WRITER MYSELF, THOUGH, BUT--
NO, YOU'RE RIGHT. AN HOUR'S DELAY IS SENSIBLE.
MY MENTALLY HANDICAPPED TWIN WILL REMAIN DEAD FOR A FEW YEARS AT LEAST. THERE'S ACTUALLY PLENTY OF TIME TO PROCEED NOW.
YOU GO ON INTO THE BATHROOM, SIR. HAND ME YOUR CLOTHES THROUGH THE DOOR.
I'LL CLEAN THEM AND TAKE CARE OF THE MESS OUT HERE.
ALL OF THE MESS OUT HERE.

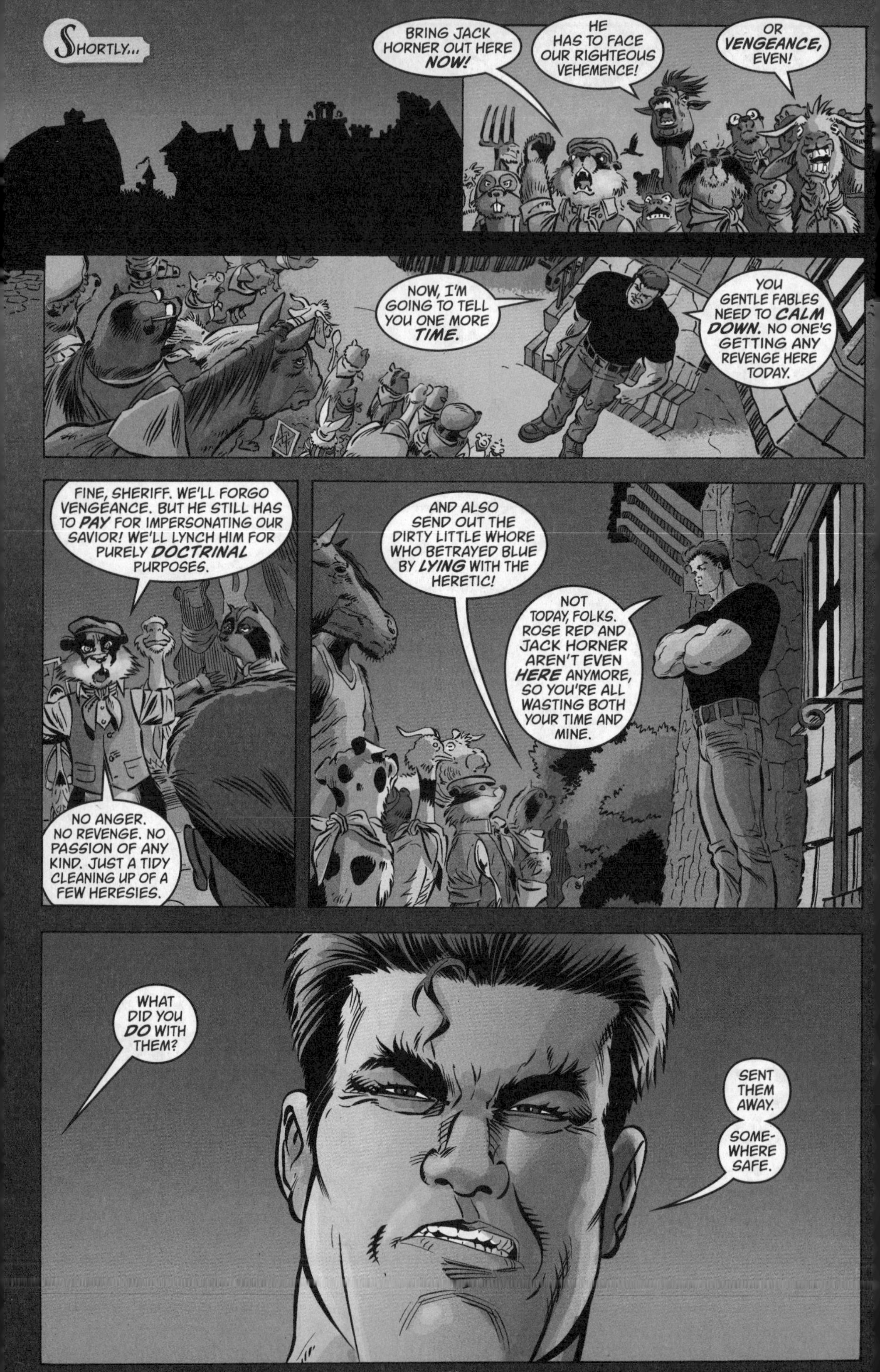
SHORTLY...
BRING JACK HORNER OUT HERE NOW!
HE HAS TO FACE OUR RIGHTEOUS VEHEMENCE!
OR VENGEANCE, EVEN!
NOW, I'M GOING TO TELL YOU ONE MORE TIME.
YOU GENTLE FABLES NEED TO CALM DOWN. NO ONE'S GETTING ANY REVENGE HERE TODAY.
FINE, SHERIFF. WE'LL FORGO VENGEANCE. BUT HE STILL HAS TO PAY FOR IMPERSONATING OUR SAVIOR! WE'LL LYNCH HIM FOR PURELY DOCTRINAL PURPOSES.
NO ANGER. NO REVENGE. NO PASSION OF ANY KIND. JUST A TIDY CLEANING UP OF A FEW HERESIES.
AND ALSO SEND OUT THE DIRTY LITTLE WHORE WHO BETRAYED BLUE BY LYING WITH THE HERETIC!
NOT TODAY, FOLKS. ROSE RED AND JACK HORNER AREN'T EVEN HERE ANYMORE, SO YOU'RE ALL WASTING BOTH YOUR TIME AND MINE.
WHAT DID YOU DO WITH THEM?
SENT THEM AWAY.
SOME-WHERE SAFE.

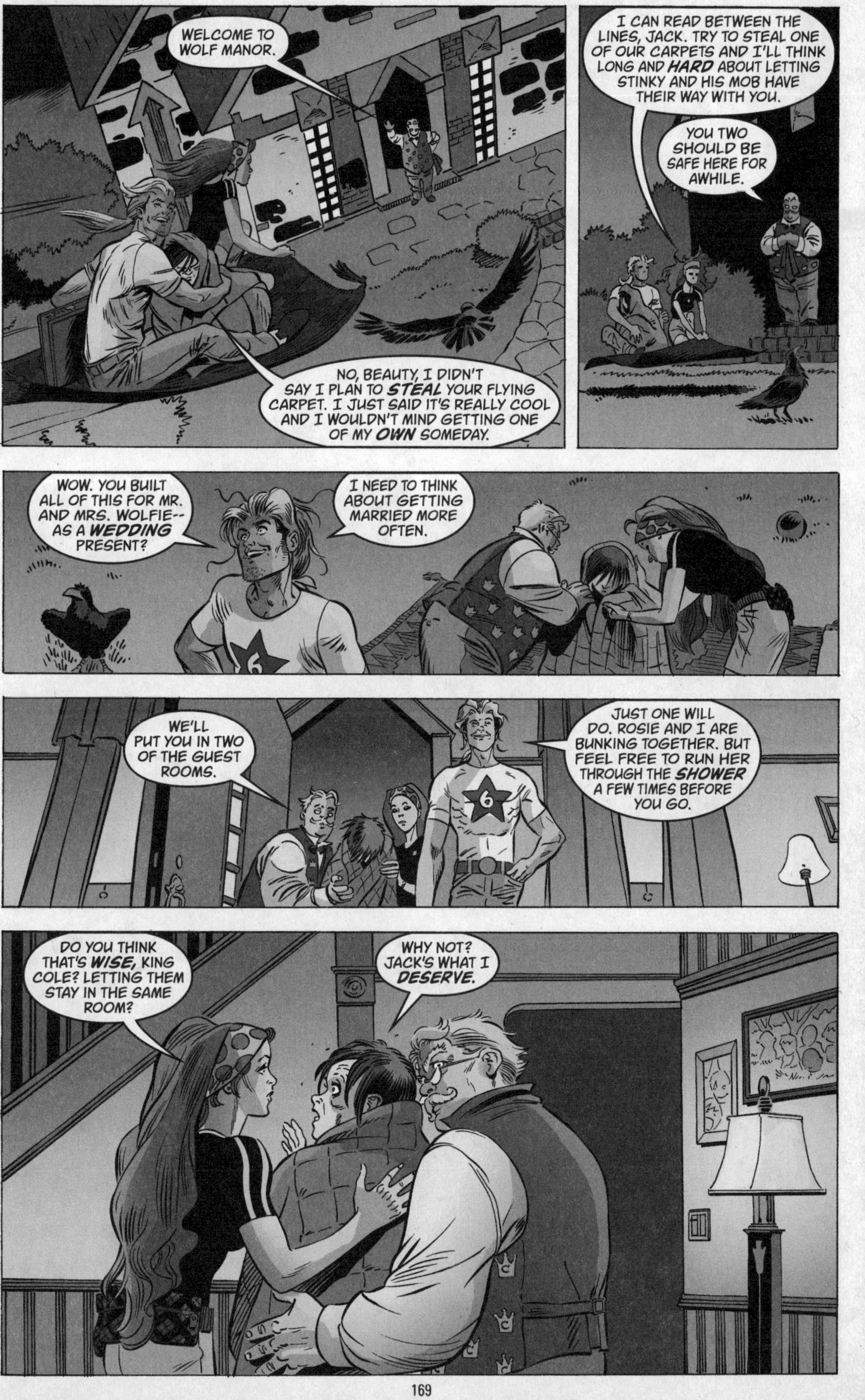
WELCOME TO WOLF MANOR.
NO, BEAUTY, I DIDN'T SAY I PLAN TO STEAL YOUR FLYING CARPET. I JUST SAID IT'S REALLY COOL AND I WOULDN'T MIND GETTING ONE OF MY OWN SOMEDAY.
I CAN READ BETWEEN THE LINES, JACK. TRY TO STEAL ONE OF OUR CARPETS AND I'LL THINK LONG AND HARD ABOUT LETTING STINKY AND HIS MOB HAVE THEIR WAY WITH YOU.
YOU TWO SHOULD BE SAFE HERE FOR AWHILE.
WOW. YOU BUILT ALL OF THIS FOR MR. AND MRS. WOLFIE-- AS A WEDDING PRESENT?
I NEED TO THINK ABOUT GETTING MARRIED MORE OFTEN.
WE'LL PUT YOU IN TWO OF THE GUEST ROOMS.
JUST ONE WILL DO. ROSIE AND I ARE BUNKING TOGETHER. BUT FEEL FREE TO RUN HER THROUGH THE SHOWER A FEW TIMES BEFORE YOU GO.
DO YOU THINK THAT'S WISE, KING COLE? LETTING THEM STAY IN THE SAME ROOM?
WHY NOT? JACK'S WHAT I DESERVE.

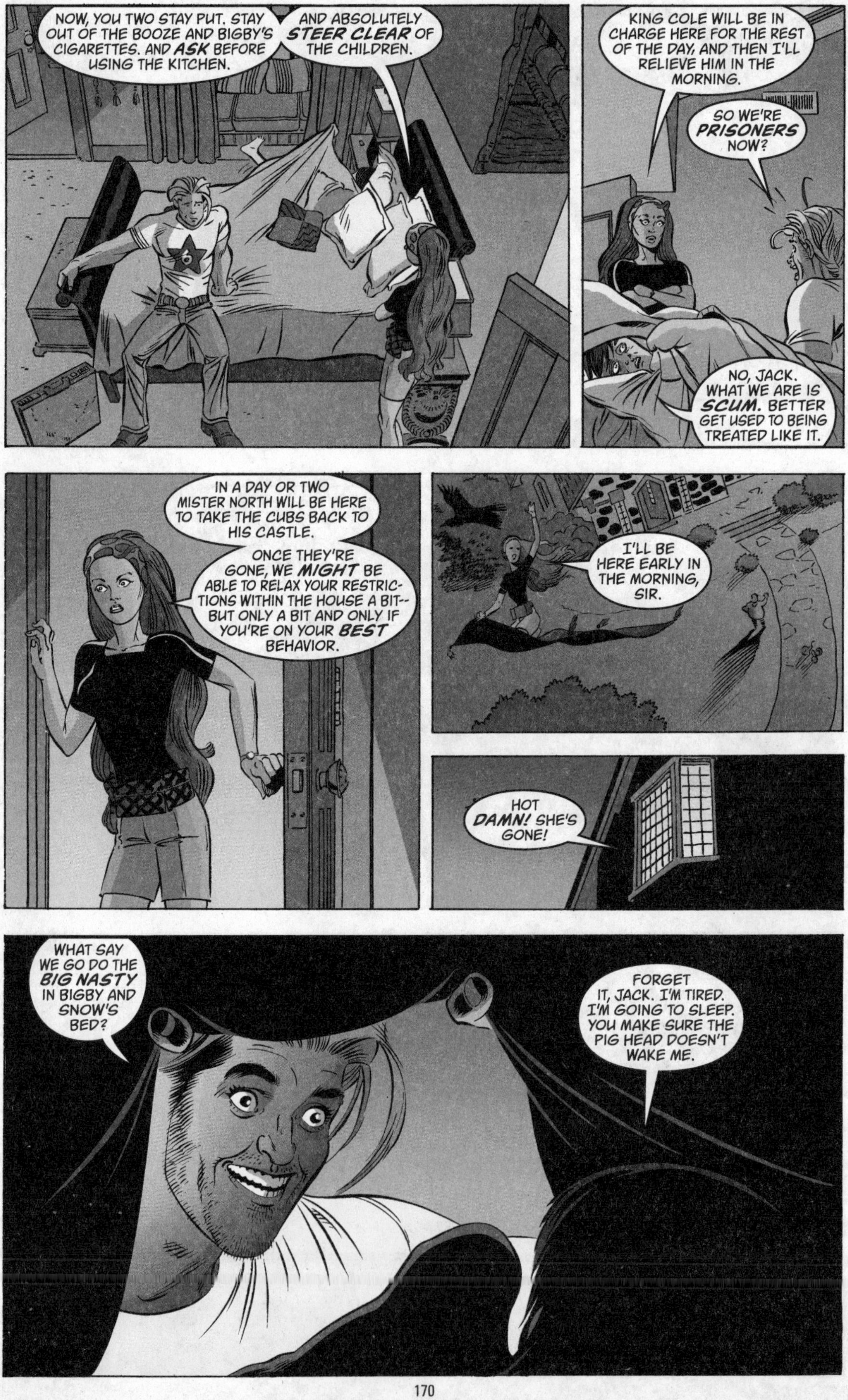
NOW, YOU TWO STAY PUT. STAY OUT OF THE BOOZE AND BIGBY'S CIGARETTES. AND ASK BEFORE USING THE KITCHEN.
AND ABSOLUTELY STEER CLEAR OF THE CHILDREN.
KING COLE WILL BE IN CHARGE HERE FOR THE REST OF THE DAY, AND THEN I'LL RELIEVE HIM IN THE MORNING.
SO WE'RE PRISONERS NOW?
NO, JACK. WHAT WE ARE IS SCUM. BETTER GET USED TO BEING TREATED LIKE IT.
IN A DAY OR TWO MISTER NORTH WILL BE HERE TO TAKE THE CUBS BACK TO HIS CASTLE.
ONCE THEY'RE GONE, WE MIGHT BE ABLE TO RELAX YOUR RESTRICTIONS WITHIN THE HOUSE A BIT-- BUT ONLY A BIT AND ONLY IF YOU'RE ON YOUR BEST BEHAVIOR.
I'LL BE HERE EARLY IN THE MORNING, SIR.
HOT DAMN! SHE'S GONE!
WHAT SAY WE GO DO THE BIG NASTY IN BIGBY AND SNOW'S BED?
FORGET IT, JACK. I'M TIRED. I'M GOING TO SLEEP. YOU MAKE SURE THE PIG HEAD DOESN'T WAKE ME.

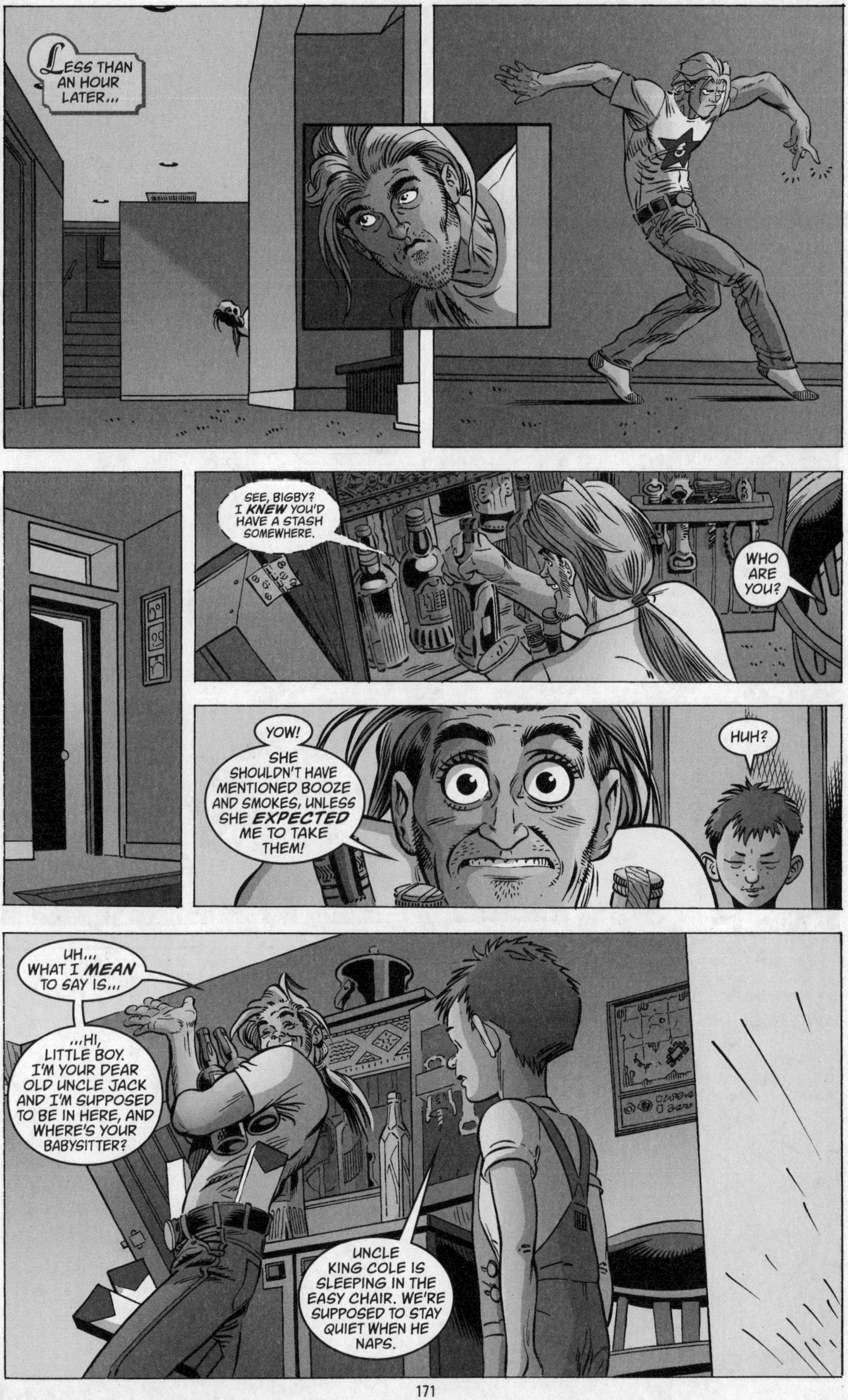
LESS THAN AN HOUR LATER...
SEE, BIGBY? I KNEW YOU'D HAVE A STASH SOMEWHERE.
WHO ARE YOU?
YOW!
SHE SHOULDN'T HAVE MENTIONED BOOZE AND SMOKES, UNLESS SHE EXPECTED ME TO TAKE THEM!
HUH?
UH... WHAT I MEAN TO SAY IS...
...HI, LITTLE BOY. I'M YOUR DEAR OLD UNCLE JACK AND I'M SUPPOSED TO BE IN HERE, AND WHERE'S YOUR BABYSITTER?
UNCLE KING COLE IS SLEEPING IN THE EASY CHAIR. WE'RE SUPPOSED TO STAY QUIET WHEN HE NAPS.

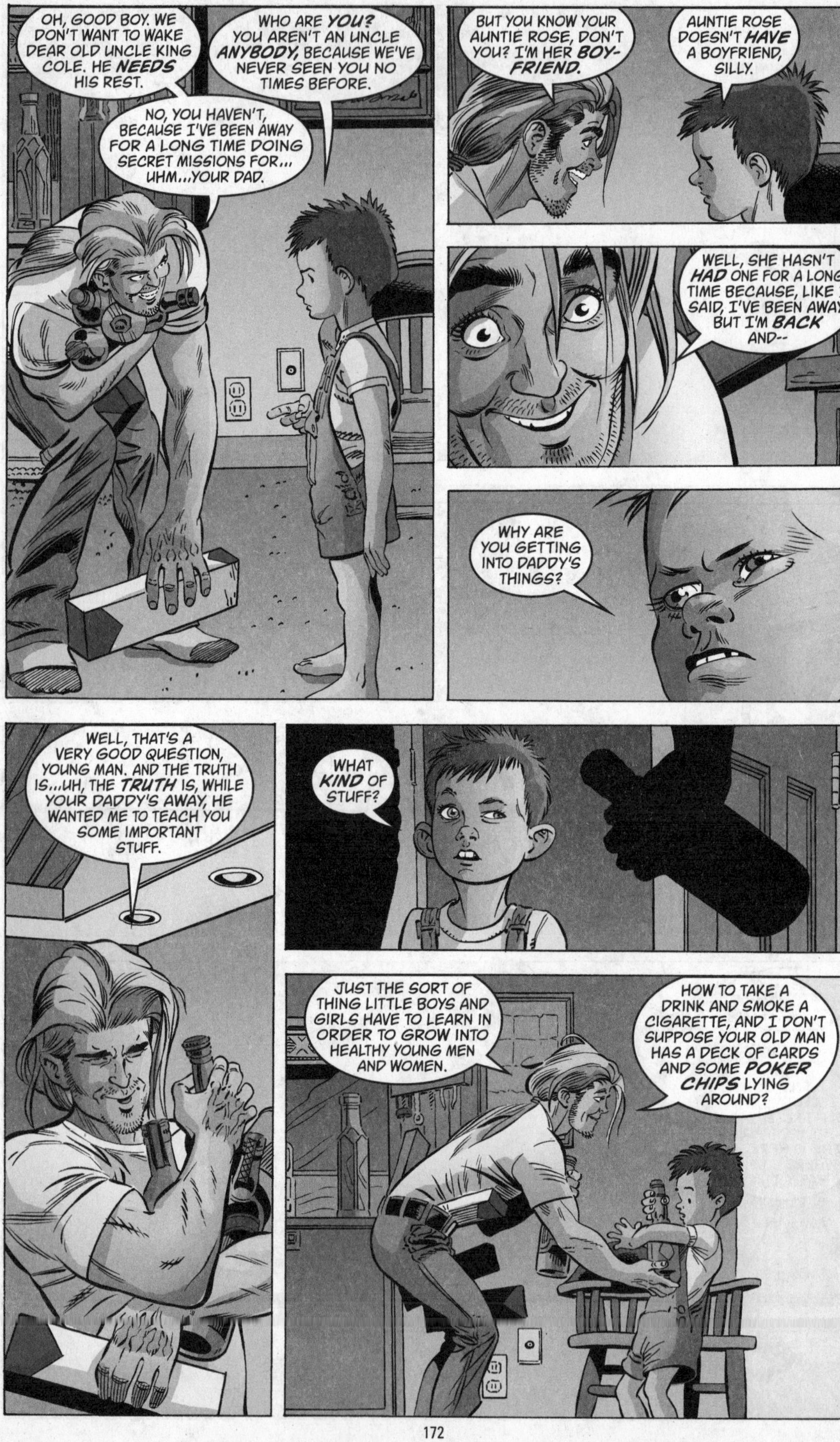
OH, GOOD BOY. WE DON'T WANT TO WAKE DEAR OLD UNCLE KING COLE. HE NEEDS HIS REST.
WHO ARE YOU? YOU AREN'T AN UNCLE ANYBODY, BECAUSE WE'VE NEVER SEEN YOU NO TIMES BEFORE.
NO, YOU HAVEN'T, BECAUSE I'VE BEEN AWAY FOR A LONG TIME DOING SECRET MISSIONS FOR... UHM...YOUR DAD.
BUT YOU KNOW YOUR AUNTIE ROSE, DON'T YOU? I'M HER BOY-FRIEND.
AUNTIE ROSE DOESN'T HAVE A BOYFRIEND, SILLY.
WELL, SHE HASN'T HAD ONE FOR A LONG TIME BECAUSE, LIKE I SAID, I'VE BEEN AWAY. BUT I'M BACK AND--
WHY ARE YOU GETTING INTO DADDY'S THINGS?
WELL, THAT'S A VERY GOOD QUESTION, YOUNG MAN. AND THE TRUTH IS...UH, THE TRUTH IS, WHILE YOUR DADDY'S AWAY, HE WANTED ME TO TEACH YOU SOME IMPORTANT STUFF.
WHAT KIND OF STUFF?
JUST THE SORT OF THING LITTLE BOYS AND GIRLS HAVE TO LEARN IN ORDER TO GROW INTO HEALTHY YOUNG MEN AND WOMEN.
HOW TO TAKE A DRINK AND SMOKE A CIGARETTE, AND I DON'T SUPPOSE YOUR OLD MAN HAS A DECK OF CARDS AND SOME POKER CHIPS LYING AROUND?

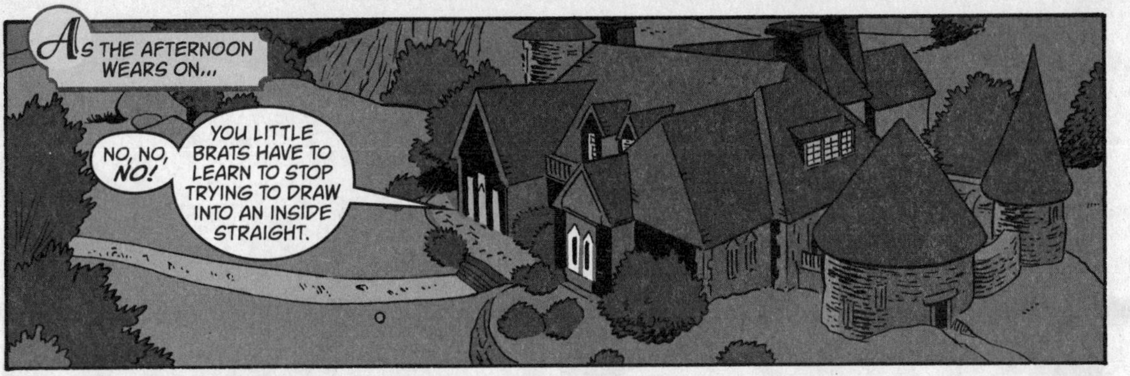
AS THE AFTERNOON WEARS ON...
NO, NO, NO!
YOU LITTLE BRATS HAVE TO LEARN TO STOP TRYING TO DRAW INTO AN INSIDE STRAIGHT.

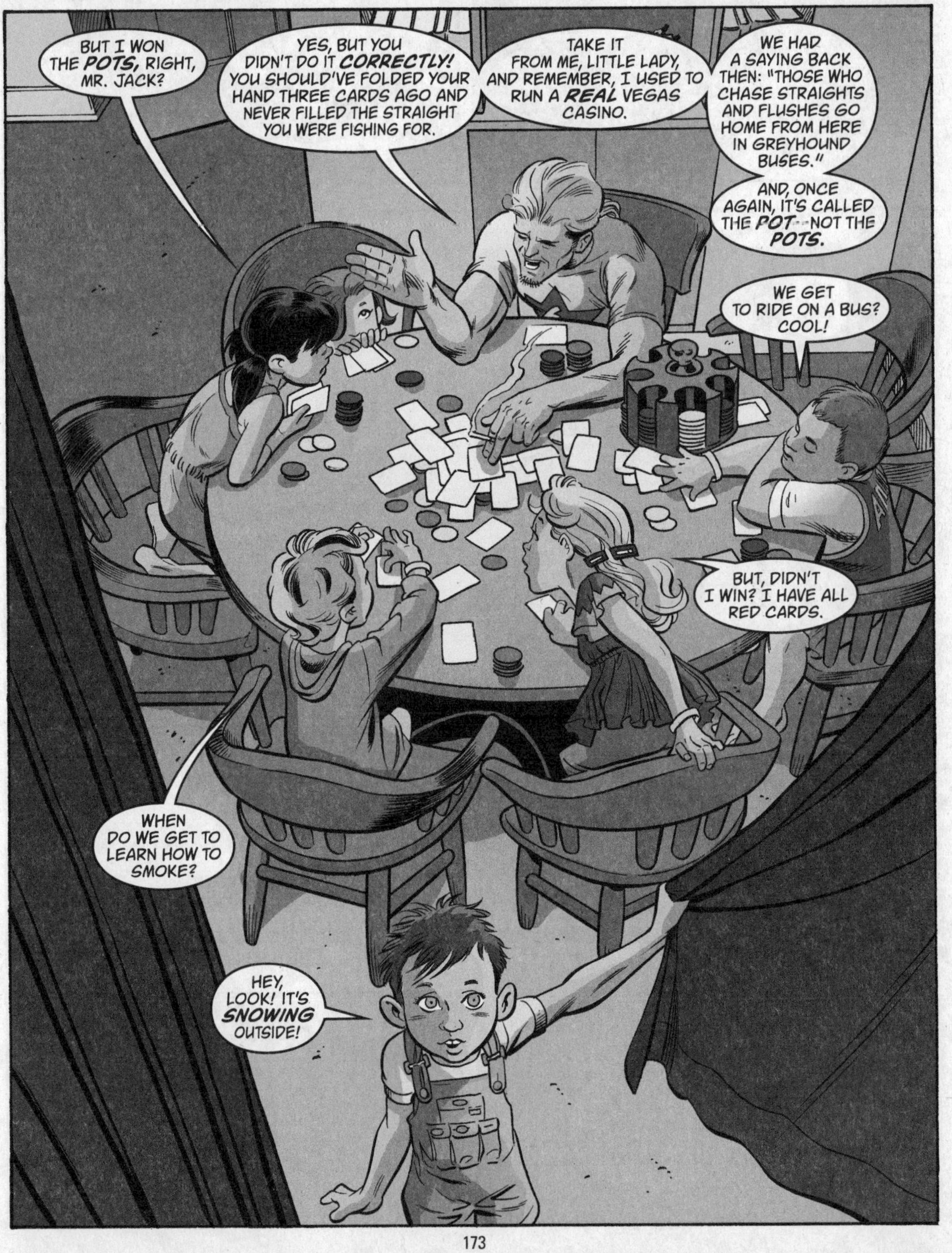
BUT I WON THE POTS, RIGHT, MR. JACK?
YES, BUT YOU DIDN'T DO IT CORRECTLY! YOU SHOULD'VE FOLDED YOUR HAND THREE CARDS AGO AND NEVER FILLED THE STRAIGHT YOU WERE FISHING FOR.
TAKE IT FROM ME, LITTLE LADY, AND REMEMBER, I USED TO RUN A REAL VEGAS CASINO.
WE HAD A SAYING BACK THEN: "THOSE WHO CHASE STRAIGHTS AND FLUSHES GO HOME FROM HERE IN GREYHOUND BUSES."
AND, ONCE AGAIN, IT'S CALLED THE POT--NOT THE POTS.
WE GET TO RIDE ON A BUS? COOL!
BUT, DIDN'T I WIN? I HAVE ALL RED CARDS.
WHEN DO WE GET TO LEARN HOW TO SMOKE?
HEY, LOOK! IT'S SNOWING OUTSIDE!

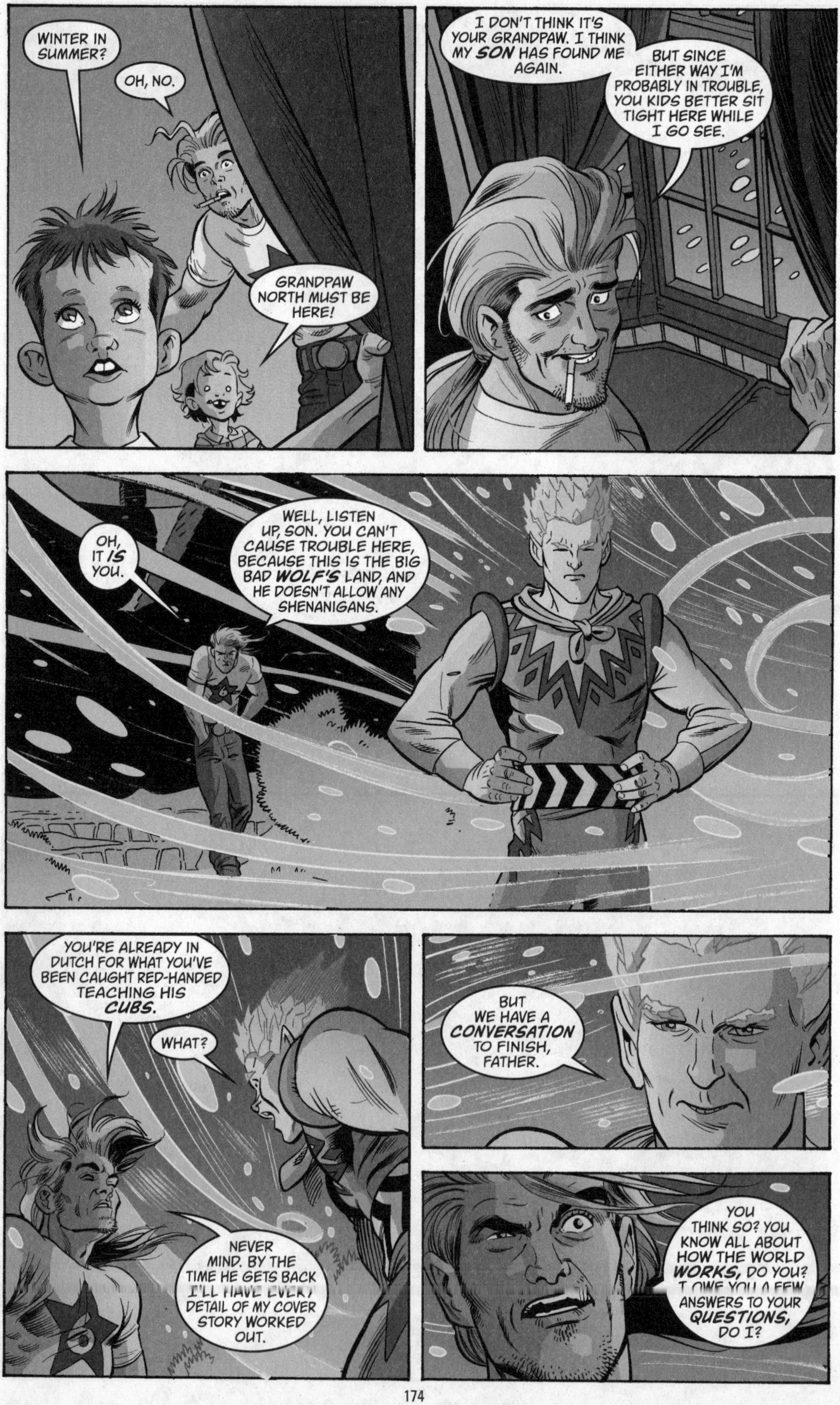
WINTER IN SUMMER?
OH, NO.
GRANDPAW NORTH MUST BE HERE!
I DON'T THINK IT'S YOUR GRANDPAW. I THINK MY SON HAS FOUND ME AGAIN.
BUT SINCE EITHER WAY I'M PROBABLY IN TROUBLE, YOU KIDS BETTER SIT TIGHT HERE WHILE I GO SEE.
OH, IT IS YOU.
WELL, LISTEN UP, SON. YOU CAN'T CAUSE TROUBLE HERE, BECAUSE THIS IS THE BIG BAD WOLF'S LAND, AND HE DOESN'T ALLOW ANY SHENANIGANS.
YOU'RE ALREADY IN DUTCH FOR WHAT YOU'VE BEEN CAUGHT RED-HANDED TEACHING HIS CUBS.
WHAT?
NEVER MIND. BY THE TIME HE GETS BACK I'LL HAVE EVERY DETAIL OF MY COVER STORY WORKED OUT.
BUT WE HAVE A CONVERSATION TO FINISH, FATHER.
YOU THINK SO? YOU KNOW ALL ABOUT HOW THE WORLD WORKS, DO YOU? I OWE YOU A FEW ANSWERS TO YOUR QUESTIONS, DO I?

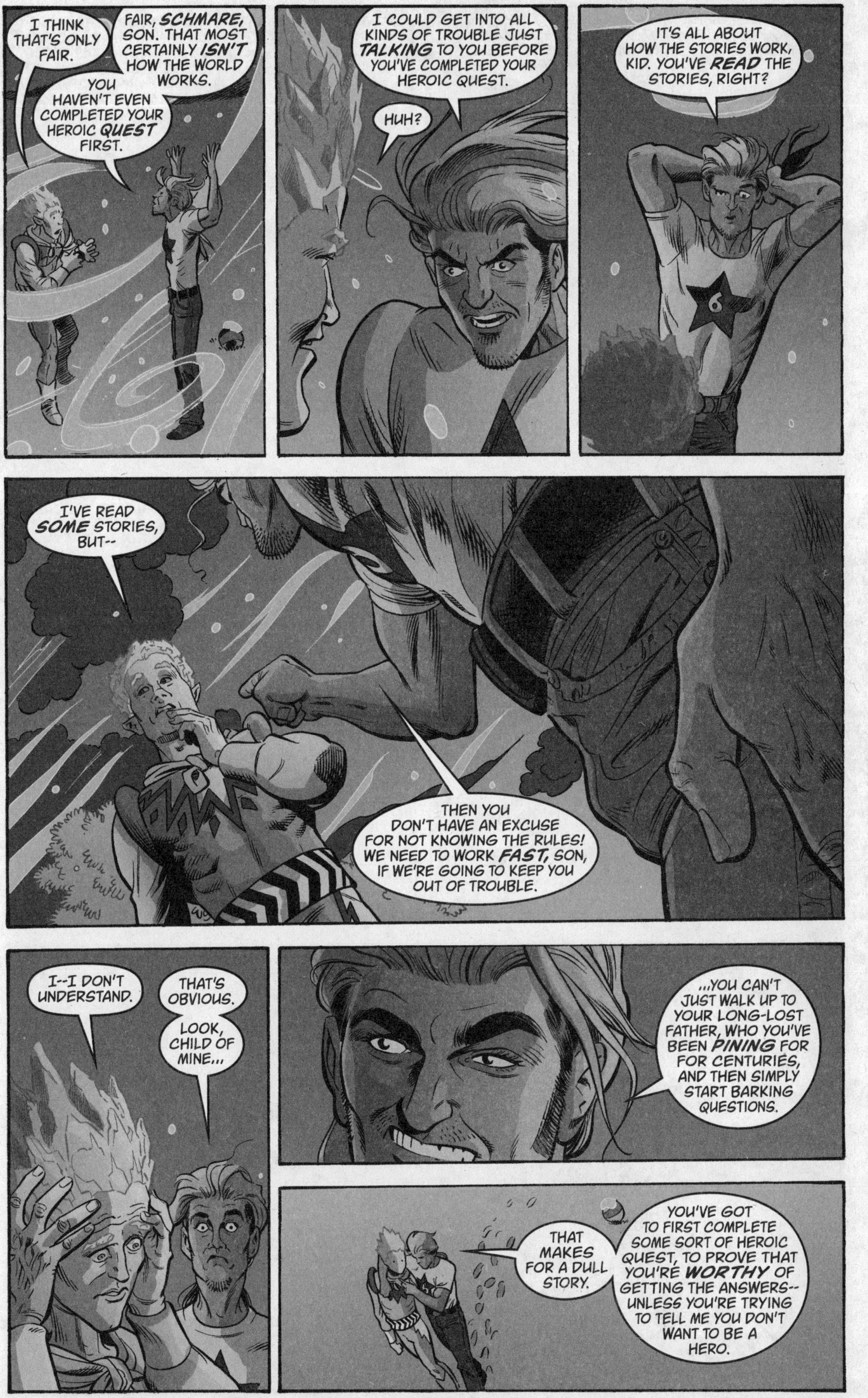
I THINK THAT'S ONLY FAIR.
FAIR, SCHMARE, SON. THAT MOST CERTAINLY ISN'T HOW THE WORLD WORKS.
YOU HAVEN'T EVEN COMPLETED YOUR HEROIC QUEST FIRST.
I COULD GET INTO ALL KINDS OF TROUBLE JUST TALKING TO YOU BEFORE YOU'VE COMPLETED YOUR HEROIC QUEST.
HUH?
IT'S ALL ABOUT HOW THE STORIES WORK, KID. YOU'VE READ THE STORIES, RIGHT?
I'VE READ SOME STORIES, BUT--
THEN YOU DON'T HAVE AN EXCUSE FOR NOT KNOWING THE RULES! WE NEED TO WORK FAST, SON, IF WE'RE GOING TO KEEP YOU OUT OF TROUBLE.
I--I DON'T UNDERSTAND.
THAT'S OBVIOUS.
LOOK, CHILD OF MINE...
...YOU CAN'T JUST WALK UP TO YOUR LONG-LOST FATHER, WHO YOU'VE BEEN PINING FOR FOR CENTURIES, AND THEN SIMPLY START BARKING QUESTIONS.
THAT MAKES FOR A DULL STORY.
YOU'VE GOT TO FIRST COMPLETE SOME SORT OF HEROIC QUEST, TO PROVE THAT YOU'RE WORTHY OF GETTING THE ANSWERS-- UNLESS YOU'RE TRYING TO TELL ME YOU DON'T WANT TO BE A HERO.

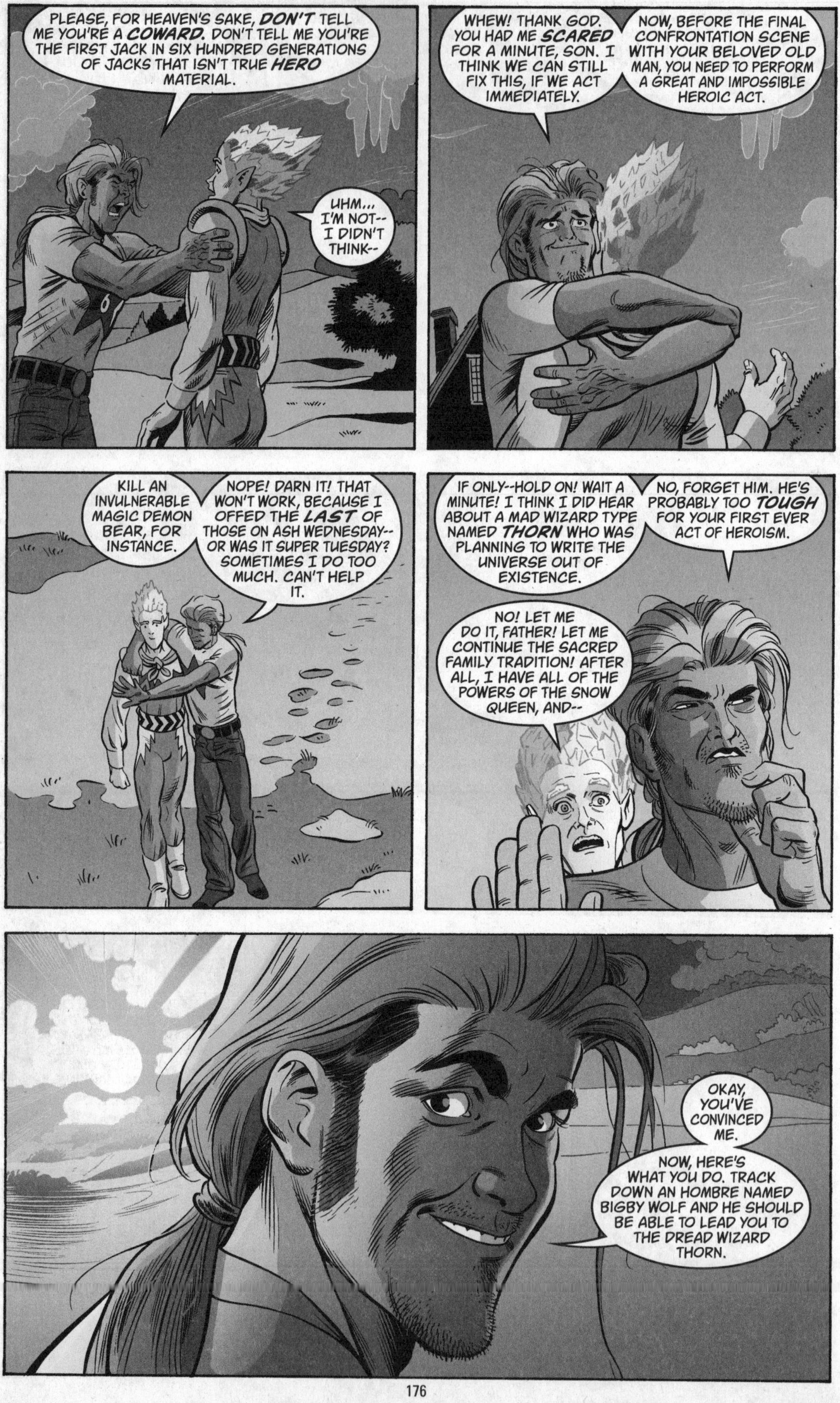
PLEASE, FOR HEAVEN'S SAKE, DON'T TELL ME YOU'RE A COWARD. DON'T TELL ME YOU'RE THE FIRST JACK IN SIX HUNDRED GENERATIONS OF JACKS THAT ISN'T TRUE HERO MATERIAL.
UHM... I'M NOT-- I DIDN'T THINK--
WHEW! THANK GOD. YOU HAD ME SCARED FOR A MINUTE, SON. I THINK WE CAN STILL FIX THIS, IF WE ACT IMMEDIATELY.
NOW, BEFORE THE FINAL CONFRONTATION SCENE WITH YOUR BELOVED OLD MAN, YOU NEED TO PERFORM A GREAT AND IMPOSSIBLE HEROIC ACT.
KILL AN INVULNERABLE MAGIC DEMON BEAR, FOR INSTANCE.
NOPE! DARN IT! THAT WON'T WORK, BECAUSE I OFFED THE LAST OF THOSE ON ASH WEDNESDAY-- OR WAS IT SUPER TUESDAY? SOMETIMES I DO TOO MUCH. CAN'T HELP IT.
IF ONLY--HOLD ON! WAIT A MINUTE! I THINK I DID HEAR ABOUT A MAD WIZARD TYPE NAMED THORN WHO WAS PLANNING TO WRITE THE UNIVERSE OUT OF EXISTENCE.
NO, FORGET HIM. HE'S PROBABLY TOO TOUGH FOR YOUR FIRST EVER ACT OF HEROISM.
NO! LET ME DO IT, FATHER! LET ME CONTINUE THE SACRED FAMILY TRADITION! AFTER ALL, I HAVE ALL OF THE POWERS OF THE SNOW QUEEN, AND--
OKAY, YOU'VE CONVINCED ME.
NOW, HERE'S WHAT YOU DO. TRACK DOWN AN HOMBRE NAMED BIGBY WOLF AND HE SHOULD BE ABLE TO LEAD YOU TO THE DREAD WIZARD THORN.

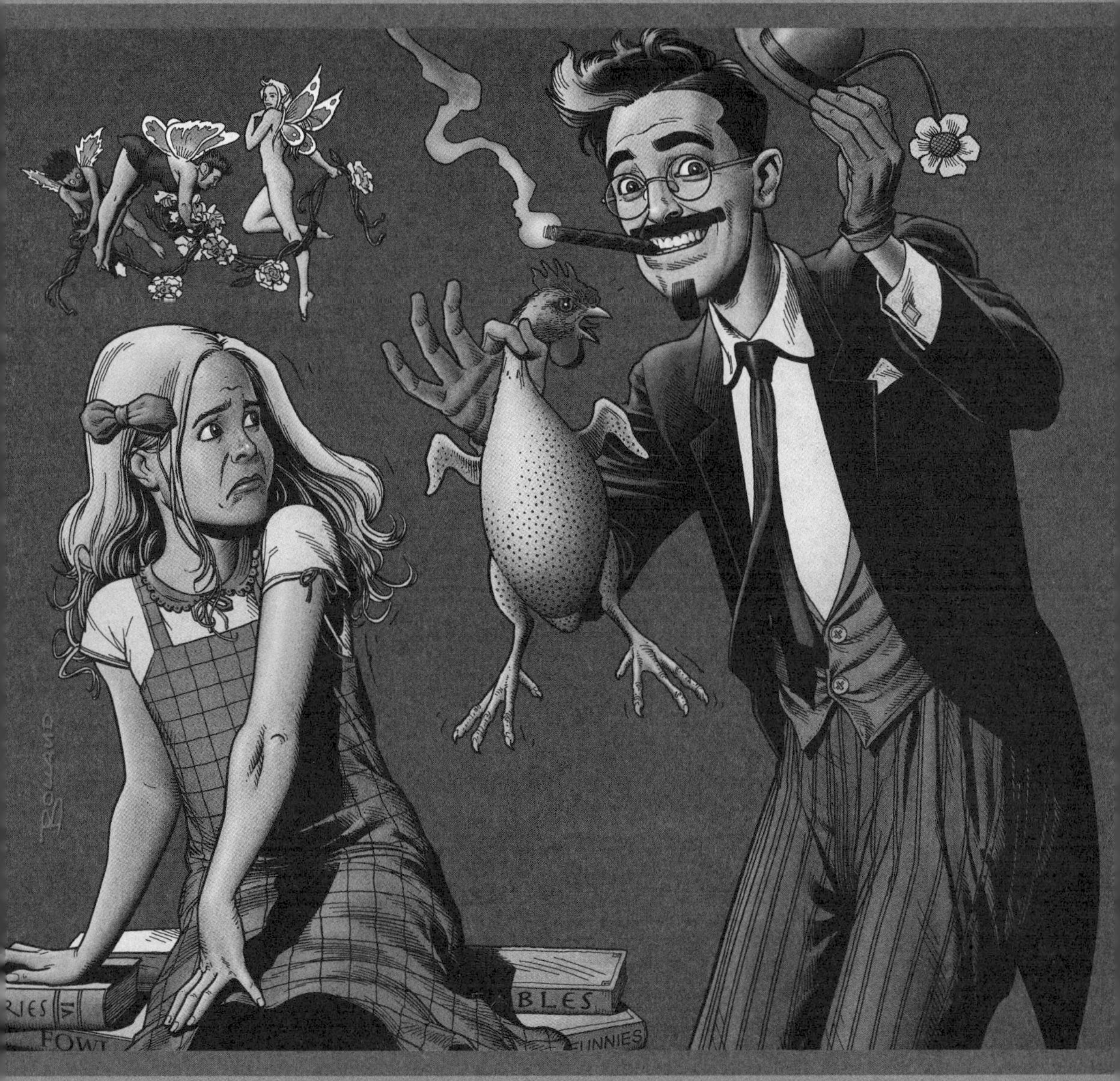
BOLLAND

"That was screaming we heard, wasn't it?"

The Great FABLES Crossover part 8 of 9

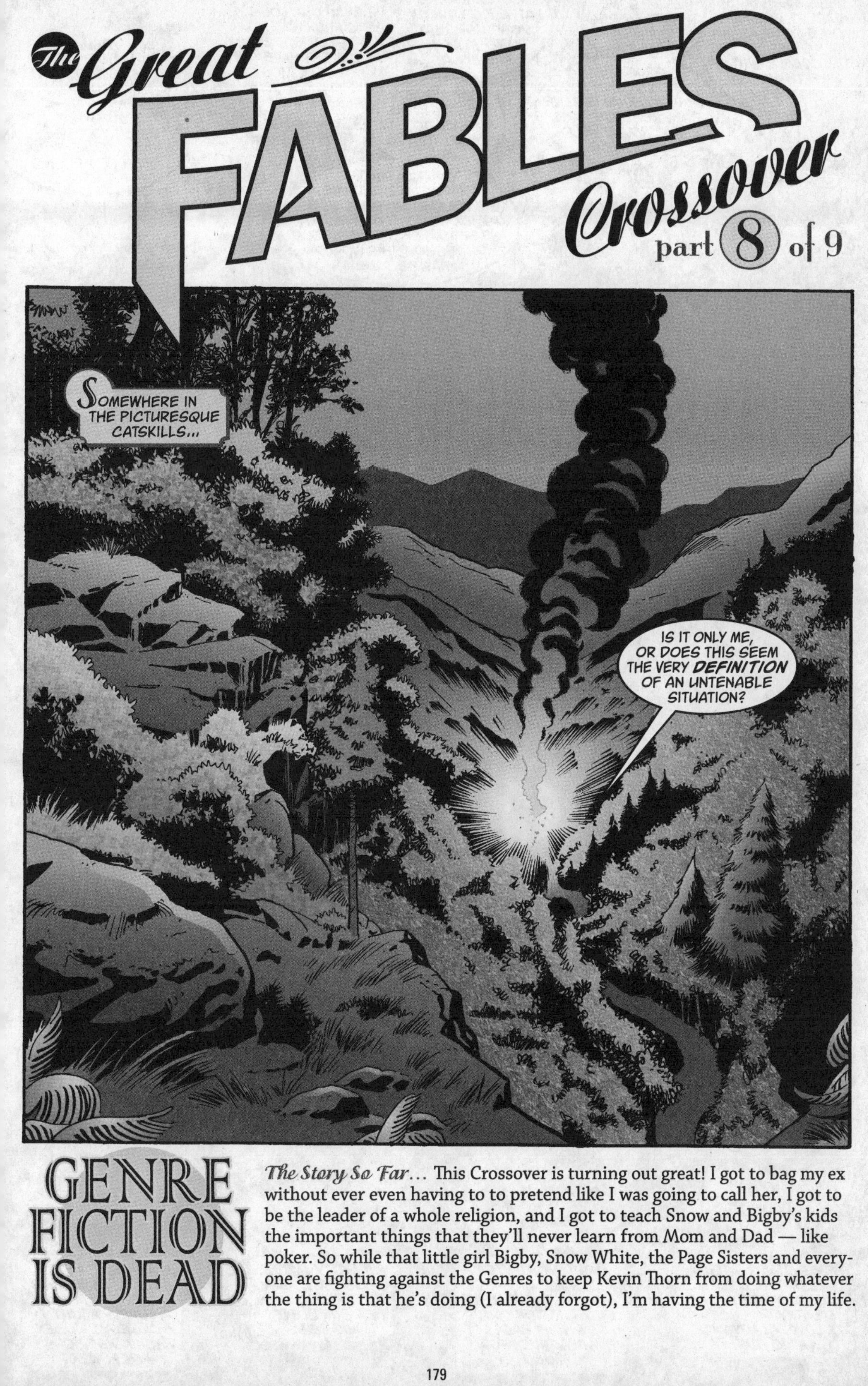
SOMEWHERE IN THE PICTURESQUE CATSKILLS...
IS IT ONLY ME, OR DOES THIS SEEM THE VERY DEFINITION OF AN UNTENABLE SITUATION?

GENRE FICTION IS DEAD

The Story So Far... This Crossover is turning out great! I got to bag my ex without ever even having to to pretend like I was going to call her, I got to be the leader of a whole religion, and I got to teach Snow and Bigby's kids the important things that they'll never learn from Mom and Dad — like poker. So while that little girl Bigby, Snow White, the Page Sisters and everyone are fighting against the Genres to keep Kevin Thorn from doing whatever the thing is that he's doing (I already forgot), I'm having the time of my life.

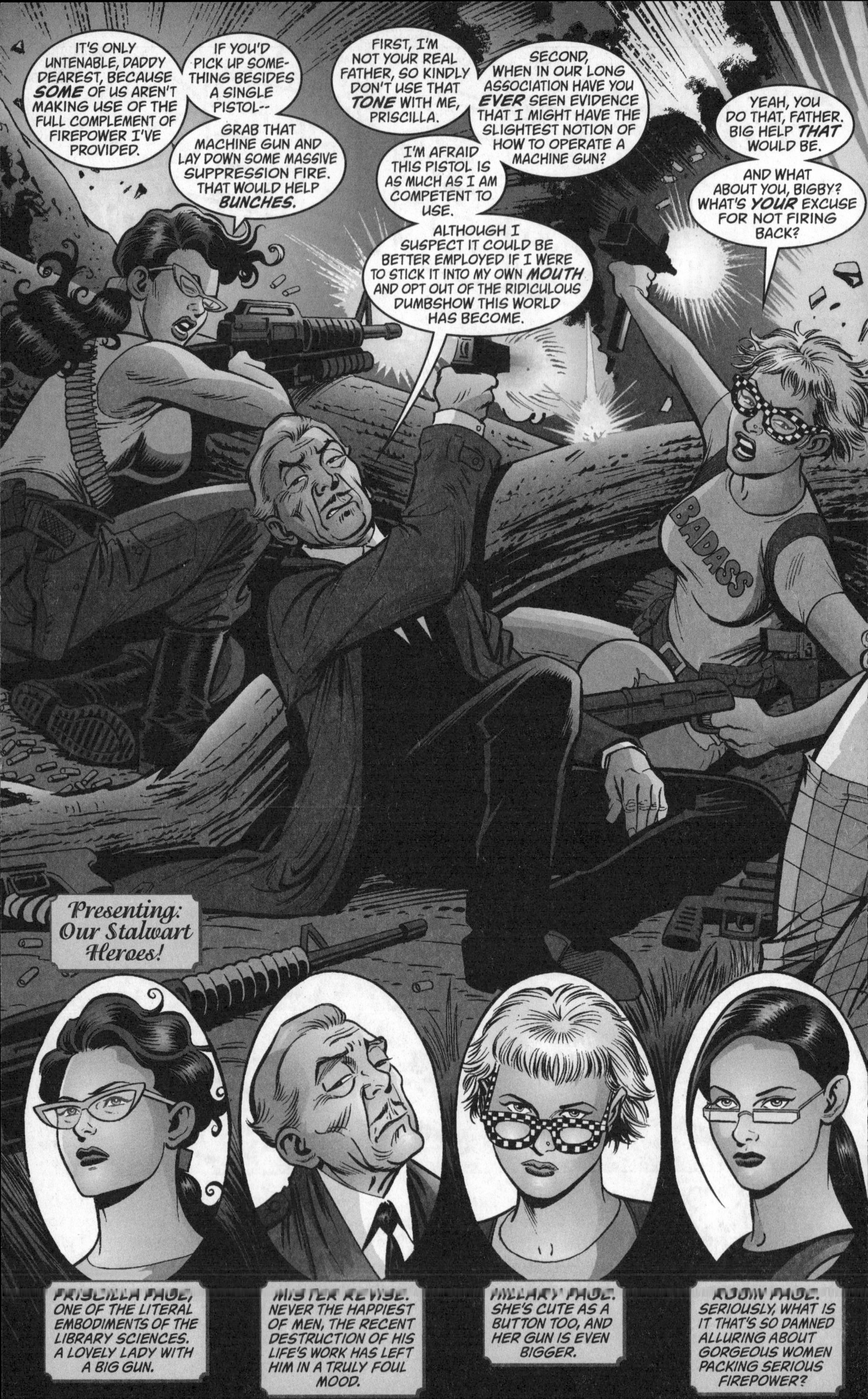

IT'S ONLY UNTENABLE, DADDY DEAREST, BECAUSE SOME OF US AREN'T MAKING USE OF THE FULL COMPLEMENT OF FIREPOWER I'VE PROVIDED.
IF YOU'D PICK UP SOMETHING BESIDES A SINGLE PISTOL--
GRAB THAT MACHINE GUN AND LAY DOWN SOME MASSIVE SUPPRESSION FIRE. THAT WOULD HELP BUNCHES.
FIRST, I'M NOT YOUR REAL FATHER, SO KINDLY DON'T USE THAT TONE WITH ME, PRISCILLA.
SECOND, WHEN IN OUR LONG ASSOCIATION HAVE YOU EVER SEEN EVIDENCE THAT I MIGHT HAVE THE SLIGHTEST NOTION OF HOW TO OPERATE A MACHINE GUN?
I'M AFRAID THIS PISTOL IS AS MUCH AS I AM COMPETENT TO USE.
ALTHOUGH I SUSPECT IT COULD BE BETTER EMPLOYED IF I WERE TO STICK IT INTO MY OWN MOUTH AND OPT OUT OF THE RIDICULOUS DUMBSHOW THIS WORLD HAS BECOME.
YEAH, YOU DO THAT, FATHER. BIG HELP THAT WOULD BE.
AND WHAT ABOUT YOU, BIGBY? WHAT'S YOUR EXCUSE FOR NOT FIRING BACK?
BADASS
Presenting: Our Stalwart Heroes!
PRISCILLA PAGE, ONE OF THE LITERAL EMBODIMENTS OF THE LIBRARY SCIENCES. A LOVELY LADY WITH A BIG GUN.
MISTER REVISE. NEVER THE HAPPIEST OF MEN, THE RECENT DESTRUCTION OF HIS LIFE'S WORK HAS LEFT HIM IN A TRULY FOUL MOOD.
HILLARY PAGE. SHE'S CUTE AS A BUTTON TOO, AND HER GUN IS EVEN BIGGER.
ROBIN PAGE. SERIOUSLY, WHAT IS IT THAT'S SO DAMNED ALLURING ABOUT GORGEOUS WOMEN PACKING SERIOUS FIREPOWER?

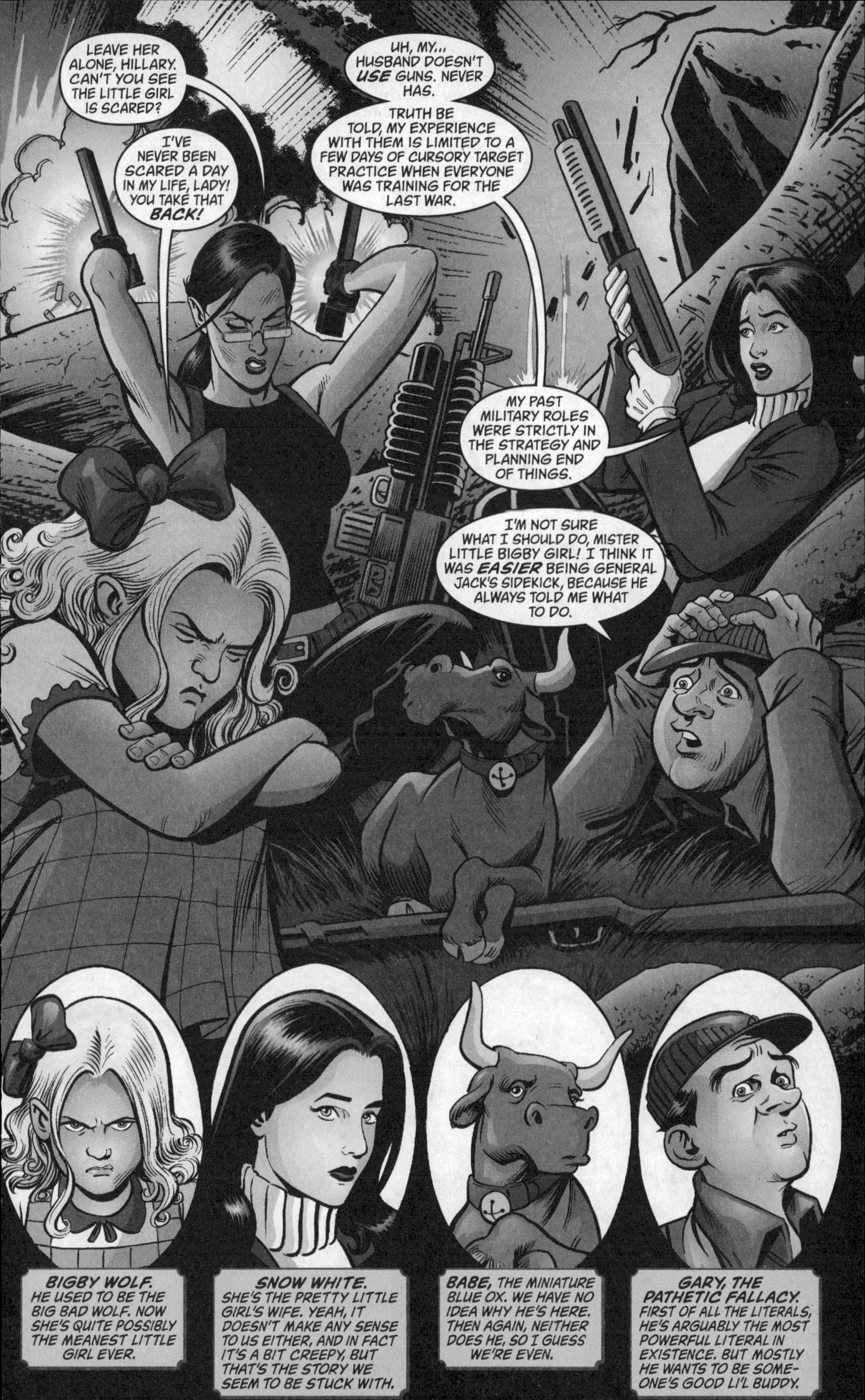
LEAVE HER ALONE, HILLARY. CAN'T YOU SEE THE LITTLE GIRL IS SCARED?
I'VE NEVER BEEN SCARED A DAY IN MY LIFE, LADY! YOU TAKE THAT BACK!
UH, MY... HUSBAND DOESN'T USE GUNS. NEVER HAS.
TRUTH BE TOLD, MY EXPERIENCE WITH THEM IS LIMITED TO A FEW DAYS OF CURSORY TARGET PRACTICE WHEN EVERYONE WAS TRAINING FOR THE LAST WAR.
MY PAST MILITARY ROLES WERE STRICTLY IN THE STRATEGY AND PLANNING END OF THINGS.
I'M NOT SURE WHAT I SHOULD DO, MISTER LITTLE BIGBY GIRL! I THINK IT WAS EASIER BEING GENERAL JACK'S SIDEKICK, BECAUSE HE ALWAYS TOLD ME WHAT TO DO.
BIGBY WOLF. HE USED TO BE THE BIG BAD WOLF. NOW SHE'S QUITE POSSIBLY THE MEANEST LITTLE GIRL EVER.
SNOW WHITE. SHE'S THE PRETTY LITTLE GIRL'S WIFE. YEAH, IT DOESN'T MAKE ANY SENSE TO US EITHER, AND IN FACT IT'S A BIT CREEPY, BUT THAT'S THE STORY WE SEEM TO BE STUCK WITH.
BABE, THE MINIATURE BLUE OX. WE HAVE NO IDEA WHY HE'S HERE. THEN AGAIN, NEITHER DOES HE, SO I GUESS WE'RE EVEN.
GARY, THE PATHETIC FALLACY. FIRST OF ALL THE LITERALS, HE'S ARGUABLY THE MOST POWERFUL LITERAL IN EXISTENCE. BUT MOSTLY HE WANTS TO BE SOME-ONE'S GOOD LI'L BUDDY.

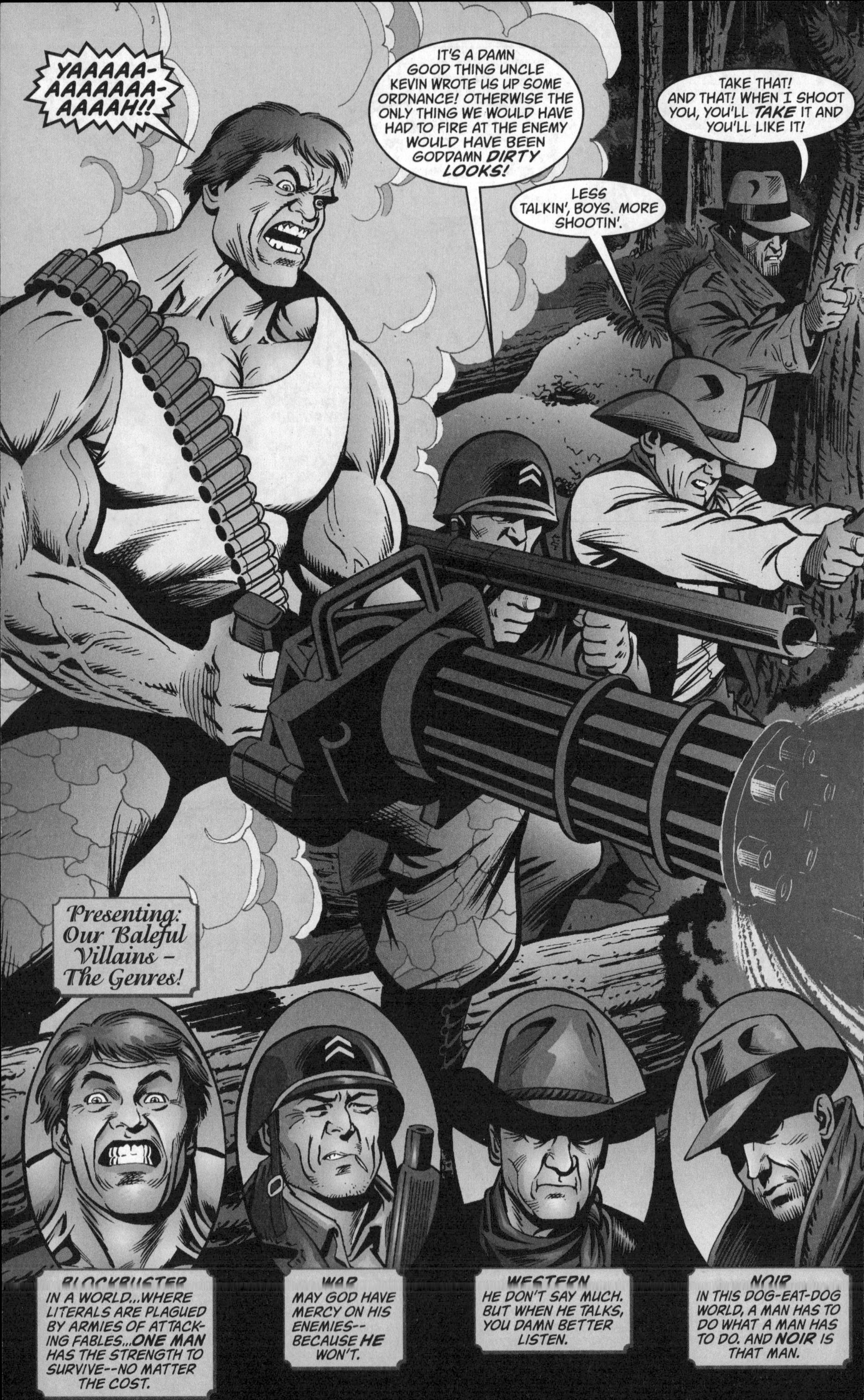

YAAAAA-AAAAAAAA-AAAAH!!
IT'S A DAMN GOOD THING UNCLE KEVIN WROTE US UP SOME ORDNANCE! OTHERWISE THE ONLY THING WE WOULD HAVE HAD TO FIRE AT THE ENEMY WOULD HAVE BEEN GODDAMN DIRTY LOOKS!
TAKE THAT! AND THAT! WHEN I SHOOT YOU, YOU'LL TAKE IT AND YOU'LL LIKE IT!
LESS TALKIN', BOYS. MORE SHOOTIN'.
Presenting: Our Baleful Villains – The Genres!
BLOCKBUSTER
IN A WORLD...WHERE LITERALS ARE PLAGUED BY ARMIES OF ATTACKING FABLES...ONE MAN HAS THE STRENGTH TO SURVIVE--NO MATTER THE COST.
WAR
MAY GOD HAVE MERCY ON HIS ENEMIES--BECAUSE HE WON'T.
WESTERN
HE DON'T SAY MUCH. BUT WHEN HE TALKS, YOU DAMN BETTER LISTEN.
NOIR
IN THIS DOG-EAT-DOG WORLD, A MAN HAS TO DO WHAT A MAN HAS TO DO. AND NOIR IS THAT MAN.

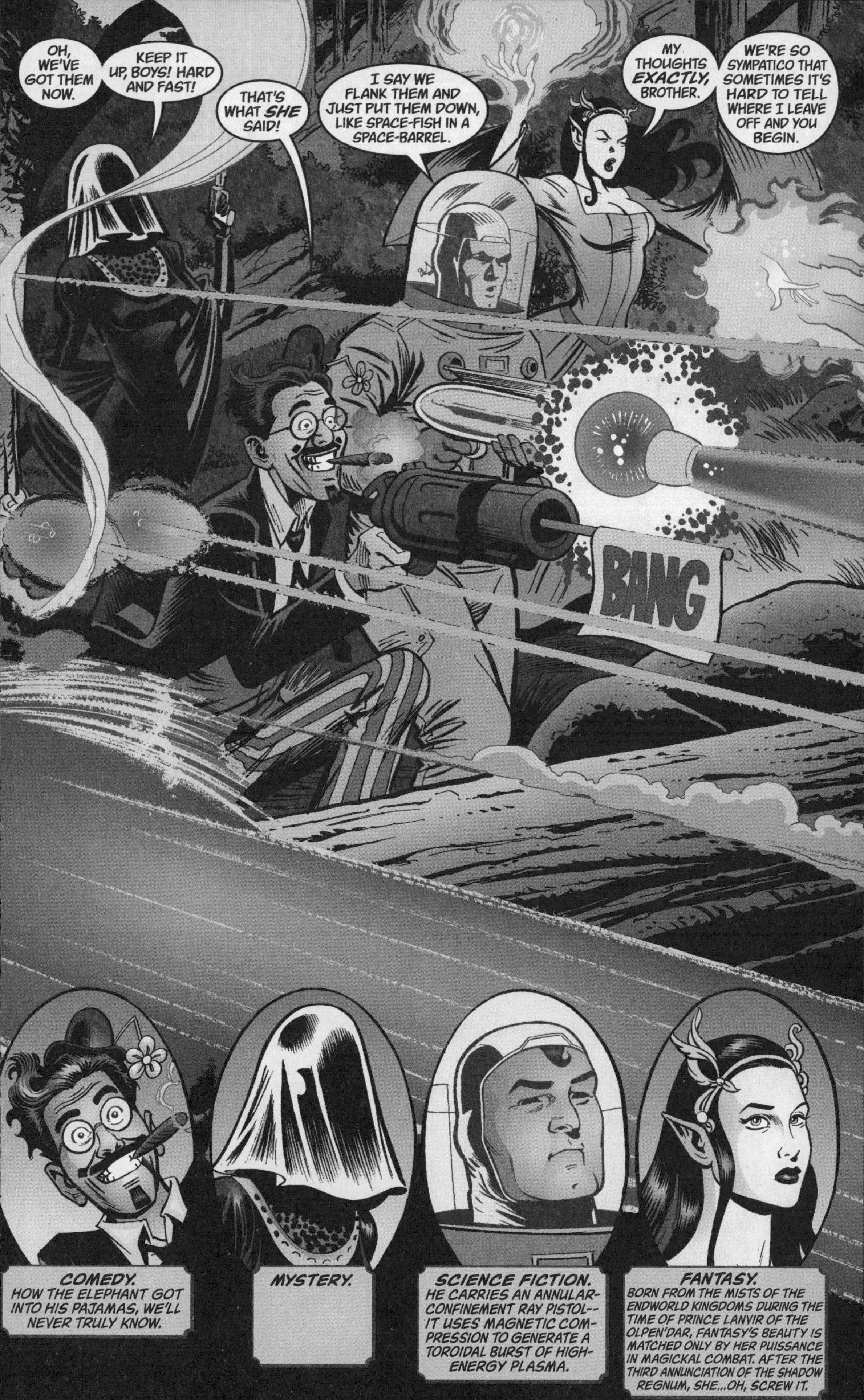
OH, WE'VE GOT THEM NOW.
KEEP IT UP, BOYS! HARD AND FAST!
THAT'S WHAT SHE SAID!
I SAY WE FLANK THEM AND JUST PUT THEM DOWN, LIKE SPACE-FISH IN A SPACE-BARREL.
MY THOUGHTS EXACTLY, BROTHER.
WE'RE SO SYMPATICO THAT SOMETIMES IT'S HARD TO TELL WHERE I LEAVE OFF AND YOU BEGIN.
BANG
COMEDY. HOW THE ELEPHANT GOT INTO HIS PAJAMAS, WE'LL NEVER TRULY KNOW.
MYSTERY.
SCIENCE FICTION. HE CARRIES AN ANNULAR-CONFINEMENT RAY PISTOL--IT USES MAGNETIC COMPRESSION TO GENERATE A TOROIDAL BURST OF HIGH-ENERGY PLASMA.
FANTASY. BORN FROM THE MISTS OF THE ENDWORLD KINGDOMS DURING THE TIME OF PRINCE LANVIR OF THE OLPEN'DAR, FANTASY'S BEAUTY IS MATCHED ONLY BY HER PUISSANCE IN MAGICKAL COMBAT. AFTER THE THIRD ANNUNCIATION OF THE SHADOW REGNUM, SHE...OH, SCREW IT.

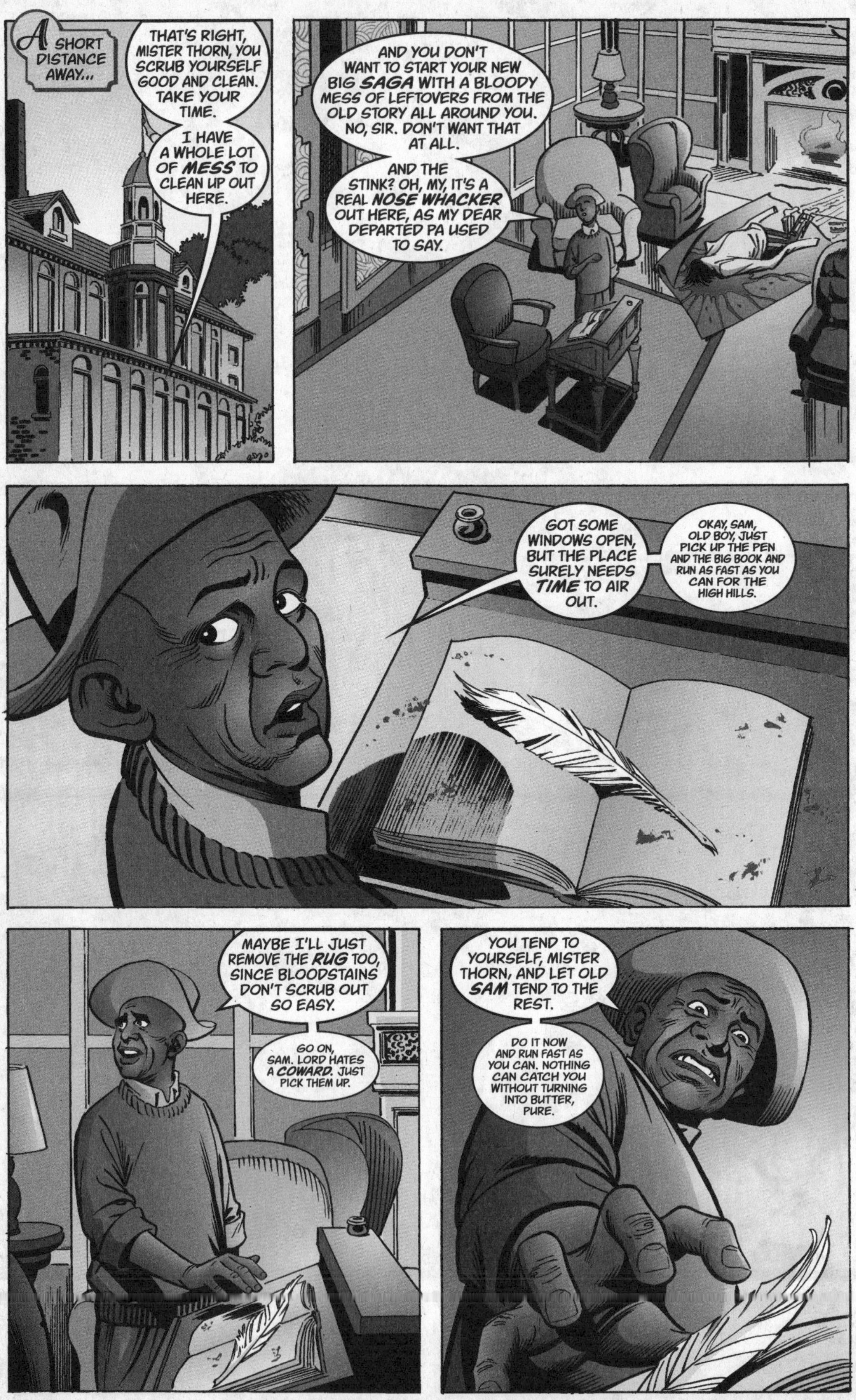
A SHORT DISTANCE AWAY...
THAT'S RIGHT, MISTER THORN, YOU SCRUB YOURSELF GOOD AND CLEAN. TAKE YOUR TIME.
I HAVE A WHOLE LOT OF MESS TO CLEAN UP OUT HERE.
AND YOU DON'T WANT TO START YOUR NEW BIG SAGA WITH A BLOODY MESS OF LEFTOVERS FROM THE OLD STORY ALL AROUND YOU. NO, SIR. DON'T WANT THAT AT ALL.
AND THE STINK? OH, MY, IT'S A REAL NOSE WHACKER OUT HERE, AS MY DEAR DEPARTED PA USED TO SAY.
GOT SOME WINDOWS OPEN, BUT THE PLACE SURELY NEEDS TIME TO AIR OUT.
OKAY, SAM, OLD BOY, JUST PICK UP THE PEN AND THE BIG BOOK AND RUN AS FAST AS YOU CAN FOR THE HIGH HILLS.
MAYBE I'LL JUST REMOVE THE RUG TOO, SINCE BLOODSTAINS DON'T SCRUB OUT SO EASY.
GO ON, SAM. LORD HATES A COWARD. JUST PICK THEM UP.
YOU TEND TO YOURSELF, MISTER THORN, AND LET OLD SAM TEND TO THE REST.
DO IT NOW AND RUN FAST AS YOU CAN. NOTHING CAN CATCH YOU WITHOUT TURNING INTO BUTTER, PURE.

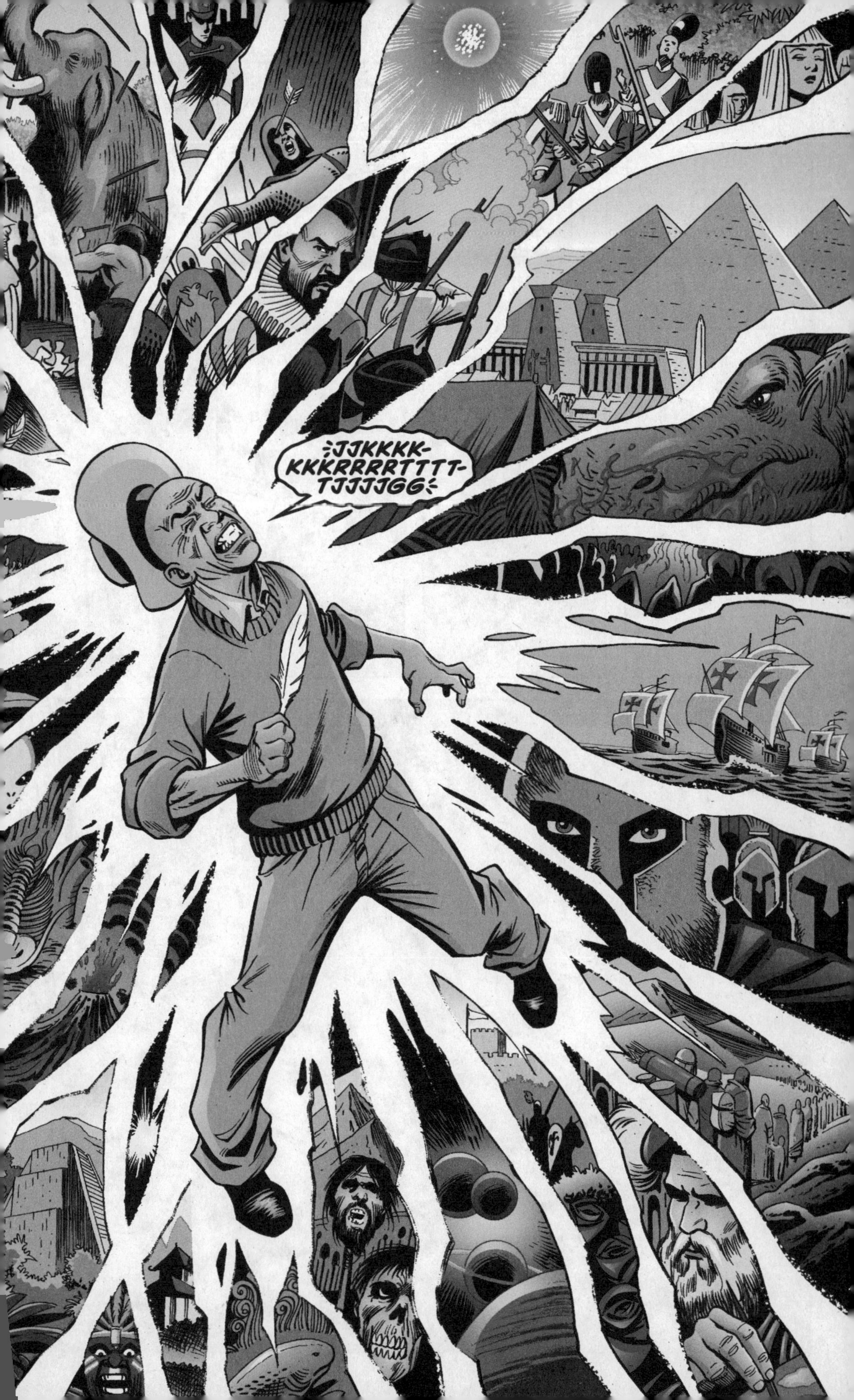
JJKKKK-KKKRRRRTTTT-TJJJJGG

♪ ...WHOLE WIDE WORLD, IN HIS PEN. ♪

HE'S GOT THE WHOLE WORLD IN HIS PEN. ♪

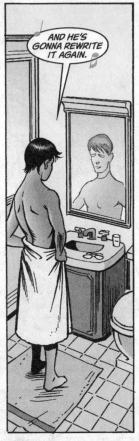

AND HE'S GONNA REWRITE IT AGAIN.

♪ HE'S GOT THE FABLES AND THE MUNDYS, IN HIS PEN. ♪

HE'S GOT THE LITERALS AND THEIR STORIES, IN HIS PEN.

♪ HE'S GOT THE MYTHS AND ALLEGORIES, IN HIS PEN. ♪

AND HE'S GONNA REWRITE IT AGAIN.

OH, SAM, YOU *FOOLISH* MAN.

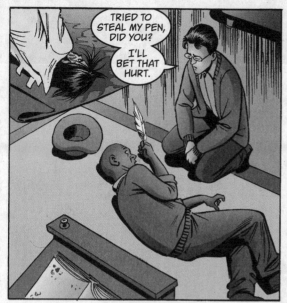

TRIED TO STEAL MY PEN, DID YOU?

I'LL BET THAT HURT.

ALL OF THAT INFORMATION, ALL THOSE *STORIES* CROWDING INTO YOUR HEAD AT ONCE.

EVERY DISASTER. EVERY CALAMITY. EVERY ACT OF CORRUPTION AND MALICE IN *ALL* OF HISTORY.

THEN AGAIN, BEING A MERE FABLE, EVEN THE VAST ACCUMULATION OF KINDNESSES MUST HAVE BEEN ENOUGH TO FRY YOUR MIND INTO A CINDER.

POOR SAM.

BUT I CAN'T LET YOU STAY LIKE THIS--BRAIN DEAD-- WHICH HAS TO BE *PEACE* OF A SORT.

I PROMISED YOU A PUNISHING END IF YOU TRIED TO INTER- FERE WITH ME AGAIN, AND I *KEEP* MY PROMISES.

EVEN IF I HAVE TO RESTORE YOU IN ORDER TO WRITE YOU A LONGER AND MORE FITTING DESTRUCTION.

NOW, WHERE DID I DISCARD MY *PRACTICE* NOTEBOOK?

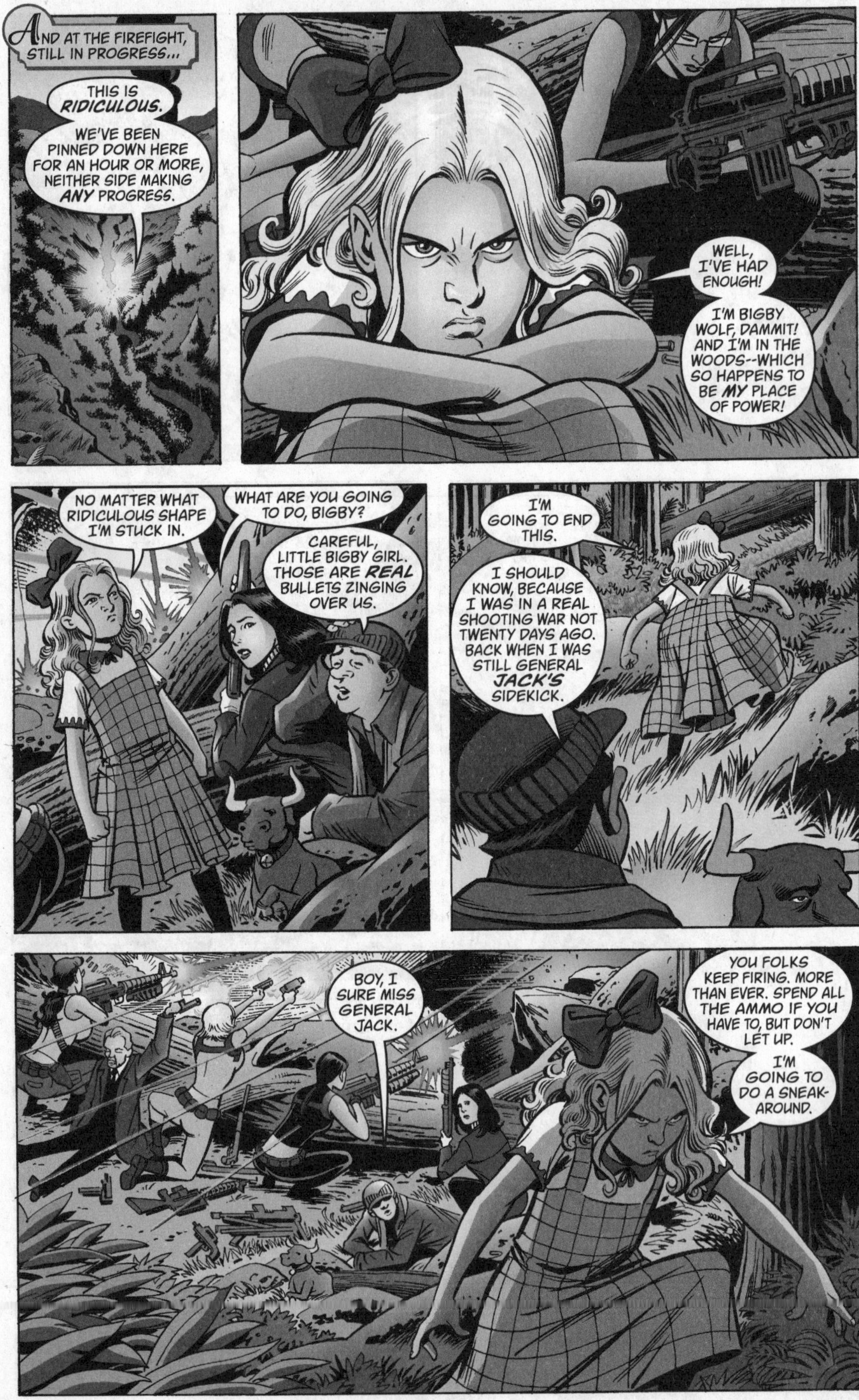
And at the firefight, still in progress...
THIS IS RIDICULOUS.
WE'VE BEEN PINNED DOWN HERE FOR AN HOUR OR MORE, NEITHER SIDE MAKING ANY PROGRESS.
WELL, I'VE HAD ENOUGH!
I'M BIGBY WOLF, DAMMIT! AND I'M IN THE WOODS--WHICH SO HAPPENS TO BE MY PLACE OF POWER!
NO MATTER WHAT RIDICULOUS SHAPE I'M STUCK IN.
WHAT ARE YOU GOING TO DO, BIGBY?
CAREFUL, LITTLE BIGBY GIRL. THOSE ARE REAL BULLETS ZINGING OVER US.
I'M GOING TO END THIS.
I SHOULD KNOW, BECAUSE I WAS IN A REAL SHOOTING WAR NOT TWENTY DAYS AGO. BACK WHEN I WAS STILL GENERAL JACK'S SIDEKICK.
BOY, I SURE MISS GENERAL JACK.
YOU FOLKS KEEP FIRING. MORE THAN EVER. SPEND ALL THE AMMO IF YOU HAVE TO, BUT DON'T LET UP.
I'M GOING TO DO A SNEAK-AROUND.

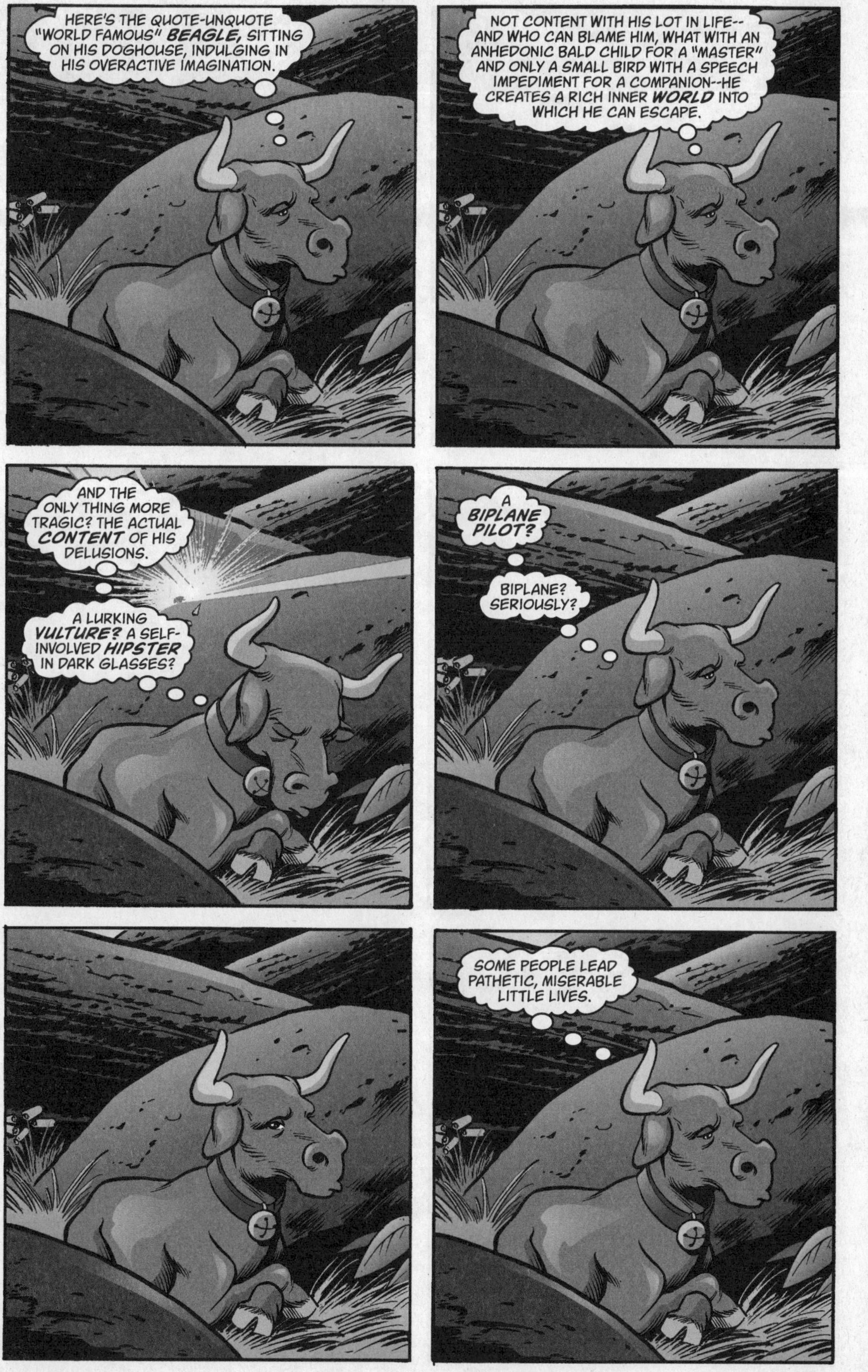
HERE'S THE QUOTE-UNQUOTE "WORLD FAMOUS" BEAGLE, SITTING ON HIS DOGHOUSE, INDULGING IN HIS OVERACTIVE IMAGINATION.
NOT CONTENT WITH HIS LOT IN LIFE-- AND WHO CAN BLAME HIM, WHAT WITH AN ANHEDONIC BALD CHILD FOR A "MASTER" AND ONLY A SMALL BIRD WITH A SPEECH IMPEDIMENT FOR A COMPANION--HE CREATES A RICH INNER WORLD INTO WHICH HE CAN ESCAPE.
AND THE ONLY THING MORE TRAGIC? THE ACTUAL CONTENT OF HIS DELUSIONS.
A LURKING VULTURE? A SELF-INVOLVED HIPSTER IN DARK GLASSES?
A BIPLANE PILOT?
BIPLANE? SERIOUSLY?
SOME PEOPLE LEAD PATHETIC, MISERABLE LITTLE LIVES.

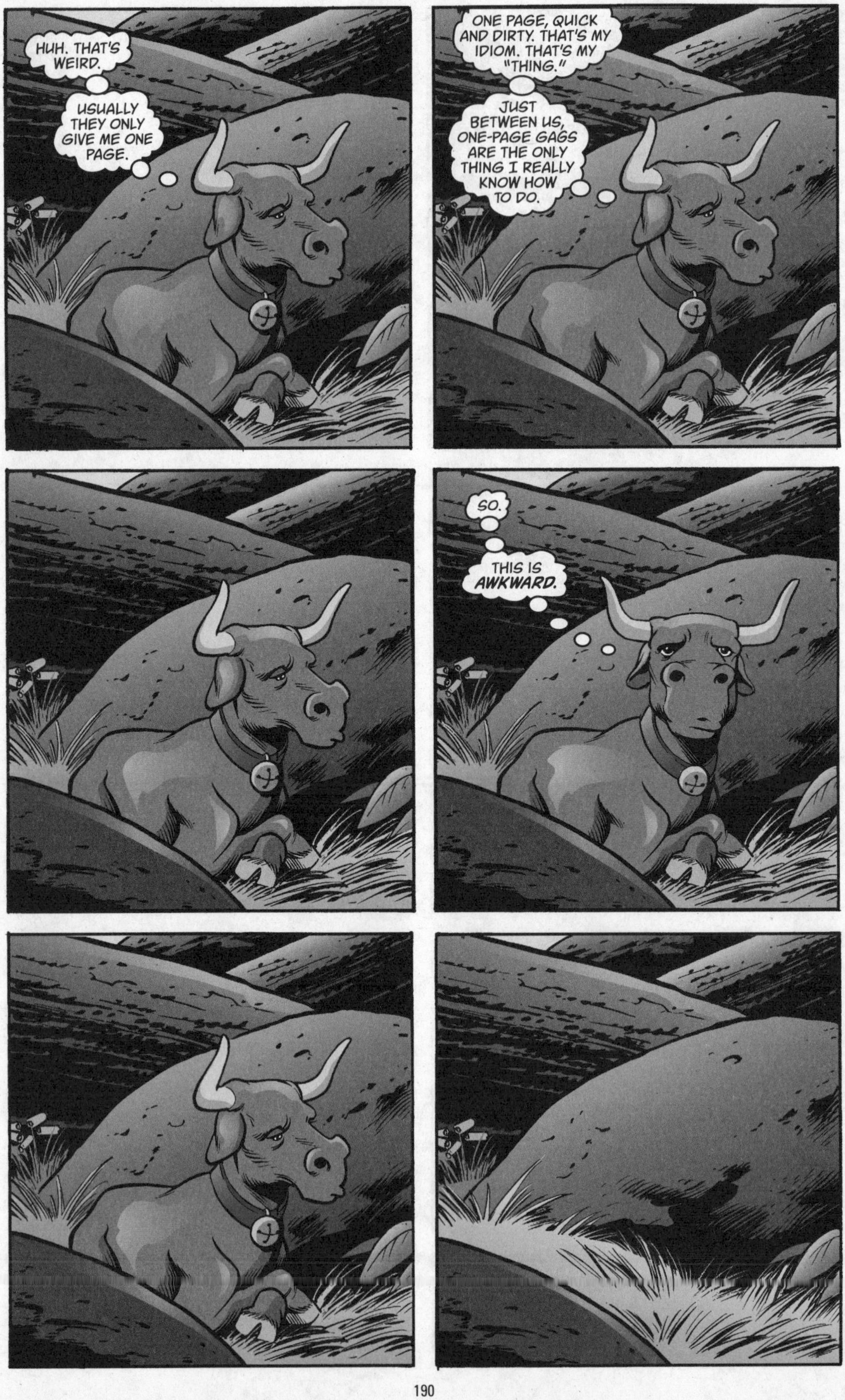
HUH. THAT'S WEIRD.
USUALLY THEY ONLY GIVE ME ONE PAGE.
ONE PAGE, QUICK AND DIRTY. THAT'S MY IDIOM. THAT'S MY "THING."
JUST BETWEEN US, ONE-PAGE GAGS ARE THE ONLY THING I REALLY KNOW HOW TO DO.
SO.
THIS IS AWKWARD.

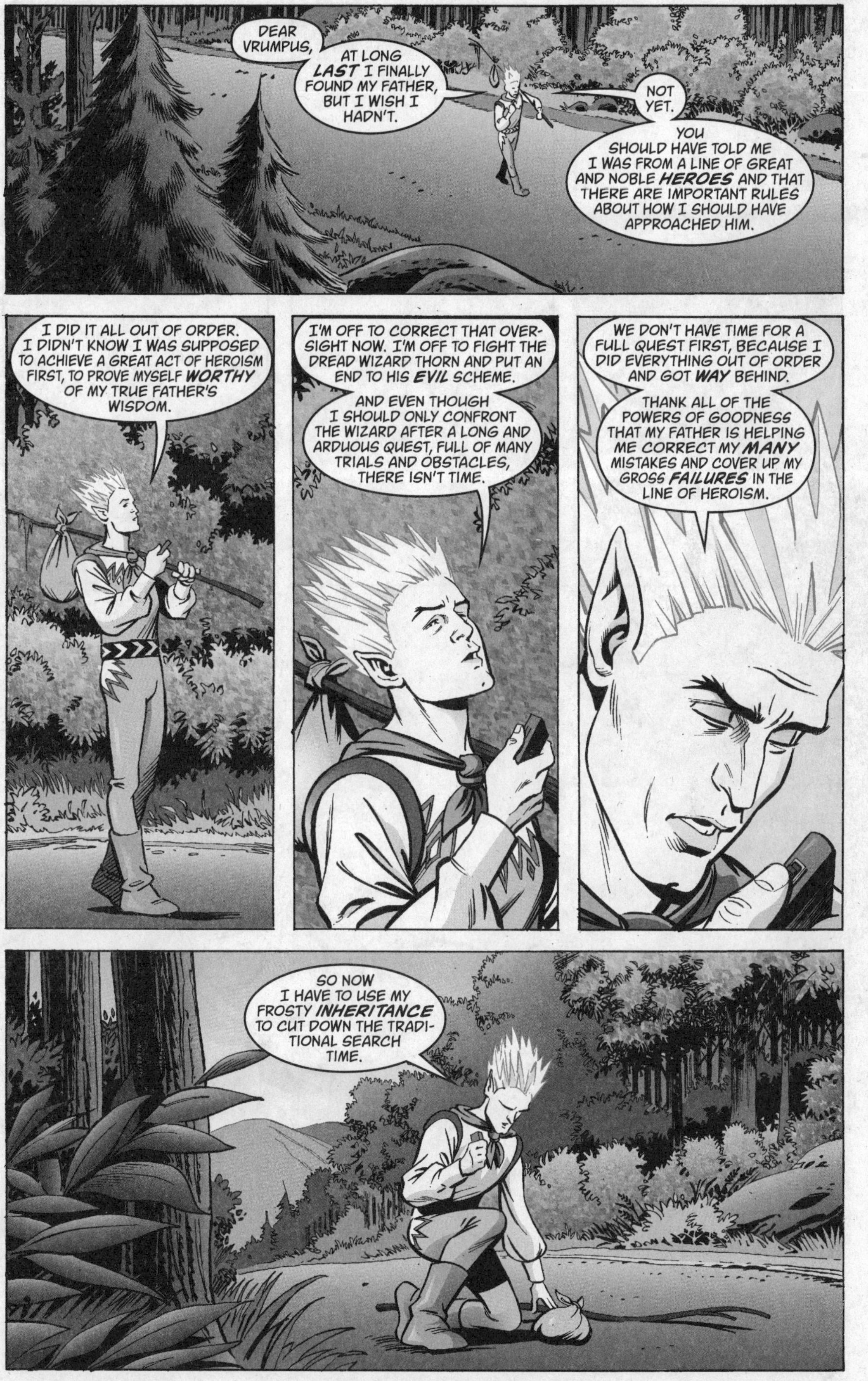
DEAR VRUMPUS,
AT LONG LAST I FINALLY FOUND MY FATHER, BUT I WISH I HADN'T.
NOT YET.
YOU SHOULD HAVE TOLD ME I WAS FROM A LINE OF GREAT AND NOBLE HEROES AND THAT THERE ARE IMPORTANT RULES ABOUT HOW I SHOULD HAVE APPROACHED HIM.
I DID IT ALL OUT OF ORDER. I DIDN'T KNOW I WAS SUPPOSED TO ACHIEVE A GREAT ACT OF HEROISM FIRST, TO PROVE MYSELF WORTHY OF MY TRUE FATHER'S WISDOM.
I'M OFF TO CORRECT THAT OVERSIGHT NOW. I'M OFF TO FIGHT THE DREAD WIZARD THORN AND PUT AN END TO HIS EVIL SCHEME.
AND EVEN THOUGH I SHOULD ONLY CONFRONT THE WIZARD AFTER A LONG AND ARDUOUS QUEST, FULL OF MANY TRIALS AND OBSTACLES, THERE ISN'T TIME.
WE DON'T HAVE TIME FOR A FULL QUEST FIRST, BECAUSE I DID EVERYTHING OUT OF ORDER AND GOT WAY BEHIND.
THANK ALL OF THE POWERS OF GOODNESS THAT MY FATHER IS HELPING ME CORRECT MY MANY MISTAKES AND COVER UP MY GROSS FAILURES IN THE LINE OF HEROISM.
SO NOW I HAVE TO USE MY FROSTY INHERITANCE TO CUT DOWN THE TRADITIONAL SEARCH TIME.

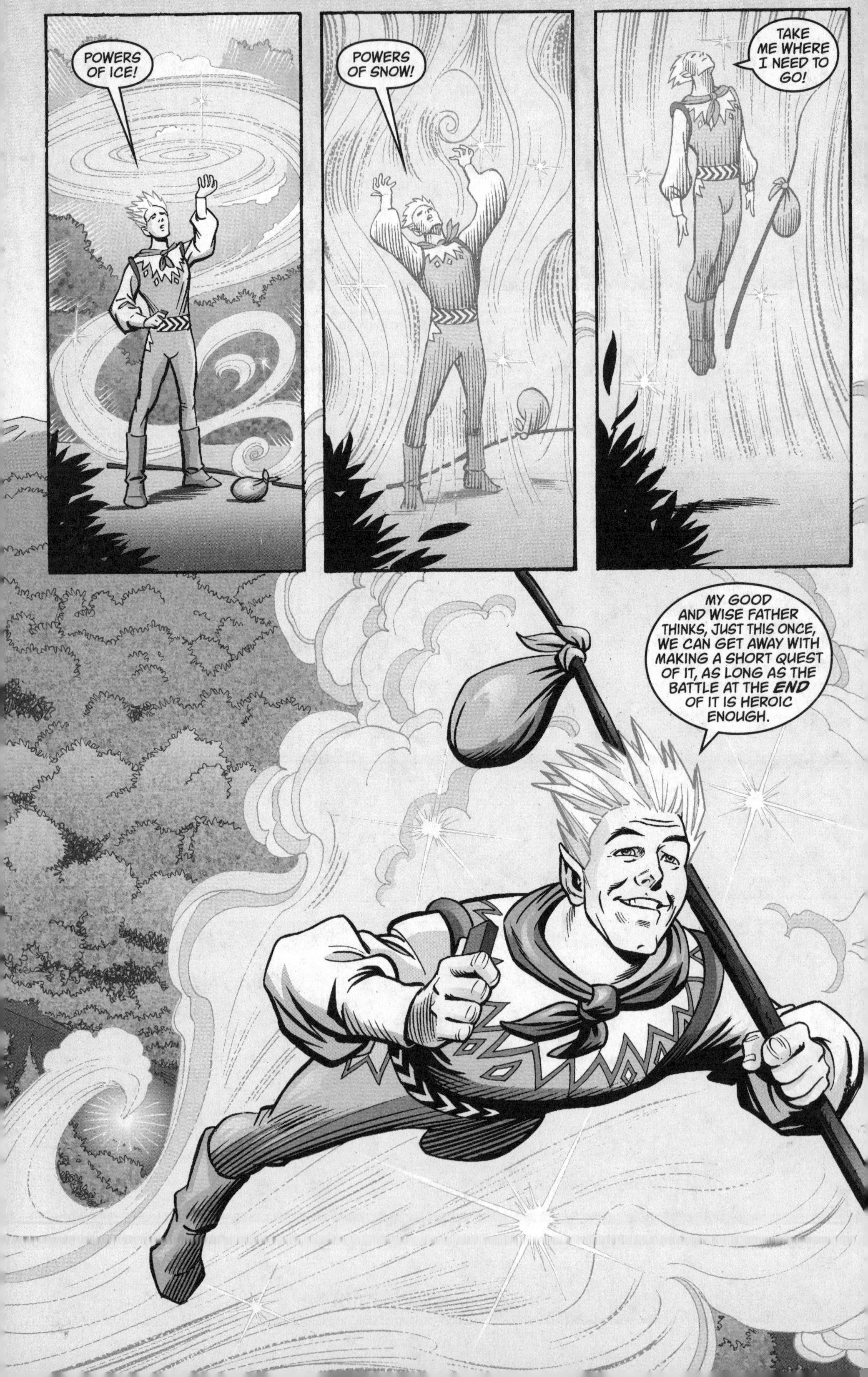
POWERS OF ICE!
POWERS OF SNOW!
TAKE ME WHERE I NEED TO GO!
MY GOOD AND WISE FATHER THINKS, JUST THIS ONCE, WE CAN GET AWAY WITH MAKING A SHORT QUEST OF IT, AS LONG AS THE BATTLE AT THE *END* OF IT IS HEROIC ENOUGH.

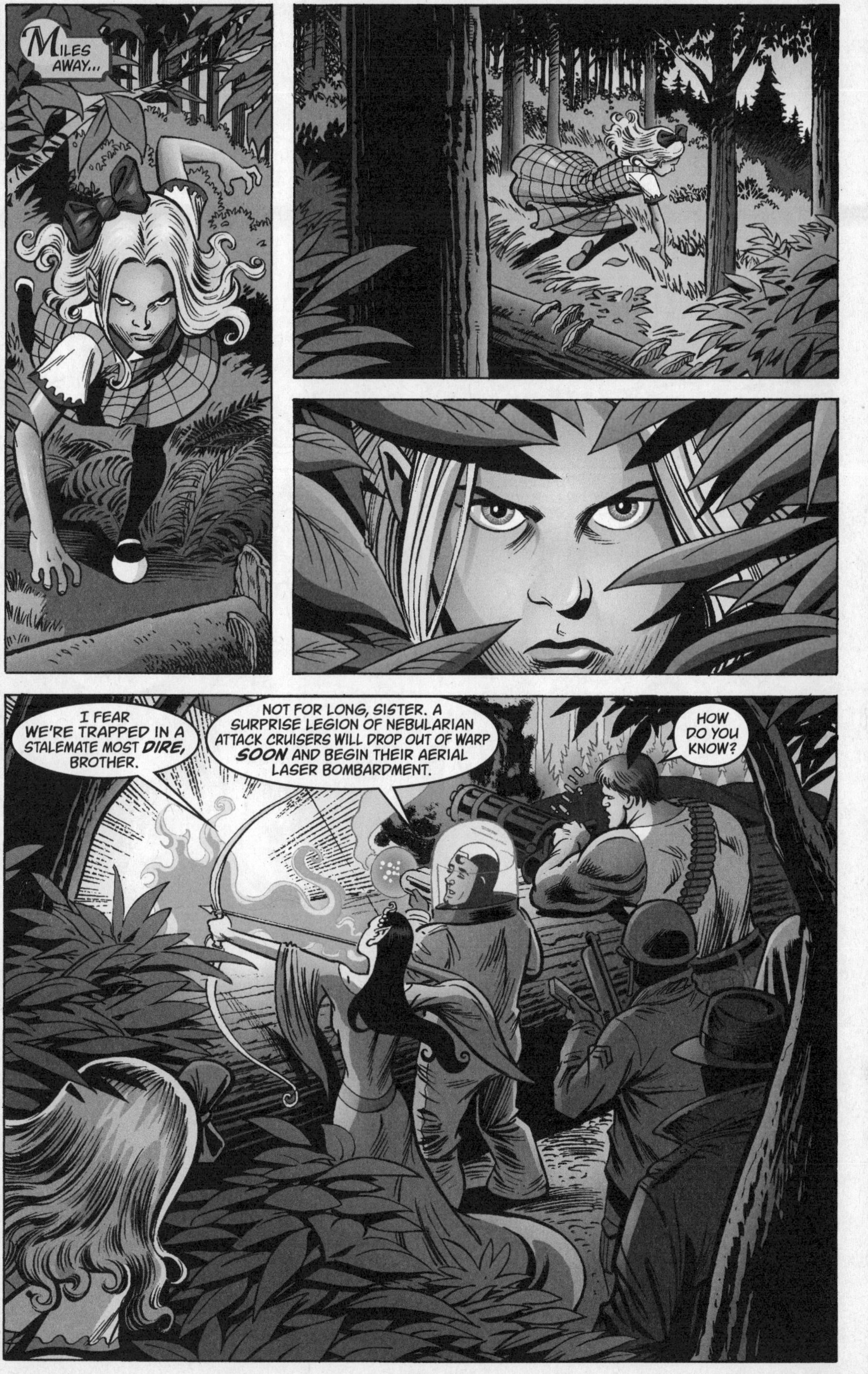
MILES AWAY...
I FEAR WE'RE TRAPPED IN A STALEMATE MOST DIRE, BROTHER.
NOT FOR LONG, SISTER. A SURPRISE LEGION OF NEBULARIAN ATTACK CRUISERS WILL DROP OUT OF WARP SOON AND BEGIN THEIR AERIAL LASER BOMBARDMENT.
HOW DO YOU KNOW?

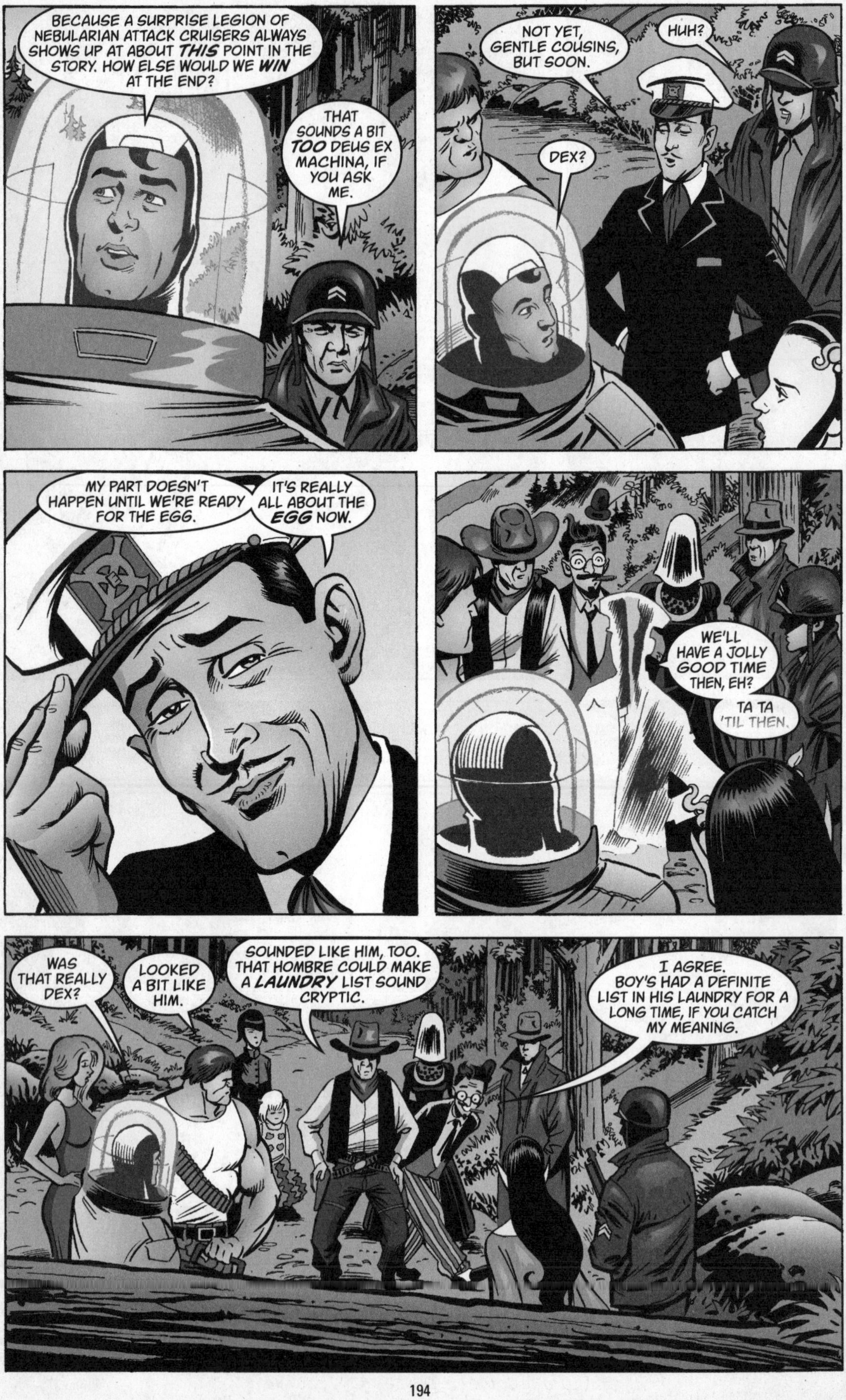
BECAUSE A SURPRISE LEGION OF NEBULARIAN ATTACK CRUISERS ALWAYS SHOWS UP AT ABOUT THIS POINT IN THE STORY. HOW ELSE WOULD WE WIN AT THE END?
THAT SOUNDS A BIT TOO DEUS EX MACHINA, IF YOU ASK ME.
NOT YET, GENTLE COUSINS, BUT SOON.
HUH?
DEX?
MY PART DOESN'T HAPPEN UNTIL WE'RE READY FOR THE EGG.
IT'S REALLY ALL ABOUT THE EGG NOW.
WE'LL HAVE A JOLLY GOOD TIME THEN, EH?
TA TA 'TIL THEN.
WAS THAT REALLY DEX?
LOOKED A BIT LIKE HIM.
SOUNDED LIKE HIM, TOO. THAT HOMBRE COULD MAKE A LAUNDRY LIST SOUND CRYPTIC.
I AGREE. BOY'S HAD A DEFINITE LIST IN HIS LAUNDRY FOR A LONG TIME, IF YOU CATCH MY MEANING.

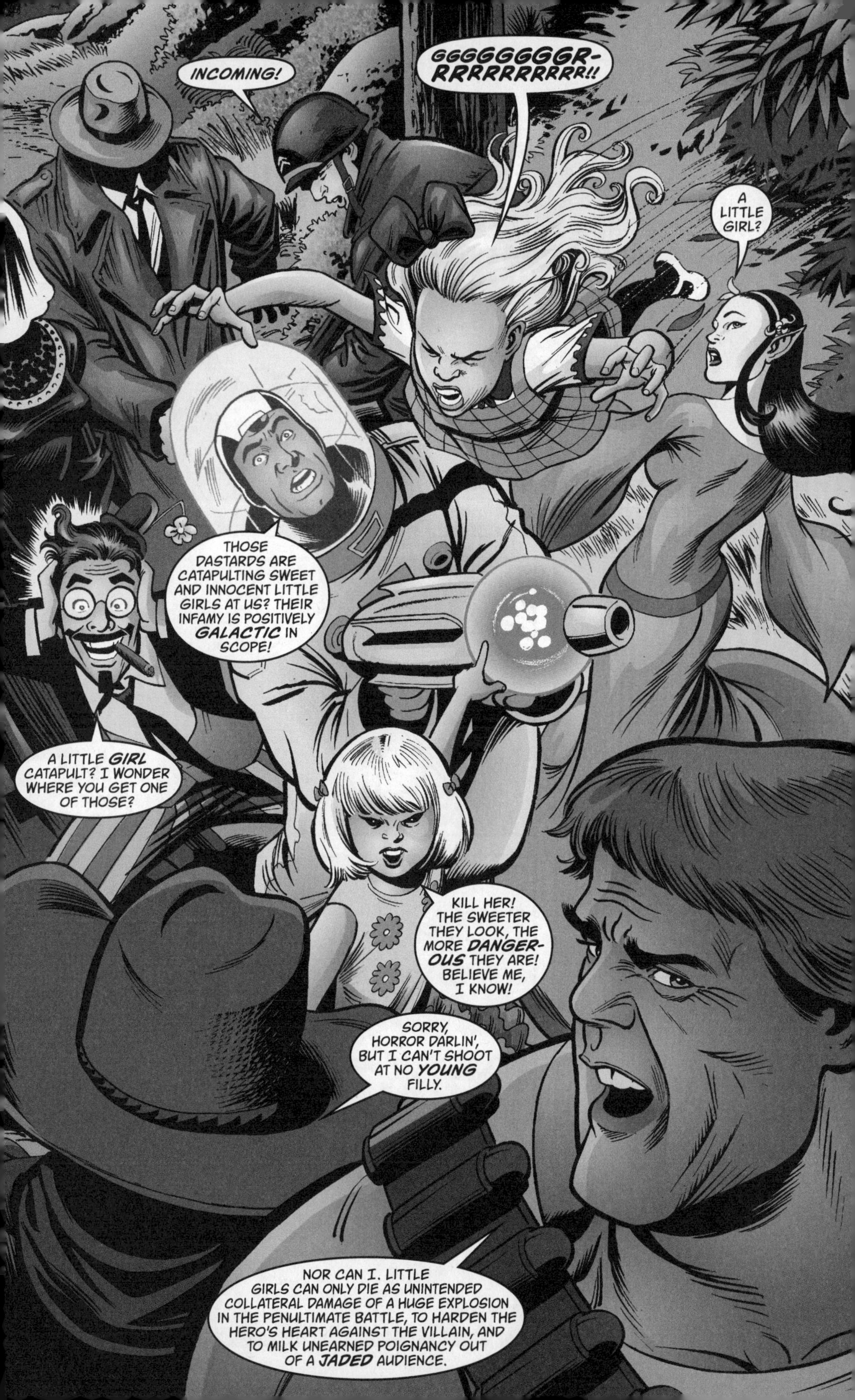
INCOMING!
GGGGGGGGR-RRRRRRRRRR!!
A LITTLE GIRL?
THOSE DASTARDS ARE CATAPULTING SWEET AND INNOCENT LITTLE GIRLS AT US? THEIR INFAMY IS POSITIVELY GALACTIC IN SCOPE!
A LITTLE GIRL CATAPULT? I WONDER WHERE YOU GET ONE OF THOSE?
KILL HER! THE SWEETER THEY LOOK, THE MORE DANGER-OUS THEY ARE! BELIEVE ME, I KNOW!
SORRY, HORROR DARLIN', BUT I CAN'T SHOOT AT NO YOUNG FILLY.
NOR CAN I. LITTLE GIRLS CAN ONLY DIE AS UNINTENDED COLLATERAL DAMAGE OF A HUGE EXPLOSION IN THE PENULTIMATE BATTLE, TO HARDEN THE HERO'S HEART AGAINST THE VILLAIN, AND TO MILK UNEARNED POIGNANCY OUT OF A JADED AUDIENCE.

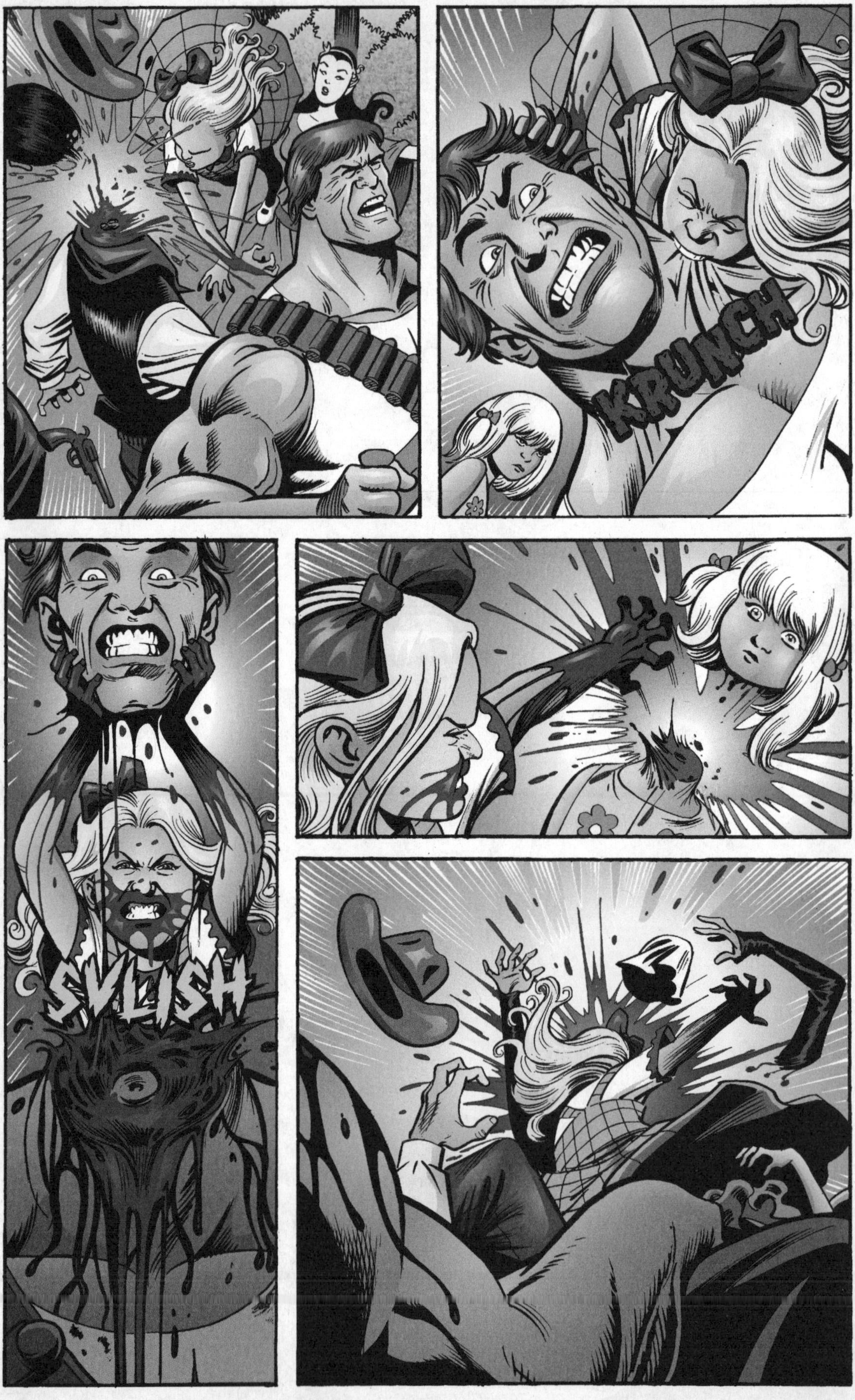
KRUNCH
SVLISH

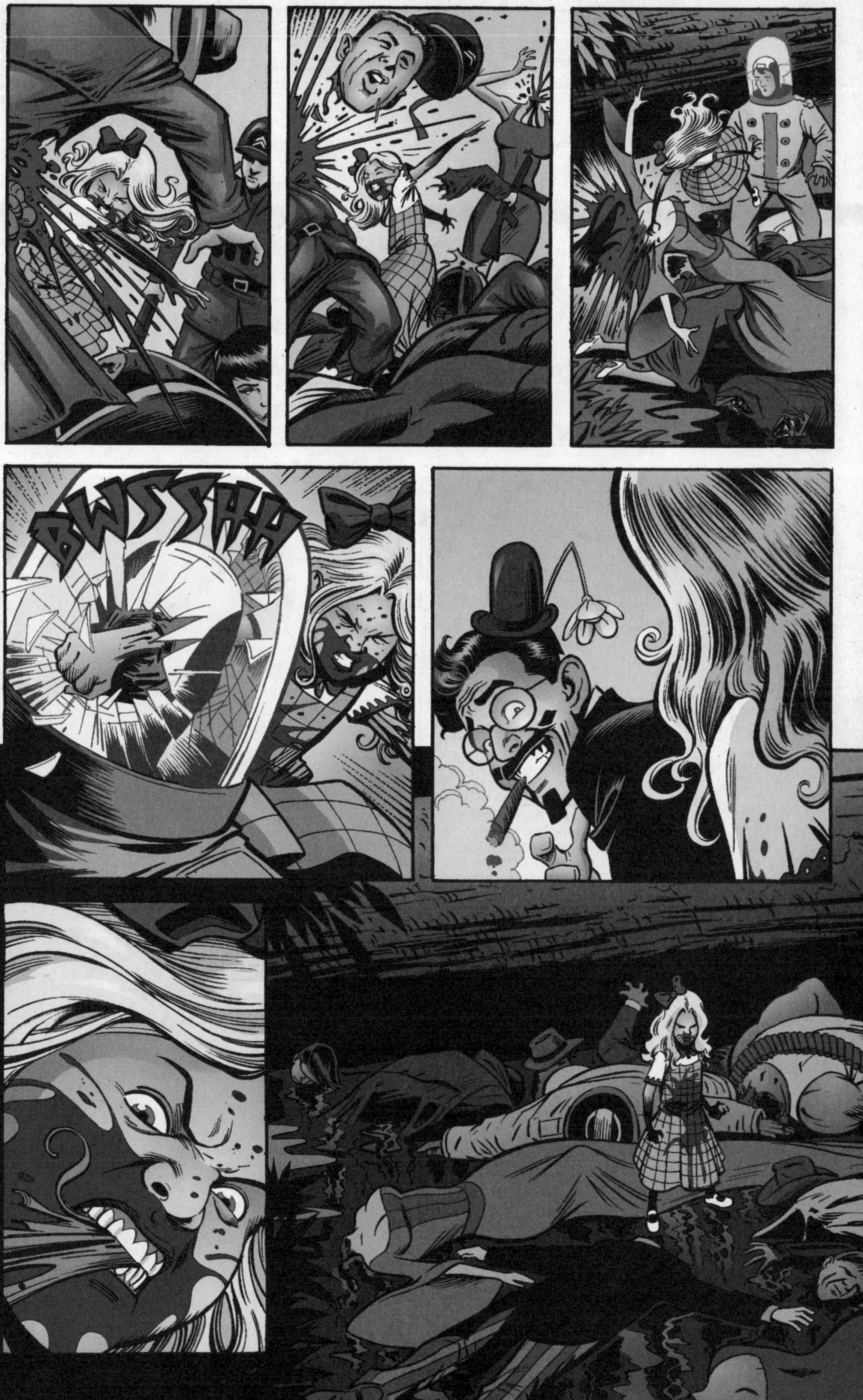
BWSSHH

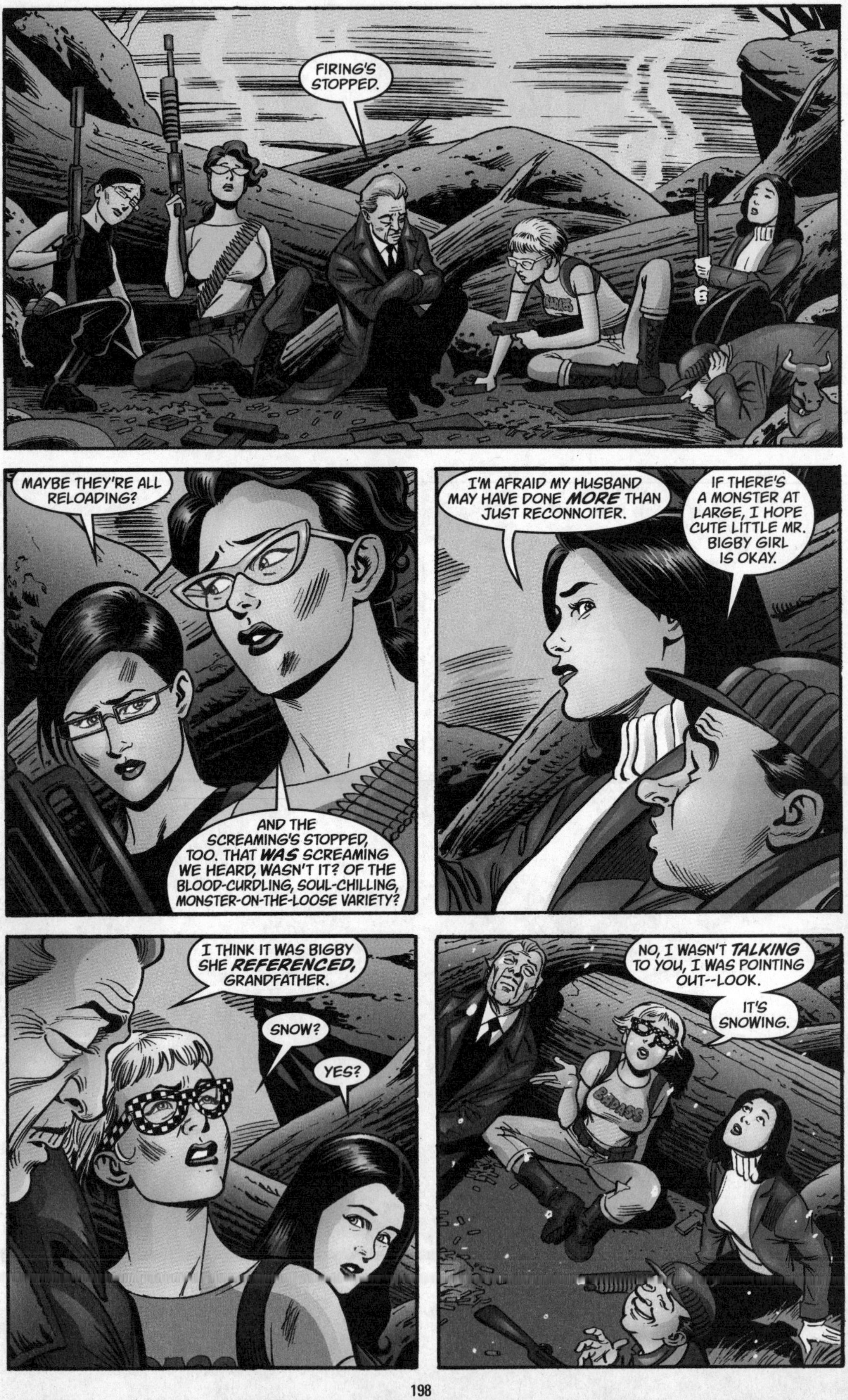
FIRING'S STOPPED.
MAYBE THEY'RE ALL RELOADING?
AND THE SCREAMING'S STOPPED, TOO. THAT WAS SCREAMING WE HEARD, WASN'T IT? OF THE BLOOD-CURDLING, SOUL-CHILLING, MONSTER-ON-THE-LOOSE VARIETY?
I'M AFRAID MY HUSBAND MAY HAVE DONE MORE THAN JUST RECONNOITER.
IF THERE'S A MONSTER AT LARGE, I HOPE CUTE LITTLE MR. BIGBY GIRL IS OKAY.
I THINK IT WAS BIGBY SHE REFERENCED, GRANDFATHER.
SNOW?
YES?
NO, I WASN'T TALKING TO YOU, I WAS POINTING OUT--LOOK.
IT'S SNOWING.

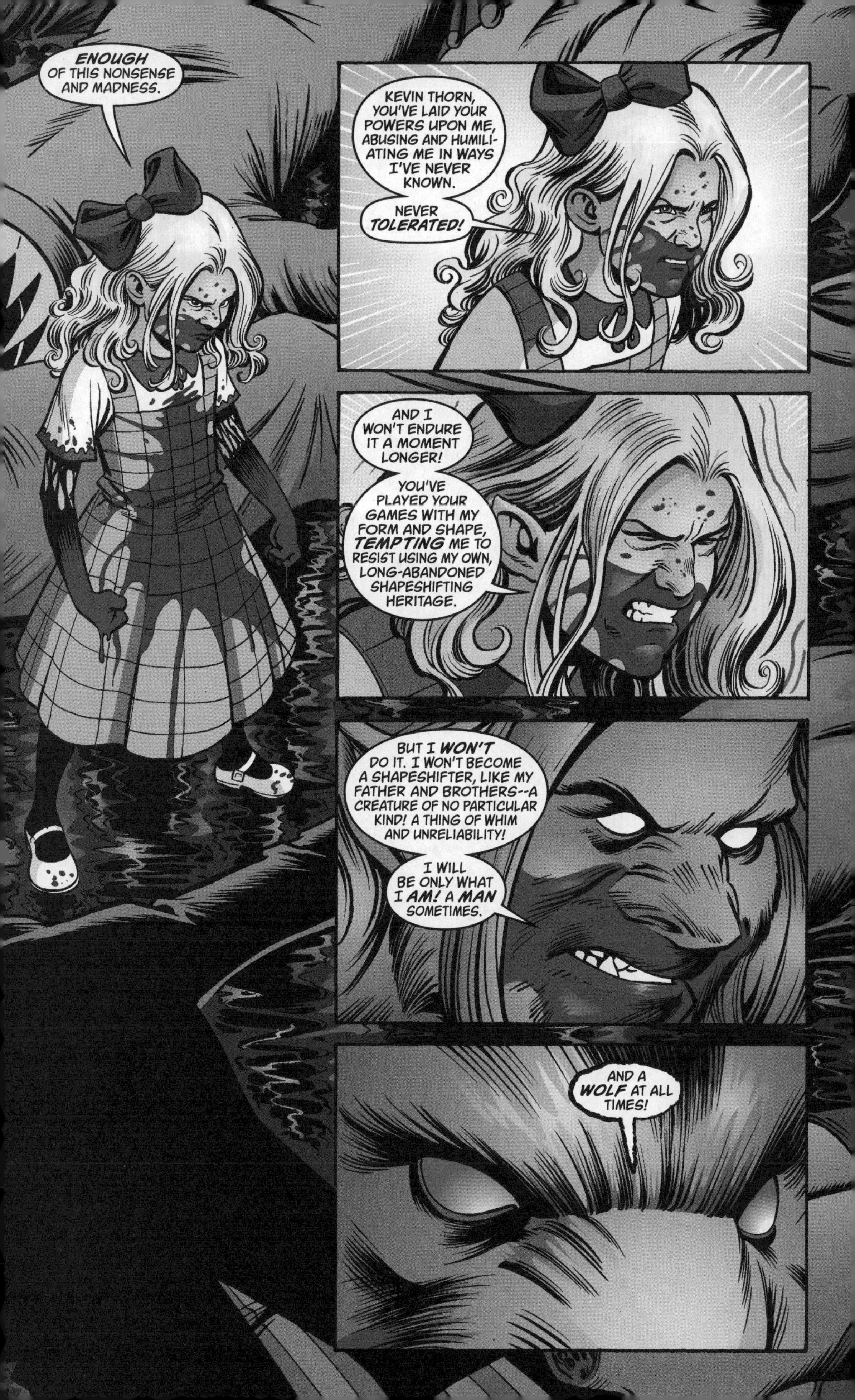
ENOUGH OF THIS NONSENSE AND MADNESS.
KEVIN THORN, YOU'VE LAID YOUR POWERS UPON ME, ABUSING AND HUMILIATING ME IN WAYS I'VE NEVER KNOWN.
NEVER TOLERATED!
AND I WON'T ENDURE IT A MOMENT LONGER!
YOU'VE PLAYED YOUR GAMES WITH MY FORM AND SHAPE, TEMPTING ME TO RESIST USING MY OWN, LONG-ABANDONED SHAPESHIFTING HERITAGE.
BUT I WON'T DO IT. I WON'T BECOME A SHAPESHIFTER, LIKE MY FATHER AND BROTHERS--A CREATURE OF NO PARTICULAR KIND! A THING OF WHIM AND UNRELIABILITY!
I WILL BE ONLY WHAT I AM! A MAN SOMETIMES.
AND A WOLF AT ALL TIMES!

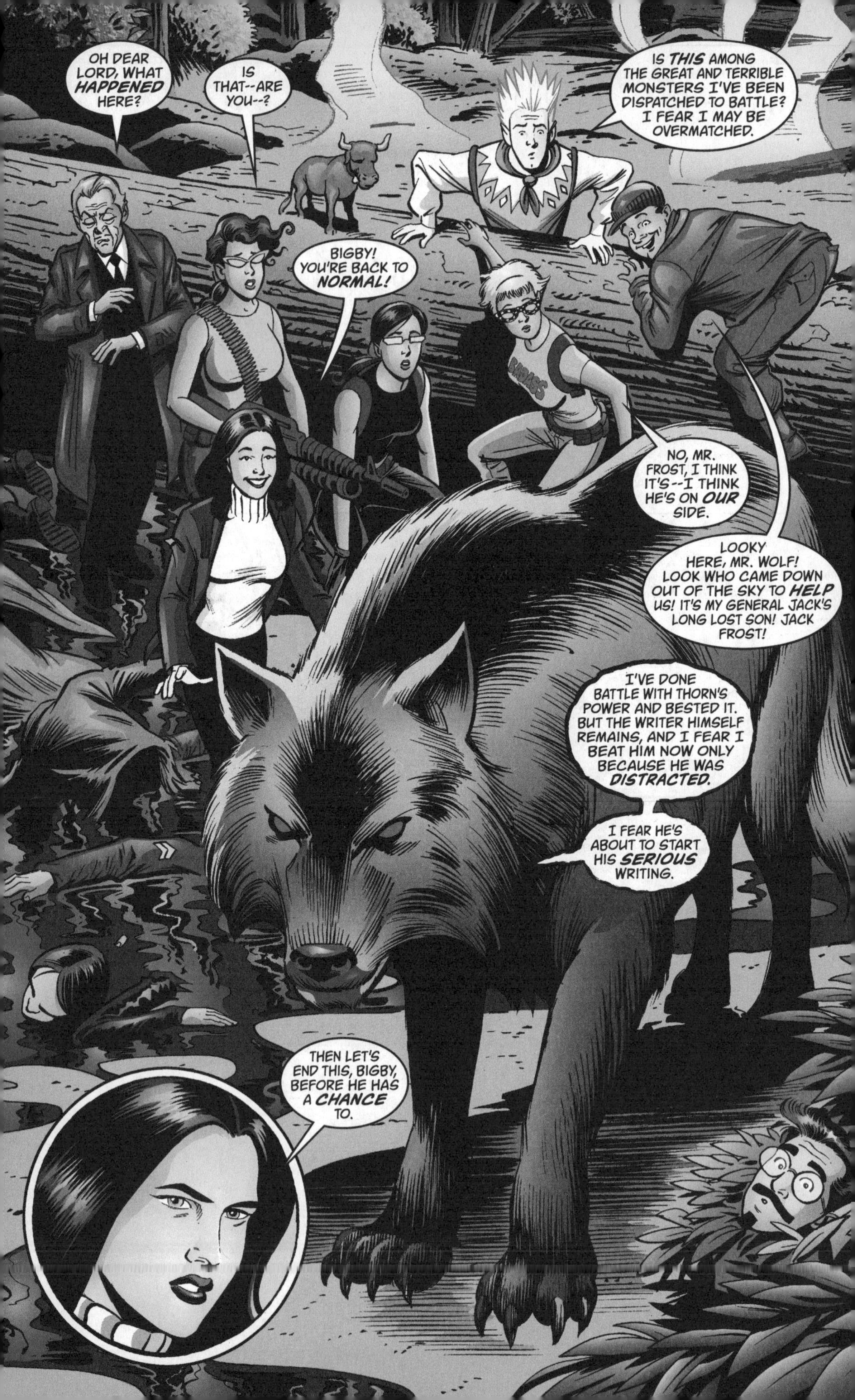
OH DEAR LORD, WHAT HAPPENED HERE?
IS THAT--ARE YOU--?
IS THIS AMONG THE GREAT AND TERRIBLE MONSTERS I'VE BEEN DISPATCHED TO BATTLE? I FEAR I MAY BE OVERMATCHED.
BIGBY! YOU'RE BACK TO NORMAL!
NO, MR. FROST, I THINK IT'S--I THINK HE'S ON OUR SIDE.
LOOKY HERE, MR. WOLF! LOOK WHO CAME DOWN OUT OF THE SKY TO HELP US! IT'S MY GENERAL JACK'S LONG LOST SON! JACK FROST!
I'VE DONE BATTLE WITH THORN'S POWER AND BESTED IT. BUT THE WRITER HIMSELF REMAINS, AND I FEAR I BEAT HIM NOW ONLY BECAUSE HE WAS DISTRACTED.
I FEAR HE'S ABOUT TO START HIS SERIOUS WRITING.
THEN LET'S END THIS, BIGBY, BEFORE HE HAS A CHANCE TO.

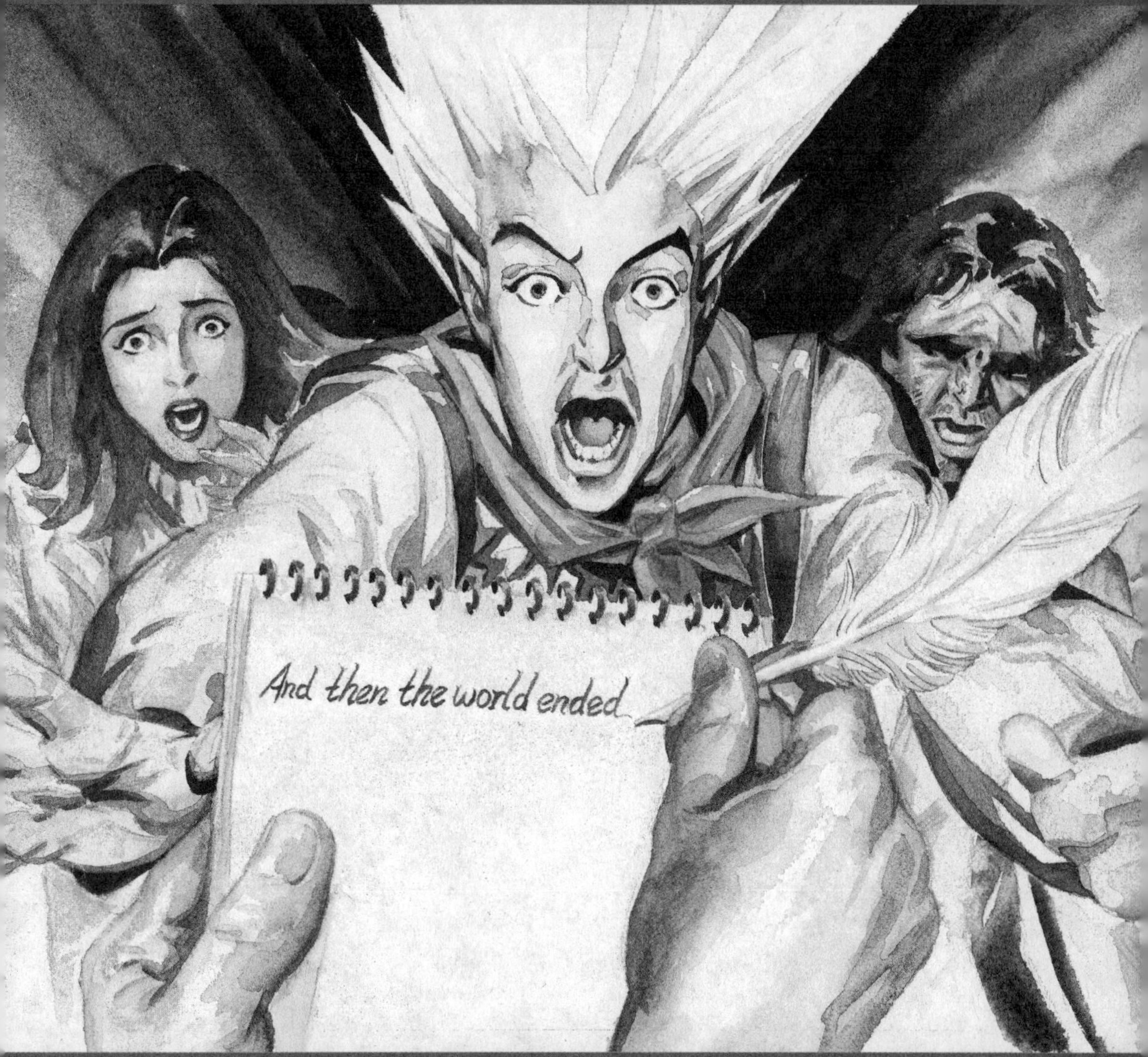
And then the world ended

"Did you imagine yourselves the noble heroes of this tale,
who'd save the day at the last second?"

The Great FABLES Crossover

part 9 of 9

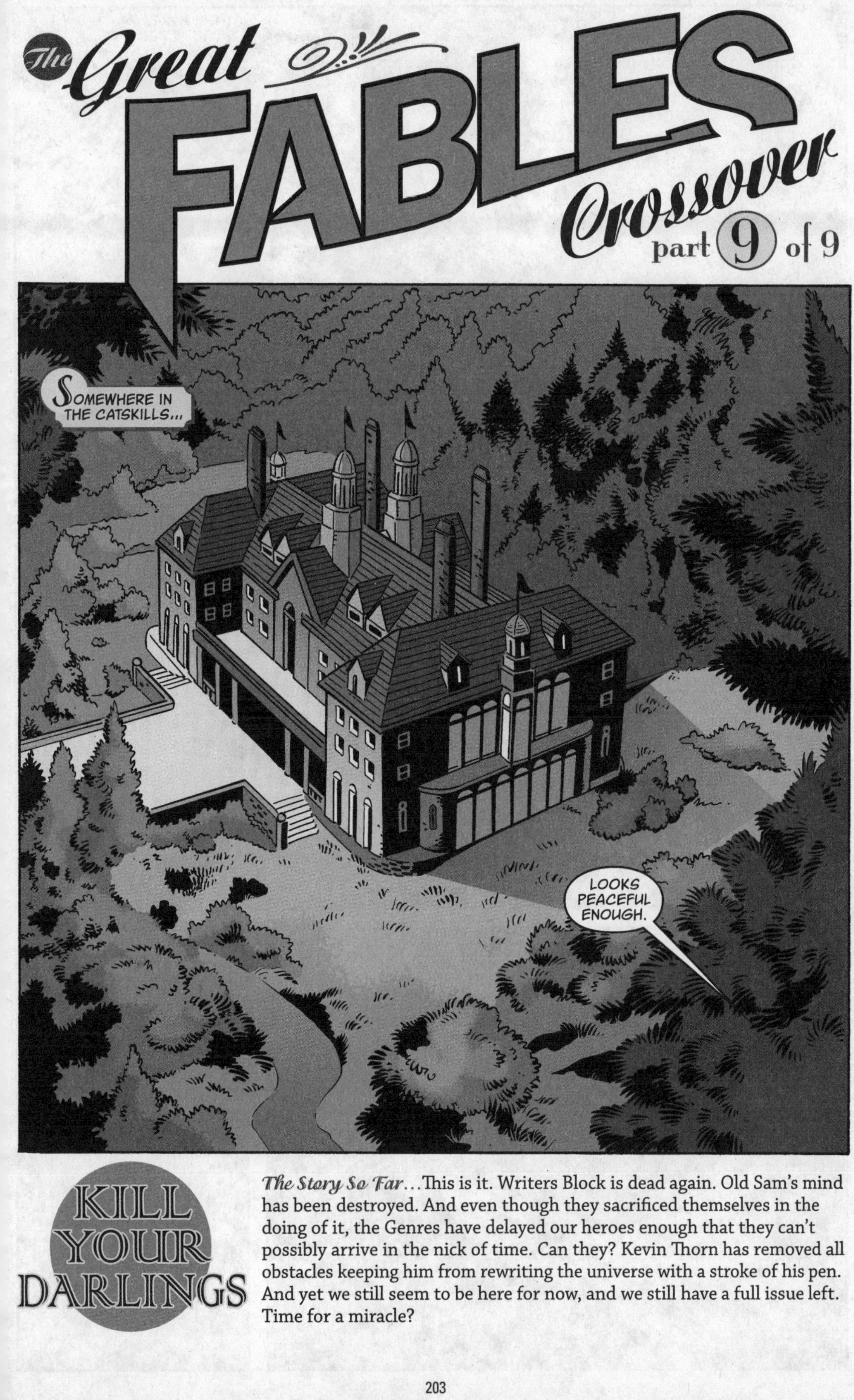

SOMEWHERE IN THE CATSKILLS...
LOOKS PEACEFUL ENOUGH.

KILL YOUR DARLINGS

The Story So Far...This is it. Writers Block is dead again. Old Sam's mind has been destroyed. And even though they sacrificed themselves in the doing of it, the Genres have delayed our heroes enough that they can't possibly arrive in the nick of time. Can they? Kevin Thorn has removed all obstacles keeping him from rewriting the universe with a stroke of his pen. And yet we still seem to be here for now, and we still have a full issue left. Time for a miracle?

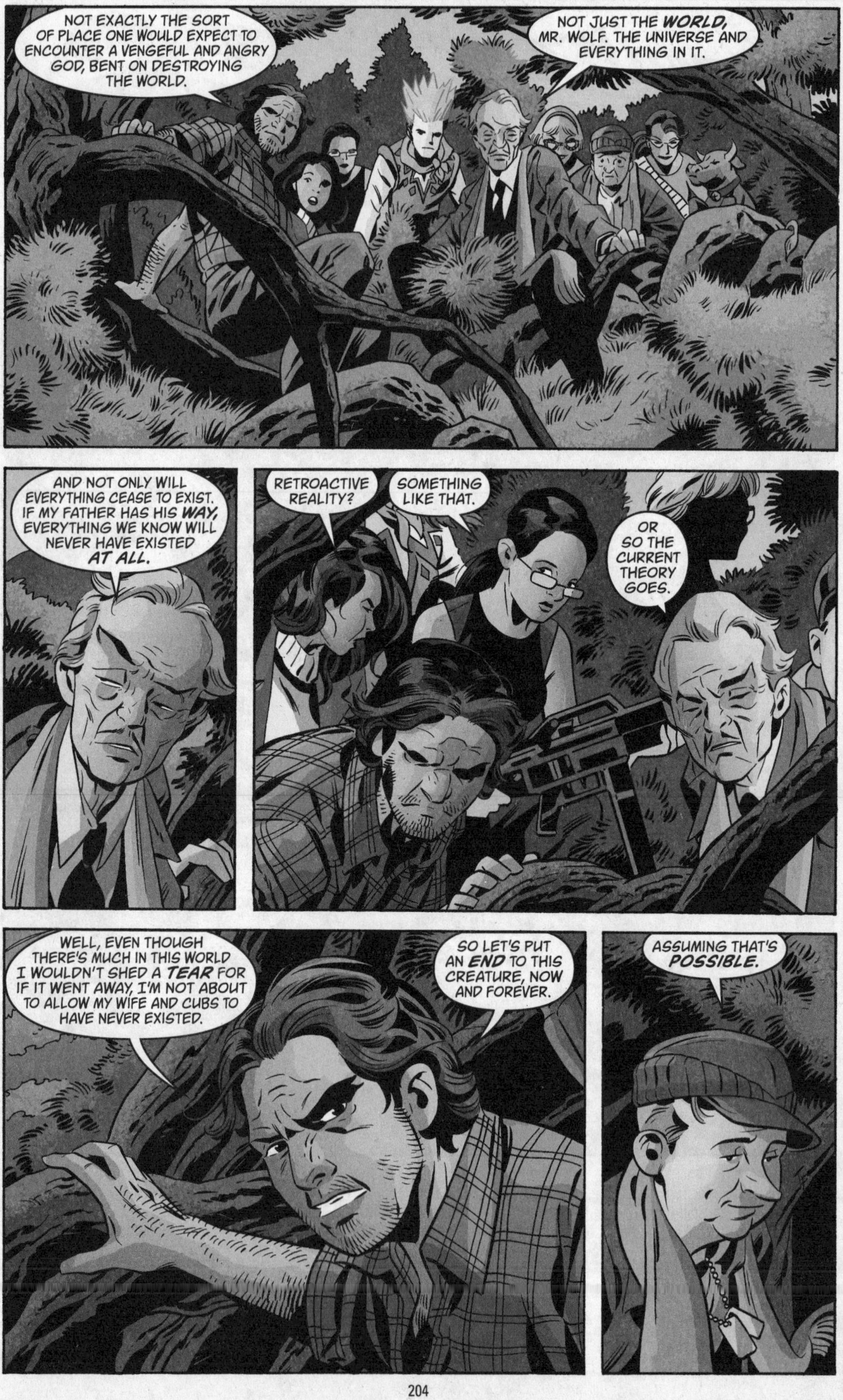
NOT EXACTLY THE SORT OF PLACE ONE WOULD EXPECT TO ENCOUNTER A VENGEFUL AND ANGRY GOD, BENT ON DESTROYING THE WORLD.
NOT JUST THE WORLD, MR. WOLF. THE UNIVERSE AND EVERYTHING IN IT.
AND NOT ONLY WILL EVERYTHING CEASE TO EXIST. IF MY FATHER HAS HIS WAY, EVERYTHING WE KNOW WILL NEVER HAVE EXISTED AT ALL.
RETROACTIVE REALITY?
SOMETHING LIKE THAT.
OR SO THE CURRENT THEORY GOES.
WELL, EVEN THOUGH THERE'S MUCH IN THIS WORLD I WOULDN'T SHED A TEAR FOR IF IT WENT AWAY, I'M NOT ABOUT TO ALLOW MY WIFE AND CUBS TO HAVE NEVER EXISTED.
SO LET'S PUT AN END TO THIS CREATURE, NOW AND FOREVER.
ASSUMING THAT'S POSSIBLE.

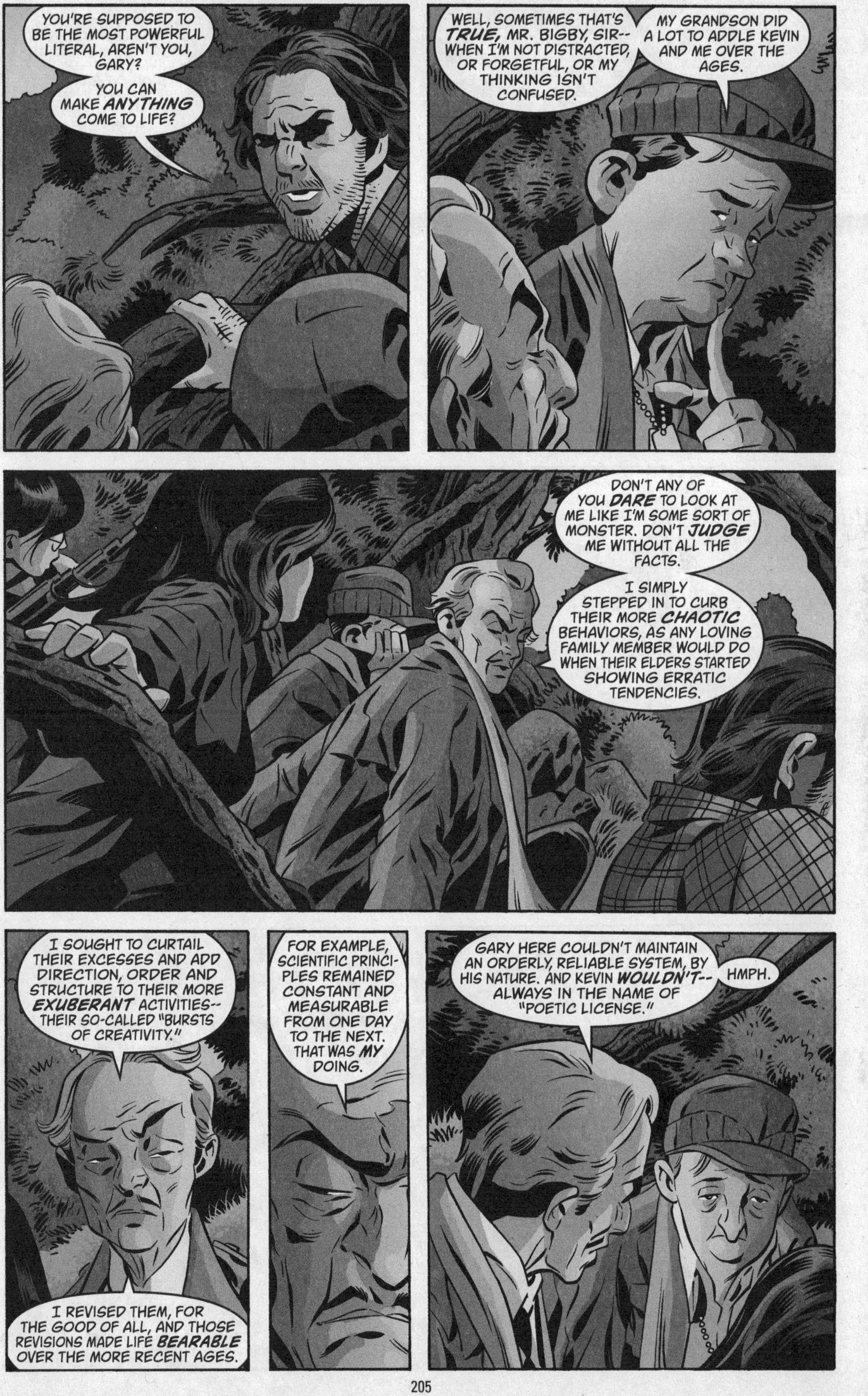
YOU'RE SUPPOSED TO BE THE MOST POWERFUL LITERAL, AREN'T YOU, GARY?
YOU CAN MAKE ANYTHING COME TO LIFE?
WELL, SOMETIMES THAT'S TRUE, MR. BIGBY, SIR-- WHEN I'M NOT DISTRACTED, OR FORGETFUL, OR MY THINKING ISN'T CONFUSED.
MY GRANDSON DID A LOT TO ADDLE KEVIN AND ME OVER THE AGES.
DON'T ANY OF YOU DARE TO LOOK AT ME LIKE I'M SOME SORT OF MONSTER. DON'T JUDGE ME WITHOUT ALL THE FACTS.
I SIMPLY STEPPED IN TO CURB THEIR MORE CHAOTIC BEHAVIORS, AS ANY LOVING FAMILY MEMBER WOULD DO WHEN THEIR ELDERS STARTED SHOWING ERRATIC TENDENCIES.
I SOUGHT TO CURTAIL THEIR EXCESSES AND ADD DIRECTION, ORDER AND STRUCTURE TO THEIR MORE EXUBERANT ACTIVITIES-- THEIR SO-CALLED "BURSTS OF CREATIVITY."
I REVISED THEM, FOR THE GOOD OF ALL, AND THOSE REVISIONS MADE LIFE BEARABLE OVER THE MORE RECENT AGES.
FOR EXAMPLE, SCIENTIFIC PRINCIPLES REMAINED CONSTANT AND MEASURABLE FROM ONE DAY TO THE NEXT. THAT WAS MY DOING.
GARY HERE COULDN'T MAINTAIN AN ORDERLY, RELIABLE SYSTEM, BY HIS NATURE. AND KEVIN WOULDN'T-- ALWAYS IN THE NAME OF "POETIC LICENSE."
HMPH.

WHAT YOU'RE SAYING IS, UNDER *YOUR* CARE MAGIC GAVE WAY TO SCIENCE?

THAT'S ONE WAY OF PUTTING IT, I SUPPOSE.

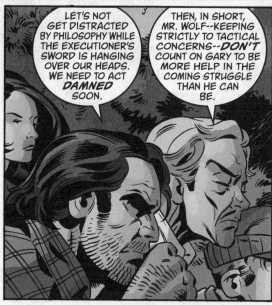

LET'S NOT GET DISTRACTED BY PHILOSOPHY WHILE THE EXECUTIONER'S SWORD IS HANGING OVER OUR HEADS. WE NEED TO ACT *DAMNED* SOON.

THEN, IN SHORT, MR. WOLF--KEEPING STRICTLY TO TACTICAL CONCERNS--*DON'T* COUNT ON GARY TO BE MORE HELP IN THE COMING STRUGGLE THAN HE CAN BE.

HIS SON KEVIN WAS *ALWAYS* MORE IMAGINATIVE THAN HE, AND WHERE OUR KIND IS CONCERNED, IMAGINATION EQUALS POWER AT ITS MOST *BASIC*.

I'LL DO WHAT I CAN, THOUGH.

THEN START DOING IT *NOW*. BUY US TIME TO GET WITHIN STRIKING DISTANCE.

JACK FROST, YOU STAY WITH ME. AND CONTINUE KEEPING THE SNOW UNDER WRAPS.

NO NEED TO TIP THE GUY OFF THAT ALL IS NOT SUNNY AND WELL SOONER THAN WE HAVE TO.

YOU KNOW WHAT TO DO. HIT HARD, FAST, AND GO FOR THE *KILL SHOT* WHEN YOU CAN.

LET'S MOVE OUT, PEOPLE.

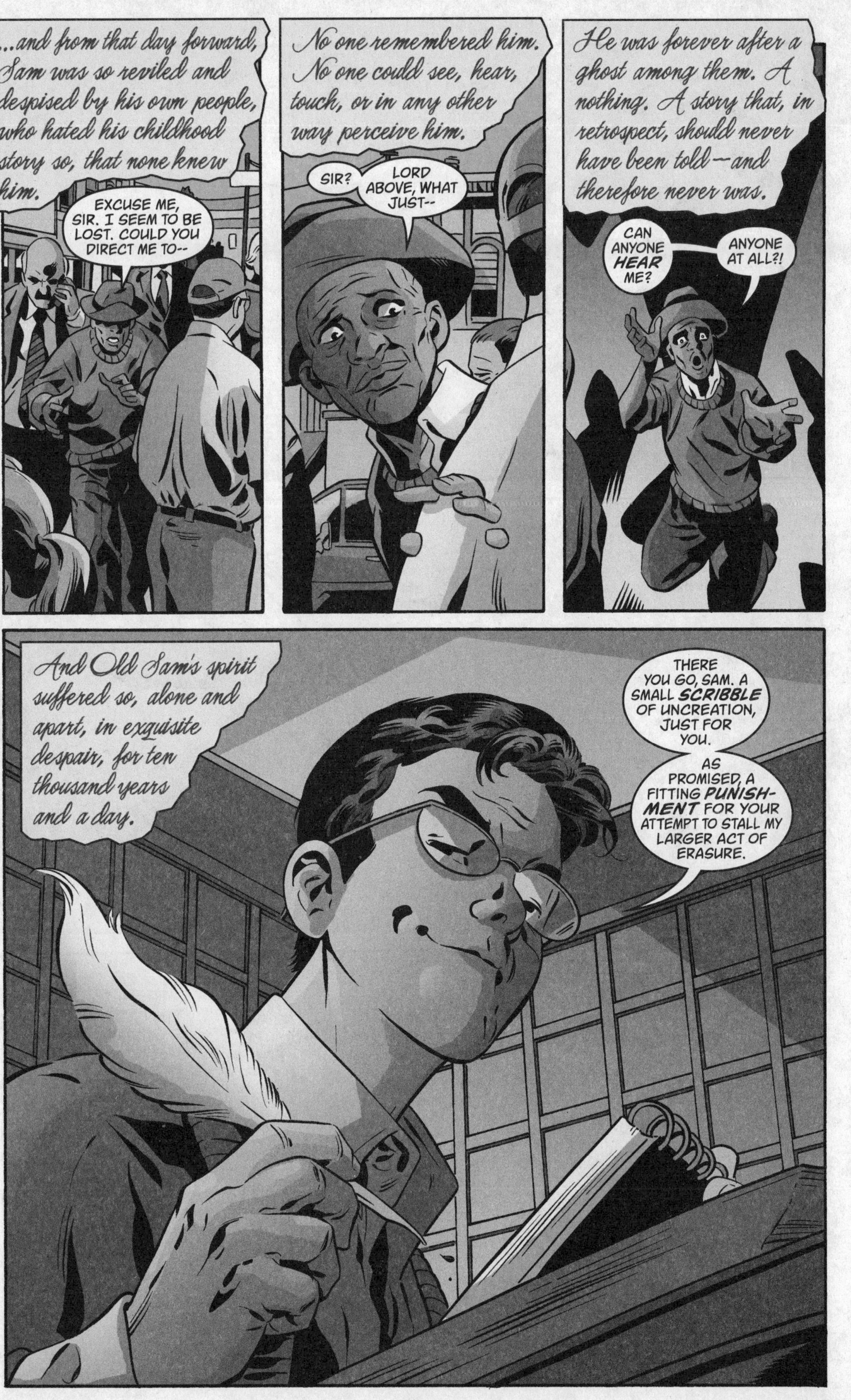
...and from that day forward, Sam was so reviled and despised by his own people, who hated his childhood story so, that none knew him.
EXCUSE ME, SIR. I SEEM TO BE LOST. COULD YOU DIRECT ME TO--
No one remembered him. No one could see, hear, touch, or in any other way perceive him.
SIR?
LORD ABOVE, WHAT JUST--
He was forever after a ghost among them. A nothing. A story that, in retrospect, should never have been told—and therefore never was.
CAN ANYONE HEAR ME?
ANYONE AT ALL?!
And Old Sam's spirit suffered so, alone and apart, in exquisite despair, for ten thousand years and a day.
THERE YOU GO, SAM. A SMALL SCRIBBLE OF UNCREATION, JUST FOR YOU.
AS PROMISED, A FITTING PUNISHMENT FOR YOUR ATTEMPT TO STALL MY LARGER ACT OF ERASURE.

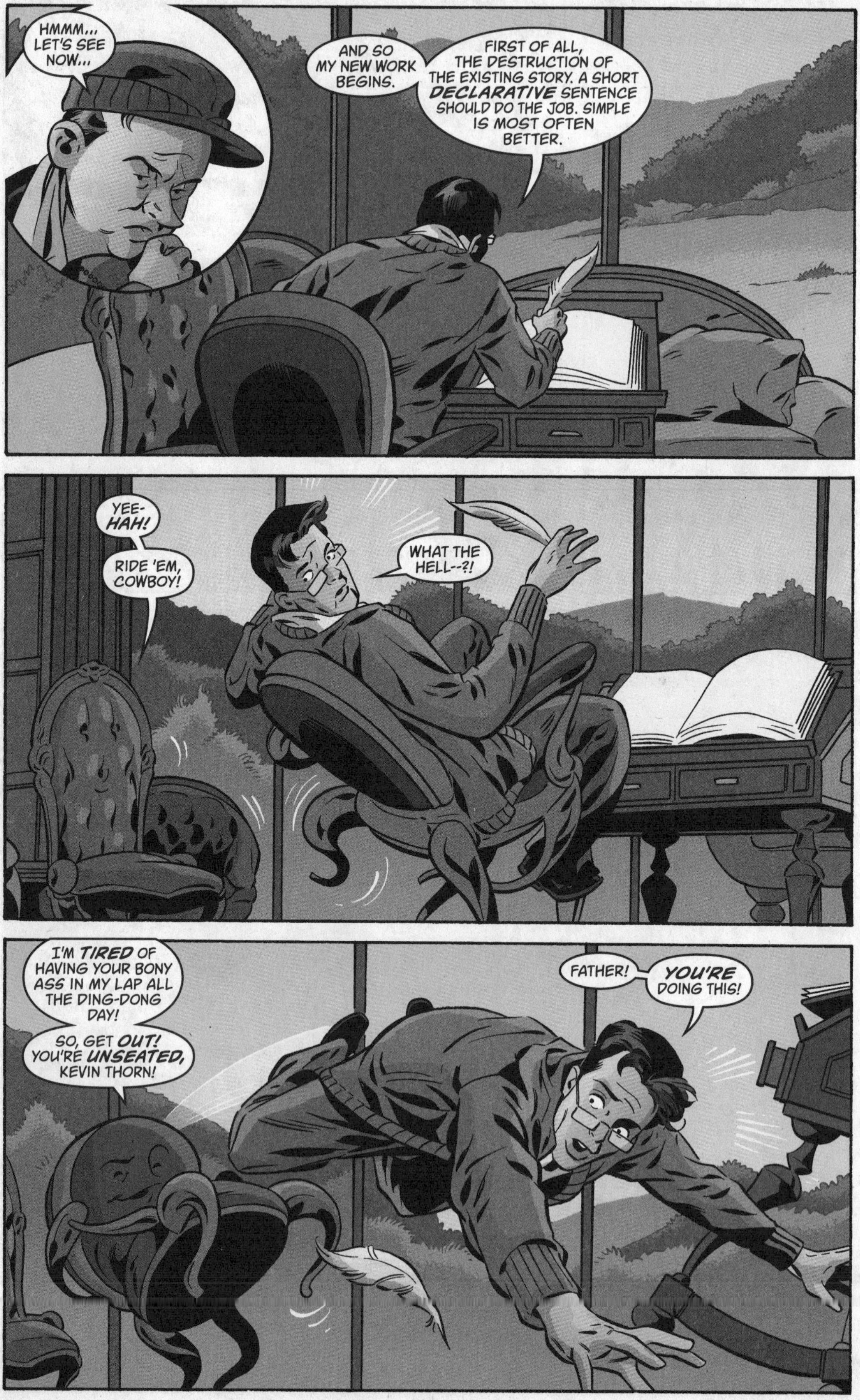
HMMM... LET'S SEE NOW...
AND SO MY NEW WORK BEGINS.
FIRST OF ALL, THE DESTRUCTION OF THE EXISTING STORY. A SHORT DECLARATIVE SENTENCE SHOULD DO THE JOB. SIMPLE IS MOST OFTEN BETTER.
YEE-HAH!
RIDE 'EM, COWBOY!
WHAT THE HELL--?!
I'M TIRED OF HAVING YOUR BONY ASS IN MY LAP ALL THE DING-DONG DAY!
SO, GET OUT! YOU'RE UNSEATED, KEVIN THORN!
FATHER!
YOU'RE DOING THIS!

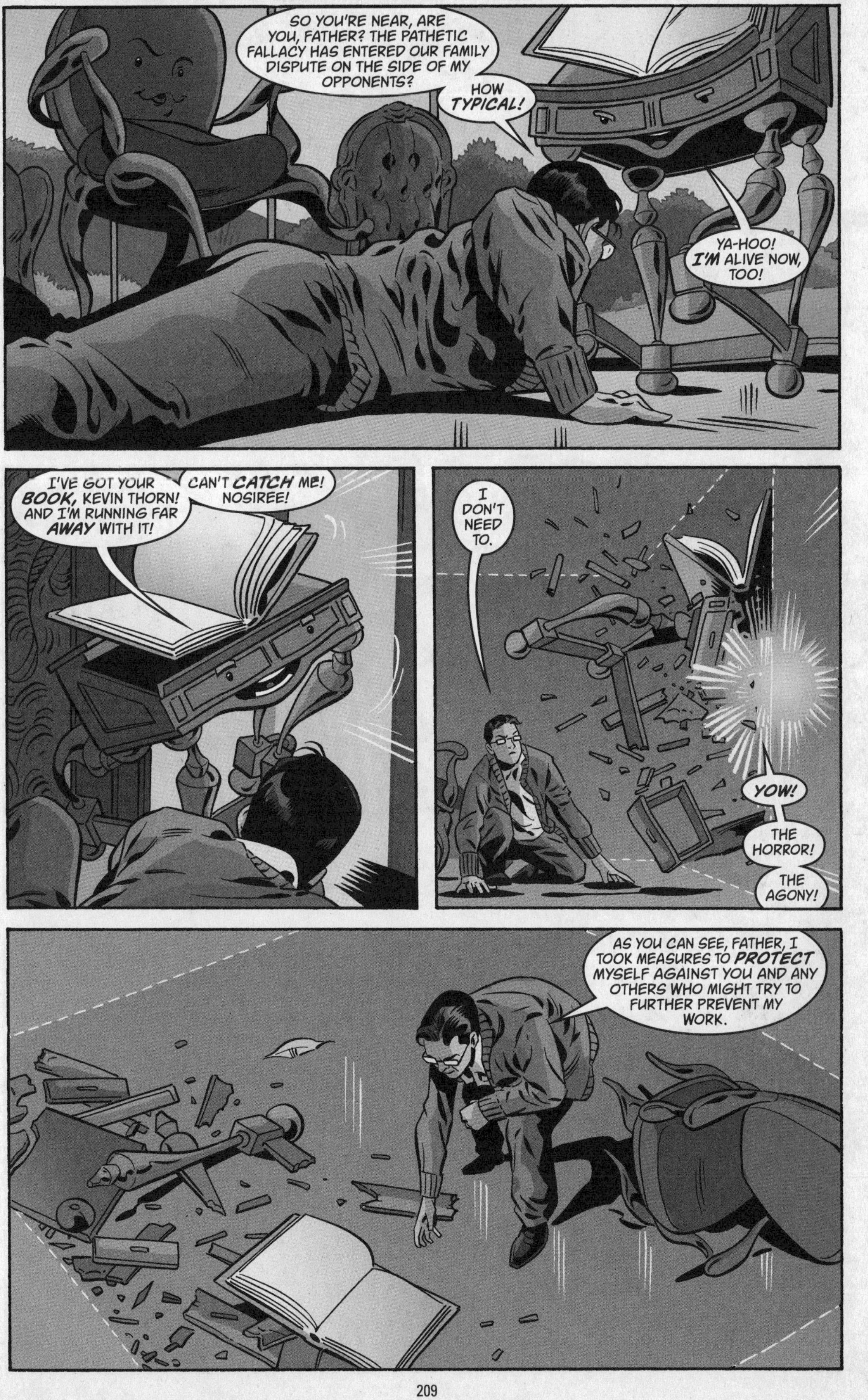
SO YOU'RE NEAR, ARE YOU, FATHER? THE PATHETIC FALLACY HAS ENTERED OUR FAMILY DISPUTE ON THE SIDE OF MY OPPONENTS?
HOW TYPICAL!
YA-HOO! I'M ALIVE NOW, TOO!
I'VE GOT YOUR BOOK, KEVIN THORN! AND I'M RUNNING FAR AWAY WITH IT!
CAN'T CATCH ME! NOSIREE!
I DON'T NEED TO.
YOW!
THE HORROR!
THE AGONY!
AS YOU CAN SEE, FATHER, I TOOK MEASURES TO PROTECT MYSELF AGAINST YOU AND ANY OTHERS WHO MIGHT TRY TO FURTHER PREVENT MY WORK.

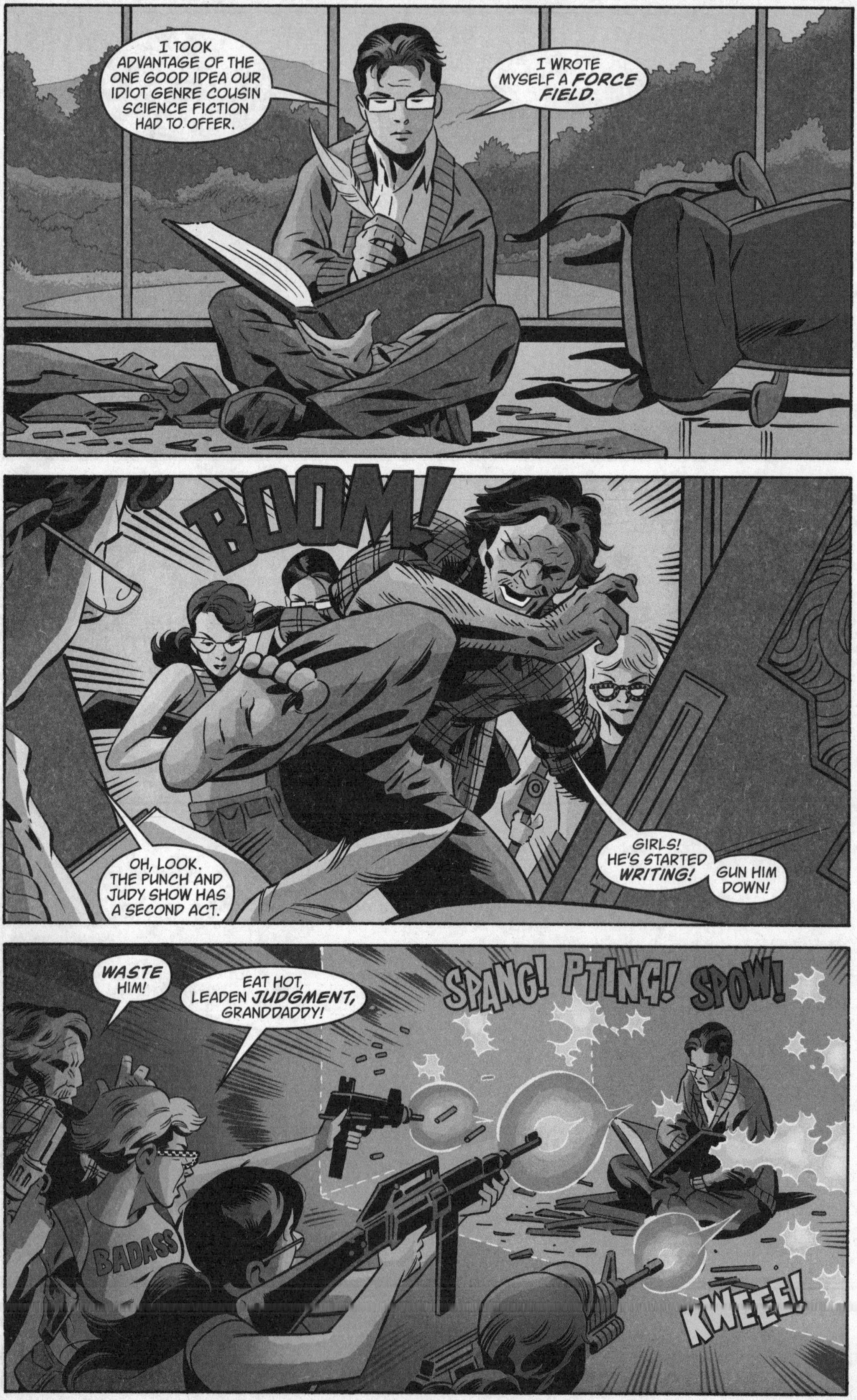
I TOOK ADVANTAGE OF THE ONE GOOD IDEA OUR IDIOT GENRE COUSIN SCIENCE FICTION HAD TO OFFER.
I WROTE MYSELF A FORCE FIELD.
BOOM!
OH, LOOK. THE PUNCH AND JUDY SHOW HAS A SECOND ACT.
GIRLS! HE'S STARTED WRITING!
GUN HIM DOWN!
WASTE HIM!
EAT HOT, LEADEN JUDGMENT, GRANDDADDY!
SPANG! PTING! SPOW!
BADASS
KWEEE!

And

IT'S SOME SORT OF--I DON'T KNOW *WHAT* IT IS, BUT I CAN'T GET THROUGH IT.

DID YOU IMAGINE YOURSELVES THE NOBLE *HEROES* OF THIS TALE, WHO'D SAVE THE DAY AT THE LAST SECOND?

YOU'VE *FAILED.* THERE ARE NO DAYS LEFT TO SAVE.

And so

WHAT HAPPENED? WHY DIDN'T YOU STOP HIM, BIGBY? WHY'S HE STILL *ALIVE* AND WRITING?

WE CAN'T. SOMETHING *IMPOSSIBLE* IS PROTECTING HIM.

YOU CAN'T STOP ME FROM WRITING YOU AWAY NOW. ALL YOU CAN DO IS WATCH *HELPLESSLY* AS I DO IT.

And so the

IF ANYONE HAS AN IDEA, NOW'S THE *TIME.*

IS THIS IT, THEN?

YES, SNOW WHITE, THIS IS IT. BUT I PROMISE IF I CHOOSE TO RECREATE YOU IN MY NEW STORY, YOU'LL GET YOUR PALACE *AND* TIARA. YOU WON'T END UP MATED TO AN ANIMAL.

JUST ONE AMONG THE MANY DISGUSTING *CHANGES* INFLICTED ON MY TALE.

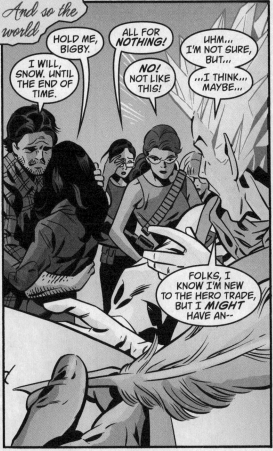

And so the world

HOLD ME, BIGBY.

I WILL, SNOW. UNTIL THE END OF TIME.

ALL FOR *NOTHING!*

NO! NOT LIKE THIS!

UHM... I'M NOT SURE, BUT... ...I THINK... MAYBE...

FOLKS, I KNOW I'M NEW TO THE HERO TRADE, BUT I *MIGHT* HAVE AN--

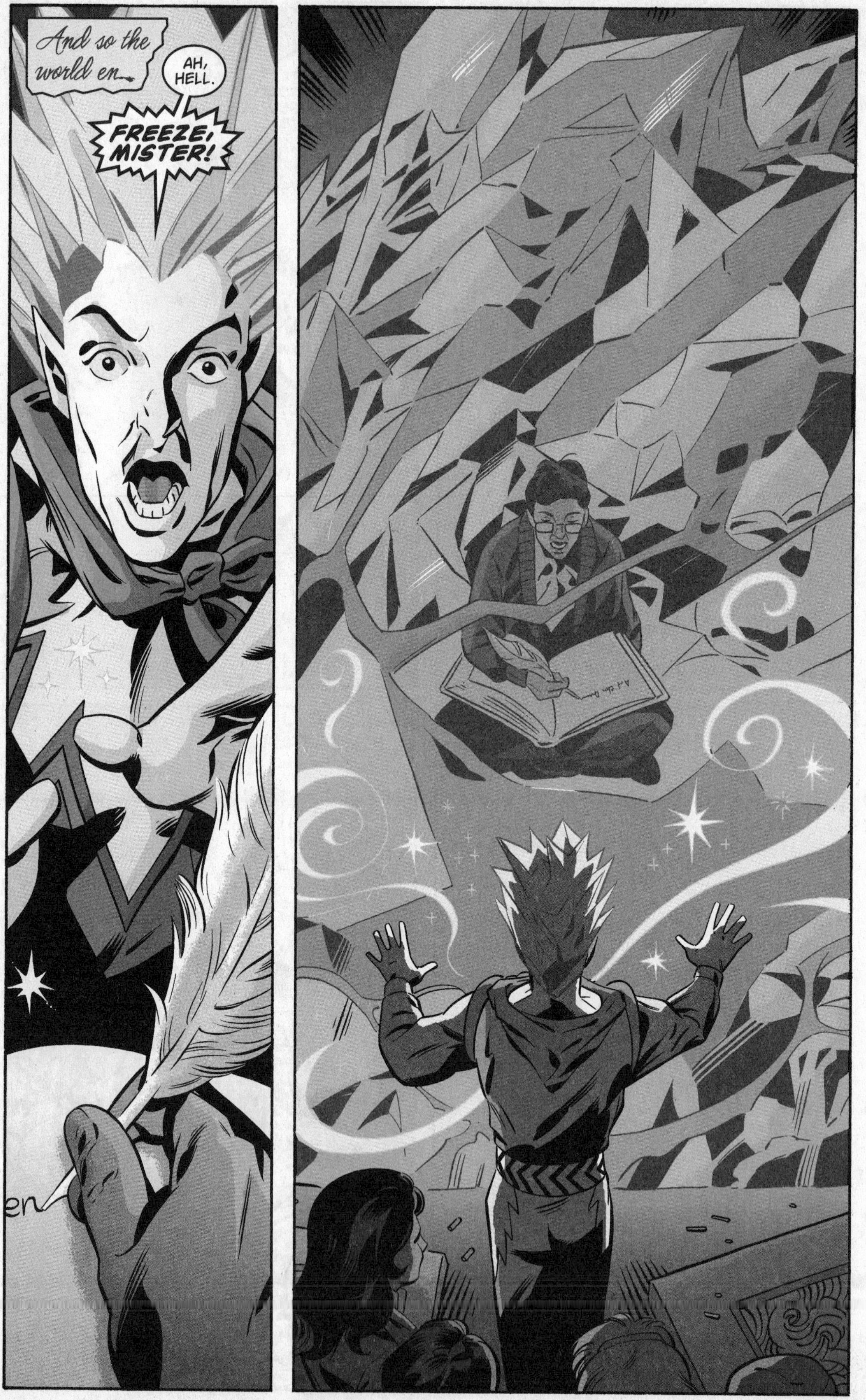
And so the world en—
AH, HELL.
FREEZE, MISTER!
en

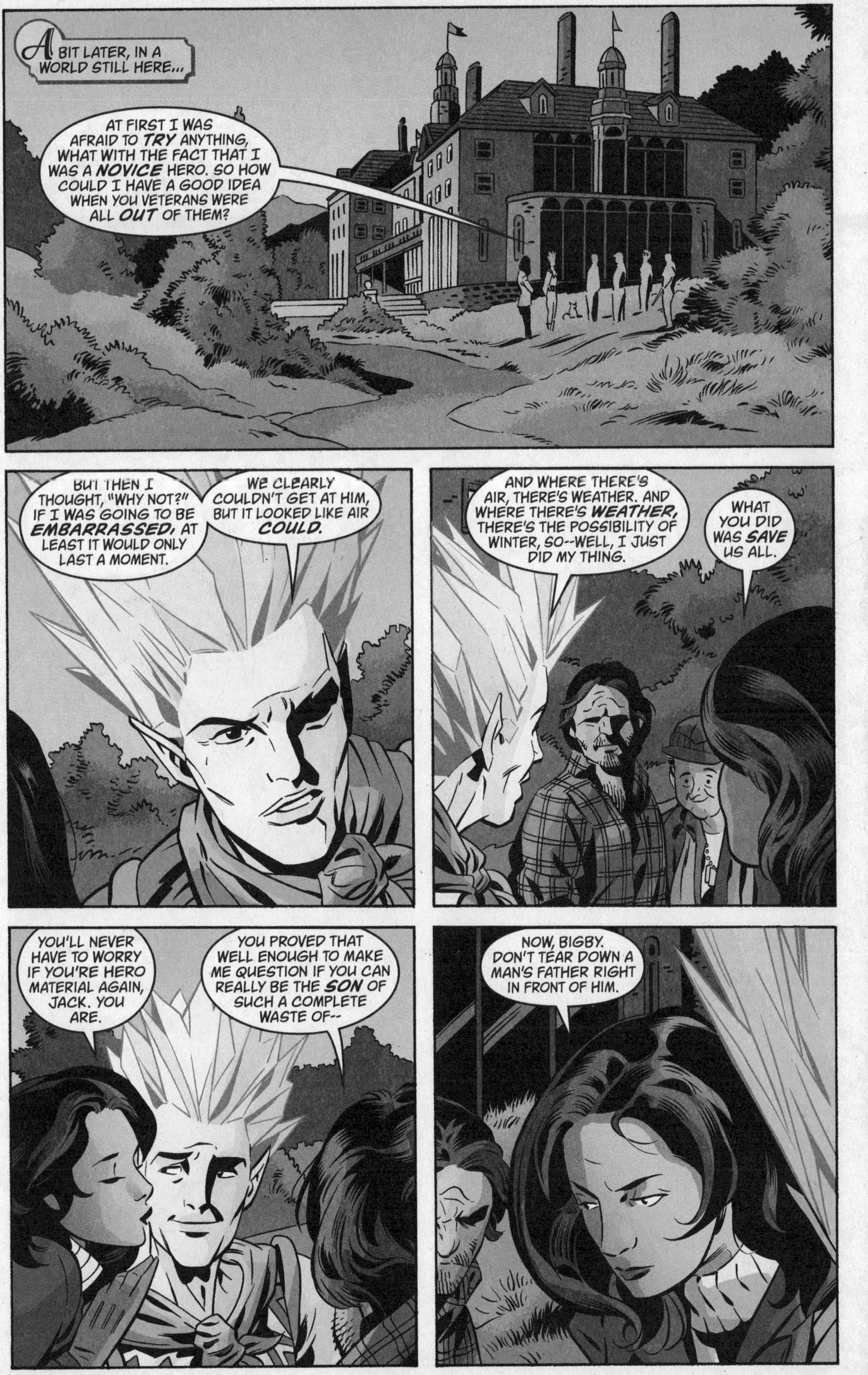
A BIT LATER, IN A WORLD STILL HERE...
AT FIRST I WAS AFRAID TO TRY ANYTHING, WHAT WITH THE FACT THAT I WAS A NOVICE HERO. SO HOW COULD I HAVE A GOOD IDEA WHEN YOU VETERANS WERE ALL OUT OF THEM?
BUT THEN I THOUGHT, "WHY NOT?" IF I WAS GOING TO BE EMBARRASSED, AT LEAST IT WOULD ONLY LAST A MOMENT.
WE CLEARLY COULDN'T GET AT HIM, BUT IT LOOKED LIKE AIR COULD.
AND WHERE THERE'S AIR, THERE'S WEATHER. AND WHERE THERE'S WEATHER, THERE'S THE POSSIBILITY OF WINTER, SO--WELL, I JUST DID MY THING.
WHAT YOU DID WAS SAVE US ALL.
YOU'LL NEVER HAVE TO WORRY IF YOU'RE HERO MATERIAL AGAIN, JACK. YOU ARE.
YOU PROVED THAT WELL ENOUGH TO MAKE ME QUESTION IF YOU CAN REALLY BE THE SON OF SUCH A COMPLETE WASTE OF--
NOW, BIGBY. DON'T TEAR DOWN A MAN'S FATHER RIGHT IN FRONT OF HIM.

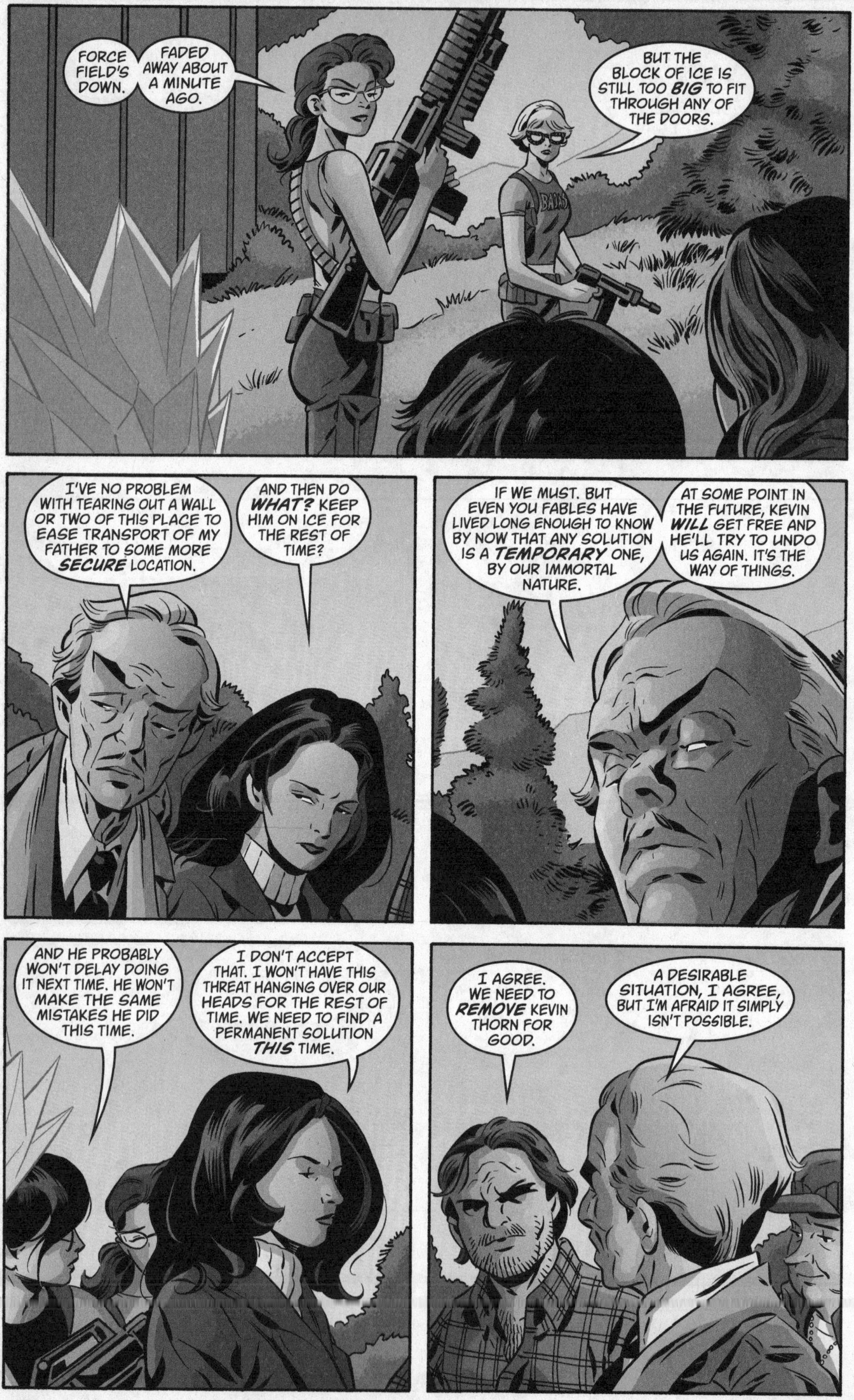
FORCE FIELD'S DOWN.
FADED AWAY ABOUT A MINUTE AGO.
BUT THE BLOCK OF ICE IS STILL TOO BIG TO FIT THROUGH ANY OF THE DOORS.
I'VE NO PROBLEM WITH TEARING OUT A WALL OR TWO OF THIS PLACE TO EASE TRANSPORT OF MY FATHER TO SOME MORE SECURE LOCATION.
AND THEN DO WHAT? KEEP HIM ON ICE FOR THE REST OF TIME?
IF WE MUST. BUT EVEN YOU FABLES HAVE LIVED LONG ENOUGH TO KNOW BY NOW THAT ANY SOLUTION IS A TEMPORARY ONE, BY OUR IMMORTAL NATURE.
AT SOME POINT IN THE FUTURE, KEVIN WILL GET FREE AND HE'LL TRY TO UNDO US AGAIN. IT'S THE WAY OF THINGS.
AND HE PROBABLY WON'T DELAY DOING IT NEXT TIME. HE WON'T MAKE THE SAME MISTAKES HE DID THIS TIME.
I DON'T ACCEPT THAT. I WON'T HAVE THIS THREAT HANGING OVER OUR HEADS FOR THE REST OF TIME. WE NEED TO FIND A PERMANENT SOLUTION THIS TIME.
I AGREE. WE NEED TO REMOVE KEVIN THORN FOR GOOD.
A DESIRABLE SITUATION, I AGREE, BUT I'M AFRAID IT SIMPLY ISN'T POSSIBLE.

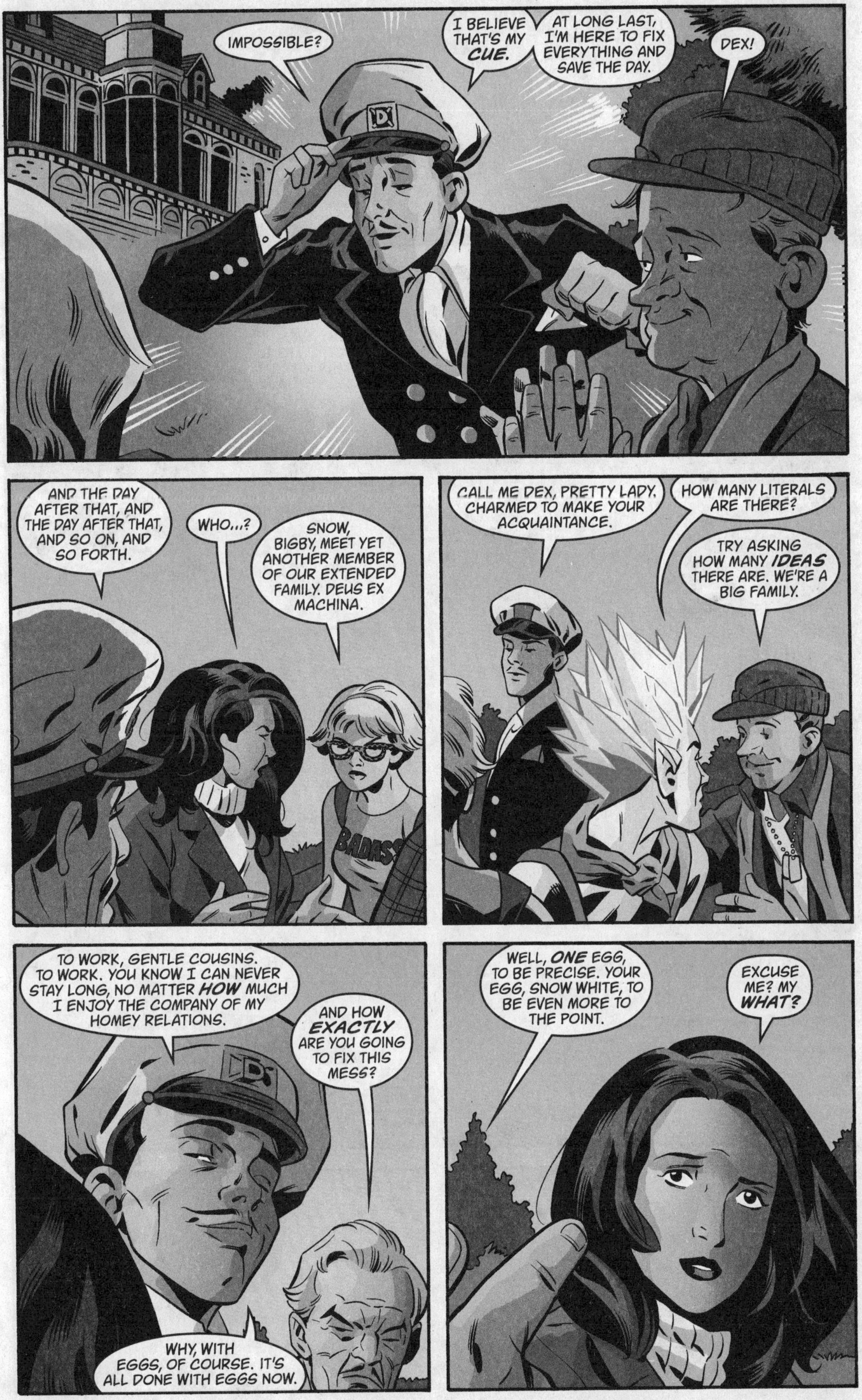
IMPOSSIBLE?
I BELIEVE THAT'S MY CUE.
AT LONG LAST, I'M HERE TO FIX EVERYTHING AND SAVE THE DAY.
DEX!
AND THE DAY AFTER THAT, AND THE DAY AFTER THAT, AND SO ON, AND SO FORTH.
WHO...?
SNOW, BIGBY, MEET YET ANOTHER MEMBER OF OUR EXTENDED FAMILY. DEUS EX MACHINA.
BADASS
CALL ME DEX, PRETTY LADY. CHARMED TO MAKE YOUR ACQUAINTANCE.
HOW MANY LITERALS ARE THERE?
TRY ASKING HOW MANY IDEAS THERE ARE. WE'RE A BIG FAMILY.
TO WORK, GENTLE COUSINS. TO WORK. YOU KNOW I CAN NEVER STAY LONG, NO MATTER HOW MUCH I ENJOY THE COMPANY OF MY HOMEY RELATIONS.
AND HOW EXACTLY ARE YOU GOING TO FIX THIS MESS?
WHY, WITH EGGS, OF COURSE. IT'S ALL DONE WITH EGGS NOW.
WELL, ONE EGG, TO BE PRECISE. YOUR EGG, SNOW WHITE, TO BE EVEN MORE TO THE POINT.
EXCUSE ME? MY WHAT?

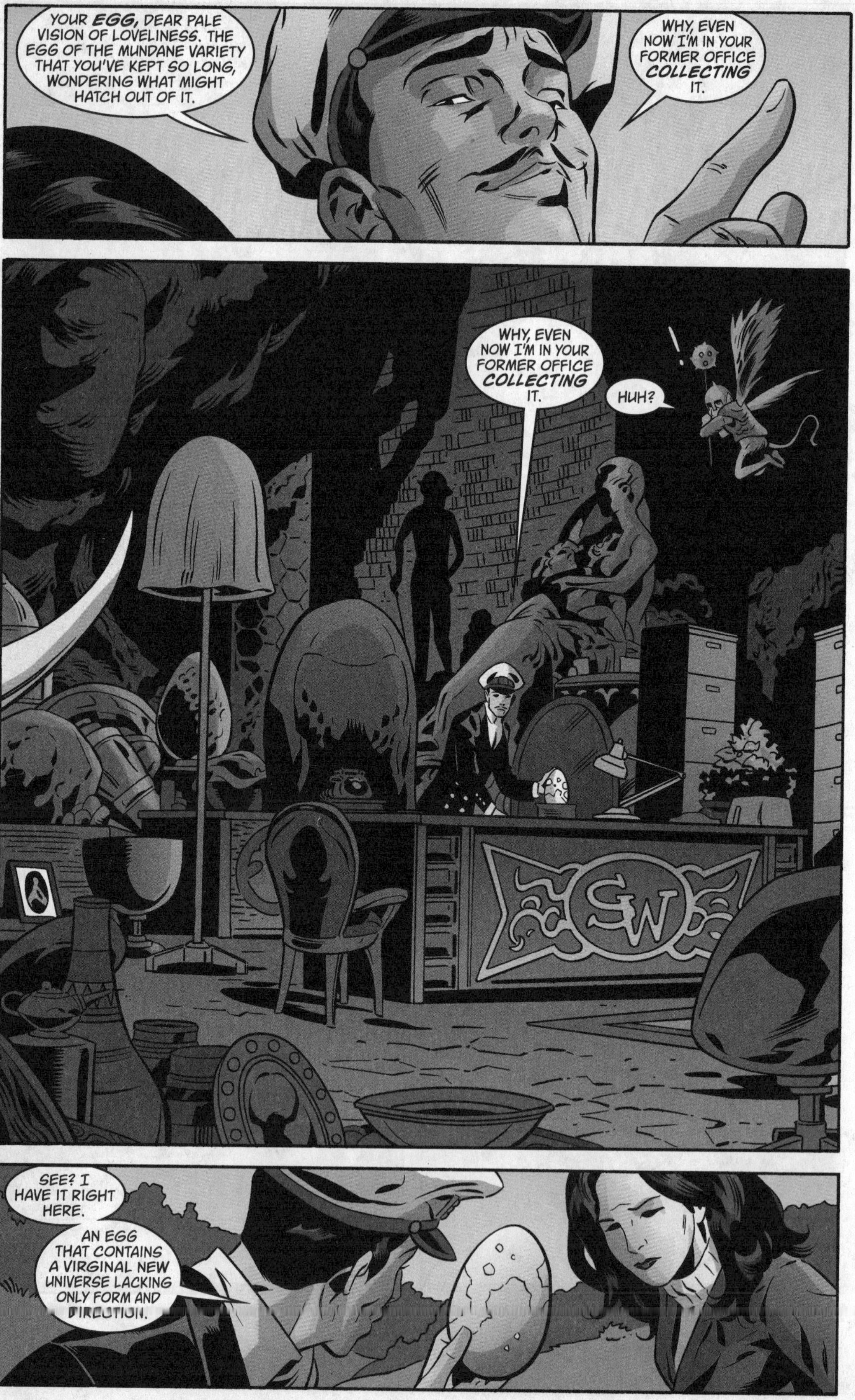

YOUR EGG, DEAR PALE VISION OF LOVELINESS. THE EGG OF THE MUNDANE VARIETY THAT YOU'VE KEPT SO LONG, WONDERING WHAT MIGHT HATCH OUT OF IT.
WHY, EVEN NOW I'M IN YOUR FORMER OFFICE COLLECTING IT.
WHY, EVEN NOW I'M IN YOUR FORMER OFFICE COLLECTING IT.
HUH?
!
SW
SEE? I HAVE IT RIGHT HERE.
AN EGG THAT CONTAINS A VIRGINAL NEW UNIVERSE LACKING ONLY FORM AND DIRECTION.

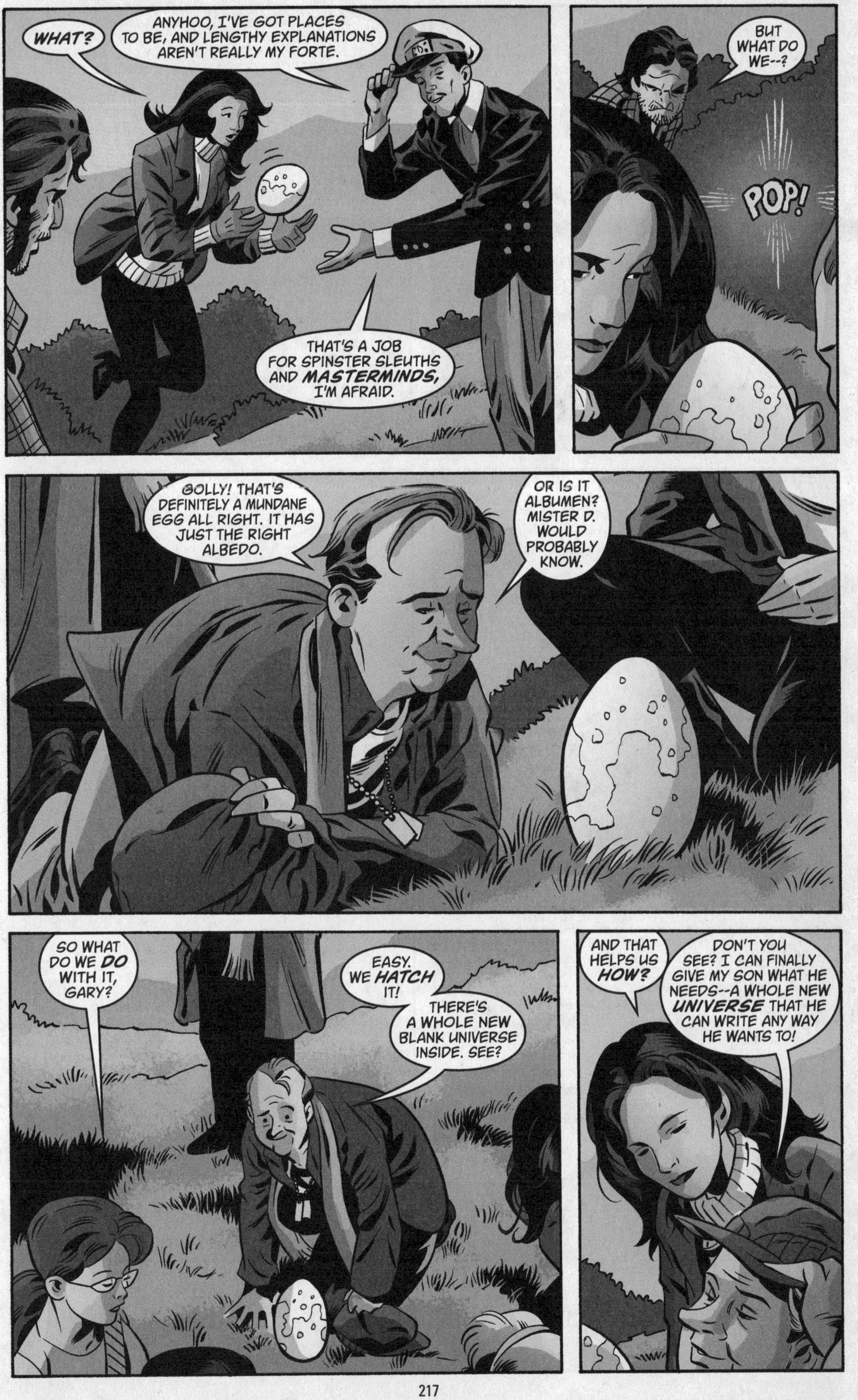
WHAT?
ANYHOO, I'VE GOT PLACES TO BE, AND LENGTHY EXPLANATIONS AREN'T REALLY MY FORTE.
THAT'S A JOB FOR SPINSTER SLEUTHS AND MASTERMINDS, I'M AFRAID.
BUT WHAT DO WE--?
POP!
GOLLY! THAT'S DEFINITELY A MUNDANE EGG ALL RIGHT. IT HAS JUST THE RIGHT ALBEDO.
OR IS IT ALBUMEN? MISTER D. WOULD PROBABLY KNOW.
SO WHAT DO WE DO WITH IT, GARY?
EASY. WE HATCH IT!
THERE'S A WHOLE NEW BLANK UNIVERSE INSIDE. SEE?
AND THAT HELPS US HOW?
DON'T YOU SEE? I CAN FINALLY GIVE MY SON WHAT HE NEEDS--A WHOLE NEW UNIVERSE THAT HE CAN WRITE ANY WAY HE WANTS TO!

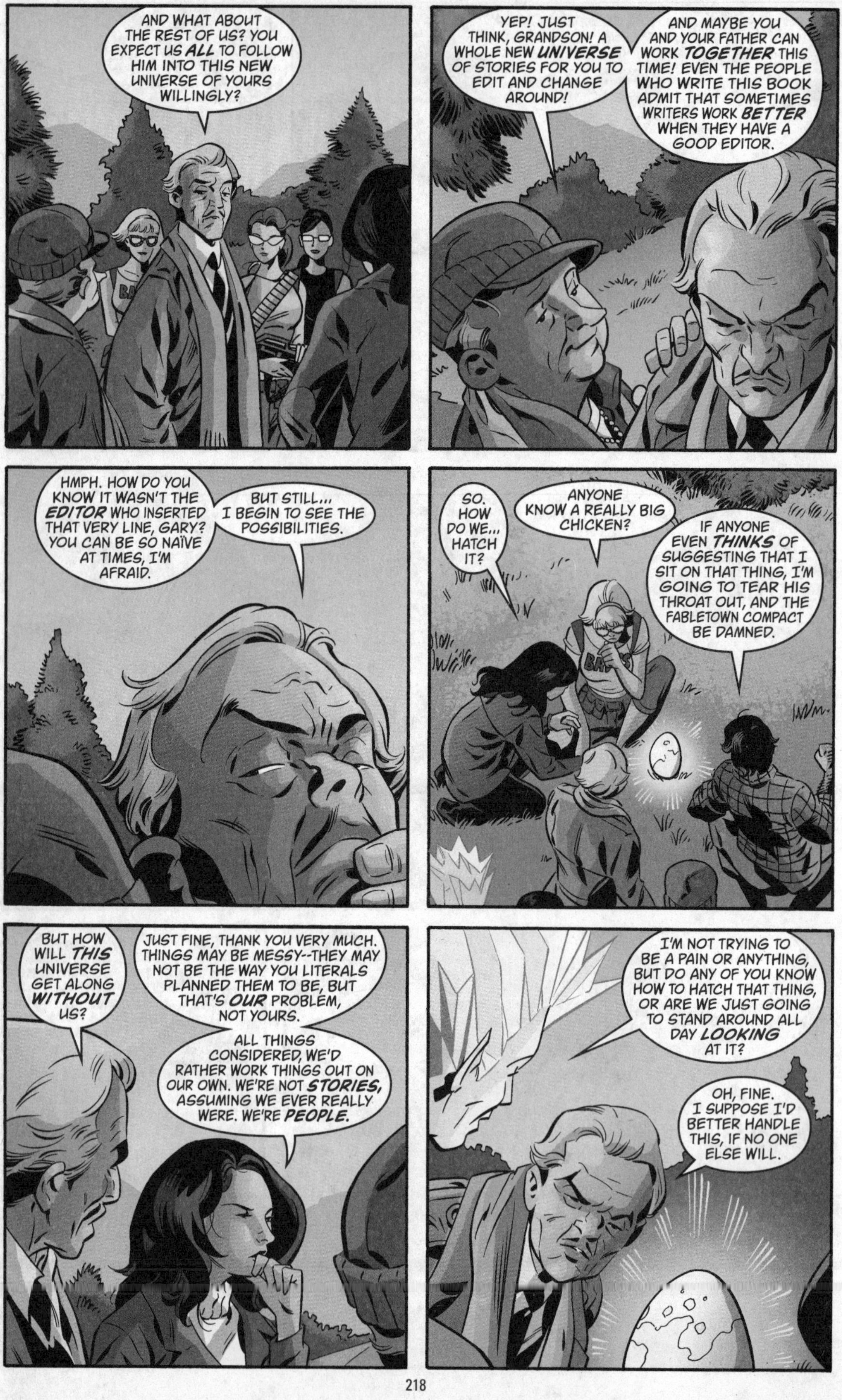
AND WHAT ABOUT THE REST OF US? YOU EXPECT US ALL TO FOLLOW HIM INTO THIS NEW UNIVERSE OF YOURS WILLINGLY?
YEP! JUST THINK, GRANDSON! A WHOLE NEW UNIVERSE OF STORIES FOR YOU TO EDIT AND CHANGE AROUND!
AND MAYBE YOU AND YOUR FATHER CAN WORK TOGETHER THIS TIME! EVEN THE PEOPLE WHO WRITE THIS BOOK ADMIT THAT SOMETIMES WRITERS WORK BETTER WHEN THEY HAVE A GOOD EDITOR.
HMPH. HOW DO YOU KNOW IT WASN'T THE EDITOR WHO INSERTED THAT VERY LINE, GARY? YOU CAN BE SO NAÏVE AT TIMES, I'M AFRAID.
BUT STILL... I BEGIN TO SEE THE POSSIBILITIES.
SO. HOW DO WE... HATCH IT?
ANYONE KNOW A REALLY BIG CHICKEN?
IF ANYONE EVEN THINKS OF SUGGESTING THAT I SIT ON THAT THING, I'M GOING TO TEAR HIS THROAT OUT, AND THE FABLETOWN COMPACT BE DAMNED.
BUT HOW WILL THIS UNIVERSE GET ALONG WITHOUT US?
JUST FINE, THANK YOU VERY MUCH. THINGS MAY BE MESSY--THEY MAY NOT BE THE WAY YOU LITERALS PLANNED THEM TO BE, BUT THAT'S OUR PROBLEM, NOT YOURS.
ALL THINGS CONSIDERED, WE'D RATHER WORK THINGS OUT ON OUR OWN. WE'RE NOT STORIES, ASSUMING WE EVER REALLY WERE. WE'RE PEOPLE.
I'M NOT TRYING TO BE A PAIN OR ANYTHING, BUT DO ANY OF YOU KNOW HOW TO HATCH THAT THING, OR ARE WE JUST GOING TO STAND AROUND ALL DAY LOOKING AT IT?
OH, FINE. I SUPPOSE I'D BETTER HANDLE THIS, IF NO ONE ELSE WILL.

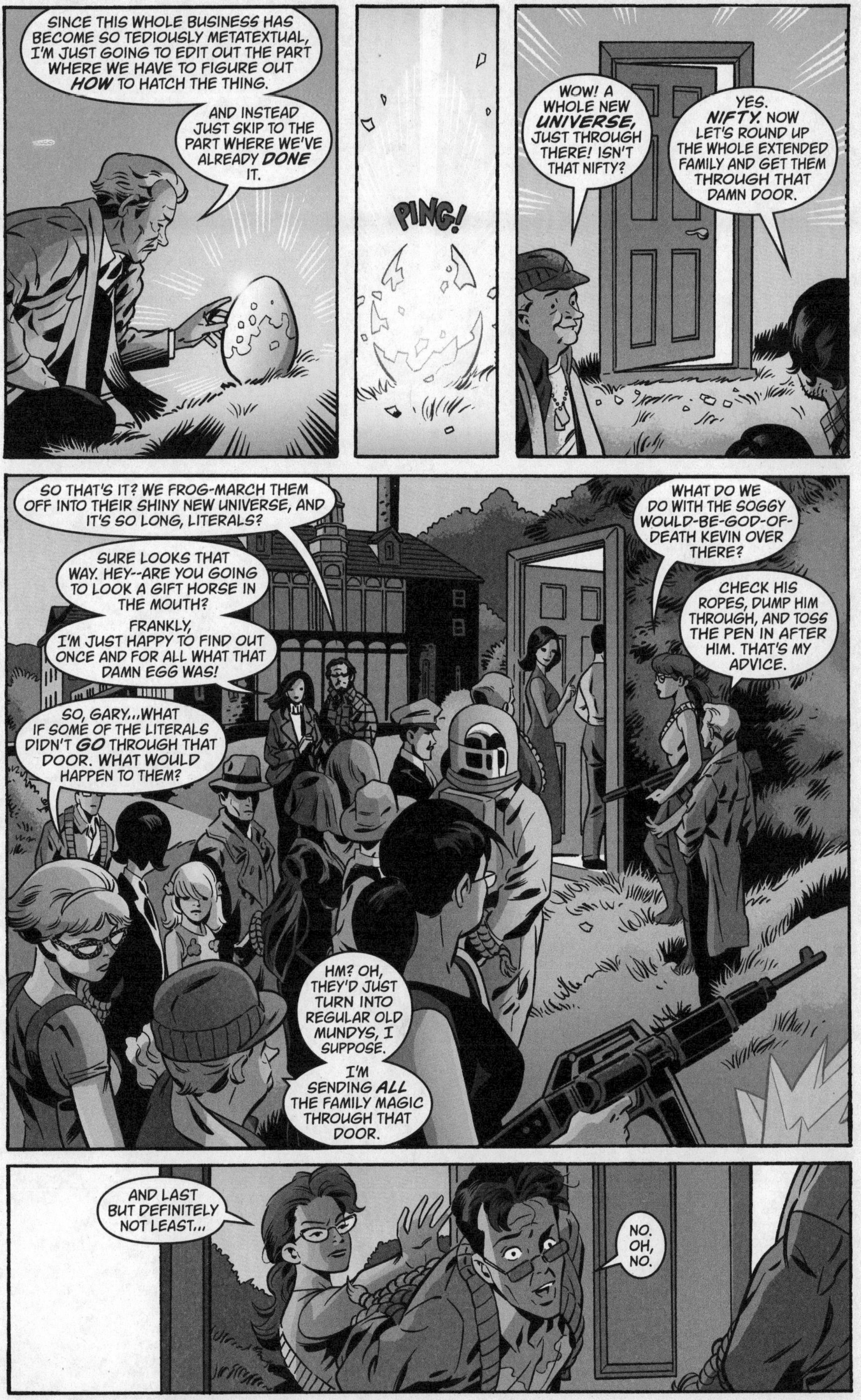
SINCE THIS WHOLE BUSINESS HAS BECOME SO TEDIOUSLY METATEXTUAL, I'M JUST GOING TO EDIT OUT THE PART WHERE WE HAVE TO FIGURE OUT HOW TO HATCH THE THING.
AND INSTEAD JUST SKIP TO THE PART WHERE WE'VE ALREADY DONE IT.
PING!
WOW! A WHOLE NEW UNIVERSE, JUST THROUGH THERE! ISN'T THAT NIFTY?
YES. NIFTY. NOW LET'S ROUND UP THE WHOLE EXTENDED FAMILY AND GET THEM THROUGH THAT DAMN DOOR.
SO THAT'S IT? WE FROG-MARCH THEM OFF INTO THEIR SHINY NEW UNIVERSE, AND IT'S SO LONG, LITERALS?
SURE LOOKS THAT WAY. HEY--ARE YOU GOING TO LOOK A GIFT HORSE IN THE MOUTH?
FRANKLY, I'M JUST HAPPY TO FIND OUT ONCE AND FOR ALL WHAT THAT DAMN EGG WAS!
WHAT DO WE DO WITH THE SOGGY WOULD-BE-GOD-OF-DEATH KEVIN OVER THERE?
CHECK HIS ROPES, DUMP HIM THROUGH, AND TOSS THE PEN IN AFTER HIM. THAT'S MY ADVICE.
SO, GARY...WHAT IF SOME OF THE LITERALS DIDN'T GO THROUGH THAT DOOR. WHAT WOULD HAPPEN TO THEM?
HM? OH, THEY'D JUST TURN INTO REGULAR OLD MUNDYS, I SUPPOSE.
I'M SENDING ALL THE FAMILY MAGIC THROUGH THAT DOOR.
AND LAST BUT DEFINITELY NOT LEAST...
NO. OH, NO.

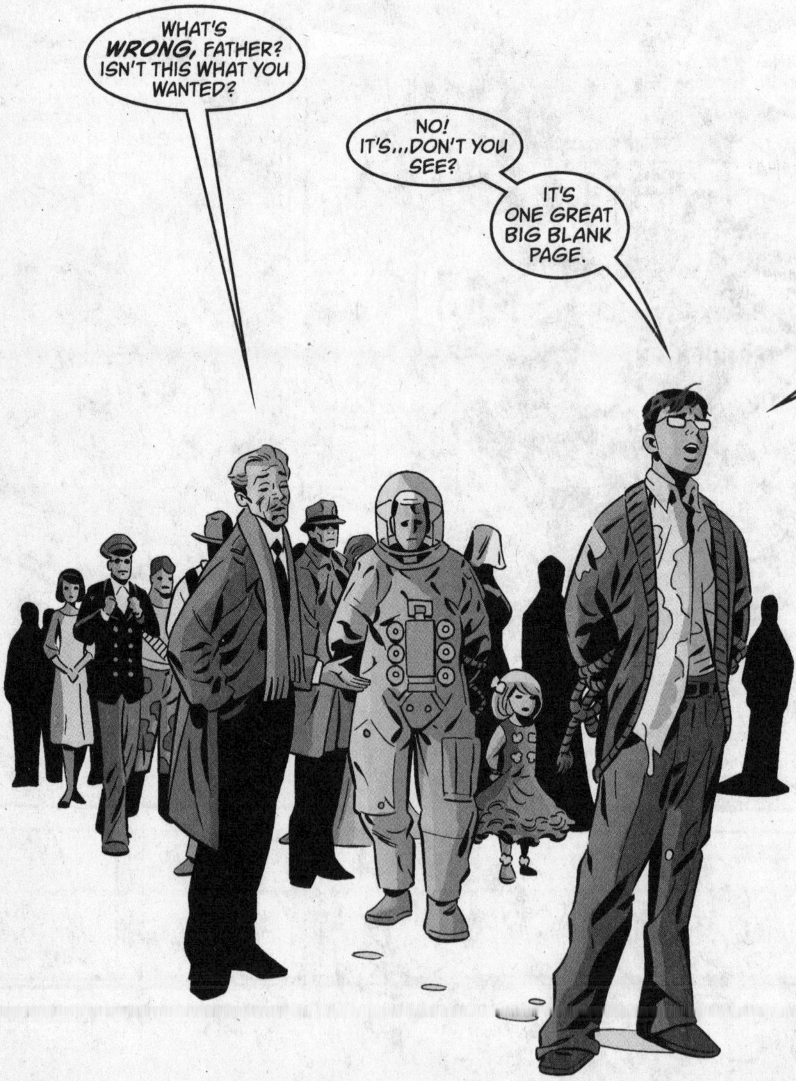
WHAT'S WRONG, FATHER? ISN'T THIS WHAT YOU WANTED?
NO! IT'S...DON'T YOU SEE?
IT'S ONE GREAT BIG BLANK PAGE.
I HAVE NO IDEA WHERE TO BEGIN!

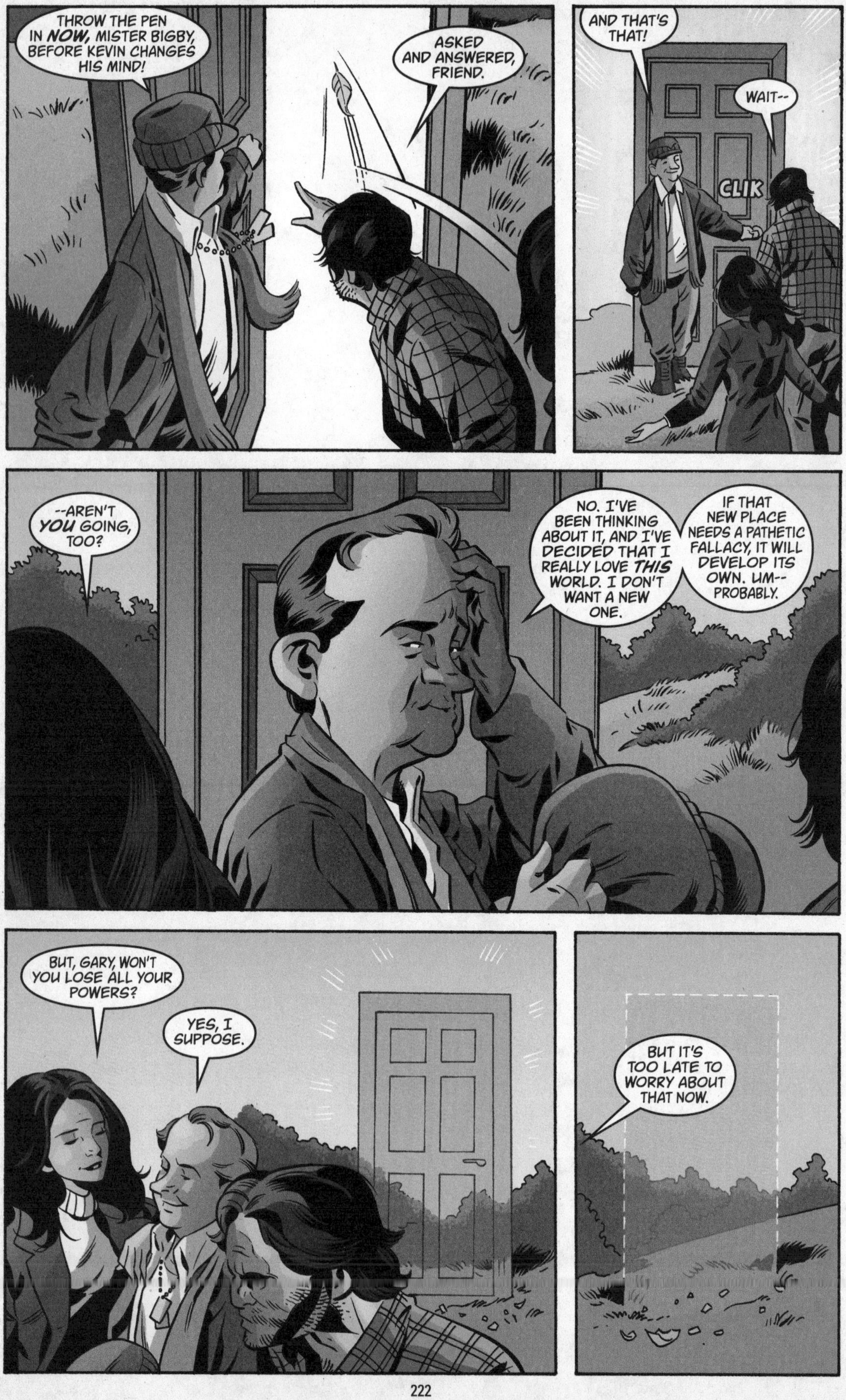
THROW THE PEN IN NOW, MISTER BIGBY, BEFORE KEVIN CHANGES HIS MIND!
ASKED AND ANSWERED, FRIEND.
AND THAT'S THAT!
WAIT--
CLIK
--AREN'T YOU GOING, TOO?
NO. I'VE BEEN THINKING ABOUT IT, AND I'VE DECIDED THAT I REALLY LOVE THIS WORLD. I DON'T WANT A NEW ONE.
IF THAT NEW PLACE NEEDS A PATHETIC FALLACY, IT WILL DEVELOP ITS OWN. UM--PROBABLY.
BUT, GARY, WON'T YOU LOSE ALL YOUR POWERS?
YES, I SUPPOSE.
BUT IT'S TOO LATE TO WORRY ABOUT THAT NOW.

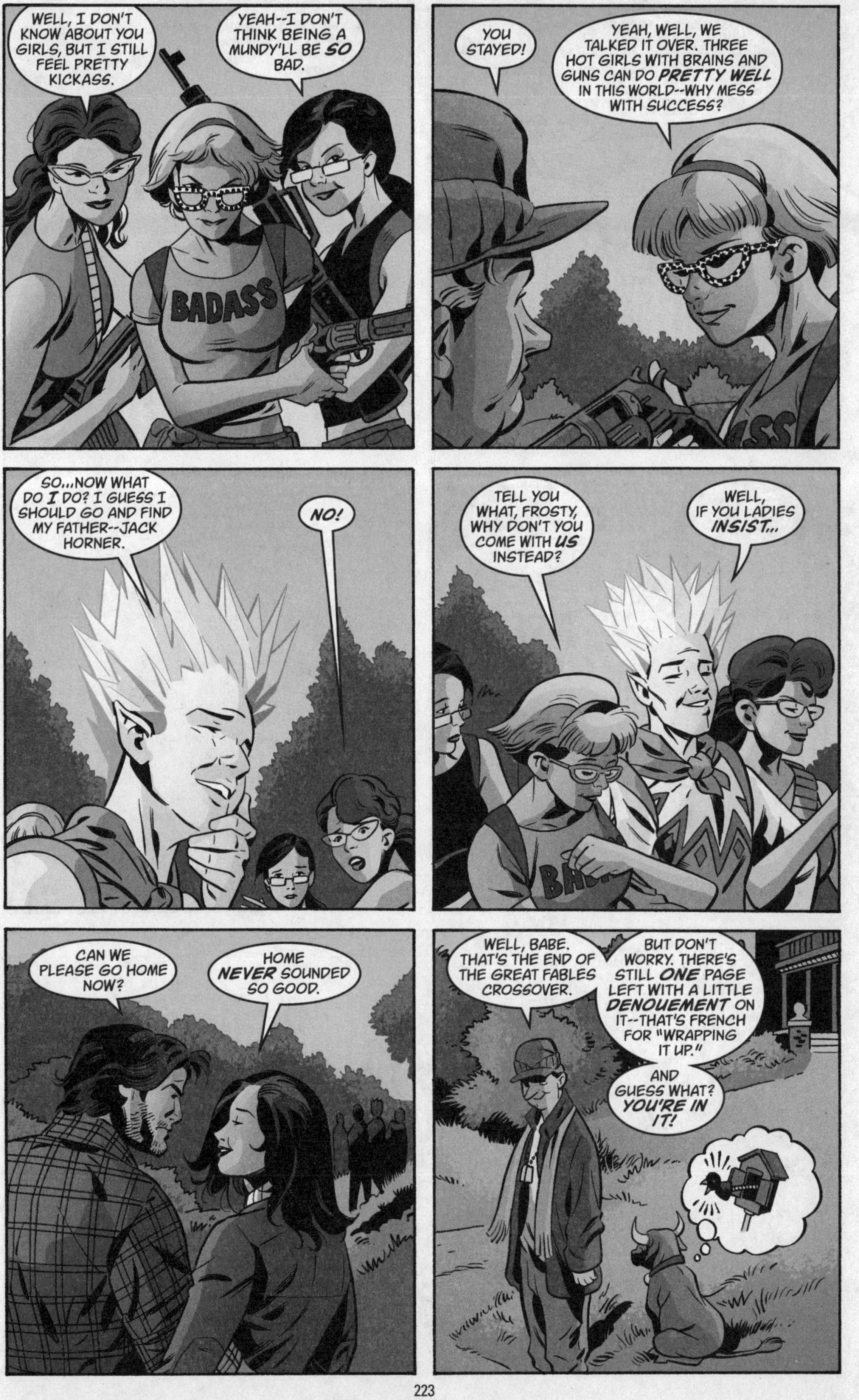
WELL, I DON'T KNOW ABOUT YOU GIRLS, BUT I STILL FEEL PRETTY KICKASS.
YEAH--I DON'T THINK BEING A MUNDY'LL BE SO BAD.
BADASS
YOU STAYED!
YEAH, WELL, WE TALKED IT OVER. THREE HOT GIRLS WITH BRAINS AND GUNS CAN DO PRETTY WELL IN THIS WORLD--WHY MESS WITH SUCCESS?
SO...NOW WHAT DO I DO? I GUESS I SHOULD GO AND FIND MY FATHER--JACK HORNER.
NO!
TELL YOU WHAT, FROSTY, WHY DON'T YOU COME WITH US INSTEAD?
WELL, IF YOU LADIES INSIST...
CAN WE PLEASE GO HOME NOW?
HOME NEVER SOUNDED SO GOOD.
WELL, BABE. THAT'S THE END OF THE GREAT FABLES CROSSOVER.
BUT DON'T WORRY. THERE'S STILL ONE PAGE LEFT WITH A LITTLE DENOUEMENT ON IT--THAT'S FRENCH FOR "WRAPPING IT UP."
AND GUESS WHAT? YOU'RE IN IT!

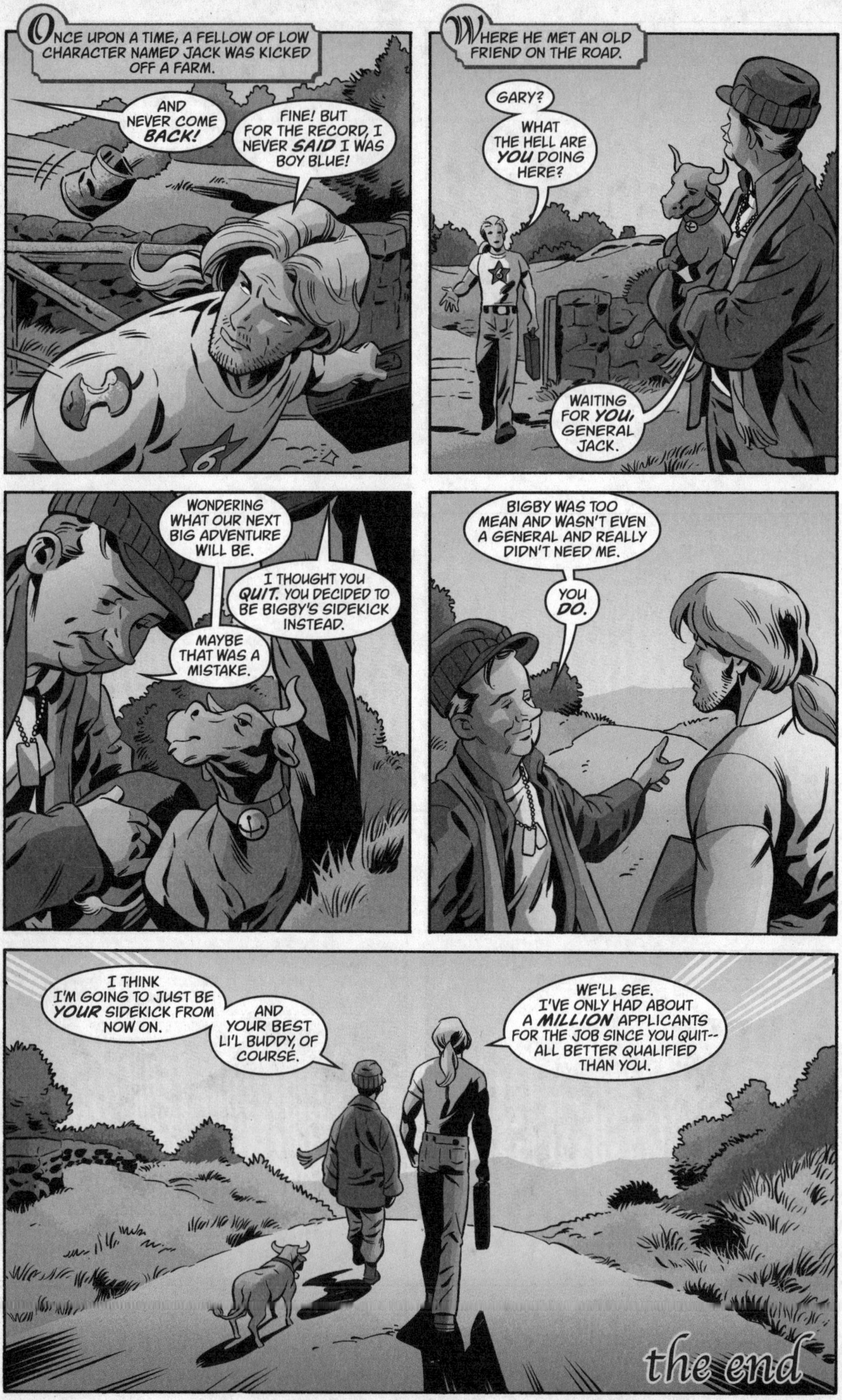

ONCE UPON A TIME, A FELLOW OF LOW CHARACTER NAMED JACK WAS KICKED OFF A FARM.
AND NEVER COME BACK!
FINE! BUT FOR THE RECORD, I NEVER SAID I WAS BOY BLUE!
WHERE HE MET AN OLD FRIEND ON THE ROAD.
GARY?
WHAT THE HELL ARE YOU DOING HERE?
WAITING FOR YOU, GENERAL JACK.
WONDERING WHAT OUR NEXT BIG ADVENTURE WILL BE.
I THOUGHT YOU QUIT. YOU DECIDED TO BE BIGBY'S SIDEKICK INSTEAD.
MAYBE THAT WAS A MISTAKE.
BIGBY WAS TOO MEAN AND WASN'T EVEN A GENERAL AND REALLY DIDN'T NEED ME.
YOU DO.
I THINK I'M GOING TO JUST BE YOUR SIDEKICK FROM NOW ON.
AND YOUR BEST LI'L BUDDY, OF COURSE.
WE'LL SEE. I'VE ONLY HAD ABOUT A MILLION APPLICANTS FOR THE JOB SINCE YOU QUIT-- ALL BETTER QUALIFIED THAN YOU.
the end

SPECIAL SNEAK PREVIEW

PETER & MAX

a FABLES novel

Chapter One

FABLES

In which Rose Red takes an early morning drive and finds our story's hero at the end of it.

FOR MOST OF HIS LONG YEARS PETER PIPER wanted nothing more than to live a life of peace and safety in some remote cozy cottage, married to his childhood sweetheart, who grew into the only woman he could ever love. Which is pretty much what happened. But there were complications along the way, as there often are, because few love stories are allowed to be just that and nothing else.

SOMEWHERE IN NEW YORK CITY there's a tiny, secretive neighborhood no one knows about except those who live there and a few scattered others in our wide world. It's a private enclave taking up only one modest block along a small side street named Bullfinch, and a few other buildings close by. It's called Fabletown by its residents and called nothing at all by anyone else, because, as we've said, they don't know of it. Fabletown has been there longer than its general location has been named the Upper West Side, and was in fact the very first settlement in that area, when all of the other dwellings were huddled together down at the southern tip of Manhattan Island. Unspoiled fields and forests were Fabletown's only neighbors at first, way back when New York was still called New Amsterdam. But the city grew up around it over the centuries, as cities tend to do, so that now Fabletown is just a small, quaint and largely ignored little side street in a much bigger enterprise, which suits them just fine.

If you were to accidentally stroll down Bullfinch Street – and it would be by accident, because strong spells of misdirection, obfuscation and "there's nothing important here" have been laid over the place, to keep outsiders out – its residents would look much like us, just normal folks in a normal place. But these people are far from normal. For one thing they've been around for awhile, some of them for millennia. The very first founders of the settlement still live there and look no older now than they did then. It's impossible to say just yet if they're immortal, because the only true test of that is to see if they're still alive at the end of time. But so far they seem to be on pace to finish that race in good position.

The Fables, which is what they call themselves collectively, are a magical people who weren't originally from this world. They arrived here long ago, over a span of years, alone or in small groups, as refugees from their own equally magical Homelands, hundreds of scattered worlds which had been overrun by the invading armies of an ambitious and merciless conqueror, who seemed determined to build himself an empire, killing all who resisted and enslaving those who didn't.

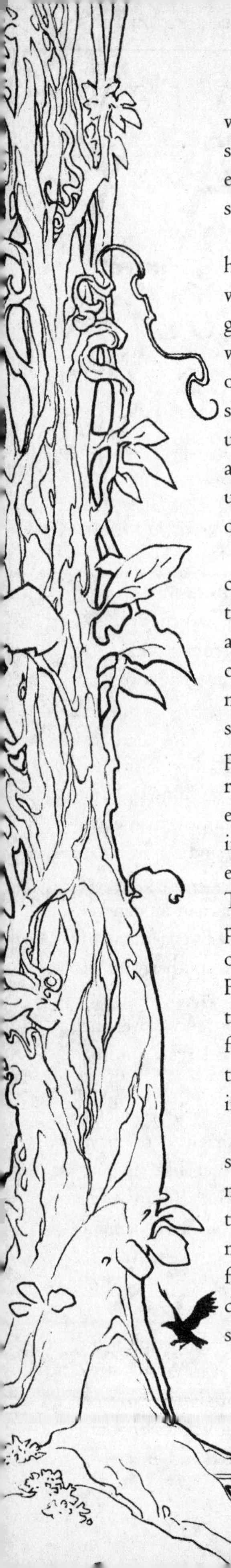

Once here they discovered their new home to be a small and humble world so excruciatingly mundane, so bereft of natural magic that the Adversary – their name for the conqueror – expressed no interest in it. All available evidence promised that they'd found a place of long-term safety. And so they settled in.

Pretty quickly they discerned a few odd things about their adopted home. Our world seemed to contain miniature versions of every Homeland world they'd originally come from. Here was a small island nation called England that mirrored the entire world they once knew as Albion. And over there was a country called Russia that was a rough sixteenth-scale sketch of the vast old world of The Rus. Ireland resembled the world of Erin, infant America slowly grew into an approximation of Americana, and so on. For some as yet undiscovered reason, or perhaps for no reason at all since some truly remarkable things do seem to be the result of mere (or possibly mighty) chance, our unimportant out-of-the-way little world turned out to be a map of sorts for all of the much grander ones they'd left behind.

Now Fables seems an odd name for any sort of people to choose to call themselves, and especially odd for this group, since the word implies that they're folks with stories to tell. They aren't. They were and continue to be adamantly secretive. But this brings us to another weird phenomenon they discovered after arriving here. It may be that when you introduce a number of very magical creatures into a decidedly unmagical environment, some of that magic seeps out, spreading by osmosis into the mundane natives (us) whom they, often pejoratively, call mundys. Perhaps the spilled magic grants the mundys some rudimentary, but unconscious, awareness of their new neighbors. Whatever the explanation, shortly after Fables arrived, mundys all over the world began telling stories about them; stories no one knew were based on actual people and everyone assumed were simply creative and occasionally clever works of fiction. These stories sometimes became distorted, as they were passed from person to person, and those that were finally written down often contained many errors of fact. But for the most part they were accurate enough that our mysterious Fable immigrants eventually realized they were being talked about. They were the subjects of many popular fairy tales – and some did indeed arrive here from the land of faeries. Their private histories were inscribed and revealed in the form of folktales, nursery rhymes, epic poems and doggerel ditties, haunting ballads, ribald songs and, of course, fables.

A thousand different mundy authors scribbled every variation on the story of Beauty and the Beast, for example; how a wicked witch cursed a nobleman with a dire enchantment, but its power was finally broken by a woman's true love. But no mundy wrote what happened next; how years after they'd married to live happily ever after, all sorts of disturbingly unhappy things befell them, until they arrived here. Now Beauty has an office job as Fabletown's deputy mayor, and her husband Beast serves as the underground community's sheriff. You've heard many tales of the dashing and heroic Prince Charming, but did you know that he's been thrice divorced and now runs Fabletown as its mayor? Elsewhere in Fabletown Cinderella runs a shoe store, the Sleeping Beauty is living off her investments, while trying not to prick her finger again, a certain famous bridge troll works as a security guard, and many a (formerly) wicked witch now resides on the thirteenth floor of the Woodland Building, which, among other things, is the community's informal city hall.

These strange and wondrous people, leaking raw and enchanted histories wheresoever they went, became known to us through conjured stories of their past adventures in abandoned lands, while their continued lives in this world remained hidden from us.

So, perhaps it was inevitable that the refugees, coming together from so many scattered lands and diverse cultures, wanting to select some collective name under which they could become a unified people, would settle on the one quality they all seemed to share in common— their tendency to become the subjects of so many stories in our mundy world. At first they tried calling themselves The Story People, but when that inevitably got shortened to Stories, it seemed a tad confusing, seeing as how both books and buildings already contained stories, and adding a third definition to so basic a word seemed overly burdensome. They tried The Folklore People for a while, but gave it up too, when it first became Folk, which was already in widespread use among the mundys, and then Lores, which never quite fell trippingly from the tongue. For similar reasons Ballads and Rhymes were also tried and discarded, leaving them ultimately with The Fabled People, which became simply Fables, which turned out to fit just fine, after a reasonable period of getting used to it.

Fables, the personification of story and song, live among us in New York and we for the most part are none the wiser. Except that some Fables don't live in the city, because they can't.

Far to the north of Manhattan and the other boroughs, deep into the wider, wilder reaches of Upstate New York, there is a vast area of largely undeveloped land known as the Farm, because some of it has indeed been cultivated. And some of it is occupied by a quaint, rural village of huts and houses, barns and stables. But most of the Farm's uncounted acreage has been left in its original wild state. The Farm is Fabletown's sister community, its upstate annex for housing all of the Fables who also fled their Homelands for this world, but who can't pass as human. Where the human-looking Fables are largely free to come and go wherever in the world they wish, Farm Fables are confined in this one place for all time – a large and comfortable prison to be sure – but a prison just the same. They're confined to the Farm because the most vital of all Fable laws strictly forbids anything that might reveal their magical nature to the mundys. And nothing is more immediately and unmistakably identifiable as magical than a talking duck, with a penchant for discussing the collected works of Jane Austen, or a moo-cow who can leap over the moon. Granted it was the moon of another land, which was both smaller and nearer than ours, but still an impressive feat, all things considered.

You can't find your way to The Farm, even more so than to Fabletown proper, because many more-powerful concealment and misdirection spells protect the place, deflecting all nosy mundys away or around it. But if you could, if you could bring yourself, by some tremendous act of will and raw, stiff-necked determination, to drive along that narrow old road, by the low, moss-covered stone wall, and turn in on the dirt track, where the tired wooden gate sags against the ancient, brooding chestnut tree, you might possibly discover that the Three Little Pigs live in a piggy-sized house of bricks (they learned their lesson long ago) just down the lane from where the Old Woman dwells in her giant shoe. Being perfectly normal looking, she could leave the Farm any time she wished, but not with her beloved shoe-house, where she'd raised so many children, so she chooses to stay where she is.

Our tale, the one that couldn't quite remain a simple love story, begins then in Fabletown and almost immediately moves up to the Farm. It happens because a witch learned something that she told to a beast, who phoned a wolf, who in turn called his wife's twin sister, who never was a princess but perhaps should have been.

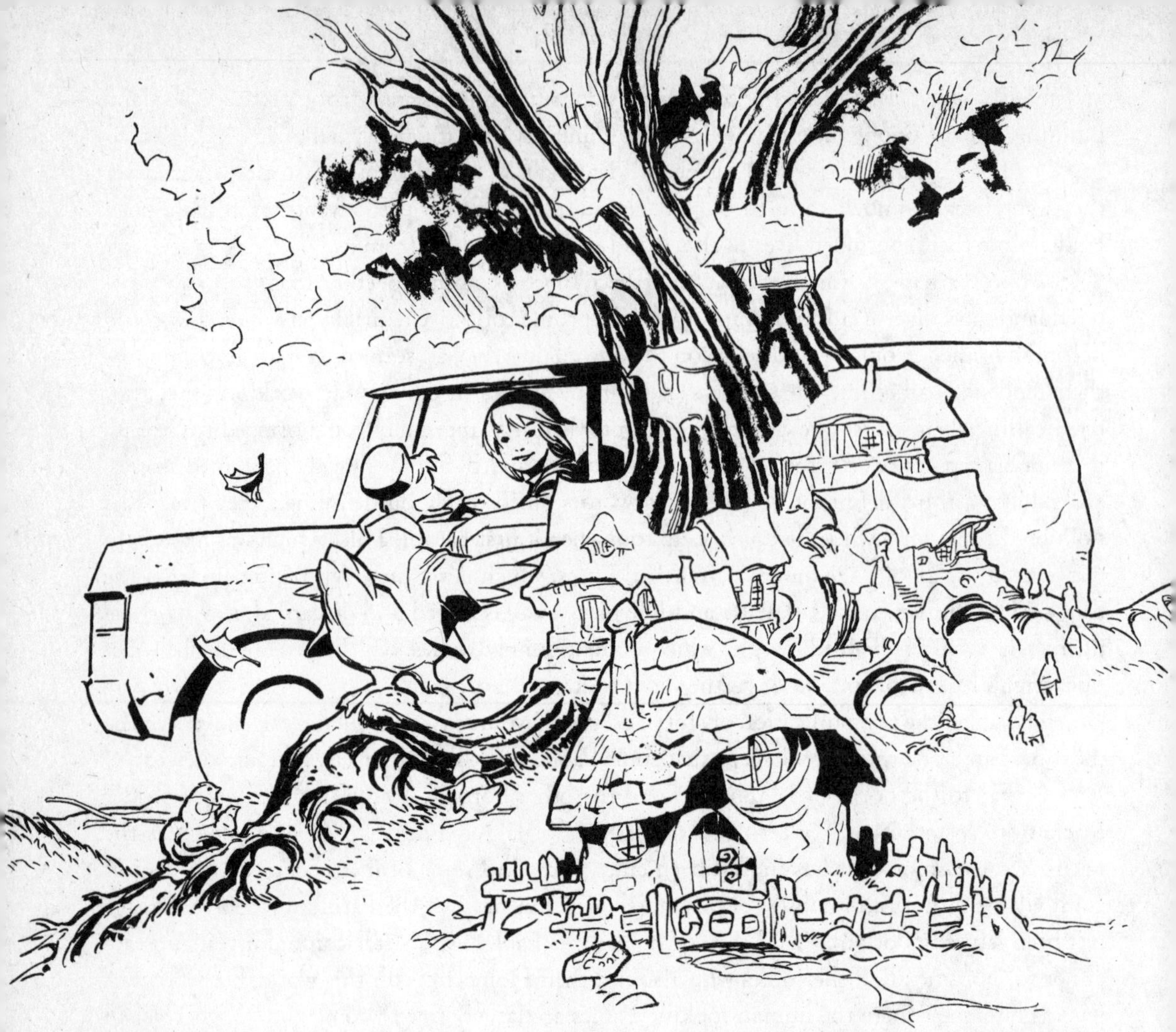

Rose Red, the no less lovely but considerably less famous sister of Snow White, wiped the sleep from her eyes as she climbed into her rust-colored Range Rover; hers at least in the sense that she ran the Farm and this was one of the vehicles owned in common by all who dwelled there. She had glossy red hair the color of fire in the daylight and dark satin at night. She wore old boots and farmer's clothes: denim pants and a flannel shirt, both of which started out in different shades of blue, but which had since been worn to the universal color of fade. Clara the raven, who'd once been a fire-breathing dragon, sat perched on the front porch railing of the main house, where Rose Red lived, and where she'd been sound asleep until just a few minutes before.

"You're out and about early," Clara said. Her breath sent a sharp flicker of fire and an attendant wisp of smoke into the brisk morning air. Having elected years ago to turn from dragon into raven, she nevertheless decided to keep the fire.

"I got a call," Rose mumbled. "Have to deliver a message."

"It can't be good news then," Clara said. "Nobody wakes someone to give out good news. Nobody civilized, anyway. Want me to go with you?" Clara served as Rose Red's personal bodyguard, a job considered necessary due to an attempted revolution against Farm authority some years back. That was why Clara thought it prudent to hold onto her fiery breath. It was a brutal and devastating weapon which served as a no-nonsense deterrent against further uprisings.

"No," Rose said. "I'm just the messenger. This business won't put me in any danger, though I can't promise the same for its recipient." With a few light curses and some pleading, Rose Red coaxed the truck's cold and reluctant engine to life. "Go back to sleep, Clara. All is well, more or less."

She drove slowly out of the village's main square, past the blacksmith's forge attached to one of the stables. She maneuvered carefully around Tom Thumb's miniature castle keep, with its tiny moat and curtain wall, and then past the goat pen, where there was a mailbox out front with the name Three Goats Gruff painted on it. An intrepid squad of mail mice was already out beginning their morning rounds. They looked dignified in their miniature frock coats, puffing important little clouds of white vapor into the cold air. And dignified they were, for it's as true among mice as among men that the swift delivery of the mail is a sacred trust. They had their delivery ladder propped against the box, and one of them was making the ascent with a letter addressed in a bold hand to one Mr. William Gruff, Esquire slung over his back. It was hard to guess which of the goats it might actually be for, since all three of the brothers were named Bill.

Rose left the village behind, driving northeast and then due north along a single-lane dirt and gravel road. After a few hundred yards of undeveloped scrubland, she entered the farmlands proper. There were cultivated fields to either side of her, newly planted winter wheat to her right and endless rows of silage corn to her left, tall yellow-green stalks, as high as an elephant's eye and groaning under the weight of their treasures. The corn harvest would have to begin in a few days, which made her wince a bit, as most of the harvester's engine was still scattered across the tractor shed floor. She'd have to get back to work on that today. To the east, the sun began peeking over the distant high hills that folks in this part of the country insisted on calling mountains. On the other side of the hills was Wolf Valley, which used to be part of the Farm, but had recently been turned over to the family of a legendary monster – her brother-in-law.

Rose came to a fork in the road and turned northwest. As she did so, the rising sun stabbed at her from her rear-view mirror. Grumbling, she angled the mirror away from her line of sight, squinted to banish the spots from her vision and drove on. The road paralleled a small but determined river for a while and then crossed it with a short wooden bridge, when the river abruptly changed direction. She left the cultivated fields behind and entered a wide rolling expanse of grasslands, where the mundy livestock were fed and fattened. Herds of cows were moved into an area to graze, bringing the grasses down to a reasonable height, then flocks of sheep were moved in after them, reducing the same grass to low stubble. A few farmhands were already in the fields, driving scattered clusters of cattle in the distance, towards fresher grass. Most of the farmhands were Fable animals earning their keep; talking horses, who talked seldom, unless they really had something to say, and talking dogs, who chattered constantly, believing that just about anything that was possible to say should be said, just in case it turned out to be important. But there were absolutely no talking cows among them. Fable cows wouldn't normally mix with mundy versions of their own species, finding the thought of their dumb cousins' eventual fate as steaks and burgers more than a little unsettling. Some of the farmhands were human Fables who lived up here because they preferred it to city life, or because they'd been caught breaking one or more Fable laws and were working off the judgments. Fabletown imposed a lot of laws on its citizens. After crossing another dozen small bridges, as the river settled into an entrenched meander, constantly turning back on itself, Rose crested a rise and looked down into a golden field full of mundy sheep being pushed around by a half dozen Fable sheep dogs, who scolded their charges with heavily accented epithets. At the far end of the field she spotted her destination, a small isolated stone and timber cottage, perched on the top of the next rolling crest and nestled under a stand of cottonwood trees. Rose was pleased to see a trail of smoke coming from the home's chimney. At least I won't be

waking anyone up, she thought. Maybe they'll even give me breakfast.

Rose pulled her truck slowly into the barely used driveway and parked it. Closer now, she noticed more details. The cottage was surrounded by a complex multi-terraced wooden porch that had all manner of ramps connecting each level. It spread out from the house in every direction and looked as if it had been added to over a large span of years. There was a green lawn and several small, well-tended flower gardens, which were also surrounded and traversed by a maze of raised wooden pathways venturing out from the porch.

As Rose stepped down from her truck, the cottage's front door opened and Peter Piper appeared in the doorway, pushing his wife Bo in front of him in her wheelchair.

"Good morning, Rose," Peter said, his wife's echo only a half beat behind him.

Then Bo said, all on her own this time, "What brings you out all the way to Casa Piper?"

They seemed cheerful at least, Rose thought. She hadn't run the Farm for very long, and hadn't lived here much longer than that. She didn't know the Pipers very well, except that they preferred to keep to themselves, way out here in their remote home, where they'd lived alone with each other, year after year, century after century, ever since escaping from the Home-lands.

"Morning," Rose answered. "I need to talk to Peter."

"Sounds ominous," Peter said. "Can Bo join in, or is this a private matter?" Bo had pale blonde hair that was nearly white in the morning sun. It was long but she wore it pulled back into a loose knot at the nape of her neck. She was lovely, as most Fable women tend to be, but hers was a wistful beauty that threatened to disappear into sadness at any moment. She wore a tan sweater and a green tartan blanket covered her legs, concealing the ruined limbs beneath. Rose had seen Bo's dead legs only once by rare accident, at one of the Farm dances, when a pair of geese, overspirited by too much dancing and too many beers, tumbled into her chair, causing her blanket to slip for a brief, terrible second. Rose had been embarrassed at how quickly she'd turned away from the sight. Bo laughed off the incident at the time and didn't seem to mind for the rest of the evening, but she never returned to the main village after that.

Peter was of average height and slim, threatening towards skinny, without quite getting there. He had dark brown hair cut short and matching brown eyes. He wore a maroon cotton shirt over a long-sleeved undershirt, khaki pants and old hiking boots.

"I'm not sure," Rose said. "I think we better make it private, until you hear what I have to say. Then you can decide if it's something you want to share. I apologize if that seems rude, Bo."

"Don't be silly," Bo said. An uncommitted smile touched her lips briefly and then vanished. "It's such a lovely morning, we were going to have breakfast out on the patio. You two have your talk while I move everything out to the picnic table. You'll join us of course."

Not waiting for an answer, she turned her chair deftly and wheeled herself back inside.

Rose and Peter walked away from the house, along one of Bo's wooden wheelchair pathways. This one led out quite a distance to where a thick wooden target had been securely propped upright. It was roughly carved into the shape of a full-grown man and had hundreds of tiny cuts and gouges in its surface.

They left the wood pathway at its farthest point and stepped down onto the turf, where the green lawn grass ended and the taller yellow livestock grass began, and then continued farther out into the fields. Itinerant gusts of wind bent the tall grass in playful

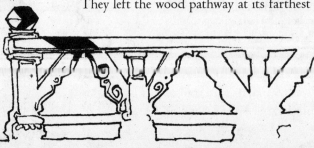

patterns. Fifty yards away a pair of energetic sheepdogs yawped and maneuvered, pushing a portion of the flock their way.

"They're good dogs," Peter said. "Good friends. They always keep a few of the sheep near our house, especially the new lambs when they come. Even after all this time, Bo still likes being near her lambs."

"Even if it means being out here so far away from anyone else?" Rose said.

"We're happy out here. Happy enough, anyway." Peter had a number of old scars on his lips and at the corners of his mouth. They were tiny and nearly invisible, except with a lucky combination of proximity and perfect light. In the distance, through the cottage's open door, they could hear the muted dry tink of porcelain cups being mated with saucers and then one quick scrape of a heavy skillet along the top of a cast iron stove.

Peter was generally a quiet man, never demonstrative, except on those rare occasions when he came into the Farm's village to play his pipe, often accompanied by Boy Blue on his horn, Seamus McGuire on his harp, and Baby Joe Sheppard on drums. And sometimes, when the mood struck, even dour old Puss would join in with his wild, screaming fiddle.

Peter would take his time getting through a sentence, punctuating even the shortest of them with one or more extended pauses. Some Fables got like that. They lived so long that they could no longer work up any sort of hurry. Urgency just faded out of them over time. His facial expressions were even more reserved than his speech, almost to the point of nonexistence. But Rose thought she could detect a contained sadness there, matching that of his wife. "Why don't you tell me what you came to say?" he said, after awhile.

"Bigby phoned me from Wolf Valley," she said. "He isn't allowed on the Farm proper, so he wants you to go see him. Today." she added.

"I guess I could do that. Long walk though."

"You can take my truck most of the way. Just drop me back home first, and return it when you're done. You'll still have to hoof it over the hills."

"That doesn't bother me. Only —"

"Only you want to know why?" Rose interrupted. "What was the part that I didn't know if your wife should hear?"

"Yes. Only that."

"Bigby can tell you more details than I can."

"All conditions, exceptions and dissembling are duly noted and acknowledged, Rose. Now please tell me the bad thing you know but don't want to say."

"Your brother is back in this world," Rose said, almost so quietly that the wind took her words.

A shadow passed over Peter's features and stayed there. He was silent for a long time. Then he said, "Someone will have to come out here and stay with Bo."

"Why? You should be back from Wolf Valley before nightfall, provided you leave right away. Even with her wheelchair and all — Well, I thought she was pretty independent."

"She is," Peter said. "She'll be fine on her own today. But later, tomorrow probably, when I leave, I'm not sure how long I'll be gone. It could be for some time, and there's always the chance I won't make it back. Someone needs to stay here with her, while I'm hunting Max."

Out in the golden fields the dogs herded sheep and the winds played their early October games, while overhead clouds gathered to spoil the blue skies.

BILL WILLINGHAM
FABLES VOL. 1: LEGENDS IN EXILE